60th Yearbook of the Literacy Research Association

Edited by

Pamela J. Dunston
Linda B. Gambrell

Kathy Headley
Susan King Fullerton
Pamela M. Stecker
Victoria R. Gillis
C.C. Bates
Clemson University

With the editorial assistance of

Chris L. Massey, Lead Assistant Editor
Clemson University

Jenny Kasza, *Editor*
Technical Enterprises, Inc.

Michelle Majerus-Uelmen, *Graphic Designer*
Technical Enterprises, Inc.

Christopher Roper, *Executive Director*
Technical Enterprises, Inc.

Published by
Literacy Research Association, Inc.
Oak Creek, Wisconsin

2011

LRA Yearbook is published annually by the Literacy Research Association, 7044 South 13th Street, Oak Creek, WI 53154, Tel: (414) 908-4924.

POSTMASTER:
Send address changes to LRA Yearbook, 7044 South 13th Street, Oak Creek, WI 53154.

SUBSCRIPTIONS:
Institutions: $80 domestic or $90 foreign (surface), per year. Individuals who are LRA members in good standing as of October 1, 2011 will receive the *Yearbook* as part of their membership. Quantity discounts available for use in university or college courses. Write for information.

PERMISSION TO QUOTE OR REPRINT:
Quotations of 500 words or longer or reproductions of any portion of a table, figure, or graph, require written permission from the Literacy Research Association, and must include proper credit to the organization. A fee may be charged for use of the material, and permission of the first author will be secured.

PHOTOCOPIES:
Individuals may photocopy single articles without permission for nonprofit one-time classroom or library use. Other nonprofit educational copying, including repeated use of an individual article, must be registered with the Copyright Clearance Center, Academic Permission Service, 27 Congress Street, Salem, MA 01970, USA. *The fee is $1.25USD per article, or any portion, or any portion thereof, to be paid through the Center. The fee is waived for individual members of the Literacy Research Association.* Consent to photocopy does not extend to items identified as reprinted by permission of other publishers, nor to copying for general distribution, for advertising or promotion, or for resale unless written permission is obtained from the Literacy Research Association.

Microfiche copy is available from ERIC Reproduction Service, 3900 Wheeler Avenue, Alexandria, VA 22304. The YEARBOOK is indexed in *Psychological Abstracts, Index to Social Sciences & Humanities Proceedings and Educational Research Information Clearing House.* The LRA Yearbook is a refereed publication. Manuscripts must be original works that have been presented at the Annual Meeting of the Literacy Research Association, and that have not been published elsewhere.

ISSN
ISBN 1-893591-13-1
Printed in the United States of America

Editorial Advisory Review Board

60th Yearbook of the Literacy Research Association

Catherine M. Kelly
St. Catherine University

Ted Kesler
Queens College, CUNY

Sharon B. Kletzien
West Chester University of Pennsylvania

Candace Kuby
University of Missouri

Amy Suzanne Johnson Lachuk
University of South Carolina

Judson Laughter
University of Tennessee, Knoxville

Christine M. Leighton
Emmanuel College

Kristin Lems
National-Louis University

Xiaoming Liu
Towson University

Sara Mackiewicz
Clemson University

Jacquelynn Malloy
George Mason University

Joyce E. Many
Georgia State University

Barbara Marinak
Penn State, Harrisburg

Susan Marshall
Westminster College

Prisca Martens
Towson University

Pamela Mason
Harvard University

Laura May
Georgia State University

Sarah McCarthey
University of Illinois at Urbana-Champaign

Jonda C. McNair
Clemson University

Carla K. Meyer
Appalachian State University

Denise N. Morgan
Kent State University

Lori A. Norton-Meier
University of Louisville

Richard M. Oldreive
Bowling Green State University

Barbara Martin Palmer
Mount. St. Mary's University

Jeanne R. Paratore
Boston University

Seth Parsons
George Mason University

Julie L. Pennington
University of Nevada, Reno

Ellen Pesko
Appalachian State University

Ray D. Reutzel
Utah State University

Mary Roe
Arizona State University

Nancy L. Roser
The University of Texas at Austin

Diane Santori
West Chester University

Diane L. Schallert
The University of Texas at Austin

Sarah E. Scott
University of Pittsburgh

Diane Carver Sekeres
The University of Alabama

Timothy Shanahan
University of Illinois at Chicago

Gerry Shiel
Educational Research Centre, St. Patrick's College, Dublin

Sunita Singh
Le Moyne College

Kristine Lynn Still
Cleveland State University

Sheelah Sweeny
Northeastern University

Allison E. Ward
George Mason University

Rachelle D. Washington
Clemson University

Patricia A. Watson
Texas Tech University/Texas Woman's University

Sarah Lohnes Watulak
Towson University

Courtney West
Texas A & M University

Dana J. Wilber
Montclair State University

Joan A.Williams
Sam Houston State University

Nancy Williams
University of South Florida

Amy M. Williamson
Angelo State University

Angela M. Wiseman
North Carolina State University

Student Editorial Advisory Board

60th Yearbook of the Literacy Research Association

Student Editorial Assistants

60th Yearbook of the Literacy Research Association

Tyler S. Bennet
Clemson University

Koti L. Hubbard
Clemson University

Melissa A. Kopec
Clemson University

Valerie L. Marsh
Clemson University

Lauren D. Phillips
Clemson University

M. Deanna Ramey
Clemson University

Colleen M. Varda
Clemson University

60th Yearbook of the Literacy Research Association

Section III: Literacy Practices In and Out of School

Section IV: New Literacies—Enriching Research and Theory

Preface

60th Yearbook of the Literacy Research Association

The Literacy Research Association was founded in 1950 as the Southwest Reading Conference for Colleges and Universities. Following the first annual meeting and for several years thereafter, the *Yearbook* was printed at Clemson University under the direction of Dr. Gordon Gray. Since that time, Clemson University faculty members have been involved actively throughout the organization's long and rich history. Two Clemson faculty members, Dr. David Reinking and Dr. Linda Gambrell, are Past-Presidents, and many other faculty members have served the association in numerous ways. Extending our service to the Literacy Research Association as editors for the 60th anniversary *Yearbook* was particularly gratifying in light of Clemson University's role in producing the first *Yearbook*. This year's editorial team included Pamela Dunston, Linda Gambrell, Kathy Headley, Pamela Stecker, Susan Fullerton, Victoria Gillis, and C.C. Bates. Our editorial team pledges to maintain the integrity and reputation of the *Yearbook* as a high-quality publication that serves as a significant outlet for scholarly work. We are committed to supporting leading scholars, midlevel scholars, and emerging scholars who engage in literacy research in traditional and nontraditional settings.

We made every effort to preserve traditional features of the *Yearbook* while at the same time adding our own touches. Toward this end, we introduce a new feature in this year's *Yearbook*, one we hope to incorporate throughout our tenure. After grouping manuscripts into topics, we invited leading scholars in the literacy field to write introductions for each section. Each luminary read manuscripts within his/her respective section and wrote a brief overview addressing the importance of the theme or line of research, contributions the papers make to the field, and/or aspects of the topic that merit consideration for future research. We believe the introductions provide succinct, insightful, and integrated overviews of manuscripts within the sections. We extend heartfelt thanks to this year's luminaries, Victoria Risko, Richard Allington, Patricia Edwards, and Donald Leu, for their thoughtful remarks and willingness to contribute to the *Yearbook* in such a meaningful way.

Like all scholarly work, this *Yearbook* was not created in a vacuum. The *Yearbook* was made possible through the support, hard work, and assistance of many people. First, we sincerely thank our Dean, Dr. Lawrence Allen, and the Director of the Eugene T. Moore School of Education, Dr. Michael Padilla, for financial support that provided us with a doctoral-student assistant, travel, release time, and tangibles necessary to our roles as editors. Their professional support was beyond measure. Second, a special word of gratitude goes to our outstanding doctoral student Chris Massey, who provided organizational and time-management skills that kept us moving forward. Chris was a tireless worker who took responsibility for tracking manuscripts, managing graduate-student editors, and communicating with advisory-board members, authors, and LRA staff members. Third, we thank Editorial Advisory Board and Student Editorial Advisory Board members who provided thoughtful and thorough reviews of the manuscripts in a timely manner. The reviewers not only guided the selection process, they provided suggestions for improving the research and writing of all the authors who submitted manuscripts for consideration. Finally, we thank all the authors who submitted manuscripts for review. Without their willingness to revise conference papers during the weeks following the conference and on the cusp of beginning a new semester, the *Yearbook* would not be possible.

Pamela J. Dunston
Linda B. Gambrell
Lead Editors

A Summary of the 60th Annual Meeting of the Literacy Research Association

December 1–December 4, 2010

Literacy Research Association members and scholarly colleagues from around the world and the United States met for the annual LRA (formerly the National Reading Conference [NRC]) in Fort Worth, Texas. This conference marked the 60th anniversary of NRC/LRA; as such, the conference theme was *Celebrate! 60 Years of Literacy Research*.

Information about the substance of the conference is provided below; but first a summary of registration and program information helps to set the stage. The conference was attended by 1,225 scholars. Over the last six years, the mean attendance was 1,203. Over the past six years, the lowest attendance was 1,081 in 2005 and the highest was 1,355 in 2007.

The number of proposals submitted for this conference was 763, about the same number as is the norm; of these, 512 were invited to present at the conference for an acceptance rate of 72.61%. Area 3, "Literacy Instruction and Literacy Learning," received the most submissions (117 submissions, with 70 accepted). Area 12, the "Study Groups," received the fewest number of proposals (21 submitted and 20 accepted). The most recently added area, "Research Theory, Methods, and Practices," received 22 proposals and 13 were accepted. The proposals are vetted by a wide array of reviewers and the LRA President Elect (the program chair) and Vice President. Each area chair and all the reviewers are listed in the annual program. In all, 13 area co-chairs (41 members) and 436 reviewer-members evaluated the proposed submissions. The LRA depends on the peer review process and the robust scholarship of its membership to make an excellent conference. By all accounts the reviewer's peer reviews and the author's presentations combined for an outstanding program.

As the program chair for this conference, I extend a heartfelt thank you to each area chair, reviewer, and presenter for their outstanding work. We stand on the shoulders of our founders and we each do our part to make the conference a scholarly treasure trove for all.

The conference also showcases the scholarship and careers of colleagues whose scholarship and service deserve special recognition. The award winners are selected by committees, which are chaired by and made up of LRA members. This year five awards were given. One annual award is the Oscar S. Causey Award. Causey was the first President of NRC/LRA and the award is given for distinguished research in literacy education. The 2010 Oscar S. Causey Award winner was Professor Lesley M. Morrow of Rutgers University. She accepted the award on Thursday morning and will speak at the 2011 conference as did Professor Barbara M. Taylor (University of Minnesota) at the 2010 conference after being awarded the Causey in 2009. Professor Taylor's presentation was titled "The Power of Collaborative Teaching with Integrity."

Another annual award is the Albert J. Kingston Award, which is for outstanding service to NRC/LRA. This year's winner was Susan L'Allier, the current LRA treasurer, of Northern Illinois University. Professor L'Allier is an exceptionally gifted officer and is treasured by the LRA membership for her exemplary outstanding service.

The Edward B. Fry Book Award was presented to Mary M. Juzwik of Michigan State University, the author of *The Rhetoric of Teaching: Understanding the Dynamics of Holocaust Narratives in an English Classroom* (Hampton, 2009). In addition, the Early Career Achievement Award winner was Leigh A. Hall of the University of North Carolina, and the Student Outstanding Research Award went to Amanda P. Goodwin of the University of Miami. Finally, the

J. Michael Parker Award went to Silvia Cecilia Nogueron of Arizona State University. These award winners represent the best of the best among our colleagues and each are to be congratulated. To nominate future awardees, please go to the LRA website and find a description of each award and the procedures for nominating.

The first day of the conference features the President's talk, which this year featured President David Reinking of Clemson University. His presentation, "Beyond the Laboratory and Lens: New Metaphors of Literacy Research," challenged us to examine the metaphors that are used to represent literacy research. His presentation is included in this volume and is destined to be required reading for literacy doctoral seminars.

The plenary presentation by Dean Lorrie Shepard (University of Colorado), "Teaching with Integrity in the Face of High-Stakes Testing," fits well with both Taylor's Causey address and Reinking's Presidential address. The three presentations make a substantial contribution to our thinking about these timely and provocatively compelling topics. The second plenary speaker, Hilary Janks of the University of Witwatersrand, South Africa, pushed participants to think about critical literacy and pedagogy. She is responsible for a powerful literacy program in South Africa and has authored and investigated curricular materials to advance critical theory.

The richness and robustness of the 2010 LRA program bodes well for the quality of the current *Yearbook*. Like you, I look forward to reading this compendium of peer-reviewed articles representing the conference and edited by the new editorial team. See you next year in Jacksonville for the annual Literacy Research Association Conference.

Patricia L. Anders
President, Literacy Research Association
2010-2011

Dr. Susan L'Allier

Albert J. Kingston Award

The annual Albert J. Kingston Service Award honors an LRA member for distinguished contributions of service to the Literacy Research Association. Established in 1985, the award was designed to honor the work of NRC/LRA's 1965-66 president, Albert J. Kingston. Professor Kingston, an educational psychologist and reading specialist, played a major role in the development of the National Reading Conference.

Dr. Susan L'Allier, Associate Professor in the Department of Literacy Education in the College of Education at Northern Illinois University, is the recipient of the 2010 Albert J. Kingston Award of the Literacy Research Association.

After receiving a BA from Macalester College and an MA from Gallaudet College, Susan taught preschool and elementary students with hearing impairments in the St. Paul Minnesota Public Schools. She then completed an MA in Educational Administration from California State University and held leadership positions in programs serving hearing-impaired students in both St. Paul and Santa Fe, New Mexico. In 1997, Susan graduated from Harvard University with an Ed.D. and began her career at the university level in Illinois. The focus of her research is on teacher education for both preservice and inservice teachers. Susan's most recent presentations and publications were on literacy coaching.

Professor L'Allier has served NRC/LRA since 1995, most notably as Treasurer, a position she assumed in 2006. During her tenure, Susan has been credited with turning the financial health of the organization around at a time when it was in crisis. To do so, she studied how funds were invested, presented her findings to the board, and proposed alternatives. Susan's recommendations led to more transparent procedures for reporting income and expenditures as well as investments that have earned money for the organization. She also initiated a Financial Advisory Committee. This committee, consisting of current and previous board members, meets three times each year to advise the Treasurer.

We extend our thanks and congratulations to Dr. Susan L'Allier, recipient of the 2010 Albert J. Kingston Award in recognition of her service to LRA.

Diane Corcoran Nielsen, Chair
Albert J. Kingston Award Committee
December 2010

Lesley M. Morrow

Oscar S. Causey Award

The Oscar S. Causey Award is presented each year at the annual conference to honor outstanding contributions to literacy research. Dr. Oscar S. Causey, the founder of the National Reading Conference, was Chair of the Executive Committee for several years, and served as President from 1952 to 1959. Individuals who are honored with this prestigious award have conducted and published research that generates new knowledge and is deemed substantial, significant, and original. The individual is also recognized as a leader in the conduct and promotion of literacy research.

Dr. Lesley M. Morrow has contributed to the field of literacy through her leadership, teaching, research, publications, presentations, and service. Dr. Morrow began her career as an early childhood teacher. She became a reading specialist and then began teaching at the university level. She received her Ph.D. from Fordham University. Her scholarship has created new knowledge in the field of early literacy. Her work is original and improved practice in reading instruction. Her research on the creation of literacy-rich environments in classrooms to motivate interest in reading is referenced in hundreds of research articles, books, and book chapters. The results of her research are evident in early childhood classrooms throughout the country and abroad. The literacy centers found in classrooms are a direct reflection of her research. The access they provide to books increases voluntary reading and enhances literacy achievement. This work led to a consultant position with a grant from Public Broadcasting Corporation and the Reading Rainbow television program to create the literacy center program in over 200 after-school and summer day care centers for 3- to 8-year-olds throughout New York City. The parent component of this project was adopted by *Highlights for Children* and called the Highlights Parent Involvement Program.

Dr. Morrow's research dealing with small group and one-one-to-one storybook reading and interactive behaviors to accompany them are well known to teachers, as is the story retelling tool she created for assessing and teaching comprehension. The retelling tool has been used in others' research included in most reading texts, and in reading programs. This work led to Dr. Morrow's invitation to participate in Head Start's Heads Up television courses for preschool teachers.

Lesley Morrow's research dealing with exemplary teaching practices resulted in invitations to Departments of Education throughout the country to be a consultant on many Reading First Projects. Her International Reading Association (IRA) preschool book collection was a new market for the IRA and is used extensively by members of the National Association for the Education of Young Children. Because of this collection she was often an invited speaker/consultant for recipients of Early Reading First Grants. She has been a consultant for many Reading First grants and state departments of education. Recently, because of her work in preschool, she was invited as a co-researcher for a funded project by the National Institute of Child Health and Human Development with Alan Mendelsohn, M.D., and his colleagues. Dr. Mendelsohn is a pediatrician and professor of pediatrics at New York University's medical school. The project is entitled Enhancing Language and Literacy Development for School Success in Primary Care Pediatrics.

The manner in which Dr. Morrow's work has spread its influence is through her extensive research, publications, and presentations. She has carried out evidenced-based research, publishes it in tier one refereed research journals, and then writes articles for classroom and pre-service teachers.

Lesley has published 35 books. Her text *Literacy Development in the Early Years* with Pearson will celebrate its 25th anniversary in 2012 and is in its 7th edition. According to her publisher, it was one of the first and best-selling texts in early literacy in the country. Her books are published with IRA, Teachers College Press, Teahouse, Guilford Publications, and Pearson to name a few.

She has 60 refereed articles in the most prestigious journals. She has published multiple times in *Reading Research Quarterly, Reading Teacher, Language Arts, Journal of Literacy Research, Early Childhood Research Quarterly, Research in the Teaching of English, Journal of Educational Psychology, Elementary School Journal,* and others.

She has published 65 book chapters and several chapters in research handbooks such as *Handbook of Reading Research, Handbook of Family Literacy,* and *Handbook of Teaching Reading and the Language Arts.* She has edited newsletters and co-edited the *Journal of Literacy Research.* She edited themed issues of *Reading Teacher* and 24 columns for *Reading Teacher* with Dorothy Strickland entitled Emergent Readers and Writers. These had a strong impact on early literacy instruction. Dr. Morrow has presented her work at more than 500 venues as an invited keynote speaker at local, state, national, and international professional conferences and in schools and universities.

Lesley has been an invited researcher, consultant, and principal investigator on grants for federally funded centers such as: the Center for the Study of Reading, the National Reading Research Center, the Center for English Language Arts Achievement, and the Center for Improvement of Early Reading Achievement and Assessment. She has had grants from the Interagency Education Research Initiative, the National Institute for Child Health and Human Development, the New Jersey Department of Education, two IRA Elva Knight grants, the National Council of Teachers of English grant, and an Eisenhower grant.

- She has been recognized for her work with the following honors and awards:

- 15 merit awards for scholarship at Rutgers University

- Rutgers Graduate School of Education's Alumni Awards for Research, Teaching, and Service

- Rutgers, The State University of New Jersey's Teaching Award

- Recipient of the Educational Press Association of America's Distinguished Achievement Award for Excellence in Educational Journalism with Dorothy Strickland

- Fordham University's Outstanding Alumni Achievement Award

- International Reading Association's Outstanding Educator of Teacher of Reading Award

- The New Jersey Reading Association's Special Service Award

- IRA's William S. Gray Award for lifetime scholarship and service to the field

- Promoted to the rank of Professor 2 at Rutgers, the highest rank at the University

- Elected into the Reading Hall of Fame and served as their president

Dr. Morrow chaired the Family Literacy Commission and published an edited a book about family literacy programs. Barbara Bush, who was First Lady at the time, wrote the foreword. Dr. Morrow worked on materials for President Clinton's America Reads initiative. She created three tutoring handbooks (with a colleague) that were published by IRA and used throughout the country to train college students to be reading tutors for children in disadvantaged communities. Dr. Morrow served as President of IRA. Her major goal was to make preschool more visible in the organization. As a result she created a team of authors who helped to write a collection of six preschool professional development books and more sessions about preschool were added to the organization's conference. Lesley is known to be efficient, hard working, productive, and an outstanding mentor to her students and young academics. She offers writing, speaking, and committee opportunities to them. Most of all, her name is synonymous with helping to shape exemplary practice in early literacy amongst both the world of academic scholars and teachers.

Deborah R. Dillon, Chair
Oscar S. Causey Award Committee
December 2010

Beyond the Laboratory and Lens: New Metaphors for Literacy Research

David Reinking
Clemson University

PRELIMINARY REMARKS

As president of the Literacy Research Association, at least for the next two days, I want to personally welcome all of you to this year's conference and to thank you for your support of my presidency during the previous year. This year's conference marks our 60th anniversary as an organization and the first as the Literacy Research Association (LRA). These twin milestones provide an opportunity to celebrate our past as the National Reading Conference (NRC) while asserting that we are a dynamic organization open to adaptation and change.

Nonetheless, many traditions continue, including the annual presidential address. I am sure that many of the former presidents in the audience today have felt the same as I do now. It is a privilege and an honor to address so many of my colleagues, and it is a humbling and intimidating opportunity to join my distinguished predecessors.

To mark our 60th anniversary and to promote our new name, as you leave this session, each of you will be given a flash drive inscribed with our new logo. I want to thank the field council, particularly Heidi Mesmer, its chair, for joining me in sponsoring this gift and memento. On the flash drive, you will find an earlier version of my talk and the accompanying slides, and several key articles that I will cite. However, to express my appreciation for this opportunity, and to honor former presidents of NRC, it also includes all of the previous presidential addresses published in the *NRC Yearbook*, thanks to the help of Jamie Colwell, my doctoral student.

INTRODUCTION

One privilege of the presidential address is having free rein to choose a topic. Former addresses fall roughly into two categories: talks that highlight some aspect of a president's research and talks that challenge the thinking or direction of the field. I have chosen the latter, perhaps riskier, approach. I was nudged in that direction for two reasons. First, our anniversary and name change inspires reflection about the past and thoughts about the future. Second, in 2005 my friend and colleague Don Leu (2006) gave a presidential talk devoted to our shared interest in how digital technologies affect literacy. He would be a hard act to follow. I urge those who remain unconvinced that we live in a revolutionary new world of literacy, as Don argued, to again read his presidential address.

Another presidential privilege is to choose, as President-Elect, the conference theme. My talk today extends the theme I chose for last year's conference entitled "Literacy Research Past, Present, and Future: Multiple Paths to a Better World." Consistent with my theme today, that title introduces a metaphor: our research as a path to a better world. As that metaphor implies, we do not engage in research for its own sake or simply to satisfy our intellectual curiosity. If you doubt that bettering the world is the central imperative of our work, I recommend reading an article in *Educational Researcher* by Karl Hostetler (2005) entitled "What is Good Education Research?"

His answer to his own question is that good research is not just theoretically and methodologically sound; it contributes to enhancing people's wellbeing. My former colleague Tom Reeves at the University of Georgia goes further (Reeves, 2006, Reeves & Harrington, 2005). According to Tom, education research not aimed directly at bettering the world is socially irresponsible, and perhaps should not be categorized as education research at all. Both articles are on the flash drive.

My talk today argues that the dominant metaphors for our research, past and present, have helped enlighten paths to a better world, but they have not been particularly well suited to building them. Specifically, the laboratory and lens metaphors suggest that our primary responsibility as researchers is to generate understanding that subsequently may be useful to others who actually build the paths to a better world. Today I propose several alternative metaphors, and an overarching one to reverse that stance. These metaphors suggest that understanding is not the precursor of actionable improvement, but a consequence of seeking it, thus making our work more useful, beneficial, and socially responsible.

Two of the plenary sessions last year highlighted the need for such a shift as well as the formidable challenges we would face operating in that frame, especially in contexts where enhancing wellbeing through literacy is desperately needed. For example, Charles Payne informed us about the complex, systemic factors that undermine reform in urban schools. He urged us to address alterable variables that could make a difference rather than finding causal ones that are only explanatory. In her Oscar Causey address, Taffy Raphael shared her and her colleagues' often unsuccessful struggles to conduct research aimed at constructive change in urban schools. As these talks illustrated, research aimed at making the world a better place is not for the faint hearted. Nor is it for those who are looking for magic bullets, prescriptions for success, or who ignore or gloss over the messiness of a complicated world. But neither is it for those satisfied to simply identify that complexity and revel in it without investing in constructive action.

THE LIMITED INFLUENCE AND EFFICIENCY OF OUR WORK

Finally, the Saturday plenary was a lively and engaging debate between two teams of leading researchers who argued opposing views on the following proposition: "Literacy researchers have not produced a base of knowledge that provides practitioners and policy makers with explicit guidance for improving literacy and literacy instruction." The decidedly mixed votes across several rounds of the debate suggested considerable ambivalence about the influence and usefulness of our work.

One somewhat depressing explanation is Labaree's (1998) argument that education research is inherently a lesser form of knowledge. Consistent with the theme of my talk today, he used two metaphors to make that distinction. Education research, he said, is a broad-ranging rural landscape, whereas research in the hard sciences is an urban landscape with skyscrapers of knowledge. I believe Labaree's point might be supported by examining almost any issue of AERA's (American Educational Research Association) journal *Review of Educational Research*. It is unlikely that you would find an article synthesizing a clear consensus from research about the ingredients of effective action aimed at improving people's wellbeing. More likely you will find a review of opposing theories and incompatible findings, an overview of disputed conclusions and interpretations, a caveat about the complexity of the issues, and a never-ending call for more research.

A new book by John Hattie (2009) supports Labaree's point, at least on the quantitative side. He analyzed 800 meta-analyses that included more than 50,000 experimental studies and 2 million students. The effect size across all of these studies was .4, not a particularly impressive figure, especially when one considers the bias toward publishing statistically significant findings and that many of the studies investigated obviously useful pedagogical practices such as providing feedback and increasing time on task. On the other hand, we might discount meta-analyses entirely, given that Gene Glass (2008), the originator of that approach, recently renounced it as a means to inform policy or practice, as noted in the following quote from his recent book: "I do not believe that [research studies aimed at shaping policy], mired as they are in debates between research methods experts, have any determinative value in shaping the current nature of public education or its future" (p. 285). The recent debate in a themed issue of *Educational Researcher* (Volume 39, Number 4) about the purpose, validity, meaning, and conclusions of the National Early Literacy Panel is a prime example of Glass' point.

My editorships of *Journal of Literacy Research* and *Reading Research Quarterly* for a total of 12 years provided a uniquely personal perspective about the limited influence and efficiency of our work. The investment of time, energy, and resources behind the 1500 manuscripts with which I had editorial contact is staggering, especially considering that overall only about one in ten were deemed worthy of publication. My years as an editor left me in awe of the productivity and the scholarly and methodological rigor of my colleagues' work. But I would be hard pressed to identify a set of studies, let alone a body of work, that has had any tangible influence on bettering the world.

I am certainly not the first to raise these issues. For example, the central theme of an article by Deborah Dillon, David O'Brien, and Elizabeth Heilman (2000) in the millennial issue of *Reading Research Quarterly* (*RRQ*) was that our work should be more pragmatic. That article, I believe, should be required reading for all literacy researchers and those who wish to become one. It is included on the flash drive that you will receive after this session.

I believe we all know in our hearts that knowledge pursued is no substitute for knowledge applied, and most of us feel at least uneasy about the longstanding gap between research and practice. However, today I am asking whether our metaphors for research may be partly responsible, and whether new metaphors might help us increase the relevance, practicality, and humanitarian influence of our work.

METAPHORS WE LIVE BY

I can trace my thinking about the limitations of our metaphors to a personal experience etched in my memory. In the early 1990s I received an Elva Knight grant from the International Reading Association to conduct a conventional experiment comparing the effects of engaging students in creating what we called multi-media book reviews on a computer instead of writing traditional book reports. From the outset, this project was a disaster, at least from the standpoint of the experimental methods in which I had been trained. For example, the school principal, at the last minute, decided to assign most of the struggling readers to an effective teacher in one of our experimental classes, which left us scrambling for statistical ways to address the inevitable imbalance. Later, a teacher in one of the control classrooms liked the online book reviews so much that she started doing them in her classroom. Both of these developments were sensible and in the best interest of students, but undermined our experiment.

However, the event I remember most was a post-project, actually a post-mortem, meeting with two of the doctoral students who had worked with me on the project. As we tried to console ourselves with an experiment gone bad and maybe salvage some supportable findings, one of the students said something that I will never forget. He commented that one reason for our failed project was that the teachers represented a nuisance variable. That observation was correct from the standpoint of experimental design, but to express that fact with such an impersonal, detached, almost disrespectful term, gave pause to all of us in the room. As our discussion proceeded, we discovered that our abject failure to conduct a valid experiment had actually revealed some useful insights about our intervention and how we might implement it better in the future.

That experience revealed the extent and power of the laboratory metaphor that put our work at odds not only with the reality of classrooms and schools, but, more importantly also with pedagogical decisions that served students. It disconnected us from the contexts in which we conducted our research and from the lives of those who we intended our work to inform.

Some of you may be thinking that naturalistic approaches guided by a lens metaphor would negate the limitations of the laboratory metaphor we were using. However, as I will point out in a few minutes, it has its own problematic entailments. You may also be thinking: Do metaphors really matter that much? Could replacing one metaphor with another really make that much difference? Actually, there is a literature suggesting that metaphors really do matter and they have subtle, but profound influence, on how we view the world.

For example, George Lakoff and Mark Johnson (1980), in their seminal book entitled *Metaphors We Live By*, pointed out that metaphors are much more than linguistic tools for explanatory or aesthetic purposes. In fact, many metaphors become unconsciously embedded in everyday language and their entailments create and sustain cultural coherency. For example, many cultures use war metaphors for argument. The entailments of the war metaphor include *attacking a position, indefensible points, a new line of attack, winning or losing, gaining ground, demolishing arguments*, and so forth. Another everyday example is time as commodity. We *spend* time, *share* it, *save* it, *waste* it, *borrow* it, *budget* it, *use it profitably* or not, and hope that some tasks don't *cost us* too much of it.

According to Lakoff and Johnson (1980), metaphors unconsciously promote one view and suppress others. For example, considering labor as a resource (e.g., as in human resources) is really a metaphor, one that promotes economic and political interests, but suppresses the distinction between meaningful and dehumanizing work. Likewise, new metaphors have the potential to redirect our conceptions and actions. For example, Lakoff and Johnson explain how a loving relationship between two partners might be conceptualized metaphorically as creating a collaborative piece of art, thus undoing ideal and unrealistic views of unending romantic love that requires no effort.

New metaphors can also be agents of power used to set agendas, to shape perceptions, and to inspire action. No Child Left Behind, and its more recent cousin, Race to the Top, are examples of such metaphors. Or, consider the Tea Party Movement. Thus, we need to consider our metaphors carefully and choose those that will most help get us where we want to go.

METAPHORS LITERACY RESEARCHERS LIVE BY

Metaphors are rife in the discourse of our field. For example, consider how we talk about reading and texts. Reading is often described metaphorically as immersion, absorption, nourishment, transportation, movement, liberation, transaction, and so forth. Texts are digested, followed, constructed or deconstructed, seminal and disseminated, wrestled with, and those who have difficulty with them struggle. Could we even talk and think about reading and texts without such metaphors? Or, how might we think differently about them if we adopted new metaphors for reading such as mirrors, music, harvesting a crop, or gifts.

In the realm of instruction, the medical metaphor continues to dominate in some quarters for conceptualizing how we view and treat (in all senses of that word) students having difficulty reading. For example, we may send them to a reading clinic for a diagnosis and a prescribed treatment. Response to Intervention (RTI) alludes to a medical metaphor, as does Reading Recovery. But, for literacy researchers the laboratory and the lens are the predominant metaphors, to which I now turn.

The Laboratory Metaphor

The laboratory embodies the highly controlled conditions and quantitative measurements that define the scientific method. Literacy researchers who invest heavily in that metaphor when they work in dynamic, real-world contexts sometimes go too far and sometimes not far enough. On the not-far-enough side, they often conveniently omit many of the laboratory metaphor's entailments. For example, scientists who actually do highly controlled laboratory experiments know that their research is often messy, riddled with unforeseen and troublesome errors, leading to erroneous findings. They know that many scientific advances are often spurious or serendipitous effects (e.g., penicillin, X-rays, and even Viagra). Some major discoveries first appeared to be measurement error (e.g., for years astronomers thought pulsars were nothing more than flaws in their observational equipment).

Real scientists are also circumspect about moving laboratory research into the real world. For example, Steven Cole, a UCLA medical researcher studying biological links between stress and physical illness, stated:

> I have to say, anytime things work out in the real world, frankly, it should be a surprise to those of us that do laboratory science. I assure you that there are many, many things that we discover that work fine in the test tube that don't work out in the real world. (see: http://chronicle.com/article/Misery-in-the-Genes-How-DNA/65335/?sid=at&utm_source=at&utm_medium=en)

Or, consider the conclusions of a scientific panel investigating the possible harmful effects of plastic containers for food and drinks:

> Given so many variables, it is difficult, if not impossible, to determine

how harmful these chemicals might be, or if they are harmful at all, or what anyone can do to avoid their effects. (see: http://www.newyorker.com/reporting/2010/05/31/100531fa_fact_groopman)

I know that many of you agree with me that the laboratory metaphor has marginal validity as a metaphor for classroom research, and perhaps a few others who may be considering leaving the room now. But, let me speak for a moment to those who largely agree. I believe that the laboratory metaphor has left some residue in our thinking, even if we have consciously rejected it. Let me give a few examples.

The fallacy of fidelity. In valid scientific experiments a treatment must be carried out with fidelity, which means, in an instructional study, that instruction must not vary. Even if that were possible, it should be contrary to every bone in an educator's body. I suppose, then, we might logically call good teaching infidelity, because it varies to accommodate students' diverse backgrounds and needs, changing circumstances, the availability of materials, and so forth. So, any inclinations any of us may have to prescribe classroom practices or even to suggest that such prescriptions are possible can, I think, be traced to the laboratory metaphor, which leads to the next example that is a close cousin.

The fallacy of "best practice." The fallacy can be revealed by trying to insert words into the blanks of the statement:

> *Considering all the possible instructional practices for teaching/developing/instilling* [insert your favorite aspect of literacy here], [insert a practice here] *is the best practice of all.*

As I have argued in published work (Reinking, 2007), if we can define best practice, it should not be any more difficult to identify worst practice, which seems nonsensical. What would the worst possible practice be? Whenever we use the term *best practice*, we implicitly further the laboratory metaphor and its limited attention to conditional factors.

The dominance of effectiveness. Another residual effect of the laboratory metaphor is the dominance of effectiveness in our research. No one would argue against striving for effectiveness in promoting literacy and seeking an understanding of how to achieve it through our research. However, the laboratory metaphor promotes disproportionate attention to measurable achievement at the expense of contextual factors, not to mention its neglect of valued outcomes that are difficult to measure. Two other practical aspects get little attention: efficiency and appeal. What good is an instructional program that is clearly effective on average if it is a logistical nightmare, a financial black hole, anathema to teachers and students, or if it produces unacceptable collateral outcomes? To the extent that we ignore or play down such factors, the laboratory metaphor is holding sway.

Playing the research card. If you have ever used research to advance or settle an argument about what should or should not be done in classrooms, or perhaps even if you remain silent while others attempt to do so, you are endorsing the laboratory metaphor. Taking that stance might be called *playing the research card.* As Bill Ayers (2006) has suggested, "In education a sentence that begins 'The research says . . .' is too often meant to silence debate. It evokes Science, which is assumed to be larger than life: The expected response is awe and genuflection. It functions as a kind of bludgeon" (p.90). As this quote suggests, laboratory science invites a posture where research is the final arbiter for making educational decisions. The periodic requests on the LRA listserv for research that counters some ill-advised instructional program in a local school district is an example of looking for research trump cards. If we choose to participate in that game, we are endorsing the laboratory metaphor. Can we imagine a world in which research is not used to win arguments? Are there metaphors that might create research that disengages us from arguing what the research does or doesn't say?

Devaluing professional wisdom. The laboratory metaphor also tacitly devalues professional wisdom. It implies a clear demarcation between researchers and practitioners, a separation that unfortunately is deeply embedded, I believe, in our self-concept. We see the task of researchers as producing the raw findings that practitioners and policy makers are expected to put into practice. For example, Labaree (2003) argued that teachers must be reprogrammed to adopt a different worldview if they are to become researchers:

> . . . students and professors in researcher training programs often encounter a cultural clash between the world-views of the teacher and researcher. . . Differences in worldview between teachers and researchers cannot be eliminated easily because they arise from irreducible differences in the nature of the work that teachers and researchers do (p. 14).

Certainly new skills and broader perspectives are necessary to become a researcher, but what does it say about our metaphors if they require would-be researchers to purge or suppress the instincts they acquired as teachers? Gerald Duffy (1994) offered a different perspective, made more poignant because it needs to be stated at all:

> Viewing research findings as something to be handed down as technical information ignores the reality that teachers must make strategic decisions about when to apply findings, how to adapt them to certain situations and even when it might be appropriate to ignore the findings altogether (p. 19).

Are there metaphors that would put effective, efficient, and appealing practice, not research, at the center of what we do, as suggested by the caption of a cartoon showing two researchers in a discussion with one saying to the other, "We know it works in practice, but will it in an experimental setting?"

Before going on, I can't resist a few challenges to those who may still cling to the laboratory as the most valid metaphor for education research. These challenges might also be useful to those who wish to confront that unenlightened view when it surfaces.

Challenge 1: What experimental research negates the findings of the nationwide first-grade studies conducted in the 1960s? Has there been research or is there something different about classrooms and instructional interventions today that call into question Bond and Dykstra's (1967) conclusions that contextual factors are more important than method or approach? As they stated, "Reading programs are not equally effective in all situations . . . factors other than method . . . influence pupil success in reading . . ." (p. 415). That interpretation actually holds as recently as the disappointing results of the equally massive data collection reported in the Reading First impact studies (Gamse, Jacob, Horst, Boulay, & Unlu, 2009).

Challenge 2: The second challenge relates to what might be referred to as *the tyranny of statistical averages.* I will give two examples. First, David Pearson (2007) has pointed out that the study of an experimental researcher's dreams is when everyone in the experimental group outperforms everyone in the control group (i.e., disjoint, non-overlapping distributions). However, in reality the distributions of treatment and control groups always overlap even when means are statistically different. In that typical case, many students do equally well in the treatment and control conditions and both may represent reasonable choices depending on the situation. Taking Pearson's point one step further: Not only do distributions typically overlap, but it is common for some students to do better in the control condition and some to do worse in the treatment condition when the distributions are skewed, as they often are. What are teachers supposed to do with those students? Or, how does knowing what works well on average inform teachers who have a whole class of students on the fringes of some statistical distribution?

A second example of the tyranny of statistics is *Simpson's Paradox*. This paradox is a little known, but not uncommon, statistical phenomenon that calls into question almost any conclusions based on statistical averages, especially when multiple variables are likely to affect outcomes. It is illustrated in Table 1, which shows the breakdown of imaginary, but not far-fetched, results from a medical experiment reporting the effects of an experimental drug on a group of patients. The box showing combined results for males and female patients (n = 80) suggests that the experimental drug was more effective than no treatment. However, when the same data for the same patients are broken down by gender, as shown in the second and third boxes, the no-treatment condition produced higher recovery rates for both males (n = 40) and for females (n = 40).

The results have been interpreted facetiously to suggest that a doctor who does not know the gender of a patient should expect better results than if gender is known. Simpson's paradox has reversed conclusions in how to treat kidney stones when the data are broken down by small or large stones, in sex discrimination cases at a major university that showed overall bias favoring males but none by any individual department, and in rating two baseball players, one of whom had a higher batting average than another player for two consecutive seasons but a lower average across both seasons. Experimental studies not only have confounding or nuisance variables, they have what have been called lurking variables that can reverse conclusions entirely depending on how aggregate data are parsed (for a portal to understanding Simpson's paradox and these findings see: http://en.wikipedia.org/wiki/Simpsons_paradox).

The third challenge is to follow in the footsteps of your elders. Several highly respected researchers in our field with impeccable credentials as experimentalists have come to the enlightened conclusion that a laboratory approach is ill suited to working in classrooms. For example, the late Ann Brown (1992; Brown

Table 1. Imaginary Results from an Experiment Testing the Effectiveness of an Experimental Drug on Recovery Rates

	Recovery	No Recovery	N	Recovery Rate
Combined Group (male and female)				
Drug	20	20	40	50%
No Drug	16	24	40	40%
Total	36	44	80	
Males Only				
Drug	18	12	30	60%
No Drug	7	3	10	70%
Total	25	15	40	
Females Only				
Drug	2	8	10	20%
No Drug	9	21	30	30%
Total	11	29	40	

& Campione, 1996) conducted laboratory-inspired research to explore the role of meta-cognition during reading comprehension. But, she abandoned those methods when she attempted to translate her laboratory findings into workable instruction in classrooms. Likewise, Michael Pressley in his final publication before his untimely passing (Pressley, Graham, & Harris, 2006) argued that we need classroom intervention research that attends to multiple theoretical perspectives, variables, and outcomes; that investigates processes across years; that uses methods that accommodate interacting variables and cross-case qualitative data; and that communicate results in a way that is useful to practitioners. At best, the laboratory metaphor works against these characteristics.

The Lens Metaphor

The lens emerged as an alternative metaphor in the early 1990s amidst tumultuous debate about whether naturalistic methods were a valid way to conduct literacy research. Some NRC members resolved that issue by voting with their feet when they formed the Society for the Scientific Study of Reading. Their allegiance to the laboratory metaphor could not be compromised. The primary entailment of the lens metaphor is that what we research, what observations we attend to, and ultimately what conclusions we draw are subjective and ideologically driven and filtered through whatever lens we use to interpret the world.

The lens metaphor offsets many of the limitations of the laboratory metaphor. Specifically, it emphasizes the inherent complexity of contexts for teaching and learning and moves us beyond perseverating on measurable achievement. Thus, inherently it offers more potential to inform practitioners and to close the gap between research and practice.

But, the lens metaphor has a fundamental limitation. Behind a lens is essentially a passive, if not ideologically neutral, observer and analyzer. The lens metaphor suggests looking studiously at interesting and complex phenomena without any specific imperative to transform what is being observed and analyzed. Research using the lens metaphor can sensitize practitioners to sometimes hidden issues and to deeper understandings affecting their practice. But it does not inherently inspire research that provides explicit guidance for day-to-day practice.

In short, the lens metaphor has no imperative for engaging in constructive action. In fact, discursive analyses and mountains of intriguing data may create what the famous sociologist Paul Lazarsfeld (1948) called a *narcotizing dysfunction* where deep and pervasive knowledge of social problems vicariously substitutes for doing something about them. Further, the theoretical underpinnings of the lens metaphor invite philosophizing and social analysis rather than action. In that regard, I believe we need a lot less Jacques Derrida and much more of pragmatic post-modernism such as that expressed by the Richard Rorty stance (as cited in Linn, 1996):

> [According to Rorty] what is needed isn't . . . reformers who pride themselves in being a proper post-modern . . . what is needed are reformers who can create a job program for kids growing up in the ghetto (p. 42).

If the curse of the laboratory metaphor is a failure to recognize and contend with the complex interacting factors operating in real classrooms, the curse of the lens metaphor is that it passively allows us to wallow in them. The result, more precisely the lack of results, is the same.

Some New Metaphors

Are there other metaphors that move us beyond the limitations of the laboratory and lens? I think so. I offer three ancillary metaphors and then an overarching one that I believe should equal the laboratory and lens in importance. None of these metaphors require new methods of data collection and analysis, only a repurposing of those methods within new metaphorical frames.

Chefs, not cooks. First, if our work is to influence practice, it may be important to have appropriate metaphors for our audience. A metaphorical distinction that I find useful is between teachers as cooks or chefs. That metaphor was inspired by a common complaint that pre-service teachers often want recipes for success. I try to convince them that their goal should not be to become a cook following recipes, but eventually a master chef who combines good ingredients into innovative and pleasing gourmet dishes often made from local ingredients. In fact, our colleagues in science education actually have a competition that uses that metaphor modeled after the televised iron chef competitions, where top chefs are challenged to create a gourmet meal built around a key ingredient. In the science education version, small teams of teachers compete to create the most interesting and effective lessons on a topic given a few objects. What if we framed our research as informing creative chefs rather than cooks who follow recipes? It might negate, for example, playing the research card and overselling the results of our research as prescriptions.

Ecology. Another supportive metaphor is ecology. It is not entirely new. Ecological validity has always been part of our research lexicon, but typically as only a potential foil to experimental validity. However, what if we framed our forays into classrooms as ecological expeditions and the introduction of new perspectives and activities as having ecological repercussions? An ecological metaphor would constantly remind us of the many complex interacting variables in classrooms.

Evolution. Evolution is a complementary, and offsetting, metaphor to ecology. Although ecosystems are complex and sometimes fragile, evolution reminds us that life forms have developed mechanisms to ensure they can adapt and survive. Thus, initiating new perspectives and activities into classrooms may be met with resistance to preserve the existing order. Educational practices and policies at all levels are the product of unique and powerful evolutionary forces designed to sustain their survival in the face of changing conditions.

For example, Chip Bruce and Andee Rubin (1993) experienced that reality in their long-term efforts to integrate a computer application they called QUILL into classrooms. QUILL was designed to engage students in more authentic purposes for reading and writing. To their dismay, teachers benignly subverted that intent by employing QUILL to address more conventional academic goals such as improving grammar and punctuation. The status quo resists change and evolution is slow and incremental. There really are no quick fixes. Authentic change typically occurs only after extended periods of trial and error.

Engineering. Finally, I propose engineering as a dominant, overarching new metaphor that I believe should stand shoulder-to-shoulder with the laboratory and lens, perhaps even subsuming them. Engineering, too, is not an entirely new metaphor as illustrated by the following quotes:

> The study of how educational interventions work can never be far removed from the task of engineering them to work better (Newman, Griffin, & Cole, 1989, p. 147).

Educational research often sits in the uneasy intersection between science and engineering (Feurer, Towne, & Shavelson, 2002, p. 28).

Some have even proposed that education research, more literally, should be considered an engineering science instead of a social science. As Figure 1 shows, Stokes (1997) framed the issue a bit differently. He created four quadrants based on whether the emphasis of research was on fundamental understanding or a consideration of use. He argued that the quadrant most often advancing scientific understanding was the one that focused simultaneously on both. He named that quadrant after Louis Pasteur, whose efforts to preserve food, led him to deep understandings of microorganisms and thus to found the field of microbiology.

Figure 1. Quadrant Model of Scientific Research

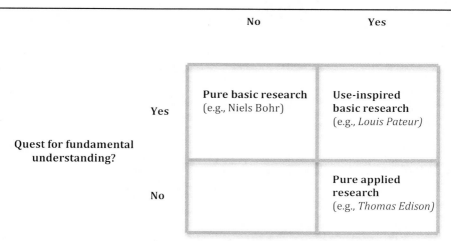

Adapted from: Stokes, D. E. (1997). *Pasteur's quadrant: Basic science and technological innovation.* Washington, DC: Brookings Institution.

Other examples illustrate that the engineering metaphor means more than simply solving problems or building things that work. For example, theoretical understanding of flight was known since Bernoulli almost 175 years before the Wright brothers. But, their genius was creating a workable flying machine with three-axis control, eventually creating the new field of aerodynamics. As Schoenfeld (2006) points out, there is a reciprocal relation between trying to build or improve something and to understanding it.

The following highlight some of the entailments of the engineering metaphor that might bring new purpose to our work and increase its influence:

- *Action* (engineering is a verb)
- *Explicit goals/ends* (presumably that better the world)
- Attention to *interacting variables in multiple contexts*
- Use of *whatever data are useful* (begs methodological debates)
- *Pragmatic stance* (begs epistemological debates)

- *Multiple solutions to the same problem* (negates the fallacy of best practice)
- *Tests and develops theory in practice*
- Employs *multidisciplinary expertise and collaboration*

Taken together, these entailments would have several other benefits. Here are a few examples:

- *Opens up new perspectives and issues for research.* For example, engineers must identify thresholds of failure. In designing a bridge an engineer must ensure that there are no conceivable conditions that would exceed its threshold of failure. Perhaps our research should specify thresholds of failure, or to use a medical metaphor, dangerous dosages and interactions?
- *Narrows the gap between research and practice.* Conducting research as engineering reasonable solutions to problems in authentic contexts is exactly what practitioners do, albeit less systematically than researchers.
- *Addresses simultaneously all major areas of education research.* According to Lagemann (2008) there are three major areas of education research: problem finding, problem solving, and translational research, but especially the latter, which she argued has been virtually absent from our research and which explains, in part, the gap between research and practice.

AN APPROACH CONSISTENT WITH NEW METAPHORS

There is a relatively new approach to research that draws on these new metaphors, particularly the engineering metaphor. It goes by many names such as *design experiments, design studies, teaching experiments, lesson studies,* or *formative experiments.* These specific variations are often subsumed by several umbrella terms such as *design-based research, design research, developmental research, and educational design research,* all of which clearly connect with the engineering metaphor. Some LRA members whose work is influenced by this approach include my frequent collaborator Barbara Bradley, Jim Baumann, Erica Boling, Karen Broadus, Susan Neuman, Doug Fisher, Nancy Frey, Robert Jiménez, Gay Ivey, Susan Lenski, Vickie Purcell-Gates, and Anna Taboada.

That approach can be understood by comparing it to experimental and naturalistic approaches. For example, experimental research uses quantitative methods and typically asks which among several competing practices *What intervention is best, on average?* Naturalistic studies use qualitative methods and ask what happens when a practice occurs, or, more simply, *What is?* Design-based research asks a different question using qualitative or mixed methods: What is necessary to allow a practice to achieve a valued goal or simply *What could be, and how do we get there?*

Put another way, imagine responses from three doctoral students who are asked what methodology they will use in their dissertation research. One traditional response is "Quantitative (or qualitative) methods because it is consistent with my world view." A second response is "Qualitative or quantitative methods depending on my question." A third, and new, response would be "Design-based research because I want to implement and understand (theoretically) an intervention that has potential to help educators achieve a valued pedagogical goal."

A defining difference, then, is that this approach, like an engineering project, originates with an explicitly stated goal—one that is valued and useful, and justifiably has potential to directly enhance wellbeing. Among several models available for conducting design research is the one I have used in my own research. It goes essentially something like this: Identify a valued pedagogical goal, justify its value, identify an intervention that has potential to accomplish the goal, implement it, modify it while gathering and analyzing data to address the following generic questions:

- What factors enhance or inhibit achievement of goal?
- In light of those factors, what modifications are useful or necessary?
- Is the environment transformed in any way?
- What are the unanticipated collateral effects (positive or negative)?
- What are the key ingredients of success or failure?
- What pedagogical theories are supported or negated?

As shown in Figure 2, data are collected and analyzed to inform cyclical modifications of the intervention. Mini-cycles occur almost daily, whereas macro-cycles occur over longer periods,

Figure 2. Data Collection, Modification, and Theory Development in Design-Based Research

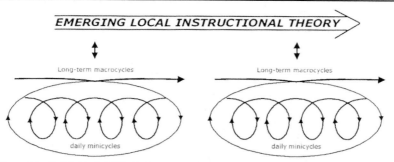

From. Gravemiejer, K., & Cobb, P. (2006). Design research from a learning design perspective. In J. Van den Akker, K. Gravemeijer, S. McKenney, & N. Nieveen (Eds.), *Educational design research* (pp. 17-51). New York, NY: Routledge.

perhaps across investigations.

The product developed is an intervention with general design specifications suggesting the key ingredients for success or failure in achieving a valued goal in specific contexts as well as across contexts. However, another product is a deep theoretical understanding of the processes and outcomes in terms of ecology and evolution. All forms of data collection and analysis that inform that process are considered and used.

In summary, design research is an approach that aims to:

- *achieve valued goals* by . . .
- *flexibly designing workable interventions* guided by . . .
- *systematic data collection* that enables . . .
- *testing, refining, and developing pedagogical theory*
- *in the crucible of authentic practice.*

I believe it is worth noting that it is the only approach to education research that originated within the field of education. All of our other approaches to research and the metaphors that sustain them are borrowed from other fields or disciplines.

MOVING FURTHER BEYOND THE LABORATORY AND THE LENS

However, new metaphors can move us beyond simply considering new approaches to research. Here are a few examples of how they might more generally influence our work:

- We could adopt what Messick (1992) referred to as consequential validity. Again, borrowing from my colleague Tom Reeves, we might replace or supplement Institutional Review Board (IRB) approvals for our research projects with an HBRB: Human Benefits Review Board. To pass the HBRB review, projects would have to explicitly specify how the proposed work would benefit people's wellbeing.
- Similarly, we might expect every published account of our research to begin with an explicit justification of its contribution to creating a better world.
- We might insist that at least one reviewer of our manuscripts be a practitioner and charge that reviewer with evaluating consequential validity. Might we invite practitioners to comment on our published work, as is becoming more common in digital publications? Such moves, which are relatively easy to implement, would, I believe, move us quickly in the direction of new metaphors and greater resolve to make a difference.
- What if LRA took a stance rejecting the premises of the "What Works Clearinghouse" advocating instead for a "What it Takes to Work Clearinghouse"? In fact, that is the recommendation of a recent working paper from the Harvard Kennedy School of Government (Smyth & Schorr, 2009). It argues that financial cutbacks have promoted more calls for accountability in social programs where only those programs showing statistical superiority on average are funded. The outcome is the cancellation of many programs that are highly effective in specific contexts even though they are below the overall mean.
- If we are going to continue to use medical metaphors, why not include Bulterman-Bos' (2008) suggestion that we follow the lead of medical researchers at research hospitals. They see patients, which keeps their research grounded in the reality of practice and people's lives. My hero in that regard is Jim Baumann; I was his department head many years ago. I recall the day he walked into my office asking me to support his decision to exchange places for one year with a second-grade teacher in a local school.

SUMMARY AND CONCLUDING REMARKS

Finally, to summarize my main points:

- Improving human wellbeing is the central imperative of education research. The deep humanitarian commitment to bettering the world that is so evident in LRA should be the reservoir from which all of our efforts emanate.

- But, our work has been marginally effective and inefficient in meeting that imperative, as evidenced by the perennial divide between research and practice and our ambivalence about the extent to which our work provides a useful base for bettering the world.

- Drawing on Lakoff and Johnson's (1980) work, I have pointed out that metaphors are pervasive elements of language and thought that influence our views, perceptions, interpretations, and actions, and that shape our identities as researchers.

- For literacy researchers the prominent metaphors are the laboratory and lens. These metaphors are not particularly well suited to furthering the central imperative of our work. The laboratory metaphor insulates us from the messiness of the real world and from the complex interacting variables that influence success or failure. The lens metaphor invites a passive observational stance that has no imperative for constructive change and that promotes abstract understanding and conclusions over concrete improvements.

- I proposed several alternate metaphors that promote instead the pursuit of valued goals in authentic contexts to gain useful understanding. Seeing the beneficiaries of our research as chefs, not cooks, helps put our research into proper perspective. Ecology and evolution remind us of the complex challenges we face, keep us humble about our work, and inspire more reasonable expectations and time frames for making a difference. Engineering opens up new ways to approach our work based on the idea that deeper understanding is developed through constructive action to achieve valued goals.

- My central argument is that our established metaphors too easily dismiss us from accountability to make a difference and do little to inspire a fervent resolve to do so. Instead, they invite a shallower focus on our next publication, our next conference presentation, or our next grant proposal. Adopting new metaphors may help us break free from a cycle of inconsequentiality and to reframe and repurpose our work without necessarily giving up our research interests, our methodologies, theoretical perspectives, and all the research activities to which we are accustomed.

So, I come to the end of my brief moment in a long history of presidential addresses. I sincerely hope that I have not unnecessarily offended any sensitivities or unintentionally denigrated anyone's research, let alone tarnished NRC/LRA's illustrious history about which there is much to be proud in this year of our 60th anniversary. At the same time, I hope I have convinced you that it behooves all of us at this historic juncture to take stock honestly of what we have and what we have not accomplished in making the world a better place, and what we want to accomplish in the next decade and beyond.

If my perspectives are wrong, misguided, off base, overstated, or all of the above, I take comfort in the advice I give to my doctoral students. I tell them that their obligation as scholars is not to always be right. On the contrary, they should expect that they will occasionally, if not often, be dead wrong, and if they never experience that sensation, they are not paying attention, not reflecting, not listening to their colleagues, or worse, engaging in demagoguery. Their only obligation, if they are wrong, is to be wrong in informed and interesting ways. The spirit of NRC in the past and I hope of LRA in the future has been an open forum for new ideas and perspectives, collegial dialogue and, when necessary, collegial correction. I hope my talk today has reflected that spirit and that it will generate responses from you, my colleagues, in the same spirit. I look forward to having the opportunity to engage in that dialog during our next few days together and beyond.

REFERENCES

Ayres, W. (2006). Trudge toward freedom: Educational research in the public interest. In G. Ladson-Billings & W. R. Tate (Eds.) *Education research in the public interest* (pp. 81-97). New York, NY: Teachers College Press.

Bond, G. L., & Dykstra, R. (1997 reprint of 1967 original). The cooperative research program in first-grade reading instruction. *Reading Research Quarterly, 32,* 348-427.

Brown, A. L. (1992). Design experiments: Theoretical and methodological challenges in creating complex interventions in classroom settings. *Journal of Learning Sciences, 2*(2), 141-178.

Brown, A. L., & Campione, J. C. (1996). Psychological theory and the design of innovative learning environments: On procedures, principles, and systems. In R. Glaser (Ed.), *Innovations in learning: New environments for education* (pp. 289-325). Mahwah, NJ: Erlbaum.

Bruce, B. C., & Rubin, A. (1993). Electronic quills: A situated evaluation of using computers for classroom writing. Hillsdale, NJ: Erlbaum.

Bulterman-Bos, J. A. (2008). Will a clinical approach make education research more relevant for practice? *Educational Researcher, 37*(7), 412-420.

Dillon, D. R., O'Brien, D. G., & Heilman, E. E. (2000). Literacy research in the next millennium: From paradigms to pragmatism and practicality. *Reading Research Quarterly, 35,* 10-26.

Duffy, G. G. (1994). How teachers think of themselves: A key to mindfulness. In J. N. Mangieri & C. Collins (Eds.), *Creating powerful thinking in teachers and students: Diverse Perspectives* (pp. 3-25). Fort Worth, TX: Harper Collins

Feuer, M. J., Towne, L., & Shavelson, R. J. (2002). Reply to commentators on "Scientific Culture and Educational Research." *Educational Researcher, 31*(8), 28-29.

Gamse, B. C., Jacob, R. T., Horst, M., Boulay, B., & Unlu, F. (2009). *Reading First Impact Study. Final Report. NCEE 2009-4038.* National Center for Education Evaluation and Regional Assistance. Accessed March 27, 2011 from http://www.eric.ed.gov/ERICWebPortal/search/detailmini. jsp?_nfpb=true&_&ERICExtSearch_SearchValue_0=ED503344&ERICExtSearch_ SearchType_0=no&accno=ED503344.

Glass, G. V. (2008). *Fertilizers, pills, and magnetic strips: The fate of public education in America.* Charlotte, NC: Information Age Publishing.

Hattie, J. A. C. (2009). *Visible learning: A synthesis of over 800 meta-analyses relating to achievement.* London, UK: Routledge.

Hostetler, K. (2005). What is "good" education research? *Educational Researcher 34*(6), 16-21.

Labaree, D. (1998). Educational researchers: Living with a lesser form of knowledge. *Educational Researcher, 27*(8), 4-12.

Labaree, D. F. (2003). The peculiar problems of preparing educational researchers. *Educational Researcher, 32*(4), 13-22.

Lagemann, E. C. (2008). Comments on Bulterman-Bos: Education research as a distributed activity across universities. *Educational Researcher, 37*(7), 424-428.

Lakoff, G., & Johnson, M. (1980). *Metaphors we live by.* Chicago, IL: University of Chicago Press.

Lazarsfeld, P. F., & Merton, R. K. (1948). Mass media, popular taste, and social action. In L. Bryson (Ed.), *The communication of ideas.* New York, NY: Harper Brothers. Also available in Marris, P. (Ed.) (2000). *Media studies: A reader* (pp. 18-30). New York, NY: New York University Press.

Leu, D. (2006). New literacies, reading research, and the challenges of change: A deictic perspective. J. V. Hoffman, D. Schallert, C. M. Fairbanks, J. Worthy, & B. Maloch (Eds.), *55th Yearbook of the National Reading Conference,* Milwaukee, WI: National Reading Conference.

Linn, R. (1996). *A teachers introduction to post-modernism.* Urbana, IL: National Council of Teachers of English.

Messick, S. (1992). The interplay of evidence and consequences in the validation of performance assessments. *Educational Researcher, 23*(2), 13-23.

Newman, D., Griffin, P., & Cole, M. (1989). *The construction zone: Working for cognitive change in school.* Cambridge, UK: Cambridge University Press.

Pearson, P. D. (2007). An endangered species act for literacy education. *Journal of Literacy Research, 39*, 145-162

Pressley, M., Graham, S., & Harris, K. (2006). The state of educational intervention research as viewed through the lens of literacy intervention. *British Journal of Educational Psychology, 76*, 1-19.

Reeves, T. (2006). Design research from a technology perspective. In J. Van den Akker, K. Gravemeijer, S. McKenney, & N. Nieveen (Eds.), *Educational design research* (pp. 52-66). New York, NY: Routledge.

Reeves, T. Herrington, J., & Oliver, R. (2005). Design research: A socially responsible approach to instructional technology research in higher education. *Journal of Computing in Higher Education, 16*, 97-116.

Reinking, D. (2007). Toward a good or better understanding of best practice. *Journal of Curriculum and Instruction.* Accessed November 2, 2010 from http://www.joci.ecu.edu/index.php/JoCI/issue/view/1

Schoenfeld, A. H. (2006). Design experiments. In J. L. Green, G. Camilli, P. B. Elmore, A. Skukauskaite, & E. Grace (Eds.), *Handbook of complementary methods in education research* (pp. 193 – 205). Mahwah, NJ: Lawrence Erlbaum.

Smyth, K. F., & Schorr, L. B., (2009). A lot to lose: A call to rethink what constitutes "evidence" in finding social interventions that work. Working paper of the Michael Wiener Center for Social Policy, Harvard John F. Kennedy School of Government, Accessed March 29, 2011 from www.hks.harvard.edu/socpol/publications_main.html

Stokes, D. E. (1997). *Pasteurs's quadrant.* Washington, DC: Brookings Institution Press.

Assessing with Integrity in the Face of High-Stakes Testing

Lorrie A. Shepard
University of Colorado Boulder

It is a great sadness that "assessing with integrity in the face of high-stakes testing" is a necessary consideration these days and requires both a conscious commitment and considerable skill on the part of teachers. The perspective I offer in this paper considers findings from a recent research project that examined how teachers use interim or benchmark assessments (Shepard, Davidson, & Bowman, 2011) within the larger context of education reform policies. I begin with a historical review of competing theories underlying standards-based reforms. Although they shared the same rhetoric, these conflicting theories of action about how the reforms were expected to work anticipate similarly dissonant theories motivating the use of interim assessments today. In the middle section of the paper, I summarize the research literatures on formative assessment and data-based decision-making, which offer quite different portrayals of assessment and its role in improving teaching and learning. Lastly, I acknowledge what I learned from literacy colleagues early on and consider what other fields might learn from the cultural practices in literacy that create more thoughtful contexts for assessment. At the same time, we should ask how the issues raised here might prompt the literacy community to further deepen some of those practices.

COMPETING THEORIES UNDERLYING STANDARDS-BASED REFORMS

To reprise, the standards movement is more than 20 years old (Goals 2000: Educate America Act, National Council of Teachers of Mathematics, 1989; Resnick & Resnick, 1992; Smith & O'Day, 1990). Listening to the talk from policymakers today, you'd think they'd just invented it, but they're actually using slogans and phrases from two decades ago. I might have picked any one of a number of policy reports to remind you of some of the salient points in that discourse. For example, the report of the National Council on Education Standards and Testing (1992), *Raising Standards for American Education*, identified the main aim of the standards movement, which was to reject and unseat the de facto, low-level, basic skills curriculum driven by textbooks and standardized tests. To accomplish this, states were advised to:

- Establish challenging standards aimed at higher-order thinking and problem-solving;
- Link standards to high-quality assessments; and
- Invest in "capacity-building" or "delivery standards" to ensure opportunity to learn.

At that time and still, I have not been a big fan of standards-based reform, mostly because the sloganeering promises too much, and invariably there is harm when the system can't live up to the rhetoric behind its mandates. Nonetheless, I agreed in the early 1990s to join a Panel of the National Academy of Education convened to examine the knowledge base that might be used to set directions for the standards reform effort (McLaughlin & Shepard, 1995). While urging caution, we pointed to findings from cognitive science research that supported the standards movement. And, we said some congratulatory things about the science underpinning the claim that "all children can learn" and attain high standards *if and when* they are provided with enriching learning opportunities heretofore reserved for only an elite track of students. Fundamental shifts in theories of learning were at the core of what some advocates were claiming for standards-based reform. Literacy researchers remember well that in the early 1990s there were new understandings about the nature of expertise and what it means to know in each of the disciplines, a still relatively new understanding of how thinking and reasoning abilities are developed (not just what one is born with), and an effort to apply these findings to support classroom practices that foster deep learning and subject matter mastery.

How People Learn (Bransford, Brown, & Cocking, 1999) is the sacred text that tells the stories and codifies these revelations from the cognitive revolution. Although the major findings set forth—such as the importance of prior knowledge in supporting new learning—are quite familiar, it is helpful to be reminded of several of the key principles:

- Learning with understanding is facilitated when new and existing knowledge is structured around major concepts and principles of the discipline.
- Learners use what they already know to construct new understandings.
- Metacognitive strategies and self-regulatory abilities facilitate learning.
- Learners' motivation to learn and sense of self affect what is learned.
- Participation in social practice is the fundamental way of learning.

We will want to consider the implications of these core principles about learning as we take up the use of assessment in classrooms, with special attention to the last of these principles focused on the sociocultural aspects of learning.

To illustrate how enormously different classroom interactions would need to be if they were responsive to findings from learning research, let me cite just one article from the many hundreds of studies summarized in *How People Learn*. Collins, Brown, and Newman (1989) proposed a "cognitive apprenticeship" model for classroom learning that was intended to overcome the decontextualized and inert ways that school knowledge is presented, which not surprisingly leads students to rely on formulaic problem solutions. It is a small wonder that students have difficulty applying what they have learned, given that what they are asked to learn has been removed from contexts of use and purpose. By contrast, when researchers study learning in apprenticeships, they note that the processes of mature practice are visible and shared. Even when the novice is completing only a part of the task, purpose and contribution to the whole are still evidenced. Building on this idea, Collins et al. proposed a cognitive apprenticeship model to transform classroom interactions. Abstract tasks should be situated in authentic contexts so that students can understand the relevance of the work; and student and teacher thinking processes must be deliberately brought to the surface to "make thinking visible."

In our report to policymakers about how they should think about standards-based reform, McLaughlin and Shepard (1995) acknowledged the scientific basis for the slogan, "All children can learn," based on countless studies like Collins et al. (1989) available to us in 1995 and later cumulated in *How People Learn*. We affirmed that claim as an important scholarly rejection of a century of believing that only certain kids could learn: "The slogan, 'high standards for all students' is fundamentally a refutation of…current educational practices…still rooted in 100-year-old-beliefs about the fixed and permanent nature of human abilities" (p. 11). Bringing to the fore the research base showing how abilities are supported and developed is critically important in helping policy leaders and the public understand how schooling typically limits opportunity, especially when it is focused on rote drill and practice, and helps to illustrate what schooling with the right opportunities and experiences could accomplish.

The National Academy of Education Panel also cautioned, however, that this was an unprecedented task, and the claim that the quality education heretofore reserved for the elite 20% was now going to be—presto!—delivered to everyone was unrealistic (McLaughlin & Shepard, 1995). We said this was a good and ambitious thing to try, but just setting high standards would not, by the miracle of high expectations, make it happen. In outlining the scholarly basis for what people were hoping to accomplish, our emphasis was on capacity-building (p. 15):

> Standards-based reform attempts to raise expectations for students throughout the system while eliminating current inequalities—all at a time when demographic shifts and declining financial support present increasing challenges for already stretched school resources and personnel. This would be a monumental goal even if the proposed content and instructional approaches were familiar to teachers and parents, and educators were prepared for the work involved in realizing them.

We reiterated that a cautious, "learn-as-you-go" approach was warranted, as long as there was adequate attention to building the capacity of the system and to on-going research and evaluation. But, there is little indication that these warnings were heeded.

While part of this paper is about understanding the theory behind reforms, it is equally important to come to an understanding of how reforms go awry. Of course, it's a problem when a reform is straightforwardly attacked. But direct attacks are not why standards-based reforms are defeated, and it's not why they have not as yet brought equity and excellence to all of our public schools. Reforms are defeated because participants do not all have the same deep understanding of the research-based arguments offered above. In fact, educators and political actors held competing theories of action about how all this was going to happen despite sharing the same rhetoric about high standards. Competing visions and superficial understandings created quite a mess in how these things played out—most especially by removing the implication that new resources would be needed to achieve the promised outcomes.

Writing for the National Research Council Committee on Title I Testing and Assessment, Elmore and Rothman (1999), called out the competing visions for reform that were evident early on in two different pieces of legislation, both passed in 1994. As represented in Figure 1, the Goals 2000: Educate America Act emphasized coherent capacity-building at all levels of the education system. So, yes, you can set high standards and, yes, you can have this idea about assessment and instruction that should be different, but it was also understood that significant effort would be required to provide professional development for teachers who would need to learn to teach in fundamentally different ways. The opposite or contending theory, characterized by a belief in incentives as the primary instruments of reform, was established in the 1994 Elementary and Secondary Education Act. Incentivizers believed that if we just create sufficient rewards and punishments, educators would figure it out. Teachers would see that they're not reaching standards. They would know that it matters, and so they would try harder, or they would ask a colleague for help, etc. The incentive theory has predominated in the discourse of test-based accountability for the past two decades and continues to permeate present-day calls for reform.

Figure 1. Two Models for the Theory of Action of Standards-Based Reform from Elmore and Rothman (1999). The expanded model adds teacher professional development and improved teaching as mediating variables

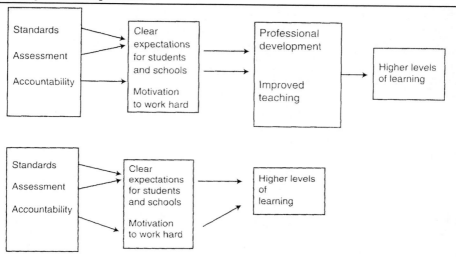

Note: Reprinted with permission from the National Academies Press, Copyright 1999, National Academies of Sciences.

The problem with the incentive theory of change was already evident to the Title I Committee (Elmore & Rothman, 1999) and has since been borne out by much more extensive studies of the effects of test-based accountability. It is a story of the rich getting richer and the poor getting poorer. For example, in examining the impacts of high-stakes testing in four states, Elmore (2003) and colleagues (Carnoy, Elmore, & Siskin, 2003) found evidence of increased sanctions but no infusions of professional development for teachers or principals. As a result, better-situated schools serving higher socioeconomic neighborhoods were more able to respond coherently to external accountability pressures. In schools that already had a good deal of knowledge and talent, and what Carnoy et al. called internal structures of coherence and accountability, educators were able to reconfigure and refocus their efforts to take those next steps. The problem is that the low-performing schools, at whom accountability legislation is directed, scurry but do not have the resources to figure out how to solve the problem. So, one of the themes that I hope you will hear now as we turn to trying to make sense of these issues, specifically as they relate to assessment, is that if the structure does not attend to substance, we cannot ensure that deep substantive work gets done. And, we have to worry about contending theories of action in the case of assessment as well.

ZONE OF PROXIMAL DEVELOPMENT VERSUS DATA-BASED DECISION-MAKING (ZPD VERSUS DBDM)

In this section, I examine the widespread use of interim assessments, which have proliferated since No Child Left Behind (NCLB). Although a bit of an oversimplification, it is helpful for the sake of argument to draw sharp contrasts between the competing theories of formative assessment, as represented in the work of Black and Wiliam (1998), versus data-based decision-making, which is more compatible with incentive theories of change. Elsewhere (Shepard, 2008b), I have offered a more balanced view of how interim or benchmark assessments might be used "formatively" for program evaluation, while still arguing that they cannot meet the interactive and self-regulation features of "real" formative assessment called for in the research literature.

The term "formative" as it is now used in formative assessment comes from Michael Scriven's (1967) distinction between formative and summative program evaluation. Bloom, Hastings, and Madaus (1971) adapted the term to apply to formative tests to be used as part of mastery learning, but given a behavioristic view of subject matter, their tests and learning materials could look quite similar to each other (Shepard, 1991). The term took on a different meaning when in 1989, Royce Sadler began talking about formative assessment the way I and a number of international colleagues understand it. Although Sadler used Ramaprasad's (1983) rather mechanical definition of feedback (identify a goal, assess where you are in relation to the goal, and use the information to close the gap), Sadler imbued the process of assessment and feedback with a much more substantive purpose, emphasizing both a shared understanding of learning goals between teacher and student and ultimately sufficient internalization of excellence criteria for a student to be able to self-monitor. Sadler had not heard of Vygotsky (1978), but I've argued that the mediation he described is entirely in keeping with the zone of proximal development and instructional scaffolding (Shepard, 2005). A shared understanding and ownership of the learning goal, support in reaching the goal, a sense of social purpose in recognizing the value of the goal, internalization, and taking over of responsibility by the learner are all closely parallel features of formative assessment and Bruner's (1975) conception of scaffolding.

Importantly, Sadler (1989) never used words like "developing identities of mastery (Lave & Wenger, 1991, p. 41)," but he talked in a very sociocultural way, bringing together cognitive and motivational aspects of learning that psychologists had kept separated for easily 50 or 100 years. Here I'm grateful to Resnick and Klopfer (1989) for suggesting that findings regarding metacognition forced learning researchers to recognize that motivation matters. And motivation is much more than just wanting to do well. Motivation to learn involves taking on an identity of mature and competent participation, which is what we have come to understand from a sociocultural theoretical perspective, so ably described by Lave and Wenger (1991). Taking on an identity of mastery occurs as learners participate in a community of practice.

From the vantage point of learning research today, we can see how specific cognitive science findings relevant to formative assessment can be embedded and interpreted in the context of a more encompassing sociocultural theory. Now we can come back to prior knowledge, back to the strategic use of feedback, and back to our understandings of transfer according to which teachers assess first what students know and then for extensions—and see all of these as examples of classroom interaction patterns likely to support learning. Similarly, we can bring together both the metacognitive and the self-regulatory aspects of self-assessment, seeing the cognitive benefits of internalizing the features of quality work but also recognizing the importance of taking on responsibility, myself, for how I am doing as a learner. To foreshadow the next discussion about data-based decision-making, let me emphasize that this way of speaking about self-regulated learning is about the substance and purpose of becoming adept at a particular skill. It is *not* about knowing my score and knowing how many more points I need to achieve a passing proficiency score. This point is critically important. In fact, if I could leave you with only one thought from the argument in this paper, it is that formative uses of assessment must focus on the *substance* of content learning, not *scores*.

The origins of data-based decision-making (DBDM) are quite different from my portrayal of a substantively focused formative assessment model. DBDM comes from Edward Deming's (1986) total quality management business model, and is intended to be recursive in very productive ways. Continuously improving organizations require measures of quality, use evidence to identify problems, and innovate to improve. In educational settings, it is possible to blend key ideas from formative assessment and DBDM; indeed, the two research literatures overlap somewhat. Therefore, I admit it is an oversimplification to say that one is good and the other bad or that one is substantive and the other not. Nevertheless, it may be useful to make explicit heretofore hidden differences in assumptions, tools, and theories of action that somehow make it possible in our current education context for DBDM to sometimes be mechanistically carried out without attention to learning processes or content.

In principle, the DBDM model assumes that what's being asked of managers examining data in a business context should parallel what's being asked of teachers in an instructional context. Unfortunately, however, business data are more direct measures of productivity than education measures are of learning. Additionally, business managers may have fewer variables to consider when trying to identify and correct the causes of poor performance. As a consequence, generic steps for effective data use—such as Deming's *Plan, Do, Check, Act* (based on lessons learned)—may not automatically be effective in educational contexts. Because proponents of DBDM are often organizational theorists who think about schooling at higher levels of aggregation, their models are typically disconnected from specific curricula and content. For example, Halverson, Grigg, Prichett, and Thomas (2005) describe six component functions in their model for a data-driven instructional system: Data acquisition, data reflection, program alignment, program design, formative feedback, and test preparation. How these components are enacted, however, will vary tremendously from one school to the next depending on the professional resources in particular schools, just as Carnoy et al. (2003) described in the case of well-resourced schools responding differentially to accountability pressures.

In promoting a culture of improvement and a habit of inquiry, DBDM models typically encourage the use of professional and collaborative communities of practice. Yet, schools have to know *how* to do this to do it well. Thus, while it is impossible to quarrel with these ambitions, it is how these reform strategies are often instantiated that causes concern. Barriers to DBDM acknowledged in the literature include lack of technology, lack of professional development, and lack of leadership. To be fair, difficulties recognized in the literature about teachers knowing how to link data back to instructional decisions are also the Achilles' heel of real formative assessment. As Joan Herman and colleagues have found, who has undertaken both types of studies, even when teachers can draw substantive insights from formative assessments, what they least know how to do is to identify next instructional steps (Heritage, Kim, Vendlinski, & Herman, 2009). Interestingly, proponents of DBDM as a central means of organizing for school improvement had in mind initially that results from end-of-year summative tests would be studied to direct improvement efforts. With NCLB, however, DBDM became the mantra for the adoption and use of interim assessments, for which there is a very limited research base. Perie, Marion, and Gong (2009) defined *interim assessments* (also called *benchmark assessments*) as "medium-scale, medium-cycle assessments falling between summative and formative assessments and usually administered at the school or district level" (p. 6). An early set of studies examining the use of benchmark assessments in the School District of Philadelphia was published in spring 2010 in a special issue of the *Peabody Journal of Education*. While the researchers in these several articles documented that the benchmark assessment results were definitely being used, the reader is struck by the limited connections between assessment results and instruction. Only in one of the schools of many that were studied was there someone they dubbed a "star principal," who helped with the sense-making and enacted the use of the benchmark assessments in the way the interim assessment literature says that everyone should be doing it. In a parallel study of teacher interviews, only two of 25 teachers were able to link the assessment results to the substance of the curriculum. As summarized by Goren (2010) in his overview commentary, it is clearly not the case that districts can just deliver the assessment system and teachers and school leaders will be able to use it to improve instruction.

For my commentary at the end of the *Peabody* special issue, I tried to capture the troubling gist of the articles with the title, "What the Marketplace has Brought Us: Item-by-Item Teaching with Little Instructional Insight" (Shepard, 2010). In the worst case, teachers would use the printouts denoting which items each child had missed and would assign an aide or a student teacher to provide extra help. Although we can't know for sure, the inference here is that the instructional response of reteaching focused primarily on specific items as opposed to teaching the content from which the items derived. Other findings similarly suggested lack of substantive insights from test results. Bulkley, Christman, Goertz, and Lawrence (2010) focused on the role of the district, noting that district leaders assumed that teachers would be able to figure out what to do by looking at the data, talking with other teachers, and reflecting on their own needs for professional development. Blanc, Christman, Liu, Mitchell, Travers, and Bulkley (2010) found that high-stakes testing talk pervaded grade-level meetings, with a special focus on the "bubble kids" who performed near the cut score for proficiency. Reteaching was the most common response to class-wide poor performance, usually with the same instructional strategies. When alternative strategies were tried, they were not informed by the assessment results. In a separate interview study, involving 25 teachers across five elementary schools, Nabors Oláh, Lawrence, and Riggan (2010) concluded that teachers were not using benchmark results to learn about their students' conceptual understanding. Rather, they tended to see incorrect items as procedural missteps and accordingly responded by reteaching problem solutions step-by-step.

A similar story has emerged from the CRESST[1] project that Brian Stecher and I undertook along with a number of other colleagues. We planned an interview study, involving 30 teachers across seven districts in two states, taking special care to use a two-stage interview process because we wanted to be able to identify specific examples of what teachers were actually doing. In the first interview, on the phone, we asked the typical general questions about how teachers use interim assessment data. At the end of the first interview, we asked respondents to bring several examples to the second interview, which would be face-to-face in each teacher's classroom, "to show the different ways that interim assessments are used." A specific goal of the study was to document substance. We really wanted to know, "What did you learn about your students' learning from these assessments, and how did you use it in your instruction?"

Two themes arose. Teachers said they used interim assessments primarily to ensure mastery of standards and to prepare for state tests. At the second interview, they brought printouts that were the familiar grids of standards mastered and items missed. They did not bring substantive examples of what they learned about their students' thinking, even though, without leading respondents too much, a probe near the end of the first interview had asked, "What did you learn about your students' thinking?" When teachers said that assessment results prompted them to modify their teaching, their reasoning was much more quantitative than qualitative. They used profile summaries to identify relative weaknesses and addressed the problem by devoting more time to these standards. Rather than providing diagnostic insight about how to change the character of what was being taught or challenge a particular misconception, poor performance simply signaled that additional teaching was needed. If a different approach was taken, it was for the sake of trying something different rather than because assessment results had suggested a more effective course of action.

These findings were disappointing, especially because we had crafted the data collection approach to try to document examples of substantive insights. After finding so few examples that warranted an "insight" code, we went back through all the interview transcripts again, searching specifically for substantive insights, but still found few. Thirteen of 30 teachers had something we could say looked like a diagnostic insight, but their examples were procedural, "It'll tell you they multiplied by 5 when they were supposed to divide by 5," or they focused on test-taking skills and strategies, "I think this student needs to slow down and check his work."

Overall, it was difficult to give a fair rendition as to whether teachers liked their districts' interim assessments and what they were learning from them. More than half of the teachers interviewed gave largely positive answers, seeming to value the information provided by the assessments. At the same time, substantially more than half used the data very little if at all. This apparent contradiction can best be explained by the teachers in the middle who thought that the data were useful, but there was just too much information and not enough time.

To better describe the few teachers who had more fully integrated the use of interim assessment results in their practice, we developed teacher cases. These four "fulsome" cases were all from different districts, so there was no indication that these more complete repertoires of use were prompted either by properties of the assessment instrument itself or by professional development provided by the district. Even these more fulsome users, however, were consistent with previous themes regarding the kind of information gained and the nature of likely interventions. Meredith (a pseudonym) is an example. She said the district interim assessment "drives planning and instruction. I mean, we teach to the test." Teachers meet to review data together, plan, and suggest new instructional strategies "where kids are really lost." "I ask myself, did they just kind of screw up on the test, or do I need to spend more time on this?" Again, even for sophisticated users we see that "the interims" identify problems but do not provide solutions, and they do not provide insights about *why* a student is struggling with a particular concept or skill.

In my presidential address to the American Educational Research Association a decade ago (Shepard, 2000), I used the image of Darth Vader and the Death Star to signify the effects of high-stakes testing on teaching and learning. That image is appropriate again. In my view, NCLB-induced interim assessments are having the same narrowing and drill-and-practice effects as end-of-year tests have been shown to have, but now they're doing it much more persistently. And, if you look at the content and technical adequacy of these products, most are worse than typical state tests, which is not surprising given how many test items must be written and implemented by test publishers, typically without field testing.

The studies and summaries of the negative effects of high-stakes testing are myriad (Herman, 2008; Shepard, 2008a). Two predominant findings—test-score inflation and curriculum distortion—were already well documented in the 1992 report, *Testing in American Schools*, from the U. S. Congressional Office of Technology and Assessment. Even most policymakers and lay citizens are aware of the curriculum distortion that occurs when the consequences attached to reading and math scores cause neglect of science, social studies, world languages, art, music, physical education, and so forth. But test score inflation is associated with a less visible and potentially more debilitating type of curricular distortion that occurs as teaching strategies for reading and math come to imitate the tests more and more closely. These patterns are clearly exacerbated by "reteaching," which is reported to be the most frequent use of interim assessment results. Some of the time reteaching is surely conceptual with new approaches trying to get at the broad domain of the standards from which items were sampled. But to the extent that specific missed items become the target for instruction, the likelihood of inflationary effects is clear, meaning that test scores will go up without commensurate increases in real learning.

In addition, the emotional and socialization effects of a testing- and score-focused learning environment are much less well documented but certainly bear mentioning. Listening as teachers talk about test scores posted in the hallway and students' awareness that two more items correct will mean a proficient score, I am alarmed that students seemed to be receiving a distorted message about what learning is *for* and what skilled performance actually looks like. These concerns are reminiscent of Lave and Wenger's (1991) description of the commoditization of learning that occurs when what you are trying to learn is removed from its context of use, hence severing all of the connections that supply meaning and purpose and draw one into participation. I am reminded as well of a review of early reading inventories many years ago by Stallman and Pearson (1990), who analyzed, in addition to the distorting effects of multiple-choice formats and taking apart of reading into componential skills, the mistaken conception of literacy that 5-year-olds are likely to draw from the test-taking experience—keeping their marker straight, filling in bubbles, and so forth. It is odd that district proponents of interim assessments and data use frequently invoke *communities of practice* as a way that teachers might come together to make sense of assessment results (Davidson & Frohbieter, 2011), but the very learning theories from which communities of practice derive are ignored when considering what participation and socially mediated learning opportunities should look like for students.

Deepening Cultural Practices in Literacy as the Context for Assessment

Given the above, what can we learn from what the literacy community has already done, and how can we further deepen our shared practice? When we say, "It takes a village," we don't just mean more adult hands, although that's certainly helpful. The meaning that is more important to me is the idea that it takes a shared set of cultural practices, which because they are shared, we can jointly reinforce, model, show, and hold as a common set of expectations. Let me remind you of several important examples here from literacy researchers, while at the same time reiterating two guiding principles. To be effective in furthering students' learning, we need both exemplary tools and a set of cultural practices in which their use is embedded. The form and content of assessment tasks must fully capture the knowledge and skills we want students to master (sometimes referenced by the term *authentic assessment*), and assessment processes and purposes must support learning and a learning orientation (addressed by formative assessment) (Shepard, 2000).

When I wrote a history of "tests and measurements" I paid tribute to literacy scholars and other subject matter experts in the early 1980s, who led the critique of standardized tests and abandoned test and measurement courses as part of teacher preparation (Shepard, 2006), saying in effect, "We don't care about reliability and validity coefficients or item analysis. We want to embed our practices in the authentic work that kids are doing. And we will assess in that context, because then we'll know directly whether students can do the very things that we want them to be able to do, and they (our students) will also know whether they can do those meaningful things in a context that conveys purpose for why you would want to be able to do them." In this spirit, Marie Clay (1985) invented assessment strategies embedded in the acts of reading. Yetta Goodman (1985) reintroduced the concept of "kid-watching." Freddy Hiebert and colleagues (Teal, Hiebert, & Chittenden, 1987) collected samples of student work to gain insight into children's thinking and to document progress over time. Emergent literacy learning continua documenting spelling stages and development of writing skills anticipated by 20 years the learning progressions that are right now so prominent in mathematics and science assessment (Duschl, Schweingruber, & Shouse, 2007). Learning progressions are important because they're substantive. They help to codify shared knowledge about natural and instructionally dependent sequences, typical impediments, and even what to do when kids get stuck. If you build learning progressions, you're building not a statistical model of growth but literally a substantive, documented model of children's skill and knowledge development.

These substantive models of increasingly proficient work need to be situated in the context of classroom practices that allow for productive assessment interactions that contribute to the furtherance of quality work. While I might have as easily selected portfolio assessment as both assessment tool and prompt for productive interactions, I find it more instructive to point to the practice of Author's Chair (Graves & Hansen, 1983), whereby children develop an understanding of themselves as authors who receive feedback as a natural part of improving. Of course, Author's Chair is not explicitly an assessment strategy, and is now so commonplace that it is being critiqued by the cognoscenti as too narrow, etc. But, it does create a context where assessment can occur, and the example is important because it is so clearly a widely shared cultural practice. Kids can learn it in second grade and still do it in third grade. Except for our negative norms of completed assignments and grading, it quite infrequently happens in our schools that there's a shared understanding—in the village—about what mature practice looks like. Through Author's Chair, kids learn that by taking on the role and thinking aloud about writing choices, it is possible to get better and better. These routines can be mapped directly on to findings from research on meta-cognition and the benefits of self- and peer assessment.

Note that these ways of talking about instructional practices in literacy are parallel to research on classroom discourse in mathematics education. If learning is a process of enculturation, then new classroom interaction patterns and social norms need to be developed that make it customary for students to explain their reasoning, challenge one another's ideas, and work together to make sense of mathematical problems and solutions. Lambert (1990), for example, sought to examine whether classroom participation structures could be shifted to more closely resemble standards of logical argument in the mathematical community. Cobb, Wood, and Yackel (1993) concluded that new social norms would need to be negotiated to overcome previously constructed norms about trying to guess the teacher's solution and avoid evaluation. Isn't it interesting that schools seem to be more able to invest in conflict resolution and peer mediation skill development than to develop new classroom norms for talking about evidence as part of mathematics and science learning?

To deepen already-thoughtful classroom routines in literacy and to teach with integrity in the face of high-stakes testing, I want to argue for more explicit recognition of the threats (from interim assessments and grading practices as well as from end-of-year accountability tests) and for greater attention by educators to the unspoken messages conveyed to students about why we think it's worthwhile to put forth effort in school. Just examining how frequently the state test is part of the talk to kids in a school would be a useful faculty discussion. If the state test is the only thing that we're trying to get good for, then we're actually doing everything that the motivation literature says is a terrible thing to do. So, just like posters in the gym about bullying, conflict resolution, or "Just say no to drugs," conscious attention to building new norms may help to combat bad habits that have become normative. For example, Lucy Calkins and colleagues (Calkins, Montgomery, & Santman, 1998) have talked about reading the test as a new *genre* requiring that students be aware of the need to develop new strategies appropriate to audience and purpose. Children are called upon to use and be aware of relevant skills they already have, and importantly, I would add, the importance of test preparation is subordinated such that the ongoing reading and writing work of the classroom is interrupted only temporarily by the bizarre demands of the test genre.

Similarly, Linda McNeil (1988) distinguished between teachers who trivialized content to prepare for proficiency testing versus those who resisted giving over to the test and explicitly helped students take notes on the real knowledge as well as the knowledge they would need for the test. In so doing, teachers helped students see the relationship between the two, one a subset of the other. Yes, it's not totally irrelevant what's on the test, but it's a slice of something bigger. The goal here is to help kids develop the metacognitive awareness of how the two relate, of being able to code-switch and have a flexible understanding rather than just a deadening drumbeat in preparation for the test. We have to take up these issues as a community and worry about what we're conveying to kids, especially kids in schools most under siege due to poor test performance.

Another example of a conversation starter among teachers in a school or colleagues in a grade-level team are simple Venn diagrams I used in a middle school collaboration several years ago. Two overlapping circles are drawn, one representing the full curricular domain guiding classroom instruction and assessment. The second circle represents the content and skills required for the accountability test. As illustrated in Figure 2, describing the relative size and degree of overlap between the two circles is itself a useful exercise, but the most important insights come from sticky notes or magic marker comments elaborating on the skills needed to do well in the region of overlap and more importantly to call out the learning goals that are an important part of the curriculum but not on the test. One way of making a conscious commitment not to let the test take over is to

Figure 2. Two Venn Diagrams Illustrating Different Degrees of Overlap Between an Accountability Test and the Full Curricular Domain Intended to Guide Classroom Instruction and Assessment

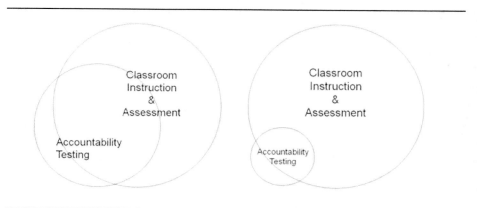

have such a discussion among colleagues about what is in the overlap and what is left out, present this information graphically or pictorially to parents, and then develop a shared understanding about how the school community is going to deal with the overlap, how much attention will be given to the small part, how it will relate to the big part, and how goals and purposes will promote student learning.

In closing, I recognize that it's a tall order to fend off the ill effects of high-stakes testing, now exacerbated by even more frequent attention to interim and benchmark assessments. To make room for formative assessment practices closely tied to research on supportive learning processes and to make feedback about ways to improve, it will also be essential to examine grading practices that misdirect student effort. Online systems such as *Infinite Campus* and other point systems that require reporting to parents weekly about grades have become the enemy because they prevent learning from a first attempt to do better on the next. Each entry in the grade book is treated like a finished product rather than as a step towards getting better and better, work done to be finished rather than to learn. Of course, teachers have to give grades. But grades should represent something substantively, and it's useful to gain some practice with the criteria, so you learn what they mean in the context of your own work. As an alternative, I've suggested things like "as if" grades. If students are still learning, why insist on recording an early summative assessment? Following this line of argument makes one want to hold off on grading to make room for formative assessment.

None of these strategies are panaceas, of course. The important thing is that discussion of these issues occur among a school's faculty, because right now educators are making decisions like, interim assessments should count some number of points towards students' grades as a motivator for students to put some effort into the tests. Do interim assessments represent attainments at the end of a unit of study, or is this another example of compliance grading, i.e., using grades to control behavior? Lots of these bad habits work against what I've argued for in advocating for formative assessment and what we know from decades of research on intrinsic and extrinsic motivation. There has to be a way that early and preliminary assessments of learning can help students get better at what they will eventually have to demonstrate for purposes of a grade. It is time that we think about the harm of current practices and think more explicitly about the potential remedies.

I ended my talk to the Learning Research Association audience with a picture of Yogi Berra in honor of his famous quotation, "Déjà vu all over again." I felt that this was a talk that I'd given many times before, even if the most recent research on interim assessments is quite new and not yet published. Once again we hear grand claims—about the use of data to improve instruction—but experience something quite different in the life of classrooms. We can draw important lessons from past reform efforts. "New" and ambitious reforms are very likely to be undone if there is not more of a conscious effort to be clear on the theoretical underpinnings and what must be done to ensure that those intentions are carried out all the way to the ground. In order that formative assessment not be just another hijacked reform, implementation efforts must attend both to the substance of what is assessed and the social processes. Data systems that routinize use of standardized assessments throughout the year, using formats that look just like the end-of-year accountability test, narrow the curriculum just as end-of-year tests have done and limit any claims that can be made about achievement gains. They harm students' understandings of what successful learning really looks like, and they must not be thought of as the first steps in implementing an assessment-for-learning vision.

REFERENCES

Black, P., & Wiliam, D. (1998). Assessment and classroom learning. *Assessment in Education: Principles, Policy, and Practice, 5*(1), 7-74.

Blanc, S., Christman, J. B., Liu, R., Mitchell, C., Travers, E., & Bulkley, K. E. (2010). Learning to learn from data: Benchmarks and instructional communities. *Peabody Journal of Education, 85*(2), 204-225.

Bloom, B. S., Hastings, J. T., & Madaus, G. F. (1971). *Handbook on formative and summative evaluation of student learning.* New York:, NY McGraw-Hill.

Bransford, J. D., Brown, A. L., & Cocking, R. R. (1999). *How people learn: Brain, mind, experience, and school.* Washington, DC: National Academies Press.

Bruner, J. S. (1975). From communication to language: A psychological perspective. *Cognition, 3*, 255-287.

Bulkley, K. E., Christman, J. B., Goertz, M. E., & Lawrence, N. R. (2010). Building with benchmarks: The role of the district in Philadelphia's Benchmark Assessment System. *Peabody Journal of Education, 85*(2), 186-204.

Calkins, L., Montgomery, K., & Santman, D. (1998). *A teacher's guide to standardized reading tests.* Portsmouth, NH: Heinemann.

Carnoy, M., Elmore, R., & Siskin, L. S. (2003). *The new accountability: High schools and high-stakes testing.* New York, NY: Routledge Falmer.

Clay, M. M. (1985). *The early detection of reading difficulties.* Auckland, New Zealand: Heinemann.

Cobb, P., Wood, T., & Yackel, E. (1993). Discourse, mathematical thinking, and classroom practice. In E. A. Forman, N. Minick, & C. A. Stone (Eds.), *Contexts for learning: Sociocultural dynamics in children's development* (pp. 91-119). New York, NY: Oxford University Press.

Collins, A., Brown, J. S., & Newman, S. E. (1989). "Cognitive apprenticeship: Teaching the crafts of reading, writing, and mathematics" (Pp. 453-494). In L. B. Resnick (Ed.), *Knowing, Learning, and Instruction: Essays in Honor of Robert Glaser* (pp. 453-494). Hillsdale, NJ: Erlbaum.

Davidson, K. L., & Frohbieter, G. J. (2011). *District adoption and implementation of interim and benchmark assessments.* Los Angeles: National Center for Research on Evaluation, Standards, and Student Testing (CRESST).

Deming, W. E. (1986). *Out of the crisis.* Cambridge, MA: Massachusetts Institute of Technology, Center for Advanced Engineering Study.

Elmore, R. (2003). Accountability and capacity. In M. Carnoy, R. Elmore, & L. S. Siskin (Eds.), *The new accountability: High schools and high-stakes testing* (pp. 195-209). New York, NY: Routledge Falmer.

Duschl, R. A., Schweingruber, H. A., & Shouse, A. W. (2007). *Taking science to school: Learning and teaching science in grades K-8*. Washington, DC: The National Academies Press.

Elmore, R. F., & Rothman, R. (Eds.) (1999). *Testing, teaching, and learning: A guide for states and school districts.* Washington, DC: National Academy Press.

Goals 2000: Educate America Act of 1994, P. L. 103-227.

Goodman, Y. M. (1985). Kidwatching: Observing children in the classroom. In A. Jaggar & M. T. Smith-Burke (Eds.), *Observing the language learner* (pp. 9-18). Newark, DE: International Reading Association and National Council of Teachers of English.

Goren, P. (2010). Interim assessments as a strategy for improvement: Easier said than done. *Peabody Journal of Education, 85*(2),123-129.

Graves, D. H., & Hansen, J. (1983). The author's chair. *Language Arts, 60*(2), 176-183.

Halverson, R., Grigg, J., Prichett, R., & Thomas, C. (2005). The new instructional leadership: Creating data-driven instructional systems in school. *Journal of School Leadership, 17*, 159-194.

Heritage, M., Kim, J., Vendlinski, T., & Herman, J. (2009). From evidence to action: A seamless process in formative assessment? *Educational Measurement: Issues and Practice, 28*(3), 24-31.

Herman, J. L. (2008). Accountability and assessment: Is public interest in K-12 education being served. In K. E. Ryan & L. A. Shepard (Eds.), *The future of test-based educational accountability* (pp. 211-231). New York, NY: Routledge.

Lampert, M. (1990). When the problem is not the question and the solution is not the answer: Mathematical knowing and teaching. *American Educational Research Journal, 27*(1), 29-63.

Lave, J., & Wenger, E. (1991). *Situated learning: Legitimate peripheral participation*. Cambridge, UK: Cambridge University Press.

McLaughlin, M. W., & Shepard, L. A. (1995). *Improving education through standards-based reform. A report of the National Academy of Education Panel on Standards-Based Reform*. Stanford, CA: National Academy of Education.

McNeil, L. M. (1988). *Contradictions of control: School structure and school knowledge*. New York, NY: Routledge.

Nabors Olah, L., Lawrence, N. R., & Riggan, M. (2010). Learning to learn from benchmark assessment data: How teachers analyze results. *Peabody Journal of Education, 85*(2), 226-245.

National Council of Teachers of Mathematics. (1989). *Curriculum and evaluation standards for school mathematics*. Reston, VA: Author.

National Council on Education Standards and Testing. (1992, January 24). *Raising standards for American education: A report to Congress, the Secretary of Education, the National Education Goals Panel, and the American people* (ISBN 0-16-036087-8). Washington, DC: U.S. Government Printing Office.

Perie, M., Marion, S., & Gong, B. (2009). Moving toward a comprehensive assessment system: A framework for considering interim assessments. *Educational Measurement: Issues and Practice, 28*(3), 5-13.

Ramaprasad, A. (1983). On the definition of feedback. *Behavioral Science, 28*, 4-13.

Resnick, L. B., & Klopfer, L. E. (1989). Toward the thinking curriculum: An overview. In L. B. Resnick & L. E. Klopfer (Eds.), *Toward the thinking curriculum: Current cognitive research* (pp. 1-18). Washington, DC: Association for Supervision and Curriculum Development.

Resnick, L. B., & Resnick, D. P. (1992). Assessing the thinking curriculum: New tools for education reform. In B. R. Gifford & M. C. O'Connor (Eds.), *Changing assessments: Alternative views of aptitude, achievement, and instruction* (pp. 37-75). Boston, MA: Kluwer Academic.

Sadler, R. (1989). Formative assessment and the design of instructional assessments. *Instructional Science, 18*, 119-144.

Scriven, M. (1967). *The methodology of evaluation*. In R. A. Tyler, R. M. Gagne, & M. Scriven (Eds.), Perspectives of curriculum evaluation (pp. 39-83). Chicago, IL: Rand McNally.

Shepard, L. A. (2008a). A brief history of accountability testing, 1965-2007. In K. E. Ryan & L. A. Shepard (Eds.), *The future of test-based educational accountability* (pp. 25-46). New York, NY: Routledge.

Shepard, L. A. (2006). Classroom assessment. In R. L. Brennan (Ed.), *Educational measurement* (Fourth Edition) (pp. 623-646). Westport, CT: American Council on Education and Praeger Publishers.

Shepard, L. A. (2008b). Formative assessment: Caveat emptor. In C. A. Dwyer (Ed.), *The future of assessment: Shaping teaching and learning* (pp. 279-303). New York, NY: Lawrence Erlbaum.

Shepard, L. A. (2005). Linking formative assessment to scaffolding. *Educational Leadership, 63*(3), 66-70.

Shepard, L. A. (1991). Psychometricians' beliefs about learning. *Educational Researcher, 20*, 2-16.

Shepard, L. A. (2000). The role of assessment in a learning culture. *Educational Researcher, 29*(7), 4-14.

Shepard, L. A. (2010). What the marketplace has brought us: Item-by-item teaching with little instructional insight. *Peabody Journal of Education, 85*(2), 246-257.

Shepard, L. A., Davidson, K. L., & Bowman, R. (2011). *How middle-school mathematics teachers use interim and benchmark assessment data.* Los Angeles: National Center for Research on Evaluation, Standards, and Student Testing (CRESST).

Smith, M. S., & O'Day, J. (1990). Systemic school reform. In S. H. Fuhrman & B. Mahen (Eds.), *The politics of curriculum and testing: The 1990 Yearbook of the Politics of Education Association* (pp. 233-267). London, UK: Taylor & Francis.

Stallman, A. C., & Pearson, P. D. (1990). Formal measures of early literacy. In L. M. Morrow & J. K. Smith (Eds.), *Assessment for instruction in early literacy* (pp. 7-44). Englewood Cliffs, NJ: Prentice Hall.

Teale, W. H., Hiebert, E., & Chittenden, E. (1987). Assessing young children's literacy development. *The Reading Teacher, 40*, 772-777.

U.S. Congress Office of Technology Assessment. (1992, February). *Testing in American schools: Asking the right questions* (OTA-SET-519). Washington, DC: U.S. Government Printing Office.

Vygotsky, L. S. (1978). *Mind in society: The development of higher psychological processes.* Cambridge, MA: Harvard University Press.

FOOTNOTE

[1]National Center for Research on Evaluation, Standards, and Student Testing (CRESST)

'May You Live in Interesting Times': Critical Literacy in South Africa

Hilary Janks

University of the Witwatersrand, South Africa

Robert F. Kennedy in his Day of Affirmation address in Cape Town (June 1966), said that 'May you live in interesting times' was an ancient Chinese curse. He was wrong about it (http://www.bbc.co.uk/dna/h2g2/A807374) being Chinese, and I leave it to you to decide, once I have told my story, whether living in interesting times is a blessing or a curse.

The Nationalist government came to power in South Africa in 1948 and it was only after the collapse of the Berlin Wall in 1989 that the demise of apartheid seemed possible. I was born after 1948 and for the first 40 years of my life lived with, and benefited from, a system based on discourses of white supremacy that infantalised or dehumanized people of colour. I was at University in the 1960s at a time when many young South Africans at the liberal English-speaking universities were committed to the liberation struggle. These were interesting times. Dangerous times. People we knew were placed under house-arrest, or in 90-day detention without trial; lecturers' offices were fire-bombed; police invaded our campuses and broke up protests with tear gas, rubber bullets, and sjamboks (whips). Members of the left-wing National Union of South African Students were recruited as police spies. Others such as Steve Biko, were arrested and died in detention from torture. The apartheid museum has a chilling display of nooses to commemorate the many prisoners who died in custody ostensibly from hanging themselves. The absurdity of the police reports on death in detention is captured in the following poem by Chris van Wyk.

In detention

He fell from the ninth floor
He hanged himself
He slipped on a piece of soap while washing
He hanged himself
He slipped on a piece of soap while washing
He fell from the ninth floor
He hanged himself while washing
He slipped from the ninth floor
He hung from the ninth floor
He slipped on the ninth floor while washing
He fell from a piece of soap while slipping
He hung from the ninth floor
He washed from the ninth floor while slipping
He hung from a piece of soap while washing.

(http://poefrika.blogspot.com/2008/12/chris-van-wyks-in-detention.html downloaded 1 May 2011)

I began teaching in the 1970s and was teaching at the time of the 1976 Soweto uprising. Protest poetry was used as a way of bringing social issues into our classrooms.

At that time the language in education policy for Bantu education was hotly contested. English and Afrikaans were the only two official languages of the country (despite the fact that the majority of the population spoke nine different African languages). Where the mission schools had enabled African families to elect either mother-tongue medium of instruction or English medium for their children's education, the apartheid State imposed mother-tongue instruction until Grade 7. Pennycoook (1994, p. 73 - 79) argues that both indigenous and colonial language policies serve the interests of colonial power—the one Orientalism, excludes Africans from the language of power; the other Anglicism provides access to English for only a few, enabling them to serve as Native Administrators who could broker relations between the colonial power and subjugated indigenous populations.

The language policy for high schools was different. From Grades 8 to 12 students had to learn half their subjects through the medium of English and the other half through the medium of Afrikaans. This became known as the 50/50 rule. Systematically disadvantaged by language in education policy, relatively few African students completed school. What sparked the Soweto uprising in June 1976 was a protest march by students to oppose the Nationalist government's decision to introduce the 50/50 rule into the last years of primary school. When police opened fire on students who were protesting peacefully, the spotlight was placed on both language and education. These were interesting times whose repercussions continue to shape language attitudes and the take-up of post-apartheid language rights. South Africa now has 11 official languages, yet most parents choose English as the medium of instruction. In a country in which urban Africans speak many languages, fluency in English has more symbolic power, and therefore more status, than multilingual competence. In South Africa language education has always been political.

Bantu education was designed to domesticate the indigenous population:

> "There is no place for [the African] in the European community above the level of certain forms of labour. It is of no avail for him to receive a training which has as its aim, absorption in the European community" (Verwoerd, speech to Parliament, 1954, cited in Rose and Tunmer, 1975).

During the Soweto uprising, slogans such as 'Liberation Before Education,' 'Say No to Gutter Education,' and 'Pass One Pass All' mobilized students to boycott classes, to destroy school buildings, and to threaten teachers. These interesting times produced what has come to be known as the 'lost generation' of young people.

The focus on curriculum change as an alternative to school boycotts spearheaded the People's Education Movement, which focused on rewriting the Curriculum in the key areas of History, English, and Mathematics. The *Critical Language Awareness Series* of workbooks (Janks, 1993a) were designed to teach students about the relationship between language and power and the ways in which 'meaning is mobilized in defence of domination' (Thompson, 1985, p. 35). Specifically conceived of as resources for People's English, they were published one year before the first democratic elections in 1994. These were interesting times.

Critical literacy in South Africa began as an overtly political and moral project and the materials that were produced were specifically designed to counter the prevailing apartheid discourses in South Africa, discourses that were used to legitimate inequality. The following activity taken from one of the workbooks is designed to undercut theories of race as biological rather than social. See Figure 1.

Figure 1. The Chameleon Dance (Janks, 1993b, p. 9)

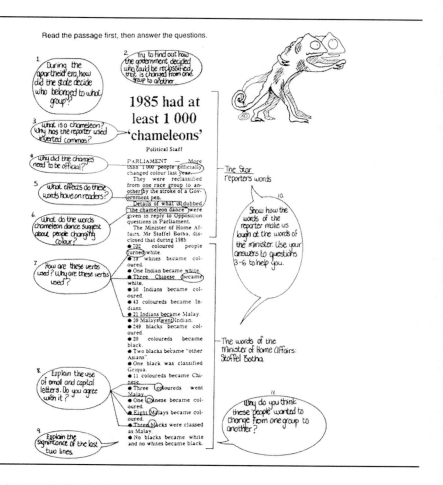

In relation to the South African context at the time, Marxist and neo-marxist theories of power which viewed power as oppressive, had explanatory power. Students were invited to consider the relations of domination and subordination in their own lives. This is captured in the classroom activity in Figure 2.

This activity on top dogs and underdogs was designed to show children that individuals are differently empowered in their different identities, Nevertheless, it reproduced a binary logic based on dominant and dominated social positions. This was pointed out by primary school students in a new arrivals class in Australia. They argued convincingly that it was also possible to be a 'middle dog' (Grant, 1999).

Figure 2. Topdogs and Underdogs (Janks, 1993b, p.12)

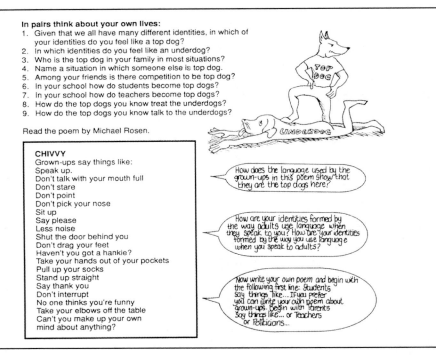

The question for critical literacy educators after 1994, under a Mandela government, was how to imagine critical literacy as a project for reconstruction, rather than deconstruction; how to imagine its contribution to establishing a new order. This question underpins the thinking that led to the construction of my interdependent model of critical literacy education that combines critique with work on identity, access, and redesign (Janks, 2010).

Foucault's theory of productive power provided a way forward. He argues against overarching conceptions of domination, 'a binary structure with dominators on one side and dominated on the other' (1980, p.142). Instead he is interested in the procedures which regulate discourses and the means by which power constitutes them as knowledge, that is, as truth. For Foucault:

> 'Truth' is to be understood as system[s] of ordered procedures for the production, regulation, distribution, circulation and operation of statements. [It] is linked in a circular relation with systems of power which produce and sustain it, and to effects of power which it induces and which extend it. A 'regime' of truth. (1980, p. 133).

This can be illustrated with an example from the United States. Under the Bush administration, quantitative psychometric research on literacy was increasingly viewed as the only valid 'scientific' research—it was the research that received government funding and informed government policy. Constructed as the 'true' discourse about literacy, this effectively excluded qualitative research based on ethnographic research methods and a socio-cultural theory of literacy. Here power was used to sustain a particular discourse and to establish its hegemony. This discourse then has effects of power, setting norms for literacy which can be surveilled, examined, and used to legitimate the No Child Left Behind policy. It is worth noting, in passing, the way in which the naming of this policy also worked to legitimate it (who in their right mind would want a child to be left behind?), to silence opponents, and to hide its practices (different and dumbed down programmes offered to at-risk children). While ostensibly designed to create equal education outcomes, this is a dividing practice that excludes.

No wonder Foucault thinks that 'discourse is the power which is to be seized' (1970, p. 110). Foucault moves away from seeing power as negative, working through the modes of 'censorship, exclusion, blockage, and repression' (1980, p. 59). Instead, he sees power as strong because it produces effects. In addition to producing effects 'at the level of desire'—and also at the level of knowledge' (1980, p. 59), power infiltrates the minutiae of daily life, affecting the 'processes which subject our bodies, govern our gestures, and dictate our behaviours' (1980, p. 97). This is clearly illustrated in the poster *Rules for Good Listening* found on the wall of a Grade 1 primary school classroom in South Africa (Dixon, 2004). This poster of a well-disciplined child sitting at her desk labels her eyes as 'watching,' ears as 'listening,' lips as 'closed,' hands as 'still,' and feet as 'quiet.'

We need to take seriously Foucault's view of power as having a 'capillary form of existence' that 'reaches into the very grain of individuals, touches their bodies, and inserts itself into their actions and attitudes, their discourses, learning processes and everyday lives' (Foucault, 1980a, p. 39). Critical literacy has to take what I have called little p politics as seriously as it does big P Politics (Janks, 2010 p. 186-188).

> The difference can be illustrated by the emblematic story of a husband, who on the occasion of his golden wedding anniversary, shared the secret of his successful marriage. 'It's easy', he said, 'my wife makes all the small decisions and I make all the big decisions.' When asked to give examples, he went on to explain, 'My wife decides things like what we should eat, who our friends should be, where we should live, how many children we should have, where they should go to school'. And what, one might ask, are the big decisions? The man said that he decided the important things: 'Who should be President of the country, whether or not to go to war, what should be done about the economy …

The story is funny because of the way in which the husband appears naively to cede power to his wife on matters that directly affect the quality of his daily life, reserving for himself matters on which he can have an opinion, but over which he can have little direct influence or control. Moreover, the story pokes fun at the gendered binary which sees the domestic domain as the disempowered domain of women, leaving worldliness to men.

Politics with a capital P is the big stuff, the worldly concerns of the husband. It is about government and world trade agreements and the United Nations; it is about ethnic or religious cleansing and world tribunals; it is about apartheid and global capitalism, money laundering and linguistic imperialism. It is about the inequities between the political North and the political South. It is about oil, the ozone layer, genetic engineering, and cloning. It is about the danger of global warming. It is about globalisation, the new work order, and sweat shops in Asia.

Little p politics, on the other hand, is about the micro-politics of everyday life. It is about the minute-by-minute choices and decisions that make us who we are. It is about desire and fear, and how we construct them and they construct us. It is about the politics of identity and place; it is about daily triumphs and defeat; it is about winners and losers, haves and have-nots, school bullies and their victims; it is about how we treat other people day by day; it is about whether or not we learn someone else's language or recycle our garbage. Little *p* politics is about taking seriously the feminist perspective that the personal is the political. This is not to suggest that politics has nothing to do with *Politics*. On the contrary, the socio-historical and economic contexts in which we live produce different conditions of possibility and constraint that we all have to negotiate as meaningfully as we can. While the social constructs who we are, so do we construct the social. This dialectic relationship is fluid and dynamic, creating possibilities for social action and change.

Gee (1990, p.142) defines big D discourses as 'speaking/writing-doing-being-believing-valuing combinations.' The hyphens are really important because they make the point that speaking and writing are fundamentally bound up with who we are and where we come from. We are produced by the ways with words of our communities, and as Heath (1983) demonstrated a long time ago, different ways with words are not equally valued. In 1972, Labov published 'The logic of non-standard English', which showed with concrete examples that African American English was as capable of producing logical and rational argument as standard English. Yet when the Oaklands School Board recognized this variety of English in 1996 in order to take it into account in teaching Standard English, there was such an outcry that the Linguistics Society of America had to pass a resolution in 1997, in support of the Board, declaring that:

> The variety known as "Ebonics," "African American Vernacular English" (AAVE), and "Vernacular Black English" and by other names is systematic and rule-governed like all natural speech varieties. In fact, all human linguistic systems —spoken, signed, and written—are fundamentally regular. The systematic and expressive nature of the grammar and pronunciation patterns of the African American vernacular has been established by numerous scientific studies over the past thirty years. Characterizations of Ebonics as "slang," "mutant," "lazy," "defective," "ungrammatical," or "broken English" are incorrect and demeaning. (http://www.stanford.edu/~rickford/ebonics/LSAResolution.html downloaded 1 May 2011)

Even where scientists argue the case for linguistic equality, social valuations produce inequality. Difference is organized in terms of power, thereby producing hierarchies. The Oaklands School Board's attempt to re-design the curriculum to provide students with access to the language of power by valuing their language and identity backfired. Access was seen as a form of Orientalism. Similarly, in South Africa parents see the use of their own languages in school as a form of ghettoisation. Parents recognize that elite languages, varieties, and discourses provide greater access and they devalue their own linguistic and cultural resources as a means to this end. This produces what I, after Lodge (1997), have called the 'access paradox':

> If you provide more people with access to the dominant variety of the dominant language, you perpetuate its powerful status. If, on the other hand, you deny students access, you perpetuate their marginalisation in a society that continues to recognise this language as a mark of distinction. You also deny them access to the extensive resources available in that language; resources which have developed as a consequence of the language's dominance (Janks, 2010, p. 139-140).

In the discussion so far three of the key terms that I have argued are crucial in conceptualizing critical literacy education: power, diversity, and access, have been considered. What makes literacy education critical is the recognition that language and literacy are shot through by relations of power. I have tried to show that sometimes this power is a form of domination and at others it is more pervasive, structured as it is by the discourses we inhabit: our naturalized ways of speaking and writing and our taken-for-granted systems of thought. This is further complicated by the fact that discourses, languages, and literacies do not just sit side by side quietly appreciating and learning from one another. Instead they compete for recognition and control of social institutions. Instead of diversity being seen as a productive resource, as the motor engine for new ideas and change, difference produces competition and conflict. Difference then translates into differential forms of access. One only has to look at the institution of schooling to see whose ways with words, whose cultural capital, whose interaction styles, whose literacies control the curriculum, making it easier for those who have access to the discourses of schooling to succeed while simultaneously working to exclude those who are Othered by these choices. To these three, I have added a fourth term—design.

Figure 3. The Redesign Cycle

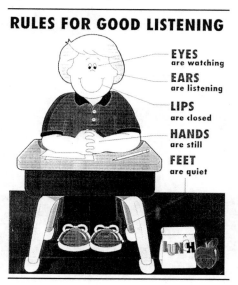

I chose the word *design* (first introduced to the field by Kress, 1995) as the term to stand for the ability to harness multi-modal resources (language, image, movement, gesture, music, etc.) for the production of meaning. This choice of this term privileges the production of meaning over reception because it is more agentive, but clearly it would be pointless designing texts if there was no one to read them—to believe them, to question them, to redesign them. Redesign is crucial, as without it, there would be no possibility of transformation and change.

In my model of critical literacy education I have argued that these four orientations—power, diversity, access and design/redesign—need to pull against each other to keep the critical literacy tent taut. One without the other produces a problematic imbalance. Elsewhere I have considered each of the key terms and systematically unpacked the implications for literacy of any one orientation without the others (Janks, 2010). All I have time for here is a sliver of this argument. Tables 1 to 4 summarise the argument that follows. (In these tables, the orientations that are the focus of each approach have been shaded, while those that are omitted have been left unshaded.)

Different approaches to literacy education can be analysed using the interdependent model (Janks, 2010) to see which, if any, of the orientations argued for in Janks' model is privileged. If they are not interdependent, what are the effects? *New Literacy Studies* (Gee, 1994; Heath, 1983; Street, 1984, Barton, Hamilton, & Ivanič, 2000) focuses on literacy variation across communities in which literacy is shaped by the specific social uses of literacy in different communities. The main argument is for the recognition and valuing of different literacies. Because diversity is at the centre here, not enough attention is given to providing students with access to the powerful forms of literacy that they nevertheless need to succeed in a knowledge economy. (See Table 1).

Table 1. New Literacy Studies

Power/domination	The fact that not all ways with words are equally resourced or valued is not taken seriously enough. (Linguistic variation)
Diversity/difference	Communities' different ways with words and with text are privileged. The approach is driven by respect for diversity.
Access	There is not enough consideration of the social goods that different literacies provide access to.
Design/redesign	The redesign of literacy resources requires a redesign of what society values and the politics of opportunity and exclusion.
Desire	Equality in the valuation of difference.

Genre approaches (Martin, Christie, and Rothery, 1987; Cope and Kalantzis, 1993), on the other hand, reverse this privileging. In over-valuing access to dominant forms, the diverse languages and literacies that children have as resources are not harnessed, nor are forms of creativity that subvert existing genres. (See Table 2).

Table 2. Genre Theory

Power/domination	Genre theory recognizes that some genres are more powerful than others.
Diversity/difference	It excludes non-dominant forms—for example, sounding or rap.
Access	This approach takes access to the dominant genres of schooling seriously.
Design/Redesign	It reifies existing genres and does not allow enough room for contestation and change.
Desire	Access to privileged forms.

Multimodal design literacies (Kress, 2010) focus on design and the play of semiotic resources largely for the stylization of self. Here the focus is the interest of the designer without attention to the ways in which these interests are shaped by power. Nor is sufficient attention paid to who gets access to the means of production. (See Table 3).

Table 3. Multimodal Design Literacies

Power/domination	The styling of self is somehow beyond critique.
Diversity/difference	Semeiosis is seen as contributing to the styling of self. Identity is at the heart of the project.
Access	Access appears to centre on access to consumption and image
Design/Redesign	The focus is on design and redesign: the infinite play of semiotic choices. What matters is the harnessing of semiotic resources for identity work.
Desire	The production of images of identity and identification.

Finally, *Back to Basics* naturalizes what counts as the basics and who decides. It does little to address the problem that some children get stuck in the basics while others forge ahead or that this correlates strongly with social stratification and class privilege. Focused on access to the basics, it ignores questions of power, difference, and redesign. (See Table 4).

Table 4. Back to Basics

Power/domination	The language and discourses of the elites determine what counts as the basics. Dominant languages, literacies, and discourses prevail and exclude all others.
Diversity/ difference	Excluded.
Access	Claimed, but in fact children *are* left behind, by dumbed-down curricula designed to drill the basics.
Design/Redesign	Redesign is conservative (back to), rather than transformative
Desire	A basic educational minimum for all.

The following sequence of critical literacy activities is offered in order to show how it is possible to engage with all four orientations in a sequence of work.

Activity 1
Research the ways in which people were treated as less than human in any of the following situations:
- The German concentration camps
- The conflict between the Hutus and the Tutsis in Rwanda
- Apartheid rule in South Africa
- 'Ethnic cleansing' in Serbo-Croatia.

Activity 2
Watch *District 9* and discuss what it teaches us about prejudice, humanity, heroism, and the relationship between us and strange others.

Figure 4. The Poster for *District Nine* (Downloaded at http://www.moviegoods.com/movie_poster/district_9_2009.htm on 1 May 2011)

Activity 3

Consider research on the negative discourses about Africa. For example, Adegoke (1999) found that 60% of reporting on Africa was negative. Topics such as:

- civil unrest and riots, corruption and crime (37%).

- foreign aid, poverty and under-development, disaster and tragedy, and health and disease prevailed (21%).

Activity 4

Then read how this is satirized in *How to Write about Africa*, by Binyavanga Wainainina (Kenya, 1992). (http://textandcommunity.gmu.edu/2009/resources/how-write.pdf).

Activity 5

Examine Figure 5 and answer the following questions:

- Who do these names refer to? Why do you think derogatory names are often used?

- What era is associated with each of these sets of 'bad guys' shown in Figure 6?

- Describe the stereotype that goes with each of these 'bad guys.'

- What is a stereotype?

- Collect photographs, headlines, words, cartoons of the people, or types of people currently constructed as the 'bad guys' in your own country or community. Redesign these stories. Begin with: How to write about ….

Figure 5. The Dangerous Other According to Hollywood

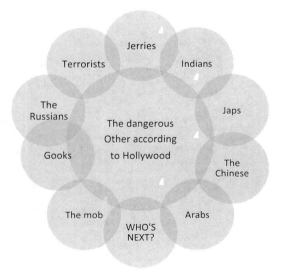

Activity 6

Read *Body Ritual of the Nacirema* (Horace Miner, 1949). http://fasnafan.tripod.com/ nacirema.pdf

Table 6 summarizes how activities 1-6 work with different power, diversity, access, and design/redesign in an integrated way.

Table 6. Integration of Power, Diversity, Access, and Design in Critical Literacy Pedagogy

	Curriculum activity	Social effects	Interdependent model
Activity 1	Lessons from history about Othering.	Dehumanization and violence on a global scale.	Interface of diversity and power in order to redesign attitudes
Activity 2	District 9: Xenophobia—tied also to language as a marker of Otherness	Language as a marker of identity. Fear of strangers.	Identity, diversity, and power. Access to resources.
Activity 2	District 9—allegory for apartheid. The use of Apartheid signage.	Who is us and who is them? Redesign that produces a design of Nigerians that needs to be redesigned.	Multimodal redesign of apartheid.
Activity 3	Adegoke's research—concrete local	Patterned representations—discourse. Systems of meaning.	Critique of representations of foreign Africans.
Activity 4	Check own newspapers—moves from the global to the local.	Discourses circulate—power to produce subjects	Power circulates—discourses affect African Americans
Activity 4	Satire—writing back	Playing with the discourses—refusing the positioning	Deconstruction; redesign
Activity 5	Othering in popular culture	Big *P* politics designs the 'bad guys'	Diversity, power, design, redesign
Activity 6	Nacirema—emic and etic perspectives	Denaturalisation of Othering.	Diversity. Who has the power to name?

I have always worked at the interface of theory and practice and have tried to show that complex social theory can be turned into lively classroom practice, whether or not the powers that be sanction what we do. The trick is to make sure that in doing so, we enable our students to outdo their peers in the mind-numbing bench-mark tests. My analysis of the PIRLS results in South Africa suggests that critical literacy approaches could improve scores (Janks, 2011).

In conclusion: If we lived in a peaceful world without the threat of global warming or conflict or war, where everyone has access to education, health care, food and a dignified life, I would argue that there would still be a need for critical literacy. In a world that is rich with difference, there is still likely to be intolerance and fear of the other. Because difference is structured in relation to power, unequal access to resources based on a multitude of social categorizations will continue to produce privilege and resentment. Even in a world where socially constructed relations of power have been flattened, we will still have to manage the little *p* politics of our daily lives. Some former critical literacy proponents, who have moved on, are now arguing that critical literacy has 'reached its sell-by date'. I want to know what perfect place they live in so that we can all go and live there too. Until then, we do what we can to create this better place in our own interesting times in our own countries, our own communities and our own classrooms.

REFERENCES

Barton, D., Hamilton, M. & Ivanič, R. (2000) *Situated Literacies*. London, UK: Routledge.

Binyavanga, Wainainina. 'How to Write about Africa', Granta: *Magazine of New Writing*. 1992. Retrieved from http://textandcommunity.gmu.edu/2009/resources/how-write.pdf on 1 May 2011.

Cope, B., & Kalantzis, M. (Eds). (1993). *The powers of literacy: A genre approach to teaching writing*. London, UK: Falmer Press.

Dixon, K. (2004). Literacy: Diverse spaces, diverse bodies? *English in Australia, 139, Number 1* (Joint IFTE issue), 50-55.

Foucault, M. (1970). The Order of Discourse. Inaugural Lecture at the College de France. In M. Shapiro (Ed.), *Language and Politics*. Oxford, UK: Basil Blackwell.

Foucault, M. (1980). P*ower/knowledge: Selected Interviews and Other Writings 1972-1977*. New York, NY: Pantheon Books.

Gee, J. (1990). *Social Linguistics and Literacies*. London, UK: Falmer Press.

Gee, J. (1994). Orality and literacy: from 'The Savage Mind' to 'Ways with Words'. In J. Maybin (Ed.), *Language and Literacy in Social Context*. Milton Keynes: Open University Press.

Grant, H. (1999). Topdogs and underdogs. *Practically Primary*, 4(3), 40-42.

Gregory, E., & Williams, A. (2000). *City Literacies: Learning to Read Across Generations and Cultures*. London, UK: Routledge.

Heath, S. B. (1983). *Ways with words*. England, UK: Cambridge University Press.

Janks, H. (1993a) (Ed) *The Critical Language Awareness Series*. Hodder and Stoughton and Wits University Press.

Janks, H. (1993b) *Language, Identity and Power*. Johannesburg, South Africa: Hodder and Stoughton and Wits University Press.

Janks, H. (2010). *Literacy and Power*. London, UK and New York, NY: Routledge.

Janks, H. (2011). Making sense of PIRLS 2006 results for South Africa. *Reading and Writing, 2*(1), pp. 27-40.

Kress, G. (1995). *Making Signs and Making Subjects: The English Curriculum and Social Futures*. Institute of Education, University of London, London, UK.

Kress, G. (2010) *Multimodality*. London, UK and New York, NY: Routledge.

Labov, W. (1972). The logic of non-standard English. In P. Giglioli (Ed.), *Language and Social Context*. Harmondsworth: Penguin.

Lodge, H. (1997). *Providing access to academic literacy in the Arts Foundation Programme at the University of the Witwatersrand in 1996 - the theory behind the practice*. Unpublished Master's dissertation, University of the Witwatersrand, Johannesburg.

Martin, J., Christie, F., & Rothery, J. (1987). Social processes of education: a reply to Sawyer and Watson (and others). In I. Reid (Ed.), *The Place of Genre in Learning: Current Debates*. Geelong: Deakin University.

Pennycook, A. (1994). *The Cultural Politics of English as an International Language*. London, UK: Longman.

Rose, B., & Tunmer, R. (1975). *Documents in South African Education. RSA: Ad.* Donker/Publisher.

Street, B. (1984). *Literacy in Theory and Practice*. Cambridge, UK: Cambridge University Press.

Family Literacy Across Time: The Field, Families, and Bradford Holt

Catherine Compton-Lilly
University of Wisconsin Madison

Family literacy, as a field, has been in existence for over 20 years. We have survived debates within the field, funding struggles, and tides of political change. Most recently, we endured a political election that fixated on middle-class economies and tax breaks for the wealthy. Notably absent were conversations related to poverty, race, diversity, and chronic unemployment that pre-dates the recent economic crisis. It is within this climate that educators and researchers interested in literacy wonder how we can make a difference.

This chapter involves the telling of two stories that draw on two very different research projects. Both studies attend to race, class, diversity, schooling, and literacy. The first is an integrative critical literature review of the field of family literacy that is being conducted by myself, Rebecca Rogers, and Tisha Lewis (in review). The second is a qualitative longitudinal research study involving a group of children who were my former first-grade students (Compton-Lilly, 2003, 2007). I have now followed seven families for 10 years as the children moved from first grade through high school and in this chapter I present an account of one student, Bradford Holt, and his family.

While these studies differ significantly in terms of their methodologies and participants, they have both turned my attention to—of all things—**time** and thus I present this chapter in reference to a timeline of events. An admittedly partial review of the field of family literacy is presented on the top. And an account of one family across the same time period is presented on the bottom. As people, we live within time, construct identities as individuals, researchers, students, readers, and writers over time and strive to use our time to make the world a better place. We draw upon our own lived pasts, the stories that circulate within our families—some that proceed our own birth—and the stories related larger historical events and shared social histories.

THE BEGINNINGS OF FAMILY LITERACY

In 1964 in the trail of the civil rights movement, President Lyndon B. Johnson introduced a "War on Poverty." I quote from Johnson's speech:

> Unfortunately, many Americans live on the outskirts of hope—some because of their poverty, and some because of their color, and all too many because of both. Our task is to help replace their despair with opportunity. . .

> For the war against poverty will not be won here in Washington. It must be won in the field, in every private home, in every public office, from the courthouse to the White House. . .

> Very often a lack of jobs and money is not the cause of poverty, but the symptom. The cause may lie deeper in our failure to give our fellow citizens a fair chance to develop their own capacities, in a lack of education and training, in a lack of

medical care and housing, in a lack of decent communities in which to live and
bring up their children. (Johnson, 1964)

Johnson's "War on Poverty" led to the creation of various initiatives including Job Corps, Project
Head Start, legal services for the poor, and various community action programs. These efforts to
address, or perhaps cure poverty, set the stage for the family literacy research that is the subject of
the first half of this talk. Before jumping into that analysis, I will take a few minutes to describe the
methodological procedures that we used to review the field.

AN INTEGRATIVE CRITICAL LITERATURE REVIEW

The complete integrative critical literature review involved four inter-related analyses. First, I
will briefly describe the two analyses that I will not draw upon in this chapter followed by a more
detailed description of our review of the citation coding analysis and the analysis of comprehensive
edited volumes that I will reference.

First, we reviewed four databases and the holdings of a major university library with
combinations of the terms "literacy," "family," "handbook," "review," and "home" to identify
articles, books, and book chapters that contained reviews of family literacy.

In addition, an *Analytic Review Template* (ART) was created and used to record qualitative
information about 213 review chapters and articles. Definitions of family literacy, the methodologies
used, theoretical frameworks, and attention to race, class, and language were among the dimensions
analyzed. Another 59 studies containing lesser reviews of family literacy were briefly summarized.

Today, I focus on the citation coding scheme that we developed to identify major contributors
to the field of family literacy. Early in the literature retrieval process, we used sample studies to
develop and refine our citation coding (CC) scheme. The following codes were recorded beside each
reference on a copy of each review's reference list.

An "L" was recorded next to studies that were presented in lists with other
references.

An "S" was recorded next to studies that were discussed in 1 - 3 sentences.

A "P" was recorded next to studies that were discussed in 4 or more sentences.

A "C" was recorded next to studies that were discussed in 1 or more paragraphs
and were central to the review's argument.

In this presentation, we focus on researchers whose work was coded at either the paragraph or
central level in a significant number of reviews. This process provided an approximation of the
centrality of researchers in the field of family literacy.

I also focus on our analysis of the tables of contents, introductory materials and editorial
statements, and chapter titles from the nine comprehensive edited volumes that focused specifically
on family literacy. These were analyzed in terms of the topics addressed, contributors, handbook
length, and terminology and each offered a different lens on these comprehensive volumes and
on the field. Analyses of tables of contents presented a sense of the scope of the texts. What was
the range of topics presented in the volumes? Analyses of introductory materials and editorial

statements allowed us to examine how the field was framed and the rationale provided for the publication of the text.

Findings Based on Citation Coding

1983 was a significant year for family literacy research. Based on our analysis of citation patterns, the two most cited scholars in the field of family literacy both published critical works in 1983. The most cited scholar in the field is Shirley Brice Heath. Her work is referenced as a major citation in 45 of the 272 reviews of family literacy (17%). This is despite the fact that Shirley Brice Heath (1983) never used the term family literacy in *Ways with Words*—by far the most cited publication in the field.

Figure 1. Thirteen Most Cited Scholars in Reviews of Family Literacy

Number of Citations	Dates of Works Cited	Name	Methods/Theory	Focus
45	1982-1995	Shirley Brice Heath	Qualitative ethnography	Language and literacy practices
41	1981-1997	Denny Taylor	Qualitative ethnography	Literacy practices
34	1988-2000	Victoria Purcell-Gates	Qualitative ethnography	Literacy practices
32	1990-2005	Luis Moll	Qualitative ethnography	ELL community practices
24	1977-2001	Catherine Snow	Quantitative Causal/Predictive	School literacy success
23	1992-1998	Trevor Cairney	Family literacy theory	Field of Family Literacy
20	1987-1995	Elsa Auerbach	Family literacy theory	Family strengths
20	1992-2006	Vivian Gadsden	Qualitative Narrative Analysis Family literacy theory	Generational literacy, race, gender Field of family literacy
19	1995-2002	M. Senechal	Quantitative Causal/Predictive	Storybook reading
17	1988-2001	G. J. Whitehurst	Quantitative Causal/Predictive	Storybook Reading
16	1987-2006	C. Delgado-Gaitan	Qualitative	Home Literacy Practices
15	1978-1987 English Publications	Lev Vygotsky	Language and Thought Theory	Culture, thought, and language
14	1991-2004	R. G. St. Pierre	Quantitative Program effects	Family Literacy Programs

That same year, Denny Taylor's (1983) introduced the term family literacy in her book's title. Denny's work is a major citation in 41 (15%) of the 272 reviews. Interestingly, the four most cited scholars in the field are all qualitative researchers whose work has documented literacy practices in diverse families. Denny Taylor and Catherine Dorsey Gaines (1988) investigated literacy practices in inner-city African American households. Luis Moll and his colleagues (i.e., Moll, Amanti, Neff, & Gonzalez, 1992) documented the funds of knowledge possessed by Mexican American children' and their families; Victoria Purcell-Gates (1995) focused on literacy practices within Appalachian families. Thus of the 14 major scholars we identified—the top four cited researchers all conducted qualitative, ethnographic studies within diverse families.

Citation coding revealed a second interesting finding. While cited less often than their early qualitative counterparts, a set of highly cited quantitative and causally oriented studies began to appear in the late 1980s (e.g., Snow, Whitehurst, St. Pierre, Senechal)—just preceding the first comprehensive edited family literacy volumes. Their work generally focused on identifying causal or predictive relationships between literacy practices and/or beliefs in families and children's school progress. Some of these researchers (e.g.,Whitehurst & Lonigan, 1998) conducted meta-analyses across existing quantitative studies. Two of these scholars focused specifically on the relationships between storybook reading and later reading achievement.

Findings from the Comprehensive Edited Volumes

We analyzed the tables of contents, introductory materials, and editorial statements from nine comprehensive edited volumes that focused specifically on family literacy. These volumes clustered around three periods 1995 to 1996 (Morrow, 1995; Benjamin & Lord, 1996), 2003 to 2005 (Anderson, Kendrick, Rogers, & Smythe, 2005; DeBruin-Parecki & Krol-Sinclair, 2003; Gregory, Long, & Volk, 2004; Wasik, 2004), and 2009 to 2010 (Dantas and Maynak, 2010; Dunsmore & Fisher, 2010; Li, 2009). The following section presents a brief analysis of the comprehensive edited volumes published during each period.

Comprehensive Edited Volumes: 1995 and 1996

Two comprehensive edited volumes focusing on family literacy were published in 1995 and 1996. Leslie Morrow edited *Family Literacy: Connections in Schools and Communities* (1995). In the *Foreword,* Barbara Bush maintained that problems such as "crime, homelessness, teenage pregnancy, hunger, and disease—would certainly be diminished if people had the literacy skills they need to help them accomplish their goals and realize their dreams" (p. ix). This emphasis on change and action was reflected in the extensive use of active verbs in chapter titles: "implementing," "combining," "encouraging," "enhancing," "helping," "linking," and "exploring." While this framing of the book could easily be read as conservative and interventionist, the book included a chapter by Auerbach, an outspoken critic of traditional family literacy programs, and the only chapter title from across all nine edited volumes that specifically references critical literacy. One chapter focused on family literacy in the United Kingdom. Others focused on adolescent mothers and teenagers, but none of the chapters identified specific cultural or linguistic communities. Eight chapters described family literacy programs.

One year later, Benjamin and Lord edited a set of papers co-commissioned by the Office of Vocational and Adult Education and Even Start entitled *Family Literacy: Directions in Research and Implications for Practice* (1996). The collection opened with an ominous message:

> Never before has education been more important to the well-being of the U.S. family, the fate of the country's economy, and the vitality of American democracy. No matter our age or socio-economic status, we all confront dramatic social, cultural, technological, and individual changes that demand more and better education for all. (p. iii)

As the report explained, "Should families beset by difficulties and deprivations be unable to master these essential skills adequately, family literacy programs offer opportunity, support and hope" (p. iii). The report was part of the first federal effort to synthesize research and life experiences into a "road map" (p. 1) that practitioners could use to help millions of Americans "become full partners in society" (p. 1). Its goal was to break the "cycle of deprivation and distress that so often accompanies lower levels of literacy skills" (p. 1).

While some chapter titles reflected efforts to help, support and perhaps remediate families (e.g., "Teaching Parenting and Basic Skills to Parents," "Meeting the Needs of Families"), other chapters recognized the interests and abilities of families. Durán's (1996) chapter description suggested that it was "essential to understand the families who are the recipients of family literacy programs" (p. 2) and Gadsden (1996) clearly stated that "families have strengths" (p. 2). This was the only edited volume that included chapters devoted to longitudinal studies of family literacy and religious diversity. Six chapters focused on family literacy programs.

While these early books were framed by discourses of intervention, remediation, and reference the goal of social change, in some ways, these volumes were also intriguingly progressive. Perhaps it is the genre of the "handbook" that begs attention to a vast range of perspectives. Nonetheless these early books are delightfully inconsistent and already attuned to major controversies in the field. Rather than presenting a field that has moved from ignorance to enlightenment or naïveté to sophisticated critique, these texts suggest that from its very conception, family literacy researchers have collectively problematized their work. Although tensions were apparent in these early volumes, changes, perhaps developments are also evident.

Comprehensive Edited Volumes: 2003-2005

Four comprehensive edited volumes were published between 2003 and 2005. Eight years after Morrow's comprehensive volume (Morrow, 1995) was published, the International Reading Association published another comprehensive volume. *Family Literacy: From Theory to Practice* (2003) was edited by DeBruin-Parecki and Krol-Sinclair (2003). Morrow wrote the *Foreword*, stating "research shows a strong link between the home environment and children's acquisition of literacy" (p. vi). While she recognized "many different forms of literacy practices," she noted that some of the literacy practices found in families from different cultures "may not influence school success" (p. vi).

Breaking from rhetoric that identified literacy as a cure for poverty, in their *Foreword*, DeBruin-Parecki and Krol-Sinclair (2003) maintained that "family literacy must be seen more as a theoretically sound field of research and practice and less as a panacea for curing multiple social and educational dilemmas" (p. 2). In the *Afterword*, they argued for multiple, situated, and local visions of family literacy and maintained that family literacy educators must decide whether their goal was to "continue to validate families' home literacy practices, cultures, languages, and values" or employ " a unilateral approach, trying to change families" (p. 308). Half of the chapters addressed family literacy programs, two focused on international programs, and others focused on fathers, adolescents, children with disabilities, and ELL students. One chapter title referenced "literacies" rather than "literacy."

Wasik's volume, the *Handbook of Family Literacy* (2004) was the longest of the comprehensive edited volumes—featuring 32 chapters. Fourteen chapters focused on family literacy programs.

Some were funded by the US Department of Education with the goal of conducting a synthesis of family literacy programs. Individuals from the Even Start office provided feedback on early drafts of research papers that eventually became chapters.

While the *Preface* described the text as a comprehensive source of information on family literacy, the contents made no mention of multiple literacies, family literacy practices, or the goals and interests of families; in addition, several topics addressed in earlier texts (e.g., special education students, adolescents, religious diversity, fathers) were not included. The book included a section on *Diversity and Culture,* addressing international issues, "Latino families," "nonmainstream children," "language-minority adults," "ESOL families," and "American Indians;" diverse populations were referenced in terms of general categories rather than specific local communities.

British and American academics, Gregory, Long, and Volk (2004), edited *Many Pathways to Literacy* (2004). This text was the first comprehensive volume that did not use the term "family literacy" in its title. It was also the first comprehensive volume that was not published by or in conjunction with either the International Reading Association or the US Department of Education. The text reflected sociocultural approaches to literacy learning. The editors argued "literacy and language development is far richer and more multidimensional than is often presumed" (p. xv). Gregory, Long, and Volk described literacy learning as involving syncretic meldings of practices from across multiple contexts. This book explicitly extended the boundaries of family literacy to include siblings and grandparents in contrast to earlier texts that tended to focus on mothers and children.

Linguistic diversity was woven throughout the chapters. Chapters addressed Puerto Rican siblings, bilingual literacy, multi-ethnic London, Latino elders, Mexican American kindergarteners, Chinese and Arabic school peers, Cantonese speaking peers, White working-class peers, Samoan American community members, Urdu Community school members, African American children, and Pueblo children. One chapter focused on children's multimedia practices. While the book recognized the multiplicity of literacy practices across families, in chapter titles the word literacy was used in its singular form. This volume did not address family literacy programs.

Like Gregory, Long, and Volk (2004), Anderson, Kendrick, Rogers, and Smythe (2005) do not use the term "family literacy" in their volume's title. The editors maintained that *Portraits of Literacy: Across Families, Communities, and Schools* "crosses traditional boundaries among the study of family, community, and school literacies" (p. 15-16) and offered a "unique global perspective on multiple literacies." Edited by a team of Canadian researchers and including chapters from Australian, British, Canadian, South African, and United States scholars highlighting literacy in South African, Pakistani, and Canadian Aboriginal communities, this book was truly international. While three literacy and family literacy projects were described, these projects involved socially and politically situated practices and critical analyses of texts and contexts.

Although not used in the volume's title, "literacies," rather than the singular term "literacy," appears prominently in section headings and highlights the multifaceted nature of literacy. In addition to traditional text-based literacies, various media practices including children's drawings, digital video, music, and graphic representations were addressed.

Comprehensive edited volumes published between 2003 and 2005 were framed less as a cure for poverty and more as human right. There was a mixed emphasis on family literacy programs and new types of programs that highlighted social, political, and situated practices that were beginning to emerge. In addition, more chapters presented expanded notions of family and referenced "literacies" rather than "literacy." These volumes addressed a wide range of local and international contexts. Discussions of multimodal and technological practices were beginning to occur.

Comprehensive Edited Volumes: 2009-2010

Three comprehensive edited volumes have been published in the last two years. *Multicultural Families, Home Literacies, and Mainstream Schooling* (Li, 2009) is the first comprehensive family literacy text to use the term "literacies" in its title. Its stated goal is to address the "need for a better understanding of literacy practices from the inside of the culturally diverse homes to ensure culturally responsive program development that will empower, not impede, all children's learning" (p. xvi). Section II addresses diversity with two chapters dedicated to African American families, Asian families, Hispanic families, and European American families, as well as a chapter focused on "Families of Mixed Heritages" (Li, 2009, p. vi). Li recognizes the danger that accompanies presenting families along racialized lines. As she explains, her intention is not to essentialize, but rather, "to draw attention to both cultural variability and universality of home literacy practices across groups and families" (p. xviii). This is the only identified edited volume that devotes chapters to White middle-class families and families of mixed heritages. Family literacy programs are not addressed. *Bringing Literacy Home* (Dunsmore & Fisher, 2010) is the result of a conversation supported by the Ball Foundation and the International Reading Association. As the editors state, this volume explicitly links home with school practices advocating for a "conversation about school-based literacy routines in which understanding the patterns and practices of home life is central to all planning for and teaching of students" (p. 1). While this book frames literacy in terms of schooling, it explicitly advocates for drawing upon home literacy practices and recognizes "new, complex, and multimodal forms of interaction with symbols and text in which home-school-community connections are myriad and changing" (p. 1). Chapters dedicated to diversity are generally limited to discussions of African American and Latino families. There is one chapter on adolescent literacy. Four of the sixteen chapters address family literacy programs.

In *Home-School Connection in a Multicultural Society*, Dantas and Manyak (2010) explicitly address deficit perspectives about children and families. They challenge educators and researchers to consider the "depth of difference" (p. 1) that exists "between families and across cultures and the significant discontinuity that children from diverse cultural groups often experience as they enter school" (p. 1). The chapters are presented in three sections. The title of the first section addresses (Dis)connections—referencing both disconnections and connections that families experience as they move between home and school. The second section moves beyond description to present tools and strategies that teachers can use to transform curricula; this is the first comprehensive volume to dedicate a section to learning from families to inform curricula and teaching. The final section includes a chapter addressing home-school-community collaborations.

The chapters present children from many different backgrounds including Sudanese, Chinese, Puerto Rican, Muslim Arab-American, Latino immigrant, and Appalachian children. Each chapter presents the words of children and adults from these communities and challenges educators to rethink assumptions that they might bring to schooling in diverse communities. The final chapter frames the book by asking readers to consider the "socio-political context" (p. 273). Rios argues for a macro-level analysis that "includes people's understanding of status and power differentials, as well as the colonizing ideologies that are used to justify them" (p. 276). This book is explicitly political and is framed not only as contributing to a conversation about diversity but also to address how diversity is treated in schools.

Our analysis of these nine comprehensive volumes revealed several patterns. First, later volumes are less focused on family literacy as a means to address social problems and more attention is focused on the relationships between home and school literacies and the ways educators can build on the home literacy practices of families. Second, with the exception of the volume edited by Dunsmore and Fisher (2010), comprehensive edited texts have increasingly focused on international and transnational contexts as well as literacy within specific local communities. References to diversity are increasingly situated in relation to specific local communities rather than general references to large groups of people. Literacy, and increasingly literacies, are treated as shared social practices within families and communities rather than as individual accomplishments or abilities. Family literacy scholars are beginning to pay more attention to technological media practices and research focused on White families and *Whiteness* is also starting to appear.

Despite these developments, comprehensive edited volumes have also narrowed the scope of diversity to refer primarily to culture, race, ethnicity, and/or language. While earlier texts referenced adolescent mothers, fathers, and children with disabilities, these groups are not represented in more recent volumes. From this analysis of the field, I move on to one family.

LITERACY IN ONE FAMILY: A TEMPORAL JOURNEY

I suspect that some readers will not be comfortable with the next story I will tell. The story does not end happily—at least not at the point I end the account presented here. Bradford's story could be read as a stereotypical account of a poor African American child—single mother, large family, struggles in school, and eventual incarceration. But I argue that his story significantly complicates these positionings—highlighting the literacy strengths of his family, the school success of his siblings, and the apparent abdication of the school district and the local community for their responsibility in educating Bradford. I do not tell Bradford's story because it is representative of low-income African American students and not all of the children in my sample had the same or even similar experiences.

CASE STUDY METHODOLOGY

Today, I follow Bradford and his family from first grade through high school. I present only an overview of the study; more detailed accounts are available elsewhere (Compton-Lilly, 2003, 2007). When the children were in first grade, I randomly chose 10 of my first-grade students and their parents to participate in the study.

The families participated during the children's first-, fourth-/fifth-, seventh-/eighth-, and 10th-/11th-grade years. In first grade, the students attended a large urban school where 97% of the students qualified for free or reduced-price lunch. Rosa Parks Elementary School was on the state's list of schools in need of improvement. Four years later, many of the students had left Rosa Parks to attend other schools in the same district. By high school, seven of the 10 students remained in the study. Four children left school without graduating; two of these students, including Bradford, left school when they were assigned to the eighth grade at age 17.

Because I was the students' first-grade teacher, the initial phase involved a rich range of data, including four interviews with children and parents, fieldnotes containing classroom observations and reflections, student portfolios and classroom assessments, and audiotaped class discussions. Phases two and three involved two interviews with students and parents, reading assessments (see Clay, 2002; Ekwall & Shanker, 1993; Leslie & Caldwell, 2006), and writing samples. The final phase of the research project involved interviews with parents and students, classroom observations, and student-created reflective texts including writing, photographs, drawings, and audio journals.

All audiotapes were transcribed and coded during each phase of the study to identify salient categories of information. During the first and third phases, data was coded into categories and contrastive analysis methods were used to organize these categories across cases to identify themes and patterns. During the second and fourth phases, data was coded separately for each case and case summaries were constructed for each family. More recently I have returned to the data to identify related codes and patterns across the phases and over time.

A SAMPLING OF FINDINGS

I last spoke with Bradford and his mother in the Fall of 2007. Ten autumns had passed since Bradford entered my first-grade class as a seven-year-old student. He was then approaching his 18th birthday and was no longer attending school. My goal in this chapter is to situate Bradford and his family within time, just as I did with the field of family literacy. In fact, Bradford and his family have inhabited the same historical period as the field of family literacy. Before Ms. Holt, Bradford's mother, was born in 1953, her parents came to this mid-sized northeastern city from "The South." As African American people growing up in the South and attending school in the 1940s, neither her mother nor father had the luxury of regular school attendance. While Ms. Holt's mother had good reading abilities, her father never learned to read.

> Like my dad he used to say, if you didn't know how to read you didn't know where you were going. . . . It's strange but he couldn't read but he was a truck driver. Anywhere in the city that he had to go, he knew. . . . She'd [Ms. Holt's mother] map out where he had to go cause he, he would know the day before where he was going the next day. He'd come home and he'd hurry to get on that table and they'd map out his route and tell him where to go and show him the letters. Cause she taught him the different letters. And how to sign his name but other than that... I'm serious, he drove a truck all for years. He couldn't read but he knew the street signs.

Ms. Holt grew up in a middle-class, integrated area of the city: "See back when I was raised up I wasn't raised up around no Blacks. My mother, she kept us you know kind of distant" (her voice trails to a whisper).

It would have been in the late 1950s when Ms. Holt attended first grade and learned to read. As she recalled, "back in my day" it was Dick and Jane:

> I still remember the dog Spot and Dick and Jane and Mom and Dad and Sally.

> . . .It was good cause they always did something different. And the words were
> kinda simple. . . You know a little short story but they [the kids] were always in
> them. Jane never did anything too much but... Dick always did.

When I asked her about the almost total absence of Black people in the stories, Ms. Holt paused, saying that she had not thought about that. Not only did her mother have copies of the "Dick and Jane Books" at home, but her mother had also purchased a complete set of SRA cards, "There were yellow, blue, green, purple—the purple was the advanced, but you started with the red and the blue." As Ms. Holt explained, these were "very expensive" but her mother considered the cards to be an investment that would benefit all her children. In fact all five of Ms. Holt's siblings graduated from high school.

Despite Ms. Holt's mother's efforts to support her children as readers, Ms. Holt's was recently reminded of the struggles she had with learning to read:

> I was asking [my older sister] about how I was when I was young, she said
> "Beverly you know when you were coming up, your reading never was that good."
> You know, I said "Really?" She said "Remember. . ." This was locked inside there
> [motions to her heart]. I said "Ok, I remember those days". . . . Couldn't try to
> make me read. . . we're talking 30, 40 years ago, something like that. And she
> [Ms. Holt's mother] was doing the best she could, she'd get so frustrated you
> know with this. . . I say "Well, that's where he [Bradford] probably gets it from
> then". . . It never even ever dawned on me that this might be what his problem
> is—[it's] hereditary.

Ms. Holt recalled a favorite third-grade teacher and borrowing books from the book mobile that visited her neighborhood. As she moved through middle school and high school in the 1960s and early 1970s, she lamented writing book reports about "Shane" and "Old Yeller." She self-identified as a "sports person" rather than as a reader.

Ms. Holt eventually had 7 children—including six sons and two sets of twins. Her oldest child was born in 1977. Between her graduation from high school in 1971 and Bradford's birth in 1990, her home burned to the ground twice and the family "lost everything." Ms. Holt worked in a dentist office for 13 years before earning her degree in food sciences and landing a job as a dining room manager.

While Bradford struggled with reading, this was not the case for all of Ms. Holt's children. At least two of her children were described as avid readers, including Bradford's older brother, Louis, who she referred to as a "bookworm" and described as learning to read at age four.

> He just got the newspaper and just started reading it. My mother-in-law, cause he
> was staying over, she said "Beverly this boy is reading the newspaper." [I answered]
> "He can't read no paper." She said "Beverly this boy is reading the paper." Cause
> then you know she got the paper [and] she put it on the table. He says [the words]
> that's right. . . [He] actually was reading the paper. He's a brilliant reader.

Despite struggling with stuttering as a child, Louis was eventually awarded a golf scholarship and became the only child in the family to graduate from a four-year school during the course of the research project.

In 1997, the year Bradford entered my classroom—after failing first grade at another school— Ms. Holt was 44 years old. While she described herself as "getting ready to retire," she was still working when the project ended 10 years later. The year before Bradford was in my class, his oldest brother was killed in a DWI accident. Bradford and his brother had been close and the death had a significant effect on Bradford, who sometimes spoke about his brother in class.

This was the year that one of Bradford's brothers left school without a diploma. A special education student, who was on the honor roll and participating in a work/study program, Bradford's brother was told in June of his senior year of high school that he would not be able to graduate. Ms. Holt was angry and her son was frustrated. He dropped out of school despite the pleas of family members, "He stopped going because they told him he wasn't going to graduate. So he was just disgusted."

In fourth grade, Bradford was placed in a special education class due to lack of progress with reading. The school district was intent on placing him in a 1-6-1 program. Ms. Holt did not believe that Bradford belonged in that setting which she referred to as the "bottom of the bucket." Her concerns about his self-esteem propelled her to enlist the help of a lawyer and an advocate. They were successful in having Bradford placed in a 1-12-1 self-contained class.

That same year Bradford took the brand new State ELA test. His mother was concerned that children in special education classes were required to take the same test as the other children, "Bradford's gonna fail that test. And guess what? You're going to demean him all his life."

Ms. Holt consistently described Bradford as a "follower" who would often be led into trouble by his peers. Bradford had experienced minor run-ins with teachers and could be uncooperative. His mother was thrilled in fifth grade when Bradford befriended James, who involved Bradford in his church. As his mother explained:

> I'm telling you he [Bradford] just accepted Christ and he started being a better person. He doesn't give me trouble that much. He had a little trouble yesterday, but that was the first time [his teacher] called me in months.

However, while Bradford's teacher was reporting to Ms. Holt "all these good qualities in Bradford" and improvements in "math and reading," his report card was all Ds. Ms. Holt was quite confused:

> He brings home all these As and B+s and then when they give him his report card they give him a D. I say what's really going on? . . . They supposed to have special classes for [children in special education]? They should not have the same standard should they?

Ms. Bradford often commented on strengths that she believed Bradford's teachers did not recognize. She described his interest in current events and noted that he watched the news with her every morning and asked "questions about it too," joking that he should be nicknamed "Channel 9 News." She argued that Bradford and his peers "ought to read books [in school] about ball players and other things that interest them."

When Bradford was in first grade, Ms. Holt did not describe herself as a reader. Four years later she had rediscovered the books by Donald Goines that she had loved in high school.

> [My daughter] came home with a couple of them [including] *Red Men*. . . She gets them out [and] we be reading them and I realize that book's all gone. (laughs) I read the whole book. Oh God, knowledge! (We both laugh)

My account of Bradford and Ms. Holt moves forward three years to the year 2003. Bradford had been placed in an eighth-grade special education classroom and things at school had gotten worse. Ms. Holt worried that teachers were not taking time with Bradford and noted that he was disengaged from school. Again, she returned to the theme of finding the right book:

> I figure if you gave him a soccer book or a baseball book, then you might have him. Couldn't you have done the same thing reading wise with a soccer book as you do with the Martin Luther King book? . . . I was thinking with [being] a special education teacher you have to kind of bend the rules a little bit more than with a regular class you've got to be able to help the child rather than do this and lose them.

Later in the same interview she noted: "Give him something that he enjoy doing and he write [about] it. You give him this book about these little animals and all this stuff. He's not interested in animals. He's afraid of most of them." She identified *Sports Illustrated* as a favorite text.

A refrain repeated at many points over the 10-year study involved access to libraries:

Ms. Holt (1997): They're closing all these libraries. . . . And they talk about they want the kids to read?

Ms. Holt (1997): And if you want my children to learn to read, put those book mobiles they had years ago.

Ms. Holt (2003): That was the worst thing they could have done, took the libraries from our children. . . . they're already in the city [schools]. . . I know that's not fair.

Ms. Holt (2004): Cause of couple times I went there [to the closest library which is on the other side of the city] and it's not open. So what good is it if it's not open?. . . So how are they supposed to learn how to read?

Ms. Holt was aware that time was passing and that things would have to change soon. Bradford was frustrated with school, no longer interested in current events, and as Ms. Holt reported, "He can't read." She explained that since "he's not disgusted yet"; she planned to enroll him in Job Corps "before he gets disgusted."

Bradford, the youngest of Ms. Holt's seven children, was the only one who had altercations with the law. Bradford and his friend James had been hanging around some older boys and were caught up in a drug bust. Bradford was sent to a juvenile detention center for a few weeks. When he returned, he was placed on probation and returned to his eighth-grade classroom. Ms. Holt believed that this probation was a good thing:

> I expect Bradford to graduate because if he got probation [for] three or four years, it'll be mandatory for him to go to school and I'll love it. . . He got to go to school EVERY day. (laughs) You know sometimes things happen for a reason.

Ms. Holt believed that Bradford's reading was his greatest obstacle, "If he had better reading skills, he'd go further in life I think. He can't read. He can't read he don't know [how]."

Between 2004 and 2006, according to his mother, Bradford and his friend James were "living the fast life"; Bradford spent over a year in a juvenile detention facility. While this was difficult for the family, Bradford did well in school:

> Going to [the detention center] was the best thing to happen to him. He went to school, he had plaques. Ms. Lilly, Bradford was making As in some classes, Bs, I

had never seen an A or B out of Bradford. I had never seen [that]. I wish I could have thanked them people, because I saved those report cards.

She also noted his excellent attendance, the trophies his soccer team had won, and his improved weight. As she reported, "He got his senses back." However, things changed when he was released and returned to his home school district.

> When he was in [the detention facility] they put him in 9th and 10th grade. And then when he came back [home], they wanted to put him in seven and eighth grade. I mean, come on now. You know Bradford, he won't go to middle school when he's like 17 years old. . . When they told him 7th and 8th grade he hit the ceiling and he ain't went back that way since.

Ms. Holt explained that she "tried to explain this to the Board of Education," but they didn't listen to her. Bradford was particularly frustrated because he believed that he was making progress in the juvenile detention center:

> When I was at the [juvenile detention center] my math was in college level. I swear to God it was. I was taking mad math and they gave you a test right before you leave. . . reading, math—and they said my math was a 12th into college [level] and my reading was like in 9th grade.

Bradford dropped out of school but planned to pursue his GED. However, school district policies required that he wait until he was over-age for high school before he could enter the GED program.

In addition to doing well in school, this was the first time in the 10 years of interviewing Bradford that he described himself as a good reader and identified texts that he enjoyed reading:

> I like magazines. I read a lot of them. Whenever they got something good I want to read, then I'll read it. When I was locked up, I was reading a couple Donald Goines books.

Notably, Donald Goines is the same author Mrs. Holt and her daughter enjoyed.

During our final interview, Ms. Holt reflected on Bradford's school trajectory:

> I don't know, they [school personnel] said they had his best interest at heart but I didn't believe that. Because he's been in that program No Kids Left Behind. They kept leaving him behind!. . . I never did understand that. I still don't. . . . Every year he was in the same [special education] class. Every year [the other children] go from one year to [the next] year and then [Bradford] is in the same class.
>
> Like I said who wants to be in the same class for nine years? . . . You don't see different kids. You see the same kids that you saw last year. Doing what? The same thing. Cutting up [misbehaving in class].

Bradford agreed with his mother:

> I think I could have did better in [a] regular class. Self-contained—you don't do nothin' there. They give you same work. . . Some stuff that I could already do they will just keep on giving it to me because I could do it and I could zip through it and they could just like huh, he gonna be done. But, they ain't never try to challenge you.

Special education, repeating grade levels, being placed in grade 8 at age 17, all of these contributed to a sense of stasis. Ms. Holt noted:

> To me it's not fair. You know they got to find another way to categorize these special needs kids. . . Most of these special needs kids they [are] dropping out of school. . . You very seldom hear about a special needs child graduating.

She reflected on Bradford as a first-grader:

> He was good. He was a good little boy. . . . he liked the kids. . . . he worked hard, he tried hard even though it didn't work out that way, he tried hard. He gave it his all. Put it that way—most [of the] time [laughs].

Bradford had dreams of opening his own business. He was thinking of a restaurant or catering service. As he reported, his mother could cook. In our final interview, I asked Bradford if there was anything that teachers might need to hear from him. Bradford replied:

> I don't know really. I can't tell them [anything]. Even though if you do tell them they probably still they won't listen. . . Some of them would. Some its obvious just come in to get their check and go home. Some of them do be here to help you and want you to succeed in life.

Bradford's story is clearly not a simple account of parental neglect. Four of his six surviving siblings graduated from high school and one received a four-year degree. It is the story of family that valued education and literacy. My question is: What is our role as family literacy educators in supporting families?

TWO STORIES ACROSS TIME

At this point it might be reasonable for readers to ask how these two stories are related. I argue that they are both connected and disconnected. I recognize connections in terms of **time.** Whether discussing academic fields or families, time references how people make sense of their worlds. Not only do ongoing events inform people's understandings, but the ways communities and families collectively make sense of their worlds affects the meanings constructed by researchers and family members. Furthermore, ongoing events and familial/community experiences are contextualized within larger social histories that bring ways of thinking, knowing, and understanding that frame people's visions of themselves and their social worlds. Recognizing academic fields and families as evolving communities complicated by tensions, acts of agency, inconsistencies, and challenges can prevent us from essentializing diverse families and groups of researchers (e.g., quantitative vs. qualitative; causal vs. descriptive). Instead, we recognize researchers and families as operating within larger social histories that involve experiences, ideologies, policies, goals, and relationships.

I argue that the juxtaposition of these two temporal accounts presents connections. First, both our review of the field and my account of Bradford's family could be read as invitations to revisit our purposes and goals as family literacy scholars. Our review of comprehensive edited volumes suggests that as a field we are less focused on family literacy as a means to address social problems and more focused on the relationships between home and school literacies and the ways educators can build on the home literacy practices of families. Just as recent comprehensive volumes focus on building on the knowledge that families bring, Ms. Holt appeals to teachers to find books that interest Bradford and draw on his knowledge of current events and sports. She advocates for testing and promotion policies that attend to Bradford's best interests rather than a narrow definition of academic and literate competency.

Second, comprehensive edited texts have increasingly focused on literacy within specific local communities. Rather than identifying prescriptive approaches that promise to universally solve literacy challenges, these approaches focus on the strengths and knowledge possessed by people within communities. A simple reading of Bradford's case might suggest a stereotypical story of a struggling single mother of seven children living in a high-poverty community. A more nuanced reading reveals a family that across generations has placed importance on high school graduation and invested significantly in literacy. We view a family in which some children learned to read at a very early age, one graduated from college, others were placed in special education, and most reading for enjoyment—sometimes the same books across generations. These accounts treat literacy, and increasingly literacies, as shared social practices within families and communities rather than as individual accomplishments or abilities.

Third, by focusing on local communities and attending to both variation and consistency within those communities, we begin to grapple with the complexities that exist at the intersection of race, class, gender, and other social markers. Rather than seeking generalizable solutions related to literacy abilities, we recognize Bradford as a male, African American youth, growing up in an economically struggling community, and attending severely underfunded schools. Race, gender, and poverty all brought historical and contemporary dimensions to the challenges Bradford's faced as a reader and as a student and to Ms. Holt's mother's challenges as a parent. The need to grapple with this intersectionality is evident in both Bradford's story and increasing nuanced and situated approaches to literacy reflected in recent edited volumes.

Despite these connections, I also argue that in others ways these stories are problematically disconnected. By viewing both fields and families as temporally bound systems, we begin to envision what might have been needed to help Bradford and that the solution might not reside in teaching Bradford's mother how to parent or how to support Bradford's literacy development. Helping Bradford and millions of other children involves addressing larger issues related to healthy communities, employment opportunities, educational opportunities for children who do not thrive in schools, channels for parental advocacy, accessible resources, changes in staffing policies that allow teachers to truly help students, individualized and focused reading instruction for students beyond the primary grades, and supporting and extending library services so that all children have easy access to books that are not traditionally available in schools. This is more than an educational issue. Social policies that allow some families to live in untenable situations and face impossible challenges are significant. Family literacy research cannot only focus on literacy for young children. So, I leave us to ponder the following questions:

- Were reading problems the simple cause of the difficulties that Bradford faced or were his unaddressed difficulties with reading a symptom of a system gone awry?
- What could have changed academic outcomes for Bradford?
- What might family literacy scholars offer families and children across time—not just as an inoculation provided during preschool years, but also as a ongoing resource?

- In what ways does diversity matter—being Black, male, and poor?
- How can family literacy scholars support teachers in recognizing and building on what all children bring?

I suspect that solutions reside in a vast range of issues related to a social contracts that allow some families to continue to live in poverty alongside inadequate school budgets. Family literacy educators need to advocate for comprehensive and longitudinal investments in families and communities. While this might appear impossible, until we can muster the determination to recognize family literacy as extending beyond young children and "deficient" parents, the educational system will fail to support students and that is untenable.

REFERENCES

Anderson, J., Kendrick, M., Rogers, T., & Smythe, S. (2005). Portraits of literacy across families, communities, and schools: Intersections and tensions. NY: Routledge.

Benjamin, L. A. & Lord, J. (1996). *Family literacy: Directions in research and implications for practice.* Washington, DC: US Department of Education.

Clay, M. M. (2002). *An observation survey of early literacy achievement.* Portsmouth, NH: Heinemann.

Compton-Lilly, C. (2003). *Reading families: The literate lives of urban children.* New York, NY: Teachers College Press.

Compton-Lilly, C. (2007). *Rereading families: The literate lives of urban children, four years later.* New York, NY: Teachers College Press.

Compton-Lilly, Rogers, & Lewis (in review). Analyzing diversity epistemologies: An integrative critical literature review of family literacy scholarship.

Dantas, M. L. & Manyak, P. C. (Eds.) (2010). Home-school connections in a multicultural society: Learning from and within culturally and linguistically diverse families.

DeBruin-Parecki, A. & Krol-Sinclair, B. (Eds.). (2003). *Family literacy: From theory to practice.* (pp. 1-6). Newark, DE: IRA.

Dunsmore, K. & Fisher, D. (Eds.) (2010). *Bringing Literacy Home.* Newark, DE: International Reading Association.

Durán, R. (1996). English immigrant language learners: Cultural accommodation and family literacy. In L. A. Benjamin and Jerome Lord (Eds.) *Family literacy: Directions in research and implications for practice: Summary and papers of a national symposium.* U.S. Department of Education Office of Educational Research and Improvement in Collaboration with the Office of Vocational and Adult Education and the Office of Elementary and Secondary Education's Even Start Program.

Ekwall, E. E., & Shanker, J. L. (1993). *Ekwall/Shanker reading inventory* (3rd ed.). Boston, MA: Allyn & Bacon.

Gadsden, V. (1996). Designing and conducting family literacy programs that account for racial, ethnic, religious, and other cultural differences. In L. A. Benjamin and Jerome Lord (Eds.) *Family literacy: Directions in research and implications for practice: Summary and papers of a national symposium.* U.S. Department of Education Office of Educational Research and Improvement in Collaboration with the Office of Vocational and Adult Education and the Office of Elementary and Secondary Education's Even Start Program.

Gregory, E., Long, S., and Volk, D. (Eds.) (2004). *Many pathways to literacy: Young children learning with siblings, grandparents, peers, and communities.* New York, NY: Routledge.

Heath, S. B. (1983). *Ways with words.* New York, NY: Cambridge University Press.

Johnson, L. B. (1964). War on Poverty Speech. Accessed on 11/20/10 at http://www.fordham.edu/halsall/mod/1964johnson-warpoverty.html

Leslie, L., & Caldwell, J. (2006). *Qualitative reading inventory - 4th edition* (QRI-4 ed.). Reading, WA: Allyn and Bacon.

Li, G. (2009). *Multicultural families, home literacies, and mainstream schooling.* Charlotte, NC: Information Age Publishing.

Moll, L. C., Amanti, C., Neff, D., & Gonzalez, N. (1992). Funds of knowledge for teaching: Using a qualitative approach to connect homes and classrooms. *Theory into Practice, 31*(1), 132-141.

Morrow, L. M. (1995). Family Literacy: New Perspectives, New Practices. In L. M. Morrow (Ed.) *Family literacy: Connections in schools and communities.* Newark, Delaware: IRA.

Purcell-Gates, V. (1995). *Other people's words: The cycle of low literacy.* Cambridge, MA: Harvard University Press.

Taylor, D., & Dorsey-Gaines, C. (1988). *Growing Up Literate.* Portsmouth, NH: Heinemann.

Taylor, D. (1983). *Family literacy: Young children learning to read and write.* Portsmouth, NH: Heinemann.

Wasik, B. H. (Ed.) (2004) *Handbook of family literacy.* Mahwah, NJ: Lawrence Erlbaum Associates.

Whitehurst, G. J. & Lonigan, C. J. (1998) Child development and emergent literacy. *Child Development, 69,* 848-872.

The Power of Collaborative Teaching with Integrity: Lessons Learned through the Journey of a Reading Researcher and Educator

Barbara M. Taylor
University of Minnesota

The primary theme of my talk is that teachers are what matter most in helping all students be motivated, successful readers. Effective instruction is not about teaching with fidelity, it is not about following a manual; it's all about teaching with integrity; teaching effectively by making informed choices to meet students' needs and by providing balanced reading instruction that motivates students and challenges them all. As much as possible, collaborative teaching with integrity is the winning strategy. Unfortunately, however, with all of the efforts directed towards improving education today, I don't think enough emphasis is being placed on professional learning for teachers that leads to more effective instruction.

Collaborative teaching with integrity is like being part of a beautiful garden. Not all gardens are the same size or shape; they don't all look the same; the flowers within each garden are not all the same; and gardens take some serious work. But a beautiful garden is a place you want to be. When I discuss teacher collaboration in this talk, think about how good teachers must feel, along with administrators, support staff, parents, and students, as members of a beautiful garden.

In this presentation, I am going to talk primarily about the efficacy of elementary teachers teaching with integrity, and do so by sharing the lessons I have learned on my 35+ year journey as a reading researcher and educator. I hope my lessons learned may give younger reading researchers and educators ideas that will help them on their professional journeys.

But to start, what have been the goals leading me throughout my professional journey? Simply stated, I have spent my career studying and researching how to improve ALL students' reading abilities, especially those who most depend on school for learning. I have focused on helping teachers improve students' reading comprehension by engaging them in high-level thinking about texts and teaching them to be strategic readers. Across my career, I have studied and researched not just the 'what' but also the 'how' of effective reading instruction, using this knowledge as I provided professional learning support to help teachers teach effectively with integrity, not fidelity.

I have been committed to conducting solid reading studies throughout my journey, using data on students as my ultimate indicator of effectiveness of the practices I have researched. In the last 15 years, I have also relied heavily on data on teacher and school effectiveness to help me help teachers and schools help their students.

Since this is the story of a researcher's journey, let me back up just a little and tell you about early interests that led to my long-standing professional goals. I have always been an avid reader, and I was an English major in undergraduate school—perhaps, as Garrison Keillor sometimes suggests, not a particularly marketable degree. But being an English major, which is all about understanding texts, is where my life-long interest came from of helping children read strategically and understand texts through engagement in high-level talk and writing about the books and other materials they read in school.

Although I did student teaching in high school English, my first job was as an assistant teacher in the intermediate grades at a private school in Atlanta where many of the students struggled with reading. There, I became interested in helping all students learn to read well, and received my elementary teaching license as I worked on a masters' degree in reading. I taught third grade in inner-city Houston for a few years, and then taught reading in sixth grade at a middle school in Appalachia while I worked on my doctorate in supervision and reading at Virginia Tech. From my teaching experiences in Texas and Virginia, I developed a passion for helping students of poverty, especially those who struggled with reading. This has been a driving force for me throughout my career. From my doctoral training, I developed a strong belief in the power of high-quality research.

I have already discussed the origins of three of my life-long professional goals: engaging in high-quality research; working with and helping children, especially poor readers, in high-poverty, diverse schools; and engaging all students in high-level thinking related to texts. What about my fourth life-long goal of helping teachers through collaborative professional learning to teach reading effectively and with integrity? This has come through my work and research in schools over many years. In the process, I've become a strong believer in teachers, not programs, as the answer to all students developing into successful readers.

To help teachers become the most effective they can be, I have spent decades focusing on collaborative, reflective professional learning in schools. Early on, I learned that as a teacher educator and researcher, I could provide valuable support to teachers and conduct useful research at the same time, but to do so I needed to get out to schools often to best understand the culture of schooling, to observe teacher's teaching and students' learning in action, and to earn teachers' trust. That is why over the past 35 years I've made a concerted effort to get into many schools and classrooms on a regular basis.

During my career, I spent about 10 years each on three lines of inquiry and research. My first decade, from 1978-1988, focused on children's comprehension of texts, especially informational texts, a continuation of what I had studied for my dissertation. I returned to research specifically on reading comprehension about 15 years later. In my second decade from 1989 to 1998, I focused on providing early reading intervention support to beginning readers through a small group approach I called Early Intervention in Reading, or EIR; I also returned to this from 2004 to the present. In my third decade, from 1997-2008, I focused on effective schools, effective teachers, and effective school-wide reading improvement through the School Change in Reading (SCR) Framework I developed and refined with colleagues, most notably David Pearson and Debra Peterson, as well as with teachers across the U.S.

During each 10-year phase, I worked with and learned from many teachers in many schools; especially during my EIR and SCR phases over the past 20 years. I didn't feel I could do quality research or help teachers help themselves become more effective teachers unless I got out to their classrooms on a regular basis.

So what happened during each of these 10+ year phases in my journey? What I did learn about effective reading instruction along the way?

STUDENTS' READING COMPREHENSION

My study of children's comprehension progressed through three stages, in which each stage provided a logical step to the next one. First, starting with my dissertation, I studied poor readers' comprehension of informational text. Then I studied the impact of teaching strategies to students to improve their comprehension of informational text, specifically through reading for main ideas and summarizing. Most recently, I studied comprehension strategies and high-level talk about text in my School Change in Reading work, that originated with the Center for the Improvement of Early Reading Achievement (CIERA), as well as in my work with colleagues Georgia Garcia, David Pearson, Kay Stahl, and Eury Bauer on an Institute of Education Sciences (IES) grant.

What did I learn from my earliest research on children's reading of informational text? I looked at fifth and sixth graders reading on a third or fourth grade level and found out that their comprehension of informational text looked very similar to that of average third or fourth grade readers, so perhaps the struggling readers did not have a processing problem, as was sometimes suggested in the literature at that time, but they were just less experienced readers (Taylor, 1979; Taylor, 1980). In general, however, I found that students in the intermediate grades had trouble reading for the main ideas in informational texts (Taylor & Samuels, 1983).

Because children had trouble understanding the main ideas of informational text, the next logical step in my research was to try to help teachers help students with this. I learned that children's reading comprehension improved more when they generated main ideas than when they selected main ideas in a multiple-choice format. I also learned that teaching students to summarize informational text improved their reading comprehension in general, as well as their ability to recall main ideas (Taylor, 1982; Taylor, 1985; Taylor & Beach, 1984).

What are lessons I learned from my study of and research on instruction to enhance intermediate grade students' comprehension of and memory for informational text? Children do better when they are taught strategies for focusing on the big picture—or main ideas of text, rather than pieces of the puzzle—or the details that they are more likely to focus upon without explicit instruction. Also, active production of main ideas by students seems to be a key factor.

When I visited schools during my comprehension phase, it seemed to me that a great deal of students' time was wasted filling out worksheets, especially when this seemed to bore them because they could already do the things they were asked to do. In one study, I found out that pretesting students on comprehension skills was beneficial. In this study, teachers agreed that those who could already complete worksheets on comprehension skills with at least 80% accuracy at a pretest phase did not have to complete more worksheets on these skills. The students still passed post-tests with 90% accuracy or better, on average, did as well as comparison students, and were freed up to do more independent reading during the reading block (Taylor & Frye, 1988; Taylor, Frye, & Gaetz, 1990).

In a second study in which fifth and sixth grade students kept logs of their time spent on reading, I found that time spent on independent reading in school contributed to gains in students' reading comprehension by spring, after controlling for their fall scores on a standardized reading test. In part, time spent on independent reading was determined by teachers, with some saying, "Read at least 10 minutes a day as one of your independent work time activities" and others saying

"Read a book if you get done with your other work." The kids in the latter situation read less. (Taylor, Frye, & Maruyama, 1990).

After the National Reading Panel report came out in 2000 with its focus on comprehension strategies, Steve Stahl invited me with others to study comprehension strategies instruction versus high-level talk and writing about texts. David Pearson, Deb Peterson, Michael Rodriguez, and I had already published a paper on the value of both aspects of comprehension instruction, but especially on the value of high level talk and writing about text on students' reading growth (Taylor, Pearson, Peterson, & Rodriguez, 2003; Taylor & Pearson, 2004). Steve in particular wondered, was it the strategy instruction per se or was it the greater involvement in the meaning of texts that made the difference? In a 3-year study of second through fifth grade students' comprehension of narrative and informational texts with colleagues across multiple institutions, we found that engaging students in high-level talk and writing about texts was at least as important as teaching them about comprehension strategies (Garcia, Pearson, Taylor, Bauer, & Stahl, in press).

My lessons learned about teaching comprehension strategies and engaging students' in high-level talk and writing about texts: You need to have a dual focus. However, as a teacher don't over focus on teaching comprehension strategies as ends in themselves; teach them as something students use as needed as they are engaged in high-level thinking about texts.

EARLY INTERVENTION IN READING

Although comprehension work has spanned my career, I came to a fork in the road in 1989. I knew there was a lot more to study and learn about students' reading comprehension, but I was excited about Reading Recovery and still concerned about getting all students off to a good start in reading. So I took the fork in the road that lead me to 10 years of research and development on Early Intervention in Reading (EIR).

I was impressed with the results of Reading Recovery in the mid to late 1980s and was doing a lot of work in schools in St. Paul and Minneapolis. I was struck by the realization in one large school I worked in (with 200 first graders) that 70 children needed an early reading intervention if they were going to learn to read in first grade. It hit me that you could not reach all of these children through Reading Recovery alone, as good as it is (Pinnell, Lyons, DeFord, Bryk, & Seltzer, 1994). So I decided to switch gears away from comprehension research and see if I could develop a small-group early reading intervention process that teachers in their own classrooms could use with a group of 5-7 children who were in need of extra reading support, without which they would likely fail to learn to read in first grade.

Although my main purpose for going into EIR was to help teachers prepare emerging readers better so they didn't end up like the intermediate grade struggling readers I had worked with earlier in my career, I also went into EIR with the goal of helping teachers focus on reading for meaning, not just decoding. Additionally, I wanted to help teachers internalize the idea that you don't need to drill on skills children can already perform.

Starting with grade 1, I was concerned about approaches that pulled out early readers without considering how to regularly support them when they were back in the classroom. I saw the need to help teachers learn how to help their struggling readers right in the classroom. Also, research suggested that many struggling readers wouldn't be 'fixed' by one model or program in one year (Hiebert & Taylor, 2000). I saw a need for continuity from kindergarten through fourth grade in supporting all struggling readers. Thus, I developed EIR models across all of these grades.

In EIR teachers use authentic, motivating literature, not dry, leveled texts that so many emergent and struggling readers are given to read. Teachers also teach and then coach students to be strategic in the use of word recognition and comprehension strategies. They focus lessons on reading for meaning and vocabulary, not just decoding accuracy and fluency. Word work is not neglected, but it is done, in part, by teaching phonic elements and by coaching students in word recognition strategies as they read. After students read, word work is reinforced through activities in which they can be actively involved. For example, in grades 1 and 2 students engage in writing words in sound boxes and in guided sentence writing, or writing for sounds.

In addition, with EIR I have always stressed ongoing professional learning sessions as an important aspect of the model. This provides teachers with the support they need from colleagues to teach EIR lessons successfully. This focus on professional learning was influenced by the year-long professional learning that is an integral part of Reading Recovery (Pinnell, Fried, & Estice, 1990).

What do teachers do in the monthly EIR professional learning sessions? Teachers engage in collaborative, reflective sharing and problem solving about EIR lessons. They talk about successes, challenges, and what to teach next as students' reading abilities develop. They engage in video sharing so they have something concrete to reflect on and talk about. It was through my 10+ years of direct experience with EIR professional development sessions that I saw the power of school-based, collaborative professional learning.

What did I find out about students' performance from the research I did on EIR? There were good results for 75 percent of struggling first graders—children who ended up reading grade-level material, independently, sight-unseen, by the end of the school year (Taylor, 2001; Taylor, 2010a; Taylor, Short, Frye, & Shearer, 1992). Typically, I also found that 94 percent of first grade EIR students were on grade level in second grade (Taylor, 2001).

But I saw the need for a model for those who came to grade 2 not yet reading independently. Thus, I developed the grade 2 model, an accelerated version of the grade 1 model. In grade 2, teachers were successful with most of the students (e.g., 25 percent of EIR students who didn't learn to read in first grade, or those who moved in) who came to second grade not yet reading. Typically, 86 percent of these EIR students were reading on grade level at the end of second grade and 92 percent were on grade level at end of third grade (Taylor, 2010a; Taylor, 2010b; Taylor, Hanson, Justice-Swanson, & Watts, 1997).

Next, I developed a kindergarten model to get all students off to a good start in emergent reading. The model includes whole-group reading lessons for all students and follow-up support for students who are the slowest to develop their emergent reading abilities. I found that by the end of the school year, most students who were in kindergarten EIR lessons had the emergent reading abilities they needed to become independent readers in first grade. I also found that EIR students outperformed control students (Taylor, 2001; Taylor 2011b).

In the grade 3 and 4 EIR models for students who come to school in the fall reading about a year below grade level, some attention is directed to decoding longer words, based on students' needs. Fluency practice comes from repeated reading of stories. But the model for these grades focuses in particular on vocabulary and comprehension of texts that are written about a year below students' grade level. Lessons stress summarizing, comprehension monitoring, and generating and answering questions—especially for informational texts in grade 4. Also, I developed this model to include a cross-age tutoring component so that the older struggling readers could, perhaps for the first time, experience a sense of pride and importance as readers as they read to and tutored younger struggling readers. In my research, I found that 94 percent of the students in EIR were successfully decoding grade-level texts by the end of the year and had more positive perceptions about themselves as readers (Taylor, 2001; Taylor, 2011c; Taylor, Hanson, Justice-Swanson, & Watts, 1997).

It was during my EIR phase that I began to visit many teachers' classrooms and became a big believer in the value of doing this regularly to personally be a better teacher educator and researcher. The regular visits helped me see what teachers were having an easy time with and what parts of the EIR teaching strategies they were struggling with; what things were working for students; and what things needed to be modified, and by modified, it usually meant accelerated. Since 1989, along with colleagues, Ceil Critchley, Barb Hanson, Deb Peterson, Rynell Schock, Karen Birhle, and others, we have provided year-long EIR professional learning support to more than 3000 teachers across the U.S. and, particularly, across Minnesota.

What have I learned about helping teachers with EIR? If I, or others on the EIR team, get into schools regularly, support teachers, help them refine their teaching, and encourage them to keep up the EIR lessons and professional learning, by February teachers are very excited about the progress they see their struggling readers are making. Also, they have greater self-efficacy as teachers, and they begin to use EIR strategies with all students based on need. In my research, I found that 75 percent of teachers continued to use EIR lessons three or more years after their initial EIR year (Taylor, 2001). Also, I could see from comments in interviews and surveys, as well as through classroom visits, that these teachers were teaching effectively with integrity, not simply following a program with fidelity (Taylor, 2001; 2010a, 2010b; 2010c; 2011b; 2011c).

One last point on early reading intervention—it works! If teachers can teach almost all struggling readers to read in first grade, it seems to me that as professional educators, we have the moral imperative to do so. No excuses.

A personal lesson I learned as a researcher: It was during my EIR phase that I saw the beauty for me professionally of combining ongoing professional development support with research. I helped teachers, I learned, I collected student data to support the efficacy of the teaching strategies teachers were working on! This was a win-win situation.

SCHOOL-WIDE READING IMPROVEMENT

Developing the School Change in Reading Framework

Things were moving along well for me with EIR. I hadn't done nearly as much research at different grade levels as I needed to, but an exciting opportunity came my way, and I took a new fork in the road. I didn't continue with EIR research, and I have had some regrets about this over the years, but instead I joined the CIERA (Center for the Improvement of Early Reading Achievement) research team—a consortium of schools, as many of you remember, including the University of

Michigan, University of Virginia, Michigan State University, University of Southern California, and the University of Minnesota. I headed up the research on effective schools and teachers, followed by research on effective school-wide reading improvement over a 5-year period from 1997-2003. I found this work to be a very rewarding choice.

With David Pearson and others, I studied effective schools and teachers in the Schools that Beat the Odds research. After learning about effective schools and teachers first hand, visiting many schools across the U.S. along the way, we turned to the development of and research on the School Change in Reading (SCR) process. The purpose was to help all teachers within schools help all students succeed in reading. We focused on high-poverty, diverse schools, reasoning that these are the students who need schools the most to become literate, and they need to have ALL teachers in their school teaching effectively to become the best readers they can be.

In the late 1990s a lot was known about school reform in general, much of it at the secondary level (many thanks to Karen Seashore at the University of Minnesota, Louis & Kruse, 1995), and in CIERA we built upon this research, as well as our work on effective schools and teachers and my work on EIR, as we developed the School Change in Reading (SCR) framework. This framework includes collaborative, reflective professional learning within schools, and the development of excellence in teaching, informed by research. Improvement of instruction focuses, in part, on our own research-based Cognitive Engagement Model: teaching for high-level thinking (including high-level talk and writing about text and strategy instruction), releasing as a teacher from explicit instruction to coaching, and maximizing students' active participation in learning (Taylor, Pearson, Peterson, & Rodriguez, 2003).

Again, I learned a great deal about how to help teachers and schools help themselves and their students by visiting schools and classroom regularly. With the CIERA project, starting with the 1997-98 school year and continuing through 2001-02 school years, I visited about 1250 kindergarten through grade 6 classrooms in 24 schools in 20 districts across 8 states. From the 2002-03 through 2006-7 school years, focusing primarily on the use of the SCR Framework in Reading Excellence Act (REA)/Reading First (RF) schools in Minnesota, I visited about 3000 K-3 classrooms in 85 schools across the state. From the 2007-08 through 2009-10 school years, I visited about 800 classrooms in grades K-6 in 15 schools.

The value of data. Data helped in so many ways in this line of work! Research data helped us better understand effective teaching and schools, which in turn helped us develop the SCR Framework (Taylor, Pearson, Clark, & Walpole, 2000; Taylor & Pearson, 2002). Research data helped us develop the Cognitive Engagement Model of teaching reading, by observing teachers, coding instruction, and using HLM (hierarchical linear modeling) analyses (Raudenbush & Bryk, 2002) to determine what practices led to or detracted from students' reading growth in grades K-6 (Taylor & Pearson, 2004; Taylor et al., 2003; Taylor, Pearson, Peterson, & Rodriguez, 2005). Research data also helped us validate the efficacy of the SCR model (Taylor et al., 2005; Taylor, Peterson, Marx, & Chein, 2007). Research data enabled the state of Minnesota to use the SCR model for the Reading Excellence Act and Reading First at a time when many states were being told by the political forces for reform in the country that they needed to follow a published program with fidelity.

Refining the SCR Framework

So what is the SCR Framework? The SCR Framework is just that—a framework, not a recipe, for school-wide reform in reading. The framework helps many participants within a school learn to work together as a collaborative community.

Goals for teachers include using research-based practices, including the Cognitive Engagement Model for teaching reading; regularly reflecting on teaching; improving instruction; and growing in self-efficacy. Goals for school staff members using the SCR Framework include learning and reflecting as a professional learning community (PLC); growing in collective efficacy; and developing ownership of the ongoing improvement effort and the school-wide reading program. Goals for external partners, such as university literacy facilitators or Department of Education colleagues, include providing research-based ideas; providing support; encouraging persistence; and releasing the reform effort to the schools. Goals for students include growing in reading; working on motivating, challenging activities; and becoming thinking, self-reliant learners. Needless to say, none of this is easy; it takes multiple years of work.

What happened in this 10-year period of research on the SCR Framework? Students consistently grew in reading; teachers grew in their ability to deliver effective reading instruction and to teach collaboratively with integrity; and schools grew in collective efficacy as true professional learning communities (Taylor & Peterson, 2008; Peterson & Taylor, in press).

In Minnesota Reading First Cohort 2 schools, students in grades K-3 saw typical growth of from 3 to 5 NCE points per year on standardized reading tests. (See Table 1.)

Teachers steadily grew in their use of research-based practices. For example, teachers on average were observed engaging in high-level questioning 19 percent of the time in Year 1 and 24 percent of the time in Year 3. Teachers on average were observed engaging in comprehension strategies instruction 7 percent of the time in Year 1 and 15 percent of the time in Year 3. (Taylor & Peterson, 2008) (See Table 2.)

Table 1. Typical Yearly NCE Growth in Reading by Grade (as Measured by Standardized Test in Vocabulary, Decoding, or Comprehension)

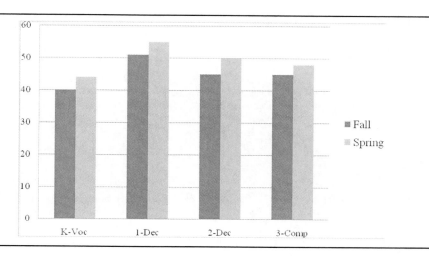

Table 2. Changes in Teaching Across 3 Years (Percentage of Time Observed for High-Level Questioning and Comprehension Strategies Instruction, Grades 2-3)

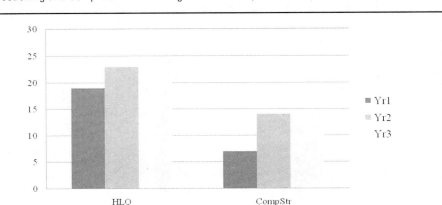

From the observation data and students' reading scores, we determined through HLM analyses that high-level questioning consistently had a positive impact on grade 2 and 3 students' growth in comprehension, vocabulary, and decoding on a standardized reading text across three years of the SCR process. In other words, the more a teacher was observed engaging in high- level questioning, the more growth was seen in her students' reading scores during a given year, compared to students in classrooms where teachers were engaged in less high-level questioning. Comprehension strategies instruction also had a positive impact on students' growth in comprehension and vocabulary. (Peterson & Taylor, in press; Taylor and Peterson, 2006, 2007, 2008) (See Table 3.)

Table 3. Reading Scores and Instruction in Comprehension*

	Comprehension	Vocabulary	Decoding
Year 1	HLQ	HLQ	HLQ
Year 2	HLQ	HLQ	HLQ
	CStr	CStr	
Year 3	HLQ	HLQ	HLQ
	CStr	CStr	CStr

* Positive relationships between grade 2 and 3 students' spring reading scores on a standardized test, after accounting for fall scores, and the incidence in which: a) high-level talk and writing about text (HLQ), and b) comprehension strategies (CStr) instruction were observed in classrooms. Score are based on approximately 3000 students and 235 teachers each year.

Schools steadily grew in collective efficacy, as measured through scores derived from interviews and surveys. Growth, determined by responses to questions on a survey using a 5-point rating scale, included increasingly positive perceptions about school climate, professional learning, effectiveness of classroom reading instruction, and effectiveness of reading interventions for struggling readers (Taylor & Peterson, 2008). (See Table 4.)

Table 4. Growth in Collective Efficacy*

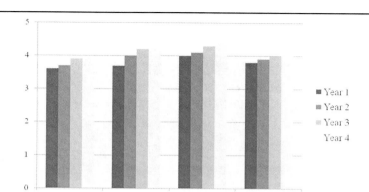

*Mean rating by individual teachers by year on perceptions (using 5-point scale where 1 = very low and 5 = very high) of 4 school dimensions of collaboration (where PD = professional development, Rdg Instr = reading instruction, and Rdg Intv = reading intervention).

One typical response from a principal during an interview illustrates these positive perceptions of school collaboration and climate, "I now understand what good reading instruction is and how to make it happen. We make sure we are having professional conversations about instruction. Teachers are teaching differently because they are more confident about their instructional choices. Also, the project has changed relationships in a good way; and it has given everyone confidence, pride, and satisfaction in their work." (Taylor, 2011a)

An excellent second grade teacher said, " We learned a lot and once you know better ways of doing things, you want to keep doing them. I've never heard so much discussion about how we're teaching and what we're noticing about the children's learning as I have these past few years. Initial support from our external partner was very helpful, but now in the third year most of the staff development is internal. We work extraordinarily well together and I'm really proud of our staff." (Taylor, 2011a)

A special education teacher in grades 1 and 2 reflected, "My lessons are more intentional. I am especially focusing on vocabulary and high-level thinking. I'm using writing as a way for students to respond. I'm also being more purposeful in relating to students' lives. I'm seeing more excitement in my students than before, and this makes me more excited." (Taylor, 2011a).

A third grade teacher commented, "I see students meeting higher standards and targets. So I am able to raise the bar and know that students will still be able to succeed. The assessments drive our instruction because we see where our students' needs are and have a study group in that area, for example comprehension strategies, to provide more effective instruction. We all take great joy in seeing the children accelerate in a way we haven't seen before."

And finally a literacy coach and teacher reported, "Because of our involvement in school-wide reading improvement, we're more reflective about our practice and more intentional about our research-based instruction. We have learned to open our doors and be more comfortable with peer observation and feedback."

What are conclusions I have drawn from the SCR work I have done? Effective teachers teaching together with integrity make a big difference for their students! And the school is the most productive unit of change!

SCHOOL-WIDE READING IMPROVEMENT: SIMILARITIES ACROSS MULTIPLE MODELS

These conclusions are not just my own. Taffy Raphael, Kathy Au, and I (Taylor, Raphael, & Au, 2010) had the good fortune to write an interpretive review on the topic of reading and school reform for the *Handbook of Reading Research*, Volume 4 (Kamil, Pearson, Afflerbach, & Moje, 2010). As with the SCR framework I have just briefly shared with you today, and the Standards-Based Change Process that Taffy Raphael shared with you last year in her Oscar S. Causey address (Raphael, 2010), we found many similarities across a number of research projects focused on professional learning as an effective path to follow for school-wide reading reform, the later most likely a "hot" topic" today and well into the future. Briefly, let me summarize for you the similarities we found across these studies (Au, Raphael, & Mooney 2008; Fisher & Frey, 2007; Lai, McNaughton, Amituanai-Toloa, Turner, & Hsiao, 2009; Lipson, Mosenthal, Mekkelsen, & Russ 2004; Mosenthal, Lipson, Torncello, Russ, & Mekkelsen, 2004; Raphael, 2010; Taylor, Pearson, Peterson, & Rodriguez, 2005; Taylor, Peterson, Marx, & Chein, 2007; Timperley & Parr, 2007).

Schools need support for organizational change. This change will come from developing vision, commitment, and ownership; developing shared leadership; using data on students, teaching, school climate, and the success of the reform effort; and becoming a collaborative, learning community—a real one, not just a school that calls itself a PLC.

Teachers need support for individual change. This change will come from engaging in collaborative, reflective professional learning. This school-based learning leads to research-based changes in content and pedagogy that in turn lead to effective teaching that focuses on differentiated, balanced, motivating reading instruction that meets all students' needs and challenges them all.

When teachers provide the opportunities, students do well with and thrive on high-level talk and writing about texts; being intellectually challenged and motivated; participating in collaborative work; and working as strategic, independent learners. I am always amazed at what students in kindergarten through grade 5 can do, say, and write if we give them opportunities that challenge and motivate them.

External partners, while helpful, need to start with the notion that they are trying to work themselves out of a job. They need to focus on visiting schools and classrooms regularly; providing ideas and support, not dogma; helping to solve problems as they arise; and releasing responsibility to schools for the reform effort and their professional learning community.

The take-away from this review, based on a number of similar, but varying models, is that reading improvement that focuses on professional learning and collaboration among teachers within schools who learn to teach with integrity is a promising approach to school-wide reading reform, effective instruction, and in turn, enhanced reading achievement for students. As I mentioned at the start of this talk, however, I worry that we are not focusing enough on quality, collaborative professional learning that leads to more effective instruction in the current era of school reform,

Race to the Top, turn-around schools, I3 grants, and the simplistic determination of teacher effectiveness through students' growth on standardized tests, irrespective of actual teaching quality.

Sustainability

But what about sustainability of a school that has become a true professional learning community, a PLC in which members feel like part of a beautiful garden? If school staff members keep working at it collaboratively and have a sound system of shared leadership in place, the school can continue as a PLC with increasingly effective instruction.

Many SCR schools do continue to get excellent results (York-Barr, 2010; Peterson, 2008). In two studies of schools in Minnesota that had come off the AYP list and fit the parameters of each study, it was discovered that more than half of the 4 or 5 schools investigated in each study had been in the SCR project (Krall, 2008; Reimer, 2010).

Unfortunately, sustainability is not easy, and research suggests that sustainability can be problematic (Giles & Hardgreaves, 2002). Nevertheless, if schools don't continue as PLCs that change all the time as needs demand, many teachers have told me, and interview and observation data substantiate, that they believe they have "changed the way they teach forever." Teachers in a reform effort like SCR say that they teach more effectively; value reflective, collaborative learning; and know that teaching with integrity, not following programs with fidelity, is what counts for students' success! These teachers will have a positive impact on many students and many colleagues for many years to come. And knowing this alone makes me feel my work has been worthwhile!

CONCLUSIONS

Looking back on my journey, I realized I stayed relatively focused across each of my 10-year research phases and benefitted greatly from visiting many schools and classrooms. These things gave me time and opportunity to develop some sense of expertise for each of the three topics I was studying. This self-efficacy in turn gave me confidence, along with knowledge, to help teachers help students. Also, visiting many classrooms and combining research and outreach to schools worked well for me professionally in fulfilling my responsibilities as a university professor and reading educator. Additionally, sound research, and with it, publications in archival journals as well as in books and articles for teachers, also helped me help teachers, schools, and indirectly, their students, and for all of these opportunities to provide assistance and support, I have been very grateful!

From Looking Back To Looking Forward

As I think about the future, I hope that general education reading researchers, like most of you in LRA, are once again leading the way in reading research and are continuing to publish in a wide variety of archival journals on reading curriculum, instruction, assessment, and school reform for the benefit of all students. Also, I hope that many of you consider partnering with colleagues in quantitative methods or educational psychology so that you continue to lend your vast expertise about schools to quantitative, or mixed methods, studies—often the types of studies that are successful when it comes to procuring grants as well as impacting policy and practice.

Before I draw this talk to a close, I want to thank everyone in LRA for all the work you do for children. This is such important work!

As for me, it has been a wonderful journey. But now I am taking a new fork in the road to a simpler life in Montana. I hope you remember my metaphor about helping teachers, administrators, support staff, parents, and most importantly, students, become part of a beautiful garden. I know my Montana flowers will keep reminding me of the many teachers and schools I have had the good fortune to work with over many years as well as you, my NRC/LRA colleagues! May your futures be bright!

REFERENCES

Au, K. H., Raphael, T. E., & Mooney, K. C. (2008). What we have learned about teacher education to improve literacy achievement in urban schools. In V. Chou, L. Morrow, and L. Wilkinson (Eds.), *Improving literacy achievement in urban schools: Critical elements in teacher preparation* (pp. 159–84). Newark, DE: International Reading Association.

Fisher, D., & Frey, N. (2007). Implementing a school-wide literacy framework: Improving achievement in an urban elementary school. *The Reading Teacher, 61*(1), 32–43.

Garcia, G. E., Pearson, P. D., Taylor, B. M., Bauer, E. B., & Stahl, K. A .D. (2011) Socio-constructivist and political views on teachers' implementation of two types of reading comprehension approaches in low-income schools. *Theory Into Practice, 58(*2) 149-156.

Giles, C., & Hardgreaves, A. (2002). The sustainability of innovative schools as learning organizations and professional learning communities during standardized reform. *Educational Administration Quarterly, 42*, 124-156.

Goddard, R. D., Hoy, W. K., & Hoy, A. W. (2004). Collective efficacy beliefs: Theoretical developments, empirical evidence, and future directions. *Educational Researcher, 33*(3), 3-13.

Hiebert, E. H., & Taylor, B.M. (1998). Beginning reading instruction: Research on early interventions." In M .L. Kamil, P. B. Mosenthal, P. D. Pearson, & R. Barr, R. (Eds.), *Handbook of reading research, Volume III* (pp. 455–82). Mahwah, NJ: Lawrence Erlbaum.

Kamil, M., Pearson, P. D., Afflerbach, P., & Moje., E. (Eds.) *Handbook of reading research, Vol. IV.* New York, NY: Routledge.

Knapp, M. S. (1995). *Teaching for meaning in high-poverty classrooms.* New York, NY: Teachers College.

Krall, L. (2008). A study of Minnesota elementary schools making adequate yearly progress in reading. Unpublished dissertation. Minneapolis, MN: University of Minnesota.

Lai, M. K., McNaughton, S., Amituanai-Toloa, S. M., Turner, R. & Hsiao, S. 2009. Sustained acceleration of achievement in reading comprehension: The New Zealand experience. *Reading Research Quarterly, 44*, 30-56.

Lipson, M. L., Mosenthal, J. H., Mekkelsen, J., & Russ, B. 2004. Building knowledge and fashioning success one school at a time. *The Reading Teacher, 57*(6), 534-542.

Louis, K. S., & Kruse, S. (1995). *Professionalism and community in schools.* Thousand Oaks, CA: Corwin.

Mosenthal, J., Lipson, M. S., Torncello, S., Russ, B., & Mekkelsen., J. (2004). Contexts and practices of six schools successful in obtaining reading achievement. *The Elementary School Journal, 41*(5), 343-367.

National Reading Panel. (2000). *Report of the National Reading Panel: Teaching children to read: Reports of the subgroups.* Washington, D.C.: U.S. Department of Health and Human Services, National Institutes of Health. (NIH Publication No. 00-4754).

Peterson, D. S., Taylor, B. M., Burnham. R., & Chein, M. (2011). Using the School Change Framework: A One-Year Follow-up Report. St. Paul, MN: Minnesota Center for Reading Research, University of Minnesota.

Peterson, D. S. & Taylor, B. (in press). Using higher order questioning to accelerate students' growth in reading. *The Reading Teacher.*

Peterson, D. S., Taylor, B. M., Burnham, R., & Schock, R. (2009). Reflective coaching conversations: A missing piece. *The Reading Teacher, 62*(6), *500-509.*

Pinnell, G. S., Fried, M., & Estice, R. (1990). Reading Recovery: Learning how to make a difference. *The Reading Teacher, 90,* 160–183.

Pinnell, G. S., Lyons, C. A., DeFord, D. E., Bryk, A. S., & Seltzer, M. (1994). Comparing instructional models for the literacy education of high-risk first graders. *Reading Research Quarterly, 29,* 8-39.

Pressley, M., Dolezal, S. E., Raphael, L. M., Mohan. L., Roehrig, A. D., & Bogner. K. (2003). *Motivating primary-grade students.* New York, NY: Guilford.

Raphael, T. R. (2010). Defying gravity: Literacy reform in urban schools. In R. T. Jiménez, V. J. Risko. M. K. Hundley, & D.W. Rowe (Eds.), *59th Yearbook of the National Reading Conference* (pp. 22-42). Oak Creek, WI: National Reading Conference.

Raudenbush, S. W. & Bryk, A. S. (2002). *Hierarchical linear models: Applications and data analysis methods. 2nd ed.* Thousand Oaks, CA: Sage.

Reimer, T. (2010). A study on the principal's role in the development of professional learning communities in elementary schools that "beat the odds" in reading. Unpublished dissertation. Minneapolis, MN: University of Minnesota.

Taylor, B. M. (1979). Good and poor readers' recall of familiar and unfamiliar text. *Journal of Reading Behavior, 11,* 375-380.

Taylor, B. M. (1980). Children's memory for expository text after reading. *Reading Research Quarterly, 15,* 399-411.

Taylor, B. M. (1982). Text structure and children's comprehension and memory for expository material. *Journal of Educational Psychology, 74,* 323-340.

Taylor, B. M. (1982). A hierarchical summarization strategy to improve middle grade students' reading and writing skills. *The Reading Teacher, 36,* 202-205.

Taylor, B. M. (1985). Improving middle-grade students' reading and writing of expository text. *Journal of Educational Research, 79,* 119-125.

Taylor, B. M. (2001). *The Early Intervention in Reading Program (EIR): Research and development spanning twelve years.* St. Paul, MN: Early Intervention in Reading Corporation. www.earlyinterventioninreading.com.

Taylor, B. M. (2010a). Catching readers: Grade 1. Portsmouth, NH: Heinemann.

Taylor, B. M. (2010b). Catching readers: Grade 2. Portsmouth, NH: Heinemann.

Taylor, B. M. (2010c). Catching readers: Grade 3. Portsmouth, NH: Heinemann.

Taylor, B. M. (2011a). Catching schools: *An action guide to school-wide reading improvement.* Portsmouth, NH: Heinemann.

Taylor, B. M. (2011b). Catching readers: Grade K. Portsmouth, NH: Heinemann.

Taylor, B. M. (2011c) Catching readers: Grades 4/5. Portsmouth, NH: Heinemann.

Taylor, B. M., & Frye, B. (1988). Pretesting: Minimize time spent on skill work for intermediate readers. *The Reading Teacher, 42,*100-105.

Taylor, B. M., Frye, B., & Gaetz, T. (1990). Reducing the number of reading skill activities in the elementary classroom. *Journal of Reading Behavior, 22,* 167-179.

Taylor, B. M., Frye, B., & Maruyama, G. (1990). Time spent reading and reading growth. *American Educational Research Journal, 27,* 351-362.

Taylor, B. M., & Beach, R. W. (1984). The effects of text structure instruction on middle grade students' comprehension and production of expository text. *Reading Research Quarterly, 19,* 134-146.

Taylor, B. M., Hanson, B., Justice-Swanson, K. J., & Watts, S. (1997). Helping struggling readers: Linking small group intervention with cross-age tutoring. *The Reading Teacher, 51,*196-209.

Taylor, B. M., & Pearson, P. D. (Eds.) (2002). *Teaching reading: Effective schools/accomplished teachers.* Mahwah, NJ: Erlbaum.

Taylor, B. M., & Pearson, P. D. (2004). CIERA research on learning to read: At school, at home, and in the community. *The Elementary School Journal 105*(2), 167-181.

Taylor, B. M., Pearson, P. D., Clark, K., & Walpole, S. (2000). Effective schools and accomplished teachers: Lessons about primary grade reading instruction in low-income schools." *The Elementary School Journal, 101,* 121-166.

Taylor, B. M., Pearson, P. D., Peterson, D. S., & Rodriguez, M. C. (2003). Reading growth in high-poverty classrooms: The influence of teacher practices that encourage cognitive engagement in literacy learning. *The Elementary School Journal, 104,* 3-28.

Taylor, B. M., Pearson, P. D., Peterson, D. S., & Rodriguez, M. C. (2005). The CIERA school change framework: An evidence-based approach to professional development and school reading improvement. *Reading Research Quarterly, 40,* 40-69.

Taylor, B. M., & Peterson, D. S. (2008) *Year 3 Report of the Minnesota Reading First Cohort 2 School Change Project.* St. Paul, MN: University of Minnesota, Minnesota Center for Reading Research.

Taylor, B. M., Peterson, D. S., Marx, M., & Chein, M. (2007). Scaling up a reading reform in high-poverty elementary schools. In B. Taylor and J. E. Ysseldyke (Eds.) *Effective instruction for struggling readers, K–6,* (pp. 216–34). New York, NY: Teachers College.

Taylor, B. M., Raphael, T. E., & Au., K. H. (2010). Reading and school reform. In M. Kamil, P. D. Pearson, P. Afflerbach, and E. Moje. (Eds.) *Handbook of Reading Research, Vol. IV,* (pp. 594-628). New York, NY: Routledge.

Taylor, B. M., & Samuels, S. J. (1983). Children's use of text structure in the recall of expository material. *American Educational Research Journal, 20,* 517-528.

Taylor, B. M., Short, R., Frye, B., & Shearer, B. (1992). Classroom teachers prevent reading failure among low-achieving first-grade students. *The Reading Teacher, 45,* 592-597.

Timperley, H. S., & Parr, J. M. (2007). Closing the achievement gap through evidence-based inquiry at multiple levels of the education system. *Journal of Advanced Academics, 19*(1), 90–115.

York-Barr, J., & Hur, J. (2010). *What happened after Reading First left?* Presentation at August Workshop. St. Paul, MN: University of Minnesota, Minnesota Center for Reading Research.

Does Meaning Matter for Reading Achievement? Untangling the Role of Phonological Recoding and Morphological Awareness in Predicting Word Decoding, Reading Vocabulary, and Reading Comprehension Achievement for Spanish-Speaking English Language Learners

Amanda Goodwin
Vanderbilt University

Currently, reading researchers are clarifying how reading may be supported by morphological awareness, or what Kuo and Anderson (2006) define as the "ability to reflect upon and manipulate morphemes [ie, the smallest units of meaning within words]" (p. 161). Identifying this relationship is difficult because of the many linguistic demands involved in morphological tasks. Researchers have used statistical techniques to try to isolate the contributions of related constructs, and while most studies suggest a unique role for morphological awareness and phonological awareness in contributing to various measures of reading achievement (Carlisle, 1995; Carlisle & Nomanbhoy, 1993; Deacon & Kirby, 2004; Mahony, Singson, & Mann, 2000; Nagy, Berninger, & Abbot, 2006; Siegel, 2008; Singson, Mahony, & Mann, 2000), questions remain because of limitations in how linguistic factors are controlled for within the research design.

At the same time, researchers have worked to improve literacy outcomes for English language learners (ELLs), who score lower on standardized tests (Menken, 2008). Morphological awareness may be particularly important for the 2 million Spanish-speaking ELLs that make up approximately three-fourths of the American ELL population (Aud, Hussar, Planty, Snyder, Bianco, Fox, Frohlich, Kemp, & Drake, 2010). To design robust instruction to close this gap, factors that contribute to components of reading must be identified by carefully controlling for related constructs.

MORPHOLOGICAL AWARENESS: A PRIMER

Morphological awareness is the manipulation of units of meaning to recognize and/or produce morphologically related words (for further discussion, see Carlisle, 2003; Kuo & Anderson, 2006). Derivational morphology, which is the construct assessed in this study, involves adding or subtracting suffixes and prefixes that change both the meaning and often the grammatical category of the word. In the word *teacher*, the morpheme *er* is added to the base word *teach* to change the meaning from a verb to a noun. Adding the morphemes *less* to *help* changes the meaning to be *without help*. Derivational morphology is more complex than relationships within inflectional morphology or compounding because of the greater number of variations involved (for example, *dark, darkness, darker, darken*, and *darkly* are derivations of *dark*) and also tends to lead to larger changes in meaning than inflectional morphology (Verhoeven & Perfetti, 2003).

POTENTIAL ROLE OF MORPHOLOGICAL AWARENESS FOR SPANISH-SPEAKING ELLS

Morphology suggests a possible, yet rarely studied support for Spanish-speaking ELLs. It would make sense that knowledge of morphological relationships and units would support reading achievement for this population because the English written language is morphophonemic and therefore communicates language through letters, units of sounds, and units of meaning (Chomsky & Halle, 1968). In fact, English is considered an opaque language with inconsistencies in phoneme grapheme conversion rules resulting from protecting the spelling of the morphological root even at the cost of sound symbol correspondence (Perfetti & Dunlap, 2008; Titos, Defior, Alegria, & Martos, 2003). For example, *breath* is pronounced with a short *e* but spelled with *ea* in order to highlight the relationship between *breath* and *breathe*.

In addition, Spanish and English share units of meaning, making some words similar in both Spanish and English. Students can access these units of meaning from their native language within English text in order to support their quest for meaning (Nagy, Garcia, Durgunoglu, & Hancin-Bhatt, 1993). For example, within the low frequency English word, *malicious*, is the Spanish high frequency word, *mal*, meaning bad. By using knowledge of their native language, ELLs can estimate that *malicious* involves a negative characteristic. Research supports the role of morphological awareness in identifying words that are similar in both English and Spanish, termed cognates, with ELLs who scored higher on morphological awareness tasks detecting more cognates (Hancin-Bhatt & Nagy, 1994).

Another reason morphology may be particularly salient for ELLs is the relationship between morphological awareness and vocabulary. Overall, ELLs perform at similar levels to their fluent English peers on decoding, word reading, and phonological tasks, yet fall behind on vocabulary and reading comprehension tasks (Lesaux & Geva, 2006). Morphology, with its connection to meaning and its established role in contributing to vocabulary outcomes, addresses these challenges (Anglin, 1993; Nagy & Scott, 2000). As Nagy and Scott (2000) assert, "It is hard to overstate the importance of morphology in vocabulary growth" (p. 275).

THE BIG PICTURE

Although the morphophonemic nature of English suggests a key role for morphology in reading, only a few general models of reading include a role for morphology. Recently, Perfetti (2009) presented a model of reading comprehension that incorporates the role of morphology as providing lexical access, which supports both word identification and accessing the word meaning. Ehri (1995) also suggests morphological units may support word identification, yet does not acknowledge differences between units of meaning and other multi-letter units such as the difference between identifying *ed* in *peeled* versus *ed* in *red*. Furthermore, Adams' (1994) theory suggests that words are made up of "interassociated sets of more primitive meaning elements... that allows us to focus on one aspect or another of a word's full meaning as appropriate in context" (p. 850-851), yet Adams does not specifically link these meaning elements to morphology.

For a morphophonemic language such as English, it seems surprising that morphology continues to either be absent or play a minor role in many general theories of reading. For example,

Gough's (1972) bottom-up model, Rummelhart and McClelland's (1986) parallel distributed processing models, and Perfetti's verbal efficiency model (1988) all highlight the processing of letters and sounds. The possible role of morpheme patterns is easy to infer from these models (ie. in Gough's model, readers may map letters onto morphemes as well as phonemes in English due to the morphophonemic nature of English; in Rummelhart and McClelland's model, the visual feature detectors may be activating units of meaning to support word identification; and in Perfetti's model, the automatic phonological and orthographic representations may also include automatic morphological representations such as affixes, suffixes, and roots), yet because the role of morphology is not overtly stated in many models of reading, researchers have been slow to examine the contribution of morphological awareness to reading.

Lexical Access Models Involving Morphological Processing

Models of morphological processing show the role of morphology within reading, yet are absent from larger general reading models. Theories of morphological processing follow the dual-route models of word recognition where morphologically complex words are stored and accessed in units and as wholes (Feldman & Basnight-Brown, 2008). According to Schreuder and Baayen's hybrid theory (1995) and Taft's activation interactive model (2004), when a stored morphologically complex word is unknown, the word is segmented into morphemes, activating and merging meanings of component morphemes to estimate the meaning of the complex word.

Growing Attention to the Role of Morphology in Reading

The relationship between reading and morphology has received increased attention over the past 30 years. In the 1990s and 2000s, researchers have examined how morphological processing supports vocabulary knowledge (Anglin, 1993), explored differences across populations (Kieffer & Lesaux, 2008), and used newer statistical models to control for related linguistic dimensions such as phonological awareness (see literature review).

Growing Attention to the Relation of Morphological Awareness (MA) to Other Linguistic Factors

Reading researchers assess morphological awareness as part of a larger construct covering phonological awareness, orthographic awareness, and semantic awareness (Kuo & Anderson, 2006). For example, some morphological relationships are transparent such that a morphological change occurs without altering the spelling or pronunciation of the root as in *grow* and *growth*, while other relationships are hidden by phonological or orthographic changes as in the example of *magic* and *magician* or *decide* and *decision*. The less transparent the relationship, the more difficult to use morphological awareness to aid decoding and meaning acquisition (Carlisle, 2000, 2003; Singson et al., 2000).

Methodological Challenges

Most measures of morphological awareness involve meta-linguistic awareness because it is difficult to untangle morphological relationships from orthographic, phonological, and even syntactic relationships. Also, tasks such as identifying, segmenting, and combining morphemes may involve similar metalinguistic skills also used in phonological recoding tasks that involve the segmenting and combining of phonemes (Singson, et al., 2000). As such, variance may be misallocated when a related predictor is not included within the model. To address this, researchers have included indicators of other types of linguistic awareness such as phonological awareness in addition to morphological awareness when predicting an outcome, yet rarely in a head-to-head comparison. Instead, researchers tend to use sequential regression or a taxonomy of regression models only allowing morphological awareness to explain any remaining variance in the outcome beyond the related linguistic constructs.

Another challenge is often the demands of the task used to control for related linguistic awareness are different from the demands in the focus task. Researchers often use a phoneme elision task involving the deletion of a phoneme, which seems different from the demands of identification of a morphological relationship when there is a change in the pronunciation of the morpheme. As a result, even when controlling for this aspect of phonological awareness, the measure of morphological awareness may still be confounded with other aspects of linguistic awareness that are required by the morphological task.

The latent variable framework of structural equation modeling provides an alternative, creating a latent variable from the overlap in shared variance from multiple indicators of morphological awareness (Kline, 2005). For example, by using indicators of morphological awareness that have varying degrees of transparency, the shared morphological awareness remains in the latent variable, whereas the confounding linguistic awareness which is not shared between tasks is put into the error term. As a result, any contribution of the latent construct is theoretically free from confounds of other types of linguistic awareness. This framework must be used with care as these latent variables with less error are at an advantage when compared with single indicators that have error (Kline, 2005).

THE CONTRIBUTION OF MORPHOLOGY TO READING ACHIEVEMENT

Overall, research suggests morphological awareness contributes to word reading, reading comprehension, and vocabulary development (for a review, see Carlisle, 2003; Kuo & Anderson, 2006), yet the field continues to develop more nuanced findings regarding the unique role of morphological awareness to reading.

Spanish-Speaking ELLs

Goodwin et al. (2011) used a similar framework to the current study, allowing latent constructs of phonological decoding and morphological awareness to predict reading achievement, although reading achievement was a latent construct defined by overlap of word reading, reading comprehension, and reading vocabulary. The pure construct of morphological awareness stemmed from overlap in indicators of varying degrees of morphological transparency, showing that when controlling for a latent construct of phonological decoding, fourth-grade morphological awareness made a moderate contribution to fifth-grade reading achievement of Spanish-speaking ELLs such that a one-standard deviation (SD)-unit increase in morphological awareness resulted in a 0.65 SD-unit increase in Reading Achievement. The significant contribution from phonological decoding to reading became non-significant when including morphological awareness, showing the importance of including multiple indicators of linguistic awareness as predictors.

In a cross-sectional study, Kieffer and Lesaux (2008) also show that fifth-grade morphological awareness explains significant additional variance in reading comprehension when controlling for phonological awareness, fluency measures, decoding skills, and vocabulary knowledge with a one-unit increase in derivational morphological awareness, resulting in a .33-.39 SD-unit increase in comprehension, although in fourth grade, the relationship was not significant. These researchers compared a baseline model without morphological awareness to a final model with morphological awareness, finding in fifth grade, including morphological awareness explained an additional 6.1%-7.8% of variance in Gates-MacGinitie comprehension and passage comprehension respectively. A phoneme elision task was used to control, but because the phonological demands in the derivational morphology task were different from deleting a phoneme, the contribution of morphological awareness continues to reflect a broader construct that includes related linguistic components.

General Population

Because the number of studies involving Spanish-speaking ELLs are small, findings involving general education populations can also provide important guiding principles. A study very similar to the present study except involving a more general population and methodological differences suggests that morphological awareness predicts decoding, reading comprehension, and vocabulary achievement for fourth through ninth graders (Nagy et al., 2006). These researchers also examined phonological recoding as a covariate in predicting reading outcomes showing morphological awareness significantly contributes to decoding assessments for all students and makes moderate to large contributions to reading comprehension across grades with a one-unit increase in morphological awareness resulting in between .58 and .76 units increase. Nagy et al. (2006) also showed a one-unit increase in morphological awareness results in between a .58 and .74-unit increase in vocabulary. Although this study uses structural equation modeling to create a latent construct of morphological awareness, only tasks with transparent relationships were used. Also, the latent was compared to a single indicator of phonological recoding, which has more error and therefore is at a disadvantage.

In a similar 2003 study with very different findings, Nagy et al. examined the relationship between morphological awareness and decoding for second- and fourth-graders at risk of developing reading difficulties. Findings show morphological awareness did not contribute significantly to decoding measures, but did contribute to 2nd-grade reading comprehension. The lack of significance in this study could stem from the presence of indicators of morphological, orthographic, and phonological awareness as predictors of reading components, therefore controlling for some of the meta-linguistic awareness that measures of morphological awareness often involve. In addition, oral vocabulary was also controlled for, perhaps hiding the contribution of morphological awareness to vocabulary which has been found by other studies (Anglin, 1993; Nagy & Anderson, 1984). Also, the latent construct of morphological awareness stemmed from overlap in three transparent tasks.

Another study, Roman, Kirby, Parrila, Wade-Woolley, & Deacon (2009), presents perhaps the most comprehensive view of how morphological awareness relates to word reading by controlling for three factors known to be related to word reading: phonological awareness, orthographic knowledge, and rapid automatized naming finding that a one-standard deviation (SD)—increase in morphological awareness results in a .27-SD unit improvement in word reading. The findings of this study could be strengthened by creating a latent variable of morphological awareness rather than using a sum score of the two morphological tasks (a morphological production task and word analogy task). Similarly, it is unclear whether phonologically opaque pairs were used in this study.

In another example, Clin, Wade-Woolley, & Heggie (2009) examined how much additional variance morphological awareness explained in reading achievement beyond phonological awareness, prosodic sensitivity, working memory, general language ability, nonverbal intelligence, and age for third-, fifth-, and seventh-grade students, finding that 6% of additional variance was explained by morphological awareness. General reading ability in this study was defined by a factor score created from reading assessments of rate, accuracy, comprehension, sight-word recognition, and decoding. The main hitch in this analysis is the use of a phoneme elision task to control for the phonological demands within the morphological production task which involved items of different degrees of transparency. Similar differences in phonological demands were found in Siegel's (2008) study which showed that morphological awareness explained between 8.7% to 17% of additional variance in various reading measures beyond phonological awareness for more than 1200 sixth-grade students (including ELLs considered fluent by their teachers and therefore different from the population of interest in this study).

Examining inflectional morphological awareness, Deacon and Kirby (2004) showed that morphological awareness scores in second grade on an 8-item measure of inflectional morphology involving regular and irregular past tense verbs contributed significantly to word identification, explaining additional 8%, 8%, and 5% of the variance in grades 3, 4, and 5 controlling for intelligence and phonological awareness. Methodologically, this study could be strengthened by reporting reliability for this short task.

THE PRESENT STUDY

This study aims to further understanding about the processes involved in reading for Spanish-speaking ELLs and add to the morphological awareness literature by exploring the unique contribution of morphological awareness to oral vocabulary, word decoding, reading comprehension, and reading vocabulary beyond phonological recoding. In addition, this study aspires to clarify how phonological recoding, defined as the "the letter-by-letter processing in sequential decoding of words" (Rayner, Foorman, Perfetti, Pesetsky, & Seidenberg, 2001, p. 40) predicts components of reading achievement when controlling for oral vocabulary and morphological awareness. Using a longitudinal sample, the following research questions were addressed for 5th-grade Spanish-speaking ELLs:

1. Does phonological recoding uniquely predict word reading, reading comprehension, and/ or reading vocabulary when controlling for morphological awareness and oral vocabulary knowledge?

2. Does morphological awareness make a unique contribution to the above components either directly or indirectly through oral vocabulary knowledge when controlling for phonological recoding?

3. Does morphological awareness contribute to oral vocabulary knowledge?

Table 1. Information on Measures Used, Including Construct and Skill Assessed, Grade, Score, Scale, Number of Items, and Reliability

Construct Assessed	Subtest	Test	Abbreviation	Grade	Skill Assessed	Score	Scale	# items	Reliability
Phonological Recoding	Word Attack	Woodcock Language Proficiency Battery	Word Attack	4	Pseudo-word decoding accuracy	Standard Scores Mean=100, SD=15	Correct/Incorrect	30[1]	.91[2]
Phonological Recoding	Nonword Accuracy	Computer Based Academic System	CAAS Non-Word Acc	4	Pseudo-word decoding accuracy	Percent of 30 total trials	Correct/Incorrect	30	.69[3]
Morphological Awareness	No Change	Extract the Base	ETB-No	4	Provide base of derived word to complete sentence	Raw Scores out of 12 points	0 (incorrect)/ 1 (partial credit)/ 2 (correct)	6	.85[4]
Morphological Awareness	Phonological Change	Extract the Base	ETB- Phon	4	Provide base of derived word to complete sentence. Word pairs are phonologically opaque.	Raw Scores out of 14 points	0 (incorrect)/ 1 (partial credit)/ 2 (correct)	7	.85[4]
Morphological Awareness	Orthographic Change	Extract the Base	ETB- Orth	4	Provide base of derived word to complete sentence. Word pairs are orthographically opaque.	Raw Scores out of 14 points	0 (incorrect)/ 1 (partial credit)/ 2 (correct)	7	.85[4]
Morphological Awareness	Both Change	Extract the Base	ETB-Both	4	Provide base of derived word to complete sentence. Word pairs are phonologically and orthographically opaque.	Raw Scores out of 16 points	0 (incorrect)/ 1 (partial credit)/ 2 (correct)	8	.85[4]
Oral Vocabulary	Picture Vocabulary	Woodcock Language Proficiency Battery	Picture Vocab	4	Naming pictured objects	Standard Scores Mean=100, SD=15	Correct/Incorrect	58[1]	.85[2]

Construct	Subtest	Instrument		Description	Items	Scores	Scoring	N	Reliability
Reading Achievement	Letter-Word Identification	Woodcock Language Proficiency Battery	Letter-Word ID	Real word decoding accuracy	5	Standard Scores Mean=100, SD=15	Correct/Incorrect	57[1]	.94[2]
Reading Achievement	Passage Comprehension	Woodcock Language Proficiency Battery	Passage Comp	Ability to read a passage and identify the word that best completes the passage	5	Standard Scores Mean=100, SD=15	Correct/Incorrect	43[1]	.88[2]
Reading Achievement	Reading Vocabulary	Woodcock Language Proficiency Battery	Reading Vocab	Ability to read words and supply a correct synonym or antonym	5	Standard Scores Mean=100, SD=15	Correct/Incorrect	79[1]	.93[2]

[1] Number of items administered varied depending on the child's performance due to basal and ceiling guidelines; [2] Spearman-Brown split-half reliability; [3] Test-retest reliability; [4] Cronbach's alpha reported for the Extract the Base (ETB) test as a whole rather than by subtest

METHODS

Participants

The study involved a longitudinal sample of 197 fifth-grade Spanish-speaking ELLs (53% female; 47% male) followed since second grade (August & Carlo, DELSS, Center for Applied Linguistics). The participants attended urban schools with a majority of ELLs and low-income students that followed the *Success for All* model of instruction and received various amounts of formal Spanish instruction in the equivalent Spanish curriculum. The students were strong word readers, but weak comprehenders and particularly poor in vocabulary knowledge.

Measures

Four constructs were assessed in this study, with three of the constructs represented by two or more indicators. Details and psychometric properties are included in Table 1. Only researcher-designed measures will be discussed in detail.

Phonological recoding. The construct of Phonological Recoding, which involves accessing the orthography, "transforming graphemes into phonemes and blending the phonemes into pronunciations" (Ehri, 1995, p. 116), was assessed in fourth grade by two individually administered pseudoword tasks: *Word Attack* (Woodcock Language Proficiency Battery/WLPB, Woodcock, 1991) and *CAAS Nonword accuracy* (Computer Based Academic Assessment System/CAAS, Sinatra & Royer, 1993). Phonological recoding was chosen because: 1) it involves both orthographic and phonological processing, and 2) other researchers have suggested phonological recoding is more appropriate at this age because phonological awareness is often mastered by this time period (Nagy et al., 2006).

CAAS nonword accuracy. This task measures accuracy in applying phonological rules to decode nonwords and, along with a response time measure, has been shown to classify grade 2-5 skilled and poor readers and predict reading comprehension achievement over time (Sinatra & Royer, 1993). Thirty monosyllabic and bisyllabic pseudowords are presented. For example, participants are shown *tet* and asked to read the target aloud. Items were scored as correct or incorrect. Scores were reported as percent correct. Based on a smaller sample of students from the larger study from which these participants were drawn, the test-retest reliability of the scores on this measure is 0.69, $p< .001$.

Morphological awareness. The second main construct measured was morphological awareness, which was assessed in fourth grade by a derivational morphological production task adapted from Carlisle (1988) named the Extract the Base task. Validation information and scoring details can be found in Goodwin et al. (in press) showing the task produces valid and reliable scores for 3rd-5th grade ELL and fluent English students.

Extract the base (ETB) no change, phonological change, orthographic change, and both change. Four indicators were created from this group administered, written task, where participants were provided with the task in writing and orally. A participant would be provided with the derived form and asked to extract the base as in: "Farmer. The cows and pigs were located on the _____." Answers were scored as 0-2 points based on the student's level of accuracy. For example, if a student just copied the given form, provided a translation, or wrote a random letter string, the student received a score of 0. A score of 1 was assigned to responses that were incorrect but showed evidence of extracting the base. A score of 2 was assigned to answers that were correct. Raw scores were used. Reliability in the form of Cronbach's alpha of the test as a whole was 0.85 for this sample of students.

The 28 items on the Extract the Base measure were split into four subtests based on the type of morphological relationship. Whereas all items involved morphological changes, some items involved phonological, orthographic, or both types of additional changes. The first subtest, ETB-No Change, included 6 word pairs with no phonological or orthographic changes such as *danger* and *dangerous*. The second subtest, ETB-Phonological Change, included 7 word pairs that have both a phonological and morphological change such as *courage* and *courageous*. The third subtest, ETB-Orthographic Change, consisted of 7 items that have both an orthographic and morphological change such as *decide* and *decision*. The fourth subtest, ETB-Both Change, is made up of 8 items that have morphological, phonological, and orthographic changes such as *muscle* and *muscular*.

Oral vocabulary. The third main construct measured in this study was fourth-grade Oral Vocabulary, which is a participant's ability to access the lexicon to determine a label for a picture assessed by *Picture Vocabulary* (WLPB, Woodcock, 1991).

Reading achievement. The third major construct assessed was reading achievement, which was measured in fifth grade by three WLPB (Woodcock, 1991) subtests: *Letter-word Identification*, *Passage Comprehension*, and *Reading Vocabulary*. These tasks assessed word reading, comprehension, and the ability to integrate vocabulary knowledge within reading of text. *Reading Vocabulary* is included within reading achievement separate from the measure of picture vocabulary because it is a measure of a participant's ability to read a word and access that word's meaning, which is an important component within major theories of reading (Adams, 1994; Ehri, 1995; Gough, 1972; Perfetti, 1988, 2009; Rummelhart & McClelland, 1986) and different than providing a label for a picture. Standard scores were calculated with a mean of 100 and a standard deviation of 15 according to test guidelines.

Data Collection

This study was part of a larger study where data was collected in five waves, although only data from waves four and five were used. Measures were administered by trained research assistants on two separate days, with all WLPB tests administered individually on the same day, and the remaining assessments administered on a different day.

Data Analysis

Models were tested using Mplus 5.1 (Muthén & Muthén, 2007). Like other longitudinal studies, missing data was present in this analysis, with 85 participants having data missing on at least one variable. Full information maximum likelihood (FIML) estimates were used to impute missing values to account for the missing data as appropriately as possible (Muthén, Kaplan, & Hollis, 1987).

Measurement models and latent variables. Measurement models representing 4th-grade Phonological Recoding and Morphological Awareness were constructed (see Figure 1). For Morphological Awareness, ETB-Phonological Change and ETB-No Change as well as ETB-Phon Change and ETB-Both were allowed to correlate based on theory. This latent variable created a

Figure 1. Results of Direct Paths Showing the Unique Contribution of Phonological Recoding and Morphological Awareness to Reading Outcomes with Oral Vocabulary as a Mediator

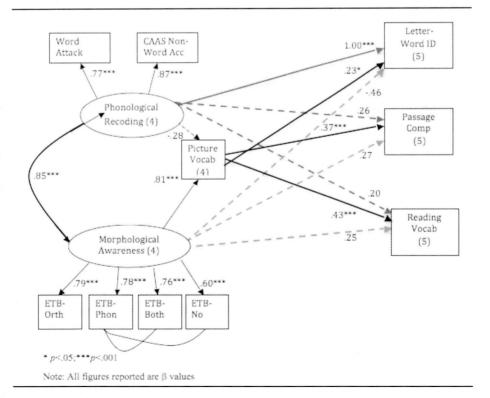

* $p<.05$;*** $p<.001$

Note: All figures reported are β values

theoretically pure construct of morphological awareness because it was created from indicators of varying orthographic and phonological transparency, and therefore, the only shared variance amongst tasks stemmed from morphological changes. Other linguistic confounds present within the ETB tasks were theoretically separated into the error terms.

Structural models. A structural model was created to determine the unique contributions of phonological recoding and morphological awareness to vocabulary and each reading component. This model represented a multiple regression of word reading (WLPB-Letter Word Identification), reading comprehension (WLPB-Passage Comprehension), and reading vocabulary (WLPB-Reading Vocabulary) on phonological recoding, morphological awareness, and oral vocabulary. This model also included a multiple regression of oral vocabulary on phonological recoding and morphological awareness, allowing oral vocabulary knowledge to act as a mediator.

Table 2. Covariance (Correlation) Structure and Descriptives of Observed Variables

Measure	WLPB-Word Attack	CAAS Non-Word Accuracy	ETB-No Change	ETB-Phon Change	ETB-Orth Change	ETB-Both Change	WLPB-Picture Vocab	WLPB-Letter Word	WLPB-Passage Comp	WLPB-Reading Vocab
WLPB-Word Attack	237.79									
	(1.00)									
CAAS Non-Word Accuracy	204.14	392.29								
	(.67)	(1.00)								
ETB-No Change	12.98	15.5	3.81							
	(.43)	(.40)	(1.00)							
ETB-Phon Change	19.56	31.79	3.26	7.52						
	(.46)	(.59)	(.61)	(1.00)						
ETB-Orth Change	19.50	26.86	2.07	3.92	5.45					
	(.54)	(.58)	(.46)	(.61)	(1.00)					
ETB-Both Change	24.50	31.81	2.79	4.07	4.69	8.95				
	(.53)	(.54)	(.48)	(.50)	(.67)	(1.00)				
WLPB-Picture Vocab	81.64	192.58	13.57	28.62	27.79	30.24	566.71			
	(.22)	(.41)	(.29)	(.44)	(.50)	(.43)	(1.00)			
WLPB-Letter Word	137.86	211.16	11.48	20.96	18.23	17.18	150.55	257.72		
	(.56)	(.66)	(.37)	(.48)	(.49)	(.36)	(.39)	(1.00)		
WLPB-Passage Comp	91.21	137.79	12.44	20.53	15.37	17.84	185.35	122.77	155.49	
	(.47)	(.56)	(.51)	(.60)	(.53)	(.48)	(.62)	(.61)	(1.00)	
WLPB-Reading Vocab	75.53	113.63	8.92	14.59	13.53	18.91	171.79	89.51	102.07	123.37
	(.44)	(.52)	(.41)	(.48)	(.52)	(.57)	(.65)	(.50)	(.74)	(1.00)
Mean	104.23	73.18	10.35	11.34	7.40	6.45	72.07	105.74	93.31	91.64
SD	15.20	19.79	1.97	2.78	2.36	3.02	23.92	16.07	12.64	11.35
N	149	168	176	176	176	176	149	167	166	163

RESULTS

Table 2 provides covariance and correlations amongst variables as well as descriptives of observed variables. Although the X^2 value was significant ($X^2(21)=34.2$, $p=0.003$), multiple fit indices (i.e., CFI = 0.98, TLI = 0.95, RMSEA = 0.07, and SRMR = 0.03) showed acceptable fit as suggested by Kline (2005). In examining direct paths (see Figure 1 and Table 3), a one-unit increase in Morphological Awareness resulted in a .81 SD-unit increase in Picture Vocabulary controlling for Phonological Recoding. In contrast, Morphological Awareness did not make a significant direct contribution to any reading outcome controlling for Phonological Recoding and Picture Vocabulary. Phonological Recoding made a significant direct contribution to Letter-Word ID but not to Picture Vocabulary controlling for Morphological Awareness, nor to Passage Comprehension or Reading Vocabulary controlling for Morphological Awareness and Picture Vocabulary.

Figure 2. Results of Total Contributions Showing the Unique Contribution of Phonological Recoding and Morphological Awareness to Reading Outcomes with Oral Vocabulary as a Mediator

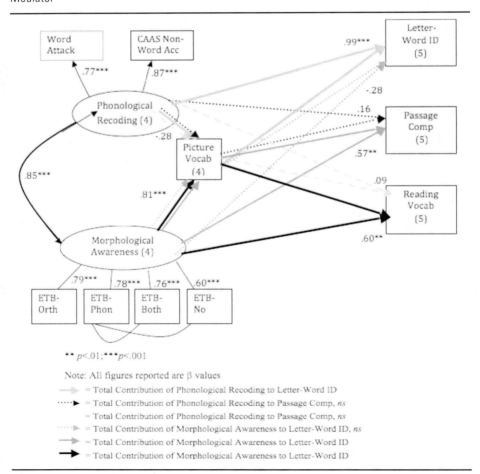

** $p<.01$; *** $p<.001$

Note: All figures reported are β values

⟶ = Total Contribution of Phonological Recoding to Letter-Word ID

····▶ = Total Contribution of Phonological Recoding to Passage Comp, *ns*

= Total Contribution of Phonological Recoding to Passage Comp, *ns*

·····▷ = Total Contribution of Morphological Awareness to Letter-Word ID, *ns*

⟶ = Total Contribution of Morphological Awareness to Letter-Word ID

➤ = Total Contribution of Morphological Awareness to Letter-Word ID

Table 3. Results showing the Unique Contribution of Phonological Recoding and Morphological Awareness to Reading Outcomes with Oral Vocabulary as a Mediator

Outcome	Contribution of Picture Vocabulary		
	Total *b* (SE), β	Direct *b* (SE), β	Indirect *b* (SE), β (via Picture Vocab)
Letter-Word ID	-------	0.16* (0.07), .23	-------
Passage Comp	-------	0.19*** (0.04), .37	-------
Reading Vocab	-------	0.20*** (0.04), .43	-------
Contribution of Morphological Awareness			
Picture Vocab	-------	10.46** (3.44), .81	------
Letter-Word ID	-2.42 (2.04), -.28	- 4.03 (2.62), -.46	1.62 (1.11), .19
Passage Comp	3.83** (1.43), .57	1.80 (1.43), .27	2.03** (0.77), .30
Reading Vocab	3.64** (1.23), .60	1.54 (1.18), .25	2.10** (0.78), .35
Contribution of Phonological Recoding			
Picture Vocab	--------	- .57 (0.52), - .28	------
Letter-Word ID	1.33*** (0.34), .99	1.42*** (0.38), 1.00	-0.09 (0.11), -.07
Passage Comp	0.17 (0.21), .16	0.28 (0.19), .26	-0.11 (0.10), -.10
Reading Vocab	0.08 (0.19), .09	0.19 (0.16), .21	-0.11 (0.11), -.12

* $p<.05$; ** $p<.01$; *** $p<.001$

According to the total paths (Figure 2 and Table 3), Morphological Awareness significantly predicted Passage Comprehension and Reading Vocabulary, but not Letter-Word ID when controlling for Phonological Recoding with a one-unit increase in Morphological Awareness resulted in a .57 SD-unit increase in Passage Comprehension and a .60 SD-unit increase in Reading Vocabulary controlling for Phonological Recoding. On the other hand, Phonological Recoding significantly predicted Letter-Word ID, but not Passage Comprehension nor Reading Vocabulary when controlling for Morphological Awareness. For example, a one-unit increase in Phonological Recoding resulted in a large and significant .99 SD-unit increase in Letter-Word ID controlling for Morphological Awareness. Oral vocabulary knowledge was a significant mediator of the relationship between Morphological Awareness and Reading Comprehension and Reading Vocabulary but not of relationships involving Phonological Recoding.

DISCUSSION

This study addresses morphological awareness as an important contributor to components of reading achievement. As Hurry, Nunes, Bryant, Pretzlik, Parker, Curno, & Midgley, (2005) states, "The role of morphology in literacy has not been extensively researched and might therefore have a relatively low profile at both levels [i.e., the national or policy level and within classrooms]" (p. 189). Because the writing system of English is morphophonemic, instruction in units of meaning could be conceivably embedded within classroom teaching across grade levels, allowing students to focus on meaning within text rather than isolated subskills.

The Role of Phonological Recoding

This study showed that phonological recoding made a unique contribution to the prediction of word reading but not reading comprehension nor reading vocabulary when controlling for morphological awareness and oral vocabulary knowledge. These results suggest that while phonological recoding may support word reading for Spanish-speaking 5th-grade ELLs, the processing of words letter by letter and sound by sound does not support reading comprehension or the integration of lexical meanings when reading texts.

This should not be interpreted to suggest that phonological recoding is not important, but rather that as prior research has suggested (Anglin, 1993; Carlisle, 2000; Deacon & Kirby, 2004; Kieffer & Lesaux, 2008; Nagy et al., 2006), developmentally by fifth grade, awareness of units of meaning and word structure play an important role in literacy achievement, perhaps because phonological recoding skills are approaching mastery, whereas morphological awareness continues to develop through high school years. Also, the latent constructs of phonological recoding and morphological awareness were highly correlated in this study, and although morphological awareness seemed to better explain variance in oral vocabulary, reading comprehension, and reading vocabulary for these 5th-grade ELLs, similar processing demands were involved in manipulating sound and meaning structures such as segmentation, elision, and blending skills. The current findings make an important contribution to the field of reading because this study suggests the need to include both morphological awareness and phonological recoding in models where these constructs are predicting vocabulary and reading outcomes.

Role of Morphological Awareness

Morphological awareness findings suggest this theoretically pure construct of morphological awareness made a moderate significant and meaningful contribution to passage comprehension and reading vocabulary controlling for phonological recoding, with most of the power of that contribution stemming from the large significant contribution of morphological awareness to oral vocabulary. Morphological awareness did not contribute to word reading.

Contribution to oral vocabulary. Morphological awareness was shown to be especially important in contributing to oral vocabulary knowledge for Spanish-speaking ELLs, which research has suggested is a particularly important area to develop for these students. As August and Shanahan (2006) state, "The research suggests that the reason for the disparity between word- and text-level skills among language-minority students is oral English proficiency...Specifically, English vocabulary knowledge" (p. 4). Snow and Kim (2007) have estimated to catch up with fluent English peers, ELLs must learn even more than 10-12 words words per day. The current study suggests that morphological awareness may contribute to the development of second language vocabulary knowledge such that by knowing the meaning of a morpheme such as *plant*, a student can estimate the meaning of *plants, planted, planting, implant, supplant, plantation, planter,* and *transplant*. In fact, Hancin-Bhatt and Nagy (1994) reported ELLs with higher levels of morphological awareness recognized more cognates.

Contribution to word reading. In this study, morphological awareness did not contribute significantly to word reading perhaps because the word reading task used (WLPB Letter-Word ID) relied more on morphologically simple words than on morphologically complex words. This is is different from estimates of typical text, which according to Anglin (1993), involve 60-80% morphologically complex words as of third grade. The use of this measure may be one of the reasons why results on the contribution of morphological awareness to word reading, controlling for phonological awareness or phonological recoding, have been mixed with some studies reporting a significant relationship (Deacon & Kirby, 2004; Fowler & Liberman, 1995; Mahony et al., 2000; Nagy et al., 2006; Singson et al., 2000) and others reporting the lack of a significant contribution (Nagy et al., 2003). Most of the studies described above did not fully control for the phonological and orthographic processing demands required by the morphological awareness task, which may explain the different results found by this study. Also, the studies above involved fluent English upper elementary students, and this current finding may suggest that morphological units play less of an important role in word reading for ELLs who, because of their low levels of vocabulary, may be paying closer attention to the orthographic rather than morphological code.

Contribution to reading vocabulary. Morphological awareness also supports reading vocabulary, perhaps because many morphemes maintain their written form even when they are pronounced differently as in the pair *know* and *knowledge*. Therefore, by recognizing the written form *know*, a student can use their knowledge of the meaning of *know* to estimate the meaning of *knowledge*. As Balmuth (1992) stated, "It can be helpful to readers when the same spelling is kept for the same morpheme, despite variations in pronunciation. Such spellings supply clues to the meanings of words, clues that would be lost if the words were spelled phonemically" (p. 207). In addition, the finding that oral vocabulary knowledge mediated the contribution of morphological awareness to reading vocabulary is consistent with findings that students with larger vocabularies are more likely to apply their knowledge of morphemes to learning words (Freyd & Baron, 1982).

Contribution to reading comprehension. This study also found that morphological awareness contributes to reading comprehension, perhaps reflecting the increasing text demands present in 5th grade and the amount of morphologically complex relationships present. According to Nagy and Anderson (1984), texts from grades 3-9 involved 139,020 transparent derived words such as *growth* compared to 49,080 semantically opaque words such as *emerge* and *emergency*, and therefore, students with higher levels of morphological awareness may be better able to estimate the meanings of morphologically related words and relate these meanings to comprehension of the text.

General Conclusions and Educational Significance

The growing attention regarding the role of morphology within reading makes it clear that it is time to develop an overall picture of how morphology contributes to reading within a morphophonemic language such as English. Evidence from predictive studies regarding the role of morphology in reading achievement is quite strong and now researchers must determine the details of the relationship. For example, future studies should determine whether the relationship between these constructs is reciprocal or unidirectional. Future research should also examine differences between the contribution of morphological awareness and phonological recoding to components of reading achievement in a student's native language versus a student's second language and whether those contributions differ depending on the nature of that language. Furthermore, differences between various populations of students such as different language or dialect groups, poor readers, and high achievers should be examined as well as changes in these relationships across time.

The findings of this study have important implications for research and classroom instruction. Understanding how morphological awareness and phonological recoding uniquely contribute to oral vocabulary, word reading, reading comprehension, and reading vocabulary helps researchers design interventions to improve achievement. Interpretation of results suggest student achievement might be supported by morphological instruction such as teaching students the meaning of affixes and roots, identifying units within morphologically complex words, and building words from morphemic units. As Nunes (2006) suggests, "Some of the most important correspondences between spoken and written language are at the level of the morpheme…The system of morphemes, therefore, is a powerful resource for those learning literacy" (p. 157).

REFERENCES

Adams, M. (1994). Modeling the connections between word recognition and reading. In R. B. Ruddell, M. R. Ruddell, & H. Singer (Eds.), *Theoretical models and processes of reading* (pp. 951-995). Newark, NJ: IRA.

Anglin, J. M. (1993). *Vocabulary development: A morphological analysis.* Monographs of the Society for Research in Child Development, *58*(10), Serial # 238.

Aud, S., Hussar, W., Planty, M., Snyder, T., Bianco, K., Fox, M., Frohlich, L., Kemp, J., & Drake, L. (2010). *The condition of education 2010* (NCES 010-028). National Center for Education Statistics, Institute of Education Sciences, U.S. Department of Education. Washington, DC.

August, D. & Shanahan, T. (2006). *Developing literacy in second-language learners.* Hillsdale, NJ: Lawrence Erlbaum Associates.

Balmuth, M. (1992). *The roots of phonics.* Timonium, MD: York Press.

Carlisle, J. F. (1988). Knowledge of derivational morphology and spelling ability in fourth, sixth, and eighth graders. *Applied Psycholinguistics, 9*(3), 247-266.

Carlisle, J. F. (1995). Morphological awareness and early reading achievement. In L. Feldman (Ed.), *Morphological aspects of language processing* (pp.131-154). Hillsdale, NJ: Lawrence Erlbaum.

Carlisle, J. F. (2000). Awareness of the structure and meaning of morphologically complex words: Impact on reading. *Reading and Writing: An Interdisciplinary Journal, 12*(3-4), 169-190.

Carlisle, J. F. (2003). Morphology matters in learning to read: A commentary. *Reading Psychology, 24*(3-4), 291-322.

Carlisle, J. F., & Nomanbhoy, D. M. (1993). Phonological and morphological awareness in first graders. *Applied Psycholinguistics, 14,* 177-195.

Chomsky, N., & Halle, M. (1968). *The sound pattern of English.* New York, NY: Harper & Row.

Clin, E., Wade-Woolley, L., & Heggie, L. (2009). Prosodic sensitivity and morphological awareness in children's reading. *Journal of Experimental Child Psychology, 104*(2), 197-213.

Deacon, S. H., & Kirby, J. R. (2004). Morphological awareness: Just "more phonological"? The roles of morphological and phonological awareness in reading development. *Applied Psycholinguistics, 25,* 223-238.

Ehri, L. (1995). Phases of development in learning to read words by sight. *Journal of Research in Reading, 18*(2), 116-125.

Feldman, L. B., & Basnight-Brown, D. M. (2008). The role of morphology in visual word recognition: Graded semantic influences due to competing senses and semantic richness of the stem. In E. L. Grigorenko & A. J. Naples (Eds.), *Single-word reading: Behavioral and biological perspectives* (pp. 85-106). New York, NY: Lawrence Erlbaum Associates.

Fowler, A., & Liberman, I. (1995).The role of phonology and orthography in morphological awareness. In L. Feldman (Ed.), *Morphological aspects of language processing* (pp. 131-154). Hillsdale, NJ: Lawrence Erlbaum.

Freyd, P., & Baron, J. (1982). Individual differences in acquisition of derivational morphology. *Journal of Verbal Learning and Verbal Behavior, 21*(3), 282-295.

Goodwin, A., Huggins, A. C., August, D., Carlo, M., & Calderon, M. (2011). The role of morphological awareness unique from phonological awareness in predicting overall reading achievement in English language learners. Manuscript submitted for publication.

Goodwin, A., Huggins, A. C., Carlo, M. C. et al. (2010). Development and Validation of Extract the Base: An English Derivational Morphology Test for Third through Fifth grade Monolingual students and Spanish Speaking English Language Learners. *Language Testing Journal.*

Gough, P. B. (1972). One second of reading. In J. F. Kavanagh & I. G. Mattingly (Eds.), *Language by ear and by eye* (pp. 331-358). Cambridge, MA: MIT Press.

Hancin-Bhatt, B., & Nagy, W. (1994). Lexical transfer and second-language morphological development. *Applied Psycholinguistics, 15,* 289-310.

Hurry, J., Nunes, T., Bryant, P., Pretzlik, U., Parker, M., Curno, T., & Midgley, L. (2005). Transforming research on morphology into teacher practice. *Research Papers in Education, 20*(2), 187-206.

Kieffer, M. J., & Lesaux, N. K. (2008). The role of derivational morphology in the reading comprehension of Spanish-speaking English language learners. *Reading and Writing: An Interdisciplinary Journal, 21,* 783-804.

Kline, R. B. (2005). *Principles and practice of structural equation modeling* (2nd ed.). New York, NY: The Guildford Press.

Kuo, L. J., & Anderson, R. C. (2006). Morphological awareness and learning to read: A cross-language perspective. *Educational Psychologist, 41,* 161-180.

Lesaux, N., & Geva, E. (2006). Synthesis: Development of literacy in language-minority students. In D. August & T. Shanahan (Eds.), *Developing literacy in second-language learners* (pp. 53-74). Hillsdale, NJ: Lawrence Erlbaum Associates.

Mahony, D., Singson, M., & Mann, V. (2000). Reading ability and sensitivity to morphological relations. *Reading and Writing: An Interdisciplinary Journal, 12,* 191-218.

Menken, K. (2008). *English learners left behind: Standardized testing as a language policy.* Clevedon, UK: Multilingual Matters.

Mplus (Version 5.1) [Computer software]. Los Angeles, CA: Muthén & Muthén.

Muthén, B. O., Kaplan, D., & Hollis, M. (1987). On structural equation modeling with data that are not missing completely at random. *Psychometrika, 52,* 431-462.

Nagy, W., & Anderson, R. (1984). The number of words in printed school English. *Reading Research Quarterly, 19,* 304-330.

Nagy, W., Berninger, V., & Abbott, R. (2006). Contributions of morphology beyond phonology to literacy outcomes of upper elementary and middle school students. *Journal of Educational Psychology, 98*(1), 134-147.

Nagy, W., Berninger, V., Abbot, R., Vaughan, K., & Vermeulen, K. (2003). Relationship of morphology and other language skills to literacy skills in at-risk second-grade readers and at-risk fourth-grade writers. *Journal of Educational Psychology, 95*(4), 730-742.

Nagy, W., García, G. E., Durgunoglu, A., & Hancin-Bhatt, B. (1993). Spanish-English bilingual students' use of cognates in English reading. *Journal of Reading Behavior, 25,* 241-259.

Nagy, W., & Scott, J. A. (2000). Vocabulary processes. In M. L. Kamil, P. Mosenthal, P. D. Pearson, & R. Barr (Eds.), *Handbook of reading research, Vol. 3* (pp. 269-284). Mahwah, NJ: Erlbaum.

Nunes, T., Bryant, P., Pretzlik, U., & Hurry, J. (Eds.) (2006). *Improving literacy by teaching morphemes.* London, UK and New York, NY: Routledge.

Perfetti, C. A. (1988). Verbal efficiency in reading ability. In G. E. MacKinnon, T. G. Waller, & M. Daneman (Eds.), *Reading research: Advances in theory and practice, Vol. 6* (pp. 109-143). New York, NY: Academic Press, Inc.

Perfetti, C. A. (2009, June). Reducing the complexities of reading comprehension: A simplifying framework. Paper session presented at the Annual 2009 IES Research Conference, Washington, D.C., 6/7-9/2009.

Perfetti, C. A., & Dunlap, S. (2008). Learning to read: General principles and writing system variations. In K. Koda & A. Zehler (Eds.). *Learning to read across languages.* (pp. 13-38). Mahwah, NJ: Erlbaum.

Rayner, K., Foorman, B. R., Perfetti, C. A., Pesetsky, D., & Seidenberg, M. S. (2001). How psychological science informs the teaching of reading. *Psychological Science in the Public Interest, 2*(2), 31-74.

Roman, A. A., Kirby, J. R., Parrila, R. K., Wade-Woolley, L., & Deacon, S. H. (2009). Toward a comprehensive view of the skills involved in word reading in grades 4, 6, and 8. *Journal of Experimental Child Psychology, 102*(1), 96-113.

Rummelhart, D. E., & McClelland, J. L. (Eds.). (1986). *Parallel distributed processing: Vol. 1. Foundations.* Cambridge, MA: MIT Press.

Schreuder, R., & Baayan, R. H. (1995). Modeling morphological processing. In L. Feldman (Ed.), *Morphological aspects of language processing* (pp.131-154). Hillsdale, NJ: Lawrence Erlbaum.

Siegel, L. S. (2008). Morphological awareness skills of English language learners and children with dyslexia. *Topics in Language Disorders, 28*(1), 15.

Sinatra, G. M., & Royer, J. M. (1993). The development of cognitive component processing skills that support skilled reading. *Journal of Educational Psychology, 85,* 509-519.

Singson, M., Mahony, D., & Mann, V. (2000). The relation between reading ability and morphological skills: Evidence from derivational suffixes. *Reading and Writing: An Interdisciplinary Journal, 12,* 219-252.

Snow, C. E., & Kim, Y. (2007). Large problem spaces: The challenge of vocabulary for English language learners. In R. K. Wagner, A. E. Muse, & K. R. Tannenbaum (Eds.), *Vocabulary acquisition: Implications for reading comprehension* (pp.123-129). New York, NY: The Guilford Press.

Taft, M. (2004). Morphological decomposition and the reverse base frequency effect. *The Quarterly Journal of Experimental Psychology, 57A*(4), 745-765.

Titos, R. M., Defior, S., Alegria, J., & Martos, F. (2003). The use of morphological resources in Spanish orthography: The case of the verb. In R. Malatesha Joshi, Che Kan Leong, & Bozydar L. J. Kaczmarek (Eds.), *Literacy Acquisition. The Role of Phonology, Morphology and Orthography* (pp. 113-118). IOS Press.

Verhoeven, L., & Perfetti, C. (2003). Introduction to this special issue: The role of morphology in learning to read. *Scientific Studies of Reading, 7,* 209-217.

Woodcock, R. W. (1991). *Woodcock language proficiency battery-revised.* Itasca, IL: Riverside Publishing.

Victoria J. Risko
Professor Emerita
Vanderbilt University

Section I:
Supporting Professional Learning of Prospective and Practicing Teachers

In the following eight papers, researchers address issues related to the effectiveness and challenges of professional development efforts. The questions they ask correspond to questions and directions of research published within the last two decades; their work contributes to a growing body of research on professional learning.

PROMISING PRACTICES

Reviews of professional development research have identified specific instructional features that hold promise for enhancing teacher development. The available evidence, for example, suggests that reading and language arts methods courses are effective for advancing teachers' pedagogical knowledge, and that applications of this knowledge are enhanced further when methods courses are accompanied by intensive and well-supervised teaching experiences in classrooms and tutoring settings (Clift & Brady, 2005; Risko, Roller, Cummins, Bean, Block, Anders, & Flood, 2008). Along with well-supervised teaching applications, feedback that is deliberate and timely, offered by professional leaders and/or peers, is reported to support teacher learning (Glazer & Hannafin, 2006). Also found effective is a collaborative apprenticeship approach to professional learning that includes experts' explicit teaching demonstrations and guided applications (Glazer & Hannafin, 2006; Risko et al., 2008).

Four papers that follow address these features of promising practices. Morgan, Zimmerman, Kidder, and Dunn report on their one-year multiple case study and implementation of a writing workshop approach to apprentice future teachers as writers. They document how narrow views of the writing process are replaced with a vision of writing as "deliberate and thoughtful" and instruction that engages teachers and students in shared writing activities. Drawing on multiple data sets, they offer an elegant case for their conclusion that "methods courses do matter."

McCarthey, Woodard, and Kang explored teachers' perceptions of the impact of PD on their writing instruction. The researchers conducted interviews and observations of the teachers across the school year. The findings of this study revealed that teachers reported that PD was most influential when there was a content focus, active learning components, and collaborative participation.

Wickstrom, Arauzo, Patterson, Hoki, and Roberts examined literacy teaching as mediated through guided and shared activity. With their goal of understanding how teachers mediate English language learners, they documented how teachers applied new collaborative writing methods to encourage their students' agency in reading and writing engagement and use of writing for bridging understandings of academic concepts with real-life contexts.

Deeney and her 16 colleagues representing multiple U.S. teacher education programs investigated the impact of tutoring on the learning of prospective teachers. They provide a strong argument for including a tutoring experience, supported with supervisors' detailed feedback and peer collaboration, as a contributor to prospective teachers' developing pedagogical knowledge. And drawing on interview data, they hypothesize that teachers are transferring this knowledge to their classroom teaching experiences.

CHALLENGES

Teacher resistance, a long-standing challenge to professional learning (Clift & Brady, 2005) and (Risko et al., 2008), is examined by several researchers in this set of papers. Risko et al. (2008) noted that resistance often followed a lack of congruence between what prospective and practicing teachers were learning in methods courses and what was expected of them in the "real world" of teaching. Conversely, congruence often ameliorated this problem.

Researchers in three papers addressed congruence. Morgan, Zimmerman, Kidder, and Dunn, as described above, noted that while there were positive changes in teachers' visions of teaching writing, teachers expressed their concerns about these methodologies when placed in teaching situations that countered their preparation. Similarly, Frambaugh-Kritzer and Stolle documented secondary teachers' resistance to interdisciplinary instruction when placed in settings where there was little to no support for its implementation. Morgan et al., Frambaugh-Kritzer and Stolle, and Vaughn and Faircloth argue that teachers need to be prepared to enact their visions of effective teaching and how to navigate difficult situations and resist institutional directions that may inhibit good teaching.

Ferguson investigated power structures and resistance from another perspective. Tracing relationships formed among teachers, literacy coaches, and administrators, Ferguson differentiated conditions contributing to resistance (top down, authorial, and evaluative forms of coaching) and those facilitative of team building (student-focused, supportive roles, collaborative and team approach to resolve students' instructional needs). Their work builds on numerous studies with similar conclusions, and aligns with recommendations for collaborative and shared learning environments that engage literacy coaches and classroom teachers in instructional planning (Glazer & Hannafin, 2006).

In the seventh paper, Albers, Vasquez, and Harste provide a compelling argument for developing teachers' critical examination of picture books and embedded power relations, intentions, and stereotypes represented. Engaging teachers in critical dialogue and within written/ spoken or art demonstrations, they describe how teachers responded to the social issues operating in the text messages and moved to setting goals for social actions.

MOVING FORWARD

As a whole, these papers contribute to a growing convergence of evidence documenting patterns of professional developments efforts affecting teacher learning. Yet needed are large-scale studies that are multi-focal, located in multiple sites, and longitudinal, and funding to support this work.

REFERENCES

Clift, R. T., & Brady, P. (2005). Research on methods courses and field experiences. In M. Cochran-Smith & K. Zeichner (Eds.), *Studying teacher education: The report of the AERA panel on research and teacher education* (pp. 309-424). Mahwah, NJ: Erlbaum.

Glazer, E. M., & Hannafin, M. J. (2006). The collaborative apprenticeship model: Situated professional development within school settings. *Teaching and Teacher Education, 22*, 179-193.

Risko, V. J., Roller, C. M., Cummins, C., Bean, R. M., Collins Block, C., Anders, P. L., & Flood, J. (2008). A critical analysis of research on reading teacher education. *Reading Research Quarterly, 43*, 252-288.

From Writing Methods to Student Teaching: Vision Development and the Implementation of Conceptual and Practical Tools by Preservice Teachers

Denise N. Morgan
Belinda S. Zimmerman
Melanie K. Kidder-Brown
Kathleen J. Dunn
Kent State University

In today's schools, teachers are challenged with helping students "compose often, compose well, and through these composings, *become* the citizen writers of our country, the citizen writers of our world, and the writers of our future" (italics in original, National Council of Teachers of English [NCTE], 2009, p. 1). Writing is an essential skill for success in the 21st century. Gallagher (2006) argues, "In an increasingly demanding world of literacy, the importance of our students leaving our schools as effective writers has magnified. The ability to write well, once a luxury, has become a necessity. Today, writing is foundational for success" (p. 4). The ability to write well and communicate ideas effectively provides students with academic advantages while lack of writing experience or writing poorly can act as a gatekeeper to students' future success in college and in the workplace (NCTE, 2008). As the National Commission on Writing for America's Families, Schools, and Colleges (2003) states, "Writing today is not a frill for the few, but an essential skill for the many" (n.p.). Learning to write well is among the most important processes taught in schools and universities. It is clear that thoughtful writing instruction matters.

When teachers first enter their own classrooms they should possess an in-depth knowledge about writing, since "what teachers do makes a difference in how much students are capable of achieving as writers" (NCTE, 2004, p. 1). Teaching writers involves "complex, informed, human judgment" (NCTE, 2004, p. 8); therefore, schools of education must provide opportunities to support, foster, and develop preservice teachers' abilities and confidence to deal with these instructional issues. A closer look at what is occurring in preparing preservice teachers pedagogically to teach writing at the university level is necessary.

RELATED LITERATURE

Writing must be taught, not assigned. Students understand the rewards and challenges of writing well when their teachers are writers (Colby & Stapleton, 2006; Graves, 1983; Whyte, Lazarte, Thompson, Ellis, Muse, & Talbot, 2007). When teachers write, the act of writing becomes demystified and teachers develop increased self-efficacy and confidence in their ability to write and to teach writing well (Graham, Harris, Fink, & MacArthur, 2001). The act of writing helps teachers become "experts on teaching writing" (Gillespie, 1985, p. 2.).

Teachers engage in an "apprenticeship of observation," (Lortie, 1975) of what writing instruction looks like based on how they were "taught" or "assigned" writing in school. For many, writing means handwriting, grammar, and spelling and not ideas, intentional crafting, and awareness of audience. Time logged as an observer and doer influences how many teachers choose to teach; they teach as they were taught unless the cycle is disrupted. Teacher education offers a space to investigate past writing experiences and beliefs and create new ones, but few universities offer courses devoted specifically to writing (Moore-Hart & Carpenter, 2008; Norman & Spencer, 2005). Writing instruction is often sandwiched into reading courses (Totten, 2005). This shortchanges a process that cannot be rushed.

Teacher educators have much to address in their methods course as many preservice teachers have had negative writing experiences or consider themselves poor writers, recalling fill-in-the-blank experiences or reporting little knowledge of the writing process (Bridge & Hiebert, 1985; Mahurt, 1998; Morgan, 2010). Teacher educators must engage preservice teachers in thoughtful new writing experiences that build confidence and develop a sense of self as a writer along with helping them understand and live the recursive nature of the writing process. National organizations call for specific coursework in writing for preservice teachers (National Commission on Writing, 2003; 2004; NCTE, 2008), as do researchers concerned with teachers' personal and pedagogical writing practices (Grossman et al., 2000). Simply put, more attention to writing is needed in teacher education.

There is reason to heed the call for focused attention to writing at the preservice teacher education level. Thoughtful deliberate writing experiences can provide preservice teachers opportunities to face firsthand the constant decisions and indecisions writers face during the act of capturing ideas on paper. Through well-crafted instruction, preservice teachers learn to be writers themselves and to develop into effective teachers of writing (Grossman et al., 2000; Whyte et al., 2007).

Teacher education is also the time to help preservice teachers develop their vision for teaching. Visions are often teachers' images of what could or might be in their classrooms (Hammerness, 2003). Langer (1995) describes vision as the formation of a vivid personal mental image, conception, or anticipation of ideas or experiences related to teaching writing not yet lived or enacted. In methods classes, preservice teachers have opportunities and experiences that can shape their beliefs and goals for teaching writing and allow them to envision how they could provide writing instruction in their classroom.

In a 3-year longitudinal study of preservice teachers who learned about writing in methods courses, Grossman et al. (2000) found preservice teachers were more likely to exhibit confidence in their ability to teach writing. Mahurt (1998) offered case study data that suggest a teacher who experienced strong preservice education about writing demonstrates those understandings in the classroom. This work suggests teacher education does make a difference in how writing is taught by teachers who received thoughtful writing instruction in methods courses.

A small number of studies (Boyd, Boll, Brawner, & Villaume, 1998; Gallavan, Bowles, & Young, 2007) focus specifically on preservice teachers' experiences with writing and their growth as teachers of writing. Even fewer studies follow preservice teachers into their student teaching experience (Grossman et al., 2000). While most studies of preservice teachers and writing have occurred within a literacy course addressing both reading and writing (Grossman et al., 2000; Street, 2003) fewer still explore preservice teachers' experiences in a course devoted entirely to writing and their subsequent student-teaching experience. By understanding the vision preservice teachers had for their student-teaching experience and how they applied their new course knowledge during student teaching, instruction in subsequent methods courses can be improved.

The purpose of this case study research is to describe the experiences of preservice teachers as they take a writing methods course. We wanted to learn about their self-growth as writers and future teachers of writers and their appropriation of pedagogical knowledge during student teaching. Specifically we wanted to know: (a) How do preservice teachers describe writing experiences prior to taking a methods course on the teaching of writing?, (b) What pedagogical knowledge do preservice teachers identify as helpful to their own learning as writers and how do they envision using that knowledge in their student teaching experience?, and (c) How do preservice teachers appropriate their knowledge learned in the methods course into their student-teaching experience?

METHOD

Context of the Methods Course

Early childhood (pre-k through third grade) preservice teachers at our university take four literacy courses; three courses focus on reading and one on writing. The first three authors have all taught the writing course. The second author was the instructor of the writing course at the time of the study. The fourth author is a doctoral research assistant. The writing methods course is designed to help preservice teachers rediscover the writer within themselves while simultaneously supporting them in developing understandings about principles, practices, theories, and research related to writing instruction. To accomplish this, we employ a unit-of-study approach to teach writing (Ray, 2006) within a writing workshop framework (Fletcher & Portalupi, 2001). The core text for the course was *About the Authors* (Ray, 2004). Students also read select chapters from the following books: *On Writing Well* (Zinsser, 2006), *Poetry Matters* (Fletcher, 2002), and *How to Write Your Life Story* (Fletcher, 2007) throughout the semester.

From the first day of class, preservice teachers live a writerly life. They are expected to write regularly in and out of class. As part of their course assignments, they engage in three separate genre studies: memoir, pattern/predictable books, and poetry. In addition, they work in small groups to develop an instructional unit of study and write a book in the genre of their choice. A predictable format was followed when studying each genre.

The instructor introduced the new genre to the preservice teachers by sharing a children's book representative of the genre under study. For example, the picture book *When I Was Young in the Mountains* (Rylant, 1982) was used to launch the memoir study, *Each Peach Pear Plum* (Ahlberg & Ahlberg, 1978) for predictable/pattern books, and *Heart Songs* (Stepanek, 2002) for the study of poetry. The preservice teachers were encouraged to notice intentional decisions the authors made and aspects of writing craft each author employed.

Once introduced to the genre, the preservice teachers read professional materials about the genre of study. For example, when studying memoir, the preservice teachers read various pieces from their course texts along with additional articles and materials from other sources the instructor gathered. Multiple books in this particular genre were available in class for preservice teachers to read and study. The preservice teachers were also encouraged to gather books from their local libraries. They worked in groups to read the books and notice and name key features of the books. For each genre, preservice teachers were expected to be able to discuss their findings to the following questions: (a) What kinds of topics do writers address with this genre and what kinds of things do they do with these topics?, (b) How is this different from other kinds of writing in the world?, (c) What kinds of work (research, gathering, reflecting, observing, etc.) does it seem like writers of this genre must do in order to produce this kind of writing?, (d) What different approaches do people take to writing in this genre?, and (e) How do writers craft this genre so it is compelling for readers? (Ray, 2006, p. 136). Thinking through these questions helped the preservice teachers to "read like writers" and provided them with specific ideas of features and crafting options they could incorporate in their own writing. In addition, the instructor led the preservice teachers in mini-lessons about the genre under study. Guided by their growing understanding of the genre through immersion in reading numerous books, class discussions, course readings, and in-class experiences, preservice teachers wrote their own book in that genre.

Time was provided in class for writing. This enabled the instructor to hold writing conferences with individual preservice teachers and also with small groups. The preservice teachers often sought help or guidance outside of class by setting up individual appointments or calling/e-mailing the instructor for feedback on their writing. Preservice teachers had opportunities to share their writing informally with others. Meanwhile, the instructor also wrote with her students, shared crafting decisions with the preservice teachers, and discussed her decision to borrow the structure from *When I Was Young In the Mountains* (Rylant, 1982) for her memoir, *When I Was a Brand New Teacher*. The instructor shared her own writing for each genre under study. At the completion of each genre study, preservice teachers shared their books in small groups. Embedded in this experience were ties to classroom teaching and the kinds of support students would need to grow and develop as writers. We wanted the preservice teachers to make connections to what supported their growth as writers and what they might offer their future students.

The preservice teachers also created a unit of study in a small group as a culminating assignment and wrote a book representative of their selected genre. At the end of the semester, each preservice teacher had written four books in different genres. We believed these regular writing experiences to be pivotal in helping preservice teachers rediscover the writer within and providing them with strong pedagogical understandings about teaching writing.

Design

We undertook a one-year, multiple-case study (Merriam, 1988) across two settings, a 16-week writing methods course, and the student teaching placement. We collected data from all preservice teachers (N = 53) enrolled in the course. We then purposefully selected seven preservice teachers to follow into their student teaching experience. We sought to "discover, understand, [and] gain insight" (Merriam, 1988, p. 48) into how preservice teachers utilized course knowledge in their student-teaching experience. For the seven cases, we selected preservice teachers that demonstrated strong to average academic ability in the methods class and were student teaching in various grade levels. We present the findings of two cases in this study.

Data Collection

Multiple data sources informed this investigation. Data collected included course work (reflective essays, genre books, and admission/exit slips), formal and informal interviews, observations, teaching artifacts, and field notes. Preservice teachers wrote five reflective essays throughout the course: an initial essay reflecting on past experiences as writers, three essays following the completion of each genre study, and a final essay highlighting what they learned about teaching writing, their growth as a writer, and what they hoped to utilize during student teaching. During student teaching, we took field notes during observations and informally interviewed preservice teachers following their lessons. We observed each preservice teacher at least twice and also conducted formal interviews at the beginning and end of student teaching. Through the use of multiple data sources and multiple investigators, we were able to triangulate data (Denzin, 1978).

Data Analysis

Data were analyzed inductively using constant comparative analysis (Glaser & Strauss, 1967). The first phase of analysis focused on preservice teachers as writers. Using data from each preservice teacher, interviews and essays were coded using an open coding system guided by the research questions (Miles & Huberman, 1994). Codes such as "writing well equals good grammar," "good writing equals good grades," and "good writing follows a formula" were employed. These initial codes allowed us to tentatively identify preservice teachers' early writing experiences. We also focused on what preservice teachers learned from the course. Examples of codes included "writing vision" and "use of the course language."

In the second phase of analysis, we coded data related to their student-teaching experience. We compared what occurred in student teaching to their imagined instruction, identifying how preservice teachers applied course material, and the challenges they faced. Codes included: (a) extrinsic management (e.g., stickers), (b) prompt writing, (c) low student engagement, (d) existing classroom practice, (e) journal writing, (f) using course language, (g) choice in writing, and (h) multiple-day writing experiences. These codes allowed us to examine how preservice teachers perceived their student-teaching experience and the instruction they wanted to offer their students. From the initial analysis, cases were developed that exemplified preservice teachers' learning and growth. We recast individual case stories as broad narratives focused on common themes across cases (Merriam, 1988).

FINDINGS

Jamie: A Bee the Size of an Elephant

Many of Jamie's memories of writing came from her primary school experiences. During this time, Jamie was "fond of reading, writing, spelling, and grammar." She shared learning to form her letters in kindergarten from a letter-of-the-week program and practicing writing each letter by completing the accompanying worksheets. Jamie believed handwriting was a good indication of her success as a young writer and commented, "handwriting was one of my strongest areas of improvement throughout the years. I was especially excited when we began to learn cursive." Thus,

Jamie's perception of writing was heavily focused on handwriting, at least in elementary school. She also acknowledged having a limited understanding of poetry. For example, she remembered "all growing up, my perception of poetry was that it had to rhyme."

Jamie remembered a book she wrote in second grade and credits her teacher for stretching her creative side. She remembered writing several drafts and finally publishing a hardbound book. Later in secondary school, Jamie lost interest in writing because it became "more of a chore, something we had to do." She said she "never felt that good at writing" because at school "we always did prompted writing. I think I went to a school that really prepared us for grammatical things" but "I wasn't totally engaged with writing."

Jamie described herself as "someone who could write but not creatively." When discussing how she believed teachers should teach writing prior to taking the course, Jamie named general goals and ideas such as "teachers need to be enthusiastic" and children should be encouraged "to take their time and never give up."

At the end of her methods course, Jamie named heart maps, poetry writing, and genre studies as instrumental to her growth as a writer and teacher. A heart map is a visual representation of the important people, places, and experiences close to one's heart that may serve as an idea bank of meaningful topics about which students can choose to write (Heard, 1999). Making a heart map helped Jamie in her personal writing and she felt it would provide students with a "good starting point when writing." She indicated this was a tool she used in creating her own books in the methods class. She noted that heart maps would help students to make a personal connection to writing and would help students generate writing ideas if they were stuck or did not know what to write. Jamie envisioned the heart map as something that "will help me help children. Instead of just asking children to write about random, non-related topics, I can encourage children to write about something that is meaningful to them." The preservice teachers wrote books from genres explored in class. Jamie identified "writing books of different genres" and creating heart maps as "the activities that impacted [her] the most." She felt she regained a sense of enjoyment for writing. She talked about sharing this enthusiasm and her rediscovered love of writing with future students. She wanted her students to experience the "sheer enjoyment" of writing a book.

Jamie's favorite course assignment, one she found "therapeutic," was poetry writing. She acknowledged poetry took time, but felt there was a payoff for her efforts in terms of greater learning and confidence. Jamie shared that "after many drafts and revisions I could feel proud of my pieces ... because so much of my heart was integrated into my writing." She elaborated, "Now that we have studied this genre of writing, my understanding has increased, and I feel comfortable with not only writing poetry, but teaching it as well." Jamie also wrote books in other genres. Jamie reflected on her experience:

> I have grown in the area of developing ideas. This has come from viewing many mentor texts and studying different genres of writing. I see the importance of becoming familiar with a variety of different genres before attempting to write a story of your own. There are so many genres that I didn't even realize were out there. With this increased knowledge, I can better expose children to these different genres and perspectives ... Now that I have more knowledge about different genres, I can be a better teacher of writing. I can expose children to many different ways of writing, all of which are engaging and [provide] hands-on experiences.

In her final reflective essay, Jamie wrote about how she had changed as a result of the course. She stated:

> After taking this course and viewing many mentor texts, I have been encouraged and have more of a desire to write. From doing many of these writing activities, my capabilities have increased and my potential has been revealed.

For Jamie, course experiences led to increased personal writing confidence as well as the development of a vision for teaching writing. She expressed the importance of offering students topic choice, rather than prompted writing so they could experience ownership of meaningful writing. She wanted her students to make heart maps, write books in different genres and write poetry like she had done. In the end, Jamie commented. "I want to offer children these experiences and encourage them that writing can be fun, creative, and an extension of who they are."

As Jamie began her student teaching in kindergarten, she struggled to negotiate with her cooperating teacher about how and when she would begin teaching writing that semester. Jamie was eager to begin taking over writing, but it was "the last thing" she was going to be allowed to do and much of what she would actually do when teaching writing was already planned. According to Jamie, writing instruction in her student-teaching classroom differed from what she learned in the methods course. The students wrote to prompts. She noticed her students would "write one sentence and they don't keep going." She had to work hard as she walked around the room "trying to get more out of them." Writing was allotted half an hour of time but often was the subject that was "bumped" during the day.

While waiting to "take over" writing, Jamie reflected on what students were doing as writers. She became concerned with a "sticker problem." Jamie worried, "How do I develop writers when they are used to getting stickers on their papers?" She was asked to have students respond to a prompt: If you had one hundred dollars, what would you do with it? After completing this task, students asked for a sticker. In past writing experiences, students received a sticker from the teacher as she walked around and read their writing. Jamie was concerned about this focus on the reward. She shared:

> I saw that they're not necessarily proud of their work. They're just looking for that reward. 'Ooo, I got a sticker. I can show my mom and dad that I did good'... So they're looking for your approval and it's not real ownership of what they're writing. They don't seem very proud of it. It is more like, 'Ok, I'm done.'

The current writing instruction in the classroom was different from Jamie's vision. Writing was often activity- and craft-based. Students wrote a short piece and completed a complimentary craft that took up the most of the allotted writing time. Another concern was the frequency with which students responded to prompts. She questioned how students could make sense of prompts such as, "What if a bee was the size of an elephant?" Prompted writing often resulted in students writing a single sentence. Jamie wondered about developing her students' ownership and voice. She wanted her students to write poetry and memoirs like she had done in class. She wanted her students to write about their own topics but worried about the "messiness and stickiness" of helping students learn how to find topics.

Eventually, Jamie did ask and was allowed to implement an author study. She led a three-week study on Eric Carle, allowing her students to "stand on the shoulders" of this author. Together the class looked for similarities and differences in books and visited his website. The class created charts depicting the author's "fingerprints" which Jamie described as, "how you would know that this was a book that Eric Carle wrote." Even though Jamie's cooperating teacher did not teach writing as Jamie had learned, she supported Jamie's author study. In fact, her cooperating teacher loved her author study and created her own binder of Jamie's materials to use in the future.

In the end, Jamie's vision of allowing her kindergartners to become more creative and expressive in their writing, creating pieces they were "really excited and proud of" was accomplished. Jamie's teaching style differed from the prompted writing she initially saw in the classroom. She was able to incorporate some ideas and instructional strategies she had learned in the writing methods course. She attributed this to the structure of the writing methods course:

> I had a great experience in that class because it wasn't just telling us how to teach kids to write a memoir, it was having us do it ourselves. I can't ask the kids to do something that I wouldn't be able to do myself.

She further reflected:

> I wouldn't want to write about elephants being bees. I would want to be able to write and …do it like when we were writing [referring to methods course] and doing genre studies… I am so thrilled with what I learned now that I actually got to put it into play.

Shannon: The Need for Authentic Writing

Like Jamie, early on, Shannon associated writing with penmanship. As she stated, "I do not remember any writing lessons or activities about writing in elementary school outside of handwriting and learning cursive." After she entered middle school, Shannon wrote research papers and had creative writing opportunities. She remembers a teacher reading her writing aloud and praising it as "an example of using extreme detail in creative writing." Consequently, Shannon viewed her strengths as creativity and the "ability to make sentences flow together."

When Shannon entered high school, she was accepted into an advanced writing class. In this class, she learned about writing essays and research papers. Her primary memory is "the first sentence in a paragraph should outline what the entire paragraph is about and that citing evidence to back up your points always makes for a stronger paper." She also commented on her challenge with spelling, "I would not be as confident in myself as a writer if I did not have spell check." Her comments underscore that prior to taking the methods course, Shannon had not yet developed a comprehensive understanding of what it means to be a writer.

Upon entry to the methods class, Shannon's vision for teaching future students was emotionally strong and instructionally vague, "I think the most important thing for teachers to do to help children write would be to provide many different types of writing opportunities and lots of feedback." This was the entirety of what she wrote in response to what she wanted to do when student teaching.

At the end of the methods course, Shannon changed her perspective of herself as a writer and developed a plan to implement these ideas in student teaching and her future classroom. Shannon credits writing poetry, writer's workshop, making books, and author studies as specific course experiences and assignments that helped her grow in knowledge and understanding. Although she considered herself a decent writer, she "never wrote for any other reason than school assignments" and felt that "the assignments and studies done in this class really changed [my] thinking of writing." She believed "...because of this class, I am no longer just a writer of scholarly essays or research papers, I am an author."

Shannon loved writing non-rhyming poetry, although she acknowledged feeling very challenged by writing an inner-poet poem (Heard, 1999). Here, preservice teachers created metaphors to describe their individual selves as writers. She "loved helping other people to figure out what their inner-poet was" yet had difficulty indentifying her own. She "speculated over this a long time," asked her friends for inspiration, and finally sought counsel from her mother. Once she and her mother established that her inner-poet was a hug, Shannon felt the idea was perfect and soon her words "just flowed like water." She felt a sense of achievement and reminisced, "I worked very hard ... and feel a strong sense of pride and accomplishment." She connected her poetry writing experience with her new role of teaching poetry to others.

> This experience really taught me a lot about the value of poetry, the ways it is presented, and how I could implement it in my own classroom. This process also taught me a lot about myself. Now that I understand more about writing poetry, I am better able to apply this knowledge in a classroom. I know what to showcase for children. I now have sources to share with them and I believe I possess the skill to help children become strong poets.

Shannon was placed in a first-grade classroom for student teaching. Shannon stated that during student teaching, she would like to employ a daily writer's workshop. She discussed the benefits, "I will implement mini-lessons and units of study. I think it is so important for children to get mini-lessons every day and to study different genres and authors." She believed "students benefit the most from authentic reading and writing experiences," cautioning that the use of worksheets and prompted writing "can put a limit on what children can do." She added students need to write what is meaningful to them in order to develop an appreciation for writing.

Shannon found the process of making books from different genres as an "assignment that helped [her] to grow the most as a writer." She said, "I was able to create beautiful works that I will always treasure" and predicted "how much [her future students] will learn and enjoy from the experience." She also described writing the books as healing to the heart. She reflected, "I never saw writing as therapy until I began to cry as I wrote my memoir or remembered my grandpa in a poem." She then conjectured, "I know that in my future classroom I will have my students make books. I believe this is a wonderful way to allow children to construct their own meaning and value writing." Shannon's comments indicate that she learned a new purpose for writing beyond school assignments; writing to understand the self. By experiencing writing first hand during the course, she was then able to visualize providing this experience for her future students as well.

Through coursework, Shannon became more secure with herself as a writer, developing a sense of self-efficacy regarding her potential to implement new ideas and processes. As Shannon explained, "Because of this class I feel confident in implementing these things. I will take with me all that I have learned and hopefully use it to develop a balanced and engaging literacy program."

During student teaching, Shannon utilized language learned in her writing methods course. Shannon referred to her students as authors and illustrators and believed this helped them "really think of themselves as authors." Prior to Shannon's arrival in the classroom, the students only completed daily prompted journal writing. Her cooperating teacher valued journal writing and had a strong focus on writing mechanics rather than content. Shannon used her knowledge about writing pedagogy to question journal writing. Shannon felt journal writing lacked luster and meaning and noticed that students seemed to be more engaged when making books. She noted:

> when they were making books they were working very hard, taking it very seriously and really showing what they knew. It wasn't like that during journal time, we had to extend our day when they were making books because they were so into it and taking so much time and effort. When journaling, they wrote a few things down and drew a picture and it wasn't as meaningful.

While completing three author studies (Eric Carle, Mo Willems, and Jack Keith), Shannon incorporated another phrase that was used during her writing methods course: "standing on the shoulders of an author." Shannon and her students created charts of what they noticed about books written by the focus author. Modeling her own writing allowed students to see what a book could look like when "standing on the shoulders of an author." From studying the authors, one specific writing technique Shannon was proud to introduce to her students was how to use dialogue effectively in their writing. After examining dialogue in author studies, the students and Shannon collaboratively created a list of ideas for incorporating dialogue into their own independent book writing.

As Shannon did additional author studies, she noticed how students' thinking deepened and evolved as they looked at a variety of texts and employed techniques discussed in class in their independent writing pieces:

> It was interesting because at first I would say, 'What do you notice about some of the stories we have been reading, do you notice any pattern?' I would try to get them thinking. At first, they were like 'Well, there are a lot of animals,' but as we did more author studies they really would pick up on things, things I didn't even notice and it became really fun to them, to identify traits that this author used and we would compare the different authors and they became really good at it. It's definitely a process for adults and children.

Fortunately, Shannon was able to try out several ideas, concepts, and strategies that she experienced in the methods course. She discovered these experiences led to student involvement in meaningful and enjoyable writing. Even though her cooperating teacher was unsure at first how Shannon's ideas would play out, in the end, her cooperating teacher was thrilled with the students' responses. Ultimately, this led to Shannon being able to create a set writing time within the class and make books more often with her students.

DISCUSSION AND IMPLICATIONS

Methods courses do matter. A writing methods course provided preservice teachers with opportunities to develop individually as writers and professionally as teachers of writers. Their apprenticeship of *observation* (Lortie, 1975) made way for an apprenticeship of *action* through specific methods-course experiences. This focused action of studying writing and writing books aided preservice teachers in developing pedagogical understandings about writing and teaching writing. The idea and power of choice became real when they were repeatedly faced with choosing a topic. The idea that writing takes time became real when they struggled to find the right words to capture their meaning. The idea of reading-like-a-writer became real when they realized how helpful it is to study how another writer has crafted something. These ideas were not ones preservice teachers merely read or heard about in passing, but rather ones they lived throughout the entire semester. These first-hand experiences contributed to preservice teachers' knowledge and vision development for teaching writers.

Their visions were specific. They wanted their students to create heart maps, write books in multiple genres, and engage in author studies— things they had not experienced fully in school. Their knowledge and vision drew heavily on their writing methods course experiences. Jamie did not speak of handwriting in her vision for the students in her student-teaching experience although it was how she marked her success as a writer in elementary school. If the preservice teachers found it powerful or helpful as writers in class, they desired a similar experience for their own students.

The preservice teachers kept their visions in mind when they entered student teaching. Both preservice teachers experienced disequilibrium between the teaching of writing in their student-teaching context and what was learned in the writing methods course. Dissonance can provide opportunities for preservice teachers to reflect more fully on concepts and practical strategies learned in coursework (Grossman et al., 2000). The preservice teachers used their course experiences and visions as a lens through which they often examined classroom practice and/or student engagement. Her experience with choice led Jamie to wonder about the use of "if a bee was the size of an elephant" writing prompt, and her experience with audience aided Shannon in looking closely at student engagement during journal writing versus writing books. The preservice teachers also initiated conversations with their cooperating teachers about implementing something specific from their writing course into their student teaching setting. Hammerness (2003) has found that teachers' visions can "inspire and motivate" as well as aid teachers in reflecting on classroom practices. For these two preservice teachers, their visions served as a critical lens through which to examine students' writing experiences and enact new learning opportunities.

Methods courses can serve as supportive contexts where preservice teachers develop complex pedagogical visions that address students' affective and instructional experiences. There is a need in teacher education to help new teachers "clarify, articulate and develop their vision" (Hammerness, 2008, p.20). Our findings show that through their experiences in a writing methods course, preservice teachers engaged in explicit opportunities that fostered and developed their own knowledge and understandings of the writing process, understandings that helped them teach writing intentionally and actively during student teaching.

REFERENCES

Ahlberg, J., & Ahlberg, A. (1978). *Each peach pear plum*. New York, NY: Penguin Group.

Boyd, P. C., Boll, M., Brawner, L., & Villaume, S. K. (1998). Becoming reflective professionals: An exploration of preservice teacher's [sic] struggles as they translate language literacy theory into practice. *Action in Teacher Education, 19*, 61-75.

Bridge, C. A., & Hiebert, E. H. (1985). A comparison of classroom writing practices, teachers' perceptions of their writing instruction, and textbook recommendations on writing practices. *The Elementary School Journal, 86*, 154-172.

Colby, S. A., & Stapleton, J. N. (2006). Preservice teachers teach writing: Implications for teacher educators. *Reading Research and Instruction, 45*, 353-376.

Denzin, N. K. (1978). *The research act: A theoretical introduction to sociological methods.* (2nd ed.). New York, NY: McGraw-Hill.

Fletcher, R. (2002). *Poetry matters: Writing a poem from the inside out.* New York, NY: HarperTrophy.

Fletcher, R. (2007). *How to write your life story.* New York, NY: HarperCollins.

Fletcher, R., & Portalupi, J. (2001). *Writing workshop: The essential guide.* Portsmouth, NH: Heinemann.

Gallagher, K. (2006). *Teaching adolescent writers.* Portland, ME: Stenhouse.

Gallavan, N. P., Bowles, F. A., & Young, C. T. (2007). Learning to write and writing to learn: Insights from teacher candidates. *Action in Teacher Education, 29*, 61-69.

Gillespie, T. (1985). Becoming your own expert: Teachers as writers. *The Quarterly, 8*(1), 1-3.

Glaser, B. G., & Strauss, A. L. (1967). *The discovery of grounded theory: Strategies for qualitative research.* New Brunswick, NJ: Aldine.

Graham, S., Harris, K. R., & Fink, B., & MacArthrur, C. A. (2001). Teacher efficacy in writing: A construct validation with primary grade teachers. *Scientific Studies of Reading, 5*, 177-202.

Graves, D. H. (1983). *Writing: Teachers and children at work.* Portsmouth, NH: Heinemann.

Grossman, P. L., Valencia, S. W., Evans, K., Thompson, C., Martin, S., & Place, N. (2000). Transitions into teaching: Learning to teach writing in teacher education and beyond. *Journal of Literacy Research, 32*, 631-662.

Hammerness, K. (2003). Learning to hope, or hoping to learn?: The role of vision in the early professional lives of teachers. *Journal of Teacher Education, 54*, 43-56. doi: 10.1177/0022487102238657

Hammerness, K. (2008). "If you don't know where you are going, any path will do": The role of teachers' visions in teachers' career paths. *The New Educator, 4*, 1-22.

Heard, G. (1999). *Awakening the heart: Exploring poetry in middle and high school.* Portsmouth, NH: Heinemann.

Langer, J. A. (1995). *Envisioning literature: Literary understanding and literature instruction.* New York, NY: Teachers College Press.

Lortie, D. (1975). *School teacher: A sociological study.* Chicago, IL: University of Chicago Press.

Mahurt, S. (1998). Writing instruction: University learning to first-year teaching. In T. Shanahan & F. V. Rodriguez-Brown (Eds.), *47th Yearbook of the National Reading Conference* (pp. 542-554). Chicago, IL: National Reading Conference.

Merriam, S. B. (1988). *Case study research in education: A qualitative approach.* San Francisco, CA: Jossey-Bass.

Miles, M. & Huberman, M. (1994). *Qualitative data analysis: An expanded sourcebook* (2nd ed.). Thousand Oaks, CA: Corwin Press.

Moore-Hart, M. A., & Carpenter, R. (2008, December). *Improving preservice teachers' attitudes toward writing: An avenue to enhanced instructional practices.* Paper presented at the annual meeting of the National Reading Conference, Orlando, FL.

Morgan, D. N. (2010). Preservice teachers as writers. *Literacy Research and Instruction 49*, 357-365.

National Commission on Writing for America's Families, Schools and Colleges. (2003). *The neglected "R": The need for a writing revolution.* Retrieved from http://www.writingcommission.org

National Commission on Writing for America's Families, Schools and Colleges. (2004). *Writing: A ticket to work...or a ticket out.* Retrieved from http://www.writingcommission.org

National Council of Teachers of English. (2004). *NCTE beliefs about the teaching of writing.* Retrieved from www.ncte.org/positions/statements/writingbeliefs

National Council of Teachers of English. (2008). *Writing now.* Retrieved from www.ncte.org/library/NCTEFiles/Resources/PolicyResearch/WrtgResearchBrief.pdf

National Council of Teachers of English. (2009). *Writing in the 21st century*. Retrieved from http://www.ncte. org/library/NCTEFiles/Press/Yancey_final.pdf

Norman, K. A., & Spencer, B. H. (2005). Our lives as writers: Examining preservice teachers' experiences and beliefs about the nature of writing and writing instruction. *Teacher Education Quarterly, 32*, 25-40.

Ray, K. W. (2004). *About the authors: Writing workshop with our youngest writers*. Portsmouth, NH: Heinemann.

Ray, K. W. (2006). *Study driven: A framework for planning units of study in the writing workshop*. Portsmouth, NH: Heinemann.

Rylant, C. (1982). *When I was young in the mountains*. New York, NY: Puffin.

Stepanek, M. J. T. (2002). *Heartsongs*. New York: Hyperion.

Street, C. (2003). Pre-service teachers' attitudes about writing and learning to teach writing: Implications for teacher educators. *Teacher Education Quarterly, 30*, 33-50.

Totten, S. (2005). Writing to learn for preservice teachers. *The Quarterly, 27*, 17-20.

Whyte, A., Lazarte, A., Thompson, I., Ellis, N., Muse, A., & Talbot, R. (2007). The National Writing Project: Teachers' writing lives, and student achievement in writing. *Action in Teacher Education, 29*(2), 5-16.

Zinsser, W. (2006). *On writing well: The classic guide to writing non-fiction*. New York, NY: HarperCollins.

Teachers Prepare Students for Careers and College: "I See You," Therefore I Can Teach You

Carol Wickstrom
Juan Araujo
Leslie Patterson
University of North Texas

with
Chieko Hoki
Texas Woman's University

Jennifer Roberts
Willamette University

Literacy educators may dismiss the recent outcry about the U. S. school "crisis" as an emotional and perhaps cynical bid for political gain and private profit, but the drop-out rate and college-going rate highlight an urgent, legitimate concern about whether all students are being served. Admittedly, multiple factors influence how and whether individual adolescents are able to negotiate various cultural, linguistic, economic, emotional, and academic challenges, many of which are clearly beyond the control of school personnel. The quality of instruction, however, is one significant factor we should be able to influence (Darling-Hammond, 2000).

Increasingly, literacy research focuses on improving our support of these students, particularly English learners, toward eventual success in the workplace and in post-secondary educational settings, but few publications specifically address the complexities inherent in writing instruction for secondary English learners. The purpose of this study is to examine two high school teachers' decisions about writing instruction, aiming to prepare students for careers and college readiness. The question addressed in this paper is, "How do two high school teachers mediate English learners' academic writing in preparation for careers and college?"

BACKGROUND OF THE LARGER STUDY

In a 3-year project funded by the National Writing Project, we investigated how middle and high school teachers enacted Culturally Mediated Writing Instruction (CMWI), a research-based approach that combined culturally responsive instruction and guided inquiry with reading/writing workshop practices (e.g., Atwell, 1998; Ball, 2006; Wilhelm, 2007). This paper reports findings from Year 2 of the study, which focused on the work of nine teachers, five in middle schools and four in high schools.

The teachers participated in a five-day institute in the summer of 2008 to engage in practices that CMWI recommends and debriefed about how and why those practices might work. Through this work, the teachers identified strategies they determined would make significant differences for their students. The following school year teachers invited the research team into their classrooms to document how they enacted the principles and practices. Through their work together, they had developed a community of practice (Lave & Wenger, 1991) that had the potential to sustain their teaching and learning throughout the year.

CONCEPTUAL ORIENTATION OF CULTURALLY MEDIATED WRITING INSTRUCTION

Like many other instructional approaches targeting English learners, Culturally Mediated Writing Instruction is compatible with culturally responsive instruction (Gay, 2000; Ladson-Billings, 1992, 1994, 1995), critical pedagogy (Freire, 1970; Giroux, 1997; Shor, 1992), and "anti-bias education" (Rebollo-Gil & Moras, 2006). We began this project with a socio-literate perspective (Johns, 1999), but have since added a broader socio-cultural framework (e.g., Vygotsky, 1978; Rogoff, 1990; Moll & Greenberg, 1990; John-Steiner & Mahn, 1996; Lantolf and Thorne, 2006).

The socio-cultural framework for writing instruction for adolescent English learners points to a number of instructional principles that undergird CMWI:

- Teachers should develop empathetic, caring, and responsive relationships with and among the students (e.g., Noddings, 2005; Freire, 1970).
- Teachers should encourage and demonstrate meaningful connections between and among ideas, texts, and experiences (e.g., Moll, Amanti, Neff, & Gonzalez, 1992; Wells, 2007).
- Teachers should provide tasks and audiences that the learners perceive as authentic (e. g., Atwell, 1998; Burke, 2003; Jago, 2008; Romano, 2000).
- Teachers should invite/expect students to take an inquiry stance toward social issues, curricular content, and literacy tasks in school (e.g., Burke, 2010; Short, Harste, and Burke, 1996; Wilhelm, 2007).
- Teachers should provide appropriate support or mediation for students as they become more confident, independent, and proficient readers and writers of English (e.g., Ball, 2006; Fitzgerald, 2006; Freeman & Freeman, 2008; Fu, 2009).

The first three principles are common to many progressive approaches to literacy instruction. First, CMWI teachers talk about their relationships with their students as being the most influential aspect of their instruction. They also share a commitment to reading and writing as meaning-making processes through which students make connections among their background experiences, the texts they are reading and writing, and the larger world. Third, they are adamant that their students must perceive the literacy tasks in the classroom as relevant and significant—authentic—in order to engage and learn from them.

Fourth, CMWI teachers frame instruction as a series of overlapping and/or nested inquiry cycles (Figure 1). This flexible cycle serves as a frame for planning long-term projects or instructional units, but it is also used as a frame for a daily lesson plan, as well as an organizational structure for writing conferences with students. This cycle operationalizes the principle concerning "inquiry stance" listed above.

Finally, as they invite students into these inquiry cycles, CMWI teachers provide a range of support (or mediation), depending on their students' backgrounds, interests, strengths, and instructional targets for growth (Patterson, Wickstrom, Roberts, Araujo, & Hoki, 2010). The

Figure 1. CMWI Inquiry Cycle

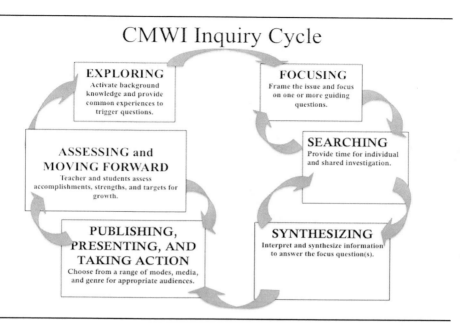

apprenticeship model (Rogoff, 1990) is useful in explaining how they mediate students' writing, but CMWI teachers also argue that familiar topics and genre serve as mediators, as well as the students' first language and various instructional tools and practices (mentor texts, anchor charts, graphic organizers, etc.).

METHODS

This report focuses on how two of the 2008-09 teacher researchers integrated CMWI principles and practices into their ongoing instruction. These cases were selected because they represent two very different school and community contexts, although both teachers voiced a passionate commitment to academic writing success for high school students. Caroline worked with students identified at risk of not passing the state-mandated test. Olivia worked with on-level 11th- and 12th-graders soon-to-transition into the workforce and/or college. Each teacher focused on one section of students for this study. Table 1 provides teacher characteristics.

Findings from the two cases presented here are based on an inductive analysis (Patterson, Wickstrom, & Araujo, 2010) of classroom observations, in-depth interviews, and teachers' reflections during 2008-09. Each of the participants selected one of their classes as the focus of this study. Research associates (who were experienced teachers) received approximately eight hours of orientation about research protocols and procedures. The first visit provided an overview of the classroom and school environment. During subsequent visits the research associates took field notes, recorded classroom lessons, collected any papers distributed to students, and conducted a follow-up interview after the observation. Student work was collected when possible. Periodic

Table 1. Teacher Characteristics

Code	Gender	Native Language	Ethnicity	Degree Level	# of Years Teaching	Years Teaching at Current Level	Grade Level of Focus Class
Caroline	F	English	Anglo	Masters	1-3	1	9th
Olivia	F	English	Hispanic	Bachelors+	11-15	11	12th

debriefings prompted additional classroom visits and further informal interviews with the teachers. To document possible changes in student writing proficiency, students in the teacher researcher classrooms did writing samples at the beginning of the year and writing samples at the end of the year. Each teacher's students are briefly described below.

The qualitative data were analyzed inductively to identify patterns in how teachers implemented the CMWI principles and practices. These preliminary categories were used to refine the codes, reconsidering relevant published research. The research team came to a consensus about the codes and categories through subsequent readings of the data and the development of a coding dictionary. The debriefing sessions with the teachers were also instrumental in affirming and refining these codes. One team member then used NVivo to organize and code all the qualitative data. Further discussion served to refine and confirm those codes, as well as helped us identify the four **language and literacy resources** which the teachers were trying to develop in their students as well as the five **instructional patterns** within and across the classrooms.

These themes allowed us to explore and explain a dimension of teaching that is critical to meeting the needs of students in today's classrooms. They helped us codify teachers' actions that otherwise might be seen as everyday conversations with students that might not be considered as teaching. In this paper, we argue that when teachers are expected to prepare students for careers and college readiness, they will take complex and *extraordinary* actions in their teaching to make that happen.

FINDINGS

Findings from the larger study suggest student writing did improve across the school year (see Appendix for comparison of scores from on-demand, pre- and post writing samples). This article, however, focuses on teachers' enactment of CMWI principles. The most significant commonality across the two cases is that each teacher connects with individual students on a personal level in order to learn what resources they bring and how best to help each student move toward academic success. The following case descriptions provide more detail about this pattern of empathy, caring, and responsiveness which emerged in the work of each teacher.

CMWI on the Texas-Mexico Border

Olivia is an experienced teacher in a rural community east of a large Texas city, a few miles from the Mexican border. The community has a population of less than 2,000, 92% of these individuals are Hispanic. In 2008, the median household income was less than $20,216 (US Census, 2005-2009).

Most students have attended these schools since the elementary grades, and Olivia knows several sets of siblings and cousins among her students. In many ways, this school context is similar to other rural schools around the country, with the exception that most of these students are bilingual in Spanish and English. Many are literate only in English although they are fluent in conversational Spanish. In 2008, the school district earned the state rating of "Academically Acceptable"; the dropout rate for 2008 was only 2.7% (Texas Education Agency, 2011). In 2007-2008, 20% (Texas Education Agency, 2011) of the students on the campus were officially identified as Limited English Proficient (LEP). All of these are receiving appropriate services, and are all native Spanish speakers (Texas Education Agency, 2011)

Olivia is currently in her 16th year of teaching, 14 of which have been in this school. Depending on campus needs, her teaching assignment varies. In the year reported here, she taught 11th- and 12th-grade English. Olivia grew up in a similar town, about 20 miles away. Olivia says she always received high grades and never doubted she would go to college and graduate. She says:

> Consequently, it was a surprise to work in a school even smaller than the one I attended and where the obstacles between the students and a college education were greater than what I had encountered growing up. However, my students and I have had many similar experiences growing up, and my understanding of their community has also helped me relate to them.

Olivia deliberately integrates this intimate knowledge of students' lives into her instruction (Ballenger, 2009). For example, Olivia and her students openly discuss the bias her students often encounter because they come from a small school and a poor, predominantly Mexican-American community. Olivia also knows religious matters are important to the community and she makes time and space for students to discuss these values when they study literature with strong religious themes, like *The Crucible* (Miller, 1959) and *Paradise Lost* (Milton & Pullman, 1992). Immigration policy and the border fence are an important part of these students' daily lives and a topic for inquiry in Olivia's classroom.

Further, Olivia knows few of her students have concrete plans to attend a college or university, and several consider the military as their only realistic option after high school. At the time of this study, Olivia was working toward a master's in English and wondered:

> What can I do, that will give them the right tools for college? When I take a class, I always look at what I can bring back, what I can apply. The theory piece, to me, was just another way of asking questions, another way of looking at texts. It seemed to just go very naturally with these other goals.

The theory piece Olivia mentioned included a range of critical lenses for literary analysis— Marxism, feminism, etc. When she learned about these in her graduate classes, she became angry that she had not been exposed to these perspectives before graduate school, and she vowed to introduce them to her students. So she obtained a class set of her college text, *How to Interpret Literature: Critical Theory for Literary and Cultural Studies* (Parker, 2008), and a number of class sets of challenging books in order to introduce her 12th-graders to these critical perspectives. For example, in 2008-09, Olivia and her 12th-graders read works by Tomas Rivera, Herman Melville, Toni Morrison, Sherman Alexie, Mary Shelley, William Shakespeare, Flannery O'Connor, John Steinbeck, John Milton, D.H. Lawrence, George Orwell, Dr. Seuss, and Kate Chopin.

These diverse texts made it possible for Olivia and her students to engage in critical examination of significant social issues. Because of their personal investment in these issues, students' enthusiastically engaged in reading, writing, and in research into related issues.

Olivia led whole-class readings of challenging novels and essays. Sometimes she began by reading aloud but, for the most part, her students read these works independently and then participated in class discussions. She focused on each critical lens and demonstrated how to use each one to make sense of what the authors were saying, and then, in their brief responses, the students experimented with these perspectives. The culminating assignment was framed as a critical essay in which students chose a theme and a critical lens; then they synthesized their critiques of relevant literature, read in class or independently, to fully explore the intent and implications of the authors' work. The students made an oral presentation of their critique, just as if they were presenting at a professional conference. Although Olivia gave these 12th-graders wide latitude in choosing an issue, developing a thesis, and selecting evidence from the literature, she also supported them through this complex process, step-by-step. In this way, Olivia invited her 12th-grade students to join the community of literary scholars, to read deeply, to inquire about connections between the literature and their lives, and to contribute their insights to the body of knowledge they were building with their classmates.

We saw Olivia mediate student learning in many ways. She read <u>to</u> the students, and she read <u>with</u> them. Her students often spontaneously worked in pairs or small groups on the tasks she gave them. The students made use of both languages. Olivia listened to students as they asked questions (often in Spanish), but she always responded to them in English. Her stated goal was for them to be able to function successfully as English speakers and writers in college courses, but she supported their use of Spanish in their responses and in their problem-solving conversations and she expected them to write their final products in English. Olivia helped the students develop informal and personal responses and successfully challenged them to use academic language and scholarly tools for literary criticism.

Olivia also took an inquiry stance, continually asking questions and posing problems to students rather than just supplying correct answers. The field notes suggest that Olivia responded to most individual student questions with deeper and more probing questions. In one exchange, a student asked Olivia a question about the *The Bluest Eye* (Morrison, 1994).

Student: "Is he trying to help her or hurt her?"

Olivia: "He does rape her."

Olivia adds, "At least he loved her enough to touch her. What kind of comment is [the character] making by saying that? What does that tell you about her?"

The student still seemed a little unsure. Olivia then said, "The only person that loved her enough to touch her did something horrible. This is the best treatment that she could get. What does that tell you about everybody else and the way they treated her?" Olivia told the student to think about it for a little while and they would talk about it. The student returned to her seat and contemplated the exchange. This instance was typical of Olivia's responses to students that challenged them to think more deeply about the texts.

Reflecting on her work in 2008-09, Olivia noted how her students embraced inquiry:

> Students' presentations of work have been consistently good this year, and students' reactions to their peers' presentations has [sic] sparked a lot of quality discussion in the class. Students have begun to question each other, including asking for justification for their responses and choices . . .I have noticed with the seniors in particular but with all students, they seem to be asking more questions in general, of me and each other.

In fact, Olivia told us about one student who relayed a story about asking questions at home. His mom wanted to know who was teaching him to ask all these questions! This is evidence that Olivia was teaching her students to inquire in the classroom and in their daily lives.

Clearly, Olivia's life experiences and her successful academic history shaped her approach to teaching. An important component of that approach was her basic respect for her students—for what they brought to the academic table—their ethnic identities, their small-town experiences, and their socio-economic realities. But Olivia did not focus exclusively on these social and cultural resources; she was just as conscious of the students' linguistic, cognitive, and academic strengths and needs. Of course, the description here is just one slice of Olivia's work, but it illustrates how well she knew her students and how she planned instruction to address all those interdependent strengths and needs in an integrated and coherent way, always with an eye on the academic challenges her students might face in the future. The 12th-graders embraced the critical perspectives that Olivia introduced, and they rose to her high expectations, moving their writing from personal response to literary analysis and critique. Their deep reading of these challenging texts served as a springboard for high-level thinking and writing. Olivia provided a complex instructional context that was particularly appropriate for these students. In the context of this inquiry, Olivia paid close attention to individual students, asked thought-provoking questions at just the right moment, and provided appropriate support for particular students.

Olivia brought her passion for learning and high expectations to her teaching, but her empathy for her students seems foundational. Not only does she know her students well, but she is able to identify with students' perspectives on their individual and collective experiences. This intimate knowledge of their shared world informs her instructional decisions.

CMWI in the Suburbs

Caroline is a young high school teacher in a suburban community located 25 miles north of a major Texas city. She grew up in this community, went to a large university in another part of the state, and then returned here to take her first teaching job. She was always a successful student and participated in dance and theater activities. Her interest in teaching evolved because of her job at her university academic assistance center where she tutored struggling students. In July of 2008, when she participated in the CMWI institute, she had just completed her first year of teaching and had just participated in the four-week National Writing Project Summer Institute.

Caroline's teaching assignment included a course entitled "Literary Genres," designed for students who had not passed the state test. This course was meant to provide flexibility to meet students' needs, but, as a first-year teacher, Caroline had struggled with its lack of structure. In addition, she was assigned to work with students (including English learners) who had previously failed ninth-, 10th-, 11th-, and 12th-grade English. Like Olivia, Caroline's explicit goal was to

Figure 2. Anchor Chart Posted in Caroline's Classroom, Traits of Good Readers

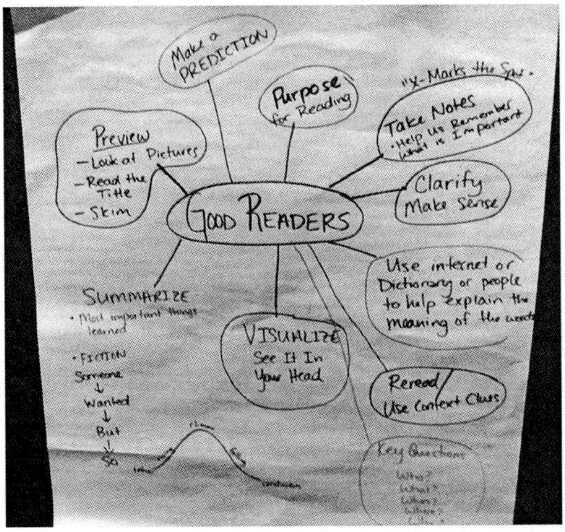

improve the students' academic literacy for career and college success. Unlike Olivia, Caroline was a new teacher searching for a framework to guide her instructional decisions.

After her 2008 CMWI institute, Caroline said she wanted to use "significant" issues as springboards for student inquiry. Caroline focused on helping students see themselves as "successful students," emphasizing study strategies, habits, and school achievement. Caroline brought atypical resources into the classroom—magazines, newspapers, websites. She took her students into the community, including a field trip to a local soup kitchen and to the local university. Caroline believed that inquiry would "arm" her students with ways to take control of their academic work. Since her students were placed in this course to build their literacy, she organized her first inquiry cycle around these questions: What do good readers do? What is the writing process?

With students' input, Caroline created the anchor charts in Figures 2 and 3, to represent "what good readers do" and "our research process."

> I wanted to know what my English IV seniors already knew about the research process, so I had them draw pictures to represent the different steps. Most of them started with a question (we had already discussed that research begins with a question or curiosity), moved on to books and/or computer, drew note cards, and finally a rough/final draft.

Figure 3. Anchor Chart Generated by Caroline's Students about Their Research Process

After completing the anchor chart about the research process, each student wrote a research proposal. During that time, the class also discussed academic writing—incorporating quotes, including analyzing, revising, and organizing.

By the end of the year, Caroline's classroom walls provided evidence of the many inquiry cycles, including the Middle Ages, the theme of revenge in literature, and academic research skills. A culminating experience in the spring semester was an inquiry project entitled, "My Life in Ten Years." Caroline designed this inquiry project to help students think about the goals they wanted to achieve. Caroline used this inquiry cycle to sustain students' engagement at the end of the year and to prepare students for college or careers.

Caroline's online postings and her interviews revealed that she understood the challenges an inquiry-based approach sets for teachers: "At the beginning of the year I wanted to help my students become expert "noticers," but I often found myself providing answers instead of letting students search and explore." In March, 2009, another of Caroline's online postings revealed her commitment to inquiry:

> At dinner tonight, I was talking to my mom about what I am doing and am planning to do with my English IV, British Literature classes. Right off the bat, she said "Oh, British literature, that is boring," and I said, "No, listen to how I am going to teach it." After I finished, I was like WOW I've figured out how I am going to teach British Literature through Inquiry! She was like "Well, that is not boring!"

Caroline was discovering that, when the teacher is excited and engaged, this enthusiasm often spreads to students. When students become enthusiastic, that, in turn, can fuel the teachers' enthusiasm. Caroline's story suggests that it takes patience and persistence, but she reports some significant successes. Here is one posting in the spring of 2009 about a book discussion:

> It was by no means a completely student-directed conversation; however it was the most back and forth conversation that has happened in this class all year. I think what was reaffirmed for me the most was that even these struggling students (many who are on the edge of not graduating) have something to say! These are the very students who sit in their classes and say nothing, yet with the right topic and some scaffolding they carried on a very passionate and insightful conversation.

Caroline's focus on "the right topic and some scaffolding" is a compelling acknowledgment that she must focus on students' perspectives.

Finally, Caroline summarizes one of her important insights after attempting to integrate CMWI into her teaching decisions in 2008-09:

> I can't say that I have been able to successfully implement inquiry units the way I had envisioned. However, I have successfully built relationships with these students and helped them to move forward academically. We continue to focus on how our literacy skills can be used for whatever we want to do in life, and they are starting to understand the work it takes to read for comprehension and write to communicate your ideas with an audience.

Although she hoped for a greater impact on the students, she felt that positive relationships with the students helped move them toward academic success. Her sincere commitment was to get to know her students—their "funds of knowledge" (Gonzales & Amanti, 1992), their interests, their literacy strengths, and targets for growth.

SUMMARY OF FINDINGS

Caroline and Olivia's case studies illustrate the power of empathy and caring—the power of seeing students for who they are, the power of caring enough about the students as individuals to try to view the world as they see and feel it. Caroline and Olivia tried to understand their students' motivations and rationales; they then planned instruction to mediate their students' development of dispositions, habits, skills, and strategies that would be more likely to bring them success in school. Each of these teachers made exceptional efforts to support the students' academic endeavors. This evidence from their classroom narratives supports the following claims about connecting teachers' empathy with students to their deep commitment to students' academic success.

- **Showing passion for academic achievement.** These teachers attended to the mandated curriculum requirements but went beyond the district's curriculum to focus on goals and content they judged as important to preparing these students for life beyond high school—both for college and for the workplace. Teachers must be passionate about their content while at the same time make the content relevant to the students so that they may become passionate about their futures.
- **Encouraging student agency.** These teachers assumed that both they and their students bring useful knowledge and skills to the classroom (funds of knowledge or knowledge capital). They expected their students to apply that capital toward particular goals that would ultimately lead to academic success.
- **Demonstrating professional risk-taking.** Not only did these teachers invest a great deal of time and energy in planning and implementing particular curricular moves, they were also willing to take the risks involved in instructional decisions radically different from the status quo on their campuses. They believed in extraordinary measures for extraordinary circumstances.
- **Leveraging today's experience into tomorrow's achievement.** These teachers grew up in communities similar to those where they now teach. They are community insiders who have achieved academic success; they demonstrate for students how to re-appropriate everyday knowledge into school wealth.
- **Working in the Zone of Proximal Development (Vygotsky, 1978).** These teachers learned specific details about their students' lives that might be relevant to instructional decisions—students' interests, expertise, family situations, culturally specific identities/ realities, and school experiences. Both Caroline and Olivia used this knowledge to orchestrate varying levels of support for individuals, sometimes stepping in to provide more guidance, sometimes stepping back to allow for independence.
- **Acknowledging multiple sites for learning (Chang, 1998, p. 181).** These teachers acknowledged that important student learning can and does happen outside of school. They took advantage of the students' ability to gain knowledge across "multiple sites"—in extracurricular activities, in after-school jobs, in hobbies, etc.

- **Making assumptions explicit.** Through their CMWI work, Caroline and Olivia acknowledged certain principles and practices that they had implicitly followed or valued but had never articulated or successfully implemented. Early in the project, they said they felt professionally unprepared and unqualified to address the students' needs. As the project progressed, as they made their goals, assumptions, and questions explicit, they gained confidence to take appropriate action.
- **Mediating through authentic texts, tasks, and contexts.** As they enacted CMWI, Caroline and Olivia searched for authentic tasks and contexts that fit their students. They acknowledged that literacy is not an asocial cognitive skill. Rather than tearing literacy from its cultural context to teach isolated skills, these teachers used students' cultural models (Lee, 2007) and other tools to mediate students' construction of new academic concepts in "real-life" contexts.

In sum, Caroline and Olivia created and sustained empathetic communities of practice where they and their students were able to learn from one other. Their students rose to the challenges that Olivia and Caroline set. Despite the students' current abilities, backgrounds, or levels of engagement, each of these teachers was adamant about preparing students for the future (O'Neill, 1995).

IMPLICATIONS FOR CLASSROOM PRACTICE

Today's students bring widely diverse views of the world so teachers must be willing to look beyond their own worlds to build empathetic and responsive relationships with students. These findings suggest implications for instruction, for professional development, and for research.

First, these findings suggest that it is possible for secondary teachers to design inquiry-based tasks that their emergent bilingual students perceive as both authentic and significant. This authentic inquiry sometimes requires teachers to make courageous decisions not to follow standardized curricular expectations. It also requires that they know their students well enough to design engaging and relevant tasks for particular students in a particular place and time, as well as to provide support and feedback that moves each student forward.

Second, teachers at all points in their careers, from the novice to the seasoned veteran, must participate in professional development that takes into account teacher knowledge and experience, student needs and interests, and curricular demands if they are to prepare students for their future. Professional development that merely addresses curriculum expectations simply addresses a limited view of the students. Thus, professional development like CMWI presents teachers with the opportunity to engage in teaching and learning that meets curriculum demands while "seeing" and capitalizing on who students are.

Finally, literacy researchers must continue to develop detailed case studies in collaboration with effective teachers of adolescent English learners. The range of differences across contexts and individual students calls for many more descriptive case studies from which researchers and teachers can begin to understand the conditions that both support and constrain academic writing progress, particularly among English learners in public schools.

This study is one contribution to that effort. These are stories of powerful teachers who see students for who they are, who care enough to explore students' perspectives, and who take courageous action to help students do whatever it takes to prepare for careers and college.

REFERENCES

Atwell, N. (1998). *In the middle: New understandings about writing, reading, learning* (2nd ed.). Portsmouth, NH: Boynton/Cook.

Ball, A. R. (2006). Teaching writing in culturally diverse classrooms. In C. A. MacArthur, S. Graham, & J. Fitzgerald (Eds.), *Handbook of writing research.* New York, NY: The Guilford.

Ballenger, C. (2009). *Puzzling moments, teachable moments: Practicing teacher research in urban classrooms.* New York, NY: Teachers College Press.

Burke, J. (2010). *What's the big idea?: Question-driven units to motivate reading, writing, and thinking.* Portsmouth, NH: Heinemann.

Burke, J. (2003). *Writing reminders: Tools, tips, and techniques.* Portsmouth, NH: Heinemann.

Cammarota, J., & Fine, M. (2008). *Revolutionizing education: youth participatory action research in motion.* New York, NY: Routledge.

Chang, J. M. (1998). Literacy in Chinese-American communities. In B. Perez (Ed), *Sociocultural contexts of language and literacy* (p. 181). Mahwah, NJ: Lawrence Erlbaum Associates.

Darling-Hammond, L. (2000). Teacher quality and student achievement. Education policy analysis archives, North America, 8. Retrieved from http://epaa.asu.ojs/article/view/392/515

Fitzgerald, J. (2006). Multilingual writing in preschool through 12th grade: The last 15 years. In C. MacArthur, S. Graham, and J. Fitzgerald (Eds.). *The handbook of writing research.* New York, NY: Guilford Press.

Freeman, Y., & Freeman, D. E. (2008). *Academic language for English language learners and struggling readers: How to help students succeed across content areas.* Portsmouth, NH: Heinemann.

Freire, P. (1970). *Pedagogy of the oppressed.* New York, NY: Continuum.

Fu, D. (2009). *Writing between languages: How English language learners make the transition to fluency, grades 4-12.* Portsmouth, NH: Heinemann.

Gay, G. (2000). *Culturally responsive teaching: Theory, research, and practice.* New York, NY: Teachers College Press.

Giroux, H. (1997). *Pedagogy and the politics of hope: Theory, culture, and schooling.* Boulder, CO: Westview Publishing.

González, N., & Amanti, C. (1992, November). *Teaching ethnographic methods to teachers: Successes and pitfalls.* Paper presented at the annual meeting of the American Anthropological Association, San Francisco, CA.

Gonzalez, N., Moll, L., & Amanti, C. (2005). *Funds of knowledge: Theorizing practice in households, communities, and classrooms.* Mahwah, NJ: L. Earlbaum Associates.

Jago, C. (2008). *Come to class: Lessons for high school writers.* Portsmouth, NH: Heinemann.

Johns, A. M. (1997). *Text, role, and context: Developing academic literacies.* New York, NY: Cambridge University Press.

John-Steiner, V., & Mahn, H. (1996). Sociocultural approaches to learning and development: A Vygotskian framework. *Educational Psychologist, 31,* 191-206.

Ladson-Billings, G. (1992). Reading between the lines and beyond the pages: A culturally relevant approach to literacy teaching. *Theory into Practice, 31,* 312-320.

Ladson-Billings, G. (1994). *The dreamkeepers: Successful teachers of African-American children.* San Francisco, CA: Jossey-Bass.

Ladson-Billings, G. (1995). But that's just good teaching! The case for culturally relevant pedagogy. *Theory into Practice, 34,* 159-165.

Lantolf, J. P. and S. L. Thorne. 2006. *Sociocultural theory and the genesis of second language development.* Oxford, England: Oxford University Press.

Lave, J., & Wenger, E. (1991). *Situated learning: Legitimate peripheral participation.* New York, NY: Cambridge University Press.

Lee, C. (2007). *The role of culture in academic literacies: Conducting our blooming in the midst of the whirlwind.* New York, NY: Teachers College Press.

Miller, A. (1959). *The crucible* (7th ed.). New York, NY: Bantam.

Milton, J., & Pullman, P. (1992). *Paradise lost.* Oxford, England: Oxford University Press.

Moll, L. C., Amanti, C., Neff, D., & Gonzalez, N. (1992*)*. Funds of knowledge for teaching: Using a qualitative approach to connect homes and classrooms. *Theory into Practice, 31,* 132-141.

Moll, L. C., & Greenberg, J. (1990). Creating zones of possibilities: Combining social contexts for instruction. In L. C. Moll (Ed.), *Vygotsky and education* (pp. 319-348). Cambridge, MA: Cambridge University Press.

Morrison, T. (1994). *The bluest eye.* New York, NY: Penguin.

Noddings, N. (2005). *The challenge to care in schools: An alternative approach to education.* New York, NY: Teachers College Press.

O'Neil, J. (1995). On preparing students for the world of work: A conversation with Willard Daggett. *Educational Leadership, 52*(8), 46-48.

Parker, R. D. (2008). *How to interpret literature: Critical theory for literary and cultural studies.* New York, NY: Oxford University Press.

Patterson, L., Wickstrom, C., & Araujo, J. (June, 2010). *Culturally mediated writing instruction* (Final Report). Berkeley, CA: National Writing Project.

Patterson, L., Wickstrom, C., Roberts, J., Araujo, J., Hoki, C. (Winter, 2010). Deciding when to step in and when to back off: Culturally mediated writing instruction for adolescent English learners. *The Tapestry Journal, 2*(1), 1-18.

Rebollo-Gil, G., & Moras, A. (2006). Defining an "anti" stance: Key pedagogical questions about engaging anti-racism in college classrooms. *Race, Ethnicity & Education, 9,* 381-394.

Rogoff, B. (1990). *Apprenticeship in thinking: Cognitive development in social contexts.* New York, NY: Oxford University Press.

Romano, T. (2000). *Blending genre, altering style: Writing multigenre papers.* Portsmouth, NH: Boynton/Cook; Heinemann.

Shor, I. (1992). *Empowering education: Critical teaching for social change.* Chicago, IL: University of Chicago Press.

Short, K., & Harste, J. (with Burke, C.). (1996). *Creating classrooms for authors and inquirers* (2nd Ed.). Portsmouth, NH: Heinemann.

Texas Education Agency. (2011). Academic Excellence Indicator System. Retrieved from http://www.tea.state.tx.us/perfreport/aeis/

US Census (2005-2009). American Community Survey 5-Year Estimates. Retrieved from http://factfinder.census.gov/servlet/ACSSAFFFacts?_event=Search&geo_id=&_geoContext=&_street=&_county=fort+hancock&_cityTown=fort+hancock&_state=04000US48&_zip=&_lang=en&_sse=on&pctxt=fph&pgsl=010

Vygotsky, L. S. (1978). *Mind in society: The development of higher psychological processes.* Cambridge, MA: Harvard University Press.

Wells, G. (2007). Semiotic mediation, dialogue and the construction of knowledge. *Human Development, 50,* 244–274.

Wilhelm, J. D. (2007). *Engaging readers & writers with inquiry: Promoting deep understandings in language arts and the content areas with guiding questions.* New York, NY: Scholastic.

APPENDIX 1

CMWI High School Mean Differences

	Pre-writing	Post-writing	Mean Change
Holistic Score			
M	2.75	3.11	0.36
SD	1.06	1.07	
N	22	22	
Content			
M	2.75	3.11	0.36
SD	1.06	1.06	
N	22	22	
Structure			
M	2.94	2.90	-0.04
SD	.93	.95	
N	22	22	
Stance*			
M	2.66	3.45	0.79
SD	1.04	1.06	
N	22	2	
Sentence Fluency			
M	3.10	3.26	0.16
SD	1.09	1.0	
N	22	22	
Diction*			
M	2.70	3.34	0.64
SD	1.19	.89	
N	22	22	
Conventions*			
M	2.61	3.20	0.59
SD	.79	1.10	
N	22	22	

Note. M = mean; SD = Standard Deviation; N = number of paired writing samples.
*Results are statistically significant (p<0.05).

Clinic Experiences that Promote Transfer to School Contexts: What Matters in Clinical Teacher Preparation

Theresa Deeney
University of Rhode Island

Cheryl Dozier
Julie Smit
Suzanne Davis
University at Albany

Barbara Laster
Towson University

Mary DeKonty Applegate
St. Joseph's University

Jeanne Cobb
Coastal Carolina University

Dolores Gaunty-Porter
Vanguard University

Debra Gurvitz
National Louis University

Stephanie McAndrews
Southern Illinois University Edwardsville

Tammy Ryan
Jacksonville University

Meagan Eeg-Moreland
Stephan Sargent
Mary Swanson
Northeastern State University

Lee Dubert
Boise State University

Aimee Morewood
West Virginia University

Tammy Milby
University of Richmond

Recently, Secretary of Education Arne Duncan took teacher preparation programs to task for "doing a mediocre job of preparing teachers for the realities of the 21st Century classroom" (Duncan, 2009). The recently released report of the Blue Ribbon Panel on Clinical Preparation and Partnerships for Improved Student Learning (NCATE, 2010) recommended revamping teacher education toward a clinical model, while acknowledging that there is currently little research investigating what makes clinical preparation effective. Darling-Hammond (2006) echoes this reality, suggesting "there has been less discussion about what goes on…inside the courses and clinical experiences that candidates encounter" (p. 303). Yet, understanding what makes clinical preparation effective is critical to designing experiences that prepare teachers to confront the complexities of their future classrooms. Our research group takes seriously the challenge of Risko, Roller, Bean, Collins Block, Anders, and Flood (2008) to engage in collaborative inquiry to better understand literacy teacher preparation because, they, and others have noted the paucity and need for this research (Anders, Hoffman, & Duffy, 2000; Darling-Hammond, 2006; Hoffman & Pearson, 2000).

As 17 teacher educators, co-researchers, and reading clinic directors located in multiple sites across the United States, we have a long history of supervising graduate-level university- and school-based reading clinics. We collaborate online and in person through writings, meetings, study groups, and retreats to share, discuss, and refine our own clinic practices. In this study, we respond to Darling-Hammond's (2006) call to unpack what happens within our reading clinics and examine what graduate students identify as important within "extensive and intensely-supervised clinical work" (p. 307). We recognize the choices we make as teacher educators are value laden (Many, 2001) and instructional decisions, both at the program and instructor level regarding content to include, impact teacher learning and development (Shulman, 1986; Zeichner, 2006). Our aim is to understand which choices in terms of experiences we provide within the clinical practicum impact graduates' development as literacy professionals who transfer clinic practices to school contexts. Our primary goal is to strengthen clinical practices for future literacy professionals. Secondarily, we hope to identify "what works" in clinical practice in graduate literacy preparation in an effort to inform policy makers as they seek to re-envision and redesign teacher-education programs.

THEORETICAL RATIONALE

Our study has its roots in social constructivism (Vygotsky, 1978) where thinking and learning are treated as processes shaped by culture and where knowledge is shared and understandings jointly constructed (Mercer & Littleton, 2007). Social constructivism is a complex phenomenon where concerns and invested activity bind together all members of the community (in this case teacher educators, graduate students, students, and families) "as they participate, in various ways, in reform-oriented education" (Windschitl, 2002, p.132). Learning "is based on conventions that we as a community have constructed and agreed upon" (Gavelek & Raphael, 1996, p.183).

In the reading clinic, instructors create learning opportunities within graduate students' zones of proximal development as they negotiate and renegotiate their understandings of teaching and learning. Vygotsky's theories are central as learning occurs through interaction with knowledgeable others for teachers as well as for children. Just as "adults cannot do the learning for the child but must enlist the child's attention and effort and provide helpful information in response to what the learner is able to do" (Clay, 2001, p. 102), so, too, teacher educators cannot do the learning for graduate students. Conversations between teacher educators and graduate students in clinic encourage critical thinking through questioning, contesting, evaluating, improving and building upon previous ideas. These conversations provide models for graduate students to engage in with children (Tharp & Gallimore, 1988). In this way, teachers (and children) see and position themselves as meaning makers and inquirers. Teachers gradually release responsibility of reading and writing development to the child to foster a self-extending system (Clay, 2001). Teacher educators also release responsibility to graduate students in the clinic setting. Graduate students grapple with understanding a learner, using multiple sources of information to design appropriate instruction, and collaborating to notice and name theirs and others' practices. For this to happen, instructors design clinical experiences to foster the reflection and problem solving needed to transform their practices (Mezirow, 2000) as teachers continue to "develop a vision of what it means to be a professional" (Bransford, Derry, Berliner, & Hammerness, 2005, p. 76).

The calls for clinical preparation to improve teacher education (Darling-Hammond, 2006; NCATE, 2010) suggest that practices learned within a clinical experience will transfer to future teaching experiences. For Perkins and Salomon (1992), "transfer occurs when learning in one context or with one set of materials impacts performance in another context or with other related materials" (p. 1). Although we expect clinic experiences to promote the more direct kind of transfer Perkins and Salomon suggest, this is inadequate if graduates solely take what they learn in clinics and apply it to classrooms and schools. Rather, in clinic, we emphasize and adopt Bransford and Schwartz's (1999) broad idea of transfer as "preparation for future learning" (p. 68). We teach for transfer, which means structuring learning environments on a "trajectory toward expertise" (p. 68), where graduates develop learner centeredness (Williams & Baumann, 2008), flexibility (Fairbanks et al., 2010), reflective stances (Zeichner & Liston, 1996), and advocacy (Johnston, 2004) needed to confront the complexities of schools.

BACKGROUND

University-based reading clinics have shifted from a medical model of literacy to a more dynamic model that includes facilitating the social and constructive aspects of learning (Laster, 1996). Clinics now encompass a variety of formats, including school-based centers that either replace or complement university sites (Allen & Leslie, 1997; Dozier, Johnston, & Rogers, 2006). Central to clinics is the supervised tutorial experience where graduate students work with children who struggle as readers and writers and tailor instruction to meet their needs (Allington, 2005; Clay, 1991, 1998; Johnston, 1997). Through supervised tutorials, graduate students gain in-depth understanding of struggling readers, focus on and teach to student strengths, increase their expectations of readers, develop a larger repertoire of instructional practices, and gain understanding of the individualization necessary for instruction that leads to student progress (Broaddus & Bloodgood, 1999; Dozier, Johnston, & Rogers, 2006).

There is some research that suggests graduates of clinic programs do transfer clinic practices to classrooms and schools (Carr, 2003; Dozier & Rutten, 2005/2006). Transfer from teacher preparation to school contexts is necessary for "teachers to understand deeply a wide array of things about learning, social and cultural contexts, and teaching and be able to enact these understandings in complex classrooms serving increasingly diverse students" (Darling-Hammond, 2006, p. 302). Building on these studies, we investigated transfer from clinic to classrooms and schools first through a broad survey of the roles and practices of 150 clinic graduates (Deeney et al., 2005). In this study, we found clinic graduates felt well prepared to understand, choose, and use a variety of instructional and assessment practices. Next, we investigated 28 recent graduates' practices within their educational contexts (Freppon et al., 2007). In this more in-depth study, we found graduates adopted and adapted clinic assessment, instructional, coaching/leadership, and collaborative practices within their classrooms and schools. Some also took active steps to change literacy teaching and learning within their schools and districts.

Our current study adds to the literature by investigating which clinical experiences influenced future literacy practices and helped graduates develop as literacy professionals. Findings presented here are part of a larger qualitative study (Deeney et al., 2010) investigating transfer from clinics to classrooms. For this paper, we address two specific questions from the larger study: What clinic experiences do graduates identify as supporting their development as literacy professionals? What clinic practices transfer to school contexts?

METHOD

Participants and Settings

The nine participants in this study are all women (8 Caucasian, 1 African-American), ranging in age from late 20s to early 50s. All are former graduate students of university programs for the preparation of literacy professionals, and all participated in an intensive supervised tutorial experience and related seminar. Among the nine participants are four elementary classroom teachers, three reading/literacy specialists, and two literacy coaches (see Table 1 for participant background information and clinic descriptions).

We selected the participants based on the following criteria: (a) all completed a graduate-level reading clinic experience as part of their preparation program, (b) participants were identified by their clinic supervisor as having demonstrated significant changes in their practices as they engaged in the clinic experience, (c) participants demonstrated through a screening interview and school-based observation that they used clinic knowledge and practices in schools and/or worked to change literacy education. Our choice of graduates who demonstrated transfer within their school contexts was deliberate and purposeful in order to better understand what and how graduates take from the clinical experience.

Data Collection

To examine our research questions, we conducted two recorded interviews, each paired with a school-based observation, and one follow-up interview with each of the nine participants during the 2009-2010 school year. While all interviews followed specific interview protocols to maintain coherence, prompts were sufficiently open ended to access each participant's experiences (Merriam, 1998). The observations followed a specific observation protocol designed for this study. As this manuscript represents a subset of the larger study, we chose to use the observation data in the current study as a means of verifying that the graduates engaged in the practices they discussed in the interviews, and as a basis for follow-up interviews.

The first interview, meant to select graduates for participation, consisted of four questions to probe ways in which graduates transferred clinic practices to classroom/schools, and clinic activities they identified as helpful in their own professional development. The second interview protocol, building on the findings of our prior studies, consisted of two parts: (a) teaching histories and demographic questions about the participants' schools and districts, (b) probes across themes

Table 1. Participants and Clinic Descriptions

Participant/ Location	Participant Role, Years out of Clinic, Years Teaching	Participant School Information	Participant Clinic Information	Clinic Experiences and Practices
Lois New York	K-5 Literacy Specialist, 4 years from clinic, 4 years teaching	Suburban K-5 elementary, 75% White, 19% Asian, 7% FRL[a]	One-semester school-based literacy lab (2x/week Fall or Spring, or 4x/week Summer), one-to-one tutoring 25 hours, 112 graduate student tutors per year, supervisor/tutor ratio 1:12-14	Written daily lesson plans, preparation, reflection; formative and summative assessments; videotaped transcript analysis of practice with group analysis, discussion, feedback; two audio-taped analyses of lessons; initial and final case report; seminar discussion of weekly readings; weekly engagement with families; ending family celebration/ presentation
Jane Rhode Island	Middle School Literacy Specialist, 6 Years from clinic, 10 years teaching	Suburban middle school, 88% White, 33% FRL	Two-semester school-based clinic (1x/week Fall and Spring), one-to-one tutoring 45 hours, 9-12 graduate student tutors per year, supervisor/tutor ratio 1:9-12	Written daily lesson plans, preparation, reflection; formative and summative assessments; assessment presentation to colleagues; videotaped transcript analysis of practice with group analysis, discussion, feedback; initial and final case report; seminar discussions on weekly topics/readings; informal weekly meetings with families; formal meeting with families; ending family literacy celebration/ presentation
Melinda Pennsylvania	Grade 1 teacher, 1 year from clinic, 1 year teaching	Suburban elementary school, 90% White, 0% FRL	Six-week university-based clinic (summer), one-to-three tutoring 78 hours, 40-46 graduate student tutors per year, supervisor/tutor ratio 1:6	Weekly guided inquiry with content; guided writing and book making; weekly underlying theme DR-TA with literature; word learning strategies integrated with literature and content intervention; administration and interpretation of assessments; progress monitoring of strategy selected based on assessments; collaborative planning of flexible grouping structure; case report; parent conference

Carla Maryland	Grade 4 teacher, 1 year from clinic, 4 years teaching	Urban elementary school, 91% African American, 66% FRL	Choice of two semesters that include university- based clinic (1x/ week Fall, Spring) and 3-week school-based clinic (summer), one-to-one tutoring 25 hours (6 hours with families), 110 graduate student tutors per year, supervisor/tutor ratio 1:5-15	Blackboard presentations based on intensive assessment and supervised instruction; reflection log; demonstration lesson (behind-the-glass or videotape) with debriefing; initial and final case reports; read/respond to 3 books (related to diverse students and family literacy); two parent workshops; two parent memos; weekly engagement with parents; family literacy project
Sylvia Florida	Instructional Coach, 5 years from clinic, 7 years teaching	Urban middle school, 41% White, 35% African American, 10% Hispanic, 45% FRL	One-semester university-based clinic (1x/wk Fall or Spring), one-to-one tutoring 20 hours, 12-15 graduate student tutors per year, supervisor/tutor ratio 2:10-12	Weekly written lesson plans and reflections; tutoring portfolio; assessment workshops; demonstrations; case study report; seminar discussions and student- selected article presentation and discussion; strategy notebooks
Michele Illinois	K-12 District Literacy Specialist, 4 years from clinic, 9 years teaching	Rural/ suburban, 99% White, 15% FRL	Two-semester university-based clinic (1x/week, one semester w/ elementary tutee/one semester middle or high school tutee), one-to-one tutoring 45 hours, 12-15 graduate student tutors per year, supervisor/tutor ratio 1:12-15	Written daily lesson plans, preparation, reflection; weekly lesson debriefings; formative and summative assessments; discussion of readings and strategy presentations; 2videotaped experiences/ transcript analyses with group analysis, discussion and feedback; 2 audio-taped analyses; case reports; weekly engagement with families; strategy and IRA standards notebooks
Pat Illinois	Literacy Coach grades K-5, 4 years from clinic, 8 years teaching	Urban ·elementary . school, 93% Hispanic, 94% FRL	Four-week school- based literacy lab (Summer), one-to- one tutoring 40 hours (20 each w/a middle and an elementary student), 18 graduate student tutors per year, supervisor/tutor ratio 1:10-12	Tutor logs with daily instructional plans, notes and evaluation of student learning; reflection; intensive assessments; strategy/ assessment notebook; initial and final reports; co-planning/ co-teaching lessons; 2 videotaped lessons with reflection and group feedback; seminar discussions; facilitate one discussion or plan/ facilitate one group tutor lesson; exchange and provide feedback to 5 tutor logs

Ivy Oklahoma	Grade 1-2 multi-age teacher, 6 years from clinic, 30 years teaching	Suburban elementary school, 19% White, 55% Hispanic, 14% Native American, 12% African American, 100% FRL	Three-semester university-based clinic (1x/week), one-to-one tutoring 57 hours, 80 graduate student tutors per year, supervisor/tutor ratio 1:20	Written lesson plans, preparation, and reflection; formative and summative assessment; behind-the-glass observations with feedback; videotaped analysis; case report; seminar discussions
Angela California	Grade 4 teacher, 4 years from clinic, 4 years teaching	Urban elementary school, 79% Hispanic, 80% FRL	One semester school-based clinic (1x/week), one-to-one or one-to-two tutoring 15 hours, 45 graduate student tutors per year, supervisor/tutor ratio 1:4	Written lesson plans (with state standards, objectives); assessments; each session audio recorded; written reflection each session/student work attached and analyzed; seminar discussion on weekly topics/readings; ongoing documented contact with parents; final literacy celebration, Readers Theater and portfolio presented to parents

[a] FRL = Percentage of students receiving free or reduced price lunch

identified within the data of our 2005 and 2007 studies (roles and responsibilities, curriculum and instruction, assessment, coaching and leadership). The third interview protocol focused on member checking (Lincoln & Guba, 1985) and included probes to clarify information researchers did not understand when coding the initial two interviews, and to follow up on practices noted within school-based observations but not discussed in interviews. (See Appendix for sample interview questions.)

Data Analysis

We created a research wikispace for the 17 researchers involved in the study to post interview transcripts, observation notes, individual case analyses, cross-case analyses, and questions generated throughout each phase of the study. To ensure coherence across the cases, we developed common analysis protocols. The extensiveness of our research group allowed us to create three research teams. Each focused on specific analyses across all interviews. The first team interviewed a graduate, transcribed the interviews verbatim, and coded the interviews using the common analysis protocols. Each member of the second team independently coded the transcripts to conduct a cross-case analysis following the common analysis protocols. The lead research team (two researchers and two doctoral students) also coded all transcripts and conducted cross-case analyses. The lead researchers met in weekly sessions to mediate discrepancies and checked all inconsistencies and questions with the respective researchers to ensure agreement. Any questions or unclear information were noted and set aside to address with graduates in the follow-up interview.

We coded and analyzed interview data in three phases using the constant comparative method (Glaser & Strauss, 1967; Strauss & Corbin, 1990). In the first phase, we identified instances within all transcripts where graduates' discussions focused on: (a) aspects of the clinic experience they identified as supportive of their development (which we term *clinic experience*), and (b) current practices in classrooms that draw from their participation in the clinic (which we term *transfer*).

In the second phase, we grouped instances from phase one into like categories and created codes that represented the relationships within the areas of *clinic experience* and *transfer*. We initially identified 18 categories of clinic experience (e.g. one-to-one tutoring, analyzing videotaped lessons, writing a detailed case report, problem solving with colleagues, course readings, writing reflections, administering a variety of assessments). We also identified 26 categories of transfer (e.g. developing a repertoire of instructional practices, collaborating with colleagues, lesson planning, focusing on students, reflecting on practices, using assessment to inform instruction, careful observations, drawing on course readings).

In the final phase, we revisited the categories within both clinic experience and transfer to test, confirm, and reconfirm these categories (Miles & Huberman, 1994). We then collapsed the categories into broader themes. We grouped the 18 categories of clinic experience into five broad experiences: (a) supervised tutoring, (b) engaging with families, (c) assessment practices, (d) collaboration, and (e) research. We grouped the 26 categories of transfer into six broad themes: (a) from one to many, (b) learning from learners, (c) assessment practices, (d) engaging and teaching learners, (e) collaboration, and (f) research. Below, we discuss findings from the research.

RESULTS

Clinic Experiences

Clinic experiences are designed to foster an understanding of literacy, teaching, and learning. Graduates identified key aspects of their clinical experiences as supporting their development as literacy professionals. The supervised tutorial, engaging with families, assessment practices, and collaboration contributed in unique ways for the nine participants.

Supervised tutoring. The intensity of the one-to-one teaching in the clinic was often new and challenging for graduate students. During the tutorial, the intent was for graduate students to focus on the learner and how the learner was taking up the instruction. In this way, they became "students of their own students" (Nieto, 2000) and of their own practices. The tutorial involved creating deliberate and purposeful plans for each session with learners. With feedback from course instructors, graduate students explored a range of teaching possibilities, reflected on their teaching decisions, and then adapted their instruction accordingly.

Angela (CA) cited the clinic focus on supporting learners as critical to her developing a learner-centered stance: "It was instilled in us to look for concrete ways we could support our students... the focus was always about the tutees." Melinda's (PA) clinic experiences focused on learning a range of strategies to help students "develop critical thinking skills." As teachers in the clinic focused first on their students, they learned the importance of engaging learners. Lois (NY) commented, "My job first and foremost is to engage them and to make sure that it is purposeful. Through lab, I felt like we met with our student and developed interaction and instruction based on each child." Graduates cited that engaging in instructional practices with their learners and reflecting on how those practices did or did not support the learner was a critical part of the clinical experience. Sylvia (FL) noted,

> We were responsible to not just read about the strategies but we actually worked through them and used them with the students in the lab. That was key...You learned to figure out what's most important. It helped me to zone in on what it is we need to focus in on.

Within the clinic, planning, reflection, and feedback were cyclical processes. Michele (IL) discussed how this reflective planning informed her practice, "I think that the detailed lesson plans, especially the reflective piece, helped me...think back on the lesson and write what I would change or modify for the next time and why." Graduates appreciated the supervision and detailed feedback from instructors. As Angela (CA) noted, "I'd say that in clinic I received lots of feedback on my practices and had opportunity to discuss what I was doing...I just kind of like having the opportunity to talk about my work."

Engaging with families. Learning from and engaging with families was also central to the clinic experience. Graduate students regularly interacted with family members to better understand the children they were tutoring (Dozier, Johnston, & Rogers, 2006). For many graduates, communicating with families, and sharing their developing knowledge about what the children accomplished during the tutorials was a new, and sometimes uncomfortable, experience. From her work in the clinic, Sylvia (FL) gained confidence to talk with families:

> It's talking through the process. I had to literally talk through the process. In the clinic parents would want to know...what's going on with their child. You would have to talk to a parent about things you've collected and you had to know the data...because a parent doesn't understand all that jargon. And so to sit down with the parent was my first real hands on experience of talking to explain what this means.

Carla (MD) found her voice through engaging with families:

> I had to develop things for the parent presentations. I had to talk to the parents of my client every night. It really taught me that I had to take the lead...And so it helped me to become more vocal about what I believe in and what I do in my classroom, and more confident in the strategies that I use.

Collaboration. In the clinic, graduate students collaborated in a range of ways when they provided feedback while watching videotapes of lessons, through observations of each other, and during shared conversations with colleagues. This collaborative inquiry prepared students for "problem-solving and theorizing necessary for refining and developing their growing repertoire as public intellectuals" (Dozier, Johnston, & Rogers, 2006, p. 25). As a community of learners, they worked together to plan, reflect, and adapt. They identified this collaboration as fostering their own learning. Lois (NY) learned from conversations with her colleagues during the video analysis of lessons when they highlighted strategies and identified instructional prompts she was not consciously aware she was using with her student, "[it was] a place for conversation with other people who were noticing things, or not noticing things." Sylvia (FL), too, benefitted from the advice of her classmates when the student she was tutoring was not improving:

> Working in the clinic with students and *not* seeing improvements yet knowing a list of things I could possibly do for interventions and having discussions with other students in class helped. Hearing how others approach things and use them helps me change things.

Through collaboration, Pat (IL) came to value the many perspectives of her classmates:

> When I look back at clinic it really made me more reflective on my practice
> as well as how to work with others where I learned to value what each person
> brought to our room. From this I became less judgmental and I think it made
> me a better leader.

Assessment. In the clinic, graduate students considered each assessment's goal, purpose, and intent and how each assessment contributed to understanding each child as a learner. Assessment was an ongoing, student-centered, recursive process rather than an act of learning to administer specific instruments. Teachers used multiple sources of data to understand students' strengths and needs (Clay, 1991; 1998; 2001). Each session with a student was a form of assessment; graduate students focused on the whole child as a reader and a writer, rather than one snapshot of one particular facet of reading and writing [IRA, 2009]. As Sylvia (FL) noted, "We would test [a student] and try to find a plan for them. It was…the process that I learned."

The clinic emphasized that the purpose of assessment was to make appropriate instructional decisions. Graduate students discussed how assessment informed instructional plans for future sessions. Michele (IL) noted, "I think I'm always using assessment to plan instruction. It always goes back to what we focused on in clinic as far as identifying strengths and needs as far as matching strategies to those things to teach them." In clinic, graduate students learned to understand a variety of assessment tools—what they do/do not do, the scores they generate, how to interpret scores, and what scores mean in the scope of a student's total literacy profile. Graduate students critically evaluated assessment tools and learned to ask—what, for whom, and when. Jane (RI) noted:

> The clinic definitely helped me understand standard scores and percentiles
> and why those are more important and accurate than age equivalents or grade
> equivalents. So I had the knowledge to say…, 'we need to look at data in a
> different way.'…I went back to the Gates [*Gates-MacGinitie Reading Tests*] and
> went into the manual and found the information that the Gates even suggested
> that age and grade equivalents weren't the best way to look at a child's needs.

Research. Our clinics focus on research as a tool to learn about literacy development, and graduates note this helps them understand research within the context of its direct application with students (Carr, 2003). In the clinical experience, graduate students read and discuss research on the nature of reading and writing, effective instructional practices, and the roles culture, language, engagement, and interest play in students' literacy learning. They discuss and use theory and research to inform their teaching. Angela (CA) commented on the research she read in clinic on English language learners,

> We read enough research to show the importance of moving from the concrete
> to the abstract when setting up our lessons, especially with the English language
> learners…With my clinic/lab experience I learned to think about ways to make
> print come alive. I mean what items could I bring in to support the lesson, what
> pictures can I bring to support the lesson, what questions I could present to
> deepen understanding.

Jane (RI) discussed research as an important tool for clinic graduates:

> I think that [research] really provided us with the knowledge when we graduated that we could go into a district and say, 'research shows.' I can cite that and I can show you that students learn best when they're working in a small group...The clinic really pushes you to ask the hard questions, and to go look for the answers.

Transfer

Through carefully constructed experiences in clinics, graduate students gain confidence and competence using a variety of instructional practices to teach children. Yet, we do not want the practices they employ during the tutorial to remain solely in the clinic. It is essential that practices transfer beyond the clinic walls. Graduates reported several aspects of the tutorial that transferred to their day-to-day lives as literacy professionals.

From one to many. The graduates' experiences in clinics across the United States demonstrated that focusing intensively on one learner has the power to transfer to classroom practices (Dozier, Johnston, & Rogers, 2006). Jane (RI) illustrates this as she describes how she transferred teaching one learner to teaching many as a middle school reading specialist:

> [the clinic experience] definitely does help you even when you go back to a group of kids. It really allows you to learn and focus your learning and practice what you're learning, and do it really well with one child, so that when you go back to your class of 26 you can start implementing those practices and do really well with all of your kids. That one child is really important in that learning curve of a reading specialist.

Ivy (OK), too, used what she learned in one-to-one tutoring in her first-/second-grade classroom, "those practices that you use one-on-one also help you [teach] whole group, they really do. They help you teach all of the children and help you look for things."

Learning from learners. Within their school contexts, graduates engage in an on-going process of learning *about* their learners *from* their learners (Clay, 1998; Clay, 2001). Their most important information comes from the students themselves when they notice and name learners' strengths, interests, and needs. Angela (CA) realized culture played a large role in her students' learning and, therefore, should play a large role in her teaching:

> As a teacher I have to be aware of the ways that culture influences the literacy skills... I mean like how [my English only and ELL students] read, what they select to read, and their responses to what they read and write.

Lois (NY) echoed the need to move beyond labels to learn about students, "I think it's real easy to say 'the kid's struggling here because his first language is Korean or Spanish or Arabic,' rather than getting to know the child and saying 'it's very possible that something else here is happening.'"

The focus on learners transferred to assessment practices within schools. Careful observations were key to learning about students in their school contexts. Jane (RI) noted:

> I can sit down with that [middle school] child and even without giving them a formal diagnostic assessment, by sitting and talking with them I feel like I can pick up on some of their issues related to reading. And that a lot of that practice comes from working in the clinic.

In Response to Intervention (RTI) meetings, Lois (NY) kept the focus on the learner central to the conversation:

> We had a conversation today about how easy it is to slide into the whole skills realm of assessing and stepping back and making sure that it's an overall picture of the child rather than zeroing on the skills. Does this kid need RTI because he or she can't rhyme or doesn't know the initial sounds or wasn't fluent? You need to keep stepping back because...it's easier to define a skill than it is to actually [define] reading and writing process.

Assessment practices. Graduates transferred a variety of clinic assessment practices to their roles in schools. They were confident to choose which instruments to administer, justify choices based on knowledge of their students, and analyze data to determine next steps (Deeney, 2009). Pat (IL) used data to match readers with appropriate texts:

> We look at the data and use the information to see what level they are independently reading so we can make sure they are reading appropriate books for independent reading time. We are choosing appropriate books for small group instruction. We are also looking at the data to see any trends.

Graduates also used assessments learned in clinic and knowledge gained to advocate for changes in assessment practices within their schools. Both Jane (RI) and Lois (NY) revamped assessments and assessment processes at their respective schools to make evaluation more expansive and to provide a more complete portrait of learners. Lois (NY) made sure her school included writing as part of their Response to Intervention protocols. Jane (RI) created an assessment protocol to guide teachers away from screening assessments toward more diagnostic measures that inform instruction.

Engaging and teaching learners. Tied closely to learning about learners was a flexible approach to engaging and teaching learners. Graduates spoke of relevance, motivation, engagement, and variety in choosing instructional practices and materials (Allington, 2005). Lois (NY) focused on students, rather than delivering instructional programs:

> I transferred in a big way the notion of relevancy and working to the student...
> It's not a program that I have to follow. It's not a script. It's meeting the child
> where the child is, finding the success and working where the child needs to go.

In meeting students' needs, Lois also focused on engaging students, "they come in [to the reading room] and they are so serious. These are the kids who are struggling and they are nervous and so we have to engage them."

Graduates also discussed transferring a broader repertoire of instructional practices, and an ability to choose from this repertoire. Michele (IL) noted, "Clinic gave me a wide variety of different strategies...when I'm working with kids." Likewise, Carla (MD) worked to "find other ways to teach the skills and strategies that I find my kids are more interested in...I have practiced and learned to modify my instruction of reading to meet the individual needs of my learners." Angela (CA) differentiated instruction in her fourth-grade classroom:

> The clinic really helped bolster the ability to see a need and quickly address that need. In the classroom, there are moment-to-moment decisions that must be made about the reading and writing of the students...I have to think

differentiation…to see how I can make the lessons so that all students feel supported in their learning.

At times, graduates' teaching was in contrast to methods and materials their districts adopted. With a broader range of instructional practices and knowledge of students, Ivy (OK) questioned her district's push toward a structured phonics program, "At this point [I] had a feel for the readers in my room…and where my kids were academically and I thought to myself, I don't think they need all that finger spelling and everything."

Collaborating. Graduates indicated the collaborative experiences encouraged in the clinic setting were powerful models and exemplars for their work in schools (Goldenberg, 2004). Pat (IL) brought a collaborative stance to her role as a k-5 literacy coach. "Clinic/Lab was an influence on grade level meetings because it taught me how important it is to collaborate with others for initiatives to happen. Teachers need time to discuss and talk about learning, instruction, students, data, assessments, etc." Sylvia (FL), in her role as a middle school instructional coach, routinely collaborated with others in her district, "In this position, it's other coaches and other schools that are my support. It's where I gather ideas and how I muddle my way through it." First-grade classroom teacher Melinda (PA) valued collaboration and helped other teachers integrate literacy centers, "One of the first grade teachers was very interested in my centers and she…adopted a lot of my centers and even my center schedule."

The collaborative relationships Pat (IL) built in the clinic remain her professional learning community:

> I still meet with a group from clinic where we meet and problem-solve our current positions. I think the time we spent during lab in seminar and informal chats built this relationship that has been going on for almost five years—a collaborative, trusting friendship as well as professional conversation.

Research. While graduates drew upon research read and discussed in the clinic, they also emphasized the importance of staying current with research to help inform their practice and advocate for change initiatives in schools. Jane (RI) used research to support her instructional decisions.

> Well they're [the clinic] good at saying, 'That's really nice but where did you get it from? Why do you think that way? Back it up with something solid.' Education can't be based on just your opinion. What does the research say? Is the research valid or applicable to what we're doing?

Clinic graduates also turned to research to think critically about district initiatives or mandates. Pat (IL) tried to reconcile recommendations for writing instruction that didn't seem to match her students:

> Once we began our writing study a…consultant provided several research articles on writing, but it really did not match our school population. Then, I remembered I had a file of writing articles that we collected throughout the program and during practicum…I used references on those articles to find additional articles on specific writing topics.

DISCUSSION AND IMPLICATIONS

In light of the current calls to increase clinical experiences during teacher preparation (Darling-Hammond, 2006; NCATE, 2010), we wanted to learn how intensive, supervised clinical experiences in nine clinic sites across the nation influenced graduates' future practices, and what experiences within the clinics mattered. Data from this study support previous research findings that demonstrate clinic graduates do transfer learning from clinic to classrooms and schools (Carr, 2003; Dozier, Johnston, & Rogers, 2006; Freppon et al., 2007), and suggest the clinical experience provides a unique and important learning opportunity for teachers.

Graduates illuminated specific experiences within the clinical settings that supported their development as literacy professionals. The understandings graduates gained through intensively supervised one-to-one tutoring transferred to teaching in the larger, more complex environments of classrooms and schools. This is an important finding—one-to-one intensively supervised experiences *do* matter. Specifically, within these tutorials, graduates learned from their learners, engaged in assessment as a process, read and analyzed research, and interacted with families. The collaborative community developed within the clinic was also significant to their learning. Graduate students engaged in jointly constructed activities jointly where they questioned, contested, and developed shared understandings (Lave & Wenger, 1991), and sought to replicate this kind of community within their schools. This finding supports the importance of providing experiences within the clinic that foster collaboration and develop community (Tharp & Gallimore, 1988). Even clinic practices graduates disliked, such as continuous reflection, intensive pacing, and detailed lesson planning, proved powerful in their lived lives within classrooms and schools. Our intentional choices of experiences within the one-to-one tutorial promoted learner centeredness, reflection, advocacy, and flexibility, and transferred beyond the clinic space.

Our graduates' voices helped us pinpoint successful clinic practices and demonstrate the importance of examining what goes on within clinic instruction and how teachers perceive and take up these experiences. Our findings raise several points to consider as teacher educators and policy makers contemplate calls for increased clinical experiences. We strongly suggest simply offering additional clinical experiences in teacher preparation is not enough. All stakeholders need to consider what happens *within* those experiences.

We believe this inquiry, along with our earlier studies researching clinical teacher preparation, provides a foundation to understand clinic practices that support literacy professionals. However, we are mindful that our sample size is a limitation. We recognize the need for both larger scale and longitudinal research following graduates over time from clinical preparation into their roles in schools to learn how clinic experiences impact school communities. We also recognize the need for more extensive observations to understand the nuanced ways in which graduates work within their schools, and the clinic's role in influencing this work. These unanswered questions and challenges will guide us as we continue research into the role of clinical experiences in literacy teacher preparation.

REFERENCES

Allen, L. & Leslie. L (1997, December). *Tutors and teachers: University-school partnerships that work for at-risk children.* Paper presented at the 47th annual meeting of the National Reading Conference, Phoenix, AZ.

Allington, R. L. (2005). *What really matters for struggling readers: Designing research-based Programs* (2nd ed.). New York, NY: Addison-Wesley Longman.

Anders, P. L., Hoffman, J. V., & Duffy, G. G. (2000). Teaching teachers to teach reading: Paradigm shifts, persistent problems, and challenges. In M. L. Kamil, P. B. Mosenthal, P. D. Pearson, & R. Barr (Eds.). *Handbook of Reading Research* (Vol. 3, pp. 719-742). Mahwah, NJ: Erlbaum.

Bransford, J. D., Derry, S., Berliner, D., & Hammerness, K. (2005). Theories of learning and their roles in teaching. In L. Darling-Hammond & J. Bransford (Eds.). *Preparing teachers for a changing world: What teachers should learn and be able to do* (pp. 40-87). San Francisco, CA: Jossey-Bass.

Bransford, J. D., & Schwartz, D. L. (1999). Rethinking transfer: A simple proposal with multiple implications. In A. Iran-Nejad & P. D. Pearson (Eds.). *Review of research in education.* (Vol. 24, pp. 61-100). Washington, DC: American Educational Research Association.

Broaddus, K., & Bloodgood, J. (1999). "We're supposed to already know how to teach reading": Teacher change to support struggling readers. *Reading Research Quarterly, 34,* 426-451.

Carr, K. C. (2003). Today's reading clinic: How relevant is the graduate reading practicum? *The Reading Teacher, 57,* 256-268.

Clay, M. M. (1991). *Becoming literate: The construction of inner control.* Portsmouth, NH: Heinemann.

Clay, M. M. (1998). *By different paths to common outcomes.* York, ME: Stenhouse.

Clay, M. M. (2001). *Change Over Time: In Children's Literacy Development.* Portsmouth, NH: Heinemann.

Darling-Hammond, L. (2006). Constructing 21st-century teacher education. *Journal of Teacher Education, 57,* 300-314.

Deeney, T. (2009). *Improving literacy instruction with classroom research.* Thousand Oaks, CA: Corwin Press.

Deeney, T., Dozier, C., Laster, B., Angell, V., Barnes, C., Carter, C., Cobb, J., Hill, M., McAndrews, S., McEnery, L., Sargent, S., Walker, B., & Freppon, P. (2005, December). *A national look at teacher preparation in reading clinics/literacy labs.* Alternative session presented at the 55th annual meeting of the National Reading Conference, Miami, FL.

Deeney, T., Dozier, C., Laster, B., Applegate, M., Cobb, J., Dubert, L., Eeg, M., Gaunty-Porter, D., Gurvitz, D., McAndrews, S., Milby, T., Morewood, A., Ryan, T., Sargent, S., Swanson, M. (2010, December). *Transfer and transformation: What reading clinic/literacy lab graduates' current practices and contexts mean for clinic/lab instruction.* Alternative session presented at the 60th annual meeting of the Literacy Research Association (formerly National Reading Conference), Fort Worth, TX.

Dozier, C., Johnston, P., & Rogers, R. (2006). *Critical literacy/critical teaching: Tools for preparing responsive teachers.* New York, NY: Teachers College Press.

Dozier, C. , & Rutten, I. (2005/2006). Responsive teaching toward responsive teachers: Mediating transfer though intentionality, enactment, and articulation. *Journal of Literacy Research, 37,* 459-492.

Duncan, A. (2009, October). Lecture presented at Teachers College, Columbia University. Retrieved from http://www.tc.columbia.edu/news/article.htm?id=7192.

Fairbanks, C., Duffy, G., Faircloth, B. He, Y., Levin, B., Rohr, J., & Stein, C. (2010). Beyond knowledge: Exploring why some teachers are more thoughtfully adaptive than others. *Journal of Teacher Education, 61,* 161-171.

Freppon, P., Deeney, T., Dozier, C., Laster, B., Barnes, C., Cobb, J., Dubert, L., Gaunty-Porter, D., Gurvitz, D., McAndrews, S., McEnery, L., Morewood, A., Patchen, C., Sargent, S., (2007, December). From clinic to mandates: The praxis of teaching reading after reading clinic literacy lab. Alternative session presented at the 57th annual meeting of the National Reading Conference, Austin, TX.

Gavelek, J., & Raphael, T. (1996). Changing talk about text: New roles for teachers and students. *Language Arts, 73,* 182-192.

Glaser, B. G., & Strauss, A. L. (1967). *The discovery of grounded theory.* Chicago, IL: Aldine.

Goldenberg, C. (2004). *Successful school change: Creating settings to improve teaching and learning.* New York, NY: Teachers College Press.

Hoffman, J. V., & Pearson, P. D. (2000). Reading teacher education in the next millennium: What your grandmother's teacher didn't know that your granddaughter's teacher should. *Reading Research Quarterly, 35,* 28-44.

International Reading Association. (2009). *Standards for the Assessment of Reading and Writing* (revised). Retrieved from: http://www.reading.org/General/CurrentResearch/Standards/AssessmentStandards.aspx

Johnston, P. H. (1997). *Knowing literacy: Constructive literacy assessment.* York, ME: Stenhouse.

Johnston, P. H. (2004). *Choice words: How our language affects children's learning.* York, ME: Stenhouse.

Laster, B. (1996). From white elephant to cutting edge: The transformation of the reading clinic. In D. Leu, C. Kinzer, & K. Hinchman (Eds.), *Literacies for the 21st century: Research and practice. 45th Yearbook of the National Reading Conference*(pp. 408-419). Chicago, IL:National Reading Conference.

Lave, J., & Wenger, E. (1991). *Situated learning: Legitimate peripheral participation.* New York, NY: Cambridge University Press.

Lincoln, Y., & Guba, E. (1985). *Naturalistic inquiry.* Newbury Park, CA: Sage.

Many, J. (2001). *Handbook of instructional practices for literacy teacher-educators: Examples and reflections from the teaching lives of literacy scholars.* Mahwah, NJ: Erlbaum.

Mercer, N., & Littleton, K. (2007). *Dialogue and the development of children's thinking: A sociocultural approach.* London, England: Routledge.

Merriam, S. (1998). *Qualitative research and case study applications in education.* San Francisco, CA: Jossey-Bass.

Mezirow, J. (2000). Learning to think like an adult: Core concepts of Transformation Theory. In J. Mezirow & Associates (Eds.), *Learning as transformation* (pp. 3-34). San Francisco, CA: Jossey-Bass.

Miles, M., & Huberman, A. (1994). *Qualitative data analysis.* Thousand Oaks, CA: Sage.

National Council for Accreditation of Teacher Education (2010). *Transforming teacher education through clinical practice: A national Strategy to prepare effective teachers.* Washington, DC: National Council for the Accreditation of Teacher Education.

Nieto, S. (2000). *Affirming diversity: The sociopolitical context of multicultural Education* (3rd ed.). New York, NY: Longman.

Perkins, D., & Salomon, G. (1992). Transfer of learning. In *International Encyclopedia of Education* (2nd ed.). Oxford, England: Pergamon Press. Retrieved from http://learnweb.harvard.edu/alps/thinking/docs/traencyn.htm

Risko, V., Roller, C., Bean, R., Collins Block, C., Anders, P., & Flood, J. (2008). A critical analysis of research on reading teacher education. *Reading Research Quarterly, 43,* 252-288.

Shulman, L. (1986). Those who understand: Knowledge growth in teaching. *Educational Researcher, 15,* 4-14.

Strauss, A., & Corbin, J. (1990). *The basics of qualitative research: Grounded theory procedures and techniques.* Newbury Park, CA: Sage.

Tharp, R., & Gallimore, R. (1988). *Rousing minds to life: Teaching, learning, and schooling in social context.* West Nyack, NY: Cambridge University Press.

Williams, T. L., & Baumann, J. F. (2008). Forty years of research on effective literacy teachers: From the process-product studies of the 1970s to contemporary explorations of classroom literacy instruction. In Y. Kim, V. Risko, D. Compton, D. Dickinson, M. Hundley, R. Jiménez, K. Leander, & D. W. Rowe (Eds.). *57th Yearbook of the National Reading Conference* (pp. 357-372). Oak Creek, WI: National Reading Conference.

Windschitl, M. (2002). Framing constructivism in practice as the negotiation of dilemmas: An analysis of the conceptual, pedagogical, cultural, and political challenges facing teachers. *Review of Educational Research, 72,* 131–175.

Vygotsky, L. S. (1978). *Mind in society: The development of higher psychological processes.* Cambridge, MA: Harvard University Press.

Zeichner, K. (2006). Reflections of a university-based teacher educator on the future of college and university-based teacher education. *Journal of Teacher Education, 57,* 326-340.

Zeichner, K. & Liston, D. (1996). *Reflective teaching.* Mahwah, NJ: Erlbaum.

APPENDIX

Sample Questions from Participant Interview Protocols

Sample Screening Interview Questions

1. Talk about any changes to your practice since you participated in clinic.

2. Talk about any ways you have transferred clinic ideas, strategies, practices, materials, or processes to your classroom or school context.

Sample In-Depth Interview Questions

1. Talk about your current position. What roles and responsibilities do you have?

2. Talk about literacy instructional practices you use *in your classroom* (if classroom teacher or reading specialist)/*in your school* (if literacy coach).

3. Discuss any ways in which your clinic experience influenced how you currently approach your own instructional practices, curriculum development, and curriculum implementation.

4. Describe assessments used in your classroom/school and how you use assessment results.

5. Talk about your role(s) in assessment at your school. Think about selection, implementation, administration, analysis, and/or professional development.

6. Discuss any ways in which your clinic experience influenced how you currently approach assessment in your classroom/school/district.

7. Talk about coaching or leadership roles you have.

8. Discuss any initiatives or changes you have brought up with teachers or administrators within your school.

9. Talk about any specific ways your clinic/lab experience helped you become a literacy leader.

(Re)conceptualizing Content Area Literacy: Encouraging Pre-Service and In-Service Teachers to Explore Interdisciplinary Instruction

Charlotte Frambaugh-Kritzer
University of Hawaii

Elizabeth Petroelje Stolle
Grand Valley State University

"When planned effectively, the possibilities are endless. I really think it [interdisciplinary instruction] gives students the opportunity to get involved in their literacy learning and make connections not only across curriculum but to life outside of school . . ." (Middle School Teacher).

This study sought to investigate how pre- and in-service teachers responded when we introduced interdisciplinary unit planning in our respective university content area literacy methods courses. Two essential notions from the content area and adolescent literacy research inspired us in this endeavor. First, Morse (2008) asserts that literacy strategies need to be taught in meaningful ways across the disciplines in our secondary schools. Second, adolescents deserve and need engaging, high-interest, critical, authentic and inter-textual curriculum coupled with multiple literacy opportunities (Moore, Bean, Birdyshaw, & Rycik, 1999). As teacher educators in secondary literacy education, we concur with these notions and think one solution to achieve this goal is the implementation of interdisciplinary unit planning in secondary education (Daniels & Zemelman, 2004).

Interdisciplinary instruction is not a new idea. While it gained considerable popularity in the 1990s, it has been implemented in the education system since the early 1900s (Weinberg & Harding, 2004). Interdisciplinary instruction allows holistic study of a given concept while providing students with authentic learning situations similar to those outside of school (Barton & Smith, 2000). However, the *No Child Left Behind* policy changed the demands of teaching—emphasizing accountability. Consequently, teachers started teaching to the test, diminishing the use of interdisciplinary instruction and leaving the curriculum segmented, isolated (Garan, 2004; Goodman, 2006; Graves, 2002), and fact-focused (Erickson, 2008). Conversely, interdisciplinary units offer a deeper concept-based curriculum that allows teachers to shift their own thinking that content serves not as an end product but as a tool to lead students to richer and more critical thinking (Erickson, 2008). While researchers continue to explore innovative ways to use and promote content area literacy (Townsend, 2009; Alvermann, Phelps, & Gillis, 2010; Lloyd, 2004; Allen, 2000), and reference interdisciplinary instruction as a topic within content area literacy (Alvermann, Phelps, & Gillis, 2010; Roe, Stoodt-Hill, & Burns, 2007), few are specifically exploring this notion of interdisciplinary units as a way to (re)conceptualize content area literacy in the present.

Traditionally, content area literacy calls educators to provide instructional support for adolescents as they interact with academic texts and disciplinary content (Alvermann et al., 2010; Santa, 2006; Vacca & Vacca, 2002). This instructional support most often materializes in the form of generalized literacy strategies. Despite efforts to teach secondary teachers how to implement content area literacy in the classroom, researchers have noted secondary teachers' resistance to taking up and engaging students in literacy within the content classroom and their disregard for these literacy strategies (O'Brien & Stewart, 1990; O'Brien, Stewart, & Moje, 1995). Based on these acts of resistance, some are exploring alternative approaches to teaching secondary teachers how to use content area literacy with students, which move from a transmissive model to a more transactional approach (Conley, Kerner, & Reynolds, 2005; Daniels & Zemelman, 2004; Morse, 2008). Others are (re)imagining content area literacy by encouraging content area teachers and literacy specialists to work in collaboration (Draper, 2010). Still others are working to (re)conceptualize content area literacy to include the larger context in which strategies are taken up and practiced, specifically thinking about disciplinary literacy instruction (Moje, 2008). That is, "literacy . . . becomes an essential aspect of disciplinary practice, rather than a set of strategies or tools brought in to the disciplines to improve reading and writing of subject-matter texts" (Moje, 2008, p. 99).

We applaud those in the field examining and rethinking how to best integrate literacy instruction and strategies in the content areas. Yet, as we consider those who have been exploring and (re)conceptualizing content area literacy over the past two decades, we offer an additional way to impact adolescent literacy learning within the content area. That is, we take up interdisciplinary instruction as the backdrop by which we engage teachers in learning about content area literacy. Interdisciplinary instruction, a valued practice that can improve student engagement, can increase teacher morale, and can raise achievement levels (Fitzharris, 2005; Kerekes, 1987; Strubbe, 1990), becomes the context in which teachers grapple, explore, challenge, question, grow in, and take up literacy as it pertains to their content area, as well as the content areas of their colleagues. In this new context, content area literacy is (re)conceptualized from a self-centered approach, looking within one's own discipline, to a holistic approach where all disciplines now recognize the literacy needs and requirements within and across the disciplines.

THEORETICAL FRAMEWORK

The theoretical framework that guided this study draws on the social aspects of learning and literacy, specifically pulling from Vygotsky (1978) and Street (1984, 2005). First, social constructivism notes that learning occurs in a sociocultural environment and learners are "active constructors of their own learning" (Mitchell & Myles, 1988, p. 162). That is, learning occurs through dialogue (Vygotsky, 1978). We learn not as isolated individuals, but as active members of society who engage in dialogue. Through dialogue, learners interact with knowledge sources in social settings as well as take an active part in reconstructing knowledge within their own minds. These notions concerning the social aspects of learning lend themselves to the nature of planning for interdisciplinary instruction, which provide teachers the opportunity to explore curriculum and learning through dialogue with colleagues.

Additionally, we looked to Street's (1984, 2005) notions that literacy is a social practice. Based on this understanding, literacy does not hold transparent, static meanings, but rather meaning is fluid and dependent on the reader's use of a given literacy for a specified purpose within a specific environment (Alvermann, Moon, & Hagood, 1999; Hagood, 2003). This concept does not simply address how literacy impacts individuals, but rather how individuals take up and use literacy. Therefore, we organized our study in such a way that the pre- and in-service teachers were encouraged to interact with ideas/knowledge in social settings, as well as reconstruct ideas/knowledge in their own minds for their unique purposes.

RESEARCH METHODS

Within this qualitative self-study, we sought to answer the following questions: (1) How do pre- and in-service teachers respond to interdisciplinary instruction?, (2) How does interdisciplinary unit planning help pre- and in-service teachers understand content area literacy?, and (3) How do we as literacy teacher educators impact the teachers' understandings about interdisciplinary instruction and content area literacy? However, for the purposes of this paper, we limit our discussion to examining the second question pertaining to teaching content area literacy through the use of interdisciplinary instruction.

Context

Forty-five participants, both male and female, from two universities voluntarily participated in this study. At one university, situated in the southwestern region of the U.S., we collected data from pre-service teachers taking an undergraduate-level content area literacy methods course. At the other university, situated in the midwestern region of the U.S., we collected data from in-service teachers taking a graduate-level reading course on adolescent literacy. At each location, the participants were placed into teams to plan an interdisciplinary unit for secondary students, which highlighted the literacy practices and strategies inherent in the learning.

As we share this study, we recognize each classroom established its own unique cultural practices and that each author took up the role of instructor/researcher in her own unique way (Fang, Fu, & Lamme, 1999). Although we shared some common materials for presenting and teaching interdisciplinary instruction (e.g., the same interdisciplinary unit plan directions, the same course text, the same PowerPoints, and the same unit examples), and our syllabi reflected similar timelines and instructional time, the students' background knowledge, expertise, needs, and desires influenced our instruction in powerful ways, thus eliminating the possibility for equal dissemination of content or symmetrical learning experiences.

The first course (taught by first author), Content Area Literacy, was taught to pre-service teachers seeking a teaching certification in Secondary Education. The content areas represented during the data collection included English, History, Social Studies, Math, Science, Art, and Dance. The second course (taught by second author), Developmental Adolescent Literacy, was taught to secondary in-service teachers (those currently teaching in a classroom) working toward a master's degree in Secondary Reading or Secondary Education and addressed the literacy needs of adolescents within the content areas. The content areas represented during data collection included English, Foreign Language, Math, Science, Social Studies, and Physical Education. Additionally, the in-service teachers' teaching assignments included sixth through twelfth grade, professional experiences varying from 1 to 19 years, and schools that were rural and urban, private and public, and high-achieving and low-achieving (as evidenced by test scores compared to state and national averages).

Within each course, we introduced interdisciplinary instruction at the beginning of the semester through the reading of the first chapter in Daniel and Zemelman's text, *Subject Matters* (2004), yet allowed students to struggle through their definitions of literacy and content area literacy for the first 3-4 weeks. Drawing on Street's (1984, 2005) work of the autonomous versus ideological model of literacy, the students' struggle allowed them to problematize traditional notions of literacy. Around the fifth week of the semester, we reintroduced interdisciplinary instruction through additional readings and direct instruction of the process. Students were then divided into interdisciplinary teams, each team having at least three different content areas represented. For the remainder of the semester, literacy practices, strategies, and instruction were taught within the context of the interdisciplinary units. That is, as we taught critical literacy, writing across the curriculum, or vocabulary learning, all topics and concepts were embedded in the interdisciplinary teams and considered and applied within the frame. With this learning, each team collaborated to create an interdisciplinary unit that highlighted the literacy practices and strategies inherent in each discipline, while organizing these practices and strategies around a common understanding. At the end of the semester, each group shared the interdisciplinary unit with the class and each student reflected on these units.

DATA COLLECTION AND ANALYSIS

In collecting our data, we had five data sources. First, we conducted systematic observations (Werner & Schoepfle, 1987), which progressed through three types of observations—descriptive, focused, and selective—to gain a complete picture of the setting. During descriptive observations, we took the stance that we knew nothing; therefore, we noted everything. As the data collection grew, we shifted to the second type of observation, focused observation. Here, we ignored irrelevant items and focused our observations on specific types of activities—those associated with interdisciplinary instruction and content area literacy. Finally, we conducted selective observations, thus concentrating on certain attributes of the various activities such as student attitudes, student understandings, and student resistance. Due to our roles as instructors, we recorded our observations immediately following each class period.

Next, we collected artifacts and class assignments from the pre- and in-service teachers. Examples include reading responses related to class readings and student reflections and evaluations of the interdisciplinary instruction assignment. Next, we collected e-mail correspondences (Tao & Reinking, 1996) in which we engaged with students, specifically collecting those related to the topic of content area literacy and interdisciplinary instruction. We also conducted an anonymous survey with the pre- and in-service teachers on the last day of class before the unit presentations. The survey specifically asked questions about the teachers' perceptions of interdisciplinary instruction as a pedagogical tool. Finally, we both kept a researcher's journal throughout the research project (Richardson, 2000). In our journals we wrote memos to: (1) record the concrete details of what we saw and heard while we were in the classroom; (2) articulate the data collection process; (3) connect what we were seeing and hearing with what we were reading professionally and wondering; (4) push ourselves to use multiple perspectives to navigate, shift, relocate, and renegotiate our thinking and analysis; and (5) record the raw feelings and emotions we experienced as researchers.

For the purposes of this paper we focused our analysis on the data pertaining to the second research question linked to content area literacy: How does interdisciplinary unit planning help preservice and in-service teachers understand content area literacy? To answer this question, we drew from various interpretive methods. First, we followed Strauss's (1995) three-step analysis using the process of open coding, axial coding, and selective coding. We started with the open coding process. This open coding process was unrestricted, and we carefully read the words to note the similarities and contradictions (Miles & Huberman, 1994). In doing so, we started to notice that many of the pre- and in-service teachers responded to interdisciplinary unit planning as it relates to their understanding of content area literacy using similar language and phrases. These phrases became specific codes (Strauss, 1995), which we used to assign units of meaning to each piece of data (Miles & Huberman, 1994). For example, many of the teachers described interdisciplinary units as *cohesive, empowering,* and *connected to real life issues.* Then we employed axial coding (Strauss, 1995) techniques to assign conceptual categories. In short, we clustered the open codes around an "axis" or point of intersection (p. 32). For example, these units described as *empowering and meaningful* then fit under the axial code of *benefits of interdisciplinary instruction and content area literacy.* Finally, we used the "selective coding" process (Strauss, 1995, p. 34) to systematically decide how the categories relate to each other and what stories they tell. Then, we linked these stories to the theoretical framework, thus coming up with our initial categories.

After we identified our categories, we compared and contrasted our findings as we wrote, which allowed us to analyze the data working from Richardson's (2000) validity metaphor of crystallization. That is, the interplay between the data sources from two different research sites allowed us to see the themes, ideas, and categories in complex ways. Taking up Richardson's (2000) writing as a method of inquiry and Erickson's (1986) data analysis method, we wrote about the themes that emerged, continuously scrutinizing what we saw and looking for supporting and disconfirming data while weighting the themes for relevance. In this way we used writing as a "way of knowing," discovering "new aspects of our topic and our relationship to it" (Richardson, 2000, p. 923).

FINDINGS

For the purposes of this paper, we would like to share three significant themes that emerged from the data: appreciation learning, conversational learning, and resistance learning.

Appreciation Learning

Throughout the data, we noted that transparency developed as the teachers started looking into each other's disciplines and understanding the literate practices within each discipline. In doing this, content area literacy was no longer *just about me* with a self-centered focus. Instead, the pre- and in-service teachers saw literacy as everyone's business. For example, one English pre-service teacher wrote, "literacy applies to all subject areas—not just my own." A science pre-service teacher also wrote, "Teaching literacy to students and even helping to deepen their love for literacy is the job of all teachers, not just the English teachers." Additionally, an in-service physical education teacher shared, "The scope and range of reading and literacy are so much larger than I imagined. By understanding the many ways we use reading in our classrooms as teachers, we can use these to actively engage students in meaningful ways." In these statements we see the teachers' understandings of literacy going beyond their own content area, thus extending into the other disciplines. In this way, the teachers learned a new appreciation for the various disciplines as they came to understand how literacy was important to all disciplines.

Daniel Pink (2006) posits that students need to be symphonic thinkers. In short, a symphonic thinker is someone who considers the entire orchestra rather than a single instrument. In our study, pre-service and in-service teachers were challenged to think in less conventional methods, to work in interdisciplinary ways, and to be symphonic thinkers who created themes that united their disciplines and provided inter-textual connections for adolescents. The data reveals that the teachers did think in symphonic ways, taking up the belief that interdisciplinary instruction is beneficial for adolescent learners because of its cohesive nature. That is, the teachers appreciated that these units make learning for adolescents more interconnected—not compartmentalized (Morse, 2008). One in-service social studies teacher shared:

> As we worked through our interdisciplinary unit I saw how important it was to have all teachers working as a team towards big concepts and understandings . . . Interdisciplinary units keep the focus on one particular topic and shows how all the subjects can be connected with it. This is like real life. Math, for example, is not a separate subject, but when combined with history and/or science it is more relevant for the student.

In this statement, this teacher notes that when working from an interdisciplinary approach, learning is more meaningful because the connections make all disciplines valuable. He demonstrates symphonic thinking, moving from a self-centered, silo approach to literacy and instruction to an interconnected approach that sees the whole picture. Another in-service social studies teacher echoes this idea, saying, "Most of the time teachers become immersed in their subject area and have little idea what other content area teachers are teaching." Through the interdisciplinary unit planning, the teachers became well versed in each other's disciplines, thus coming to appreciate the literate practices necessary for student success. A math in-service teacher continues in this vein saying, "The experience was beneficial to me primarily in that I can better understand the teaming process of my fellow staff members." In other words, disciplines outside of math became more transparent through the process, opening her eyes to the needs of the other disciplines.

Conversational Learning

As literacy educators, we gave the teachers space to socially construct their knowledge of content area literacy and interdisciplinary instruction through dialogue (Street, 1984, 2005; Vygotsky, 1978). That is, the pre- and in-service teachers rehearsed the conversations around content area literacy through the interdisciplinary unit planning. Our goal was not necessarily about the perfect unit plan, but rather engaging the teachers in conversation and thinking about the possibilities.

One pre-service social studies teacher explained:

> Being able to work together and create our own interdisciplinary unit and present it in class was priceless . . . (Sharing) comments about other groups on-line was valuable in thinking of other variations and ideas about how interdisciplinary units could be used.

Another in-service foreign language teacher echoes this, saying:

> Despite the fact that my teaching experience does not lend itself to this kind of teaching with a team, I now have a shared experience with teams who have tried it and resources for those who might want to give it a try. Thinking through an IDU (interdisciplinary unit) from its beginning to the end was a good experience.

These teachers' reflections highlight this notion of rehearsal; the benefit is seen in the rehearsal. As the foreign language teacher articulates, although she can't currently apply interdisciplinary instruction within the classroom, she values the shared experience, the engagement in dialogue, and the potential she now holds. With that, we note Vygotsky's (1978) notions of dialogue, and recognize how the social aspects of learning within the interdisciplinary unit planning teams moved the teachers to think in more complex ways.

For many of the pre-service teachers, this was not only their first opportunity to create interdisciplinary units, but also their first exposure to the idea. In this context, many of the pre-service teachers noted that they attended traditional middle and high schools where they never experienced this kind of curriculum. While the prospect of interdisciplinary teaching was exciting for many, it was also difficult for some to imagine when they never experienced it first hand. However, by working in interdisciplinary teams, they began to see they are not alone in creating important curriculum that adolescents deserve. In the words of one science pre-service teacher, "I think this unit plan is a combination of everything we have learned this semester. We have integrated not only all the literacy practices, but now all the content areas can execute this in one cohesive unit of study." This notion represents the social learning theories we employ as literacy educators, helping teachers of various backgrounds to collaborate around meaningful instruction. We believe that curriculum development should be a shared experience between students and teachers and not prescribed by textbook companies. Indeed, the pre-service teachers appreciated this freedom, as they were encouraged to think outside the box and beyond the textbook.

Additionally, the rehearsals in conversation also highlighted the teachers' approximations and reflections. For example, one history pre-service teacher reflected, "I am proud of our team's plan…we never resorted to worksheets, multiple choice tests or the textbook in our unit plan." Yet, this same student recognized that if he were to teach this unit some day, he would like to make refinements and commented, "I noticed that I resort to the jigsaw strategy a lot; I need to be less dependent on jigsaw in this unit plan." This is a reminder that the pre-service teachers are novices teaching the literacy practices within their discipline. In that, they are trying new strategies and, at times, over relying on familiar ones. Through dialogue, the teachers could reflect on their learning and pedagogical decisions, thus refining their approximations and gaining confidence in what is best for students.

Resistance Learning

This study was not exempt from participant resistance. That is, a number of pre-and in-service teachers shared some apprehension and skepticism regarding interdisciplinary instruction and content area literacy. However, in our analysis of this resistance, we see that the teachers in our study did not necessarily resist on a conceptual level (they all see the benefits); however, their resistance comes from an imposed resistance they sense from the structures and individuals within schools. For example, one in-service science teacher spoke about the colleagues with whom he works, saying:

> We have a few of these (teachers who are unable to see how literacy is important to their discipline) . . . Teaching with colleagues across a theme is awesome, but restrictions on time and resources cause a lot of problems that people would rather avoid (interdisciplinary instruction). It's easier to just do things yourself.

This teacher's thoughts represent many of the teachers in our study who felt limited in their ability to implement interdisciplinary instruction and infuse literacy practices within their discipline due to these outside forces of resistance.

One reason this resistance seems legitimate to the teachers in our study is due to constraints seen in secondary schools. The teachers asked critical questions regarding the implementation of interdisciplinary instruction and the practical need for literacy in the content. For example, one pre-service teacher asked, "When will we really get a chance to implement these units in schools—especially when so many middle and high school teachers do not share students in common?" Moreover, the teachers reported that they rarely see this type of curriculum instruction in middle and high schools, thus leaving them without effective models/inspirations. Still, the teachers are hopeful to implement these units in classrooms someday. In fact, every in-service teacher within the study commented in some form that they would like to use interdisciplinary instruction and teach the literacy practices within their discipline. With that, all of the in-service teachers could readily take up the instruction of literacy practices. However, only three of these teachers saw immediate opportunities for interdisciplinary instruction. The others felt inhibited by the resistance of colleagues and schedules.

Another interesting intersection of resistance was some teachers' limited knowledge of interdisciplinary instruction and content area literacy. That is, many of the teachers were not schooled within this paradigm, so it was difficult to think in this manner. For example, one pre-service teacher wrote, "The interdisciplinary unit was by far the most challenging for me: academically as well as personally." Adding to that, one in-service physical education teacher shared, "I had little understanding of how to put it all together in a structured manner. Before this project I thought of interdisciplinary teaching as each teacher doing his or her own part." This teacher goes on to share his thinking on literacy, saying:

> When I started this class I imagined myself actually teaching students how to read a book . . . I learned that reading is really about thinking and comprehending words, ideas, and thoughts . . . the scope and range of reading and literacy are so much larger than I imagined . . . there are so many ways in which we utilize literacy in the classroom.

Through team collaboration and dialogue, the teachers came to understand interdisciplinary instruction and content area literacy in new and complex ways, despite their misgivings or notions of resistance.

DISCUSSION

These three themes highlight the complex issues faced by secondary pre-service and in-service teachers as they think about and use interdisciplinary instruction to enhance learning within the frame of content area literacy. The findings provide key insights into how we can encourage interdisciplinary instruction as we push forward in (re)conceptualizing content area literacy.

Using interdisciplinary instruction in the university classroom to teach content area literacy challenges teachers to think in less conventional ways. As we stated earlier, most of our participants had experienced fairly traditional schooling in their own journeys, so the introduction to interdisciplinary planning met some resistance. This did not surprise us due to the traditional, linear-designed curriculum that is pervasive in many schools today, and the resistance to literacy within the content classroom documented in the literature (O'Brien & Stewart, 1990; O'Brien, Stewart, & Moje, 1995). However, intersdiciplinary instruction coupled with content area literacy offers a deeper concept-based curriculum that allows teachers to shift their own thinking to see content as a means for leading students to richer and more critical thinking (Erickson, 2008), while understanding the role literacy plays in that leading.

As seen in one pre-service teacher's testimony regarding the academic and personal challenges encountered in planning interdisciplinary instruction, for some teachers this is difficult work. Kucer, Silva, and Delgado-Larocco (1995) caution that if assumptions from the traditional curriculum are appropriated and repackaged to an interdisciplinary framework, tensions will arise for teachers and students. This is why Duerr (2008) asserts, "…interdisciplinary units cannot be delivered off the cuff. They require careful planning and review of grade-level standards, learner characteristics, and teacher objectives" (p. 179). Within our courses, the pre- and in-service teachers were given the time and resources to do the challenging work of planning for interdisciplinary instruction. With that, we encouraged the teachers to carefully think beyond traditional notions of content instruction. We built on Duerr's assertions, believing teachers need to understand the strong connections between literacy and content area instruction so meaningful learning can occur within the classroom. Using interdisciplinary instruction while teaching content area literacy provided a space for teachers to recognize and make sense of these connections.

Specifically, interdisciplinary instruction provides an opportunity for teachers to be symphonic thinkers (Pink, 2006). A symphonic thinker views learning as a social construct. That is, learning takes place in a sociocultural environment (Au, 1997) where teachers are members of a school community in pursuit of the same goals. This symphonic thinking emerged as the teachers communicated about literacy learning. Through dialogue the teachers gained several new understandings about literacy learning, thus highlighting the benefits of learning and working in teams. Crow and Pounder (2000) found that teachers working in teams show "internal work motivation, growth satisfaction, general job satisfaction, work efficacy, and professional commitment" (p. 225). That is, when teachers engage in social learning situations, they feel empowered. This is critical today when content is often segmented and learned in isolation, leaving teachers disempowered by a curriculum that dictates what is taught and disengaged students who experience confusion as they jump class-to-class, isolated skill to isolated skill (Kucer, Silva, & Delgado-Larocco, 1995). When this segmented curriculum occurs, Kucer, Silva, and Delgado-Larocco (1995) argue, "Lost is literacy as a powerful cultural tool for mediation and learning" (p. 3). However, interdisciplinary instruction allows teachers time to converse, making great gains in seeing how literacy is the business of all content areas and important to student learning.

As we consider the participants in our study, and the learning that occurred, we are encouraged and excited. However, we do recognize the unique characteristics of both types of participants— pre- and in-service teachers. In our data analysis, we uncovered the same themes from both the pre-service teachers and the in-service teachers. Still, we note a specific variation evident in the teachers' learning connected to the collaborative nature of the class and the assignment of creating interdisciplinary units that incorporate literacy practices within the content areas. That is, as we drew on Vygotsky's (1978) notions of learning through dialogue, providing space for teachers to learn from each other within our university classrooms, background knowledge impacted how students collaborated and learned from each other.

Background knowledge, which relates to the "mental resources that enable us to make sense" of what is going on around us (Smith, 2004, p. 13), varied from the pre-service to the in-service teachers. As noted, many of the pre-service teachers found it difficult to conceptualize interdisciplinary instruction and/or content area literacy based on their limited exposure to both within the school setting. As would be expected, their limited background knowledge both in interdisciplinary unit planning and disciplinary knowledge restricted their ability to conceptualize the potential of interdisciplinary instruction along with content area literacy on student learning. Still, the pre-service teachers put in the thought and effort, eventually creating effective interdisciplinary units that incorporated literacy practices to assist in the content learning, thus fulfilling the course requirements.

Unlike the pre-service teachers, the in-service teachers' background knowledge of interdisciplinary instruction, deeper discipline knowledge and content area literacy varied from an advanced understanding to a naive understanding. That is, eight of the in-service teachers were well versed in incorporating literacy into content learning while three of the in-service teachers had direct experience teaching within an interdisciplinary frame. Therefore, these particular in-service teachers were able to offer practical insights and first-hand experiences, thus assisting their team members with limited exposure to the concepts of interdisciplinary instruction and content area literacy. We find this difference in background knowledge significant. Through dialogue with a more knowledgeable other, the in-service teachers with limited background knowledge were able to grow in their understandings. However, in the undergraduate-level course, the knowledgeable other was the instructor (first author). In contrast, in the graduate-level course, there were multiple knowledgeable others—both the instructor (second author) and the other in-service teachers within the class. This difference impacted the social learning environment. Even still, we observed both types of participants—pre-service teachers and in-service teachers—work in teams to create innovative units incorporating literacy in effective ways. Collaboration proved powerful and meaningful within our university classrooms, but as noted, we saw it work in different ways between the pre- and in-service teachers.

CONCLUSIONS

Based on our findings, we believe interdisciplinary instruction has the potential to (re) conceptualize content area literacy instruction for pre-and in-service teachers. However, we acknowledge that our work only studies teacher learning in these two university courses. Although our findings are encouraging, we cannot fully assume they translate into improved classroom instruction. That is, following the teachers into their teaching assignments and observing their classroom instruction would benefit our work, thus noting if this coursework focused on interdisciplinary instruction within the content areas actually influences the work of the teachers and the learning of students. With this in mind, we see important research yet to be conducted.

Although all curriculum programs have positive aspects and drawbacks, we believe teacher educators can lead and guide pre-and in-service teachers toward new understandings and paradigms as we seek to evolve and reform secondary curriculum. In the end, even if the participants in our study do not implement the actual unit plans developed in our courses, we trust the hallmarks and thinking behind this learning experience provide individual teachers the best road map to design future unit plans in their own individual classrooms.

REFERENCES

Allen, J. (2000). *Yellow brick roads: Shared and guided paths to independent reading 4-12.* Portland, ME: Stenhouse.

Alvermann, D. E., Moon, J. S., & Hagood, M. C. (1999). *Popular culture in the classroom: Teaching and researching critical media literacy.* Newark, DE: International Reading Association.

Alvermann, D. E., Phelps, S. F., & Gillis, V. R. (2010). *Content reading and literacy: Succeeding in today's diverse classrooms* (6th ed.). Boston, MA: Allyn & Bacon.

Au, K. H. (1997). A sociocultural model of reading instruction: The Kamehameha Elementary Education Program. In S. A. Stahl & D. A. Hayes (Eds.), *Instructional models in reading* (pp. 181-202). Hillsdale, NJ: Erlbaum.

Barton, K. C., & Smith, L. A. (2000). "Themes or motifs? Aiming for coherence through interdisciplinary outlines." *The Reading Teacher, 55*, 54-63.

Conley, M. W., Kerner, M., & Reynolds, J. M. (2005). Not a question of "should," but a question of "how": Integrating literacy knowledge and practice into secondary teacher preparation through tutoring in urban middle schools. *Action in Teacher Education, 27*(2), 22-32.

Crow, G. M., & Pounder, D. G. (2000). Interdisciplinary Teams: Context, Design and Process. *Educational Administration Quarterly, 36*(2), 216-254.

Daniels, H., & Zemelman, S. (2004). *Subjects matter: Every teacher's guide to content area reading.* Portsmouth, NH: Heinemann.

Draper, R. J. (2010). *(Re)Imagining content-area literacy instruction.* New York, NY: Teachers College Press.

Duerr, L. (2008). Interdisciplinary instruction. *Educational Horizons, 86*, 173-180.

Erickson, F. (1986). Qualitative methods in research on teaching. In M. Wittrock, (Ed.), *Handbook of Research on Teaching* (3rd ed., pp. 119-161). New York, NY: Macmillan.

Erickson, H. L. (2008). *Stirring the head, heart and soul: Redefining curriculum, instruction, and concept-based learning.* Thousand Oaks, CA: Corwin Press.

Fang, Z., Fu, D., & Lamme, L. L. (1999). Rethinking the role of multicultural literature in literacy instruction: Problems, paradox, and possibilities. *The New Advocate, 12*, 259-276.

Fitzharris, L. (2005). Making all the right connections: Curriculum design helps teachers see the bigger picture that students experience, then see the logical connections. *Journal of Staff Development, 26*(1), 24-28.

Garan, E. (2004). *In defense of our children: When politics, profit, and education collide.* Portsmouth, NH: Heinemann.

Graves, D. (2002). *Testing is not teaching.* Portsmouth, NH: Heinemann.

Goodman, K. (2006). *The truth about DIBELS: What it is and what it does.* Portsmouth, NH: Heinemann.

Hagood, M. (2003). New media and online literacies: No age left behind. *Reading Research Quarterly, 38,* 387-391.

Kerekes, J. (1987). The interdisciplinary unit: It's here to stay! *Middle School Journal, 19*(4), 12-14.

Kucer, S. B., Silva, C., & Delgado-Larocco, E. (1995). *Curricularconversations: Themes in multilingual and monolingual classrooms.* York, MA: Stenhouse Publishers.

Lloyd, S. (2004). Using comprehension strategies as a springboard for student talk. *Journal of Adolescent and Adult Literacy, 48*(2), 114–124.

Moore, D., Bean, T., Birdyshaw, D., & Rycik, J. (1999). Adolescent literacy: A position statement. *Journal of Adolescent and Adult Literacy, 43*(1), 97-112.

Miles, M. B., & Huberman, A. M. (1994). *Qualitative data analysis,* (2nd ed). Newbury Park, CA: Sage.

Mitchell, H., & Myles, F. (1988). *Second language learning theories.* London: Arnold.

Moje, E. B. (2008). Foregrounding the disciplines in secondary literacy teaching and learning: A call for change. *Journal of Adolescent and Adult Literacy, 52*(2), 96-107.

Morse, L. (2008). Under the big top: Using the Hartford Circus Fire of 1944 to teach literacy strategies to Connecticut's content area teachers. *Journal of Adolescent and Adult Literacy, 52*(4), 296-307.

O'Brien, D., & Stewart, R. (1990). Preservice teachers' perspectives on why every teacher is not a teacher of reading: A qualitative analysis. *Journal of Reading Behavior, 22,* 101-107.

O'Brien, D., Stewart, R., & Moje, E. (1995). Why content literacy is difficult to infuse into the secondary school: Complexities of curriculum, pedagogy, and schoolculture. *Reading Research Quarterly, 30,* 442-463.

Pink, D. (2006). *A whole new mind: Why right-brainers will rule the future.* New York: NY: Penguin.

Richardson, L. (2000). Writing: A method of inquiry. In N. K. Denzin & Y. S. Lincoln (Eds.) *Handbook of Qualitative Research* (2nd ed., pp. 923-948). Thousand Oaks, CA: Sage.

Roe, B. D., Stoodt-Hill, B. D., & Burns, P. C. (2007). *The content areas: Secondary school literacy instruction.* Boston, MA: Houghton Mifflin Company.

Santa, C. M. (2006, March). A vision for adolescent literacy: Ours or theirs? *Journal of Adolescent and Adult Literacy, 49,* 466-476.

Smith, F. (2004). *Understanding reading*(6th ed.). Mahwah, NJ: Lawrence Erlbaum.

Strauss, A. (1995). *Qualitative analysis for social scientists.* New York, NY: Cambridge University Press.

Street, B. V. (1984). *Literacy in theory and practice.* Cambridge, UK: Cambridge University Press.

Street, B. V. (2005). Recent application of new literacy studies in educational contexts. *Research in the Teaching of English, 39,* 417-423.

Strubbe, M. (1990). Are interdisciplinary units worthwhile? Ask students! *Middle School Journal, 21*(3), 36-38.

Tao, L., & Reinking, D. (1996). *What research reveals about email in education* [Electronic version]. Paper presentation at the 40th annual meeting of the College Reading Association, Charleston, SC.

Townsend, D. (2009). Building academic vocabulary in after-school settings: Games for growth with middle school English-language learners. *Journal of Adolescent and Adult Literacy, 53,* 242-251.

Vacca, R. T., & Vacca, A. L. (2002). *Content area reading: Literacy and learning across the curriculum* (7th ed.). Boston, MA: Allyn & Bacon.

Vygotsky, L. S. (1978). *Mind in society.* Cambridge, MA: MIT Press.

Weinberg, A., & Harding, C. (2004). Interdisciplinary teaching and collaboration in higher education: A concept whose time has come. *Washington University Journal of Law and Policy, 14,* 15-48.

Werner, O., & Schoepfle, G. M. (1987). *Systematic fieldwork: Vol.1. Foundations of ethnography and interviewing.* Newbury Park, CA: Sage.

Understanding Teacher Visioning and Agency during Literacy Instruction

Margaret Vaughn
University of Idaho

Beverly S. Faircloth
University of North Carolina at Greensboro

> I've been told not to do my centers any more. I don't pay them any attention. When the administration comes in I have the students run and do whole group instruction.
> *-Patricia, 2nd grade teacher*

Current research suggests that effective teachers adapt their instruction in order to meet the needs of their students (Bransford, Darling-Hammond, & LePage, 2005; Duffy, Miller, Kear, Parsons, Davis, & Williams, 2008). The ability to 'speak back' against institutional directives that restrict teaching adaptively, as illustrated by the above teacher, may be an essential skill for many teachers today. However, the current political climate may be making it even more difficult for teachers to teach adaptively in order to meet the needs of their students. Obstacles teachers face (i.e., emphasis on test preparation, the growth of scripted programs, the pressure teachers feel to comply with scientifically based research programs) often appear to stifle teachers' abilities to adapt and modify the curriculum as needed by their students (Duffy & Hoffman, 1999; Valencia, Place, Martin, & Grossman, 2006).

As difficult as contemporary obstacles to teaching adaptively are to overcome, there is some evidence that teachers with a clear *vision* for their teaching may be more likely to have the strength of purpose required to adapt their instruction and to teach responsively (Achinstein & Ogawa, 2006; Duffy, 2002; Hammerness, 2001; 2003; 2006; Turner, 2006; Parsons, Massey, Vaughn & Scales, 2010). Teachers with a clear vision are described by Duffy (2002) as 'effective,' often able to "adjust, modify, and invent; they do not [merely] emulate" (p. 333). However, possessing a vision alone may not sustain teachers in contexts that challenge their teaching convictions. Teachers must possess a vision for teaching *and* the ability to *act* upon it. The term teacher agency has been applied to teachers who, rooted in their professional convictions or visions, work to actively challenge restrictive policies and practices and teach according to their beliefs (Achinstein & Ogawa, 2006; Paris & Lung, 2008). In this paper, we explore the relationship between visioning and teacher agency through the voices of two in-service teachers. We suggest that visioning and agency work in tandem, guiding teachers' decisions as they work to implement change in often-restrictive environments which limit teacher adaptability and creativity.

VISIONING AND AGENCY

Many educators today feel pressure to comply with district standardization and accountability measures despite the fact that these measures may not be the most effective ways of teaching their students (Valencia, Place, Martin, & Grossman, 2006). Theory suggests that teachers who possess a vision may be more likely to adapt their instruction based on the needs of their students (Duffy,

2002; Mascarenhas, Parsons, & Burrowbridge, 2010). A teacher's vision has been characterized as an integration of teachers' "passions, their hopes, cares, and dreams with their knowledge about how and what children should be learning" (Duffy, 2002, p. 24).

Teachers with a clear vision are aware of what Maxine Greene (1988) calls a "personal reality" regarding teaching, developed in part, through experiences, interests, and often based on moral convictions. That is, teachers with a vision have a "particular standpoint" and are "conscious, interested and committed" to that viewpoint (p. 26). Duffy (2002) suggests that visioning links "the inner teacher and independent thinking" (Duffy, 2002, p. 334). Similarly, Shulman and Shulman (2004) argue that teachers with a vision may be more likely to reflect on their practice; evaluating their instruction based on what their students need. The vision of what could be may also allow teachers to imagine other possibilities (Hammerness, 2001). Consequently, the construct of visioning may be essential to understanding how and why some teachers have a sense of purpose (vision) that guides them in restrictive climates. However, as Hammerness (2001) suggests, given the complexities of teaching, there may remain a gap between a teacher's vision and their actual classroom practice.

We suggest that to bridge this gap, teachers must develop a sense of agency (the ability to act on their vision), negotiating obstacles in order to achieve their goals. Agency has been conceptualized as the "starting place of doing" (Oakeshott & Fuller, 2001, p. 35) and underscores individuals' abilities and efforts to act upon their beliefs and convictions (Daneilewicz, 2001; Bandura, 2001). Holland, Lachicotte & Cain (1998) contextualize agency, as the ability to actively engage in one's environment and respond to one's surroundings. As teachers harness a sense of agency, they use their vision and "act upon their world purposefully and reflectively in order to remake the world (or community) in which they live" (Inden, 1990, p. 23).

Although there may be a gap between a teacher's vision and their practice, those teachers who harness a sense of agency *act upon* their vision and persist in the face of perceived obstacles. For example, Paris and Lung (2008), in their study of 18 novice teachers, found that the participants contested restrictive instructional policies and programs which ultimately veered away from their vision of what they believed worked best for their students. These teachers were "fueled by their beliefs and took effective action" against the required curriculum; thereby demonstrating a sense of agency. Similarly, Danielewicz (2001) found that teachers with an established vision demonstrated a sense of agency by working against district-wide mandates and argued that teachers must have the will "to act, to make decisions, and to participate" (p.163).

OUR RESEARCH

Although many teacher education programs encourage teachers to become 'change agents' and to enact a sense of agency and to persist in the face of obstacles, research suggests that such teaching is relatively rare (Paris & Lung, 2008). It was the goal of the current exploratory study to investigate how teachers view and approach perceived obstacles to their vision. Through the examination of teachers' visions, their perceptions of obstacles to enacting their visions, and the agentic acts they engage in to confront those obstacles, we hoped to begin to glimpse ways in which some teachers are able to resist curricular pressures and teach according to their beliefs. As part of a larger study, two in-service teachers were interviewed to understand the authentic challenges of their particular setting and how they navigated obstacles. The following research questions were explored:

(1) What aspects of teachers' visions do they report as salient to their current teaching?

(2) What obstacles to teaching according to their vision do teachers identify?

(3) What agentic acts do teachers report taking in order to counter obstacles?

METHODS

This study used a multiple-case study design (Yin, 2009) to explore two teachers' visions and the ways in which they demonstrated a sense of agency by negotiating a variety of obstacles to the enactment of their visions. These teachers were intentionally selected from the population of a larger research project because they reported the most restrictive school climates. Yin (2009) demonstrates how case studies are appropriate for understanding relationships among such complex phenomena. The two participants were in-service teachers taking a master's course on differentiated instruction at a mid-sized university in a southeastern state.

Patricia (all names are pseudonyms) is an African American female in her mid-20s. She was a third-year teacher, who taught second grade in a diverse Title I school. She attended a different university for her pre-service preparation than she was attending for her master's degree. As part of her teacher preparation at her other university, she received training on how to teach and work in communities with high-needs students. She described her student teaching experience as working at a high-poverty, rural school with a large African American and Hispanic population.

Leeann is a Caucasian female in her early 30s, teaching in a Title I school. She studied teacher education at a major university other than the one she was attending for her master's degree. She described her teacher preparation as relatively sheltered and one in which she did not receive adequate training in working with diverse populations. At the time of the study, she was a fourth-year teacher who was teaching a large English Language Learner (ELL) population.

Participant interviews were the primary data for the study. Teachers were interviewed three times during the course of the semester (14 weeks) about what obstacles to teaching according to their vision confronted them at their school and what actions they took to enact their vision given the particular constraints their school climate presented. The first interview occurred during the second week of the course, the second interview occurred during the eighth week of the course, and the third interview occurred during the 15th week of the course. Each interview was audiotaped and transcribed for analysis. To answer our research questions, a semi-structured interview protocol was employed (What is your vision?; What is it that you want your students to accomplish?; Describe your school context.; Describe your teaching practices.; Why do you teach in this way?; What obstacles may prevent you from enacting your vision?; What are some ways you negotiate these constraints?)

A grounded theory approach (Glaser & Strauss, 1967) was used to analyze the transcribed interviews. A research team comprised of two professors and two doctoral students read the interview transcripts individually. After transcripts were read independently, the researchers discussed themes that emerged. For the purposes of this study, a teacher's vision may include a teacher's beliefs, ideals, and goals for instruction or for future development as a teacher. An agentic act was defined as an act rooted in the teacher's vision.

The following codes emerged during the analysis of data as dimensions of *teachers' visions*: student empowerment, creating critical thinkers, lifelong learners, risk takers, motivation, collaboration, and skill development. Teachers' responses to *obstacles* were specific to: obstacles in the classroom and obstacles in the school and district. The majority of obstacles pertained to school and district where the following subcategories emerged: curricula mandates, administrative support, scheduling, resources, testing pressures, and difficult colleagues. Teachers' responses about the ways they *negotiated obstacles* were then examined to see to what extent these responses reflected their vision.

FINDINGS

In this section, we report each of the two cases investigated in this study including the teacher's visions, the obstacles, and the agentic acts.

Case 1: Patricia

Patricia mentioned different aspects of her vision but maintained a focus on motivating her students. She stated that she wanted her students to become interested in learning and that her vision was "to motivate my kids to actually want to learn." During her second interview, she described developing an interest in reading in her students: "…It is very important for me to find ways that kids actually want to go back and read and the more they read, the more fluent they get, the smoother their reading gets and then that just builds." As the study progressed, Patricia's vision included motivating students in their out-of-school lives. She states, "Reading is necessary. To me I just want them to see that it actually does apply outside of my classroom."

Patricia taught within a school where teachers had minimal autonomy and were expected to teach from scripted curricula for math and literacy instruction. Patricia's school did not make adequate yearly progress in state tests leading her administration to enforce "teach to the test" practices at her school. Quite interestingly, although Patricia taught in a non-testing grade (2nd grade), she was pressured to teach test-taking skills to her students using worksheets which outlined specific targeted skills—a practice which she described as "not even going to work with my kids." Such "teach to the test" tactics were in direct conflict to her vision for teaching as well. She described that these test-taking practices would not motivate her students; she emphasized the need to develop lessons pertinent to students' lives.

> I think it's a lot harder to teach kids anything if they're not motivated to learn it—especially my kids—they've been through a lot. It's about getting them to think about what's around them. It's about getting them to see beyond this little wall and see outside.

Although this school climate created Patricia's primary obstacle to enacting her vision of promoting students' interests in reading and learning, she creatively and covertly resisted that pressure. When she was encouraged to teach whole-group instruction using a scripted basal series, she supplemented her reading program with real-world texts like *Weekly Reader* and other small trade books she believed would be of interest to her students. She added materials like this to get her students interested and motivated to learn—a salient aspect of her vision. Patricia continued to provide small-group instruction to her students, although this was in direct conflict with what was widely promoted at her school.

Perhaps not surprisingly, over the course of the study, as the school calendar approached standardized testing, the obstacles to implementing her vision became greater in number. "Actually things have gotten worse because it's so close to testing time even though I'm not in a testing grade. There is a huge push to get them ready for testing." Throughout the study, she continued to describe her school's emphasis on testing as her primary obstacle.

> It's all about test scores, deep into knowing how to take the tests. We need to train them, let them know this is what you're going to see next year. In some schools it's more free thinking—let the kids maybe find out how they come up with the answers, whereas at my school we're supposed to basically train them to how to take the test.

These obstacles were especially challenging for Patricia because they were directed by an administration that closely monitored teachers as they taught. She described the difficulties of enacting her vision in such a restrictive climate.

> I've been told to not let my students get up and move to do their small-group learning stations, because I'm right next door to a third-grade classroom and because it needs to be really quiet in our room, so then I'm supposed to have my students do a lot more seat work.

However, Patricia continued to enact her vision despite directives like this from her administration. Because administrators could see into her classroom, she blocked her door with paper so that she could continue providing engaging, differentiated literacy stations while she conducted individualized reading instruction for her students; a practice which was in direct conflict with her school's recommendations of providing whole-group instruction using a common basal text. When asked why she covered her door, she said, "I had to do this because I've been told not to do my centers anymore. It was the only way—now only really tall people can look in (and my principal isn't tall)."

Patricia reported other ways she negotiated constraints to attain her vision. She described incorporating authentic activities in math to support her vision of motivating her students. Such a practice was in opposition to the kinds of scripted math instruction also recommended by her administration.

> I just did this McDonald's activity which, of course, they loved because they know McDonalds' and they can see it—when I leave here I think counting money is pretty important because McDonalds' is their favorite restaurant. They're trying really hard when it's something they want to learn because they want to be able to use it.

Given the emphasis on testing, scripted programs, and whole-group instruction, Patricia was faced with a wide gap between her vision and the practices promoted by her school. She described the challenges of motivating her students with scripted test-taking materials. Her agentic acts were in response to the gap between her vision and practice. She demonstrated a sense of agency as she effectively negotiated these obstacles to teach according to her vision (of motivating her students), often veering away from school mandates in the process. She challenged school-wide practices using her vision as a guide to implement practices she believed would best meet the needs of her students, which was her ultimate priority.

Case 2: Leeann

Leeann's vision focused on wanting her students to be able to voice their opinions in any situation they may experience in their lives. The following statement was taken from her initial interview: "My vision for my students is for my students to be able to speak and defend their own answers." Throughout the course of the study, this aspect of her vision remained salient. During her second interview she described how she wanted her students to develop their own voice and to feel as though they were important members of the classroom:

> My vision is for every child in my classroom to feel independent and able to defend whatever they think and to appreciate their own background …and whatever knowledge they have—to feel like they are a vital part of the classroom.

During her third interview, she anchored her vision statement in students' goals for reading. She described wanting her students to be able "to get information from books that they need and use it for their own purposes."

Leeann also taught within a school that emphasized test-taking skills and strict adherence to district pacing guides. She explained how her vision was at odds with these perspectives, for example, in conflict with the school's recommendation to teach 'to the test.'

> The school emphasizes assessment data and places importance on test scores. They want you to break everything down into score grids—basically the administration is looking at skills instead of understanding.

Like Patricia, Leeann explained that since her vision emphasized students' individuality, viewing students as groups in scoring grids was difficult. She stated, "I think that my kids need to be viewed as individuals and be able to learn how to read for a real purpose—not for taking tests. With that said, they need to be allowed to do that on their own schedule—not the school's." As the study progressed, she continued to emphasize the need for her students to develop skills at their own pace.

> I want my students to be seen and treated as individuals—not on some scale and some prescribed schedule of being able to do certain things at certain times.

Perhaps not surprisingly given her vision, the testing climate in which Leeann taught proved to be her primary obstacle, creating a significant gap between her vision and the practices expected by her school. Leeann exercised a sense of agency and persisted to enact her vision despite the restrictions placed on her. Such agentic acts included incorporating more open-ended discussion questions in her instruction (a practice not supported by her school) in order to provide opportunities for her students to voice their opinions. Although the administration monitored her to ensure that she was teaching certain skills and then moving on to other skills, she enacted a sense of agency by structuring her class so her students would have more opportunities to choose and make decisions about the curriculum. In order to enact her vision, she modified the literacy program and created opportunities in her classroom where students created research projects based on their own interests. When asked about what the administration would think, she stated, "I just say I am doing what they want and then I close the door and do what I want to do." Her story describes the challenges of trying to teach according to one's vision given such a restrictive climate. Similar to Patricia, she exercised agency as she enacted practices to teach according to her vision. Both teachers expressed that their schools emphasized what and how they should teach. However, Patricia and Leeann contested many directives promoted school-wide because such directives did not support their visions.

LIMITATIONS

An initial exploration into the important intersection of teacher vision and agency this study focused on gaining an understanding through teacher voices (specifically through interviews) among a small sample of teachers (2). It is essential that both this data and methodology be expanded as this work continues. Other data sources may include a larger pool of teachers as well as school administration to strengthen findings. Additional methodologies that would be beneficial to these efforts would include teacher observations and teacher journals to reflect more explicit and authentic (real-time) teacher perspectives and experiences. Moreover, more concentrated examination of why some teachers choose agency will add important insight to our understanding. Future work should definitely attend to these research possibilities.

SIGNIFICANCE

The ability to teach adaptively and according to one's vision has become an even more challenging task given the complexities of classroom instruction and current public school policy mandates. Many teachers are stifled by educational policies and programs that aim to control and thereby limit teacher creativity and restrict adaptive instructional practice. However, despite these limitations, some teachers who possess a clear vision use this to negotiate obstacles and to act upon their vision. Teachers like Patricia and Leeann harnessed a sense of agency toward their vision to span the gap between their vision and practice. But why did these particular teachers enact their visions in the face of the repressive contexts of which they taught? Interestingly, their visions for teaching related to the specific needs of their students—and they ultimately demonstrated a sense of agency to bridge the gap between their vision and practice. They argued that teaching according to their vision was essential if they were going to meet the specific needs of their students. Thus, these teachers' agentic acts emerged from their convictions to teach according to their visions. We suggest that these teachers used their vision of what they believed would benefit their students to sustain them through difficult times (Hammerness, 2008). Without their vision of what could be, these teachers perhaps would have folded and yielded to the restrictive pressures the high-stakes accountability climate has demanded.

However, since many teachers struggle to respond to obstacles in this way, it may be that teacher education programs do not adequately prepare teachers to develop a sense of agency in light of the many obstacles within education today. Teacher education programs should include coursework that includes developing and promoting visioning and how to best enact such a vision given the challenges the current educational climate presents. Given the current political climate, such an emphasis may be essential to help teachers withstand and thrive in the profession.

This article highlighted the cases of two teachers who negotiated obstacles, often against standardization practices adopted by their school district, in order to implement their vision within their classrooms. The purpose of this article was to highlight the ways in which teachers enact their visions, thereby demonstrating a sense of agency, despite constraints that often restrict their ability to be creative and adaptive in the classroom today. These teachers demonstrated a sense of agency, rooting their decisions in their visions of what they believed worked best for their students. Examining such stories may provide an avenue through which pre-service teachers may gain insight into the potential of their own ability to agentically and effectively enact their vision for teaching. Moreover, it is our hope that examining such stories may provide key information in the development of such resilience in developing teachers. An important step for our future research is to discern whether these stories might be effective in helping other teachers develop a sense of agency.

REFERENCES

Achinstein, B. & Ogawa, R. T. (2006). (In)fidelity: What the resistance of new teachers reveals about professional principles and prescriptive educational policies. *Harvard Educational Review, 76*, 30–63.

Bandura, A. (2001). Social cognitive theory: An agentic perspective. *Annual Review of Psychology, 52*, 1-26.

Bransford, J., Darling-Hammond, L., & LePage, P. (2005). Introduction. In L. Darling-Hammond & J. Bransford (Eds.), Preparing teachers for a changing world: What teachers should learn and be able to do (pp. 1-39). San Francisco, CA: Jossey-Bass.

Danielewicz, J. (2001). *Teaching selves: Identity, pedagogy and teacher education.* Albany, NY: State University of New York Press.

Duffy, G. G. (2002). Visioning and the development of outstanding teachers. *Reading Research and Instruction, 41,* 331-344.

Duffy, G. G. & Hoffman, J. V. (1991). In pursuit of an illusion: The flawed search for a perfect method. *Reading Teacher, 53,* 10-17.

Duffy, G. G., Miller, S. D., Kear, K. A., Parsons, S. A., Davis, S. G., & Williams, J. B. (2008). Teachers' instructional adaptations during literacy instruction. In Y. Kim, V. J. Risko, D. L. Compton, D. K. Dickinson, M. K., Hundley, R. T. Jiménez, K. M. Leander, & D. W. Rowe (Eds.), *57th Yearbook of the National Reading Conference* (pp. 160-171). Oak Creek, WI: National Reading Conference.

Glaser, B. G., & Strauss, A. L. (1967). *The discovery of grounded theory: strategies for qualitative research.* Mill Valley, CA: Sociology Press.

Greene, M. (1988). *The dialectic of freedom.* New York, NY: Teachers College Columbia University.

Hammerness, K. (2001). Teachers' visions: The role of personal ideals in school reform. *Journal of Educational Change, 2,* 143-163.

Hammerness, K. (2003). Learning to hope, or hoping to learn? The role of vision in the early professional lives of teachers. *Journal of Teacher Education, 54,* 43-56.

Hammerness, K. (2006). *Seeing through teachers' eyes: Professional ideals and classroom practices.* New York, NY: Teachers College Press.

Hammerness, K. (2008). "If you don't know where you are going, any path will do": The role of teachers' visions in teachers' career paths. *New Educator, 4,* 1-22.

Hammerness, K., Darling-Hammond, L., Bransford, J., Berliner, D., Cochran-Smith, M., McDonald, M., & Zeichner, K. (2005). In L. Darling-Hammond & J. Bransford (Eds.), *Preparing teachers for a changing world: What teachers should learn and be able to do* (pp. 358-389). San Francisco, CA: Jossey-Bass.

Holland, D., Lachiotte, W., Skinner, D., & Cain, C. (1998). *Identity and agency in cultural worlds*. Cambridge, MA: Harvard University Press.

Inden, R. (1990). *Imagining India*. Oxford: Blackwell.

Mascarenhas, A., Parsons, S. A., & Burrowbridge, S. C. (2010). Preparing teachers for high needs schools: A focus on thoughtfully adaptive teaching. *Bank Street Occasional Papers, 25*, 28-43.

Oakeshott, M., & Fuller, T. (2001). *The voice of liberal learning: Michael Oakeshott on education*. New Haven, CT: Yale University Press.

Paris, C., & Lung, P. (2008). Agency and child-centered practices in novice teachers: Autonomy, efficacy, intentionality, and reflectivity. *Journal of Early Childhood Teacher Education, 29*(3), 253-268.

Parsons, S. A., Massey, D. D., Vaughn, M., Scales, R. Q., Faircloth, B. S., Howerton, S., Griffith, R. R., & Atkinson, T. S. (2010). Developing teachers' reflective thinking and adaptability in graduate courses. *Journal of School Connections*.

Shulman, L. S., & Shulman, J. (2004). How and what teachers learn: A shifting perspective. *Journal of Curriculum Studies, 36*, 257-271.

Turner, J. D. (2006). "I want to meet my students where they are!": Pre-service teachers' visions of culturally responsive literacy instruction. In J. V. Hoffman, D. Shallert, C. Fairbanks, J. Worthy, & B. Maloch (Eds.), *55th Yearbook of the National Reading Conference* (pp. 309-323). Oak Creek, WI: National Reading Conference.

Valencia, S., Place, N., Martin, S., & Grossman, P. (2006). Curriculum materials for elementary reading: shackles and scaffolds for four beginning teachers. *The Elementary School Journal, 107*, 93–120.

Yin, R. K. (2009). *Case study research: Design and methods* (4th ed.). Los Angeles, CA: Sage.

Examining the Relationships of Power and Resistance in Literacy Coaching in Three School Contexts

Kristen Ferguson
Nipissing University

Literacy coaching is a popular initiative in schools across the United States and Canada; however, it has been well documented that there is only a limited research base for literacy coaching (Casey, 2006; Dole & Donaldson, 2006; Rodgers & Rodgers, 2007). Moreover, while the research often cites resistance as a problem for literacy coaching (e.g. Lynch & Ferguson, 2010; Dole & Donaldson, 2006), there is scant literature that details the relationships among the players in literacy coaching programs. This paper is a part of a larger study that investigated the role of the literacy coach, the social relationships in literacy coaching, and the successes and barriers of literacy coaching in three schools in Ontario, Canada. In this paper, I present a portion of the research, the relationships among teachers, literacy coaches, and principals, and specifically, I will discuss the issues of teacher resistance and power that emerged from the study.

LITERATURE REVIEW

Teachers may be resistant to participating in literacy coaching and working with the coach (Dole & Donaldson, 2006; Morgan et al., 2003). There are suggestions in literacy coaching guides about how to lessen teacher resistance, such as working with willing teachers first, supporting teachers in any way possible, and being knowledgeable about the change process (Allen, 2006; Casey, 2006; Toll, 2005). Another suggestion is for literacy coaches to avoid being seen as evaluators or as experts who are perfect teachers and, instead, assume the role of a teacher resource (Fisher, n.d.; Swafford, Maltsberger, Button, & Furgerson, 1997).

Demonstration lessons, observations of teaching, and giving feedback to teachers is the most frequently cited literacy coaching model in the literature (e.g. Toll, 2005; Dozier, 2006) but this model may impact teacher resistance. For instance, Rodgers and Rodgers (2007) caution literacy coaches about demonstration lessons since they may create a sense of inadequacy among teachers and perceptions of "'I'll never be able to do that'" (p. 82). Toll (2005) states that literacy coaches should not observe teachers because, despite attempts to be non-evaluative, the coach is still put in the position of a judge, possibly creating a sense of mistrust on the part of the teacher. Joyce and Showers (1996; 2002) believe that providing feedback about an educator's teaching forces coaches to be evaluators and breaks down collegial attitudes. Poglinco et al. (2003) also find some literacy coaches are uncomfortable with giving feedback, feeling that they are "policing" teachers (p. 24). Thus, perhaps the popular coaching model of demonstration, observation, and feedback is contributing to teacher resistance towards literacy coaching.

While it is important for administrators to be involved with and supportive of literacy coaching (Elish-Piper, L'Allier, & Zwart, 2009; Steckel, 2009), there are some contrasting views about the role of administration in literacy coaching. Elish-Piper et al. (2009) believe principals should follow up with teachers and take the role of enforcing the initiatives. Burkins (2007) disagrees, stating that principals may probe the coach for information about teachers and this may be detrimental to the teacher/coach relationship. Poglinco, Bach, Hovde, Rosenblum, Saunders, & Supovitz (2003) also report that, in some cases, teacher resistance increased when teachers felt they were unfairly rebuked by the principal for noncompliance.

While resistance has been noted in the literature, there is only the work of Gibson (2006) and Rainville and Jones (2008) that delves deeper into the relationships within literacy coaching and explores issues of power. These studies indicate that power is negotiated between the literacy coach and the teacher, and both parties can be in positions of power. Gibson (2006) concludes that the relationship between the teacher and literacy coach should be empowering for both individuals while maintaining a focus on effective instruction and student achievement. Rainville and Jones (2008) find that the literacy coach's power is dependent on the teacher/coach relationship. In some relationships, the coach retained power as an expert in literacy, but in others, the coach's identity as an expert was challenged by teachers, and the literacy coach had no control or power.

THEORETICAL FRAMEWORK

According to Foucault (1977/1990; 1977/1979), power is a complex overall effect stemming from the inequalities of relationships, and knowledge is a product of power. Foucault (1977/1988) also states that where power exists, so too will resistance to power. Arendt (1958) writes that passive resistance may be the most powerful form of resistance.

Using Foucault's theory (1977/1979), those in power roles can change a person's behavior using three methods of "correct training:" hierarchical observation, normalizing judgment, and the examination (p. 170). First, in hierarchical observation, individuals in power roles can observe those whose behavior is to be corrected. The second method is normalizing judgment, where nonconformance is punishable, and the fear of being thought abnormal creates a sense of conformity. Finally in the examination, the person in power documents observations about an individual, turning the individual into a case to be compared with others. A central feature of corrective training is the metaphor of the prison panopticon, which allows supervisors to view all prisoners at once without being seen by the prisoners themselves. Thus, if people believe they are being watched, they will behave in the normative and correct way.

Fullan's (2001) work presents three phases of educational change. The first phase is initiation, the decision to initiate the change, and it can generate a variety of emotions including confusion and alienation. Lasting two or three years, phase two is implementation, during which educators can experience an "implementation dip," a time when things get worse before they get better and when people grapple with change (p. 92). The last phase is institutionalization in which the change either becomes a part of the system or is discarded. Fullan also argues that both pressure and support are required for educational change because pressure without support can lead to resistance.

METHODS

The guiding question for this paper is: what social relationships exist in literacy coaching, and what is the effect of these relationships? To answer this question and achieve a holistic picture of coaching, qualitative methods are appropriate (Bogdan & Biklen, 1998; Frankel & Wallen, 2003). This multi-case study explores literacy coaching in three schools (Yin, 2003) and uses qualitative research methods: observing, interviewing, and collecting artifacts and documents (Merriam, 1988). Since relationships in coaching develop over time, interviews are important because participants can reflect and provide a retrospective not possible through observations or artifact collection. Thus, the results presented in this paper are mainly based on data from interviews. Observations and document and artifact collection are helpful, however, as they help triangulate the data gleaned from interviews (Patton, 1990).

School Contexts and Participants

This Ontario school board was in its third year of literacy coaching. Most schools had a part-time (0.33) literacy coach who was also a classroom teacher in the same school. There were also three full-time district literacy coaches who provided guidance and professional development for the school literacy coaches. There was no written job description for the coaches; instead, the roles and responsibilities were to be determined at the school level by the principal and literacy coach. There were a number of literacy initiatives being mandated for implementation by the Ontario Ministry of Education and the board including: balanced literacy, reading comprehension strategies, teacher collaborative marking, and literacy-based Professional Learning Communities (PLCs).

I used reputational sampling (McMillan & Schumacher, 2001; Miles & Huberman, 1994) to select the schools for the study. The district literacy coaches were asked to nominate three schools experiencing exemplary literacy coaching with the purpose of selecting schools with well-developed coaching that would provide rich data (Patton, 1990). All three nominated schools agreed to participate and all were kindergarten to Grade 8 schools with populations of 220, 221, and 475 pupils. Two of the literacy coaches were first-year coaches but had previously worked as teachers in these schools. Both worked part-time as coaches and spent the remainder of their day as classroom teachers. The third coach was a district literacy coach. She had been coaching for three years and worked half-time at her school and half-time at the board office. In previous years, she was a part-time coach in this same school. All coaches were female and two possessed additional qualifications in literacy. Three literacy coaches, four principals (three principals and one vice-principal), and 27 teachers participated in the study. Because the school board had been focusing literacy coaching in the primary grades (kindergarten to Grade 3), at the board's request, only primary teachers were a part of the study.

Data Collection and Data Sources

This study used interviews to collect data about the feelings, attitudes, and experiences of the participants (Gay & Airasian, 2000). Literacy coaches, principals, and teachers were interviewed once using a structured interview format (see Appendix for the interview protocols). Interviews were conducted wherever the participants felt most comfortable, such as in the library or in their classrooms. Depending on the participants' preference, interviews were audio recorded or I took notes, and then were transcribed. Literacy coaches also participated in informal unstructured interviews; these brief interviews were spontaneous and were informal conversations to clarify and provide insight into observations.

I observed literacy coaches by shadowing them for over 110 hours over an eight-week period. Coaches were observed during their regular literacy coaching time and during other times when they were working in a coaching capacity, at PLCs for example. In order to observe a variety of situations, when possible, I rotated the days of the week that I observed in each school. One coach was observed for 31.41 hours, the second for 27.48 hours, and the third for 51.70 hours. For a detailed account of the day-to-day roles of the literacy coaches, see Ferguson (2011). In summary, literacy coaches were observed performing three main tasks in their role. First, they acted as school literacy organizers, performing tasks such as ordering resources and organizing the bookroom. Second, they took on some of the leadership role in the school by conducting professional development sessions for teachers and leading PLCs. Finally, they were a support system, providing content knowledge, resources, and affective support for teachers and principals. Literacy coaches occasionally worked individually with teachers, but most often worked with groups of teachers during PLCs. The coaches did not use the coaching model of demonstration lessons, observations, and feedback (e.g. Casey, 2006; Dozier, 2006). Instead, the coaches used Hasbrouck and Denton's (2007) student-focused coaching model, which centers on student achievement rather than on changing teaching practices. Following Hasbrouck and Denton's model, coaches and teachers would set goals for student achievement, plan teaching strategies, then follow-up on how the students were doing at future PLCs (Ferguson, 2011).

I also collected artifacts and documents, including school literacy documents and minutes from meetings. By the end of the eight weeks, data collection reached saturation (Flick, 2006) as data became repetitive and revealed no new information. My role was observer-as-participant (Fraenkel & Wallen, 2003). I identified myself a researcher and used my judgment about when to participate in the activities observed (Bogdan & Biklen, 1998). Having worked previously as a teacher in this board, I had prior knowledge of board literacy initiatives and had established relationships with some of the participants in the study. This was an advantage because having rapport with participants may better position the researcher to collect data (Bogdan & Biklen, 1998).

Data Analysis

The answers to interview questions resulted in rich data about the relationships among the players in literacy coaching. The data gained from observations of literacy coaching helped triangulate and corroborate the data from interviews. Using the data analysis strategy outlined by Bogdan and Biklen (1998), I read through all interviews, observations, and artifacts making comments, notes, and a list of preliminary categories based on emerging broad themes. Next, I examined my categories and collapsed categories that were similar, made new categories, and also made subcategories. Then, using Microsoft Word, I read through all data again, giving each category and subcategory a numerical code. For instance, #6 was the category for the broad theme of relationships and thus codes beginning with 6 were related to relationships; for example, 6.2 was "informal relationships with the coach" and 6.3 was "friends outside of school." Finally, I reread all coded categories, subcategories, and raw data an additional five times, collapsing some subcategories and recoding some pieces of data. The subcategory "the powerlessness of literacy coaches," for example, was similar to "literacy coaches in the middle," and thus these two subcategories were combined. During this process, I used a constant comparative method, continually comparing data so it could be placed into appropriate categories (Gay & Airasian, 2000).

RESULTS

A number of themes emerged as categories during the data analysis. The categories of pressure, change, the role of the principals, relationships with the coach, and barriers to literacy coaching, contained data concerning the relationships within literacy coaching and thus help answer the guiding question, what social relationships exist in literacy coaching, and what is the effect of these relationships? I compiled the data from these categories and present four main findings in this paper: the literacy coach/teacher relationship, the literacy coach/principal relationship, literacy coaches in the middle between teachers and principals, and teacher resistance.

Literacy Coaches' Relationships with Teachers

When asked during interviews, most teachers described their relationship with the literacy coach as informal, consulting with the coach as needed, such as in the hall or at the photocopier, rather than scheduling a time with the coach. Teachers' relationships with the literacy coaches were also personal, and they were observed digressing from coaching conversations to chat about friends, family, and their personal lives. Some teachers felt that having an established relationship with the coach quickened the process of gaining trust. One teacher told me, "We have been friends for a long time…so I was very comfortable with her, but I think a lot of people weren't at the beginning." Teachers also felt that the literacy coach must trust their professional abilities to teach and be nonjudgmental because teachers did not want to be told what to do or that they were doing something "wrong." Teachers stated that coaching was successful because the coach "wasn't a big authority figure," and she "wasn't bossing us around."

During observations, coaches and teachers all appeared to work well together and generally appeared collegial during coaching conversations and PLCs. Many teachers and literacy coaches referred to themselves as a "team." With all the new initiatives, one teacher told me, "really we only had each other to kind of float." All three literacy coaches expressed pride in their relationships and the sense of "team" they had established in their schools. One coach stated, "We've always maintained that we can do any of it together…Nobody gets left behind."

Literacy Coaches' Relationships with Principals

All principals also stated during interviews that they felt that they worked well with the coach as a team. Coaches and principals stated that regular communication with each other is important so they can maintain "a common vision" and continue "goal setting" and that their relationship should be reciprocal, based on mutual respect. One principal stated, "It is very important that your literacy coach is comfortable enough to ask you for help when they need it, and as principal, that you are comfortable enough to ask for their help." I observed principals consulting with the coaches about literacy strategies and working together to plan upcoming PLCs.

In all three schools, principals stated that they have communicated to teachers that the literacy coach takes direction from the principals. By having the principals in the power position, principals felt that teachers were more likely to feel comfortable working with the coach. Principals took the role of enforcing initiatives; as one principal told me, "I'm the heavy, really . . . I'm just sort of the backup henchman," and another principal stated, "My job is ensuring that everyone is pulling their weight." Principals often conducted classroom walk-throughs, looking for "evidence" that teachers were doing what was asked of them. Teachers were aware that the principal was enforcer of initiatives. One teacher told me, "she's [the principal] the muscle behind it, you know?" While teachers did not always like the power exerted by the principals, teachers knew that principals were also being pressured by the school board and the Ontario Ministry of Education to implement changes in their schools. One teacher stated bluntly: "We have a job to do; she has a job to do." I also observed principals in their enforcer role, restating board and Ministry of Education goals at PLCs, and conducting classroom walk-throughs.

Literacy Coaches in the Middle between Teachers and Principals

It was "a fine balance" for literacy coaches to remain a peer to teachers and not be perceived as taking on the power role of an administrator. During interviews, the coaches explained their uneasiness about being in a position that felt somewhere in the middle between teachers and the administration. This was made particularly difficult because, under union guidelines, a coach cannot evaluate a teacher's performance in any way. This put literacy coaches in an awkward position: they had to report to the principal about what was occurring in a nonevaluative manner; it was then up to the principal to follow up with teachers and enforce change if necessary. Teachers agreed that the roles of the principal and coach should be distinct; as one teacher said, "It should be the principal putting the pressure and the literacy coach providing the support." One teacher summed up this precarious position of the literacy coach as a middleman, "Our literacy coach is a communication between teachers, students, and the administration . . . She's not an administrator; she's not a teacher . . . It's almost like an arbitrator, like you know?"

Literacy coaches treaded carefully not to overstep their position of a peer. As one teacher said, a coach can ask teachers to do something, "but what recourse do you have? You can't force them." And, indeed, literacy coaches were observed gently suggesting that teachers try new strategies or engaging in conversations in hopes of shifting attitudes towards literacy. No coach, however, was ever observed evaluating teachers or enforcing change. Moreover, the literacy coaches did not want to be a part of the administration, stating that it is "not their job" to do follow-up or enforcement with teachers and they told me that they made a conscious effort to remain a teacher first and foremost.

Teacher Resistance towards Literacy Coaching

Teacher resistance was mentioned by participants during interviews as a barrier for literacy coaching. Teachers often reflected on resistance; however, it was usually in the past tense, as if it was a barrier that had been overcome. One teacher reflected on this change in attitude: "If you had been here three years ago; the complaining, the refusal to cooperate . . . But when you look at what's happening now, it's so totally different now. Like, we're a team." Other teachers said, "We're really strong now compared to what we were," and "This year seems to be the best of all, everybody is just right on board." Teachers generally felt that they needed three years to change and become comfortable with new initiatives. Comments such as "It's actually all coming together now," "I find it a lot better this year," and "This is the first year I can honestly say that I'm very comfortable" were made by teachers to describe this third year of change. For teachers, it seemed natural that change would take time and that there would be a period of resistance; one teacher explained, "When a change happens, there's not going to be the nice flow that people want." Some teachers also attributed diminished teacher resistance to a type of peer pressure. As one teacher said, "It's really obvious if somebody's not doing something." New teachers were under particular pressure to change; "You're parked in the middle of people who have been doing this and believe in it and it's important. And you can't say no."

Literacy coaches felt teacher resistance to change had improved. One coach explained during an interview that "there was much more resistance in year one and year two." This coach credited the diminished resistance to the creation of trust with teachers, developing relationships with teachers, and increases in student achievement: "I think in year three, there's that trust, and I think the resistance has diminished because we see the success we're having with our students." Teachers empathized with the literacy coaches whose job was to support teachers to adopt change. One teacher stated teacher resistance is difficult for the coach: "It's hard to get excited, motivated, and to plan things and have these meetings if you've got people who you feel have a little bit of negative attitude towards it, right?" While all principals believed that teacher resistance had lessened, they still felt it was a problem. One principal simply stated, "Resistance is still an issue."

Teachers were aware that the coach's role was to support the initiatives and did not seem to openly resist the coach herself. I observed little overt resistance to literacy coaching; no teacher was unwilling to work with the coach and during interviews, all teachers thought literacy coaching was a positive experience. However, it is significant to note that some teachers worked with the coach more than others, and this could be a form of resistance. Some teachers scheduled one-on-one time with the literacy coach while others only worked with the coach at PLCs. For some teachers, however, this may be a preferred learning style; one teacher said, "I'm kind of a do-it-myself person, so she [the coach] doesn't push herself on me . . . when I do need her, she's there. She can read that very well."

I did observe resistance within the larger coaching context, focusing on principal enforcement of initiatives and the initiatives themselves. For example, teachers did not generally like creating bulletin board displays that showed "evidence" of a specific initiative. If the initiative at a PLC was a reading comprehension strategy, for instance, all teachers would have to teach that strategy and display student work on a classroom bulletin board. Principals would then conduct walk-throughs looking for these bulletin boards. One teacher called it "demeaning" to her professionalism to have this type of "homework assignment." At a PLC, I observed a teacher challenging the principal by inquiring about the value of the bulletin boards. I later asked that teacher about the bulletin boards at an interview and the teacher told me that principal enforcement was "absolutely necessary" because teachers would not follow through with the initiatives. Other teachers simply disliked some of the board and Ministry initiatives; for example, during interviews some teachers expressed their disdain for certain reading assessments.

DISCUSSION

Power and resistance within the relationships in literacy coaching were a common link within the themes that emerged from the data analysis and presented in the findings. These themes (the relationships among coaches, principals, and teachers, literacy coaches in the middle between teachers and principals, and teacher resistance) can be interpreted using Foucault's (1977/1979, 1977/1988) theory on knowledge, power, resistance, and correct training, Arendt's (1958) position on resistance, Fullan's (2001) ideas on educational change, and the existing literature on literacy coaching.

Dynamics of Power in Literacy Coaching

According to Foucault (1977/1979), one in a power position has knowledge that others do not. Literacy coaches supported teachers in learning the normative teaching practices and had expert knowledge in literacy, possibly putting them in a power position as Rainville and Jones (2008) report and using Foucault's (1977/1979) theory of knowledge and power. But overall, my findings show that coaches had little power and, instead, I argue that the principals had power in the three literacy coaching contexts. The Ontario Ministry of Education and the school board had normative methods which they insisted that teachers adopt, and this method of getting teachers to change teaching practices can be interpreted using Foucault's theory of correct training (1977/1979). Principals were in enforcement roles and principal walk-throughs acted as a panopticon because teachers knew that principals would be observing them. Teachers had to change teaching practices or experience the constraint of conformity, a sort of "peer pressure" to adopt the initiatives (Foucault 1977/1979). The literacy coach appeared to remain on the outside of this power hierarchy and instead stayed in the gray area as mediator between teachers and the administration. Moreover, two of the literacy coaches were still teachers teaching literacy, and they too were subject to principal observation, entrenching them as a trusted peer to teachers (Steckel, 2009).

While teachers did not like having power exerted over them, power did create change in their practices, and teachers were able to acknowledge this. Teachers felt that someone had to be the "tough nut" and that change would not have occurred if the principals had been more relaxed. Teachers also believed that support from the administration was important in the change process, and the coach was viewed as the main component of support. This aligns with Fullan's (2001) theory that support and pressure are necessary for educational change, as pressure leads to action and support prevents resistance. But this runs contrary to the finding of Poglinco, et al., (2003), who report that some literacy coaches experienced resistance from teachers because of principal enforcement. I argue that in this study, the teacher/coach relationship was strengthened by principal enforcement because the coach maintained a position of a supportive peer. Burkins (2007) and Poglinco et al. (2003) note that if principals gain information about teachers from the literacy coach, it may have negative effects on the teacher/coach relationship. However, in this study, principals were not able to use information from coaches to evaluate teachers because union rules prevented coaches from taking on a supervisory role. These union rules, while making coaching awkward at times, limited the power of the coaches and possibly helped the coach maintain positive relationships with teachers. There appears to be no other research which examines how union guidelines impact literacy coaching.

Resistance towards Literacy Coaching

Teacher resistance to working with the literacy coach is well documented in the literature (Dole & Donaldson, 2006; Morgan, Saylor-Crowder, Stephens, Donnelly, DeFord, & Hamel, 2003). In my study, there were teachers who utilized the coach more than others, possibly because some teachers might have been too busy, some might have preferred other types of professional development, and perhaps some were less enthusiastic about coaching, and this avoidance could be a form of resistance. This final possibility supports Arendt's (1958) idea that resistance may be a refusal to participate. However, no teachers had any negative comments to say about the literacy coaches or their work, and negative opinions that did arise focused on the initiatives or the enforcement of initiatives. Because of their role as the enforcer of change, "the backup henchman," so to speak, principals had a different perspective on teacher resistance and it is likely that principals would be the ones to see overt resistance. Teachers thus seemed able to separate the literacy coach from the enforcement of the initiatives, embracing a sort of "don't shoot the messenger" attitude towards coaching.

While resistance did not appear to be a current barrier to literacy coaching, resistance appeared to be a major barrier in the past, and there are a number of possible reasons for this diminished resistance. First, time helped overcome teacher resistance; teachers felt that they needed time to learn and to change teaching practices, a finding supported in the research (Garet, Porter, Desimone, Birman, & Suk Yoon, 2001; Wildman & Niles, 1987). Coaches also need time to develop positive relationships with teachers, since building trust and rapport is important for successful literacy coaching (Dole & Donaldson, 2006; Shaw, 2006).

Second, teachers believed that the coaches were their peers and together they were a team, a factor important in decreasing resistance (Moxley & Taylor, 2006; Walpole & McKenna, 2004). This strong feeling of teamwork was evident as schools "rallied" together to support each other during times of change. The coaches and teachers were also friends outside and these types of relationships can also assist in breaking down the barrier of teacher resistance (Rainville & Jones, 2008).

The coaching model may also have helped decrease resistance. Coaches used Hasbrouck and Denton's (2007) model of student-focused coaching, which centers on student achievement rather than changing teaching practices. The three coaches were observed working with teachers both one-on-one and in PLCs examining student assessments, setting goals for specific students, and following up on students (Ferguson, 2011). Perhaps not using the demonstration, observation, and feedback model improved relationships between literacy coaches and teachers, as is suggested by Joyce and Showers (1996), Rodgers and Rodgers (2007), and Toll (2005) because coaches are not in a power or quasi-supervisory role. Observation and feedback use Foucault's (1977/1979) elements of correct training. First, hierarchical observation would occur when coaches observe teachers teaching, as would normative judgment since a coach's goal would be to change teachers' practices to the normative method. Teachers may conform and change their practices in fear of being a "bad teacher." Finally, observation and feedback would use what Foucault (1977/1979) calls "the examination," where teachers are made into a "case" that requires treatment (p. 170). Literacy coaches often take notes (e.g. Dozier, 2006) while observing teachers, and from these notes, the coach turns the teacher into a case with specific goals for improvement (Foucault, 1977/1979).

Foucault (1978/1990) writes, "where there is power, there is resistance" (p. 95). Because literacy coaches did not use the observation and feedback model, coaches were not in a power role of correct training and would not likely face teacher resistance.

A perception of improved student learning is another possible reason for diminished teacher resistance. It was believed by the participants that literacy coaching had a significant and positive impact on teaching and student learning. Teachers told me that they felt that their level of teaching had been "raised" and that literacy coaching was an "easy sell" for them because of student success. This supports the findings of Morgan et al. (2003), who report that in South Carolina, as student achievement increased, so did the demand for literacy coaches and their services.

A final plausible explanation for the diminished resistance towards literacy coaching is that the schools were working through the change process. Fullan's (2001) model of change includes initiation, implementation, and institutionalization, and the schools appear to have entered the institutionalization phase; teachers were generally implementing the initiatives with independence. Years one and two when teachers were learning new methods would have been the implementation phase when teachers tend to struggle with change. The coaches acted as a support system during the change process, and this support from the coach would help decrease resistance (Fullan, 2001).

It is significant to note that, unlike teachers, the literacy coaches did not resist the initiatives or the enforcement of initiatives, and I propose a number of reasons for this finding. First, the schools were nominated as having exemplary literacy coaching, and it is likely that these schools had coaches who followed the initiatives. The coaches may have felt that implementation was their job and not question authority. Another possible reason is that after three years of pressure and implementation, the coaches were also normalized by the administration into using the correct method. It is also possible that literacy coaches, like teachers, presented an appearance of compliance but may have had doubts about the initiatives and were covertly resistant (Hargreaves & Dawe, 1990). A final possibility is that the coaches genuinely felt that the initiatives were beneficial. The coaches told me a number of times that teaching and learning had improved in their schools. Steckel (2009) writes, "the proof is in the pudding" (p. 19). Thus, perhaps the coaches saw success in their schools and, therefore, believed in the initiatives.

Limitations and Implications for Research and Practice

The study is limited by its small sample size, and a larger sample in other contexts would provide a wider perspective on relationships in literacy coaching. In addition, the schools that participated were nominated as having exemplary literacy coaching, and it is plausible that this characteristic impacted the relationships among teachers, coaches, and principals. It would be beneficial to study literacy coaching in schools where coaching is not exemplary and compare issues of power and teacher resistance to this study. This study was also conducted over eight weeks, a relatively short period of time to observe relationships and school change. Participant interviews did help fill the gaps of the observations and provide a retrospective into what had occurred in the three schools before the study. Longitudinal studies, however, would shed a new light on literacy coaching and how coaching unfolds as schools change practice.

Due to the small sample, the results of the study should be generalized with caution. However, there are a number of suggestions gleaned from this study that may be useful to those implementing literacy coaching. First, the roles of the principal and literacy coach should be clear, ensuring that coaches are in support roles and principals in pressure and evaluator roles. Without these roles, teacher resistance may occur because literacy coaches cannot form nonthreatening supportive relationships with teachers (Steckel, 2009; Sturtevant, 2004). I also suggest that the model of teacher observation, feedback, and demonstration be carefully considered. As suggested by the research (Joyce & Showers,1996; Rodgers & Rodgers, 2007; Toll 2005), these activities may put literacy coaches in an expert role who informally evaluate teachers, leading to a power imbalance between coaches and teachers. Other coaching models, such as Hasbrouck and Denton's (2007) model of student-focused coaching which centers on improving student achievement, could be considered as alternatives. Finally, it appears coaching takes time to work. Participants felt that it took three years to build relationships and see success with literacy coaching. If less time is dedicated to coaching, it is possible it will be deemed ineffective and will be regarded simply as another fad in education.

CONCLUSION

There has been a gap in the research that investigates the camaraderie, power, and resistance among teachers, principals, and literacy coaches and how these relationships impact literacy coaching. This paper has presented new findings about these relationships, demonstrating that it is possible, with principal support and enforcement of initiatives, a nonsupervisory coaching model, and time, that literacy coaches can create positive and supportive relationships as peers with teachers. Moreover, these collegial teacher/coach relationships may decrease teacher resistance towards coaching.

REFERENCES

Allen, J. (2006). *Becoming a literacy leader: Supporting learning and change.* Portland: Stenhouse.

Arendt, H. (1958). *The Human condition.* Chicago: The University of Chicago Press.

Bogdan, R. C., & Biklen, S. K. (1998). *Qualitative research for education: An introduction to theory and methods* (3rd ed.). Boston: Allyn and Bacon.

Burkins, J. M. (2007). *Coaching for balance: How to meet the challenges of literacy coaching.* Newark, DE: International Reading Association.

Casey, K. (2006). *Literacy coaching: The essentials.* Portsmouth: Heinemann.

Dole, J. A., & Donaldson, R. (2006). "What am I supposed to do all day?" : Three big ideas for literacy coaches. *The Reading Teacher, 59*(5), 486-488.

Dozier, C. (2006). *Responsive literacy coaching: Tools for creating and sustaining purposeful change.* Portland, OR: Stenhouse.

Elish-Piper, L., L'Allier, S. K., & Zwart, M. (2009). Literacy coaching: Challenges and promising practices for success. *Illinois Reading Council Journal, 27*(1), 10-21.

Ferguson, K. (2011). Exploring the role of literacy coaches: A case study of three schools in Ontario. Manuscript submitted for publication.

Fisher, D. (n.d.). *Coaching considerations: FAQs useful in the development of literacy coaching.* Literacy Coaching Clearinghouse. Retrieved from http://www.literacycoachingonline.org/briefs/Coaching ConsiderationsFinal020707.pdf

Flick, U. (2006). *An introduction to qualitative research: Theory, method and applications* (3rd ed.). London, UK: Sage.

Foucault, M. (1979). *Discipline and punish: The birth of the prison.* (A. Sheridan, Trans.). New York, NY: Vintage Books. (Original work published in 1977).

Foucault, M. (1988). Power and sex (D. J. Parent, Trans.). In L. D. Kritzman (Ed.), *Politics, philosophy, culture: Interviews and other selected writings 1977-1984* (pp. 110-124). New York, NY: Routledge. (Original work published in 1977).

Foucault, M. (1990). *The history of sexuality Volume 1: An introduction.* (R. Hurley, Trans.). New York, NY: Vintage Books. (Original work published in 1978).

Fraenkel J. R., & Wallen, N. E. (2003). *How to design and evaluate research in education* (5th ed.). New York, NY: McGraw Hill Higher Education.

Fullan, M. (2001). *The new meaning of educational change* (3rd ed.). New York, NY: Teachers College Press.

Garet, M. S., Porter, A. C., Desimone, L., Birman, B. F., & Suk Yoon, K. (2001). What makes professional development effective? Results from a national sample of teachers. *American Educational Research Journal, 38*(4), 915-945.

Gay, L. R., & Airasian, P. (2000). *Educational research: Competencies for analysis and application* (6th ed.). Upper Saddle River, NJ: Prentice-Hall.

Gibson, S. A. (2006). Lesson observation and feedback: The practice of an expert reading coach. *Reading Research & Instruction, 45*(4), 295-318.

Hargreaves, A., & Dawe, R. (1990). Paths of professional development: Contrived collegiality, collaborative culture, and the case of peer coaching. *Teaching and Teacher Education, 6*(3), 227-241.

Hasbrouck, J., & Denton, C. A. (2007). Student-focused coaching: A model for teaching coaches. *The Reading Teacher, 60*(7), 690-693.

Joyce, B., & Showers, B. (1996). The evolution of peer coaching. *Educational Leadership, 53*(6), 12-16.

Joyce, B., & Showers, B. (2002). *Student achievement through staff development* (3rd ed.). Alexandria, VA: Association for Supervision and Curriculum Development.

Lynch, J., & Ferguson, K. (2010). Reflections of elementary school literacy coaches on practice: Roles and perspective. *Canadian Journal of Education, 33*(1), 199-227.

McMillan, J. H., & Schumacher, S. (2001). *Research in education: A conceptual introduction* (5th ed.). New York, NY: Addison Wesley Longman.

Merriam, S. B. (1988). *Case study research in education: A Qualitative approach.* San Francisco: Jossey-Bass.

Miles, M. B., & Huberman, A. M. (1994). *Qualitative data analysis: An expanded sourcebook* (2nd ed.). Thousand Oaks, CA: Sage.

Morgan, D. N., Saylor-Crowder, K., Stephens, D., Donnelly, A., DeFord, D., & Hamel, E. (2003). Managing the complexities of a statewide reading initiative. *Phi Delta Kappan, 85*(2), 138-145.

Moxley, D. E., & Taylor, R. T. (2006). *Literacy coaching: A handbook for school leaders.* Thousand Oaks, CA: Corwin Press.

Patton, M. Q. (1990). *Qualitative evaluation and research methods* (2nd ed.). Newbury Park, CA: Sage.

Poglinco, S. M., Bach, A., Hovde, K., Rosenblum, S., Saunders, M., & Supovitz, J. A. (2003). The heart of the matter: The coaching model in America's Choice schools. Philadelphia, PA: University of Pennsylvania, Consortium for Policy Research in Education. Retrieved from www.cpre.org/Publications/AC-06.pdf

Rainville, K. N., & Jones, S. (2008). Situated identities: Power and positioning on the work of a literacy coach. *The Reading Teacher, 61*(6), 440-448.

Rodgers, A., & Rodgers, E. M. (2007). *The effective literacy coach: Using inquiry to support teaching and learning.* New York, NY: Teachers College Press.

Shaw, M. L. (2006*). A response to the IRA survey of reading/literacy coaches. Reading Today, 23*(6), 13.

Steckel, B. (2009). Fulfilling the promise of literacy coaches in urban schools: What does it take to make an impact? *The Reading Teacher, 63*(1), 14-23.

Sturtevant, E. G. (2004). *The literacy coach: A key to improving teaching and learning in secondary schools.* Washington, DC: Alliance for Excellent Education. Retrieved from http://www.all4ed.org/publications/LiteracyCoach.pdf

Swafford, J., Maltsberger, A., Button, K., & Furgerson, P. (1997). Peer coaching for facilitating effective literacy instruction. In C. K. Kinzer, K. A. Hinchman, & D. J. Leu (Eds.), *Inquiries in literacy theory and practice: Forty-sixth yearbook of the National Reading Conference* (pp. 416-426). Chicago, IL: National Reading Conference.

Toll, C. A. (2005). *The Literacy coach's survival guide: Essential questions and practical answers.* Newark, DE: International Reading Association.

Walpole, S., & McKenna, M. C. (2004). *The literacy coach's handbook: A guide to research-based practice.* New York, NY: Guilford Press.

Wildman, T. M., & Niles, J. A. (1987). Teachers reflect on change. *Educational Leadership, 44*(5), 4-10.
Yin, R. K. (2003). *Case study research, design and methods* (3rd ed.). Thousand Oaks, CA: Sage.

APPENDIX

Interview Protocol for Literacy Coaches

1. Tell me briefly about your teaching experience and how you became a literacy coach.
2. What are some of the activities you do in your role as a literacy coach?
3. As a literacy coach, how do you view success in your literacy coaching program?
4. What makes for an effective literacy coaching program?
5. Are there any barriers to success that the literacy coaching program encounters?
6. Have you been able to deal with these barriers?
7. Tell me about your relationship with the teachers you coach in regard to literacy coaching.
8. Tell me about your relationship with the school principal in regard to literacy coaching.
9. How do these relationships impact your role as a literacy coach and the literacy coaching program in the school?
10. How could literacy coaching be improved?
11. Is there anything about literacy coaching that I have not asked you that you would like to comment on?

Interview Protocol for Principals

1. Tell me briefly about your experience teaching and also as a school principal.
2. What are some of the literacy coaching activities you participate in?
3. As a principal, how do you view success in the literacy coaching program?
4. What makes for an effective literacy coaching program?
5. Are there any barriers to success that the literacy coaching program encounters?
6. Have you been able to deal with these barriers?
7. What is the principal's role in a literacy coaching program?
8. Tell me about your relationship with the literacy coach in regard to literacy coaching.
9. Tell me about your relationship with the teachers in regard to literacy coaching.
10. How do you think these relationships impact the literacy coaching program in the school?
11. How could literacy coaching be improved?
12. Is there anything about literacy coaching that I have not asked you that you would like to comment on?

Interview Protocol for Teachers

1. Tell me briefly about your teaching experience.
2. What are some of the literacy coaching activities you participate in?
3. As a teacher, how do you view success in the literacy coaching program?
4. What makes for an effective literacy coaching program?
5. Are there any barriers to success that the literacy coaching program encounters?
6. Have you been able to deal with these barriers?
7. Tell me about your relationship with the literacy coach in regard to literacy coaching.

8.   Tell me about your relationship with the school principal in regard to literacy coaching.
9.   How do you think these relationships impact the literacy coaching program in the school?
10. How could literacy coaching be improved?
11. Is there anything about literacy coaching that I have not asked you that you would like to comment on?

Interrupting Certainty and Making Trouble: Teachers' Written and Visual Responses to Picturebooks

Peggy Albers
Georgia State University

Jerome C. Harste
Indiana University

Vivian Vasquez
American University

Picturebooks continue to play a significant role in the English language arts classroom as a way through which children learn about and experience worlds outside their own. Access to this knowledge is through both written text and visual images. It is imperative that teachers consider both the visual and the written when conducting discussions that matter with their students around picturebooks. Sumara (2002) argues that literature study should involve "reformulating the already formulated, interrupting certainty, [and] making trouble" (p. 46). We argue that using picturebooks that address strong social issues in literature studies encourages critical readings, and provides readers with opportunities to "interrupt certainty," and disrupts commonplace beliefs. As a result, readers are positioned to "make trouble" by challenging certainty, disrupting inequity, and repositioning themselves for social action (Keis, 2006).

This study involved two groups of inservice teachers from two urban cities who studied, in common, three picturebooks identified as addressing difficult social issues: *Willy and Hugh* (Browne, 2000), *Sister Anne's Hands* (Loribecki, 2000), and *Into the Forest* (Browne, 2005). We identified these three as being particularly useful in creating space for critical literacy in that teachers could speak to what we saw as definable social issues presented in each book. Specifically, this study focused on helping teachers unpack, or identify and critically analyze, power relations, intentions, and stereotypes embedded within the visual and written language in these picturebooks. One group of teachers was asked to respond to these picturebooks primarily through written language. The other was asked to respond primarily through art. By asking two groups of teachers to respond in two different ways, we could explore similarities and differences in their responses. We see this study as a kind of "making trouble," an invitation for teachers to explore social issues within children's literature, in hopes of engaging them in critical dialogue and social action. Additionally, we view this study as contributing specifically to the significance of art as a semiotic system to position issues and people in ways often attributed only to written language. In designing the study as we did, we wanted to explore visual responses as critically as we do written/spoken responses.

We understand the exploration of social issues and social action as essential goals for teacher education in the 21st century, and see this study as a demonstration of how critical approaches to teaching literature might become an everyday part of literacy instruction. Research questions for this study were: (a) To what explicit or implicit messages, issues, or stereotypes in the picturebooks did participants attend?, (b) When positioned to respond through language (written/spoken) or art, how did participants respond to the systems of meaning operating in picturebooks that contained definable social issues?, and (c) To what extent did participants' responses reflect their growing understanding of critical literacy as represented through word and image?

These questions locate the analysis of this study within semiotics, and more specifically, critical social semiotics (Albers, 2007; Hodge & Kress, 1988). Not only are all texts socially constructed semiotic events (Fairclough, 2003), all texts are constructed through multiple semiotic systems (Anstey & Bull, 2000; Hodge & Kress, 1988), and mediated through these systems. Reality is, therefore, textually mediated not just by written language but also by images, sound, space, movement, and so on (Harste, 1994). This study contributes to a deeper understanding of how discourses around social issues are constructed through texts, and how such constructions may or may not be reified by geography. That is, certain beliefs about an issue may not be situated only in the experiences of readers in "The South" or "The North," but across boundaries. A critical approach to children's literature encourages readers to *talk back* to certainties in texts, to interrupt through written and visual languages, and "make trouble" by challenging the interpretations they and others construct.

OVERVIEW OF THE STUDY

This interpretive study evolves from our years of careful and critical investigation both of written and visual texts produced by students and teachers in classroom settings (Albers, 2004; Harste, Short, & Burke, 1988), especially focused on interpretations and discussions around children's literature that promote social justice (Albers, Vasquez, & Harste, 2011; Vasquez, 2004). Analytical work that focuses on close readings of picturebooks is significant for several reasons. First, picturebooks are most often used to teach young children to read and consider aspects of their world, and through which cultural values, historical information, symbolic interpretations, and so on are conveyed (Enciso, 1999; Short, 2009; Wolf, 2004). A number of scholars have worked with critical literacy and picturebooks (Harste, Lewison, Leland, Ociepka, & Vasquez, 1999; Jewett, 2007; Souto-Manning, 2009). They found that when children read and studied social issues in picturebooks, they desired to participate in social action and inquiry. Second, two primary systems of meaning, written and visual, comprise picturebooks, and as such, both systems must be interrogated (Serafini, 2009). Specifically, art comprises much of literacy learning for both younger and older students. The younger student depends on image to read the language in text (Kiefer, 1995), while the older student often depends on image for content information, clarification, confirmation, and/or symbolic connections (Alvermann & Phelps, 2004). As Kist (2005) and Kress (2003) have argued, the visual mode is fast becoming the source through which many read, experience, and build beliefs about the world. For those who are learning to read the world through image, understanding the visual structures that exist within picturebook images is as important to the shaping of beliefs as the written word. This understanding must be interrogated as rigorously as we have interrogated print-based literacies (Harste, 2003). Third, as Albers, Harste, and Holbrook (2010) argued, teachers cannot do for their students what they themselves do not do. With this mind then, when readers—including teachers—can systematically read and interpret image alongside written text, they are better able to read implicit messages as well as explicit, and the cultural values and associations connected to art and design elements.

This study's significance lies in the analysis of tensions between the desired readings and viewers' own interpretation of picturebooks. Such readings, we suggest, offer insight into how readers can generate new understandings about the position(s) from which they engage with texts. Additionally, analyses of relationships between and among objects within a picturebook, along with a holistic reading of the overall text, provide information about how texts position readers, and encourage them to take on certain identities, values, and ideologies other than their own. The net result of such analyses is an emerging understanding of a culture's everyday literacy practices, and how these practices position individuals and groups within that culture.

Theoretical Framework

As English language arts teachers our goal has always been to create a literate citizenry. Along with other scholars (Comber, 2001; Edelsky, 1999; Luke & Freebody, 1997), we wish to argue that despite this lofty goal, for the 21st century, our aim has to be higher. Our goal must be to create a critically literate citizenry. This means we are not abandoning universal literacy but rather framing it from a different theoretical perspective. In essence, we want universal literacy plus, with the plus being critical literacy.

By critical literacy we mean a citizenry that can identify and critically address the implicit and explicit messages conveyed in text. We use the word "text" broadly to include spoken, written, or depicted language, including that which is electronically transmitted. We want learners to understand that no text is neutral and that all texts are created from particular ideological perspectives. We also want them to understand that our response or reaction to text is never neutral, and that as we encounter them, we do so from particular ideological positions based on our past experiences and the discourses through which we have engaged. Our goal, then, is to work with learners to become citizens who understand the ideological nature of texts, and be able to read, respond, and produce texts from a critical perspective. We want to create a citizenry who are agents of texts rather than victims of text.

In concert with critical literacy, we suggest that visual discourse analysis (VDA) (Albers, 2007), both a theory and method of analysis, enables researchers to study the discourses that present themselves within visual text, as well as the viewers' identification with these discourses. The visual text is a communicative event, one that elicits and invites viewers to participate (or not) vicariously in the lived worlds of those represented or objects featured. Informed by Gee's (2005) discourse analysis, several semiotic principles underpin visual discourse analysis. First, visual language is reflexive in that it has the capacity both to create and to reflect the context and reality in which it was created. The viewer is implicated to the degree of her or his familiarity with the context, as well as visual messages sent and interpreted by the viewer. Second, language allows for situated meanings to occur. That is, interpretations of visual texts are produced in a given context and based upon previous experiences. Third, language is composed of many different social languages (Bakhtin, 1981), and visual designers and artists use different tools or media through which to communicate or carry out their intended message. Fourth, there are units of analysis within visual texts, including graphic, structural, semantic, pragmatic, and tactile, that engage viewers into noticing particular aspects of a visual text more than others (symbol, metaphor, size, color, etc.). For us, critical literacy and visual discourse analysis provide frameworks around which to study the written and visual interpretations and responses generated by teachers as they read picturebooks that encourage critical readings.

Design of the Study

We intentionally designed this interpretive study with two separate groups of teachers in mind. One was asked to respond in writing to three picturebooks that conveyed difficult social issues, and the other was asked to respond visually to the same three books. In their own settings, participants read together and responded in order to these picturebooks: *Willy and Hugh* (Browne, 2000), *Sister Anne's Hands* (Loribecki, 2000), and *Into the Forest* (Browne, 2005). *Willy and Hugh* focuses on the friendship between two unlikely characters after a bullying incident. *Sister Anne's Hands* addresses the racism that erupts when an African American nun teaches at a Catholic grade school. *Into the Forest* is a highly imaginative tale in which a boy wakes up to find his father gone. Like Little Red Riding Hood, he is sent to take goodies to his grandmother who is sick, only to find his father attending to her needs.

Procedures

Within the 2009-2010 academic year, researchers undertook this study with two groups of urban teachers (N=41). We align ourselves with Janks (2000) and Edelsky (2006), who argued that we must intentionally bring issues of social justice to the forefront of our discussions, centralizing the significance of social action as part of a democratic citizenry. As such, we took a critical stance in this study, and introduced picturebooks we believed would elicit responses that encouraged critical dialogue and action about social issues.

Participants across both groups ranged in age from 25–65, and most were full-time teachers. Their enrollment in these university programs demonstrated both an interest in critical literacy and visual methods of analysis. Participants in Group 1 (N=30) were inservice teachers in a literacy master's program at a major university in the North. The group met monthly from September 2009–October 2010, during which time data for this study were collected. Participants read widely on critical literacy, and implemented critical literacy engagements in their own classrooms. They also had opportunities to engage in critical readings of visual texts using visual discourse analysis. Members of the group produced and analyzed a range of visual and media texts including picturebooks, advertisements, and Public Service Announcements among others. During these monthly meetings, participants were introduced to children's literature that presented clear social issues for the purpose of supporting them in learning to identify and critically analyze the implicit and explicit social systems of meaning, which they saw operating in a story. We read each picturebook aloud to Group 1. After the reading, we asked participants to record their responses to the picturebook on 4" x 6" index cards that we then collected. This was followed by a whole class discussion of the book.

Participants in Group 2 (N=11) were enrolled in a major university in the South in a semester-long graduate literacy course, Visual Methodologies. The focus of this course was to teach students to analyze a range of visual texts primarily using the grammar of visual design (Kress & van Leeuwen, 2006), visual discourse analysis (Albers, 2007), and multimodal interaction (Norris, 2004). Nine participants were inservice teachers and two were principals. Participants met weekly and, as part of the course, they read and analyzed visual texts using methods introduced in professional readings. They also produced visual texts and used these same methods to study their own visual work. Group 2 read each picturebook aloud in the same order as Group 1, followed by a large group discussion. Participants were then asked to respond visually to the picturebook, and to bring their visual texts to class the following week. They presented their visual texts to the whole group, drawing upon their ongoing knowledge of visual methods. After this, the rest of the group added analysis they saw going on in these texts. At the end of the semester, participants were asked to bring their visual texts to class and to reread and reanalyze their visual responses produced across the semester. This exercise enabled us to better understand Group 2's evolving ability to use visual methods to interpret and analyze visual information.

Data Collection and Analysis

Data were collected over the year in Group 1 and over a semester in Group 2. For Group 1, we collected 90 written responses (one response/3 picturebooks x 30) on notecards. For Group 2, we collected 33 visual responses (one response/3 picturebooks x 11). Researchers also kept notebooks in which we recorded comments, questions, and thoughts that emerged in the large group discussions. For Group 2, we photographed their visual responses. Photographs enabled us to study the organizational structures and art and design elements evident in participants' texts (see, for example, Albers, 2007; Albers, Frederick, & Cowan, 2010). Additionally, we videotaped Group 2's explanations of their visual texts to study the interaction between the participant and her/his visual text. Videotapes allowed us to engage in multiple viewings of participants' analyses, as well as implement multimodal interaction analysis (Norris, 2004) to study participants' verbal and nonverbal responses about theirs and their colleagues' visual texts: types of gestures, eye movements, vocal inflections and pauses, spatiality, and so on.

Data analysis was complex as it concerned written, spoken, and visual data elicited within and across Group analysis. Because data were collected over time, we were also interested in whether participants in both Groups were growing in their ability to identify implicit and explicit visual and/or written messages. We were specifically interested in whether and how participants were able to identify messages directly signed by words or pictures in each picturebook (explicit), and whether and how they were able to identify messages not directly signed (implicit). For the written data (Group 1), we initially identified explicit systems of meaning operating or were on offer in each picturebook: *issues* at play, *stereotypes* represented, and *underlying messages* in both image and word. We identified 21 explicit messages within these systems in *Willy and Hugh*, 18 in *Sister Anne's Hands*, and 16 in *Into the Forest*. We then went through each participant's responses and recorded directly signed words and pictures (explicit). We coded them in the following way: "bullying," "racism" (*issues*); "bullies are big," "nerds are weak and small" (*stereotypes*); and "little people need big people too," "difference is bad" (*underlying messages)*. We then went through and recorded responses that were implicit, or messages not directly signed by pictures or words. Examples of this coding included the following: "racism is somehow 'very American,'" "the relationship between apes and monkeys parallel the relationship between bullies and nerds" (*underlying messages)*; "As teachers, nuns are very strict;" "Men (boys) don't cry" (*stereotypes)*. Some responses were coded in several systems of meaning: "Cities tolerate differences better than small communities" (*issues; underlying messages)*. For each picturebook, we tallied the number of explicit and implicit messages identified by participants, divided by the number of messages we had initially identified, and found the average number of messages identified by participants. For example, participants identified a total of 103 explicit/implicit messages (hits) in *Willy and Hugh*, for which we had initially identified 21 messages. For this book, on average, each participant identified 4.91 messages. Because we identified a different number of messages in each of the books, and each book drew a different total number of hits from participants, we were able to use these statistics to look across the books using the same metric.

For Group 2 we used visual discourse analysis (Albers, 2007) to study participants' visual responses. Each visual text was studied in relationship to the picturebook, guided by the following questions: What's s/he doing? (Attention to actual use of technique); How's s/he doing it? (Attention to grammar of visual design); What choices is s/he making? (Attention to materials, affordance, canvas space, object size/volume, color); How does s/he organize visual information? (Quadrants of information); How does s/he use the canvas? (Use of space, size and placement of objects, position of viewer); What does s/he reveal about herself or himself? (Attention to discourses and systems of meaning that underpin the visual text). We further studied each visual text for the explicit messages that were overtly signed by image or object (e.g., "Teachers support diversity:" drawing of open hands with TEACHER written across them, and a heart above with the words "OPEN HEART." We also looked for implicit messages that were not overtly signed by image or object (e.g., "We had to take the back roads to avoid being lynched;" visual depiction of Sister Anne kneeling under a lynched African American). We then looked across the Group's visual texts to identify common or unique objects, colors, organizational structures, and discourses that emerged. For example, with *Sister Anne's Hands*, participants visually depicted hands reaching up, reaching towards each other, hands in an opened position, hands in prayer, all of which reflected discourses of importance of unity, diversity, and desire to achieve, or to reach for, this unity.

We also studied the spoken comments by participants in Group 2 and triangulated those with the visual elements evident in their text. For example, David remarked that he used particle board to symbolize how "relationships are heavy at times." The materiality (the heavy board) reflected David's intention to express the underlying message of relationships in the book, between Sister Anne and her students, the school, the parents, and society in general.

Our initial analysis of data was conducted independently. We then met to discuss our findings. When we could not confirm a finding, we returned to and discussed the data. When we could collectively confirm a finding, we recorded it as such.

Findings for Group 1

Although we met with participants monthly and critically analyzed the issues, stereotypes, and underlying messages in one children's book each time we met, we only collected data at the beginning (September 2009), middle (May 2010), and end of the school year (September 2010). Because we were interested in the growing ability of participants to identify explicit and implicit messages in children's books, findings are presented in the order that data were collected.

The first book we read was *Willy and Hugh*. Of the 21 issues, stereotypes, and underlying messages we identified in this text, only one underlying message, "Don't judge people by their appearance," was not identified by participants. In their written responses, we found that participants identified 103 total messages within these three systems of meaning. Stereotypes were most often cited: "Nerds are little" (N=12), "Bullies are big" (N=11), "Bullies disrupt belonging which causes marginalization" (N=11). Three participants identified stereotypes and underlying messages that we ourselves had not seen: "Jocks are bullies" (N=1) and "The relationships between apes and monkeys parallel the relationship between bullies and nerds" (N=2). After data collection, participants shared the messages they had identified. These discussions reflected a depth of thinking and concern we found hopeful. Lori, for example, commented, "Willy never got to be strong on his own. He was strong only in Hugh's presence." On the average, 4.91 issues, stereotypes, or underlying messages were identified per participant in this text. Because these data were collected at the beginning of the school year, these findings constituted baseline data.

Sister Anne's Hands was the second book we read. Participants identified 85 underlying messages. The most salient were: "Being a minority member in a dominant culture causes problems" (N=13); "Teachers should be of the same ethnicity as the students they teach" (N=12); "Powerful institutions, like churches, have a particular social responsibility to wash their dirty laundry in public rather than sweep it under the rug" (N=11). Participants were indignant with this text and the values that the author assumed readers would take on. One participant, Patrick, said, "I felt aligned with the narrator <u>despite</u> the fact that her values did not agree with me....perhaps it is harder to be critical when...the 'storyteller' is a vulnerable child." Lilly commented, "What I'm made to accept is that when people don't like something, they just 'leave,' they don't 'act.'" Catherine observed, "The children...feel guilty when Sister Anne reacts with silence to the airplane, but I think her gentleness and forgiveness is atypical. I think it also suggests that it's okay to treat black people in this manner because they will accept and forgive." On the average, participants identified 4.73 issues, stereotypes, and/or underlying messages in this text, a slight decrease from their reading of *Willy and Hugh*.

The last book we read was *Into the Forest*. The dominant message that participants gathered from this book was that "Intact families give children security; single-parent families, absent families, or broken families are associated with fear, anxiety, and insecurity" (N=16). The two next dominant messages identified were "Fairy tales often play with the notion of children left to their own devices, and often have characters that act like wolves," and "Adults reinforce fears by not offering explanations." Participants identified three underlying messages which we had not ourselves identified: "Children in certain cultural groups are more likely to be raised in absent-father families than are children in other cultural groups" (N=2); "Children are vulnerable" (N=1); Men (boys) don't cry" (N=1). Of the 91 messages participants identified, all were explicit, and the average number of messages identified was 5.69 per participant. After data collection, their comments during the whole class discussion were often pointed. Many took the author to task saying that he was picking on non-dominant family patterns. Nor were they happy with his allusion to fairy tales. Michael said, "Expecting a wolf, but instead just got a few irresponsible grown-ups!!" while Kris quipped, "Sketchy places always have sketchy people."

Group 1 overall findings. As a Group, participants did read picturebooks more critically over the course of the year. Nonetheless, growth was slow and minimal. Initially, they were able to identify between 4 and 5 issues, stereotypes and/or underlying messages in a text. This increased to between 5 and 6 messages by the end of the year. No participant was outstanding. While the class average was between 4 and 5, one participant, Paddy, averaged 6.67 across the three data collection points. Participants as a group were much better at identifying explicit messages in text (those signed by either words or pictures) than they were at identifying implicit messages. There is an old Cree saying, "To say the name is to begin the story." Participants initially did a lot of naming of issues—bullying, racism, abandonment—without fully articulating the systems of meaning or stereotypes they saw operating. Discussions of the books after data collection were rich in that participants often seemed better able to articulate verbally their critiques of books than write about them. This may have been due to their ability to build off each other's comments or that, like many of us, their rhetoric got ahead of their ability to apply what they intuitively were coming to understand.

Findings for Group 2

Several key findings emerged from the study of Group 2's visual responses. Although these findings cut across representations, each finding will be explained through a single picturebook to more clearly illustrate the finding. First, participants often used explicit elements from the book to talk to the discourses they saw operating in the picturebook, and often they saw only a single discourse emerge (bullying, racism, absent parent). They recreated this discourse through a range of media including photocopied images from the book, recreations of these images in pencil color, charcoal, or construction paper, Photoshopped images, or mixed media. In *Willy and Hugh*, for example, friendship visually emerged as a single discourse, with friendship perceived as a solution to bullying. Participants used objects and symbols commonly associated with friendship (clutched hands and hearts, a bridge, hands touching, strong gazes between characters) to express this discourse.

Participants' verbal responses confirmed their visual metaphors and symbols: "The design comes from the sweater pattern [on Willy's sweater]" (Figure 1); "The two together show that there is strength in numbers" (clutched hands, gazes between characters) (Figure 2). One participant photographed two hands clutching, one white, one brown, and Photoshopped them over a

Figure 1. Participants' representations of *Willy and Hugh:* Participants' uses of explicit objects from the text to represent friendship.

Figure 2. Participants' representations of *Willy and Hugh:* Participants' uses of explicit objects from the text to represent friendship.

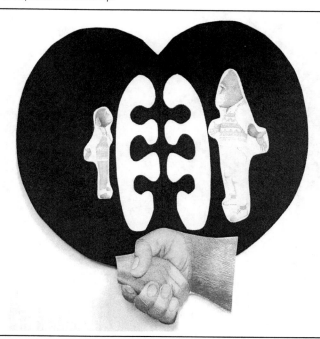

compass. She stated, "Difference made them friends. I overlaid a speckled pattern and a moral compass that guided them…I wanted no words; I resisted words. They are not needed here." One participant commented that friends always have one's "back," and represented this message by a human bridge framed by the pattern on Willy's sweater, similar to that shown in Figure 1. For participants, human bridges, clutching hands, direct gazes, hearts, and playful scenes represented friendship. Solutions around bullying were visually framed with friendship images. The use of

Figure 3. Participants' representations of *Sister Anne's Hands:* Participants' use of hands to signify participants' interest and discourse around resolving racism.

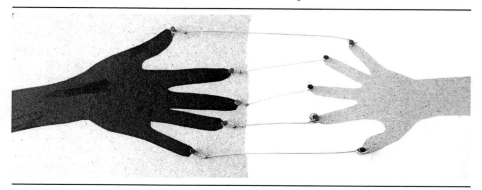

Figure 4. Participants' representations of *Sister Anne's Hands:* Participants' use of hands to signify participants' interest and discourse around resolving racism.

symmetry as an organizational structure confirmed the reciprocity that is expected with friendship. Friendship was the discourse, a declarative sentence, a full stop, and the means to a favorable end.

Second, participants spoke to explicit underlying messages (racism, discrimination, hatred, bullying, absent parent) in their presentations. In *Sister Anne's Hands*, for example, they saw messages of racism and the need for racial unity as the underlying messages. Interestingly, they interrupted these certainties visually. That is, rather than locate their visual texts within the issue of racism, they located their interest in solving racism, evidenced through their use of recognizable, cultural symbols.

Figures 3 and 4 present two of seven images in which participants used hands—multicolored, reaching out or up, fingers spread and open—to signify that issues such as racism can be overcome with the touch of a hand, a teacher's hands, Christ's hands, or

Figure 5. Participants' representations of *Sister Anne's Hands:* Participants' use of hands to signify participants' interest and discourse around resolving racism.

Sister Anne's hands. Additionally, two participants created tightly composed collages, comprised primarily of overlapping black and white photos and written text like "We Shall Overcome," all of which represented scenes of racism. In Figure 5, the overarching metaphors of an angel's wings located resolution of racism in religion. The other participant saw resolution through multi-colored hands that reach into a 3-dimensional red wire heart centered in the visual text ("X" marks the spot). Both participants signified their desire to place more importance on solving racism. Like in *Sister Anne's Hands*, visually and across texts, participants positioned themselves as problem-solvers who could take action on what they considered an important social issue.

Third, participants' visual texts spoke to the complexity of a social issue through their material choice, size, organization, art, and design elements. Participants resisted using written text within and across their texts. With their ongoing knowledge of visual discourse, including the grammar of visual design (Kress & van Leeuwen, 2006),

Figure 6. Participants' representations of *Into the Forest:* Participants' visual texts spoke to the complexity of a social issue through their material choice, size, organization, art, and design elements.

participants represented across media, and often used multimedia to represent their understandings. Specifically, they played with text (e.g., pop-ups, particle board, torn paper) to symbolize emotions that underpinned a social issue (e.g., *Sister Anne's Hands*: somber, sad, heavy; *Willy and Hugh*: surprise, happiness; *Into the Forest*: confusion, fear). For example, one participant created a pop-up text to represent the surprise that awaited the boy when he reached his grandma's house at the end of *Into the Forest*. He stated, "Behind these doors is fear." (Figure 6)

Others saw fear of the unknown and represented this through object selection and organization. One participant commented, "This is the path that the character took… "The bird is Mother Goose, twisted and dark, but it's all saccharine at the end. The torn paper signifies the jagged journey—everything around it is scary" (Figure 7). Another commented, "This is me walking down the path of life, guided by my dad's wisdom." Media choices were deliberately and consciously chosen: "Something is dark in the story, and there's something about the house with the wolf's ears sticking out. Something about the grandma is wrong."

Figure 7. Participants' representations of *Into the Forest*: Participants' visual texts spoke to the complexity of a social issue through their material choice, size, organization, art and design elements.

In 7 of the 11 visual texts, participants saw fear as the underlying message. Materiality and size afforded them a way to express this message. For example, David's piece (Figure 3) was a 36"(L) x 24" (H) while Rick's was 24" (H) x 12" (W) (Figure 6), and Jackie's was 40" (L) x 24" (W) (Figure 5). Participants used size as a way to emphasize the fear the young boy felt in his journey to his grandmother's house. Participants also used a variety of art media (graphite, oil pastel, photography, charcoal, construction paper, collage) that signaled their interest in particular aspects of their representation. David, for example, intensified the outlines of his Mother Goose with black charcoal, an ominous foreboder of doom (Figure 7). Lynn used lead pencil to highlight special moments she remembered with her father. Her only use of color is to define her father, further emphasizing the importance of her relationship with him. Margaret emphasized through color crayon the wolf's ears on the grandmother's house.

Cross-Group Findings

We found that those in Group 1 and those in Group 2 shared similar responses to the underlying messages within the picturebooks, represented in their conversations and expressed visually. In Figure 8, we present one example of the number of similarities that we saw in how Group 1 and Group 2 expressed their ideas about social issues at play in the picturebook.

We highlight this as an important finding as it situates the social issue not in the picturebook, but contextualized in the situations, backgrounds, and experiences of both groups of participants. For example, in *Sister Anne's Hands*, nearly half of the participants in Group 1 identified the explicit message of "Being a minority member in a dominant culture causes problems." The social issue at play not only was racism, but also the lack of power of those in minority populations like Sister Anne. Visually, participants in Group 2 also expressed this message through a tightly composed

Figure 8. Cross-analysis of Group 1 and 2's responses. Participants in Group 1 and 2 shared similar responses to underlying messages within the picturebooks, represented in their conversations, and expressed visually.

Picturebook	Underlying Message in Group 1	Visual Representation of Underlying Message in Group 2
Sister Anne's Hands	Being a minority member in a dominant culture causes problems	
Willy and Hugh	Unlikely characters can have meaningful relationships	
Into the Forest	Forests are dark and scary where bad things happen	

collage of black and white images of hate, signs that collectively signal how the power of the dominant culture sees civil rights as a problem. In *Willy and Hugh*, Group 1 identified that unlikely characters can be friends. Visually, Group 2 represented this same issue by positioning Willy and Hugh as back-to-back (another expression of having one's "back"). With the added symmetry of both pieces, these relationships are meaningful and reciprocal. In *Into the Forest*, Group 1 responded that forests are dark and scary places where bad things happen. Represented visually, participants in Group 2 suggested this through their use of charcoal and the anthropomorphic rendering of the wolf onto the grandmother's house. Both features signal fear, fright, and danger. We note these occurrences between both groups to suggest that participants in different locations identified similar underlying messages, stereotypes, and issues. Even though both groups live a thousand miles apart, they found common elements across books, and articulated similar concerns about the issues that affect both spaces.

DISCUSSION

We see this study as significant for a number of reasons. First, part of the work of education is to think ethically about what discourses of difference, visibility, and choice mean in pedagogy and the refusal to recognize difference as disruption, whether in curriculum or pedagogy (Britzman, 1995; Janks, 2010). Janks writes that the word "critical" "signal[s] analysis that seeks to uncover the social interests at work, to ascertain what is at stake in textual and social practices. Who benefits? Who is disadvantaged? In short, it signals a focus on power, on the ways in which meanings are 'mobilised in the defence of domination'" (p. 12-13). In this study, participants identified messages and discourses within picturebooks, and demonstrated their interest in interrupting the certainties of power both in written and visual ways. They made written and visual choices that positioned them ethically to read and respond to issues of social justice. They took a stand and spoke against issues that marginalize some and give power to others. By interrupting the certainty often afforded to those in power, these participants interrupted this power through written and visual language. In essence, their responses gave them voice to "make trouble," an experience they were encouraged to try with their own students with the goal to create space for them to think differently about social issues and to move toward social action.

Second, that participants across both groups identified underlying messages, issues, and stereotypes suggests that they were able to see that larger discourses are at play in picturebooks. Specifically, the participants live a thousand miles apart and yet they identified similar messages. This suggests that such issues cut across geographic boundaries and affect lives across borders. In both groups, participants moved toward solutions and problem solving. This move toward problem solving is the first step towards social action, according to Janks (2010). Further, their responses demonstrated their interest in social justice and equity—a single touch, memories of parenting experiences, or cutout hearts are calls for society to overcome such issues. As teachers they saw their ability to make such changes, especially in their classrooms, indicated visually by a teacher's hands rising upward (Figure 4).

Third, our data suggest that critical literacy, including the move from critique to social action, can start with the reading of picturebooks addressing social issues. Even though there was no steady rise in their identification of messages across books, Group 1 did show an increase in their ability to read picturebooks critically at the end of the academic year. This finding suggests that teachers must have sustained and multiple experiences reading, talking, and responding to social issues in picturebooks in order to evolve in their own political stance against social injustice.

Teachers must also have opportunity to represent meaning across semiotic systems. Even though Group 1 could name issues, their responses were often short and somewhat limited. As educators we were interested in having participants understand crictical literacy as both critique and social action. However, when participants were asked to respond to text in writing, rather than in art, they stayed at the level of critique. The production of art allowed participants to move to social action. In other words, those in Group 2 conveyed a richer and more developed sense of the issues in the book and how they saw themselves working towards a resolution.

When space is opened for other forms of representation, including art, we see the extent to which readers have taken on a critical stance. When participants were invited to produce art in response to picturebooks with difficult social issues, their responses reflected a personal as well as political response. This study offers evidence that the taking on of a critical stance is supported by opportunities to interpret picturebooks semiotically. Moving to art allowed participants more to fully explore the complexity of social issues as well as resolutions. Significantly, this study supports the notion that the production of art objects pushes students to think about critical literacy as social action rather than be satisfied with a definition of critical literacy that stops at critique.

CONCLUSION

Lankshear and Knobel (2006) argue that truth no longer exists in our society. "What seems to count, they say, "is the stories that you spin" (p xii). While this is a powerful assertion in its own right, when it is added to Kress's observation (2003) that the visual image is overtaking print as the dominant means of communication in society, the implications for education are great. In order not to be duped by 21st century literacies, students and teachers must be able to analyze stories critically and to understand the ways in which, as Hilary Janks (2010) says, "texts have designs on us" (p. 8). Because we argue that teachers cannot do for children what they themselves have not experienced, creating a critically literate citizenry for the 21st century must begin in our teacher education classes. This study shows that while this work is not easy and while we cannot take this work for granted, over time and with the analytical tools we now have available to interpret and study written and visual texts, teacher educators can make a difference. Importantly, given this study, we see one conclusion that seems irrefutable: Teachers must have opportunities to analyze issues critically through both language and art in order to identify the implicit and explicit issues, stereotypes, and underlying messages in picturebooks with difficult social issues. When offered such opportunities, teachers can see and understand the value and complexity that both communication systems afford as well as the importance of sharing these insights with students.

REFERENCES

Albers, P. (2004). Literacy in art: A question of responsibility. *Democracy and Education, 15,* 32-41.

Albers, P. (2007). Visual discourse analysis: An introduction to the analysis of school-generated visual texts. In D. W. Rowe, R. T. Jiménez, D. L. Compton, D. K. Dickinson, Y. Kim, K. M. Leander, & V. J. Risko (Eds.), *56th Yearbook of the National Reading Conference* (pp. 81-95). Oak Creek, WI: National Reading Conference.

Albers, P., Frederick, T., & Cowan, K. (2010). Visual conversations: A study of the visual texts of elementary grade students. In R. T. Jiménez, V. J. Risko, M. K. Hundley, & D. W. Rowe (Eds.), *59th Yearbook of the National Reading Conference* (pp. 201-215). Oak Creek, WI: National Reading Conference.

Albers, P., Harste, J. C., & Holbrook, T. (2010). Talking trade: Literacy researchers as practicing artists. *Journal of Adult and Adolescent Literacy, 54,* 164-171.

Albers, P., Vasquez, V., & Harste, J. C. (2011). Making visual analysis critical. In D. Lapp & D. Fisher. *Handbook of research on teaching the English language arts* (3rd ed.) (pp. 195-201). New York, NY: Routledge.

Alvermann, D. E., & Phelps, S. F. (2004). *Content reading and literacy: Succeeding in today's diverse classrooms.* Boston, MA: Allyn & Bacon.

Anstey, M., & Bull, G. (2000) *Reading the visual.* Sydney, Australia: Harcourt.

Bakhtin, M. (1981). *The dialogic imagination.* Austin, TX: University of Texas Press.

Britzman, D. (1995). Is there a queer pedagogy? Or, stop reading straight. *Educational Theory, 45,* 151-161.

Browne, A. (2000). *Willy and Hugh.* Sydney, Australia: Red Fox.

Browne, A. (2005). *Into the forest.* London, England: Walker Books Ltd.

Comber, B. (2001). Negotiating critical literacies. *School Talk, 6*(3), 1-3.

Edelsky, C. (1999). *Making justice our project: Teachers working toward critical whole language practice.* Urbana, IL: National Council of Teachers of English.

Edelsky, C. (2006). *With literacy and justice for all.* Mahwah, NJ: Erlbaum.

Enciso, P. (1999). Gender representations: Reaching beyond the limits we make. *The New Advocate, 12,* 285-297.

Fairclough, N. (2003). *Analyzing discourse: Textual analysis for social research.* New York, NY: Routledge.

Gee, J. (2005). *An introduction to discourse analysis: Theory and method* (2nd ed.). Abingdon, England: Routledge.

Harste, J. C. (1994). Literacy as curricular conversations about knowledge, inquiry, and morality. In R. B. Ruddell, M. Rapp Ruddell, & H. Singer (Eds.), *Theoretical models and processes of reading* (4th ed.), pp. 1220-1242. Newark, DE: International Reading Association.

Harste, J. C. (2003). What do we mean by literacy now? *Voices From the Middle, 10*(3), 8-12.

Harste, J. C., Lewison, M., Leland, C., Ociepka, A., & Vasquez, V. (1999). Exploring critical literacy: You can hear a pin drop. *Language Arts, 77*, 70-77.

Harste, J. C., Short, K. G., & Burke, C. (1988). *Creating classrooms for authors: The reading-writing connection.* Portsmouth, NH: Heinemann.

Hodge, R. & Kress, G. (1988). *Social semiotics.* Cambridge, UK: Polity Press.

Janks, H. (2000). Domination, access, diversity and design: A synthesis model for critical literacy education. *Educational Review, 52*, 175-186.

Janks, H. (2010). *Literacy and power.* New York, NY: Routledge.

Jewett, P. (2007). Reading knee-deep. *Reading Psychology, 28*, 149-162.

Keis, R. (2006). From principle to practice: Using children's literature to promote dialogue and facilitate the 'coming to voice' in a rural Latino community. *Multicultural Perspectives, 8*(1), 12-19.

Kiefer, B. K. (1995). *The potential of picturebooks: From visual literacy to aesthetic understanding.* Englewood Cliffs, NJ: Prentice Hall.

Kist, W. (2005). *New literacies in action: Teaching and learning in multiple media.* New York, NY: Teachers College Press.

Kress, G. (2003). *Literacy in the new media age.* New York, NY: Routledge.

Kress, G. & van Leeuwen, T. (2006). *Reading images: The grammar of visual design* (2nd ed.). New York, NY: Routledge.

Lankshear, C. & Knobel, M. (2006). *New literacies: Everyday practices and classroom learning.* Maidenhead, England: Open University Press.

Loribecki, M. (2000). *Sister Anne's hands.* New York, NY: Puffin Books.

Luke, A., & Freebody, P. (1997). Shaping the social practices of reading. In S. Muspratt, A. Luke, & P. Freebody (Eds.), *Constructing critical literacies* (pp. 185-223). Cresskill, NJ: Hampton Press.

Norris, S. (2004). *Analyzing multimodal interaction: A methodological framework.* New York, NY: Routledge.

Serafini, F. (2009). Understanding visual images in picturebooks. In J. Evans (Ed.), *Talking beyond the page: Reading and responding to contemporary picturebooks* (pp. 10-25). London, England: Routledge.

Short, K. G. (2009). Critically reading the word and the world. *Bookbird, 47*(2), 1-10.

Souto-Manning, M. (2009). Negotiating culturally responsive pedagogy through multicultural children's literature: Towards critical democratic literacy practices in a first-grade classroom. *Journal of Early Childhood Literacy, 9*(1), 50-74.

Sumara, D. J. (2002). *Why reading literature in school still matters: Imagination, interpretation, insight.* Mahwah, NJ: Erlbaum.

Vasquez, V. (2004). *Negotiating critical literacies with young children.* Mahwah, NJ: Erlbaum.

Wolf, S. A. (2004). *Interpreting literature with children.* Mahwah, NJ: Erlbaum.

Teachers' Perceptions of Professional Development in Writing

Sarah J. McCarthey
Rebecca L. Woodard
Grace Kang
University of Illinois at Urbana-Champaign

In her recent review of professional development (PD) studies employing various methodologies, Desimone (2009) identified five critical features for teacher learning: (a) a *content focus* (i.e., activities that focus on subject matter content and how students learn that content); (b) *active learning* (i.e., teachers engage in knowledge construction); (c) *coherence* (i.e., the extent to which teacher learning is consistent with teacher's knowledge and beliefs); (d) *duration* (i.e., sufficient span of time over which activity is spread and number of hours spent on activity), and (e) *collective participation* (i.e., arrangements that encourage interaction and discourse). Desimone (2009) also created a conceptual framework for evaluating the effectiveness of PD in three main areas—increases in teacher knowledge or skills/changes in attitudes or beliefs, changes in instruction, and improvements in student learning. The work of this study is focused on how particular PD experiences in writing influence teachers' knowledge and beliefs.

Categorizing Professional Development in Literacy

In his case study of the effective PD efforts of New York City's Community School District 2, Elmore (1997) found that we know little about how to organize successful PD to affect practice in large numbers of schools. While recognizing that categorizing has limitations, it is important to investigate how particular structures or forms of PD influence teachers' attitudes and instruction. For this study, we organized PD in writing into four categories: (a) university/school partnerships (e.g., National Writing Project), (b) district-level PD (e.g., lab sites and networks where inter-visitations can occur), (c) school-based PD (e.g., literacy coaches and professional study groups), and (d) self-directed PD (e.g., professional literature, graduate programs, professional organizations/National Board Certification).

University-school partnerships. University-school partnerships, particularly those focused on school-wide reform, are increasingly common. Research on university-partnership professional development projects such as the National Writing Project (Lieberman & Wood, 2003; National Writing Project & Nagin, 2006; Whitney, 2008), the School-Based Change approach (Au, Raphael, & Mooney, 2008), the Master Teacher Program (Crawford, Roberts, & Hickman, 2008), and professional study groups (Godt, 2007) are overwhelmingly in favor of such pairings. They cite benefits such as changing the mindsets of teachers (Crawford, Roberts, & Hickman, 2008), increasing teacher confidence (Godt, 2007; Whitney, 2008), and creating on-going professional networks for teachers "[by treating] teachers as creators—not just receivers—of curriculum" (Au, Raphael, & Mooney, 2008, p. 182).

The National Writing Project (NWP), envisioned by James Gray in 1974, has received much attention for its PD networks that are embedded in school-university partnerships (Lieberman & Wood, 2003). Whitney (2008) found that many teachers who participated in the NWP described their experiences as "transformative" both personally and professionally. A key feature of all 200 sites is the 20-day Summer Institute in which teachers conduct staff development activities.

District-level professional development. Traditional district-level PD structures have received extensive criticism (Crawford et al., 2008; Hawley & Valli, 1999). These skill-training workshops where outside experts come in for a short period of time to train teachers on administrative-chosen topics usually emphasize individual activity, passivity, and immediate results.

In contrast, Elmore's (1997) case study of Community School District 2 in New York City documents this exemplary district's use of PD to mobilize knowledge in system-wide instructional improvement reform. However, Elmore concluded that:

> It may be less important for other districts to imitate what District 2 is doing than for them to shift the purposes and activities of the system to focus more centrally on instructional improvement and sustain that commitment long enough for people in the system to begin to internalize it and start engaging in problem-solving consistent with it. (p. 30)

School-based professional development. School-level professional development in literacy has become a focus in recent years, as evidenced by the fact that many states, districts, and schools are moving toward the literacy coach position as a model of PD (Dole, 2004). Numerous researchers now incorporate all facets of reading and writing by relabeling reading coaches as literacy coaches (Bean, Swan, & Knaub, 2003; Hall, 2004; Walpole & Blamey, 2008). The strength of literacy coaching is the accessibility of change agents in the schools who have relationships with the staff; they are more apt to have a long-lasting impact on teachers (Desimone, Porter, Garet, Yoon, & Birman, 2002; Parise & Spillane, 2010). Literacy coaching has been described as "hot" in recent international reports (Cassidy & Cassidy, 2008) and has had an impact on teacher efficacy (Cantrell & Hughes, 2008). Recent research indicates that literacy coaching is responsible for significant improvements in students' literacy learning (Biancarosa, Bryk, & Dexter, 2010) as well as improvements in teachers' knowledge and quality of their language and literacy practices (Neuman & Wright, 2010). However, variability in the amount of time coaches spend with teachers can affect students' levels of proficiency (Bean, Draper, Hall, Vandermolen, & Zigmond, 2010). Factors such as collaboration with teachers, coaching for differentiation, and leadership support are related to teachers' instruction (Walpole, McKenna, Uribe-Zarain, & Lamitina, 2010). Teachers value collaboration with the coaches, on-going support, and instructional strategies they learn through coaches' work in their classrooms and in study groups (Vanderburg & Stephens, 2010); yet, coaching can be filled with tensions between teachers' goals and improving literacy instruction (Ippolito, 2010). In Walpole and Blamey's (2008) two-year study of an intense staff development program, coaches identified themselves as having multiple roles, including: assessor, curriculum manager, formative observer, modeler, teacher, and trainer. The participants typically identified coaches as either directors (i.e., "change coaches") or mentors ("content coaches").

Teacher inquiry groups and professional study groups are also a growing area for school-supported professional development (e.g., Bissex, 1987; Godt, 2007; Hubbard & Power, 2003). Benefits from participation in professional study/inquiry groups include helping teachers understand the students' points of view, providing teachers with a foundation for practice, and inspiring the work of teachers and students (Hubbard & Power, 2003).

Self-directed professional development. Technology has created unprecedented access to knowledge and PD, particularly for isolated teachers. Professional literacy organizations are beginning to offer self-directed professional development for teachers. For example, the National Council of Teachers of English (NCTE) online Pathways program, "offers sustained and intensive professional development at an affordable price" to individual teachers, schools and districts, and university classes (NCTE, 2009). No research has yet documented the results of organized online programs for self-directed teacher professional development.

Membership and participation in professional organizations is another type of self-directed professional development for teachers. Researchers cite many potential ways that professional membership may enhance teacher professionalism. For example, professional membership provides teachers with an independent professional community, the capacity to advance and disseminate specialized knowledge, opportunities for ongoing PD, and advocacy for members (Bauman, 2008; Hargreaves, 2000; Roen, Goggins, & Clary-Lemon, 2008). However, "The place of teachers' professional associations remains nearly invisible in the mainstream professional development literature" (Little, 1993, p. 135). Few empirical studies in education have focused on the effects of professional membership on teacher beliefs and practices or on reform movements (Little, 1993).

While there have been a number of studies cited above that have established the benefits of PD on teachers' practices, few studies have investigated how different types of PD structures affect teachers' perceptions in writing instruction. With the exception of Whitney's study, few studies have focused on teachers' experiences of PD in writing. Thus, our guiding question for this study was: What are teachers' perceptions of the impact of PD on their writing instruction?

METHODS

The study is part of a larger study examining professional development and writing instruction with 20 teachers, from four different districts, who were involved in a variety of professional development activities.

Participants and Selection

The current study focused on 10 elementary teachers (6 White, 3 African American, 1 Asian American; 8 female and 2 male) from the same district in which the *Units of Study* (Calkins, 2003) was a mandated writing curriculum. It is a consolidated district with 11 elementary schools, three middle schools, and two high schools, which is located in a small urban community near a large state university. There is a diverse student population: 45.7% are White, 37.3% are Black, 6.8% are Hispanic, 9.8% are Asian, .3% are Native American, .1% are multi-racial, and 47.1% qualify for free or reduced lunch. Initially, about 15 teachers (from five schools) were nominated by a combination of educators involved in several university-school partnerships, including leaders at the local NWP site. Then all teachers at the five participating schools were invited by the principals to participate and were offered a little stipend from a small research grant. From this pool, 10 teachers volunteered to participate; they had various levels of teaching experience and opportunities for professional development.

Data Collection/Analysis

Three researchers conducted interviews and observations of participating teachers over the course of one school year. Each researcher focused on three teachers (one researcher focused on four teachers), conducting observations of writing instruction followed by interviews (e.g., Round 1: September/October; Round 2: January-March; Round 3: April/May) to capture changes in perceptions of PD and writing practices. Due to space restrictions, the researchers present only the findings from the interview data for this article; an analysis of teachers' practices and the ways they integrated the PD, primarily using the observational data, is in preparation. Focusing on teachers' perceptions of PD lays the groundwork for examining how PD influenced their practices.

The semi-structured interviews focused on curriculum, student work, and professional development. Protocols for the second and third rounds were developed to follow up on information gained from the first round; thus, questions were added to elicit teachers' views of technology, their philosophies of writing, and their views of themselves as writers. For this analysis, the researchers focused on the professional development section of each of the protocols (see Appendix for compilation of questions focused on PD). The protocols included questions with specific probes about professional development opportunities and teachers' perceptions of their effectiveness and impact on writing practices.

In addition, we interviewed a University Curriculum Specialist (UCS), Claire (all names are pseudonyms), and the district-level language arts coordinators, Jane and Barbara. Claire worked extensively with the school district and with seven of the ten teachers in this study, so we interviewed her about her role and perceptions of the district writing curriculum. The two language arts coordinators were interviewed together about the role of coaches in schools and the selection of the *Units of Study* curriculum.

Interviews were transcribed by the researchers or verbatim by a professional transcriber. Data analysis began by combining the responses related to professional development from all three interviews for each of the ten teachers and placing them into one document to facilitate closer analysis. Then the team summarized each teacher's responses and created charts to represent the opportunities they had to participate in different types of professional development within the last three years. The charts included four main categories of professional development taken from the literature: (a) university-school partnerships, (b) district-level workshops, (c) school-level opportunities, and (d) self-initiated activities.

Once we established the opportunities each teacher had, we categorized their perceptions into: (a) benefits, and (b) disadvantages of each type of professional development. We used their responses to questions about major influences on their writing instruction to understand the potential impact of professional development on their instruction. Representative quotations were selected to present in the findings section. Interviews from the UCS and district-level coordinators were used to provide context for the writing programs, role of the coaches in buildings, and perceptions of effectiveness of implementation.

FINDINGS

Our findings suggested that there were many K-12 professional development opportunities in the district including: (a) the Summer Academy (SA), a week-long, intensive experience on the university campus involving keynote speakers and school-based teams who plan curricular implementations; (b) 7 University Curriculum Specialists (UCS) who work in local schools modeling in classrooms and collaborating with teams of teachers on either math or literacy; (c) the local site for the National Writing Project with a 20-day Summer Institute focused on writing with technology; (d) district literacy coaches who had variable roles (e.g., working with children, providing resources, or acting as mentors) in elementary buildings; and (e) district-run workshops with release time for all teachers to attend. In addition, some of teachers were in the master's program at the university and several discussed self-initiated professional development such as National Board Certification.

Table 1 presents an overview of the professional development activities in which the 10 teachers in the study participated. All teachers were involved in *some* type of professional development; however, not all teachers participated in *all* professional development activities. Furthermore, not all types of professional development were available to all teachers since only some schools and teachers had a UCS or were invited to participate in the Summer Academy.

In the next section we: (a) describe the types of professional development, (b) indicate the numbers of teachers who had access to that type of PD, and (c) communicate teachers' perceptions of the impact of various types of professional development on their teaching of writing.

University School Partnerships

Three different types of university-school partnerships occurred in this urban district. Teachers who participated in these activities reported having positive experiences with the PD offered.

Table 1. Participation in Professional Development

Teacher	University-school Partnerships			School-based		District-level	Professional Literature			
	Summer Academy	University Curriculum Specialists	NWP Summer Institute	Literacy Coach	Colleagues	District Workshops	Professional Literature	Masters Program	Professional Membership	National Board Certified
Tamara			X	x		x				
Mandy	x			X	X	x				x
Jocelyn	x			x	X	x		x		
Vicky	x	X		x	X	x		x		
Dana		X	X	x		x		x		
Ellen	x	X		x	x	x				
Wanda	x	X		x			x	x		
Mike	x	X		x		x				
Tara	x	X		x		X				
Jackson		X		x		x		x		
Total	7	7	2	10	4	9	1	5	0	1

Note. Lower case x = PD in which teachers participated. Upper case X = PD that was most influential on teachers' writing instruction.

University Curriculum Specialists. There were 7 UCS working in two districts on literacy and math at the elementary and secondary levels. Only one of these, Claire, worked in the focal district as an elementary literacy UCS. She had been in this role for three years working with groups of teachers at individual schools on their literacy curriculum in 4-6 week cycles. Claire described her work in this way, "It's a combination of co-teaching and modeling and then planning and debriefing." She found that over the course of the three years her role had shifted:

> I've been taking more of a leadership focus with teachers. I think at the beginning it was a lot of working in classrooms, just to kind of get a feel for who leaders were in buildings...I purposely chose teachers that I felt would be able to move forward a little bit and co-teach with me...I definitely have noticed that the modeling part is a lot less and the co-teaching and planning and debriefing is a lot more.

Claire thought that the major benefits of her work with teachers were providing support for teachers and working with children in the classroom context:

> I think the advantage is that you have ongoing support, obviously, through the year. Then, it's contextualized in the classroom, which is a big one, because I think that curriculum is just really hard when it's not contextual. So, I think it's helping people navigate that. I think that at least what having a (UCS) does is it helps people reflect and think back to what they're doing and what they're teaching...I think that a lot of our conversations are more student focused, so it's not necessarily about, "Why is Lucy Calkins making us do this?" kind of thing, but it's more like, "Let's see what these kids are doing," and that conversation has been really good.

The seven teachers who had the opportunity to work with Claire commented on the importance of her being in the classroom to model lessons and discuss writing; they all reported that she had a major impact on their curriculum. Ellen described how Claire worked with teachers:

> She would meet with all of the teachers, K-1 group at the time, and give us some overview, some challenges...We would go into a classroom and observe. Then we got to conference with kids so the kids got the benefit of having all these teachers in the room. Then we would go back and debrief. They (interactions) were very positive and we all learned from them because we could ask questions or make comments about what we noticed.

Vicky had the opportunity to have Claire twice the year before, "It was so helpful to watch her with kids," and stated that the UCS, "is like a master at teaching writing." Dana's most influential professional development was working with Claire, who helped her adapt the Calkins curriculum, "The way she comes in, and models, it is wonderful to watch her teach. It is inspiring to me. It makes you feel freer than sticking with a program that does not fit your teaching style." Mike reported that the partnership serves as a "liaison between public schools" and "The university can really bridge that divide." Wanda's comments indicated the value of working with Claire, "A lot of things that I didn't try last year or I didn't even know how to try—she showed me how to do it. She would do it and then ask me if I was comfortable enough to do it on my own." Ellen found the collaboration valuable because others shared her concerns, "I was not alone, I had struggles and questions. Across grade levels we had different needs and yet a lot of us had the same questions—

how to motivate a writer?" Jackson also had the opportunity to work with Claire and found it helpful because, "It forces you to look in the mirror…Things are tangible and if it does not work, you tweak it." Tara also had a positive experience with the UCS; she noted that her long-standing relationship with Claire facilitated their interactions with students.

Summer Academy. The Summer Academy (SA) was supported by the administrators of the university for five years to bring teachers to campus in an effort to improve local schools. The SA then became a part of a larger initiative to bring the university and schools together with the seven UCSs playing roles in leading it. Claire described her role in the SA:

> The focus of it is that they're actually doing their own work and thinking about something that's relevant and pertinent to their building and taking something concrete back with them…How that looks has definitely evolved, because at first it was more of a, "Change your whole building and change the world," kind of philosophy…And we realized that was a little bit lofty and not doable. And what we saw through the year is that people were really excited during the SA, but then nothing really came of it through the year. So, then we kind of changed it a little bit the year after, where we asked them to work on a literacy plan for their building. That gained some momentum in some schools and didn't in others.

Claire elaborated on how the SA evolved into the development of professional learning communities where the teachers focused on assessment, examining student work, and reflective practice within their own schools.

Seven of the ten teachers had opportunities to be part of the SA in the past three years. Although the focus was not specifically on writing, most reported gaining confidence in their writing instruction due to the emphasis on differentiated instruction. Vicky described her experiences in this way, "The first year it was focused on differentiated instruction but it was everything—writing, math, how to take curriculum and tailor it to the needs of different students—whether they are low achieving or high achieving." The SA helped her become "more aware that I have 34 students with varying abilities…It is going to change the way I am going to assess. I am looking more for growth in my students than I ever was. And that comes from differentiated instruction." She reported that the next year they used the RTI model, "We talked about RTI and intervention, that is still new to me so it is another new thing, I am still getting differentiated instruction down and now we are talking about intervention at all different levels." Most important to participating teachers was the opportunity to work with colleagues from their schools to differentiate their curriculum for students of varying abilities. Ellen said, "I look at learners as individuals instead of everybody needs to write a paragraph." However, two teachers were not so enthusiastic about the SA, especially Wanda, who felt that she could not use the SA curriculum because it was idealized, "Like if I had the perfect class that were all on grade level." Wanda preferred working with Claire, who personalized the writing curriculum to Wanda's students, so she could see "immediate results" with students improving their writing.

Summer Institute of NWP. The local site of the NWP was established in 2008 using the following components consistent with the NWP model: individual writing time, peer writing groups, demonstrations of teaching lessons, literature discussion groups, and a focus on technology where teachers each had their own laptops and learned to create imovies, blogs, webpages, and digital portfolios to enhance their own writing and writing instruction. The two teachers who had participated in the local NWP noted their involvement enhanced their own writing and instruction; in particular, they valued the focus on technology. Dana explained, "It is a time of immersion, what you need, that immersion is amazing. At the beginning I thought I can't do this. It was not the writing; it was the technology for me." She found the experience "life changing. . .you come back at the top of your game, using everything you learned." Tamara noted that she gained many ideas for writing, including quick writes and writer's notebooks. The NWP helped her consider technology outside of the computer lab; currently, she was working with a parent to help her second-graders present projects using technology.

District-Level Professional Development

The school district offered six "School Improvement" days in which students were released from school and teachers took part in mandatory professional development activities. Teachers had choices about which district-sponsored activities they wanted to attend; however, the programs were not content-specific and tended to be programs such as "Nurtured Heart" (building students' self-efficacy). The teachers found these to be somewhat valuable, but only loosely related to their writing instruction. However, five years before the study began, the district adopted the Calkins curriculum and offered workshops for interested teachers. Trainers from Teachers College came to school sites to work with teachers. Of the participating teachers, only one had attended the workshops.

School-Level Professional Development

School-level professional development had two inter-related aspects: coaching and working with colleagues. The district-level coordinators described the coaching model at the elementary schools as "evolving" over the last several years. A coach split his or her day between working with students for half of the day and "providing job-embedded professional development for teachers" for the other half of the day. The district leaders (Jane and Barbara) found that the implementation "depends on the building and how coaching has been introduced ...It is a little different in each school—there is not a single model." Barbara found that the coach "can wear many hats, providing resources, helping a teacher to plan, facilitating a discussion about data, co-teaching in the classroom." Jane suggested that the most successful models were in schools where the teachers were open to working with the coaches, and the principals communicated effectively about their roles rather than assigning coaches to work with ineffective teachers. The coordinators were strong supporters of the coaching model and believed that the advantages included:

> It is on-site embedded, it is right there; it is much different than having people come after school to a workshop. It is working with someone and it is very applicable. It is not just theory; we are into the classroom living it, breathing it. Another benefit of having coaches in the building is being able to organize and bring data, facilitate discussion around data. (Barbara)

They found that it was more effective than the "one-shot workshop;" teachers were less interested in attending PD after school as the demands of their jobs increased in the current standards and testing era.

There was variation in how literacy coaches interacted with teachers from building to building. Teachers were somewhere along the continuum from simply receiving resources from their coach to meeting often for co-planning sessions and having lessons modeled by their coach. Many teachers indicated that if they initiated working with the coach, she was always responsive, but it usually required the teacher to be proactive to start working with the coach. All 10 teachers had literacy coaches in their buildings; however, some teachers worked with the coach primarily on reading and some teachers had never even worked with the coach. Vicky indicated that she had a coach, but the coach mainly worked with her struggling readers outside of the classroom. Wanda contacted her coach to meet, but had never heard back from her. And Mike commented, "The literacy positions in this district have changed a lot this year, more than any other year I've seen." He elaborated that most of the support the coach provided was pull-out, but he preferred push-in.

Seven of the ten teachers had a positive perception of working with the coach because it was meaningful, collaborative, and contextualized. Tamara worked with the coach every week for reading groups and was beginning to collaborate with the coach on other aspects of literacy. Mandy valued any chance she had to work with her coach and expressed that she would like to have more opportunities to co-plan and co-teach with her and for the coach to model lessons in her classroom. She found these coaching sessions to be the most significant, "It is the most meaningful form of professional development because it's a long-term relationship and it's ongoing." Dana's coach pushed in during writing workshop to confer with students and she felt that the coach made district mandates accessible to the teachers. Ellen commented that the coach came into her classroom twice a week and they both conferred with students, "I really depend on her." Tara enjoyed the workshops her literacy coach provided for her school and she expressed that the coach was a great resource and if she had questions, she knew her coach would have the answers. Jackson found his literacy coach an invaluable resource, "(Names coach) is awesome. It's a mutual trusting relationship. Anything you need she provides you, any support you need, she'll come in and do a mini-lesson, do it with you. She'll provide you with resources."

The majority of the teachers did not mention working with colleagues as a form of professional development; however, those who did found it to be significant. Four teachers mentioned working with colleagues, but two of them were working with Claire as well. Two other teachers who were on the same grade level team at their school reported it as one of the most influential forms of professional development. Mandy noted that she met often with Jocelyn for team planning and that she found "tons and tons of collaboration" extremely meaningful. She also continued, "I mean you can get ideas from the conferences, but if you don't come back and talk about how to implement those ideas, the ideas will work (only) for a particular group of students. . . I mean these guys are totally different from last year's students." Jocelyn realized that teaching writing was a weakness, "[Meeting with colleagues] it helped me to become better at it and where to even start with this, because I would have had no idea." She elaborated, "You don't have to collaborate, but I choose to."

Self-Initiated Professional Development

Teachers were involved in a variety of self-initiated professional development activities from being a part of master's degree programs at the university to reading professional literature or writing on their own. Five teachers were in a master's degree program (one pursuing an administrative credential and four pursuing EdMs); only one of these teachers found it to be a major part of her growth as a teacher. Dana named particular professors who had been part of the Summer Institute as well as teaching courses. She integrated her work with the UCS, the NWP, and her coursework:

> I can't say enough how my connection with the university has made a difference with me. (Names professors.) There's just been a lot of wonderful input, theory, practice—I can't advocate for that enough. You feel like you're very theory grounded. You feel like you're current. And then I don't feel like I'm just trying what I think might be a good idea. I'm trying what I think might benefit my students, and that is all about professional development.

However, the other teachers did not find that their coursework related to writing or was a factor in their attitudes toward writing.

Other types of self-initiated professional development that teachers stated had some impact on their writing instruction included: National Board Certification (one teacher), professional literature (one teacher), and a workshop at Teachers College in NYC (one teacher). Most surprising was that the teachers did not cite involvement in professional organizations even when specifically asked, and they were not connected to the local or national organizations available in the community.

DISCUSSION

Although the district had multiple types of professional development, access varied. All teachers who worked with the UCS named this PD experience as the most significant influence on their instruction. In particular, Claire was instrumental in helping teachers adapt the Calkins curriculum to their own settings. Teachers reported the other university-school partnerships, such as the Summer Academy and local NWP, had an impact on their writing instruction. School-based coaching played a varied role in teachers' practices. While some reported working closely with the coach on literacy in general and writing in particular, others had little access to or did not take advantage of their building coaches. Our data found consistency between what the UCS and district-level language arts coordinators reported about goals and impact and the teachers' perceptions. The professional development activities (e.g., UCS, NWP, SA, literacy coaches) that teachers cited as influential on their writing instruction fit the model proposed by Desimone (2009)—they had a content focus, active learning components, coherence, duration, and collective participation.

One issue raised by most of the participating teachers was the desire for even more time with the UCS. Claire had developed close relationships with many of the teachers and those relationships appeared to motivate teachers to implement writing strategies in their classrooms. However, some teachers did not have access to the UCS, who was asked to serve a large number of teachers in a school district with 11 elementary schools. Developing close professional/personal relations was also a factor in teachers' reports about the influence of literacy coaches on their instruction—those who had close relations valued the coaches' work; this finding expands the research on coaching by identifying developing close relationships between coaches and teachers as a major factor in teachers' willingness to engage in reflective practice (Bean, Swan, & Knaub, 2010; Walpole et al., 2010).

A limitation of the study is that the selection of participants may have reflected bias since most of the participants had worked closely with the UCS or coach and were encouraged by their principals (who likely viewed them as leaders) to be part of the study. This raised another issue about the models of PD implemented—they all appeared to focus on establishing leaders in the building who could model and support writing for others. Little attention was paid to those teachers who may be weak instructors and need more intensive assistance in teaching writing.

One contribution of this study is the attention paid to teachers' voices by asking about their perceptions of PD; often the focus is on effectiveness of implementation or viewing PD as something that is done "to" teachers. The study demonstrated that teachers have positive views of coherent, contextual, and ongoing models of PD; thus, the next step is to observe the effects of coherent models of PD on teachers' practices.

REFERENCES

Au, K. H., Raphael, T. E., & Mooney, K. C. (2008). What we have learned about teacher education to improve literacy achievement in urban schools. In L. Wilkinson, L. Morrow, & V. Chou (Eds.), *Improving literacy achievement in urban schools: Critical elements in teacher preparation* (pp. 159-184). Newark, DE: International Reading Association.

Bauman, S. (2008). To join or not to join: School counselors as a case study in professional membership. *Journal of Counseling and Development, 86*, 164-177.

Bean, R. M., Swan, A. L., & Knaub, R. (2003). Reading specialists in schools with exemplary reading programs: Functional, versatile, and prepared. *The Reading Teacher, 56*, 446-455.

Bean, R. M., Draper, J. A., Vandermolen, J., & Zigmond, N. (2010). Coaches and Coaching in Reading First Schools: A Reality Check. *Elementary School Journal, 111*, 87-114.

Biancarosa, G., Bryk, A. S., & Dexter, E. R. (2010). Assessing the Value-Added Effects of Literacy Collaborative Professional Development on Student Learning. *Elementary School Journal, 111*, 7-34.

Bissex, G. L. (1987). What is a teacher-researcher? In G. Bissex & R. Bullock (Eds.), *Seeing for Ourselves: Case-Study Research by Teachers of Writing* (pp. 3-6). Portsmouth, NH: Heinemann.

Calkins, L. M. (2003). *The units of study for primary writing: A yearlong curriculum.* Portsmouth, NH: Heinemann.

Calkins, L. M. (2006). *Units of study for teaching writing, grades 3-5.* Portsmouth, NH: Heinemann.

Cantrell, S. C., & Hughes, H. K. (2008). Teacher efficacy and content literacy implementation: An exploration of the effects of extended professional development with coaching. *Journal of Literacy Research, 40*, 95-127.

Cassidy, J., & Cassidy, D. (2008). What's hot for 2008. *Reading Today, 25*(4), 1-11.

Crawford, P. A., Roberts, S. K., & Hickman, R. (2008). All together now: Authentic university-school partnerships for professional development. *Childhood Education, 85*, 91-95.

Desimone, L. M. (2009). Improving impact studies of teachers' professional development: Toward better conceptualizations and measures. *Educational Researcher, 38*, 181-199.

Desimone, L. M., Porter, A. C., Garet, M. S., Yoon, K. S., & Birman, B. F. (2002). Effects of professional development on teachers' instruction: Results from a three-year longitudinal study. *Educational Evaluation and Policy Analysis, 24*, 81-112.

Dole, J. A. (2004). The changing role of the reading specialist in school reform. *The Reading Teacher, 57*, 462-471.

Elmore, R. F. (1997). *Investing in teacher learning: Staff development and instructional improvement in community school district #2, New York City* (Report). New York: National Commission on Teaching and America's Future.

Godt, P. T. (2007). Leadership in reading. *Illinois Reading Council Journal, 35*, 60-66.

Hall, B. (2004). Literacy coaches: An evolving role. *Carnegie Reporter, 3*, 10-19

Hargreaves, A. (2000). Four ages of professionalism and professional learning. *Teachers and Teaching: History and Practice, 6*, 151-182.

Hawley, D. W., & Valli, L. (1999). The essentials of effective professional development. In L. Darling-Hammond & G. Sykes (Ed.), *Teaching as the learning profession: Handbook of policy and practice* (pp. 127-150). San Francisco, CA: Jossey-Bass Inc.

Hubbard, R. S., & Power, B. M. (2003). *The art of classroom inquiry.* Portsmouth, NH: Heinemann.

Ippolito, J. (2010). Three ways that literacy coaches balance responsive and directive relationships with teachers. *Elementary School Journal, 111,* 164-190.

Lieberman, A., & Wood, D. R. (2003). *Inside the National Writing Project: Connecting network learning and classroom teaching.* New York, NY: Teachers College Press.

Little, J. W. (1993). Teachers' professional development in a climate of educational reform. *Educational Evaluation and Policy Analysis, 15,* 129-151.

National Writing Project, & Nagin, C. (2006). *Because writing matters: Improving student writing in our schools.* San Francisco, CA: Jossey-Bass.

National Council of Teachers of English. (2009) *Pathways professional development program.* [audio podcast] Retrieved from http://www.ncte.org/pathways.

Neuman, S. B., & Wright, T. S. (2010). Promoting language and literacy development for early childhood educators: A mixed-methods study of coursework and coaching. *Elementary School Journal, 111*(1), 63-86.

Parise, M. L., & Spillane, P. J. (2010). Teacher learning and instructional change: How formal and on-the-job learning opportunities predict change in elementary school teachers' practice. *The Elementary School Journal, 110,* 323-346.

Roen, D., Goggins, M. D., & Clary-Lemon, J. (2008). Teaching of writing and writing teachers through the ages. In C. Bazerman (Ed.), *Handbook of research on writing: History, society, school, individual, text* (pp. 347-364). New York, NY: Erlbaum.

Vanderburg, M., & Stephens, D. (2010). The impact of literacy coaches: What teachers value and how teachers change. *Elementary School Journal, 111,* 141-163.

Walpole, S., & Blamey, K. L. (2008). Elementary literacy coaches: The reality of dual roles. *Reading Teacher, 62,* 222-231.

Walpole, S., McKenna, M. C., Uribe-Zarain, X., & Lamitina, D. (2010). The relationships between coaching and instruction in the primary grades: Evidence from high-poverty schools. *Elementary School Journal, 111,* 115-140.

Whitney, A. (2008). Teacher transformation in the National Writing Project. *Research in the Teaching of English, 43,* 144-187.

APPENDIX

Professional Development Protocol

Round 1 (September/October)

1. How has your writing instruction changed over the last 3 years?
2. What have been the significant influences on your instruction?
3. What types of professional development activities have you been involved in over the last 3 years? (probe for the following)
   a. District Workshops?
   b. National Writing Project?
   c. University Curriculum Specialists*? (*program name changed to protect confidentiality)
   d. Summer Academy*?
   e. Other?
   f. Courses at the local universities?
4. What effects have the professional development activities had on your teaching of writing?
5. What effects (benefits? disadvantages?) do you see of each type of professional development activity?

Round 2 (January/February/March)

1. What opportunities have you had for professional development since we last talked?

2. What effects have the professional development activities had on your teaching of writing?

3. Is there a literacy coach in your building and if so, how do you work with him/her?

4. What do you do on your professional development days/inservice times [e.g., district required with release time]?

5. Are you a member of any professional organizations? And if so, what is your involvement in them?

Round 3 (April/May)

1. What opportunities have you had for professional development since we last talked?

2. What effects have the professional development activities had on your teaching of writing?

3. What kind of professional development opportunities are you looking for or might you want in the future?

Richard L. Allington
Professor
Reading Education
University of Tennessee, Knoxville

Section II: Effective Instruction Fostering Meaning-Making

We have learned much in the past century about the effective teaching of reading. But we still have much to learn. We know, for instance, much about the important role that a student's vocabulary plays in becoming a successful reader and successful learner. We also know that little exemplary vocabulary instruction is observed in the classrooms students attend. A similar situation exists with reading comprehension. Some of this lack of effective instruction may be due to the design of commercial reading curriculum materials (Brenner & Hiebert, 2010; Dewitz, Joes, & Leahy, 2009; McGill-Franzen, Zmach, Solic, & Zeig, 2006) and the press some teachers feel to implement these curricula with fidelity. Truth is, little of what we know about effective vocabulary or comprehension instruction can be found in any of the core reading programs. But some of the lack of effective instruction can be laid at our feet because there remains much we just simply do not know (Biancarosa & Snow, 2006).

In this section, Honig explores just how we might facilitate the acquisition of scientific vocabulary in primary grade classrooms. While she reports the successful use of one science curriculum, her results also suggest that children's knowledge of domain-specific words in isolation "is significantly distinct from children's ability to use such language to express ideas." In other words, while students' knowledge of vocabulary words in isolation nearly doubled, there was less evidence in a more contextualized task that students had acquired the deeper meanings of technical words included in the materials they studied.

Ford-Connors examines the instructional talk of three urban middle school teachers, each using the same vocabulary development curriculum framework in their classes. Even with the same curriculum materials, teacher talk was widely variable across these classrooms, with one teacher spending far more time engaged in talk than the other two teachers. However, what we don't know is just why these common lessons featured such different patterns of talk. However, Ford-Connors concludes that the teacher who was least faithful in implementing the curriculum framework was the one most successful at fostering vocabulary growth.

Chisholm reports on the classroom discussion that three students participated in during an English 12 class. Discussion is one of those other things we know too little about (Nystrand, 2003). Too often commercial curriculum materials present only an interrogational format for the teacher to follow both while and after the students read a text. These interrogational questions, of course, have answers that are typically literal and text-based. Thus, the correct "answer" to the question can be displayed for the teacher and repeated to the students when necessary.

Of course, any attempt to "script" an authentic discussion in a commercial program's teacher manual would be foolhardy because every discussion follows individual responses. One might craft "discussion" questions, typically open-ended questions, but attempting to suggest how students will respond to those questions is likewise foolhardy (and if the answers are in the manual then it can hardly be considered "discussion"). What Chisholm does though is examine both student-to-student discussions as well as student responses to the teacher's discussion questions. What he demonstrates is how a multimodal class assignment fosters rich discussion that allows students to think differently about MacBeth, the "hero" of the text they have been reading.

Kinzer, Hoffman, Turkay, Gunbas, and Chantes present what seems to be a surprising finding—that both interest in and understanding of a narrative presented in three formats (an electronic game, a graphic novel, and traditional book versions) was highest in the traditional book version. This finding seems to go against the grain today, where there are many proponents of integrating technologically based curricula in our schools. But as Kinzer and his colleagues point out, we simply do not know very much about how to create such curricula so that learning is greater than when students simply read the assigned text. Given the problems that scholars have had in developing technologically-based curricula for reading or mathematics that work even as well as standard classroom lessons (Trotter, 2007), it seems clear that we have a lot to learn about technology and effective lesson designs.

Or, consider the case of the gender gap in reading. While it is well established that girls read better than boys, literally across the world, few studies have explored just why we have this outcome. Dunn and Rudd interviewed adolescent boys from two urban high schools, a suburban high school, and a suburban middle school. The interviews asked these boys to comment on how they felt about the activity of reading. A central theme in the interviews (with two-thirds of the respondents noting this) was the lack of choice in determining what they were to read both in and for school. In other words, boys do not much like what they are assigned to read in schools. There were varying complaints from the overemphasis on reading narratives to reading short passages and then answering a number of questions about what was just read. Others have noted that it isn't that boys don't read, rather it is more that they are less likely to read texts assigned in schools than are their female classmates (Smith & Wilhelm, 2002).

So, as you read these reports, think a bit about how little we actually know about effective classroom practices supporting topics such as vocabulary development, text comprehension (including comprehension of narratives presented in different formats), the effect of powerful discussions in classrooms, and the gender gap that continues to grow when it comes to literacy proficiencies. None of these papers provides anything close to a "final answer" on the aspects of instruction they observed. But each represents progress towards a better understanding of what effective instruction might look like in the schools we have.

REFERENCES

Biancarosa, G., & Snow, C. (2006). *Reading next—A vision for action and research in middle and high school literacy: A report to Carnegie Corporation of New York* (2nd ed.). Washington, DC: Alliance for Excellent Education.

Brenner, D., & Hiebert, E. H. (2010). If I follow the teachers' editions, isn't that enough? Analyzing reading volume in six core reading programs. *Elementary School Journal, 110*, 347-363.

Dewitz, P., Jones, J., & Leahy, S. (2009). Comprehension strategy instruction in core reading programs. *Reading Research Quarterly, 44*, 102-126.

McGill-Franzen, A., Zmach, C., Solic, K., & Zeig, J. L. (2006). The confluence of two policy mandates: Core reading programs and third-grade retention in Florida. *Elementary School Journal, 107*(1), 67- 91.

Nystrand, M. (2006). Research on the role of classroom discourse as it effects reading comprehension. *Research in the Teaching of English, 40*, 392-412.

Smith, M. W., & Wilhelm, J. D. (2002). *Reading don't fix no Chevy's: Literacy in the lives of young men.* Portsmouth, NH: Heinemann.

Trotter, A. (2007). Federal study finds no edge for students using technology-based reading and math products. Retrieved from http://www.edweek.org/ew/articles/2007/04/04/32software_web.h26.html?qs=federal+study.

Primary-Grade Children's Scientific Vocabulary Knowledge Before and After Language-Enriched Science Instruction

Sheryl Honig
Northern Illinois University

Children come to school expert in many language practices. They are adept at code-switching as they move across settings and purposes in their lives in the world. As they move from bedtime conversations to mealtime conversations, and from cooking conversations to grocery shopping conversations, young children use a variety of vocabulary and linguistic patterns to signify situated and culturally constructed meanings. They become fluent in many life-world discourses through the social interaction and scaffolding of other participants. However, such everyday language use can be problematic for these young learners when they confront the academic, domain-specific language of the classroom (Gee, 2004; Halliday & Martin, 1993; Newkirk, 1987). By fourth grade, children are required to read, comprehend, and write informational text, even though research shows that they have not had many experiences in informational genres. (Duke, 2000; Kamberelis & Bovino, 1999; Moss & Newton, 2002). This article reports on an exploratory study in which Language Enriched Science Instruction was developed to support children's acquisition of the domain-specific language and vocabulary of the science topic "life cycle of the seed plant."

THEORETICAL FRAMEWORK

Importance of Language in Learning

Central to this study is the complex link between thought and language. The mediational role of discourse in children's learning is the focal point of recent developments in educational and developmental theories (Hicks, 1996; Vygotsky, 1987). Learning is being reconceptualized as a dialectic between the individual and his or her social world (Applebee, 1996; Driver, Asoko, Leach, Mortimer, & Scott, 1994; Fairclough, 1992; Nystrand, 1997; Rommetveit, 1987; Wells, 1999, 2001). Through social interactions, children construct meaning and language simultaneously. Vygotsky (1987) argued that thinking and speaking work together in development; thinking about an idea and being able to talk about the idea are interrelated. According to Vygotsky's (1987) theory of the reciprocal nature of thought and language, children's very use of language transforms their thinking as they grapple with scientific ideas:

> …the structure of speech is not a simple mirror image of the structure of thought. It cannot, therefore, be placed on thought like clothes off a rack. Speech does not merely serve as the expression of developed thought. Thought is restructured as it is transformed into speech. It is not expressed but completed in the word. (p. 250)

This suggests that, for children to appropriate multimodal scientific discourse, and to develop scientific conceptual understanding, models of ways to "talk about" scientific ideas are just as crucial as models of ways to "enact" scientific activities.

Instruction in science occurs in many social contexts including hands-on explorations, discussions, and read-alouds. Children's appropriation of scientific discourse is necessarily a social phenomenon. Recent research reflects a social, cultural perspective of development that defines learning as a transformation in the learner's appropriation of ways of participation in specific social practices within specific communities (Gee, 1996; Rogoff, 1990, 2003; Rogoff & Wertsch, 1984; Vygotsky, 1987; Wells, 2001; Wenger, 1998; Wertsch, 1991). From this view, psychological functions are considered to have social origins (Valsiner, 1987) and learning is as much about what happens between people rather than what happens inside minds (Gee, 1996). Development, then, is the process of internalization of social experience (Bazerman, 2004; Kamberelis & de la Luna, 2004; Kress, Jewitt, Ogborn, & Tsatsarelis, M., 2001; Rogoff, 1990, 2003; Wells, 2001; Wenger, 1998). This perspective suggests that children do not acquire scientific understandings only by encountering cognitive dissonance and attaining equilibrium by interacting, along with peers, with natural phenomena. In addition, children need to be introduced to the cultural tools of the domain by an expert other, and then need to be provided scaffolding through dialogic processes as they make sense of empirical evidence in the context of theoretical frameworks (Driver, et al., 1994; Metz, 1995, 1997).

Gee (1996) argued that children are apprenticed in school-based languages such as scientific discourse by being immersed in reading, writing, and hands-on activities, all of which are set in the context of rich discussion and rehearsal of ideas. This kind of discussion is reminiscent of Barnes & Todd's (1995) notion of *exploratory talk* in which children have multiple contexts in which to try out the language of a domain to reason through the ideas of the domain. Mercer, Wegerif, and Dawes (1999) described *exploratory talk* as "an 'educated' way of using language to construct knowledge which one would expect to be fostered by school experience" (p. 98). As children participate in social activities, they not only appropriate new understandings and language practices, but also acquire a stance toward the social activities themselves. Children learn how to *be* participants in the social events and learn how to position themselves to the specific discourse (Gee, 1996; Pappas & Zecker, 2001).

Domain-Specific Nature of Scientific Language

Comprehending science text on the life cycle of the seed plant is qualitatively different than comprehending a history text about the industrial revolution. Scientific discourse represents a distinct way of knowing and thinking (Gee, 2004; Lemke, 1990; Ogborn, Kress, Martins, & McGillicuddy, 1996; Pappas, Kiefer, and Levstik, 2006), and therefore particular vocabulary and linguistic elements for conveying ideas to others (Goldman & Bisanz, 2002; Halliday & Martin, 1993). Scientific discourse functions to describe, classify, and explain, and these functions are mediated by specialized vocabulary. Therefore, scientific discourse is characterized by elements such as Topic Presentations, Descriptions of Attributes, Characteristic Events, Category Comparisons, Experimental Ideas, Results, Final Summaries, (Pappas, 2006), and Explanation (Lemke, 1990; Ogborn, et al., 1996). Further, scientific language has linguistic characteristics such as general nouns (e.g., *mammals*), present tense verbs (e.g., *bears hibernate)*, nominalization (in which complex processes are referred to with the use of a noun, *[precipitation can result in erosion])*, and technical vocabulary (Halliday, 2004; Halliday & Martin, 1993; Hasan, 1985). Finally, academic scientific text is written from an authoritative distance from the reader (Christie, 1989), in a "serious" register

(Wollman-Bonilla, 2000), or *paradigmatic* genre (Bruner, 1966) that precludes the use of familiar, everyday language. This means that facts are presented objectively, without explicit evidence of the author's opinion of the value of the facts.

The decontextualized language of narrative text is highly supported in primary grades. However, narrative and everyday languages are different from the academic, content-area language of the intermediate elementary classroom (Gee, 2004; Halliday & Martin, 1993; Newkirk, 1987). Once in these grades, children are required to read, comprehend, and write informational text, even though research shows that they have not had many experiences in informational genres (Duke, 2000; Moss & Newton, 2002; Scott, 2005; Walsh, 2003). While scientific discourse may be new and challenging to some children, it is not the case that young children are unable to learn informational discourses, nor is it the case that children find such discourse to be unappealing. Research shows that young children respond to and take up informational discourses quite readily, when socially supported in those discourses (Honig, 2010b; Pappas, 1993). The point is that many children do not come to school with fluency in academic languages.

Vocabulary Learning

Vocabulary is a key aspect of scientific discourse. Vocabulary knowledge is a strong predictor of reading comprehension (National Reading Panel, 2000), and word learning has been linked to overall academic success (Baumann, Kame'enui, & Ash, 2003; Chall, Jacobs, & Baldwin, 1990). Research suggests that very little explicit vocabulary instruction occurs in elementary schools (Biemiller, 2006; National Reading Panel, 2000), and most of it is in relationship to storybooks, rather than informational books. This is problematic for two reasons. First, by the end of second grade, the number of words children know varies from 4,000 to 8,000 words, with a gap of 2,000 words being approximately equal to two grade levels; this suggests that more vocabulary instruction is necessary for many children (Biemiller, 2006). Second, by fourth grade, children are required to comprehend and write informational (e.g., science or social studies) text, even though they have had very little experience with it during grades K-3 (Duke, 2000; Moss & Newton, 2002; Walsh, 2003). With the intense focus in primary grades on reading and spelling skills, content area vocabulary instruction is neglected in primary classrooms, and children typically do not receive explicit instruction in the vocabulary and language structures that serve science (Biemiller, 2006; Halliday & Martin, 1993; Rothery, 1989).

While vocabulary learning in primary grades has received minimal recent attention, there is research that suggests that explicit vocabulary instruction, such as teacher explanations of new vocabulary words during story reading, can increase vocabulary learning in classroom settings (Biemiller, 2006; Graves, 2006; Beck & McKeown, 2004, 2007; Robbins & Ehri, 1994; Silverman, 2007). In addition, teacher use of questions that elicit students' own use of new words increases acquisition of story language vocabulary (Sénéchal, 1997; Walsh & Blewitt, 2006). Further, opportunity for discussion has been shown to have positive effects on story language acquisition (Zevenbergen, Whitehurst, and Zevenbergen, 2003). Research suggests that, although a child's ability to learn new vocabulary through *incidental* vocabulary exposure depends on extensive prior vocabulary knowledge, *explicit* vocabulary instruction results in gains for children with both minimal and extensive prior vocabulary knowledge (Biemiller, 2006). This in turn suggests that children with different vocabulary resources may learn differently.

In this body of research, little is documented regarding scientific word acquisition beyond multiple-choice definition or picture-pointing tests (Best, Dockrell, & Braisby, 2006). Research is needed to examine children's vocabulary knowledge in deeper and broader terms than forced choice definition tests. Children's ability to comprehend as well as produce specialized vocabulary needs to be addressed in assessment as well as instruction (Best, et al. 2006; Read & Chapelle, 2001). While it is a complex endeavor to identify a child's reading level and math skills, it is perhaps even more complex to measure the size and depth of a child's vocabulary knowledge. Acquisition of a new word occurs incrementally, as a result of multiple, diverse, multimodal experiences with the new word (Marzano, 2004; Nagy & Scott, 2000). With such experiences, a child comes to know the word in more and more complex ways. In order for researchers to determine which instructional approaches are effective at increasing the complex construct of children's vocabulary knowledge, they need a way to measure *growth* in breadth and depth of vocabulary knowledge before and after instruction.

This article reports on an exploratory study in which Content Area Vocabulary Assessment (CAVA) was used to measure children's expressive and receptive vocabulary knowledge before and after Language Enriched Science Instruction, in which the traditional textbook was replaced by language rich science instruction around hands-on activities and tradebooks. This work also examined the relationship of prior vocabulary knowledge on vocabulary learning. As discussed above, children with varying levels of vocabulary knowledge acquire new words in different ways and therefore may respond differently to certain types of instruction. Finally, related to children's success in science is that women are under-represented in science (National Science Foundation, 2000). For this reason, the study examined the relationship between gender and prior knowledge of science vocabulary, as well as gender and gains in science vocabulary knowledge.

RESEARCH QUESTIONS

In this exploratory study, the author used a 5-part Content Area Vocabulary Assessment to measure children's expressive and receptive science vocabulary knowledge before and after instruction on "Life Cycle of the Seed Plant." Questions included the following: (a) Was there an increase in the number of domain-specific words children could name, identify, and use in connected written and spoken text after instruction?; (b) Were children able to *use* newly acquired vocabulary words to express relationships among ideas in connected spoken and written text?; (c) To what extent were they able to use these vocabulary words in extended text?; (d) In which linguistic global elements did children use domain-specific vocabulary words?; (e) Was gender related to CAVA scores?; (f) Was gender related to gains after instruction?; (g) Was gender related to the frequency, range, and density with which children use key scientific vocabulary in their writing?; and, (h) Was prior knowledge related to the frequency, range, and density with which children use key scientific vocabulary in their writing? These questions explore the extent of and nature of children's vocabulary development in the context of instruction that intentionally scaffolds the language of science.

METHODOLOGY

Design

The design of this exploratory study of 32 children's science vocabulary knowledge before and after instruction included both qualitative and quantitative analyses. Student results on the five subtests of CAVA were analyzed quantitatively (e.g., how *many* science vocabulary words did they use in their writing/talking), and qualitatively (e.g., for what *purposes* did children use science vocabulary words in their writing/talking). Within-subject correlational analyses were used to determine relationships between scores before and after instruction. Between-subject correlational analyses were used to determine relationships: (a) between gender and vocabulary knowledge; (b) between prior knowledge and gains; and (c) among subtests.

Content Area Vocabulary Assessment

The purpose of this study was to measure—in authentic, meaningful ways—children's receptive and expressive vocabulary knowledge about the life cycle of a seed plant before and after Language Enriched Science Instruction. The construct of vocabulary knowledge was considered both as receptive knowledge and expressive knowledge. Further, the construct of vocabulary knowledge was viewed as more complex than children's ability to select a correct definition of a word, or to point to a picture of a word. Of interest in this study was the child's *use* of specialized vocabulary words. Read and Chapelle's (2001) framework for assessing vocabulary knowledge was used to define the construct. First, vocabulary knowledge was viewed as an *interactional* construct—student tasks therefore were designed to infer student ability to *use* domain-specific vocabulary about plants when writing and talking about plants. Second, five separate tasks (see Table 1 and Figures 1, 2, 3, and 4) were conceived to reflect various aspects of vocabulary knowledge, such as Embedded (as opposed to Discrete), Comprehensive (as opposed to Selective), and Context Dependent (as opposed to Context Independent).

Table 1. Content Area Vocabulary Assessment Subtests

Subtest	Description	Focus	Construct		Scoring
CAVA 1	Quick Write of terms, based on picture prompt	Expressive, written	Discrete X Select ContInd X	Embed XCompr ContDep	Quantity of domain-specific words
CAVA 2	Oral brainstorm of terms, based on picture prompt	Expressive, oral	Discrete X Select ContInd X	Embed XCompr ContDep	Quantity of domain-specific words
CAVA 3	Matching picture based on picture prompt	Receptive, oral	Discrete X Select X ContInd X	Embed Compr ContDep	Quantity of correct responses
CAVA 4	Written extended text	Expressive, written	Discrete Select ContInd	XEmbed XCompr XContDep	-Range -Quantity -Density of terms
CAVA 5	Oral explanation of #4	Expressive, oral	Discrete Select ContInd	XEmbed XCompr XContDep	-Range -Quantity -Density of terms

Figure 1. Example of CAVA 1 Student Artifact (Given Pre- and Post)

Plants
rootz
dort
seeds
shoot
soil
leaves
Water
grow
Sun

Figure 2. Example of CAVA 2 Score Sheet (Given Pre- and Post)

leaf
root
stem
air
rain
big
seedling
germinate
small
soil
grass
bugs
snail
pollen
center

Figure 3. Example of CAVA 4 Student Artifact (Given Post)

in side a Plant

In side of a plant is a
Pistil. On top of the Pistil is
the Stigma. It is very sticky
EHH!

Figure 4. Example of CAVA 5 Student Transcript (Given Post)

First it starts out like a little seed.
Then it starts making roots out into the grow
and then it makes it longer,
and then after a few weeks it makes a little plant.
The seed coat is opened
and a little plant is coming up.
It starts sprouting up and out
and the roots get much bigger
and then the seed leaves come out
and it starts budding out.

CAVA 1, 2, and 3 measured knowledge of words in isolation, and therefore reflect relatively discrete knowledge, whereas CAVA 4 and 5 measured words (how many and for what purposes) used in extended text. CAVA 3 measured knowledge of 20 select science words that were selected as a result of a review of state curriculum, district science textbook, and 47 trade books, and included words like *seed coat, stem, pollen*, and so forth. In contrast, CAVA 1, 2, 4, and 5 allowed for much more comprehensive evidence of children's word knowledge, as the "science words" were not limited to a list, but included a wide range of specialized vocabulary about plants from children's background knowledge (e.g., words like *stigma, soil, seed coat* were counted as domain-specific words, while words like *dirt, green, bug* were not). CAVA 3, the picture-pointing task, reflects a context-independent view of a child's word knowledge, whereas CAVA 1 and 2 provide a *more* context-dependent view, and CAVA 4 and 5 an even *more* context-dependent view as children's extended writing and talking were situated within a complex context of communicating ideas. These five tasks, or subtests, were conceived of as a way to provide multiple points of data about a child's ability to *use* scientific vocabulary about plants, thereby creating a valid evaluation of a child's vocabulary knowledge.

Further construct validity was considered in terms of utility. For the picture-pointing task, CAVA 3, vocabulary words for the topic of plants were taken from a range of leveled children's trade books about plants, reducing the chance of a ceiling or floor effect. Known-group validity was addressed by comparing native English children's scores to those of children whose native language was not English. Concurrent measure validity was addressed by using correlational analyses to establish relationships among subtests. Because of the construct characteristics of each subtest, it was expected that CAVA 1, 2, and 3, which reflect discrete, context-independent knowledge, would be moderately correlated. Moreover, it was expected that the correlation of CAVA 1, 2, and 3 with CAVA 4 and 5 would be low.

Reliability, Validity, and Utility of Content Area Vocabulary Assessment

The CAVA measurement tool was successfully administered, and was neither too easy nor too difficult for this age group. Scores were normally distributed and it was sensitive enough to show change in student ability after ten days of instruction (see Table 3). Inter-rater reliability was tested on CAVA 1 (student-written list of domain-specific words) and CAVA 2 (student- spoken list of domain-specific words) and was found to be high. Pearson r ranged from .728 to 1.000. Test-retest reliability for CAVA 1 was high (r .948). In addition, Chronbach's alpha procedure showed a high internal item consistency (.837) on CAVA 3 (the only subtest with "items").

The Pearson Correlation procedure indicated that post-tests of CAVA 1, 2, and 3 were moderately correlated (ranging from .525 - .676, $p < .01$); this suggests that they may measure a similar underlying construct of vocabulary knowledge.

The Pearson Correlation procedure indicated that post-test of CAVA 1 and CAVA 4 (Length, Range, Density) were not significantly correlated; thus, it appears that it may measure a different construct than do CAVA 1, 2, and 3. This supports the idea that isolated knowledge of words does not necessarily transfer to ability to use the words to express extended ideas.

Setting and Participants

This study was implemented in April, in a second-grade classroom in a school district in a small Midwestern city. This school serves a predominantly low-income (71% free/reduced lunch), diverse population (33% White, 6% Black, 53% Hispanic), including children for whom English is a second language. 32 second-grade children, including eight English Language Learners, participated. The researcher, rather than the classroom teacher, provided Language Enriched Science Instruction (LESI). It is important to note that up to this point in the school year science had been taught somewhat irregularly and consisted exclusively of whole-class teacher-led instruction and individual workbook work. Instruction did not regularly include hands-on demonstrations or activities but included teacher or individual child reading aloud of the textbook. This textbook contained minimal text on each domain. For example, the life cycle of a seed plant consisted of three pages with a total of 31 words, and vocabulary words such as *germinate, stem, root,* etc., appeared only one or two times. Student talk during these lessons was typically limited to one- or two-word answers in response to teacher questioning.

Instruction: Language-Enriched Science Instruction

Children received 15 lessons of LESI. Instructional time during a LESI lesson consisted of approximately 33% whole-class activities and 66% partner work. Whole-class activities included: (a) seed plant model demonstration, (b) read-aloud with "Vocabulary Visit" (Blachowicz & Obrochta, 2005) and Idea Chart, and (c) dramatic enactment of the life cycle of the seed plant (Honig, 2010a). Partner activities included: (a) planting and observation of seeds and plants, (b) partner reading of multiple trade books on plants, and (c) co-planning individual journal entries in response to book reading. On most days, children spent about 20 minutes engaged in partner-reading multiple trade books. Some children re-read books and others sought out new titles each day. These children encountered words like *pollination, stigma, germination, seedling,* and *seed coat* in multiple contexts. Children used journals on most days to write: (a) data-level text regarding observations of seed plants and (b) theoretical-level text that described attributes and characteristic events of seed plants, explained sequence of life cycle, explained processes in the life cycle, and compared categories of plants. Children consistently talked with a partner about: (a) observations of seed plants, (b) information from books, and (c) writing ideas. Importantly, such instruction illustrates the intentional focus on the domain-specific nature of academic scientific language found in informational books (see Table 2).

Data Sources

Pre-test measures included CAVA subtests 1, 2, and 3. CAVA 1 was administered in a whole-class setting. The researcher provided a large poster of pictures of multiple aspects of the life cycle of a seed plant and asked children to brainstorm and write as many words as they could think of that would go with the ideas and objects in the pictures. CAVA 2 and 3 were administered in a one-on-one interview setting. Post-tests of CAVA 1, 2, and 3 were administered again during three days following instruction, using the same procedures. CAVA subtest 4 was administered in a whole-class setting during two class sessions, after instruction was completed. Children were asked to write a book about the life cycle of a seed plant. CAVA subtest 5 was administered during three days following instruction, in a one-on-one interview, in which children were asked to explain everything they knew about the life cycle of a seed plant.

DATA ANALYSIS

Pre- and post- CAVA subtests 1 and 2 were scored for number of domain-specific words. In order to determine what would "count" as a domain-specific word, these criteria were established: (a) the word must be directly related to the life cycle of the seed plant and (b) "everyday" synonyms would not be counted, such as *dirt* (for *soil*) or *bug* (for *insect*). Three readers scored 20% of the data, met to discuss discrepancies among readers, and came to agreement on how to score. As a result of this process, inter-reader reliability on pre- and post- CAVA subtests 1 and 2 ranged from Pearson $r = .728$ to Pearson $r = 1.00$.

Pre- and Post- CAVA 3 subtests were scored for number of correct items. Quantitative analysis of CAVA 4 and 5 artifacts were conducted in order to describe children's use of domain-specific words in connected text. Raters counted the following: (a) the number of different key words used in individual children's artifacts and (b) the number of times key words were used in an artifact.

Table 2. Three Days from Unit, "Life Cycle of the Seed Plant"

Day	Instructional Activity	Language Focus
1	Vocabulary Visit	
	• Display Plant Poster with multiple images	Domain-specific Vocab
	• Brainstorm vocabulary words that reflect images	
	• Teacher writes each word on Post-It note	
	• Student places Post-It notes on poster	
	• As work continues, Post-Its may be grouped according to semantic links among words	
	Read Aloud: Informational Trade Book 1	Domain-specific Vocab
	• Record student ideas on Idea Chart	Theoretical Language:
	• Set purpose for reading	*Description of Attributes,*
	• During reading, children listen for more words to add to poster	*Characteristic Events, Category* *Comparison Explanation*
	• Teacher provides explanation of words	
	Response to Literature	Domain-specific Vocab
	• As children share learned information on Idea Chart, teacher records each response by sorting responses as "Description of Attributes," "Characteristic Events," etc.	*Description of Attributes,* *Characteristic Events, Category* *Comparison Explanation*
2	Vocabulary Visit (see above)	
	Seed Planting	Domain-specific Vocab
	• Discussion during planting	Data-Level Language: *Observation & Procedures*
	Journal Writing	Domain-specific Vocab
	• With partner, plan journal entry about seed planting	Data-Level Language: *Observation & Procedures*
	• Write journal entry and read to partner	
3	Read Aloud Informational Trade Book 2 (see above)	
	Partner Reading of Informational Trade Books	Domain-specific Vocab
	• Students select from multi-level	Theoretical Language:
	• Informational trade books and explore books with partners	*Description of Attributes,* *Characteristic Events, Category* *Comparison Explanation*
	Journal Writing	Domain-specific Vocab
	• With partner, plan journal entry about text read with partner	Theoretical Language: *Description of Attributes,* *Characteristic Events, Category*
	• Write journal entry and read to partner	*Comparison Explanation*

In addition, qualitative analysis of CAVA 4 and 5 artifacts were conducted. Reflecting the model of vocabulary learning in the framework of this article, it is relevant to identify children's use of specialized words (e.g., *stigma*) in more specific terms than "right" or "wrong." Because vocabulary knowledge involves the ability to form relationships among words of a domain, a child's word use can be examined in terms of his/her ability to link some key words to others. To this end, a rating scale (1-5) was developed to describe the complexity of word use. This scale is discussed briefly in Table 3 below.

Vocabulary rating scale. Using this scale, it is possible to gain a better idea of the extent to which child was able to *use* a specific vocabulary word in extended written or spoken text to show *interrelatedness* with other vocabulary words.

Table 3. Vocabulary Rating Scale

Rating	Definition	Example
1	Incorrect Use	*Roots hold up the flower.*
2	Correct Isolated Use	*A leaf is green.*
3	Use in a "thought unit" to show relationship among components or processes	*The roots take up water and minerals in the soil.*
4	Use in two consecutive "thought units" that show relationship among components or processes	*The roots take up water and minerals in the soil so the plant can grow.*
5	Used in more than two consecutive "thought units" that show relationship among components or processes	*Roots grow down into the soil. The roots take up the water and minerals in the soil so the plant can grow.*

It is also possible to compare children's use of *new* words in extended text to their use of *familiar* words in extended text. To this end, pre- and post- CAVA 1 and 2 were used to identify which words individual children were already familiar with, and which words individual children gained after instruction.

Finally, children's written artifacts were examined to determine which types of scientific ideas children expressed. Artifacts were examined for global elements of scientific text: (a) Description of Attributes, (b) Characteristic Events, (c) Category Comparison, (d) Procedure, (e) Explanation, (f) Definition, (g) Sequence, (h) Topic Presentation, and (i) Final Summary. Table 3 below provides examples.

Examples of global elements. Repeated Measures ANOVA procedure was used to determine whether there was a significant difference between pre- and post-CAVA results. Correlational analysis (*r*) was used to determine the relationships between: (a) prior knowledge and CAVA scores, (b) gender and CAVA scores, (c) gender and prior knowledge, and (d) range/density of vocabulary use and gender.

RESULTS

Effects of Instruction

The purpose of this study was to examine changes in children's vocabulary knowledge after participation in LESI. Repeated Measures ANOVA procedure showed a strong significant increase in student CAVA 1, 2, and 3 scores. This suggests that instruction was effective in increasing student receptive and expressive vocabulary knowledge of domain-specific words about plants (see Tables 4 and 5).

Effects of Prior Knowledge

Pearson Correlation procedure indicates that CAVA 1 pre-test scores were significantly related to post-scores of CAVA 1, 2, but not 3 (r = .518, .438, and .209, respectively). However, Pre CAVA 1, 2, 3 scores were not significantly related to, respectively, CAVA 1, 2, 3, gain scores (r = -.117, -.073, and -.119, respectively). This suggests that, while the level of knowledge children had at the beginning of instruction did moderately predict their knowledge after instruction, it did not predict their gains. Pre CAVA 1 scores were not significantly related to CAVA 4 scores (only given post-instruction) in terms of length (r = .105), range of target vocab (r = .185), or density of target vocabulary (r = -.188). In other words, the number of domain-specific words a child was able to list before instruction did not predict the *length, range, or density* of his artifact after instruction.

Table 4. Summary of Scores of Content Area Vocabulary Assessment Subtests 1-5

	N	Min Score	Max Score	Mean Score	St. Deviation
CAVA 1: Number of Brainstormed Words Written in List					
Pre:	31	1	19	9.58	4.478
Post:	30	7	30	17.67	6.194
CAVA 2: Number of Brainstormed Words Spoken in List					
Pre:	30	2	16	8.63	3.399
Post:	32	4	30	15.94	5.679
CAVA 3: Picture Point					
Pre:	29	30%	78%	51.21%	11.562
Post:	31	43%	100%	74.10%	14.748
CAVA 4: Length of Artifact					
Post:	28	17	370	151.86	89.866
CAVA 4: Range of Words in Artifact					
Post:	28	4	31	13.43	5.882
CAVA 5: Length of Oral Explanation					
Post:	30	11	371	154.17	87.437
CAVA 5: Range or Words in Oral Explanation					
Post:	30	4	30	13.43	5.882

Table 5. Effect of Instruction: CAVA 1 Scores

CAVA 1 Pre Mean Score	CAVA 1 Post Mean Score
9.6	17.7

$F(1, 28)$ = 67.305, p < .01

Effect of Instruction: CAVA 2 Scores

CAVA 2 Pre Mean Score	CAVA 2 Post Mean Score
8.6	16.0

$F(1, 28)$ = 109.045, p< .01

Effect of Instruction: CAVA 3 Scores

CAVA 1 Pre Mean Score	CAVA 1 Post Mean Score
50.4%	74.1%

$F(1, 28)$ = 169.252, p<.01

Effects of Gender

Pearson Correlation procedure indicates that gender was not significantly (at the .01 level) related to pre- CAVA 1, 2, or 3 ($r = -.271$, $.223$, and $.432$, respectively), or post-scores of CAVA 1, 2, or 3 ($r = -.401$, $-.137$, and $-.170$, respectively). This suggests that gender does not predict a child's vocabulary knowledge before instruction. Moreover, gender was not significantly related to gains made after instruction on CAVA 1, 2, or 3 ($r = .093$, $.188$, and $-.072$, respectively). This suggests that instruction was equally effective for boys and for girls. Finally, gender was not significantly related to CAVA 4 in terms of length ($r = .066$), range ($r = -.030$), or density ($r = -.236$).

Using CAVA for Qualitative Information about Children's Use of Vocabulary Words in Connected Text

Beyond providing evidence of significant increases in number of words children could write and say, CAVA provides qualitative evidence of patterns in which children used domain-specific vocabulary. For example, while it is significant that children increased the number of specialized vocabulary words they could write and match with pictures after instruction (CAVA 1, 2, and 3), it is important to consider the extent to which children were able to use this language in connected written text.

The average number of *new* domain-specific vocabulary words that children used in their written texts about plants was 3.67. The average number of *already familiar* domain-specific vocabulary words that children used in their written texts about plants was 10. This suggests that

Table 6. Global Elements in Children's Written Texts about the Life Cycle of a Seed Plant

Global Element	Example	Frequency of Use
Description of Attributes	Pods are full of seeds.	209
Characteristic Events	The flower falls off.	157
Topic Presentation	This is a flower.	75
Category Comparison	Strawberries are a type of fruit.	11
Procedures	Plant the seed in the dirt.	10
Final Summary	And that's how it grows.	4
Definition	Pollination is when bees move pollen to a flower.	2
Sequence	First comes the seed. Second comes the roots. Third comes the shoot. Fourth comes the leaf.	18
Explanation (how or why)	The sun makes the water heated Then when it is so hot it evaporates. into the sky. The water can only vaporate when it's warm out, not cold out. It can't evaporate when it is cold out because the air needs to be warm or hot.	3
Value Statements (not characteristic of Scientific Discourse)	I just love flowers.	75
Personal Narrative (not characteristic of Scientific Discourse)	My dad dug a hole.	15

children were able to *list* more "new" words than they were able to *use* in connected text to express ideas. Further, the average *rating* of children's *new* words in their written text was the same (2.7) as the average *rating* of children's familiar domain-specific words. In other words, when children *did* use new words in their writing, they used them as well as they did words that were familiar to them.

Finally, children overwhelmingly used domain-specific words for the purpose of expressing the linguistic elements of Description of Attributes and Characteristic Events (see Table 6). Explanations, sequences, definitions, category comparisons, final summaries, and topic presentations were rare.

DISCUSSION

A possible limitation of this study is that the researcher implemented the instruction instead of the children's regular classroom teacher. While it is true that this could have created a Hawthorne Effect, it is also important to note that the interactional instructional activities used by the researcher were unfamiliar to the students, and could, in fact, have limited children's ability to engage fully in learning content. Another limitation of this study is that there was no pre-assessment of children's general vocabulary knowledge. Further research could examine the relationship between children's general vocabulary knowledge and their response to LESI. A third limitation is that this study does not provide evidence that LESI is *better* than the classroom's regular science instruction. The purpose of this study was to validate LESI as an effective instructional approach and to determine the utility and reliability of using and scoring CAVA. Further research could include a quasi-experimental design to compare LESI to a district's regular science program.

The results of this study suggest that LESI is, in fact, effective in promoting growth in vocabulary knowledge. As a result of instruction, students nearly doubled their scores, on average, when asked to list target words, or when identifying pictures of target words. This is not surprising in light of our understanding of vocabulary development. Children who participated in LESI had explicit instruction in and multiple exposures to domain-specific vocabulary by engaging in Vocabulary Visits each day, by hearing the teacher read new text every day, by encountering domain-specific vocabulary in multiple books, and by engaging in talk around planting and observing seed plants. LESI was effective, even in this context in which children were not previously accustomed to partner work, or expressing science ideas verbally in extended talk, or navigating informational trade books in a relatively loosely controlled environment.

Further, subtests 1, 2, and 3 of CAVA were indeed useful in capturing the increase in children's expressive and receptive knowledge of isolated words by measuring children's ability to list, orally and in writing, domain-specific vocabulary and to identify pictures of domain-specific entities (e.g., *stem*) and processes (e.g., *germinate*). CAVA 1, 2, and 3 scores were significantly related; this suggests that these three subtests measure a similar underlying construct of vocabulary knowledge. However, CAVA 1, 2, and 3 scores did *not* correlate significantly to CAVA 4 and 5 scores. CAVA 4 and 5 measured children's use of domain-specific words to express ideas in connected text; this suggests that children's knowledge of domain-specific words in isolation is significantly distinct from children's ability to *use* such language to express ideas. This is important if the goal of instruction is to increase children's fluency in a domain-specific language. It suggests that instruction and assessment must account for this more complex construct of vocabulary use in connected text to express ideas.

Integrated analysis of pre- and post-CAVA 1 and 2 results along with CAVA 4 and 5 results provide evidence that children who participated in LESI were more likely to use *already familiar* words to express scientific ideas, but that when they did use *newly acquired* vocabulary, they used them at the same level of complexity as they did familiar words. This suggests that LESI was effective in scaffolding children's ability to use new vocabulary to make meaning in science. Moreover, CAVA 4 and 5 showed that children predominantly expressed ideas about isolated attributes and events, minimally using complex functions of language such as explanations, sequences, or definitions. This is not unexpected, as research suggests that textbooks, tradebooks, and teacher discourse reflect this preference for isolated science facts (Newton & Newton, 2000). However, it is an important finding, as it relates to the construct of "systems thinking" (Assaraf & Orion, 2010). In this study, children's predominant expression of isolated facts reflects a low level of systems thinking, pertaining to "components" and "process" of the domain. Further research could be conducted to investigate ways to support children's ability to engage in more complex systems thinking that includes explanations of processes, reference to cycles, and integration of multiple cycles over time.

Finally, neither gender nor prior science vocabulary knowledge was significantly related to children's pre, post, or gain scores. This suggests that explicit instruction in domain-specific language is effective for children of either gender, and for children with differing prior vocabulary knowledge. The participants in this study included predominantly low-income children of minority ethnicity; these results are especially relevant because research suggests that such populations have limited exposures to academic language and content at home and in school (Hart & Risley, 1999; Lee, 1999; Lee & Avalos, 2002).

There is very little research that links domain-specific language and conceptual knowledge in primary grade science. As the content of elementary school curricula narrows (most dramatically in low income, minority schools), research that features content- and language-rich instruction is essential. Further research might include a quasi-experimental study comparing the effects of LESI to other approaches. In a quasi-experimental study, qualitative and quantitative results of CAVA 4 and 5 could be used to compare the effects of LESI to other instructional approaches on children's fluency in domain-specific language. Moreover, further analysis of such data could be undertaken to examine children's conceptual understandings in science.

IMPLICATIONS

LESI is an instructional approach in which teachers promote student talk and attention to language within the context of choice and multi-modal simultaneous activities during a lesson. While all children engage in these activities, they engage at diverse levels and paces. Not all children read identical texts. For these reasons, LESI may seem a risky venture. Yet, in this context of direct participation in talk around books, plants, and journals, vocabulary learning occurred. It is vital that informational discourses be better supported in the primary grades, especially since the decontextualized and theoretical language of science texts becomes increasingly central in mediating scientific knowledge in intermediate and middle school years and since prior knowledge and vocabulary knowledge are key components of comprehension. This study provides evidence that supports the idea that, when socially supported in the use of multimodal language of science, children increase their ability to talk about and write about scientific ideas. Such instruction is especially necessary for children who come to school with limited fluency in content area languages. The ultimate goal of such instruction is to support the full participation of all children in the field of science.

REFERENCES

Applebee, A. N. (1996). *Curriculum as conversation: Transforming traditions of teaching and learning.* Chicago, IL: University of Chicago Press.

Assaraf, O. B., & Orion, N. (2010). System thinking skills at the elementary school level. *Journal of Research in Science Teaching, 47,* 540-563.

Barnes, D., & Todd, F. (1995). *Communications and learning revisited.* Portsmouth, NH: Heinemann.

Baumann, J. F., Kame'enui, E. J., & Ash, G. (2003). Research on vocabulary instruction: Voltaire redux. In J. Flood, D. Lapp, J. R. Squire, & J. Jensen (Eds.), *Handbook of research on teaching the English language arts* (2nd ed., pp. 752-785*).* New York, NY: Macmillan.

Bazerman, C. (2004). Speech acts, genres, and activity systems: How texts organize activity and people. In C. Bazerman & P. Prior (Eds.), *What writing does and how it does it: An introduction to analyzing texts and textual practices* (pp. 309-339). Mahwah, NJ: Erlbaum.

Beck, I. L., & McKeown, M. G. (2004). Direct and rich vocabulary instruction. In J. F. Baumann & E. J. Kame'enui (Eds.), *Vocabulary instruction: Research to practice* (pp. 13-26). New York, NY: Guilford Press.

Beck, I. L., & McKeown, M. G. (2007). Increasing young low-income children's oral vocabulary repertoires through rich and focused instruction. *The Elementary School Journal, 107,* 251-271.

Best, R., Dockrell, J. E., & Braisby, N. (2006). Real world word learning: Exploring children's developing semantic representations of a science term. *British Journal of Developmental Psychology, 24,* 265–282.

Biemiller, A. (2006). An effective method for building meaning vocabulary in primary grades. *Journal of Educational Psychology, 98,* 44-62.

Blachowicz, C., & Obrochta, C. (2005). Vocabulary visits: Virtual field trips for content vocabulary development. *The Reading Teacher, 59,* 262-268.

Bruner, J. (1966). *Toward a theory of instruction.* Cambridge, MA: Belknap Press.

Chall, J. S., Jacobs, V. A., & Baldwin, L. E. (1990). *The reading crisis: Why poor children fall behind.* Cambridge, MA: Harvard University Press.

Christie, F. (1989). Language development in education. In R. Hasan & J. R. Martin (Eds.), *Language development: Learning language, learning culture* (pp. 152-256). Norwood, NJ: Ablex.

Driver, R., Asoko, H., Leach, J., Mortimer, E., & Scott, P. (1994). Constructing scientific knowledge in the classroom. *Educational Researcher, 23,* 5-12.

Duke, N. K. (2000). 3.6 Minutes per day: The scarcity of informational texts in first grade. *Reading Research Quarterly, 35,* 202-223.

Fairclough, N. (1992). *Discourse and social change.* Malden, MA: Blackwell Publishers.

Gee, J. (1996). *Social linguistics and literacies: Ideology in discourses* (2nd ed.). New York, NY: Routledge.

Gee, J. (2004). Language in the science classroom: Academic social languages as the heart of school-based literacy. In W. E. Saul (Ed.), *Crossing borders in literacy and science instruction: Perspectives on theory and practice* (pp. 13-32). Arlington, VA: National Science Teachers Association.

Goldman, S. R., & Bisanz, G. L. (2002). Toward a functional analysis of scientific genres: Implications for understanding and learning processes. In J. Otero, J. A. Leon, & A. C. Graesser (Eds.), *The psychology of science text comprehension* (pp. 19-50). Mahwah, NJ: Erlbaum.

Graves, M. F. (2006). *The vocabulary book.* New York, NY: Teachers College Press.

Halliday, M. A. K. (2004). *An introduction to functional grammar.* London, UK: Edward Arnold.

Halliday, M. A. K., & Martin, J. R. (1993). *Writing science: Literacy and discursive power.* Pittsburgh, PA: University of Pittsburgh Press.

Hart, B., & Risley, T. R. (1999). *The social word of children: Learning to talk.* Baltimore, MD: Brooks.

Hasan, R. (1985). The structure of a text. In M. A. K. Halliday & R. Hasan (Eds.), *Language, context, and text: Aspects of language in a social-semiotic perspective* (pp. 52-69). Deakin, Australia: Deakin University Press.

Hicks, D. (1996). *Discourse, learning, and schooling.* New York, NY: Cambridge University Press.

Honig, S. (2010a). A framework for supporting scientific language in primary grades. *Reading Teacher, 64,* 23-32.

Honig, S. (2010b). What do children write in science? A study of the genre set in a primary science classroom. *Written Communications, 27,* 88-119.

Kamberelis, G., & Bovino, T. D. (1999). Cultural artifacts as scaffolds for genre development. *Reading Research Quarterly, 34,* 138-170.

Kamberelis, G., & de la Luna, L. (2004). Children's writing: How textual forms, contextual forces, and textual politics co-emerge. In C. Bazerman & P. Prior (Eds.), *What writing does and how it does it: An introduction to analyzing texts and textual practices* (pp. 96–115). Mahwah, NJ: Erlbaum.

Kress, G., Jewitt, C., Ogborn, J., & Tsatsarelis, M. (2001). *Multimodal teaching and learning: The rhetorics of the science classroom.* London, England: Continuum.

Lee, O. (1999). Equity implications based on the conceptions of science achievement in major reform documents. *Review of Educational Research, 69,* 83–115.

Lee, O., & Avalos, M. (2002). Promoting science instruction and assessment for English language learners. *Electronic Journal of Science Education, 7,* 64-75.

Lemke, J. L. (1990). *Talking science: Language, learning, and values.* Norwood, NJ: Ablex.

Marzano, R. J. (2004). The developing vision of vocabulary instruction. In J. Baumann & E. Kame'enui (Eds.), *Vocabulary instruction: Research to practice* (pp. 15-45). New York, NY: Guilford Press.

Mercer, N., Wegerif, R., & Dawes, L. (1999). Children's talk and the development of reasoning in the classroom. *British Educational Research Journal, 25,* 95-111.

Metz, K. E. (1995). Reassessment of developmental constraints on children's science instruction. *Review of Educational Research, 65,* 93-127.

Metz, K. E. (1997). On the complex relation between cognitive developmental research and children's science curricula. *Review of Educational Research, 67,* 151-163.

Moss, B. & Newton, E. (2002). An examination of the informational text genre in basal readers. *Reading Psychology, 23,* 1-13.

Nagy, W., & Scott, J. (2000). Vocabulary processes. In M. Kamil, P. Mosenthal, P. D. Pearson, & R. Barr (Eds.), *Handbook of reading research* (Vol. 3, pp. 269-284). Mahwah, NJ: Erlbaum.

National Reading Panel. (2000). *Teaching children to read: An evidence-based assessment of the scientific research literature on reading and its implications for reading instruction.* Washington, DC: National Institute of Child Health and Human Development.

National Science Foundation. (2000). *Women, minorities, and persons with disabilities in science and engineering* (NSF 00-327). Arlington, VA: National Science Foundation.

Newkirk, T. (1987). The non-narrative writing of young children. *Research in the Teaching of English, 21,* 121-144.

Newton, D. P., & Newton, L. D. (2000). Do teachers support causal understanding through their discourse when teaching primary science? *British Educational Research Journal, 26,* 599-613.

Nystrand, M. (1997). *Opening dialogue: Understanding the dynamics of language and learning in the English classroom.* New York, NY: Teachers College Press.

Obgorn, J., Kress, G., Martins, I., & McGillicuddy, K. (1996). *Explaining science in the classroom.* Bristol, PA: Open University Press.

Pappas, C. C. (1993). Is narrative primary? *Journal of Reading Behavior, 25,* 97-129.

Pappas, C. C. (2006). The information book genre: Its role in integrated science literacy research and practice. *Reading Research Quarterly, 41,* 226-253.

Pappas, C. C., Kiefer, B. K., & Levstik, L. S. (2006). *An integrated language perspective in the elementary school: An action approach.* Boston, MA: Pearson.

Pappas, C. C., & Zecker, L. B. (2001). *Transforming literacy curriculum genres: Working with teacher researchers in urban classrooms.* Mahwah, NJ: Erlbaum.

Read, J., & Chapelle, C. (2001). A framework for second language vocabulary assessment. *Language Testing, 18,* 1-32.

Robbins, C., & Ehri, L. C. (1994). Reading storybooks to kindergartners helps them learn new vocabulary words. *Journal of Educational Psychology, 86,* 139-153.

Rogoff, B. (1990). *Apprenticeship in thinking: Cognitive development in social context*. New York, NY: Oxford University Press.

Rogoff, B. (2003). *The cultural nature of human development*. New York, NY: Oxford University Press.

Rogoff, B., & Wertsch, J. V. (1984). *Children's learning in the zone of proximal development*. New York, NY: Jossey-Bass.

Rommetveit, R. (1987). Meaning, context, and control: Convergent trends and controversial issues in current social-scientific research on human cognition and communication. *Inquiry, 30*, 77-99.

Rothery, J. (1989). Learning about language. In R. Hasan & J. R. Martin (Eds.), *Language development: Learning language, learning culture* (pp. 199-256). Norwood, NJ: Ablex.

Scott, J. A. (2005). Creating opportunities to acquire new word meanings from text. In E. Hiebert & M. Kamil (Eds.), *Teaching and learning vocabulary* (pp. 69-91). Mahwah, NJ: Erlbaum.

Sénéchal, M. (1997). The differential effect of storybook reading on preschoolers' acquisition of expressive and receptive vocabulary. *Journal of Child Language, 24*, 123–138.

Silverman, R. (2007). A comparison of three methods of vocabulary instruction during read alouds in kindergarten. *The Elementary School Journal, 108*, 97-113.

Valsiner, J. (1987). *Culture and the development of children's action*. Chichester, England: Wiley & Sons.

Vygotsky, L. S. (1987). Thinking and speech. (N. Minick, Trans.). In R. W. Rieber & A. S. Carton (Eds.), *The collected works of L. S. Vygotsky: Vol 1. Problems of general psychology* (pp. 37-285). New York, NY: Plenum.

Walsh, K. (2003). Basal readers: The lost opportunity to build the knowledge that propels comprehension. *American Educator, 27*, 24-27.

Walsh, B. A., & Blewitt, P. (2006). The effect of questioning style during storybook reading on novel vocabulary acquisition of preschoolers. *Early Childhood Education Journal, 33,* 273-278.

Wells, G. (1999). Language and education: Reconceptualizing education as dialogue. In W. Grabe (Ed.), *Annual review of applied linguistics* (Vol. 19, pp. 45-56). New York, NY: Cambridge University Press.

Wells, G. (Ed.). (2001). *Action talk and text: Learning and teaching through inquiry*. New York, NY: Teachers College Press.

Wenger, E. (1998). *Communities of practice: Learning, meaning, and identity*. New York, NY: Cambridge University Press.

Wertsch, J. W. (1991). *Voices of the mind: A sociocultural approach to mediated action*. Cambridge, MA: Harvard University Press.

Wollman-Bonilla, J. E. (2000). Teaching science writing to first graders: Genre learning and recontextualization. *Research in the Teaching of English, 35*, 35-65.

Zevenbergen, A. A., Whitehurst, G. J., & Zevenbergen, J. A. (2003). Effects of a shared-reading intervention on the inclusion of evaluative devices in narratives of children from low-income families. *Applied Developmental Psychology, 24*, 1–15.

Examining Middle School Teachers' Talk During Vocabulary Instruction

Evelyn Ford-Connors
Boston University

Students' vocabulary development has been a focus of research and instructional attention for several decades, as both researchers and educators have recognized vocabulary's essential role in reading comprehension and reading proficiency (Anderson & Freebody, 1981; Beck, McKeown, & Kucan, 2002; Cunningham & Stanovich, 1998; Davis, 1968). Research has shown that students with large vocabularies demonstrate stronger reading comprehension and score higher on standardized achievement tests than their peers with smaller vocabularies (Stahl & Fairbanks, 1986). Furthermore, vocabulary knowledge is closely linked to students' long-term academic achievement (Cunningham & Stanovich, 1997; National Reading Panel, 2000).

Knowledge of word meanings and skill in efficiently accessing that knowledge become progressively more important for listening and reading comprehension as students advance into higher grades (Chall, 1983). To access the information contained in texts from one grade to the next while keeping pace with increasing academic demands, students' knowledge of words and their associated concepts must continually grow.

Recognizing this dynamic relationship between vocabulary and comprehension, researchers have studied classroom instruction that develops students' vocabulary knowledge and have identified a number of essential elements. These include engaging students in wide reading; offering direct instruction of individual words to build knowledge networks and connect to students' background knowledge; providing explicit instruction in word analysis and word identification; investigating the multi-dimensional nature of word meaning; developing students' 'word consciousness,' i.e., their interest in and awareness of words and their meanings; and immersing students in rich oral language (Beck, McKeown, & Kucan, 2002, 2008; Graves, 2006; Scott, 2005; Stahl, 2005).

Classroom discussions have been defined as productive instructional contexts for students to examine word meanings and explore the relationships of words to ideas (Stahl & Vancil, 1986; Nagy, 1988; Beck, et al., 2002, 2008). Classroom discussions promote students' learning, in large part, through teachers' skilled facilitation and strategic use of talk. By employing authentic questions that invite open response and reasoning while practicing uptake and revoicing of student ideas, teachers encourage students' active engagement and critical thinking about the content. Furthermore, teachers' instructional emphases assist students in identifying essential information (Applebee, 1996; Nystrand, Wu, Gamoran, Zeiser, & Long, 2003; O'Connor & Michaels, 1996; Wolf, Crosson, & Resnick, 2005). However, discussions as contexts for word learning are relatively uncommon (Scott, Jamieson-Noel, & Asselin, 2003), especially in classrooms with older students where many teachers continue to use traditional instructional methods that focus on dictionary searches and definition writing (Blachowicz, Fisher, Ogle, & Watts-Taffe, 2006). Moreover, even when teachers initiate discussion, there is substantial variability in their effectiveness in facilitating productive discussions (Adler, Rougle, Kaiser, & Caughlan, 2003/2004; Murphy, Wilkinson, Soter, Hennessey, & Alexander, 2009).

It is widely recognized that vocabulary expands and improves over a lifetime, and several recent studies have provided insight into instructional interventions that support vocabulary development in older students (Kucan, Trathen, Straits, Hash, Link, Miller, & Pasley, 2007; Snow, Lawrence, & White, 2009; Lesaux, Kieffer, Faller, & Kelley, 2010). Despite these important understandings, the particular effects of teachers' talk as a strategic instructional tool in vocabulary instruction for adolescents remains understudied.

To better understand the kinds of talk that teachers use to promote students' vocabulary knowledge, and in turn, to understand the type of support teachers might need to improve their instruction, I investigated middle school teachers' talk during their vocabulary instruction. Instruction took place within the context of Word Generation (WG), a vocabulary development program whose primary objective is to develop middle-school students' knowledge of academic words and encourage word use during discussions of high-interest topics (Strategic Education Research Partnership, 2008/2009). Each week, five new, high utility words, taken from the Academic Word List, e.g., investigate, compile, distribution, are introduced within the context of a reading passage that deals with a controversial issue of interest to adolescents, e.g., "Should junk food be sold in the school cafeteria?" These words then reappear on subsequent days during related lessons, with each subject-area teacher at a particular grade level taking responsibility for instruction once per week.

This study examined how teachers used talk in whole-class discussions of new words and related ideas. Each differed in background, teaching style, and in the make-up of the class I studied. My inquiry was guided by two questions:

1. How do middle school teachers use classroom talk during vocabulary instruction?
2. What is the relationship between teachers' talk and students' participation and use of the focal vocabulary and concepts?

METHODOLOGY

Setting

This study took place in the classrooms of three experienced teachers in two urban middle schools. The schools were both ethnically diverse (58%-65% Hispanic; 27%-38% African American, 3%-5% White, 1%-3% Asian, Native American, or "unknown"; and both schools served students from high-poverty families (83%-85% eligible for free or reduced lunch).

Participants

Teachers were selected by convenience sampling and volunteered to take part in this study during their schools' implementation of Word Generation (WG). All three teachers taught mathematics and spoke English as their first language. Ms. Sol (pseudonyms are used for all participants) was licensed in general and special education. She had been teaching general education math for 3 years and had been a paraprofessional for 6 years beforehand. When asked to describe her students, she said that they were "a very quick, very bright group." Ms. Callahan also had dual certification as a general education and special education teacher; she had 9 years of experience teaching in both general and special education classrooms. She described her students as "a group of talkers" who were "not the top kids in terms of their academic achievement." Ms. Jenson had certification in elementary education with 10 years of experience in elementary and middle schools. When asked to describe her students, she explained that her first class was an "inclusion class" in which 13 of the 26 children were on Individualized Education Programs (IEPs); and the second class was a "regular, mixed-ability math class." Data were drawn from one class each taught by Ms. Sol and Ms. Callahan and two of Ms. Jenson's classes.

Each of the teachers participated in professional development during the first year of their schools' implementation of WG. Ms. Sol and Ms. Callahan participated in 2 hours of professional development that focused on Word Generation and essential principles of vocabulary learning. Ms. Jenson participated in 2 hours of similar professional development at the beginning of the school year, with a one-hour follow-up session in the winter, and a second session in the spring.

Table 1. Teacher Talk Codes

Code	Description	Examples
Questioning/ eliciting	Questions, invitations, and prompts to draw out students' ideas or manage student participation	*Do you have a sentence?* *How do you become **eligible** to pass the 6th grade?*
Responding	Replies to students' utterances that include revoicing, repeating, acknowledgement, and providing the correct answer	*Good, nice.* *Okay, so I'm hearing stuff about fairness, about people being allowed to play, not being allowed to play. I'm hearing some stuff about in case if you get injured, you need a career 'cause if you get hurt, what are you going to do with your life?*
Organizing/ giving instructions	Procedural or routine aspects that structure the lesson or regulate students' behavior	*Alright, let's move on.* *Let's go on to the next word.*
Presenting/ explaining	Talk that explicates the lesson content or builds on students' ideas as they relate to the topic	*So your **prerequisite** for entering 7th grade is that you have an understanding of how to do the 6th-grade stuff. So it's not just passing, it's not just doing your homework, it's really understanding the standards and the goals and knowing all the 6th-grade stuff, and sometimes we even sneak in some older-grade stuff.*
Evaluating	Clearly evaluative remarks, either positive or negative	*I like it, thank you.*
Sociating	Strategies that engage students in the lesson or hold the floor for reluctant students	*We're still stuck. So Jason, help me out. We're trying to decide the difference between affect with an **a** and effect with an **e**.*
Word Use	Frequency of focal word use during whole-class discussion	*Oh, you **maintain** speed. So, if I was maintaining the legal speed on the highway, what would I be going?*

Data Collection and Analysis

Teachers were asked to conduct instruction as they normally would during their WG lessons. Instruction was audio-taped and/or videotaped during teachers' weekly implementation of the WG vocabulary curriculum and later transcribed for analysis. Data included transcripts from 10 audiotaped lessons: 6 from Ms. Sol's classroom and 4 from Ms. Callahan's classroom; together, these transcripts totaled approximately 500 minutes of vocabulary instruction and discussion. Data also included transcripts from three videotaped lessons from Ms. Jenson (approximately 150 minutes). Other data sources included field notes taken during classroom observations (10 observations across 3 classrooms) and notes from my informal conversations with teachers following each observation.

Transcripts were coded at the level of teacher and student utterances, according to the types of teacher moves (e.g., questioning, contextualizing) and student responses (e.g., assent, elaborated answers). A total of 36 codes emerged to represent the range of teacher talk and 17 codes captured students' talk. A second rater helped establish the reliability of this coding schema; we worked with one transcript from each classroom, representing 23% of the 13 total transcripts in the study. After independently coding the first transcript, we compared codes, and I revised the schema. We next used the revised codes to independently code two additional transcripts and achieved 90% agreement. I then coded the remaining 10 transcripts.

After all transcripts were coded, I grouped similar codes into six broad categories of teachers' classroom talk (Table 1), using categories previously established by Berry & Kim (2008) in their analysis of teachers' instructional talk. To these general categories, I added Word Use, to mark the frequency with which teachers used target vocabulary during their instruction.

Similarly, I collapsed student talk codes into broad categories (Table 2), based in part on those used by Alvermann & Hayes (1989). To these categories, I added Reads Definitions and

Table 2. Student Talk Codes

Code	Description	Examples
Simple Answer	An affirmative, negative, or brief answer with few words	T: Corel, if I am **eligible** to go to an event without writing a letter, what must my status be? Corel: Independent.
Elaborated Answer	An answer that contains some explanation or builds on ideas of others	"You're not necessarily going to school to learn, like, traditional work like math, English or social studies. You're training for your career."
Definitional Talk	An answer that uses focal words, defines or gives meaning of focal words, or provides an example of word use.	"I **compiled** all the parts from the junkyard to make my bike. And I compiled data to find the class's favorite color."
Questions	Queries related to the content	"Are you kind of trying to say, each of them are the same but you use it in different ways?"
Reads Definition	Reads the text	"It means (reads WG definition) to put together or to collect."
Incomplete, Incorrect, or Doesn't Know	Answers that are incomprehensible, off-task, or wrong.	"Um, uh."

Definitional Talk to mark the specific kinds of student talk that occurred relative to discussions about words and their definitions.

In addition to analyzing individual teacher and student talk moves, I also segmented each session into instructional episodes. I considered the series of teacher and student turns that centered around each word to be an instructional episode, and I analyzed each episode in terms of its duration, the extent of student participation, and the teacher's predominant instructional focus. I characterized instructional episodes as either Abbreviated, Extended, or Elaborated, with designations based on the numbers of words spoken, turns, and student participants per episode (Table 3).

Table 3. Instructional Episodes to Establish Word Meanings

Type of Episode	Components
Abbreviated	• student reads definition or restates the meaning • student gives an example or uses word in a sentence • exchange involves fewer than 3 students • minimal related conversation (may be sparse or irrelevant)
Extended	• student reads definition or restates the meaning • student gives an example or uses word in a sentence • teacher offers synonyms, explanations of the word's meaning, connects to student experience, or provides multiple examples of a word's use • student(s) may make a connection or observation • may involve multiple students • some teacher-student turn taking, although exchanges may be brief
Elaborated	• student reads definition or restates the meaning • teacher provides multiple examples of use and • creates a context for exploring word meaning or • analyzes word parts • may also connect meaning to a text, an academic task, to other content/concepts or convey word's multiple meanings • engages more than 3 students • multiple teacher-student turns

Finally, I categorized teachers' instruction according to its predominant focus (i.e., Definitional or Contextual) (Table 4).

Table 4. Teachers' Predominant Instructional Emphasis Around Words

Definitional Talk	Conversations about words with a primary focus on the elements found in a dictionary, i.e., the word's definition and at least one of its meanings; one or more examples of a word's use in a sentence; and possibly its grammatical function.
Contextual Talk	Conversations about words that focus on building students' knowledge of word meaning through examples that link words to familiar contexts and ideas. Talk likely links word information to students' experiences. While this kind of discourse may include a reference to a word's definition, the primary instructional focus is to locate the word within a familiar framework.

In all but one of the 13 total lessons, teachers followed a similar format as they implemented the Word Generation curriculum: they first established the meaning of focal vocabulary words; then solved the math problems; and finally, engaged students in discussions about the math questions presented at the end of the WG lessons. Although I analyzed classroom discourse throughout the Word Generation lesson, for this paper, I focused exclusively on the first segment of each class as teachers worked with their students to establish the meaning of new target words.

FINDINGS

Findings are presented in two sections. The first section presents a quantitative view and includes numbers of teacher and student words during discussions of word meaning, as well as the patterns of turn-taking and numbers of student participants. The second section presents a qualitative view to examine the nature of the talk in each classroom, including teachers' instructional foci and the patterns of elicitation and response that came to characterize each teacher's instruction.

A Quantitative View of the Talk

I first determined quantities of student and teacher talk in each classroom, levels of participation, and time devoted to this task. As the data in Table 5 indicate, Ms. Callahan and Ms. Jenson devoted substantially more time than did Ms. Sol to the task of establishing the meaning of target words. They also had more to say about each target word and engaged more students in their discussions than did Ms. Sol.

To reconcile differences among teachers in time spent on this task so that meaningful comparisons could be made, I calculated mean quantities of classroom talk as well as teacher-student turn-taking per 5-minute increments of instruction (Figures 1 and 2). These calculations allowed a view of classroom discourse during equivalent timeframes.

Figure 1. Mean Number of Student Turns and Words per Turn in Five Minutes of Discussion of Word Meaning

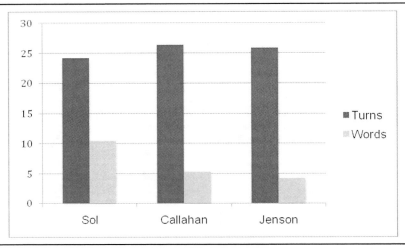

Although the number of student turns was similar across the three classrooms, students in Ms. Sol's classroom had more to say, per turn, than did students in either Ms. Callahan's or Ms. Jenson's classrooms. On average, Ms. Sol's students uttered nearly twice as many words in a 5-minute period of instruction as students in either of the other two classrooms.

Figure 2. Mean Number of Teacher Turns and Words per Turn in Five Minutes of Discussion of Word Meaning

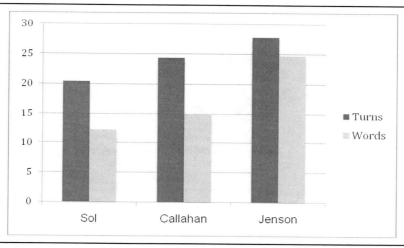

Analyses of teacher talk (Figure 2) indicate more talk from Ms. Jenson during these 5-minute periods than from the other two teachers. Since Ms. Jenson's students also said fewer words per turn than in other classrooms, I wondered if differences in classroom talk related to Ms. Jenson's control of the conversation and subsequent limits on students' talk. Similarly, I wondered if the greater number of words per turn among Ms. Sol's students signaled a more balanced classroom discussion, a characteristic often associated with higher levels of student academic achievement (Langer, 2001; Nystrand, Gamoran, & Heck, 1993). To answer these questions, I next examined the nature of the talk during discussions of words.

A Qualitative View of the Talk

Teachers' varying instructional approaches and patterns of elicitation and response during discussions became evident during my qualitative analysis of discussion. Similarly, variation emerged across classrooms in the predominant patterns of student talk. These differences are described in the following section.

Ms. Sol's Classroom. To establish word meanings, Ms. Sol followed the same instructional format in every lesson: she asked students to read the definitions from the WG materials, to restate the meanings in their own words, and to use each word in an original sentence. The largest proportion of Ms. Sol's talk during this segment consisted of questioning/eliciting, primarily by prompting students to participate (mean of 3.8 instances per 5 min.) and eliciting student examples of each word's use (mean of 2 instances per 5 min.). Ms. Sol's talk also focused on organizing the discussion by calling on volunteers to share their sentences using the words (mean of 5.6 instances per 5 min.). On average, Ms. Sol used target words nine times per lesson and occasionally offered an example of the target word's use in a sentence of her own. Generally absent from Ms. Sol's talk, however, were explanations of word meanings or attempts to help students refine their examples.

In response to Ms. Sol's emphasis on definitional talk, students' talk was also predominantly definitional; that is, students read aloud the definitions contained in the WG materials, put these definitions into their own words, and called upon their understanding of each word's meaning to create original sentences that they shared with the class, as in the following example with the target word **compile**:

T:	*Another word? The words we have on the board for today? Someone want to give me the definition? And a sentence? Michaela?*
M:	Compile?
T:	*Compile.*
M:	It means (reads WG definition) to put together or to collect.
T:	*to put together or collect.*
M:	I have two sentences.
T:	*Okay.*
M:	One is about math and one is not.
T:	*Okay.*
M:	I compiled all the parts from the junkyard to make my bike. And I compiled data to find the class's favorite color.
T:	*To find what?*
M:	The class's favorite color.
T:	*The class's favorite color. Good. My example would be: Miss Farrell asked the students to choose five of their favorite books on Tuesday. And on Wednesday, she compiled the data to find out what the favorite books were. Okay? Anybody else have a good sentence for compile? No? For compile?*
S1:	Well, I used it in my discussion question as, the amount compiled in pure [unintelligible] may become regulative over time.
T:	*Good, nice. Justin?*
J:	My word, the sentence was, we compiled our brainstorm to get one great idea.
T:	*We compiled?*
J:	our brainstorm to get one great idea.
T:	*Compiled our brainstorm…*
S2:	Maybe our brainstorming ideas, compiled our brainstorming ideas?
T:	*Right. Yeah, that sounds better. Can you say that to him?*
S2:	We compiled our brainstorming ideas to get one good idea?
T:	*Good.*

For the most part, Ms. Sol responded to children's contributions by acknowledging and affirming their participation with a simple "okay," or "good;" however, there were few additional teacher-student exchanges, evidenced by the predominance of abbreviated instructional episodes (13 of the 22 episodes, or 59%). All remaining episodes were extended (41%) with no elaborated episodes.

Ms. Callahan's Classroom. Data analysis revealed a similar, definitional focus during Ms. Callahan's lesson. As she facilitated discussions of word meaning, Ms. Callahan's utterances consisted predominantly of elicitations and responses. Within these two major categories, primary elicitations consisted of prompting (mean of 3.4 instances per 5 min.), questioning (mean of 2.3 per 5 min.), and soliciting examples (mean of 1.4 instances per 5 min.); and responses consisted mostly of repeating students' contributions (mean of 3 instances per 5 min.), simple acknowledgements or assent (mean of 1.4 instances per 5 min.), and revoicing to clarify or elaborate a student's utterance (mean of 1.3 instances per 5 min.).

Like Ms. Sol, Ms. Callahan structured her instructional episodes by reading the WG definitions and soliciting students' examples of each word's use. Student talk during this segment of the lesson consisted mostly of definitional talk (mean of 7.2 instances per 5 min.) and simple answers (mean of 4 instances per 5 min.) with a strong emphasis on defining words and using the words in sentences.

However, unlike Ms. Sol, Ms. Callahan's responses to students' contributions often included some further explanation or refinement:

T:	***Compile***, *what does it mean? Shaneen?*
Sh:	(reads WG definition) Collect.
T:	*Collect. And I heard something—I heard Gregory use it in a sentence. Compile.*
G:	I had compiled Biandre's notebook back together.
T:	*That means put back together. So some of you have your notebooks falling apart, okay? What do you have to do each week?*
S3:	Compile them.
T:	*Compile them. Put it back together. Compile it.*
G:	That's what I just said.
S4:	I compiled a puzzle.
T:	*Compiled a puzzle? Put it together? It's like to put BACK together. A puzzle isn't really put together.*
S5:	I compiled a computer.
SS:	[laughter]
T:	*I don't know about that. I think it's better to be used with paper, or compiled a list of names of people in the classroom. I don't know about compiled a computer...*

During many instructional episodes, Ms. Callahan extended the conversation with a follow-up question, reference to an alternate meaning, or a brief connection to students' experiences or conceptual knowledge. These utterances, which followed students' contributions, promoted some further classroom talk about a word's meaning. Moreover, Ms. Callahan often noted when students' examples differed from the definitions, and she attempted to explain where the meaning and the example diverged.

In addition, of the three teachers in the study, only Ms. Callahan referred to target words' mathematical meaning, which she did on three occasions, thus acknowledging the polysemic nature of some of the words:

T:	*Okay. Prime. Somebody else? David?*
David:	(reads WG definition) The best or most important.
T:	*… and in math it has a different definition than that. Prime number. Who can tell me what a prime number is, not five though. Isaac?*
Isaac:	Seven.
T:	*Seven. How come it's a prime number?*
I:	Because one and itself, one and itself only goes into it.
T:	*Right.*

Although her explanations sometimes lacked sufficient precision to clarify the meaning or to help students improve their examples, Ms. Callahan was more likely than Ms. Sol to embed additional explanations and ask students to say more. When she used these talk moves, she often extended the discussion of target words, evidenced by the presence of 5 elaborated instructional episodes out of 17 total episodes (29%). Seven of the remaining episodes were abbreviated (41%), and 7 were extended (41%). During each lesson, Ms. Callahan used focal vocabulary words an average of 24 times.

Ms. Jenson's Classroom. Ms. Jenson also began her discussion of words by inviting students to discuss each word's meaning. However, Ms. Jenson structured these discussions differently from the other two teachers. Although she referred students to the WG materials and asked students to read the definitions, she quickly moved beyond the definitions to construct familiar contexts around the words. This contextual talk became the predominant feature of Ms. Jenson's talk during this segment of lesson and reflected her emphasis on building bridges between new words and students' existing knowledge and experience.

In contrast to the other two teachers who framed their instruction using students' examples of target word use, Ms. Jenson often initiated an instructional episode by proposing examples for students' responses, engaging in a type of "scenario-building" (Stahl & Nagy, 2006) to collaboratively construct one or more contexts around each target word. As she did so, she consistently connected the word to students' knowledge or experience. Ms. Jenson engaged students in scenario-building by relating the new word to a familiar experience. As students responded and contributed their ideas, she revoiced or repeated each idea and followed it with a brief explanation or a question that asked students to explain how the idea related to the concept being discussed. She often used hypothetical sentence constructions like "What if" or "If…then" to either initiate scenarios or to maintain the discussion and encourage additional ideas. The following excerpt from an elaborated instructional episode about the word eligible illustrates this process:

T:	*What were some of your vocabulary words that were new this week? Vidraia?*
V:	**Eligible?**
T:	*What is it?*

V:	**Eligible**.
T:	*Eligible. What is **eligible**, Vidraia?*
V:	Like to be able to do it?
T:	*To be able to do it. So, I can tie my shoes. Am I **eligible** to tie my shoes?*
SS:	Yes.
T:	*Really? Do I say, "I am **eligible** to tie my shoes!"*
SS:	No, that would not make sense.
T:	*Who can use **eligible** in a different way? Because **eligible** does mean "to be able," but it's got a little bit of a twist in its meaning...Magdalena?*
M:	I am **eligible** to pass the 6th grade.
T:	*How do you become **eligible** to pass the 6th grade?*
M:	By paying attention.
T:	*By paying attention? What kinds of things do you have to do to be **eligible**? Do you want to call on somebody to help you out?*
S6:	Homework and class work.
T:	*And what does your homework and class work help with? Armana?*
A:	To be **eligible** also has something to do with requirements.
T:	*Okay, so requirements. So what are the requirements for passing 6th grade? Ivan?*
I:	To do your homework everyday.
T:	*To do your homework every day? And what does doing your homework every day allow you to do? What do you get 4 times a year? Regina?*
R:	Good grades?
T:	*Good grades. So if I gave homework every single day, and somebody did it every day, then they would get what?*
SS:	Good grades. As. Passing.
T:	*They'd be passing, they'd get good grades, they'd get As and Bs, they'd do all their class work, they'd pass all their tests,*
S:	Make honor roll.
T:	*They'd make honor roll. They would definitely be **eligible** to pass 6th grade. If they didn't do their homework, that would mean they didn't understand the work, which means they didn't understand the tests, which means they didn't do well. What kind of grades would that person get?*
SS:	Fs.
T:	*If you get Fs, you wouldn't be **eligible**.*
S:	for sports
T:	*not only for sports, but*
SS:	to pass

T: *for me to put my stamp of approval on you, and to say this child is **eligible** to*
                enter the 7th grade, they know, they have met the requirements to get into 7th
                *grade? What else, Isaiah? What was your example of **eligible**?*

As this discussion continued, students generated additional examples of appropriate contexts for the word *eligible*. Over the course of this episode, Ms. Jenson used the target word 17 times and placed it within familiar contexts that connected to students' experiences.

Ms. Jenson's talk during this segment of the class was characterized by three major categories: questioning, responding, and explaining. Within each of these larger categories, she used a broad repertoire of talk moves to elicit students' thinking and encourage participation. In addition to asking questions (mean of 2.2 instances per 5 min.), Ms. Jenson prompted students (mean of 3.8 instances per 5 min.), and probed for greater elaboration (mean of 2.3 instances per 5 min.). She also responded to students' utterances by repeating (mean of 4.9 instances per 5 min.) or revoicing their utterances to clarify or extend their ideas (mean of 5.2 instances per 5 min.). Finally, Ms. Jenson explained/presented information about words, mostly by making connections (mean of 4.4 instances per 5 min.) and elaborating (mean of 1.6 instances per 5 min.). Her explanations also incorporated definitional talk (mean of 3.9 instances per 5 min.) through which she gave examples, analyzed parts of words, and provided or amplified word meanings.

Ms. Jenson's approach engaged students in sustained discussions of each word (mean of 3.3 minutes per word) and encouraged participation among numerous students; student participation ranged from 3 to 13 per instructional episode, with a mean of 8. All of Ms. Jenson's 10 instructional episodes were either extended (40%) or elaborated (60%), and she used focal words an average of 37.5 times per lesson.

An analysis of student talk codes revealed a predominance of simple (mean of 9 instances per 5 min.) and extended (mean of 6 instances per 5 min.) answers, as students responded to Ms. Jenson's questions and scenarios. Students also applied definitional talk (mean of 4 instances per 5 min.) as they used the words, talked about the meanings, and offered relevant examples.

DISCUSSION

I set out in this study to understand how middle school teachers used classroom talk during their vocabulary instruction and to examine the relationships between teachers' talk and students' responses and participation. Despite teachers' use of a common curriculum (Word Generation), quantitative analyses indicated important differences, not only in the amount of class time devoted to establishing words' meaning, but also in the amount of talk each teacher used to accomplish this instructional task, with one teacher clearly dominating the discussion. This finding prompted a closer, qualitative examination to understand what was transpiring during these conversational exchanges among teachers and their students.

I found that instructional differences stemmed from teachers' predominant instructional focus, whether definitional or contextual, as well as their principal patterns of talk, with resultant differences in students' responses and participation across the three classrooms. Teachers especially varied in the quantity and quality of prompts and feedback they used to sustain productive discussions of words.

In particular, Ms. Sol's strict focus on definitional information limited productive discussions. Throughout this segment of the lesson, she relied on the definitions presented in the lesson materials and on students' examples to structure her instruction. Rather than explore meanings, extend students' examples, or engage in word analysis to clarify meaning, she often let pass opportunities to relate target words to concepts or other contexts. In addition, she used a relatively limited repertoire of talk moves to facilitate the discussion, with little uptake (Collins, 1982) of students' ideas or examples. Students' responses were similarly limited to definitional information, and the discussion seldom moved beyond these tight boundaries to allow more productive exploration of target vocabulary.

Similarly, Ms. Callahan maintained a predominant focus on definitional information about words as she facilitated discussions. While she often asked a question or added further explanation, her responses were fairly limited and did not consistently generate additional talk about the words or lead to further exploration of target words' connections to related concepts or familiar contexts. However, when on occasion she added contextual information or made connections to students' experiences, she fostered further discussion as students generated additional examples of the words' uses.

Ms. Jenson was the most skilled at orchestrating discussions, and her predominant focus on contextual talk created numerous, rich conversations that connected words to students' existing knowledge and experience. She encouraged classroom talk in several ways, including "scenario-building," a process through which she engaged students in collaboratively constructing contexts around words. Ms. Jenson's process was similar to that proposed by Stahl & Nagy (2006) in which they suggested asking students to write brief stories, or scenarios, and embed new words; in addition, she seemed to deliberately connect each new word's meaning to students' background and experience as a way to construct a student-friendly context.

Ms. Jenson's instructional episodes were structured by a recursive process in which she invited and incorporated students' ideas, responded with explanations or clarifications of their contributions, and then asked a follow-up question that encouraged students to articulate how their ideas related to the emerging context or scenario. This combination of talk moves elicited students' additional ideas about the words and prompted their consideration of meaning within relevant contexts.

This collaborative construction process prompted broad student participation and the generation of a more complete understanding of the word than would have emerged from a single student example. Posing questions and revoicing students' ideas further positioned students as active participants in developing word meaning, even when their initial knowledge of target words was partial or tenuous. As she revoiced students' utterances, Ms. Jenson clarified and recast their ideas, affirming their roles as active contributors while making their ideas accessible to others. Moreover, her contextual focus created the opportunity for formative assessment through which she could obtain a "quick read" of students' understanding. Evidence of students' growing knowledge emerged from the relevance and quantity of their contributions while building meaning, and this information helped her structure each instructional episode. Her decisions about the length and specificity of each episode were then based on her appraisal of students' levels of understanding.

As in previous studies (e.g., Stahl & Fairbanks, 1986; Stahl & Vancil, 1986; Beck, et al., 2002, 2008), the data in this study affirm the value of providing both definitional and contextual information to build students' word knowledge. When teachers engaged in this type of instruction, periods of student engagement were longer and greater numbers of students participated. The sustained discussions presented an important byproduct: As students talked more and used the words in more varied ways, teachers were afforded greater opportunity to observe students' misconceptions about word meanings and address them comprehensively. In contrast, when teachers relied on definitional information alone, discussions were brief and afforded little opportunity to develop students' conceptual understanding. In addition, students were less likely to apply the new information to familiar contexts.

IMPLICATIONS

Despite a strong research base about effective principles for developing students' vocabulary knowledge, productive vocabulary instruction is rare in many classrooms (Blachowicz, et al., 2006; Hedrick, Harmon, & Linerode, 2004). While this instructional gap may stem from teachers' limited knowledge of best practices (e.g., connecting words to students' existing schema, investigating the multi-dimensional nature of word meaning, raising students' word consciousness, etc.), it may also result, in part, from limited understanding of the specific talk moves that facilitate productive discussions to deepen and extend students' vocabulary knowledge. This study suggests the presence of both difficulties for two of the three teachers, as evidenced by their narrow instructional focus and relatively limited repertoire of talk moves, making clear the need for more comprehensive support as teachers implement vocabulary instruction.

Productive directions for future research include investigations of professional development that deepens teachers' knowledge of the full array of factors that influence student vocabulary development and strengthens teachers' ability to translate this knowledge into effective classroom practice through more strategic use of talk. In addition, further examinations of the role of teachers' talk in facilitating students' explorations of word meaning that include student outcome data would extend the research base and support teachers' practice.

REFERENCES

Adler, M., Rougle, E., Kaiser, E., and Caughlan, S. (2003/2004). Closing the gap between concept and practice: Toward more dialogic discussion in the language arts classroom. *Journal of Adolescent and Adult Literacy*, 47, 312-322.

Alvermann, D. E. & Hayes, D. A. (1989). Classroom discussion of content area reading assignments: An intervention study. *Reading Research Quarterly*, 24, 305-335.

Anderson, R. C., & Freebody, P. (1981). Vocabulary knowledge. In J. T. Guthrie (Ed.), *Comprehension and teaching: Research reviews* (pp. 77-117). Newark, DE: International Reading Association.

Applebee, A. N. (1996). *Curriculum as conversation: Transforming traditions of teaching and learning*. Chicago, IL: University of Chicago Press.

Beck, I. L., McKeown, M. G., & Kucan, L. (2008). *Creating robust vocabulary: Frequently asked questions and extended examples*. New York, NY: Guilford.

Beck, I. L., McKeown, M. G., & Kucan, L. (2002). *Bringing words to life: Robust vocabulary instruction*. New York, NY: Guilford Press.

Berry, R. A. W. & Kim, N. (2008). Exploring teacher talk during mathematics instruction in an inclusion classroom. *The Journal of Educational Research, 101*, 363-377.

Blachowicz, C. L. Z., Fisher, P. J., Ogle, D., & Watts-Taffe, S. (2006). Vocabulary: Questions from the classroom. *Reading Research Quarterly, 41*, 524-539.

Chall, J. S. (1983). *Stages of reading development.* New York, NY: Harcourt Brace.

Collins, J. (1982). Discourse style, classroom interaction and differential treatment. *Journal of Reading Behavior, 14*, 429-437.

Cunningham A. E. & Stanovich, K. E. (1997). Early reading acquisition and its relation to reading experience and ability 10 years later. *Developmental Psychology, 33*, 934-945.

Cunningham, A. E., & Stanovich, K. E. (1998). What reading does for the mind. *American Educator 22*(1-2), 8-15.

Davis, F. B. (1968). Research in comprehension in reading. *Reading Research Quarterly, 3*, 499-545.

Graves, M. F. (2006). *The vocabulary book: Learning and instruction.* New York, NY: Teachers College Press.

Hedrick, W. B., Harmon, J. M., & Linerode, P. M. (2004). Teachers' beliefs and practices of vocabulary instruction with social studies textbooks in grades 4-8. *Reading Horizons, 45*(2), pp. 103-125.

Kucan, L., Trathen, W. R., Straits, W. J., Hash, D., Link, D., Miller, L. & Pasley, L. (2007). A professional development initiative for developing approaches to vocabulary instruction with secondary mathematics, art, science, and English teachers. *Reading Research and Instruction, 46*, 175-195.

Langer, J. A. (2001). Beating the odds: Teaching middle and high school students to read and write well. *American Educational Research Journal, 38*, 837-880.

Lesaux, N. K., Kieffer, M. J., Faller, S. E., & Kelley, J. G. (2010). The effectiveness and ease of implementation of an academic vocabulary intervention for linguistically diverse students in urban middle schools. *Reading Research Quarterly, 45*, 196-228.

Murphy, P. K., Wilkinson, I. A., Soter, A. O., Hennessey, M. N., & Alexander, J. F. (2009). Examining the effects of classroom discussion on students' comprehension of text: A meta-analysis. *Journal of Educational Psychology, 101*, 740–764.

Nagy, W. E. (1988). *Teaching vocabulary to improve reading comprehension.* Newark, DE: International Reading Association.

National Reading Panel (2000). *Report of the National Reading Panel: Teaching children to read: An evidence-based assessment of the scientific research literature on reading and its implications for reading instruction.* National Institute of Child Health and Human Development (NIH Publication No. 00-4769). Washington, DC: U.S Government Printing Office.

Nystrand, M., Gamoran, A., & Heck, M. J. (1993). Using small groups for response to and thinking about literature. *The English Journal, 82*(1), 14-22.

Nystrand, M., Wu, L. L., Gamoran, A., Zeiser, S., & Long, D. A. (2003). Questions in time: Investigating the structure and dynamics of unfolding classroom discourse. *Discourse Processes, 35*, 135-198.

O'Connor, M. C. & Michaels, S. (1996). Shifting participant frameworks: Orchestrating thinking practices in group discussion. In D. B. Hicks (Ed.), *Discourse, Learning, and Schooling,* pp. 63-103. Cambridge, England: Cambridge University Press.

Scott, J. A. (2005). Creating opportunities to acquire new word meanings from text. In E. H. Hiebert and M. L. Kamil (Eds.), *Teaching and learning vocabulary: bringing research to practice,* pp. 69-91. Mahwah, NJ: Lawrence Erlbaum Associates.

Scott, J. A., Jamieson-Noel, D., & Asselin, M. (2003). Vocabulary instruction throughout the day in twenty-three Canadian upper-elementary classrooms. *The Elementary School Journal, 103*, 269–283.

Snow, C., Lawrence, J., & White, C. (2009). Generating knowledge of academic language among urban middle school students. *Journal of Research on Educational Effectiveness, 2*, 325-344.

Stahl, S. A. (2005). Four problems with teaching word meanings (and what to do to make vocabulary an integral part of instruction). In E. H. Hiebert & M. L. Kamil (Eds.), *Teaching and learning vocabulary: Bringing research to practice,* pp. 95-114. Mahwah, NJ: Lawrence Erlbaum Associates.

Stahl, S. A. & Fairbanks, M. M. (1986). The effects of vocabulary instruction: A model based meta-analysis. *Review of Educational Research, 56*(1), 72-110.

Stahl, S. A. & Vancil, S. (1986). Discussion is what makes semantic maps work in vocabulary instruction. *Reading Teacher, 40*, 62-69.

Stahl, S. A., & Nagy, W. E. (2006). *Teaching word meanings.* New York, NY: Routledge.

Strategic Education Research Partnership Institute, Washington, D.C. Word Generation Website: http://www.
    serpinstitute.org/tools-and-resources/word-generation.php
Wolf, M. K., Crosson, A. C., & Resnick, L. B. (2005). Classroom talk for rigorous reading comprehension
    instruction. *Reading Psychology*, *26*, 27-53.

A Profile of Three High School Students' Talk about Literature during Multimodal Instructional Activities and Whole-Class Text-Based Discussions

James S. Chisholm

Morehead State University

For quite some time, scholars across disciplines have revealed the central role that teacher and student talk plays in promoting or precluding learning opportunities (Cazden, 1988; Rex et al., 2010). Literacy researchers have continued to enhance our understanding of the relationship between classroom talk and student learning through the development of innovative analytical instruments that illuminate aspects of classroom talk that shed new light on how meanings are constructed in classrooms (Nystrand, Wu, Gamoran, Zeiser, & Long, 2003). Particularly, researchers who have explored the characteristics of classroom talk that have facilitated students' content learning have provided practitioners and policy makers with robust data that could be used to inform the structure of talk in classrooms, as well as the development of rigorous standards to which classroom talk should aim.

Due in part to the growing body of research that has uncovered the importance of classroom talk as it relates to student learning, the *Common Core State Standards (CCSS) for English Language Arts and Literacy in History/Social Studies, Science, and Technical Subjects* (2010) have highlighted the important roles played by different types of discussions in promoting students' understanding of the English language arts (ELA) curriculum. The CCSS speaking and listening standards for students in grades 11-12, for example, articulate how students should "initiate and participate effectively in a range of collaborative discussions (one-on-one, in groups, and teacher-led) with diverse partners on grades 11–12 topics, texts, and issues, building on others' ideas and expressing their own clearly and persuasively" (p. 50). The language of this grade-specific standard recognizes the diverse discourse contexts that exist for students to discuss ideas (e.g., one-on-one, in groups, and teacher-led), the role of interactional awareness (Rex & Schiller, 2009) in "building on others' ideas," and, finally, the opportunity that talk offers for students to support their own particular stances toward curricular topics. Despite the inclusion of such language in the CCSS and the range of research perspectives and educational policy briefs that identify and support the role that talk plays in leveraging students' learning, many teachers and adolescents continue to struggle to talk about content in ways that enhance students' literacy learning (Applebee, Langer, Nystrand, & Gamoran, 2003; Kamil, Borman, Dole, Kral, Salinger, & Torgensen, 2008).

In the spirit of Applebee's (1996) conceptualization of the "curriculum as conversation," this paper examines how a series of instructional activities, co-designed with a secondary English teacher and grounded in 21st-century and transactional theories of learning in ELA contexts, facilitated secondary English students' talk and literacy learning. I present a profile of three secondary English students who engaged in a multimodal instructional activity prior to participating in a whole-class discussion of a challenging piece of literature. In this study, multimodality refers to students' uses of more than one semiotic system to represent their interpretations of literary texts. I chose to examine the potential relationship between collaborative multimodal instructional activities and classroom talk because of the pervasiveness of the multiple modes through which many adolescents make meanings during social interactions in their in-school and out-of-school lives (Cope & Kalantzis, 2000; Hull & Schultz, 2001). Despite the ubiquity of multimodality in adolescents' lives, schools remain essentially verbocentric (Siegel, 1995). The present study sought to address the gap between the multiple ways in which students make meanings and the ways of knowing that are valued in schools.

The model of learning that I propose in this study centralizes the mediating role of classroom talk in leveraging students' multiple literacies and learning of the academic content of the ELA curriculum (see Figure 1). Talk is only one aspect of one sign system; yet, talk, for many students and teachers, is how education happens. Literacy, however, is a "multimodal social practice with specific affordances in different contexts" (Larson & Marsh, 2005, pp. 20-21). Thus, social interaction and talk mediate students' learning of the content of the ELA curriculum, *and* social interaction and non-linguistic modes of meaning-making mediate classroom talk. From a literacy-as-multimodal-social-practice perspective, the relationship between classroom talk and the learning of the content of the ELA curriculum is dialectical; talk shapes the learning of the curriculum, which, in turn, shapes the nature of subsequent classroom talk. If talk can shape the learning of the ELA curriculum in such consequential ways, then the inclusion of multiple sign systems into the

Figure 1. A Multimodal Model of Learning for the ELA Curriculum

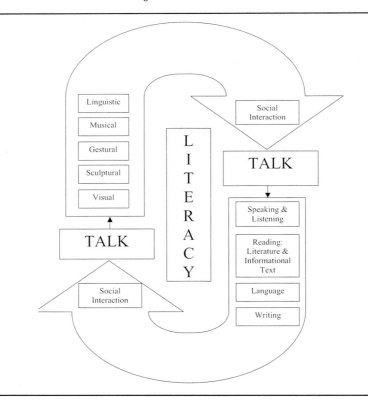

ELA course of study could provide equally robust learning opportunities for students, since students may use these sign systems, as I will discuss below, to extend the potential for meaning-making across texts (Zoss, 2009).

Although many studies have considered the nature of students' multimodal composing (e.g., Coiro, Knobel, Lankshear, & Leu, 2008), few studies have investigated how multimodal composing shapes academic literacy learning through moment-by-moment interactions in classrooms (Jewitt, 2008), and no study has researched how multimodal instructional activities inform talk about texts in which students build on and transform each other's ideas in secondary English contexts. The following research question sought to build on the promising but isolated findings on talk and multimodal activities in secondary English classrooms: How does student talk during a collaborative multimodal instructional activity shape the interpretations that students make about literature during small group and whole-class text-based discussions?

REVIEW OF LITERATURE AND THEORETICAL PERSPECTIVE

The present study is grounded in multimodal social semiotic theory (Kress & van Leeuwen, 2001), which considers as pedagogically central the vast repertoires of meaning-making modes that teachers and students use in their everyday classroom practices. By considering, for example, the linguistic as well as the gestural, sculptural, and visual modes through which students may make and transform meaning, multimodal social semiotic theory provides a useful lens through which to study classroom interaction. In particular, multimodal social semiotic theory is "concerned with how human beings make meaning in the world through using and making different signs, always in interaction with someone" (Stein, 2008, p. 875).

Within ELA research, the concept of transmediation—the recasting of meaning from one sign system into another (Berghoff, Egawa, Harste, & Hoonan, 2000; Siegel, 1995; Suhor, 1984)—is a process that can be promoted by students' engagement with multimodal instructional activities. Recently, for example, researchers have shown how students who recast their interpretations of literary texts across semiotic systems expanded their perspectives and extended the interpretive potential of literary texts (Short & Kaufmann, 2000; Zoss, 2009). Inquiry-based models of instruction depend on students' generating ideas and creating meanings between texts (Siegel, 1995). The question taken up in this study asks whether or not students who engaged in a multimodal instructional activity that promoted transmediation actually produced and analyzed texts in ways that reflected "generative" (Siegel, 1995) ideas about content matter.

Since the first empirical investigations of talk in educational settings were conducted more than 150 years ago, a substantial body of knowledge on the role of talk in promoting students' literacy learning has developed (Nystrand, 2006). Classroom talk that has been related to student achievement often resembles naturally occurring conversation or dialogue between teacher and students (Nystrand & Gamoran, 1991). Talk in many secondary English classrooms, however, continues to be characterized by teachers who pose closed questions that have pre-specified answers and students who ask questions not as a primary means of learning content, but in order to reveal an already-developed understanding of the teacher's preferred response (Greenleaf & Freedman, 1993). Lacking in such a pattern of classroom discourse are the features of naturally occurring dialogues that make conversations about literature enjoyable and insightful, including students' taking up others' responses while teachers "incorporate, probe, and honor students' multiple voices" (Juzwik, Nystrand, Kelly, & Sherry, 2008, p. 1116).

METHODS

Context of the Investigation

Data for this study were taken from a larger corpus of data collected over a 15-week semester in one English 12 classroom. In the larger study, the classroom teacher, Mr. Smith (a pseudonym, as are all student and school names used throughout this study), implemented three cycles of multimodal project work, followed by whole-class discussions of three literary texts. This paper reports on *one* small group's work during *one* instructional cycle of Shakespeare's *Macbeth*. During multimodal instructional activities, students addressed a series of interpretive questions through small group deliberation and by completing a project that required them to use an extra-linguistic mode, such as a film, painting, or sculpture, to compose their responses. Directions for this project guided students to: (a) engage in conversation about the text, (b) use the text as a resource, and (c) interpret meanings based on shared understandings of the text. Students had one 60-minute class period to plan and execute their project.

Mr. Smith was a second-year teacher at River Valley High School, a large suburban school in the eastern United States. He completed a graduate degree and his teacher education at a large research institution where he was also a student in a methods course that I facilitated. That course drew heavily on the Junior Great Books model for literary discussions called "shared inquiry" (The Great Books Foundation, 1999) and focused on planning, leading, and assessing text-based discussions in ELA classrooms. Although Mr. Smith regularly incorporated a multimodal project into his literature courses, he looked forward to "working multimodality into everyday classroom instruction" (personal communication, April 30, 2009).

Participants

All students in Mr. Smith's 12th-grade literature class completed an inventory that inquired into students' experiences during discussions in ELA as well as their out-of-school and in-school multimodal literacy practices, such as whether or not, and how frequently, if so, students participated in multiplayer videogames, or could read sheet music and play an instrument, for example. Small groups were configured heterogeneously according to the number of multimodal literacy practices that students identified on this inventory. I established three ranges for inventory scores: *novice* (0-5 multimodal literacy practices), *intermediate* (6-8 multimodal literacy practices), and *expert* (9 or more multimodal literacy practices). I formed each small group by selecting participants whose scores represented each range. The small group featured in this paper, then, was composed of one novice, Nick; one student, Leonard, rated for an intermediate level of participation in multimodal activities; and one expert, Louise. These focal students (LeCompte & Preissle, 1993) were selected at the beginning of the semester after it was confirmed that all three of these students attended class meetings regularly.

Nick's responses to discussion-based inventory questions focused on understanding content. The primary way that Nick characterized his participation in discussion was through "answering and asking questions on the topic" to promote reading comprehension. This stance toward discussion was not uncommon among his classmates; 80% of students in his class also identified reading comprehension as the primary purpose for discussion. Leonard, on the other hand, contended that the purpose of literature discussions was "to help everyone understand the meanings of literature; when more than one person discusses something it gives more than one point-of-view." This acknowledgement of the value of multiple perspectives was not common among his peers. Finally, Louise was the only student in her class who not only identified the ways in which discussion can improve comprehension, but also characterized the purposes of discussion in terms of its potential for application: "To understand, find a deeper meaning, and apply it to real life." These focal students, therefore, like all students, represented both shared and singular experiences and perspectives on schooling, learning, and literature.

DATA SOURCES AND DATA ANALYSIS PROCEDURES

Data sources in this study included the following: (a) video files and transcripts from the focal group's multimodal instructional activity, (b) students' multimodal project work, and (c) video files and transcripts from one whole-class discussion of *Macbeth*.

Classroom discourse analysis (Bloome, Carter, Christian, Otto, & Shuart-Faris, 2005; Rex & Schiller, 2009) was the analytical tool that I used to compare the data against my research question. Transcripts of students' talk during the multimodal instructional activity and whole-class discussion were segmented into turns at talk. I drew on a rich body of literature about text-based discussions in ELA classrooms that identified teacher and student discourse strategies, such as *uptake* and the use of *authentic questions*, to develop a coding scheme that was complex enough to differentiate between inquiry-based and transmission models of classroom talk, yet simple enough that another researcher could learn the coding rubric and arrive at a comparable evaluation of each transcript. I coded each teacher or student turn and then identified *rich interactions*; that is, I set aside for further analysis interactions that were characterized by high concentrations of effective student *and* teacher discussion moves.

I generated a list of eight teacher moves to devise a coding scheme to operationalize and analyze *teacher talk* during classroom discussions. Drawing primarily on the body of research assembled by Nystrand and his colleagues (Applebee et al., 2003; Christoph & Nystrand, 2001; Nystrand & Gamoran, 1991), I coded the discussion for the following features of teacher talk: (a) using revoicing to create a shared understanding of a text (O'Connor & Michaels, 1996); (b) posing questions that do not prompt pre-specified answers (Nystrand & Gamoran, 1991); (c) coaching students and scaffolding student talk (Kong & Pearson, 2003; Maloch, 2002); (d) establishing interpretive and exploratory discourse norms (Whitin, 2005); (e) making intertextual connections to previous class discussions or texts to create curricular coherence (Applebee, 1996); (f) providing "just in time" information for students as they ask for it (McIntyre, Kyle, & Moore, 2006); (g) modeling interpretive thinking (Christoph & Nystrand, 2001); and (h) taking up students' responses to extend discussion (Nystrand, 1997).

I coded *student talk* based on the following list of 11 moves that researchers have related to students' learning through discussions of literary texts: (a) challenging classmates to consider alternative perspectives (Keefer, Zeitz, & Resnick, 2000); (b) using positive metatalk that encourages others to participate (Almasi, O'Flahavan, & Arya, 2001); (c) exploring possibilities and using tentative textual interpretations (Langer, 1993); (d) elaborating on prior knowledge to extend current thinking (Langer, 1993); (e) warranting claims using evidence (Hadjioannou, 2007); (f) making intertextual connections (Bloome et al., 2005); (g) making nonstrategic concessions (Keefer et al., 2000); (h) participating in open discussion (student-to-student discussion for more than two talking turns) (Nystrand & Gamoran, 1991); (i) posing student-generated questions (Nystrand et al., 2003); (j) using reasoning that is hypothetical, personal, based on events, characters, or language that supports textual interpretations (Keefer et al., 2000); and (k) taking up others' ideas to extend discussion (Nystrand, 1997). A doctoral candidate in the learning sciences was employed to learn the coding rubric and code a subset of transcripts. Inter-rater reliability was established at the level of .70 for coding these features of student and teacher talk during discussions. Finally, students' multimodal product was analyzed to triangulate findings from the classroom discourse analyses described above. All of the codes used to analyze the nature of classroom talk in this study, the operational definition for each code, an example of the code as it was applied to the transcripts, and the scholarly sources from which the codes were derived, can be found in Appendix A.

FINDINGS

Discourse analyses suggested that students' co-construction of a multimodal product facilitated their interpretive talk about *Macbeth*. Students actively engaged one another in text-based interpretations that recast meanings from the linguistic sign system of the text into the visual sign system of a painting. Furthermore, one student profiled in this paper drew on the multimodal product in ways that mediated his participation in a whole-class discussion of literature. Finally, focal students *connected* ideas that were generated during their small group multimodal instructional activity to extend and deepen a whole-class literary discussion.

Macbeth *Multimodal Instructional Activity*

Pushing reasoning. Leonard, Louise, and Nick mediated their interpretations of *Macbeth* during the multimodal instructional activity by: (a) pushing each other to reason through the text as they completed their projects, and (b) actively deliberating meanings based on the text. Students realized and transformed their own and each other's thinking through speaking. In the excerpt below, students grappled with the question, "What is Macbeth's tragic flaw?" by making new meaning about the text as evidenced by their rethinking of ideas (turns 5, 7, and 8), authentic questions about the text (turn 8), and internalized discourse norms (turn 10) (see Appendix B for transcript conventions):

1. Louise: Okay. What is Macbeth's tragic flaw? I would say greed.
   Nick: Greed and a weak heart.
   Louise: (*to Leonard*) What do you think?
   Leonard: I'm trying to think of this word right now…Gullible.

5.   Louise: Why would it be, oh yeah, that would be...

      Leonard: That would be key. Because of the three witches, that's why he's gullible....That's why he did everything.

      Louise: I could see that. But I could also see, but even if he was gullible, greed is one of the reasons. There's a lot of 'em we could do.

      Leonard: I wonder if we could do something about gullible turning into greed or like something like that.

      Louise: You probably could, just, I mean, probably.

10. Leonard: (*whispering*) How is that tied together, though?

During this brainstorming session, students engaged in multiple perspectives (turn 7), valued each person's contribution (turn 3), and attempted to synthesize the information meaningfully (turn 10). Students considered Macbeth's tragic flaw using their own language ("greed," "weak heart," "gullible") and approached the question as if it were being asked for the first time by reasoning through ideas (turn 6) and exploring possibilities in the text (turn 8).

Co-constructing meaning. In the following extended excerpt, students actively co-constructed the meaning that they were making in response to their chosen prompt, "Construct something using the materials provided to you that captures a theme of *Macbeth*." Important to notice in this excerpt are the non-linguistic ways in which students communicated meaning to one another (turns 4, 6, 7, 11, 16, 17, 20, 24, 26, 27). Leonard connected (turn 3) the small group's consideration of overreaching ambition as a theme to explore in the text with the group's earlier talk about the complementary forces of greed and gullibility evidenced by Macbeth's actions in the play (turns 7 and 8 above). In this section, the focal students, in effect, imagined and acted out the scene that they eventually created (see Figure 2):

1.   Leonard: (*reading*) "Construct something using the material provided to you that captures the theme of *Macbeth*." We should do over...

      Nick: Overreaching ambition?

      Leonard: Yeah that one. That would tie in with the gullible thing.

      Louise: He's like held to a tree and like ahhh (*stretches her right arm up and out while her left arm stretches down and back*).

5.   Leonard: With a crown, actually. That'd be pretty (cool?).

      Louise: Yeah, just like (*stretches her right arm up and out while her left arm stretches down and back*).

      Leonard: Or, like have his head in this arm (*signals toward Louise's left arm*). Could you draw that?

      Louise: Yeah I could.

      Leonard: Then do it.

10. Louise: (*shrugs shoulders*) Geet it!

      Nick: (*reaches his right hand upward*) I could sort of see a shadow coming in and overreaching like that=

      Louise: =Shut your mouth. Just kidding. We want your input.

Figure 2. Multimodal Product of the Focal Students' Collaborative Activity: "Macbeth's Overreaching Ambition"

Leonard: Oh my god, wait a second.

Nick: It's like the crown=

15. Leonard: =Actually we don't want your input.

Nick: =with a white outline (*shapes his hands as if he were holding a crown and raises his hands upward*) and with like shadows and it's leaning on him (*brings both hands down to the desk*). And he's sitting there tryin' to reach for it (*raises right hand upward, grasping*). I don't know. It's a real vivid picture in my head.

Leonard: Can we kinda do like a before and after thing? Is it possible for you to do that? To tie in gullible and greed. We can have like a before thing, (*sketches a rough scene on a piece of paper in front of him*) before the three witches telling him what he wants to hear.

Louise: (*laughing*) That is a beautiful drawing.

Leonard: I'd figure I'd make it even more interesting. I thought you were about to add to it. I saw your pencil, and I was like "Get out of here." But then after you could do your part where the dude is holding the other dude's head, trying to reach the crown.

20. Louise: I don't know. I think if we just did that that would just be like before and after could show like deep, like I don't know. It's just real like. Like it makes sense, but I think we should do like that (*gestures with arms outstretched in front of her and behind her*).

Leonard: But it kinda brings in like the play as it is, like the play as a whole. Because it is about Macbeth taking what they say to become king. Then it also ties in both of our tragic flaws that we think he had.

Louise: Alright.

Nick: Shouldn't you have like a bunch of bodies around him, like since he killed a bunch of people?

Leonard: He has a dude's head in his hand (*holds up an imaginary head*).

25. Nick: I'm just sayin'.

Louise: (*holds her own imaginary head in her left hand and leans her head to the left as if to say: "Look at what I've got!"*)

Leonard: That's my point. You gotta have 'em like this (*pretends to hang himself*) with his tongue like (*tongue extending out of his mouth*).

Louise: I love that.

This extended passage revealed a deep engagement with understanding the play. Students grappled with the ways with which they might represent both an overarching theme in the play as well as how they might create non-linguistic meaning through their talk about visual symbols (turns 4-6), shadows (turn 16), and spatial arrangement (turn 17). Students' end product (Figure 2) represented the meaning that they made about the theme of the text that was not constrained by what students believed to belong to the "grammar" of the visual mode. That is, students engaged each other and the text in order to generate a novel, visual interpretation of *Macbeth*.

The quality of the final product reflected the quality of the talk that occurred during the small group activity (see Figure 2). On the left hand side of the painting, the three witches look on as Macbeth reaches for the king's crown, holding in his other hand the head of the slain King Duncan. The figure of Macbeth is surrounded by darkness; he stands upon those he killed to reach the "light of the crown." The brushstrokes sweep downward, representing, perhaps, the "fall" of the tragic hero from light to darkness. This painting illustrates how students recast meanings from the linguistic system of the text to the visual system of the painting. The end product provided a perspective on the play that did not exist in the linguistic system alone.

Macbeth *Whole-Class Discussion*

Open discussion. The following excerpt represents the type of talk that characterized students' participation in the whole-class discussion of *Macbeth* that occurred during class on the day after the multimodal instructional activity. Important to note during this section of the discussion are the following characteristics: (a) Mr. Smith's single question and relative absence from the discussion (turn 1); (b) the length of Leonard's initial response (turn 2); and (c) students' "heavy lifting"; that is, students co-constructing their interpretive responses by drawing on textual evidence and providing reasons based on inferences (turns 5, 8, 13, and 14).

1.   Mr. Smith: So take a minute here and think about the other themes, overreaching ambition, gender roles, virtue versus evil, reason versus passion—see if you can use any of those to talk about why Macbeth connects to being a tragic hero as well. If you have other examples of other tragic heroes that might connect, maybe you could try to help us understand that as well.

Leonard: I had overreaching ambition….So, in the beginning, he was fine and everything like that. And then he committed one killing, and after that he just kept kinda going with it. 'Cause he kinda started freaking out, because how he had someone sent to kill Macduff, but instead they killed the son and the mother. You know, that's just saying that he's panicking. He didn't just go for men in the line of kings; he went for anyone around him.

Thomas: Didn't he kill Macduff's son because Macduff went to England?

Nate: He killed the guards, too. I totally forgot about that. He killed the guards, too. They were innocent.

5. Leonard: He killed the king. He had to do that so that no one would see it.

Tony: Why didn't he just sneak up behind them and knock 'em out?

Brad: He tried to.

Leonard: He couldn't take the risk of that=

Louise: =Yeah, I mean people can connect the dots easily, like=

10. Tony: =I'll (leave) the dots.

Louise: Alright.

Leonard: But what if you just knock 'em out….if he did not kill those guards the way he did it…

Louise: There wouldn't have been anyone to blame the murder on.

Leonard: Exactly. It would have just been the murder of Duncan and like a ghost did it or something like that. He had to kill the guards in order to frame the guards for the murder. He couldn't have just knocked them out and framed them for it.

In this excerpt, Mr. Smith invited students to consider the ways in which some of the themes that they had identified as a class in *Macbeth* might connect to Macbeth's status as a tragic hero. Rather than asking students multiple leading questions and completing most of the interpretive work around the text, Mr. Smith structured his invitation to inquiry in such a way so that it would be difficult for students to respond with only one word. Instead, as Leonard demonstrated in turn 2, students were asked to think about the interpretive possibilities that existed within the text that could support or challenge Macbeth's status as a tragic hero.

Leonard's response in turn 2 illustrated the value of *talking-to-learn* during whole-class discussions of literature. First, Leonard began his response by identifying the theme that he had been working with in his small group during their multimodal project ("overreaching ambition"). He described how Macbeth's life unraveled before him after he killed the king. As Leonard continued to speak, however, he made a new interpretation about Macbeth—"he's panicking"—which connected the theme of overreaching ambition with a useful description of the behavior of the tragic hero. Thus, Leonard's talk about the text mediated his thinking about *Macbeth* to the extent that he recognized the role of panic in order to explain Macbeth's behavior in the text.

Perhaps most interesting about this excerpt, however, was the way in which it promoted other students' participation (who may have had a less thorough understanding of the text than Leonard did) to begin to explicate particular passages from *Macbeth*. Thomas asked a question about the text, which did not require an inference in order to be answered (line 3). That is, the text supplied the answer to this question because it was basic stated information (Hillocks & Ludlow, 1984). Nate, who provided two entire turns at talk during all of the class discussions that I observed over the course of a semester, realized that Macbeth had slaughtered people—the king's guards—who were entirely "innocent" (line 4). This prompted a series of exchanges about Macbeth's alternatives to killing the guards (lines 6, 7, 8, 12) before the ultimate point was reached: Macbeth had to kill the guards and not simply injure them because he needed to set up the scene to make it look as if the guards had actually killed the king (turns 13 and 14). Students' interactions during this extended period of multiple student-to-student exchanges about ideas in the text, what researchers in ELA have referred to as "open discussion" (Applebee et al., 2003, p. 700), illustrated how discussion mediated thinking and promoted student engagement.

Generative transmediation. During the whole-class discussion of *Macbeth*, Leonard responded to the final discussion question (Why do people do evil knowing that it's evil?) by drawing on the product of the previous day's multimodal project. That is, Leonard seemed to recast his understanding of the visual composition he co-created into the linguistic mode of discussion, functioning as a generative instance of transmediation (see Figure 2):

> I think people are blind to the evil in the sense that anyone who's about to do an evil deed, the person who has come to them to talk to them about it has influenced them enough for them to only see the good in the outcome and not the bad. They know the bad things that will happen…and [Macbeth] looked past the fact that he was going to kill the king, and he was going to have to kill people to become king. He just said, "I'm gonna think about the good of it and that's it."

Leonard's reference to "the person who has come to them to talk to them about it has influenced them enough for them to only see the good in the outcome and not the bad" constituted the verbal expression of the visual image of the "collective person" (the three witches) in the left side of the painting in Figure 2. The witches influenced Macbeth to "only see the good" (the crown of the king) in the top right side of the painting and "not the bad" (the former king's decapitated head and the dead bodies of those Macbeth murdered) at the base of the image. In essence, Leonard's response recast the meaning of the painting from the visual sign system into the linguistic sign system of the whole-class discussion.

Discourse analyses revealed how students actively co-constructed meaning during the multimodal instructional activity. These students primed their own interpretive thinking by using ideas generated during their small group work to respond to others' ideas during whole-class discussions. In fact, 17 separate ideas—12 from Leonard and 5 from Louise—were elicited during the whole-class discussion that could be traced to the talk that occurred during the focal group's collaboration. This suggests that the learning that took place during the multimodal instructional activity shaped students' participation during the whole-class discussion in consequential ways. For example, Leonard used the multimodal product as a thinking device (Lotman, 1988) as he re-shaped his response to a text by leaning on the product of the multimodal task to respond to an interpretive question during the whole-class discussion.

The value of the multimodal instructional activity for Nick was not as clear, however. Nick, a "novice" in terms of the multimodal literacy practices with which he identified, and whose understanding of the purpose of discussion was "reading comprehension," only volunteered one response during the whole-class discussion of *Macbeth*. In response to Mr. Smith's question: "What is so different about the murder of Duncan?" Nick replied, "'Cause Duncan was sort of pure; he was a good person, and he was good-hearted. Killing him was just (out of whack?)." Nick seemed to treat the question as if it only had one correct response by beginning his reply with the word "'cause." Furthermore, analysis of the discussion transcript revealed that Nick had raised his hand to participate on two separate occasions, but never "gained the floor." Although Mr. Smith encouraged students to respond freely throughout the semester by reminding students that they didn't have to be called upon in order to contribute to the inquiry-based discussion, not calling on Nick might have discouraged his participation.

Although his ideas during the small group activity were taken up by his group members (e.g., the inclusion of the dark shadow that divides the painting and the depiction of the bodies upon which Macbeth stands), Nick's role during the small group discussion was not defined. While Louise painted the canvas and Leonard wrote the caption that described the work, Nick interjected his interpretations, which Louise and Leonard dismissed playfully, only to incorporate them later into the multimodal product. A more clearly defined role for Nick during the small group activity might have promoted his recasting of meaning across sign systems, in addition to the reading comprehension that this activity may have offered him.

CONCLUSION

Although these findings are limited to the profiles of three high school students in one classroom, they illustrate some of the ways in which multimodal instructional activities can inform literature and literacy learning. Inquiry-based discussions diverge from the default patterns of discussion in most secondary English classrooms (Nystrand et al., 2003). Preparing students to participate in such discussions might require more than an explanation of how to participate in a new pattern of classroom discourse. Understanding the multiple modes through which students make meaning and students' particular perspectives on the value of multimodal and academic literacy practices, such as inquiry-based discussions, can inform how educators facilitate such activities so that students can "prepare for and participate effectively in a range of conversations and collaborations with diverse partners, building on others' ideas and expressing their own clearly and persuasively" (CCSS, 2010, p. 50).

In this case, the multimodal instructional activity facilitated students' engagement with multiple perspectives on a literary text—a primary goal advocated by current ELA scholars of literature instruction (Beach, Appleman, Hynds, & Wilhelm, 2010). Nick, whose participation during the whole-class discussion of *Macbeth* compels many additional questions, might have participated differently had he had a more clearly defined role, a different group configuration, or additional experience with inquiry-based discussions. As the "novice" in the group, Nick might have hesitated to take on the roles that seem to have informed Leonard's and Louise's participation. It is also important to note that the novelty of this instructional activity may have shaped the particular nature of the small group talk. Students in this study were engaging for the first time in such a multimodal instructional activity in their English class. Further research on the potential links between multimodality and classroom talk in other areas of the ELA curriculum may reveal additional affordances and limitations that can be used to structure literacy learning opportunities in secondary English classrooms.

By examining how classroom talk shaped and was shaped by students' participation in multimodal instructional activities, this study identified important ways in which transmediation informed students' participation in a whole-class text-based discussion of literature. Ultimately, students' participation in multimodal instructional activities seemed to expand the interpretive potential of *Macbeth*, which, in turn, enhanced the inquiry involved during the whole-class discussion. The findings from this study support the use of multimodal instructional activities to mediate students' talk about texts and to promote students' literary interpretations. which can support students' meaning-making across the curriculum (Carnegie Council on Advancing Adolescent Literacy, 2010). Understanding how the uses of multiple modes of instruction, including the visual, sculptural, and gestural modes leverage students' learning is critical for adolescent literacy—a wide field that is experiencing what some scholars have identified as a paradigmatic shift toward multimodality (Alvermann & McLean, 2007; Darling-Hammond, 2009).

REFERENCES

Almasi, J. F., O'Flahavan, J. F., & Arya, P. (2001). A comparative analysis of student and teacher development in more and less proficient discussions of literature. *Reading Research Quarterly, 36*, 96-120.

Alvermann, D. E., & McLean, C. A. (2007). The nature of literacies. In L. S. Rush, A. J. Eakle, & A. Berger (Eds.), *Secondary school literacy: What research reveals for classroom practice* (pp. 1-20). Urbana, IL: National Council of Teachers of English.

Applebee, A. N. (1996). *Curriculum as conversation: Transforming traditions of teaching and learning.* Chicago, IL: University of Chicago Press.

Applebee, A. N., Langer, J. A., Nystrand, M., & Gamoran, A. (2003). Discussion-based approaches to developing understanding: Classroom instruction and student performance in middle and high school English. *American Educational Research Journal, 40*, 685-730.

Beach, R., Appleman, D., Hynds, S., & Wilhelm, J. (2010). *Teaching literature to adolescents* (2nd ed.). Mahwah, NJ: Lawrence Erlbaum Associates.

Berghoff, B., Egawa, K. A., Harste, J. C., & Hoonan, B. T. (2000). *Beyond reading and writing: Inquiry, curriculum, and multiple ways of knowing.* Urbana, IL: National Council of Teachers of English.

Bloome, D., Carter, S. P., Christian, B., Otto, S., & Shuart-Faris, N. (2005). *Discourse analysis and the study of classroom language and literacy events: A microethnographic perspective.* Mahwah, NJ: Lawrence Erlbaum Associates.

Carnegie Council on Advancing Adolescent Literacy. (2010). *Time to act: An agenda for advancing adolescent literacy for college and career success.* New York, NY: Carnegie Corporation of New York.

Cazden, C. (1988). *Classroom discourse: The language of teaching and learning.* Portsmouth, NH: Heinemann.

Christoph, J. N., & Nystrand, M. (2001). Taking risks, negotiating relationships: One teacher's transition toward a dialogic classroom. *Research in the Teaching of English, 36*, 249-286.

Coiro, J., Knobel, M., Lankshear, C., & Leu, D. (Eds.). (2008). *Handbook of research on new literacies.* New York, NY: Lawrence Erlbaum Associates.

Common Core State Standards Initiative. (2010). *Common core state standards for English language arts and literacy in history/social studies, science and technical subjects.* Retrieved from http://www.corestandards.org/the-standards.

Cope, B., & Kalantzis, M. (2000). *Multiliteracies: Literacy learning and the design of social futures.* New York, NY: Routledge.

Darling-Hammond, L. (2009). President Obama and education: The possibility for dramatic improvements in teaching and learning. *Harvard Educational Review, 79*, 210-223.

Greenleaf, C., & Freedman, S. W. (1993). Linking classroom discourse and classroom content: Following the trail of intellectual work in a writing lesson. *Discourse Processes, 16*, 465-506.

Hadjioannou, X. (2007). Bringing the background to the foreground: What do classroom environments that support authentic discussions look like? *American Educational Research Journal, 44*(2), 370-399.

Hillocks, G., Jr., & Ludlow, L. H. (1984). A taxonomy of skills in reading and interpreting fiction. *American Educational Research Journal, 21*, 7-27.

Hull, G., & Schultz, K. (2001). *School's out! Bridging out-of-school literacies with classroom practice.* New York, NY: Teachers College Press.

Jewitt, C. (2008). Multimodality and literacy in school classrooms. *Review of Research in Education, 32*, 241-267.

Juzwik, M. M., Nystrand, M., Kelly, S., & Sherry, M. B. (2008). Oral narrative genres as dialogic resources for classroom literature study: A contextualized case study of conversational narrative discussion. *American Educational Research Journal, 45*, 1111-1154.

Kamil, M. L., Borman, G. D., Dole, J., Kral, C. C., Salinger, T., & Torgesen, J. (2008). *Improving adolescent literacy: Effective classroom and intervention practices: A Practice Guide* (NCEE #2008-4027). Washington, DC: National Center for Education Evaluation and Regional Assistance, Institute of Education Sciences, U.S. Department of Education. Retrieved from http://ies.ed.gov/ncee/wwc.

Keefer, M. W., Zeitz, C. M., & Resnick, L. B. (2000). Judging the quality of peer-led student dialogues. *Cognition and Instruction, 18*(1), 53-81.

Kong, A., & Pearson, P. D. (2003). The road to participation: The construction of a literacy practice in a learning community of linguistically diverse learners. *Research in the Teaching of English, 38*, 85-124.

Kress, G., & van Leeuwen, T. (2001). *Multimodal discourse: The modes and media of contemporary communication.* New York, NY: Hodder Arnold.

Langer, J. A. (1993). Discussion as exploration: Literature and the horizon of possibilities. In G. E. Newell & R. K. Durst (Eds.), *Exploring texts: The role of discussion and writing in the teaching and learning of literature* (pp. 23-43). Norwood, MA: Christopher-Gordon Publishers.

Larson, J., & Marsh, J. (2005). *Making literacy real: Theories and practices for learning and teaching.* Thousand Oaks, CA: Sage Publications.

LeCompte, M. D., & Preissle, J. (1993). *Ethnography and qualitative design in educational research.* San Diego, CA: Academic Press.

Lotman, Y. M. (1988). Text within a text. *Soviet Psychology, 26*(3), 32-51.

Maloch, B. (2002). Scaffolding student talk: One teacher's role in literature discussion groups. *Reading Research Quarterly, 37*, 94-112.

McIntyre, E., Kyle, D. W., & Moore, G. H. (2006). A primary-grade teacher's guidance toward small-group dialogue. *Reading Research Quarterly, 41*, 36-66.

Nystrand, M. (with A. Gamoran, R. Kachur, & C. Prendergast) (1997). *Opening dialogue: Understanding the dynamics of language and learning in the English classroom.* New York, NY: Teachers College Press.

Nystrand, M. (2006). Research on the role of classroom discourse as it affects reading comprehension. *Research in the Teaching of English, 40*, 392-412.

Nystrand, M., & Gamoran, A. (1991). Instructional discourse, student engagement, and literature achievement. *Research in the Teaching of English, 25*, 261-290.

Nystrand, M., Wu, L., Gamoran, A., Zeiser, S., & Long, D. (2003). Questions in time: Investigating the structure and dynamics of unfolding classroom discourse. *Discourse Processes, 35*, 135-198.

O'Connor, M. C., & Michaels, S. (1996). Shifting participant frameworks: Orchestrating thinking practices in group discussion. In D. Hicks (Ed.), *Discourse, learning, and schooling* (pp. 63-103). New York, NY: Cambridge University Press.

Rex, L. A., & Schiller, L. (2009). *Using discourse analysis to improve classroom interaction.* New York, NY: Taylor and Francis/Routledge.

Rex, L., Bunn, M., Davila, B. A, Dickinson, H. A, Carpenter Ford, A., Gerben, C., & McBee Orzulak, M. J. (2010). A review of discourse analysis in literacy research: Equitable access. *Reading Research Quarterly, 45*(1), 94-115.

Short, K. G., & Kauffman, G. (2000). Exploring sign systems within an inquiry system. In M. A. Gallego & S. Hollingsworth (Eds.), *What counts as literacy: Challenging the school standard.* New York, NY: Teachers College Press.

Siegel, M. (1995). More than words: The generative power of transmediation for learning. *Canadian Journal of Education, 20*, 455-475.

Stein, P. (2008). Multimodal instructional practices. In J. Coiro, M. Knobel, C. Lankshear, & D. J. Leu (Eds.), *Handbook of research on new literacies* (pp. 871-898). New York, NY: Lawrence Erlbaum Associates.

Suhor, C. (1984). Toward a semiotics-based curriculum. *Journal of Curriculum Studies, 16*, 247-257.

The Great Books Foundation. (1999). *Introduction to shared inquiry: A handbook for Junior Great Books leaders.* Chicago, IL: The Great Books Foundation.

Whitin, P. (2005). The interplay of text, talk, and visual representation in expanding literary interpretation. *Research in the Teaching of English, 39*, 365-397.

Zoss, M. (2009). Visual arts and literacy. In L. Christenbury, R. Bomer, & P. Smagorinsky (Eds.), *Handbook of adolescent literacy research* (pp. 183-196). New York, NY: The Guilford Press.

APPENDIX A

Teacher and Student Talk Coding Scheme

Code Label	Definition	Transcript Example	Source
Revoicing	Teacher and students collaboratively create understandings of a text that serve to develop students' reasoning and facilitate the communication of students' thinking. In collaborating with students in this way, teachers often "revoice," or repeat all or part of a student's utterance and ask the student to verify the interpretation.	Joe: [The witches] boosted his ego, and said like "Go do it and you'll be king." Mr. Smith: So you don't think he was ever going to be able to be patient and do things the right way? Is that kind of what I'm hearing?	(O'Connor & Michaels, 1996)
Authentic Questions	Questions posed that do not prompt pre-specified answers. Authenticity depends on context (cannot be determined by words alone).	Mr. Smith: Could Macbeth have gone about becoming king in any other way? Was he, sort of, locked into the path that he took, or did he have some other choice?	(Christoph & Nystrand, 2001; Nystrand, 1997)
Coaching/ Scaffolding	Teacher talk that explicitly facilitates student talk by encouraging participation in literary discussions through direct instruction on discussion norms, reminding students about their roles, and providing language about discussion. To scaffold how students negotiate interpretations, teachers may focus on the text, refer students to the text, provide a concept map to guide discussion and model analysis within the text.	Mr. Smith: Look at this question here, number 4: In what ways do any of the themes of the play make Macbeth seem more or less like a tragic hero? For example, since the tragic hero always goes through a downfall in a play like this, the increasing disorder in Macbeth's life and the world of the play, in general, signifies his descent from goodness and order, right? So, as he does more to show himself as being that tragic hero figure—falling from a high position, becoming more evil—the world in general becomes more and more disordered.	(Maloch, 2002; Kong & Pearson, 2003)
Challenge	Student pushes back constructively against either another student's use of evidence or another student's line of reasoning.	Tony: Why didn't [Macbeth] just sneak up behind [the guards] and knock 'em out?... Leonard: He couldn't take the risk of that... Louise: There wouldn't have been anyone to blame the murder on.	(Keefer et al., 2000)

Code Label	Definition	Transcript Example	Source
Classroom Culture	Student talk that builds the collaborative culture of the classroom environment by encouraging participation through positive interactions with peers.	Louise: All of the things that happened were going to happen, [the witches] just... Malcolm: Stretched the truth. Louise: I guess you could say that...I just think they manipulated what they were saying to use him, but I don't think they actually lied. Malcolm: They exaggerated the truth. Louise: Exaggerated would be a good word to use.	(Almasi et al., 2001; McIntyre et al., 2006)
Explore Possibilities	Students consider potential meanings in the text tentatively in order to gain information to form an understanding of the characters and events in the text.	Ian: I just don't get why—they weren't pure enemies—why would you kill someone he was close, who he respected before all of this happened?	(Langer, 1993)
Extending/ Elaborating	Students build on prior knowledge and elaborate on that knowledge in order to extend their current understanding.	Louise: The people that [Macbeth] was killing before were fighting back. [Macbeth] was killing someone in his sleep; and even though all of those other things might come before, ... to murder someone in their sleep is a very dirty and snakelike thing to do.	(Langer, 1993)
Evidence Source	Students back up or warrant their claims with evidence based on the (a) text, (b) students' prior knowledge, or (c) students' interpretations or inferences.	Mr. Smith: So does Macbeth represent someone who murders because fate (through the witches) tempts him? Because his wife pushes him into it? Or because he is overly ambitious?... Louise: Yeah, because fate tempts him. He even specifically said in the book that he never even thought that being king was a possibility until the witches told him that.	(Hadjioannou, 2007; Keefer et al., 2000)

Code Label	Definition	Transcript Example	Source
Interpretive/ Exploratory Discourse Norms	Teacher postpones judgment, uses tentative language, entertains multiple points of view, hypothesizes issues, values students' contributions, revisits ideas, tolerates ambiguity, and seeks connections to build interpretations.	Leonard: And [Macbeth] feels that everyone knows exactly what happened, and he's scared, so that's why he puts the spies out in everyone's home. Mr. Smith: That's an interesting point, right. He's dealing with the guilt over the first [murder]—he already felt so bad about that. Why does he continue killing more people?	(Hadjioannou, 2007; Whitin, 2005)
Intertextuality	Teacher or student juxtaposes texts (including written texts, conversational texts, and nonverbal texts) by referring to common features across texts, common referents among texts, or historical relationships between texts.	Mr. Smith: So take a minute here and think about the other themes— overreaching ambition, gender roles, virtue versus evil, reason versus passion—see if you can use any of those to talk about why Macbeth connects to being a tragic hero as well. If you have other examples of other tragic heroes that might connect, maybe you could try to help us understand that as well.	(Bloome et al., 2005)
Just In Time Information	Teacher talk that provides contextually relevant information to students as they request it	Thomas: Was Macbeth a real person? Mr. Smith: He was a real person, but he didn't do any of those things. He was the king for a short time, but...	(McIntyre et al., 2006)
Modeling	Teacher explicitly talks about how she or he is thinking about the content of a particular passage by considering, among other things, historical context, etymology, or reading strategies that could be used to make an inference.	Leonard: Didn't the head say, "What have you done?" or whatever? Or "Why would you have done this?" Isn't that kinda like "Why did you go and do this?" Mr. Smith: Well, this is something that I'm wondering right now. We know the second set of prophecies—about not of woman born and the forest moving—we know that those were definitely meant to mislead him.	(Christoph & Nystrand, 2001; Kong & Pearson, 2003)
Nonstrategic Concession/ Rethinking	During the course of discussion, students make voluntary or spontaneous changes in their reasoning based on the quality of the dialogue that arises.	Thomas: Didn't he kill Macduff's son because Macduff went to England? Nate: He killed the guards, too. I totally forgot about that. He killed the guards, too. They were innocent.	(Keefer et al., 2000)
Open Discussion	Student-teacher interactions in which an open exchange of ideas occurs among students and/or between at least three students and the teacher.	Ian: The witches also said what would happen when he died, so how could it be true? Louise: ...They didn't lie to him, they just manipulated what they were saying. They just manipulated him by saying things...like by saying things in a very vague way. Leonard: Cryptic messages. They made him believe a lie.	(Applebee et al., 2003)
Student Questions	Students spontaneously pose an authentic question without being asked to do so by the teacher.	Louise: I do have a question about this play, though. Like you said before, usually in the play, like a tragedy, you feel bad like for the person at the end, but Macbeth didn't really seem to have like, you didn't really feel bad for him. He deserved everything that he got. I don't know, are there different kinds of tragedies, or is this like an odd kind of...?	(Nystrand et al., 2003)

Code Label	Definition	Transcript Example	Source
Reasoning	Student provides (a) hypothetical, (b) personal, (c) event-based, (d) character-based, or (e) language-based examples to support an interpretation of a text.	Ian: I think he would become crazy knowing that he would become king one day, but not knowing when that time is. He probably would've done it at a (later hour?) if he wouldn't have done it then.	(Keefer et al., 2000)
Uptake	When a participant in a discussion uses another participant's utterance to extend or deepen the discussion. Uptake is often marked by deictic references, or the use of pronouns that refer back to previous answers.	Joe: He just feels like everyone's gonna stab him in the back and rat on him. Leonard: Just to elaborate on him: you can never be too careful when it comes to something like that...Like you could kill one person and think you killed one and then he's actually alive or something—he knows what happened. Or someone saw through like a door or a doorway or something like that, that could easily just ruin him right there.	(Nystrand, 1997; Nystrand et al., 2003)

APPENDIX B

Transcript Key

(words)	guess at speech
=words=	immediately connected speech
words	researcher's comments for clarification
(...)	pause in speech

Exploring Motivation and Comprehension of a Narrative in a Video Game, Book, and Comic Book Format

Charles K. Kinzer
Daniel L. Hoffman
Selen Turkay
Nilgun Gunbas
Pantiphar Chantes
Teachers College Columbia University

This study investigates the effects of narrative presentation format on sixth-graders' comprehension of and motivation for reading a story. Digital games have become increasingly popular for school-aged children (Pew Research, 2008), and several researchers suggest that video games and game play involve important literacy skills (e.g., Gee, 2003; Squire, 2005) and may be viewed as a "constellation of literacy practices" (Steinkuehler, 2007, p. 302). Acknowledging that the format of narratives, delivered via comic books, graphic novels, traditional print, video games, and so on can affect motivation and comprehension, a study was designed in which 67 sixth-grade students in New York City were presented with a similar story in three formats: within a Nintendo DS adventure game (Game Group, GG, n = 23); as a comic book (Comic-book Group, CG, n = 23), and as a book (Book Group, BG, n = 21).

It was hypothesized that a narrative-based video game format could generate high motivation scores due to the popularity of video games in general as well as the novelty of playing a video game in a school setting. In addition, the video game used in this study includes challenges that rely on a need to read and understand its narrative as a central element of game play. This could also enhance motivation and interest in the narrative, and provides an overt sense of purpose for reading. Further, the supportive graphic elements in a video game and in comic books could enhance both literal and inferential understanding.

However, most statements about the motivational value and possible learning outcomes of playing video games is often done is sweeping terms, without important caveats that video games represent many genres (e.g., first-person shooters, role-playing games, multiplayer games, adventure games), are played in many contexts and on many platforms (e.g., in schools, at home, with friends, on mobile devices, on large screens), and that factors such as free choice of game vs. forced choice may all influence motivation to play and learning outcomes. In short, research is needed to carefully examine games in their specific contexts, as related to claimed learning outcomes. Being mindful, therefore, that, "Not everyone is a gamer... and assuming that games can be lumped into one genre and that all students enjoy playing video games is not appropriate" (Kinzer, 2010, p. 55) this study examines outcomes related to narrative understanding and motivation to play within a specific game genre (an adventure game played on a mobile, Nintendo DS platform), compared to outcomes from a more traditional, narrative text and the same narrative presented in a comic book/graphic novel.

Following a brief discussion of relevant background, subsequent sections of this paper present the study's results and discuss their implications relative to two central research questions:

(1) Is there a difference in motivation and perceived story interest when it is presented within a popular and commercially available video game, a comic book, or a traditional novel?, and (2) Is there a difference in the comprehension of a narrative when it is presented within a popular and commercially available video game, a comic book, or a traditional novel?

BACKGROUND

According to Luke (2000), traditional forms of literacy remain necessary though not sufficient for effective participation in a network society, as facility with digital forms of literacy become fundamental for participation and communication. Similarly, Kellner (2006, p. 5) argues that traditional print literacy becomes increasingly important in the digital age, Kamil, Borman, Dole, Kral, Salinger, & Torensen (2008) suggest that far more advanced literacy skills are required of current (and future) generations compared to previous generations, and strong arguments have been made to redefine literacy to include but go beyond conceptions of print-based literacy practices (e.g., Leu, 1997; Kinzer & Leander, 2003; Ito, Baumer, Bittanti, Boyd, Cody, Herr-Stephenson, & Tripp, 2009). Central to all such arguments is the acknowledgment of the need to understand what is read at both literal and inferential levels (Leu, Zawilinksi, Castek, Banerjee, Housand, Liu, & O'Neil, 2007; see also, Partnership for 21st Century Skills, 2009).

Data continue to indicate that reading proficiency in elementary school children is of great concern. For example, the 2009 National Assessment of Educational Progress in reading reported that 68% of eighth-grade students fell below the proficient level in their ability to comprehend the meaning of a text at their grade level (National Center for Educational Statistics, 2010). In response, a wide variety of approaches, strategies, curricula, teaching methods, teaching materials, and administrative structures have been investigated in hopes of improving the nation's literacy rate, in both traditional texts and in online reading. Of these important lines of research, two are most relevant to the current study: (1) recommendations to "increase student motivation and engagement in literacy learning" (e.g., Kamil et al., 2008, p. 9), and (2) recommendations to focus on the integration of literacy and technology as teaching tools and to understand required reading practices in digital environments (e.g., Leu et al., 2007).

Thus, the current study is centered on three premises. The first premise is that motivation is a crucial aspect of literacy; students need to be motivated to read and motivation has an effect on comprehension. The second premise is that children like playing video games. Statistics show that most middle school students, from a wide variety of backgrounds, enjoy playing video games. The third premise is that many types of video games require a great deal of literacy in order to play, due to their reliance on narrative conventions.

Motivation to Read

Motivation is a key component of reading. Research has shown that a person reads a word or comprehends a text not only because she can do it, but because she is motivated to do it (Guthrie & Wigfield, 2000); one has to be able to read as well as *want* to read. Motivation factors play a critical role in the development of literacy skills in middle childhood and beyond (Guthrie, Wigfield, Metsalaet, & Cox, 1999). Unfortunately, a growing body of evidence suggests that students in the middle school grades are lacking in motivation to read and engage with texts.

Many factors have been shown to influence students' motivation to read. One is how interesting the text is to the reader, based on purpose for reading and personal engagement. If a book is personally significant and/or if a purpose for reading is established and accepted, it is likely to be rated as interesting (Schraw, Bruning, & Svoboda, 1995). For example, Ivey and Broaddus (2001) focused on what makes sixth-grade students want to read in reading and language classrooms. The students in their study sent a strong message about the need to read personally interesting materials and about having some control over what they read in school. This finding, coupled with the recommendation to make literacy experiences more relevant to students' interests and experiences in everyday life (Guthrie, Wigfield, & VonSecker, 2000) acknowledge the importance of exploring innovative ways to motivate students to read.

Narrative in education. Bruner (1990) argues that narrative is a form of thought that is innate in human beings. Perhaps this is why it is often used in education (Dettori & Paiva, 2009). Although there are "various narrative practices" (see Conle, 2003, p. 3), in this context we use the term narrative to mean "story," which Genette, Lewin, and Culler (1980, p. 25) defines as a "succession of events" that "tell what happened" and "who did what to whom and why" (Calfee & Drum 1986, p. 836). Put another way, narratives are a form of speech that do not describe the here-and-now but rather the there-and-then (Peterson, Jesso, & McCabe, 1999). When narratives are involved, a proficient reader attempts to explain *why* events in the text occur and *why* the author explicitly mentions particular information in the text (Graesser, McNamara, & Louwerse, 2003). Such explanations include motives of characters' actions, causes of events, and justifications of claims. In addition to the content, the vocabulary load of the text and its linguistic structure, discourse style, and genre also interact with the reader's knowledge (Sweet & Snow, 2003). Therefore, narratives presented in different formats, such as in video games, comic books, or traditional books, may well affect motivation and comprehension of the story.

As educational tools, narratives are effective because they are often believable, memorable, and entertaining (Neuhauser, 1993). Of course, the ability to read and comprehend written material is a "cross-curricular competence and an important prerequisite for success in school" (Artelt, Schiefele, & Schneider, 2001, p. 364). Such skills become increasingly important as students enter the middle school grades, where there is considerable emphasis on new vocabulary, connecting and summarizing ideas, and organizing and remembering information (Readence, Bean, & Baldwin, 2004). In science, for example, there have been many calls to leverage the explanatory power of narratives (Norris, Guilbert, Smith, Hakimelahi, & Phillips, 2005) in order to allow "nonscientists, who [do not] share the conventions of formal scientific monologue" (Smolin, 1998, p. 6) to communicate ideas and make ideas "coherent, memorable, and meaningful" (Millar & Osborne, 1998, p. 13).

In 1998, Milne identified four different types of science stories in science textbooks. These story types include heroic, discovery, declarative, and politically correct stories, all of which, Milne argues, promote a particular set of philosophical assumptions about science. Others have argued for the use of historical narrative as a means of providing a context to address science content in a humanistic and more authentic manner (for an overview see Metz, Klassen, McMillan, Clough, & Olson, 2007). In short, understanding narratives is important both in its own, "traditional" domain of stories and literature, and in content-area subjects.

Nontraditional Texts

Given the documented importance of providing interesting texts to young readers, a natural follow-up question is what area(s) of popular culture are students interested in that might provide some sort of reading experience? Multimodality of Internet technologies (Leander & Lewis, 2008), electronic books like the Amazon Kindle family, comic books, video games, and even mobile phones can be motivating ways to promote students' reading and writing (Black, 2006; Ito et al., 2009; Jenkins, 1992). Is there some way to harness adolescents' interest in video games to promote traditional literacy development? Drawing upon students' out-of-school interests to promote literacy development is supported by a number of researchers. For example, Alvermann and Hagood (2000) argue that using fandom of popular cultural texts, such as music, can get students interested in school literacies while providing teachers with insight into students' out-of-school lives. Chandler-Olcott and Mahar (2003) argue that acknowledging fan fiction or other text forms privileged by students, but often marginalized by teachers within formal learning communities, can increase student engagement and achievement in literacy.

Another possibility lies in comic books and graphic novels. Comic books are extremely popular because of their relationship to popular movies (Wax, 2002), the popularity of Japanese animation (Toku, 2001), and their increasing artistic and literary achievements (Gardner & Dillon, 2004). In a study of young readers of Archie comics, Norton (2003) concluded that the pleasure children derive from comics is associated with a sense of ownership of text, which in turn provides the confidence to engage "energetically and critically" (p. 145) with the comic book. The Comic Book Project, an arts-based literacy initiative for urban youth, used comic books to address specific literacy skills. Working with 733 children, the pilot program reported that participants processed a wealth of information related to the creation of comic books while including State learning standards (Bitz, 2004).

According to Schwarz (2002) the term graphic novel includes fiction as well as nonfiction text with pictures—"comics" in book format. These novels appeal to young people, are useful across the curriculum, and offer diverse alternatives to traditional texts as well as other mass media. Lavin (1998) suggests that reading graphic novels may require more complex cognitive skills than the reading of text alone. In this vein, Weiner, Weiner, and Royal (2010) suggest that graphic novels are multimodal texts that combine traditional text literacy with visual literacy, requiring multimodal literacy. Gardner and Dillon (2004) argue that just as with early readers, the correlation of pictures and text helps encourage the reluctant teen reader to engage with text in order to plumb the depths of a story.

Video games as texts. Adolescents play and enjoy video games—a national survey of school-age children found that they devote about seven hours per week to playing video games (Woodard & Gridina, 2000). Gentile, Lynch, Linder, and Walsh (2004) reported that eighth and ninth grade students averaged nine hours per week of video game play overall, with boys averaging thirteen hours per week and girls averaging five hours per week. Given the popularity of video games among adolescents, we might consider them as texts to promote traditional literacy practices in the way that comic books, graphic novels, and fan fiction have been used.

Although not present in all games, narrative is a critical element in most modern video games. According to Onder (2002) typical narrative devices in video games include backstory, cut scenes, flashbacks, foreshadowing, cliffhangers, and red herrings. Advocates of narrative in game design argue that a strong narrative line creates more immersive and engaging game play (Adams, 2001). Schneider (2004) notes that some games offer a more complete narrative that provides a storyline and a justification for the actions taken during the game, thus making a more interactive, immersive and involving experience, while Frasca (2003) argues that a better understanding of the elements shared by games and stories, such as characters, settings, and events, is needed. Graesser and colleagues (2003, p. 84) emphasize multiple levels of dialogue in narrative, stating, "Not only are there explicit speech acts between characters in the plot, but there are implicit acts of communication between characters, implicit dialogues between the narrator and audience, and implicit dialogues between writer and reader." In short, video games (1) are extremely popular with adolescents, and (2) include strong narrative elements that are often critical to successful game play. The game chosen for use in this study includes both features.

RESEARCH DESIGN, PARTICIPANTS, AND PROCEDURE

This study was designed to examine the impact of narrative presentation format on the learning outcomes and motivation of 67 (27 female and 40 male, average age 11.6) public school students in New York City. They were randomly assigned to one of three groups: Game Group (GG, $n = 23$), Comic-book Group (CG, $n = 23$), and text-only Book Group (BG, $n = 21$).

Data were collected in two sessions on two consecutive days. In the first session, subjects were introduced to the study and asked to complete a comprehension assessment and a brief survey about their familiarity with and play habits regarding video games. Students' standardized reading test scores were also made available by the school. These assessments were used to examine equivalence across groups in terms of general reading proficiency and comprehension, and in experience with video games and the Nintendo DS.

In the second session, subjects (previously randomly assigned into groups) were separated into different rooms, introduced to the task, and given one of three versions of the narrative. A research assistant explained that the name of the book/comic/game was *Blood Edward Island Memories* and that they had 45 minutes to complete the first chapter of the story. Subjects were also told that they would be asked to answer questions about what happened in the story without being able to go back to the story. During the 45-minute period, after 10 and 20 minutes, subjects rated their interest and desire to continue the story on a 4-point Likert scale and then continued with the story. After 45 minutes, subjects were told to stop reading/playing, even if they had not finished, and were given the comprehension measures described below.

INSTRUMENTS AND MEASURES

The Narrative/Text

The narrative used in this study was from *Trace Memory* (released outside of North America as *Another Code: Two Memories*), a 2005 adventure video game developed by CiNG and published by Nintendo for the Nintendo DS. In an adventure game, the player assumes the role of a protagonist in an interactive story driven by exploration and puzzle solving instead of physical challenge

(Adams, 2006). The protagonist in *Trace Memory* is Ashley Mizuki Robbins, a 13-year-old girl, searching for her father on Blood Edward Island. Nintendo's website describes the storyline of *Trace Memory* as follows:

> While researching human memory for the government's secret lab, scientists Richard and Sayoko Robbins suddenly disappear and are presumed dead. Ten years later, their daughter, Ashley, receives a letter from Richard, telling her that he is still alive and sequestered in a lab on Blood Edward Island. Ashley traces the letter to the island to find the truth behind her parents' mysterious disappearance. Once there, she discovers that her parents had been working on a memory-generating computer called Trace, but the connection between Trace and their disappearance remains unclear.

> While searching for Richard, Ashley befriends a ghost named D, who is looking for answers of his own. Having lost all his memories and any recollection of his death, D is destined to remain in limbo and wander the island until he recovers them. Together, they set off to find the truth of their pasts. (from http://www.nintendo.com/games/detail/909a0218-3a62-4d6f-a290-cb07ff26fa3c, accessed 2/6/11)

Trace Memory was chosen for several reasons. The first was practical: It was unlikely that sixth grade students in 2010 had played an adventure game released in 2005. Second, the game is story-driven. It was described as a "touchable mystery novel" with "lengthy conversations" (StaffReviewer, 2005; Hruschak, 2006). Other reviewers claimed it was "well-written" with a "good amount of suspense" (Harris, 2005; Parish, 2005). Finally, the protagonist of the story is a 13-year-old, a similar age to the target audience of the study.

Using the narrative within the *Trace Memory* adventure game, comic-book and text-only versions of the story were created. The goal was to create identical versions of the story with the same title, cover art, text, and (in the comic-book version), graphics. To create the comic-book, over 800 screen shots of the game were captured from a computer monitor while running the game using Nintendo DS emulator software. These screen shots were used to extract dialogue sequences and graphics from the video game. The comic was then assembled using the comic publishing software *Comic Life* (plasq, 2010). The result was a full-color, 8.5 x 11, double-sided, 72-page spiral-bound comic book with a transparent plastic sleeve and a custom cover page that read "Blood Edward Island Memories." All images in the comic were taken directly from the DS adventure game and were presented in the same order as a player would see them in the game. In both the comic and book, all dialogue and scene descriptions were taken word-for-word from text displayed in the game. Figure 1 shows samples of the three versions.

The third version of the narrative was an all-text "book" version. To assemble this version, a word processor was used. The result was a 42-page novel titled *Blood Edward Island Memories*. As with the comic book, a spiral plastic binding that included a transparent plastic cover page was used. Because the original game version of the story includes graphics to convey some story-related information about the setting and time, appropriate scene descriptions were added. For example, where the game might show a setting sun to establish time of day, the book version would incorporate the phrase "at sunset" into the narrative.

Figure 1. Sample Comic Book Pages (Top), Book Page (Left), Nintendo DS "Pages" (Right)

Subjects in the GG played the first chapter of *Trace Memory* on Nintendo DS Lites. Each student was given a Nintendo DS, headphones, and the console's original stylus. They were given instructions on how to launch the game, which was preloaded. Subjects in the other two groups were given the comic book and book version, respectively, and asked to read the story.

Comprehension Measures

At the end of the second 45-minute period, all subjects were given a comprehension assessment designed by the authors to measure both literal understanding of the story as well as higher-order comprehension of the story. In total, there were eleven literal comprehension questions, such as "Who did Ashley meet at the cemetery?", and "Why did Ashley come to the island?" The eight higher-level questions were all short-answer, write-in questions, ranging from "How do you think the boat captain feels about the island?", to "Briefly, summarize the story in your own words." Subjects were encouraged to answer as many questions as possible. They were also told it was ok to guess if they didn't know the answer.

Motivation Measures

Two forms of motivation measures were used: a series of two during-intervention questions and a post-task survey. The two during-intervention motivation-related questions were asked of subjects at 10 and 20 minutes during the 45 minutes subjects played the game/read the narrative. At those times, research assistants recorded each students' responses on two, 4-point Likert scale questions: 1) How *interested* are you in this story?, and 2) How much do you want to *continue* this story? The 4-point Likert-scale ranged from 1 ("not at all") to 4 ("very much").

The post-intervention motivation measure included four questions, one each in the area of enjoyment ("How much did you like the game/book/comic?"), overall interest ("How interesting did you find the story?"), concentration ("How well did you concentrate on the game/book/comic?") and perception of task difficulty ("How hard was it for you to read the story in the game/comic/book?"). Each of these areas is linked to motivation (Ryan, Koestler & Deci, 1991). Responses were provided on a 5-point Likert-scale from 1 (not at all) to 5 (very much).

Measures Exploring Equivalence Between Groups

After subjects had been randomly assigned into the three groups, two measures examined equivalence across groups. First, as a pre-task measure of comprehension proficiency, subjects completed a paper-based comprehension measure used by the Teachers College Reading and Writing Project, *Abby Takes Her Shot* (Dyckman, 2001). Eleven students were absent for this measure, thus this comprehension measure was completed by 56 students. However, absent students were equally, and randomly, distributed across groups (4 in BG, 4 in CG, 3 in GG). There was no statistically significant difference ($F(2,53) = 0.696$, $p = 0.503$) between groups on this measure, thus implying group equivalence.

Second, by the time students in New York City schools are in the sixth grade, they have completed several standardized tests in the area of English Language Arts (ELA). For each student, the cumulative score on their past three standardized tests was obtained. Because not all had taken all three prior ELA tests, available scores for each student were averaged. There was no statistically significant difference in averaged standardized test scores across groups. We also examined possible differences in video game experience (e.g., number of hours spent playing video games, familiarity with video adventure games, owning gaming consoles). There was no statistically significant difference in any of these categories, and the 47 students who stated that they owned and used the Nintendo DS or DSi were equally distributed across groups (17 in GG, 15 in CG, 15 in BG). Cross-group equivalence is thus implied in these areas as well.

FINDINGS

Table 1 shows the mean and standard deviation statistics for all measures.

Motivation Findings

The first research question investigated the impact of presentation and format of a narrative on motivation/interest. Responses to a 4-point Likert scale question asking "How *interesting* is this story?" were not statistically significant after 10 minutes ($F(2, 64) = 1.660$, $p = .197$). However, a

Table 1. Means and Standard Deviations for the Measures Used in Each Condition

MEASURE	CONDITION					
	Book Group (BG; n = 21)		Comic Group (CG; n = 23)		Game Group (GG; n = 23)	
	Mean	SD	Mean	SD	Mean	SD
Interest						
after 10 minutes	3.62	0.50	3.14	0.99	3.10	0.89
after 20 minutes*	3.90	0.31	3.09	1.19	3.43	0.60
Desire to Continue						
after 10 minutes	3.67	0.73	2.95	1.13	3.14	0.79
after 20 minutes*	3.95	0.22	3.09	1.19	3.52	0.81
Likeability	4.57	0.98	4.30	0.97	3.78	1.04
Overall Interest						
at end of task	4.43	0.98	4.43	0.90	3.78	1.16
Concentration	4.45	0.76	4.26	0.76	3.61	1.23
Task Difficulty	2.62	0.87	2.00	1.13	2.78	1.04
Literal Comprehension	9.43	1.57	9.70	1.40	8.13	1.91
Inferential Comprehension						
accuracy	6.76	1.26	6.48	1.85	6.70	1.22
number of details	2.06	0.55	1.99	0.86	1.94	0.44
word count	16.16	11.90	13.85	8.58	10.69	4.87

* Students who finished before 20 minutes were not asked to complete this measure. Thus, for the 20-minute assessments BG = 20, CG = 22, GG = 21.

statistically significant overall difference was found after 20 minutes ($F(2, 60)$ = 6.891, p = 0.002, n^2 = .19). Post hoc comparisons using the Tukey Honestly Significant Difference (HSD) test indicated that the mean score for the BG was significantly different than the CG ($p < 0.001$) but there was no difference between the BG and the GG. A comparison between the GG and the CG did not reveal a significant difference after 20 minutes.

Within-group comparisons were also made for subjects' reported story interest, to determine whether a given group's score changed significantly from 10 to 20 minutes. None of the groups showed a significant increase in their interest ratings from 10 to 20 minutes.

The second during-intervention motivational measure recorded desire to continue, assessed on a 4-point Likert scale question, "How much do you want to *continue* this story?" An overall comparison of desire to continue was statistically significant after 10 minutes ($F(2, 64)$ = 3.529, p = .035, n^2 =.10), and also after 20 minutes ($F(2, 60)$ = 5.276, p = .008, n^2 = .15). Post hoc comparisons using the Tukey HSD test indicated that the mean score for the BG was statistically significant when compared to the CG ($p < 0.05$) for desire to continue, after 10 minutes, and also after 20 minutes ($p < 0.01$). There was no statistically significant difference in the desire to continue between the

GG and the CG after 10 or 20 minutes, although the GG group's desire to continue was slightly higher in both instances.

Within-group comparisons were also made for subjects' desire to continue the story. Although the reported desire to continue increased slightly for each group as the task went on, the change was not statistically significant within any group.

After subjects experienced (read or played) the narrative for 45 minutes, data were collected asking how much they liked the story (henceforth "likeability") and about their interest, concentration, and perception of task difficulty through questions using a five-point Likert scale from 1 (not at all) to 5 (very much). A mean score comparison found a significant difference across groups in reported likeability at the end of the intervention ($F(2, 64) = 3.579$, $p = 0.034$, $n^2 = 0.1$). Post hoc comparisons using the Tukey HSD test showed that the BG vs. GG mean score comparison was statistically significant ($p < 0.05$), implying that the book group liked the story more than the video game group.

A mean score comparison of all three groups' story interest ratings at the end of the 45 minute task approached statistical significance ($F(2, 64) = 3.054$, $p = .054$, $n^2 = .08$), with the GG reporting the lowest rating in how much subjects liked the story.

A mean score comparison of the three groups found a significant difference between reported concentration on the task ($F(2, 64) = 4.266$, $p = .018$, $n^2 = .11$). Tukey HSD post hoc comparisons of the three groups indicated that the mean score for the BG was statistically significant when compared to the GG ($p < 0.05$) but not the CG, implying the lowest concentration scores on the task for game group.

A mean score comparison of all three groups' rating of task difficulty found a statistically significant difference ($F(2, 64) = 3.729$, $p = .029$, $n^2 = .10$). A post hoc analysis using Tukey HSD revealed that participants in the CG reported the lowest task difficulty, which was significantly different from the GG ($p < 0.05$), but not the BG.

Comprehension Findings

The second research question investigated the impact of the presentation format of a narrative on middle school students' comprehension of the story. Two types of comprehension questions were analyzed: literal and higher-order questions. In total there were eleven, one-point multiple choice literal questions, and eight higher-order questions. A one-way between subjects ANOVA conducted to compare the total correct responses on the eleven multiple-choice questions found a statistically significant effect of presentation format on literal comprehension score at the $p = < .05$ level for the three groups [$F(2,64) = 5.93$, $p = .004$, $n^2 = .15$)]. Post hoc comparisons using the Tukey HSD test indicated that the mean score for the GG was statistically significantly different from the CG ($p < 0.05$) and the BG ($p < 0.05$). However, the CG condition did not differ significantly from the BG.

To analyze the higher-order questions, three different aspects were coded for each answer to the eight, open-ended, questions: accuracy, level of detail, and word count. For example, consider the following questions and responses: *Q:* How would you describe the relationship between Jessica and Ashley? *R1:* It was complicated. At first Ashley liked her <u>because she thought Jessica was helping her</u>, but then Ashley didn't like her <u>because Jessica lied</u>. *R2:* It was complicated. At first Ashley liked her, but then she didn't like her.

Accuracy was coded in a binary fashion; each answer was either correct or incorrect. Both responses in the above example are correct in their inferences about the relationship and would receive one point for accuracy. However, a simple accuracy score masks additional important information. Level of detail was scored by giving one point for an accurate and relevant descriptor, or an appropriate reason. In the aforementioned example, details are underlined and each would receive one point. Details were thought to be a potential differentiating feature between the three groups, as each condition provided different information with regard to how details could enhance inferences. For example, in the comic and video game conditions, graphics of body position, posture, and hand movements could help indicate how the two characters were interacting and felt about each other. This would not be true in the text condition, where all such information would have to be inferred from the text itself.

The word count measure was also used within the inferential comprehension analysis, as the provision of more details would be confirmed by a higher number of words used. Thus, in the above example, scores would be as follows: *R1*: accuracy = 1, details = 2, word count = 24; *R2*: accuracy = 1, details = 0, word count = 14. While both responses are accurate and exhibit inferential understanding of the relationship in question, *R1* provides more depth and sophistication, as shown in its number of details and words. Two graduate students independently scored the responses to each question for accuracy and details. Both raters had to agree, in terms of a response's accuracy score and its detail score, for inter-rater agreement to be coded as matching. Comparing their scores across both aspects for each response yielded a 92% inter-rater reliability rating; disagreements were resolved by a third reader.

A one-way between subjects ANOVA was conducted on each of the three score types: accuracy, number of details, and word count. There was no statistically significant difference found in any of these areas across the three groups (accuracy [$F(2, 64) = .224$, $p = .800$]; number of details [$F(2, 64) = .193$, $p = .825$]; word count [$F(2, 64) = 2.144$, $p = .126$]).

DISCUSSION

Two research questions were explored in this study. The first concerned the format of a narrative and how a respective format impacts middle school students' motivation to read a provided narrative, as indicated by students' perceptions of a story's interest level, their desire to continue reading, and how much they liked the story. The second question explored the impact of narrative format on the comprehension of a story. To address these questions, 67 middle school students were presented with a narrative in one of three formats: a video game, a comic book, or a book.

Results from this study reveal that narrative format may indeed impact middle school students' motivation to read, although perhaps somewhat counterintuitively. We felt initially that a narrative presented in a video game format might be the most interesting, be perceived as the most liked story, and would elicit the highest ratings in terms of desire to continue playing/reading given the documented interest children in this age range tend to show toward video game play. However, the results presented here indicate otherwise and argue for more research in this area.

For example, although there was no difference in reported perception of story interest between the three groups after 10 minutes, at the 20-minute mark statistically significant differences emerged. Subjects in the book group ranked the story as more interesting than the comic group, although there was no difference between the book and game groups. Results regarding interest at the end of the 45-minute period approached statistical significance ($p = 0.054$), with the book group reporting the most interest and game group reporting the least. Statistically significant results indicate that the book group liked the story more than the game group, and that desire to continue with the activity was higher in the book group than the game group after both 10 and 20 minutes; there was no difference in desire to continue the story between the game and comic groups.

A similar pattern was seen in literal comprehension scores. The book group significantly outperformed the game group and the comic group; there was no statistically significant difference between the game and comic groups. There were no statistically significant differences in the three measures (accuracy, number of details, and word count) associated with the inferential comprehension questions.

These findings are somewhat puzzling, given the evidence suggesting middle schools students' interest in video games. Logical follow-up questions include, Why would the book group show the highest desire to continue the task? Why, with the support of graphics in the game and comic groups, would literal comprehension scores favor the book group, and why would the task demands that require an overt purpose for reading in the game not result in a gain over the other groups?

Perhaps the subjects' prior experience with the various narrative formats was a mitigating factor. For example, it is possible that narratives in book form are most familiar and thus the narrative within a video game is not the central focus during game play, even when the narrative is integrated into the game and is a central part of game play. We note that the game group reported that they concentrated less on the task than did the other two groups. Perhaps the game group concentrated on game play rather than on the narrative. This, of course, has important implications for those attempting to use games as instructional vehicles—one might not assume that the motivational value or interest in out-of-school endeavors will be automatically beneficial when used for in-school tasks. Co-opting students' leisure activities for instructional purposes may not always result in optimal outcomes (e.g., see Kinzer, 2010; Ito et al., 2009).

Additional explanations for our findings might include our subjects' expectations for the game itself. While the game we chose was popular, it is possible that the students had more experience with, and liked, faster-paced games such as action/fighting and racing genres. If this was the case, the relatively slow, plot-driven adventure game might have been disappointing or unfamiliar to the subjects. *Trace Memory* has a lengthy introduction with dialogue between characters. Perhaps, to some subjects, *Trace Memory* may not have felt like a game. While it is an adventure game on the Nintendo DS, *Trace Memory* is similar to a graphic novel, though with puzzles/challenges interspersed within its dialogue.

We note that the game group reported higher task difficulty scores than the other two groups. Perhaps their interest and likeability ratings were influenced by how difficult they found the task. Perhaps there is a tension between the narrative and the interactivity of the game. As Costikyan (2000, p. 45) notes, "There is a direct, immediate conflict between the demands of a story and the demands of a game. Divergence from a story's path is likely to make for a less satisfying story;

restricting a player's freedom of action is likely to make for a less satisfying game." Juul (2001) similarly argues that games and stories do not translate to each other as do some of the more traditional media, such as movies and books.

With regard to the comprehension results, a possible explanation is that the puzzles interspersed throughout the game, rather than focusing the player on the narrative to gain clues to apply to the puzzles, distracted students. In addition, the need to navigate Ashley through the in-game world required some concentration on the part of the player. Perhaps students processed fewer story details due to the additional tasks involved in playing the game: holding the console, selecting and pressing the appropriate buttons, navigating Ashley through the in-game worlds, and so on. From a cognitive perspective, these additional tasks might cause a form of dual-task interference (Pashler, 1994) that ultimately impacts subjects' ability to process the narrative fully. This explanation seems consistent with the finding that subjects in the game group reported the highest level of task difficulty.

Taken together, the results of this study point to a need for well-designed research that examines the roles and effects of narratives in video games. This study used one genre of video game—an adventure game. The effects on motivation and comprehension in other video game genres may well be different. It remains necessary to explore the role of narrative understanding in game play, and the ways that game-based narratives might serve as vehicles for learning. This is not to say that learning cannot or does not occur in and through games. However, all games are not the same, and coming to understand optimal narrative environments for specific learning tasks within games is still woefully unexplored. We urge others to take up the challenge and closely examine the interrelationships between game play, game design, educational goals, game mechanics, and learning mechanics, especially as these might inform the teaching and learning of literacy and the exploration of literacy practices both in and out of school settings.

ENDNOTE

This work was funded in part by Microsoft Research through the Games for Learning Institute. The content and opinions herein are the author's and may not reflect the views of Microsoft Research, nor does mention of trade names, products, or organizations imply endorsement.

REFERENCES

Adams, E. (2001). Replayability, Part One: Narrative: *Gamasutra*. Retrieved December 10, 2010, from http://www.gamasutra.com/view/feature/3074/replayability_part_one_narrative.php

Adams, E. (2006). *Fundamentals of Game Design* (Second ed.). Berkeley, CA: New Riders.

Alvermann, D., & Hagood, M. (2000). Fandom and critical media literacy. *Journal of Adolescent & Adult Literacy, 43*(5), 436-446.

Artelt, C., Schiefele, U., & Schneider, W. (2001). Predictors of reading literacy. *European Journal of Psychology of Education, 16*(3), 363-383.

Bitz, M. (2004). The comic book project: Forging alternative pathways to literacy. *Journal of Adolescent & Adult Literacy, 47*(7), 574-587.

Black, R. W. (2006). Language, culture and identity in online fanfiction. *E-Learning and Digital Media, 1*(3), 170-184.

Bruner, J. (1990). *Acts of meaning: Four lectures on mind and culture*. Cambridge, MA: Harvard University Press.

Calfee, R., & Drum, P. (1986). Research on teaching reading. In M. C. Wittrock (Ed.), *Handbook of research on teaching* (Vol. 3, pp. 804-849). New York, NY: Macmillan.

Chandler-Olcott, K., & Mahar, D. (2003). Adolescents' anime-inspired "fanfictions:" An exploration of multiliteracies. *Journal of Adolescent & Adult Literacy, 46*(7), 556-566.

Conle, C. (2003). An anatomy of narrative curricula. *Educational Researcher, 32*(3), 3.

Costikyan, G. (2000). Where stories end and games begin. *Game Developer, 7*(9), 44-53.

Dettori, G., & Paiva, A. (2009). Narrative learning in technology-enhanced environments. In N. Balacheff, S. Ludvigsen, T. de Jong, A. Lazonder, & S. Barnes (Eds.), *Technology-Enhanced Learning* (pp. 55-69). Dordrecht, Netherlands: Springer.

Dyckman, S. M. (2001). *Abby takes her shot.* Raleigh, NC: North Carolina Testing Program, North Carolina State Board of Education.

Frasca, G. (2003). Simulation versus narrative: Introduction to ludology. In M. Wolf & B. Perron (Eds.), *The video game theory reader* (Vol. 1, pp. 221-236): New York, NY: Routledge.

Gardner, C., & Dillon, C. (2004). The Challenge of New Media. *Virginia Libraries, 50*(2), 2-3.

Gee, J. P. (2003). *What video games have to teach us about learning.* New York, NY: Palgrave.

Genette, G., Lewin, J., & Culler, J. (1980). *Narrative discourse: An essay in method.* Ithaca, NY: Cornell University Press.

Gentile, D., Lynch, P. , Linder, J., & Walsh, D. (2004). The effects of violent video game habits on adolescent hostility, aggressive behaviors, and school performance. *Journal of Adolescence, 27*(1), 5-22.

Graesser, A., McNamara, D., & Louwerse, M. (2003). What do readers need to learn in order to process coherence relations in narrative and expository text? In A. P. Sweet & C. E. Snow (Eds.), *Rethinking reading comprehension* (pp. 82–98). New York, NY: Guilford Publications Press.

Guthrie, J., & Wigfield, A. (2000). Engagement and motivation in reading. In M. Kamil, P. Mosenthal, P. Pearson, & R. Barr (Eds.), *Handbook of reading research* (Vol. 3, pp. 403–422). Mahwah, NJ: Lawrence Erlbaum Associates.

Guthrie, J., Wigfield, A., Metsala, J., & Cox, K. (1999). Motivational and cognitive predictors of text comprehension and reading amount. *Scientific Studies of Reading, 3*(3), 231-256.

Guthrie, J., Wigfield, A., & VonSecker, C. (2000). Effects of integrated instruction on motivation and strategy use in reading. *Journal of Educational Psychology, 92*(2), 331-341.

Harris, C. (2005). Trace Memory: The DS interactive mystery finally hits the US. Was it worth the wait? *IGN.* Retrieved January 1, 2011, from http://ds.ign.com/articles/652/652873p1.html

Hruschak, P. (2006). Player 1: A DS double whammy. *CiN Weekly.* Retrieved January 1, 2011, from http://web.archive.org/web/20060603141054/http://www.cinweekly.com/apps/pbcs.dll/article?AID = /20060111/ENT09/601110350/1063

Ito, M., Baumer, S., Bittanti, M., Boyd, D., Cody, R., Herr-Stephenson, B., & Tripp, L. (2009). *Hanging out, messing around, and geeking out: Kids living and learning with new media.* Cambridge, MA: The MIT Press.

Ivey, G., & Broaddus, K. (2001). Just plain reading: A survey of what makes students want to read in middle school classrooms. *Reading Research Quarterly, 36*(4), 350-377.

Jenkins, H. (1992). *Textual poachers: Television fans and participatory culture.* New York, NY: Routledge.

Juul, J. (2001). Games telling stories? A brief note on games and narratives. *Games Studies, The International Journal of Computer Game Research, 1.* Retrieved February 2, 2011 from http://gamestudies.org/0101/juul-gts/>

Kamil, M., Borman, G., Dole, J., Kral, C., Salinger, T., & Torgesen, J. (2008). *Improving adolescent literacy: Effective classroom and intervention practices. A practice guide (NCEE #2008-4027).* Washington, DC: National Center for Education Evaluation and Regional Assistance, Institute of Education Sciences, U.S. Department of Education.

Kellner, D. (2006). Technological transformation, multiple literacies, and the re-visioning of education. In J. Weiss, J. Nolan, J. Hunsinger, & P. Trifonas (Eds.) *The international handbook of virtual learning environments* (pp. 241-268). Dordrecht, Netherlands: Springer.

Kinzer, C. K. (2010). Considering literacy and policy in the context of digital environments. *Language Arts, 88*(1), 51-61.

Kinzer, C. K., & Leander, K. (2003). Technology and the language arts: Implications of an expanded definition of literacy. In J. Flood, D. Lapp, J. R. Squire, & J. M. Jensen (Eds.), *Handbook of research and teaching the English language arts* (pp. 546-566). Mahwah, NJ: Lawrence Erlbaum Associates.

Lavin, M. (1998). Comic books and graphic novels for libraries: What to buy. *Serials Review, 24*(2), 31-45.

Leander, K. M., & Lewis, C. (2008). Literacy and Internet technologies. In B. Street & N. H. Hornberger (Eds.), *Encyclopedia of Language and Education* (2nd ed., Vol. 2, pp. 53-70). Heidelberg, Germany: Kluwer Academic Publishers.

Leu, D. J. (1997). Caity's question: Literacy as deixis on the Internet. *The Reading Teacher, 51*(1), 62-67.

Leu, D., Zawilinski, L., Castek, J., Banerjee, M., Housand, B., Liu, Y., & O'Neil, M. (2007). What is new about the new literacies of online reading comprehension. In L. S. Rush, A. J. Eakle, & A. Berger (Eds.), *Secondary school literacy: What research reveals for classroom practices.* Urbana, IL: National Council of Teachers of English.

Luke, C. (2000). Cyber-schooling and technological change: Multiliteracies for new times. In B. Cope & M. Kalantzis (Eds.), *Multiliteracies: Literacy learning and the design of social futures* (pp. 69-91). New York, NY: Routledge.

Metz, D., Klassen, S., McMillan, B., Clough, M., & Olson, J. (2007). Building a foundation for the use of historical narratives. *Science & Education, 16*(3), 313-334.

Millar, R., & Osborne, J. (1998). *Beyond, 2000: Science education for the future.* London: King's College School of Education.

Milne, C. (1998). Philosophically correct science stories? Examining the implications of heroic science stories for school science. *Journal of Research in Science Teaching, 35*(2), 175-187.

National Center for Educational Statistics. (2010). *The nation's report card:Reading 2009.* Retrieved February 5, 2011 from http://nces.ed.gov/nationsreportcard/pubs/main2009/2010458.asp.

Neuhauser, P. (1993). *Corporate legends and lore: The power of storytelling as a management tool.* New York: McGraw-Hill.

Norris, S., Guilbert, S., Smith, M., Hakimelahi, S., & Phillips, L. (2005). A theoretical framework for narrative explanation in science. *Science Education, 89*(4), 535-563.

Norton, B. (2003). The motivating power of comic books: Insights from Archie comic readers. *The Reading Teacher, 57*(2), 140-148.

Onder, B. (2002). Storytelling in level-based game design. In F. D. Laramee (Ed.), *Game design perspectives* (pp. 291-299). Hingham, MA: Charles River Media, Inc.

Parish, J. (2005). Nintendo presents: My First Adventure Game. Retrieved January 1, 2011, from http://www.1up.com/do/reviewPage?cId = 3144099&did = 1

Pashler, H. (1994). Dual-task interference in simple tasks: Data and theory. *Psychological Bulletin, 116*(2), 220-224.

Partnership for 21st Century Skills. (2009). *P21 framework definitions.* Tucson, AZ: Author. Retrieved April 12, 2010, from www.21stcenturyskills.org.

Peterson, C., Jesso, B., & McCabe, A. (1999). Encouraging narratives in preschoolers: An intervention study. *Journal of Child Language, 26*(01), 49-67.

Pew Research (2008). *Teens, video games and civics: Teens' gaming experiences are diverse and include significant social interaction and civic engagement.* Retrieved July 10, 2009 from http://www.pewinternet.org/PPF/r/263/report_display.asp.

Plasq (Producer). (2010). *Comic Life.*

Readence, J., Bean, T., & Baldwin, R. (2004). *Content area literacy: An integrated approach.* Dubuque, Iowa: Kendall Hunt Publishing Company.

Ryan, R. M., Koestner, R., & Deci, E. L. (1991). Varied forms of persistence: When free-choice behavior is not intrinsically motivated. *Motivation and Emotion, 5*(3), 185-205.

Schneider, E. (2004). Death with a story. *Human Communication Research, 30*(3), 361-375.

Schraw, G., Bruning, R., & Svoboda, C. (1995). Sources of situational interest. *Journal of Literacy Research, 27*(1), 1-17.

Schwarz, G. (2002). Graphic novels for multiple literacies. *Journal of Adolescent & Adult Literacy, 46*(3), 262-266.

Smolin, L. (1998). *The life of the cosmos.* New York, NY: Oxford University Press, USA.

Squire, K.D. (2005). Toward a theory of games literacy. *Telemedium. 52*(1-2), 9-15.

StaffReviewer. (2005). GamesMaster deciphers the latest fiendish puzzler for DS. Retrieved January 1, 2011, from http://web.archive.org/web/20051218083941/www.gamesradar.com/?pagetypeid = 2&articleid = 36514&subsectionid = 1608

Steinkuehler, C. (2007). Massively multiplayer online gaming as a constellation of literacy practices. *eLearning, 4*(3), 297-318.

Sweet, A., & Snow, C. (2003). *Rethinking reading comprehension: Solving problems in the teaching of literacy.* New York, NY: Guilford Publications, Inc.

Toku, M. (2001). What is manga? The influence of pop culture in adolescent art. *Art Education, 54*(2), 11-17.

Wax, E. (2002, May 17). Back to the drawing board: Once-banned comic books now a teaching tool. *The Washington Post*, p. B01.

Weiner, R., Weiner, S., & Royal, D. (2010). *Graphic novels and comics in libraries and archives: Essays on readers, research, history and cataloging.* Jefferson, NC: McFarland & Co.

Woodard, E., & Gridina, N. (2000). *Media in the home, 2000: The fifth annual survey of parents and children.* Philadelphia, PA: The Annenberg Public Policy Center of the University of Pennsylvania.

"Dudes don't read, Ms. Rudd": The Voices Behind the Statistics

Lynn L. Rudd
Kent State University

Kathleen Dunn
Kent State University

"Guys think it's [reading] not a cool thing to do; it's kinda nerdy. A good amount of guys do read; it's just usually different. Girls read novels. Guys read magazines, things online" (David, personal communication, March 17, 2010).

Is it true that boys just don't read? What do boys have to say about their reading motivations and perceptions? Our research group investigated these questions with 62 male adolescents; their responses surprised and challenged us.

Surprisingly, many of these young men do read varying amounts; however, the reading in which they engage may not be considered 'school' reading or the definition of reading they've acquired throughout their lives. Many of them, 54% in this study, say that they do indeed, read. In fact 25% of the young men admit to enjoying reading. What do the voices behind the statistics say about adolescent males and reading? How can we understand their current viewpoints, values, and paradoxes about reading in and out of school? Furthermore, how can classroom teachers positively impact the way young males engage with text?

OUR STUDY

Five researchers examined the question of how male adolescents view their own reading attitudes and habits. We understood that much of the quantitative research such as NAEP (2003 & 2005) and Coles & Hall (2002) found that girls consistently performed better on reading tests than their male peers. We knew the literature, but we wanted to hear the situated voices of the young men in our current classrooms and schools. We then began asking the questions of what did or did not motivate them about reading and wondering what we as teachers could do to impact their points of view.

We begin by investigating what research says about motivation and its connection to gender and reading. We then focus on studies that address the perceptions and performances males have when they read. Finally, we describe our study and offer suggestions to prompt male adolescents to increase their reading efforts.

RELEVANT LITERATURE

General convention would say that having a greater ability in an activity and surrounded by others who are positively impacted most likely creates a positive attitude toward that activity (Logan & Johnston, 2009). When people are successful in an activity, they tend to pursue that activity which then encourages intrinsic motivation (Guthrie, McRae, & Klauda, 2007). Intrinsic motivation is based on curiosity and personal challenge, whereas external motivation is based on factors such a grades and recognition (Marinak & Gambrell, 2010). When readers are good at reading, they feel good about their ability; they have a high sense of self-efficacy and are therefore more likely to be motivated to engage in challenging activities and have more intrinsic motivation. Consequently, frequent readers will be more likely to employ additional reading activities (Wigfield & Guthrie, 1997; Schunk, 1995). Unfortunately, for many young males, as they observe their immediate surroundings, they do not see their male peers reading or being compelled to read. Often their affinity group (Gee, 2007), those peers who share common interests, only read for compliance or actively resist reading. This does not build motivation in male individuals or groups.

Gender and Motivation

Logan & Johnston (2009) found that girls are more likely to be interested and have a better attitude towards reading than boys. When considering why some students succeed and others do not, a variety of factors such as class, culture, and ethnicity are considerations (Coles & Hall, 2002). However, gender seems to be a consistent area of differentiation that needs to be understood and analyzed, especially as it relates to adolescents. Coles & Hall (2002) found that girls continually outperformed boys beginning at ages five to seven and the gap increased with age.

Many studies have also found that boys consistently score lower in reading ability than their female counterparts. Large-scale assessments such as the National Assessment of Education Progress (NAEP) (2009), the Program for International Student Assessment (PISA) (2006), and British governmental studies such as one conducted by the Office for Standards in Education have consistently found that boys struggle with reading in ways that girls generally do not (Louie & Ehrlich, 2008; Marinak & Gambrell, 2010). "Across all theories, findings indicate girls' and boys' motivation-related beliefs and behaviors continue to follow gender role stereotypes, and boys are very protective of their male persona" (Meece, Glienke, & Burg, 2006, p. 351).

Besides interest, boys' motivational levels may be affected by expectancy-value. In other words, their perception of success in an activity such as reading matters. The more likely one is to succeed in the activity, the more likely one will engage in it (Atkinson, 2009). Therefore, if a reader thinks that s/he will not be successful at reading a specific text, or reading in general, s/he will not engage in reading. Given that girls outperform boys in reading and writing assessments, one could infer that boys' motivation falls below that of girls (Meece, Glienke, & Burg, 2006). Further disheartening studies point to the fact that all students' motivation levels decrease as they progress to higher grades (Guthrie & Davis, 2003).

Boys' Reading Preferences

The nature of the reading material affects whether or not boys will be interested in reading. Carnell (2005) indicates that a high percentage of boys' reading ranges between science fiction and fantasy, sports-related books, war and spy stories, comic and joke books, and humorous fiction. Atwell (2007) and Coles and Hall (2002) extended this research by adding that boys tend to read less fiction than girls. They also read texts with more technical information than narrative structure. Merisou-Storm (2006) suggests that:

> Boys prefer to read for a purpose. For example, they read about how to fix something, how to help people or to get specific information on a topic, texts that

have a purpose: getting information, making things, and helping others (p. 113).

In his research, Kendrick (1999) recommended that educators, teachers, and parents have to invest in the genres that are popular with boys. These genres include science fiction, biographies of famous people, mysteries, sports stories, and survival/adventure stories. Other reading material that piques boys' interest revolves around mystery, humor, and danger (Weih, 2008).

Boys and School Reading

The current literature indicates that boys differ from girls in their attitude, motivation, and beliefs in reading and school-related reading, which therefore impacts their performance. Logan & Johnston (2009) assert that attitude toward school and attitude toward reading are causally related; therefore, boys who have negative attitudes toward school may have a negative attitude toward reading. They also looked at the interplay of factors, including attitudes, beliefs, and reading ability relating to school and support structures, as opposed to only studying an isolated factor such as reading ability. Their results supported the idea that boys need to feel achievement and success for a positive attitude to grow. Their motivation and attitudes seem to influence their reading achievement levels.

Oakhill and Petrides (2007) found that boys tended to do better on assessments connected to texts they preferred reading. While girls had strong preferences, they seemed to score in similar fashion on any text they encountered, while boys' reading comprehension and achievement was influenced by their preferences. In addition, females generally have been found to have higher self-efficacy in all types of reading and read more for enjoyment and to alleviate boredom (Marinak & Gambrell, 2010).

Coles and Hall (2002) found that as boys age, they want to differentiate themselves from girls and the culture that surrounds them. Teachers' overemphasis on fictional texts may lead to boys rejecting reading, especially if that activity is perceived as disconnected from the reading that they enjoy. This disassociation appears to be directly connected to boys' preferences for reading. If boys' preferences are not addressed, motivation may suffer.

Male Reading Models

In accordance with Vygotsky (1978), learning is a social experience. The acquisition of knowledge in children is mediated by others, by their actions, and through language. Both oral and semiotic mediation can stretch a child's intellect. Those who surround a student often serve as reading models. Models can be family members, modern-day heroes, teachers, and peers. Some of the influences can be positive while some can be negative.

Hamston & Love (2005) found that the practices of a family over time greatly affect the reading habits of children. Horton (2005) agrees, "The greatest influence on young people who read is family and friends" (p. 30). Boys generally spend more time reading recreationally when they have a father who sometimes reads and a mother who reads on a consistent basis (Woolcott Research Pty. Ltd., 2001). Boys look to fathers to model behavior for them. Boys, generally, do observe their fathers engaged in reading a newspaper, often the sports section and the statistics therein, which is reading, but not necessarily the type that is valued in the classroom.

Male role models are especially important because boys view reading as a feminine activity. Sports figures and action heroes socially demonstrate to boys how men should act. These high-profile male figures are kinesthetically engaged and prefer "doing" an activity rather than reading about it (Giles, 2008). In fact, Sullivan (2004) suggests that boys should be physically active while reading, for example, by acting or talking. However, as mentioned above, these are not the activities often connected to school reading, which is often illustrated by novels and study guides.

Teachers' influence on boys' reading habits and the gender of teachers is important. Statistics evidence that female teachers far outnumber male teachers, comprising 71% of the American teaching force (US Department of Census, 2004). These statistics may make a difference in the selection of classroom reading materials. As a result, these teachers are the ones who choose books that often have heroines and are about girls such as *Little House on the Prairie* and *Charlotte's Web* (Scieszka, 2003) and are also the ones who generally read aloud to boys (Giles, 2008). Unfortunately, when there is a lack of material that boys find interesting, such as informational books, books with facts, and biographies, they distance themselves from reading itself (Farris, Werderich, Nelson, & Fuhler, 2009).

Boys also look to other boys to see what their peers are reading or not reading. Male adolescent peers often negatively influence boys' reading behaviors. Negative labels are often given to boys who read (Atkinson, 2009), and although there are examples of innovative book clubs developed for boys (Weih, 2007), boys will not often find readers among their friends (Smith & Wilhelm, 2002). Their affinity group (Gee, 2007), so important to adolescents, often doesn't include reading; therefore, the practice is not seen as important.

Among influences that can positively affect boys' reading interest and present heroic role models are a series of male archetypes that Brozo (2002) details in his book *To Be a Boy, To Be a Reader: Engaging Teen and Preteen Boys in Active Literacy*. He delineates 10 archetypes that embody strong, time-honored male characteristics: the pilgrim, the patriarch, the king, the warrior, the magician, the wildman, the healer, the prophet, the trickster, and the lover. Each of these archetypes displays strength of character in compassionate, brave, wise, and playful ways. Brozo indicates that these positive male archetypes starkly contrast with the mass media's "spurious and injurious conception of masculinity" (p. 24). The archetypes in the literature that Brozo suggests convey what it means to be "male" and serve as role models for boys in today's pop culture, which too often portrays many males as negative stereotypes.

There are a variety of factors that impact boys' reading achievement. Our investigation is framed by the research history of this field while we attempt to hear the voices in the situated context of three Northeastern Ohio secondary schools. We wish to hear their stories in order to better articulate how adolescent males perceive reading practices and reading achievement to balance our current understandings.

DESIGN

Our research team designed our study to describe how boys feel about reading. We hoped to allow the voices of adolescent males to further shape the understanding and general knowledge for educators and those who have stake in adolescent males' lives. To do this, we conducted interviews in three public high schools and one middle school located in northeastern Ohio. Two high schools were urban; the remaining high school and middle school were suburban. Participants were volunteers who agreed to be a part of the research study when invited by a classroom teacher, school administrator, or one of our research team members. The 62 male adolescents, aged 14-18, were questioned using brief, semi-structured, one-on-one interviews.

Parts of the interview protocol were based on the Carolyn Burke Reading Interview (Rhodes, 1993). Other segments of the interview protocol were developed by the group, and we used them to guide the interview process. (See Appendix A for interview questions.)

Throughout the interviews, each research team member took extensive notes, and after the individual interview data were collected, each group member indexed and partially transcribed each interview. Audio tapes were used to clarify and supplement the notes and further the insights for the transcriptions. Individual results were then collected, collated, and thematically examined using constant comparison and a grounded theory methodology (Glaser & Strauss, 1967).

Throughout the data analysis stage, each research team member used his/her own results and compared those responses with the group. After coding each question individually, larger categories were developed across responses. During numerous group meetings, each member was involved in crafting the conceptual and thematic developments across all responses. Throughout the entire stage of data analysis and coding activities, the members were continuously verifying concepts and themes and coding with each other.

FINDINGS

Despite the variety of personalities, settings, and ages of the young men we interviewed, the theme of choice was prevalent in all their responses. Their lack of ability to choose their own reading material was connected to their self-reported motivation, and we also saw this thematic topic as connected to their limited definition of reading, their gendered reading role models, as well as a particular paradox we found as we analyzed our interviews. Here are the connections we found within their thoughts. After the themes are discussed, we attempt to integrate creative tips for teachers as they struggle with this complex issue.

Choice Matters

As stated above, the impact of choice was a theme that permeated a great majority of the responses. For example, when asked what they would change about reading in school, 64% of the young men wanted more choice in their reading. They reported that their motivation was greatly impacted by their ability to choose what they read. Regardless of the specific question they were asked, the young men repeatedly agreed that they would read more if they had broader choices.

"When I feel like reading, I can read for a long time. If it's a good book or a magazine, whatever, if it catches my eye. If it's boring, I'm like, nah, I'm not reading this at all" (Jett, personal communication, March 22, 2010).

Some of the high school seniors who were interviewed wanted to tell freshmen that they should choose the books they read. Grant's advice was, "Pick a book that interests yourself" (personal communication, March 22, 2010). Deon agrees by saying, "Pick up a book that you like" (personal communication, March 22, 2010).

A majority of the boys perceived that they had not been given sufficient reading choices in school. This impacted how much they read independently and the level of motivation they had when engaging with texts they were assigned.

Definition of Reading

When asked what counted as reading, 36 responses centered only on actual materials that were used for reading. For example, many participants simply responded by listing books or magazines. They didn't expound on the activity that was actually done with the materials. Forty-eight percent of the young men supplied simplistic definitions of reading and 42% recalled specific reading that was required for class. Of those with skill-based definitions, only 10 responses included any mention of reading with technology.

Like many other participants, two seniors, Jett and Grant, only referred to a list of things you might use for reading. They cited a good novel, newspapers, or magazines as their answers. They didn't mention skills and/or connection to how reading could impact their lives through learning new information.

Their definition for reading within school wasn't any more profound. For example, Caden, a senior, had this to say about school reading. "School reading is the little passage and then answering the question" (personal communication, March 8, 2010).

Jacob, also a senior, seemed to indicate in-school reading was narrow and non-motivating, "In school they want more fiction which I'm not a big fan of. It's more or less pointless. You learn how to read better, but there's nothing else to get from it" (personal communication, March 8, 2010).

Sustained Silent Reading (SSR) programs were integrated into three of the four schools involved in the study; however, there was little difference in the definition of school reading. Some of the boys did describe their SSR experiences, yet once again, the boys who were able to choose what they preferred to read had better reports of the effectiveness of SSR.

Gendered Readers

The participants believed that the women they quoted as good readers read a lot and read quickly, while many men in their lives didn't read or only read for pragmatic reasons. The young men repeatedly offered women as reading role models in their lives. They often cited mothers, sisters, or grandmothers as 'good readers.' In fact, 55% of all the good readers who were reported were female. A few of the young men did specify that their male teachers were good readers. This impression was mainly based on oral reading completed within their English classrooms. This section is limited in the reported data, as sometimes the boys would say that a friend was a good reader but did not specify the gender of the reader.

The Paradox

Despite their lack of reading motivation, which they reported was connected to a lack of choice, 32 of the 62 respondents (approximately 52%) said they believed they were good readers because they could understand 'big' words, they could comprehend most of what they read, and/or they read a lot. However, bringing some discrepancy to their self-reported descriptions, a majority of the young men believed they needed to improve in the key area of amount of reading. They also reported needing improvement in comprehension, rate or fluency of reading, and vocabulary knowledge. Another complicating factor in this paradox is the way the young men described the good readers. For example, Casey cited that his mother was a good reader because she read a lot and she understood a wide variety of texts. Later in the interview, Casey also described himself as a good reader; however, he admitted that he didn't read a lot independently.

Another paradox was found in the responses regarding the level of comprehension and vocabulary a 'good reader' has. Will believed his parents were good readers. "They're able to read faster because they've been reading so much and they have a wider vocabulary. They analyze text" (personal communication, March 17, 2010). Again, they believed a wider vocabulary and increased vocabulary will result in more success with reading.

TIPS FOR ENGAGING MORE ADOLESCENT MALES IN READING

The young men involved in our study did not self-report that they read very much; however, they still believed they were fairly proficient readers. This is in juxposition to their belief that good readers read a lot. Classroom teachers have the ability to redirect and refine this type of paradoxical thinking in young adolescent males.

First, choice was the biggest issue for the young men. Our young men assert that they need to be provided with choices in classroom and independent reading. They believed that ability to choose would dramatically impact their motivation for reading, yet many of them were not able to enjoy this opportunity within their school experiences. Programs such as SSR, which have been incorporated into three of four of our secondary school districts, often do not actively change preconceived notions of reading. Although SSR has been linked to improved vocabulary and reading comprehension (Krashen, 2004); it appears to do little to change young men's reading motivation if their need for choice is not fulfilled. Our data seem to indicate that young adolescent males ought to be given choices of reading materials.

To be most successful, choices they are offered must extend beyond just a myriad of titles. Young males must be validated in their interests regarding different types of genres such as non-fiction, true crime, or even graphic novels and magazines. Reading technical information needs to be accepted and validated also. Our young men seemed to prefer reading that had pragmatic value in their mind. Allowing them access to these types of texts, whether via technology or more traditional, technical texts seem important in broadening their views of what reading is and the role they could play in their lives. If young men were able to set their own purposes for reading and then fulfill those purposes individually, they may learn to define reading in more complex terms.

Second, many of our young men were unable to identify other males as good readers. As a result, male teachers have an opportunity to model good reading habits for their students. This includes reading books of all sorts, magazines, and even technology-based texts. Infusing these reading habits and information into their classrooms will allow more young men to identify reading with males. This need for male reading role models extends to not only secondary teachers but also to elementary teachers and administrators. For example, if a school district does implement some type of SSR initiative, all teachers, but especially male teachers, must model reading while their students read.

Schools could also encourage more male reading role models within families with other unique initiatives and programs targeted at this specific need. Classroom teachers could engage more young males to read via collaborative, small-group work with independent texts. Having conversations centered on text might invite more adolescent males to connect reading to their male peers and thus change the reading experience. Positive experiences can impact and broaden the understanding young men have toward the benefits and influences of reading (Smith & Wilhelm, 2002, p. 7).

Third, many of our participants seem to prefer pragmatic, informational reading to fictional texts. Unfortunately, language arts classrooms are often centered on longer stories and/or novels that feel removed from the young men's experience. It may behoove teachers and schools to incorporate more inquiry-based projects into their curriculum so that young men are encouraged to find answers to their own meaningful questions. This would allow them to perceive a measure of control, choice, and personal connection to reading material (Smith & Wilhelm, 2002). Perhaps even adding more of a pragmatic or inquiry-based element to an SSR program would elevate the motivation of young men and invite more of their participation.

Finally, although it is somewhat of an abstract element to measure, it would seem that our participants would benefit from schools and teachers who widen the definition of reading. With the infusion of technology, teachers have the ability to guide students through many different types of texts for many different reasons. These choices will benefit young male readers. For example, reading a novel through an IPad application might be more inviting to an adolescent male due to the variety of ways he could interact with the text. In addition, reading and researching online would seem to offer male students to ability to choose materials and resources while designing their own projects. Online reading, with its nonlinear trajectory and individual structuring, can be a positive way to reshape the definition of reading and invite more males into the practice.

CONCLUSION

As teachers, there are many lessons we want our students to learn. Perhaps the most dynamic concept our adolescent males can learn is that reading can be an important part of their own lives in ways they never imagined; however, to introduce them to this possibility, we must allow them to choose their reading engagement and broaden their definition of what 'counts' as reading. By doing this, more young men will self-identify as readers and become role-models for other males.

REFERENCES

Atkinson, C. (2009). Promoting high school boys' reading engagement and motivation: The role of school psychologist in real world research. *School Psychology International, 30*(3), 231-254.

Atwell (2007). *The reading zone*. New York, NY: Scholastic Press.

Brozo, W. G. (2002). *To be a boy to be a reader: Engaging teen and preteen boys in active literacy*. Newark, DE: International Reading Association.

Carnell, E. (2005). Boys and their reading: Conceptions of young people about the success of the full on magazine. *Curriculum Journal, 16*(3), 363-389. doi: 10.1080/09585170500256461

Coles, M., & Hall, C. (2002). Gendered readings: Learning from children's reading choices. *Journal of Research in Reading, 25*(1), 96-108.

Farris, P. J., Werderich, D. E., Nelson, P. A., & Fuhler, C. J. (2009). Male call: Fifth-grade boys' reading preferences. *Reading Teacher, 63*(3), 180-188.

Gee, J. (2007). *What video games have to teach us about learning and literacy.* New York, NY: Palgrave Macmillan.

Giles, G. (2008). Wanted: Male models. *School Library Journal, 54*(12), 48-49.

Glaser, B. G., & Strauss, A. L. (1967). *The discovery of grounded theory: Strategies for qualitative research.* Chicago, IL: Aldine Publishing.

Guthrie, J. T. & Davis, M. H. (2003). Motivating struggling readers in middle school through an engagement model of classroom practice. *Reading & Writing Quarterly, 19,* 59-85.

Guthrie, J. T., McRae, A., & Klauda, S. L. (2007). Contributions of concept-oriented reading instruction to knowledge about interventions for motivations in reading. *Educational Psychology, 42*(4), 237-250.

Hamston, J., & Love, K. (2005). Voicing resistance: Adolescent boys and the cultural practice of leisure reading. *Discourse: Studies in the Cultural Politics of Education, 26*(2), 183-202.

Horton, R. (2005). Boys are people too: Boys and reading, truth and misconceptions. *Teacher Librarian, 33*(2), 30-31.

Kendrick, M. (1999). *Middle Grade Boys: Reading Habits and Preferences for a New Millennium.* US Department of Education. Retrieved from ERIC. (ED 429274).

Krashen, S. (2004, April). *Free voluntary reading: New research, applications, and controversies.* Paper presented at the RELC Conference, Singapore.

Logan, S. & Johnston, R. (2009). Gender differences in reading ability and attitudes: Examining where those difference lie. *Journal of Research in Reading, 32*(2),199-214.

Louie, J., and Ehrlich, S. (2008). *Gender gaps in assessment outcomes in Vermont and the United States* (Issues & Answers Report, REL 2008–No. 062). Washington, DC: U.S. Department of Education, Institute of Education Sciences,

National Assessment of Educational Progress. (2003, 2005, 2009). Retrieved from http://nces.ed.gov/nationsreportcard/

Logan, S., & Johnston, R. (2009). Gender differences in reading ability and attitudes: Examining where those differences lie. *Journal of Research in Reading, 32*(2), 199-214.

Marinak, B. A., & Gambrell, L. B. (2010). Reading motivation: Exploring the elementary gender gap. *Literacy Research and Instruction, 49,* 129-141. doi: 10.1080/19388070902803795

Meece, J. L., Glienke, B. B., & Burg, S. (2006). Gender and motivation. *Journal of School Psychology, 44,* 351-373.

Merisuo-Storm, T. (2006). Girls and boys like to read and write different texts. *Scandinavian Journal of Educational Research, 50*(2), 111-125.

National Assessment of Educational Progress (2007). http://Nationsreportcard.Gov/Reading.

Oakhill, J. V., & Petrides, A. (2007). Sex differences in the effects of interest on boys' and girls' reading comprehension. *British Journal of Psychology, 98,* 223-235.

Program for International Student Assessment. (2006). Retrieved from http://nces.ed.gov/surveys/pisa/

Rhodes, L., & Shanklin, N. L. (1993). *Windows into literacy: Assessing learners, K-8.* Portsmouth, NH: Heinemann.

Schunk, D. H. (1995). Self-efficacy in education and instruction. In J. E. Maddux (Ed). *Self-efficacy, adaptation, and adjustment: Theory, research, and application.* New York, NY: Plenum Press.

Scieszka, J. (2003). Guys and reading. *Teacher Librarian, 30*(3), 17-19.

Smith, M. & Wilhelm, J. (2002). *"Reading don't fix no chevys": Literacy in the lives of young men.* Portsmouth, NH: Heinemann.

Sullivan, M. (2004). Why Johnny won't read. *School Library Journal 50*(3), 36-39.

United States Department of Census. (2004). Retrieved from http://www.census.gov/www/eeoindex/page_c.html

Vygotsky, L. S. (1978). *Mind in society.* Cambridge, MA: Harvard University Press.

Watson, A., Kehler, M. & Martino, W. (Feb. 2010). The problem of boys' literacy under-achievement: Raising some questions. *Journal of Adolescent & Adult Literacy, 53*(5), 356-361.

Weih, T. (2008). A book club sheds light on boys and reading. *Middle School Journal, 40*(1), 19-25(5), 356-361.

Wigfield, A., Guthrie, J. T., Tonks, S., & Perencevich, K. (2004). Children's motivation for reading: Domain specificity and instructional influences. *Journal of Educational Research, 97*(6), 299-309.

Wigfield, A. & Guthrie, J. T. (1997). Relations of children's motivation for reading to the amount and breadth of their reading. *Journal of Educational Psychology, 89*(3), 420-432.

Woolcott Research Pty. Ltd. (2001). *Young Australians Reading: From keen to reluctant readers.* Retrieved from www.slv.vic.gov.au/about/information/publications/policies_reports/reading.html.

APPENDIX A: THE INTERVIEW QUESTIONS

(modified from the Burke Reading Interview, [Rhodes & Shanklin], 1993)

1. What do you think counts as reading?
2. What do you think counts as reading in school?
3. Who do you know that is a good reader?
4. What makes that person a good reader?
5. Do you consider yourself a good reader? Why?
6. What would you like to do better as a reader?
7. If you could change anything about reading in school, what would it be?
8. Is there anything else you'd like to say about guys and reading?

Patricia A. Edwards
Distinguished Teaching Professor of Teacher Education
Michigan State University

Section III: Literacy Practices In and Out of School

> With some shared understanding of their commonalities and differences, schools and homes should be able to work together to support each other in the development of a literate populace. (Corno, 1989, p. 41).

Lyn Corno's quote reminds us of the importance of the connectedness between home and school. Unfortunately, creating such connections/partnerships isn't easy. Almost three decades ago, Heath's (1983) seminal research highlighted this disconnect between the rich, but often different, kinds of literacy practiced in home compared to mainstream school settings. Here is where our job as educators can either offer a bridge that connects home and school literacies, or create a divide that essentially shuts out the home literacy.

While traditional forms of home-school interactions, such as conferences, ice cream socials, and back-to-school nights are positive pathways to communication, they do not build the types of connections that we need with parents in order to coordinate home and school literacy environments. We need many more examples of teachers, parents, and schools that are rolling up their sleeves and building relationships that provide a foundation of success for their children (Edwards, 2007). Examples of success in urban schools, and in other culturally and linguistically diverse settings, are particularly critical.

We know that parents, and the home literacy environments they create, are significant factors in the development of children's literacy and academic achievement. Also, we know that as Sara Lightfoot (1978) has reported, "many mothers are distressed about releasing their child to the care of a distant person because they fear the external judgments made about their parenting during the first five years of the child's life (p. 87). Many of these mothers are distressed, according to France and Meeks (1987), because they may lack some basic skills. The articles in this section provide explicit examples of classroom and family literacy practices that open the dialogue between homes and schools.

Matthews, Dooley, and Cziplicki's article examines parents' support for a young literacy learner from a young age. The authors document parental involvement in literacy in a way that will inform teachers interested in making the connections between home and school. This article offers a foundation for thinking about the ways that teachers can include home literacies as part of their everyday practices.

Worthy, Consalvo, Russell, and Bogard's article focuses on how one exemplary second-grade teacher works to open spaces for dialogue around personal concerns, which provides opportunity for students to engage more critically around issues that matter to them. Through the use of dialogue, reading and writing workshops, and getting to know your students, teachers can provide more equitable opportunities for learning and create more inclusive classrooms.

Ten years ago, Duke (2000) noted the scarcity of informational texts in first-grade classrooms, both in physical availability of texts and time spent with these texts. Here, Maloch's article reports that while there is some indication that informational texts are increasing in availability, she warns that informational texts are still not readily available or prioritized in many primary classrooms. Her study shares promising practices for actively engaging students to interact socially around informational texts, again with a focus on engaging students around issues that interest and motivate them.

Rush, Ash, Saunders, Holschuh, and Ford's article presents two perspectives on text selections for English/Language Arts courses in the upper grades. They share views from the Common Core State Standards for English/Language Arts (Common Core State Standards, 2010), and from findings of a recent survey of English teachers on text choices (Stotsky, 2010a). The authors share recommendations for educators working with the complicated issues around selecting texts for individual students' needs, considering text complexity, and finding available resources.

FUTURE RESEARCH

The articles presented in this section lead the way for teachers and researchers thinking about the following issues. We know that "parental literacy beliefs have been correlated with academic achievement, but we need to know more about how parental beliefs are correlated with child beliefs" (Scher & Baker, 1994, p. 2). As well, we need "to look at ways in which schools do and do not/can and cannot build on whatever abilities and beliefs children bring with them to achieve educational parity across class, race and ethnicity" (Purcell-Gates, 2000, p. 867).

How do we bring parents into the learning process in ways that respect their contributions to their child's literacy development (Edwards, McMillon, & Turner, 2010). These questions, along with others raised in each article, provide a possible roadmap for future research on issues that will help bridge home and school literacies.

REFERENCES

Corno, L. (1989). What it means to be literate about classrooms. In D. Bloome (Ed.), *Classroom and literacy* (pp. 29–52). Norwood, NJ: Ablex.

Duke, N. K. (2000). 3.6 minutes per day: The scarcity of informational texts in first grade. *Reading Research Quarterly, 35*, 202-224.

Edwards, P. A. (2007). Home literacy environments: What we know and need to know. In M. Pressley, A. Bilman, K. Perry, Kelly Refitt, & J. Reynolds (Eds.), *Shaping literacy achievement: Research we have, research we need* (pp. 42-76). New York, NY: Guilford Press.

Edwards, P. A., McMillon, G. M. T., & Turner, J. D., (2010). *Change is gonna come: Transforming literacy education for African American children.* New York, NY: Teachers College Press.

France, M. G., & Meeks, J. W. (1987). Parents who can't read: What the schools can do. *Journal of Reading, 31*, 222-227.

Heath, S. B. (1983). *Ways with words: Language, life, and work in communities and classrooms.* New York, NY: Cambridge University Press.

Lightfoot, S. (1978). *Worlds apart: Relationships between families and schools.* New York, NY: Basic Books.

Purcell-Gates, V. (2000). Family literacy. In M. L. Kamil, P. B. Mosenthal, P. D. Pearson, & R. Barr (Eds.), *Handbook of reading research* (Vol. III, pp. 853-870). Mahwah, NJ: Erlbaum.

Scher, D., & Baker, L. (1994). *Attitudes toward reading and children's home literacy environments.* (ERIC Documents Reproduction Service No. ED 418 757).

Using Parents' Perceptions to Gain Insights into a Young Child's Emergent Literacy Journey: A Phenomenological Case Study

Mona W. Matthews
Caitlin McMunn Dooley
Karen Cziplicki
Georgia State University

Emergent literacy theories place the beginning of children's literacy journey at birth (Clay, 1991; Teale & Sulzby, 1986). These theories replaced ones suggesting that children had to be determined "ready to learn" to read before they received reading instruction (Teale & Sulzby, 1986). In response to this expanded conception of literacy learning, many emergent literacy researchers turned their attention to the contexts in which children spent most of their time for insights into the experiences children participated in that supported their literacy learning (for example, Teale, 1986). This is the context of the study reported herein. Specifically, the study provides a detailed analysis of interviews with the parents of one young European American literacy learner, Darin (a pseudonym), conducted across three years beginning when their son was two years old and ending when he was five. The interviews were part of a three-year longitudinal investigation, conducted in two child development centers, that focused on how young learners make literate meaning, a process we reference as emergent comprehension (Dooley & Matthews, 2009). From these interviews, we gained insights into the ways the family spent time together and their son's interest and participation in these family events. To guide our analysis of the interviews, we merged precepts from socio-cultural theories with insights from family and emergent literacy studies. Then, we used Alexander's (2006) lifespan model of reading to map Darin's non-print interactions within a favorite family event, onto elements considered essential for print-based literacy development. In the next section, we describe the theories and research that ground our study.

THEORETICAL FRAMES AND RELEVANT LITERATURE

Why examine young children's experiences with families and other important others for insights into literacy development?

Clay's (1991) "emergent literacy" theory proposes that literate behaviors, such as the ability to recognize letter names and sounds or the ability to know how to hold a book, emerge over time with multiple experiences. She (2001) further theorizes that children, during their early years, develop processing systems for understanding their world. These include the syntax of oral language; meanings of words; knowledge of the visual forms of objects, pictures, scenes; the sense of daily activities; and understanding stories. The content and form of those processes reflect children's unique life experience; histories that Clay asserts should function as a bridge to formal school literacy instruction.

Emergent literacy researchers who assume a socio-cultural stance place the beginnings of literacy within the home and community in which the children live (Clay, 1991, 2001). Within the home, children's approaches to literate activities begin as approximations of activities they witness within social groups. Heath (1982) along with others (e.g., Barton, Hamilton, & Ivanic, 2000) pointed out how children's different social groups provide distinct models for their children. Add to these various experiences a child's propensity for approximation, and we must draw conclusions that children are progressing toward disparate models of culturally defined convention. Due to the situated nature of learning, witnessing a child's interactions within social groups provides clues to what the child finds meaningful (Tomasello, Carpenter, Call, Behne, & Moll, 2005).

The rituals or routines within a family serve as important learning contexts for the young learners in those families. "Rituals are repeated behaviors or interactions that have symbolic value beyond the experiences themselves" (Sugarman, 2005, p. 126). For example, the practice of blowing out candles on a birthday cake symbolizes luck in U.S. society, just as the daily routine of family dinners signifies togetherness and caring in other families. Family rituals embody cultural meanings and manifest that family's social values (Jackson, 2005). Children learn the significance of and the expected ways to interact in family rituals from observation and imitation (Rogoff, 2003).

What connections can be made between young children's experiences during their early years to provide insights into the development of conventional literacy?

Alexander's (2006) lifespan model of reading provided a recognized reading framework we could use to map non-print behaviors onto elements considered essential for reading development. In Alexander's model, literacy develops across three stages: acclimation, competence, and proficiency/ expertise with the development marked in changes in the learners' interest, knowledge, and strategic processing. Interest, both situational and individual, drives readers' motivation to read. A learners' knowledge of reading and knowledge of language and concepts are critical to reading development. Strategic processing guides readers to know how to approach texts and construct meaning.

The developmental, lifespan nature of Alexander's (2006) model complements emergent literacy theories because it conceptualizes reading as a developmental process that occurs "from womb to tomb." As a developmental process, precursors to later conventional expressions of reading reside in children's behavior expressed in print and non-print forms (Clay, 1998). Alexander's model places children, such as Darin, within the Acclimation stage because they are becoming acclimated to the unique demands of reading.

To summarize, as emergent-literacy researchers, we assume a socio-cultural stance. Therefore, we view families as key architects of the social and cultural environments in which their children live and we focus on the routines family and children practice to reveal what the family considers meaningful. Our in-depth analysis of family events, in which children acquire knowledge of the values of extant culture, is grounded in Wells' (1999) work as a socio-cultural theorist and researcher. Clay's (2001) description of processing systems supports our focus on Darin's non-print behaviors as potential bridges to more formal literacy learning. Finally, Alexander's (2006) model enabled us to examine non-print behaviors for evidence of key elements in reading development.

This phenomenological case study adds to the literature in several important ways. First, this study examined the non-print behaviors of an emergent literacy learner for evidence of elements considered essential for print-based reading development. Much of the research that investigates children's emergent literacy learning has focused on children's early book-related experiences (Doake, 1985; Dooley, 2010; Ferreiro & Teberosky, 1982; Goodman & Goodman, 2009; Strommen &

Mates, 1997; Sulzby, 1985, 1991). Although these early studies of readers offer important insights, their focus is restricted to print-related events.

Second, the study uses parents as key informants of their son's behavior. This provided important information into their son's behavior at home, in contexts familiar to him while participating in events meaningful to him. Research informs us of the influential and foundational role the family plays in children's view of what is meaningful in their world. Therefore, descriptions of children's interactions at home participating in events that represent day-to-day family routines and rituals are essential to a robust description of emergent literacy development.

Third, the data analyzed in this study were collected across a three-year period, beginning when this young learner was two years old until he was five. As a developmental process, early expressions of literacy do not resemble the expressions of older learners. Thus, to reveal the diversity that exists in emergent learners' expressions, more descriptions are needed of them participating in familiar events.

METHODOLOGY

This section lays out the process used to collect and analyze the data to answer the research question, *What can a family's perceptions of their son's interactions tell us about his emergent literacy learning?* A phenomenological case study was used. This case study provides an in-depth phenomenological perspective (Crotty, 1998) of what parents' perceptions of their son's interactions during important family routines can tell us about his emergent literacy learning. Phenomenological case studies explore the lived experiences as they relate to extant theories and can result in new knowledge construction (van Manen, 1990). Notably, a limitation of this methodology is that one case cannot represent all situations; however, the purpose of phenomenology is to shape the on-going formation of theory through accumulation of cases, not through generalization.

Background

Data reported herein were collected during a three-year longitudinal investigation of how young learners make meaning and how their early experiences contribute to their literacy development. The study utilized a naturalistic methodology via systematic observations, time-logs, interviews, and video-recordings of children's activities both at school and in their homes. The children were two years old at the beginning of the study and four and five at its conclusion. There were 38 children total, 12 of whom we had a complete data set for all three years. (For more information about the study see Dooley, 2010; Dooley and Matthews, 2009; and Dooley, Matthews, Matthews, and Champion, 2009.)

We selected Darin, a European American male from a middle-class home, as a focal case study for several reasons. One, his data set was complete, thereby, providing a rich, triangulated set of data across all three years. Two, both his mother and father attended the interviews, allowing multiple perspectives on his home activities. Three, his parents provided detailed descriptions of Darin's actions, yielding insight to their "lived experience" (van Manen, 1990).

Darin's mother and father are writers and readers. His mother has a graduate degree; his father has a college degree. Darin's older stepbrother lives part-time with the family. Darin exhibited deep interests in stereotypically "boyish" things like trains, cars, and puzzles. A parent read nightly to

Darin and every three weeks the family visited the local public library. Whereas Darin enjoyed being read to, during his free time, he usually preferred to play with his trains, legos, or puzzles. One interest, however, dominated his attention during the three years of the larger study—watching NASCAR racing. For 10 months, two to three times a week, Darin and his family watched NASCAR racing. Supported by a confluence of theories and research, we viewed Darin's participation in this valued family routine as a rich venue for Darin's emergent literacy learning. Intrigued by changes that occurred in Darin's participation in this event across the three years, we view these as the potential the changes implied by Alexander's (2006) lifespan model.

Data Sources

For this study, we analyzed transcripts of six parent interviews across the three years of the study. Two time logs and two video-recordings of family routines were also collected and used to inform the interviews. We interviewed Darin's mother and father at home each time, except for the final time during which we interviewed his mother at Darin's child development center. Time logs and video-recordings of family activities were collected and analyzed and informed the interviews iteratively. The second author conducted the first interview; a graduate research assistant conducted other interviews. Although the family was informed the study was about the beginnings of literacy, they were asked to discuss any important family routines (thereby, encouraging discussion of non-print focused events).

The interviews focused on the parents' perceptions of family routines and rituals, their intentions and perceptions about those routines and rituals, and their child's interests and participation in these events. Interviews 2 and 6 focused on video-recordings of Darin as he participated in what his parents' selected to represent typical family events. To give some indication of family routines, twice we asked parents to complete time logs of family events. One time log was completed at the onset of the study and another during year 3 near the conclusion of the study. Parents were instructed to list all activities, whether typical or not, that occurred during a five-day period, including at least one weekend day. These logs were used to prompt questions during the initial parent interview, questions such as: "Tell about a typical week day" and "Tell about something your family traditionally does together?" This discussion then led to an invitation for the parents to video-record experiences described in the time log. Darin's family took a video-recorder home for two weeks to record. In follow-up interviews, the family watched those videotapes with the interviewer and answered questions such as, "What's going on here?" "How often does your family (or Darin) do this?" "What do you intend for Darin within this activity?" "What are your goals?" Some of the video-taped events selected by Darin's family included: Darin playing with a toy train set, the family playing a card game together, Darin playing with toy cars while NASCAR is on the TV in the background, and Darin reading with his older brother. After the first interview, each subsequent interview began with a summary of the routines and rituals identified by the parents in the previous interview and their comments related to their son's interests. Parents discussed changes in their routines and rituals and their perceptions of their son's current interests. Each interview was transcribed shortly after it occurred.

Data Analysis

Data analysis proceeded in three phases and followed an inductive process, common in phenomenological studies. Procedures described by Corbin and Strauss (2008) guided the analysis. During Phase One, we identified and prepared the data for analysis. First, we culled from the corpus of data six transcripts of interviews with Darin's parents. Then, beginning with the first interview transcript and progressing to the sixth, each transcript was read multiple times. From these readings, we realized the transcripts provided a chronological, descriptive record of his parents' conceptions of their son's interests in several key events.

During Phase Two, we proceeded with open coding. We continued to read the transcripts multiple times, noting in memos potential salient elements in the data. After multiple readings, salient elements were revealed in the parents' perceptions of family routines and their son's during those events. This led to the identification of patterns, that is, concepts that delineate consistent blocks of data (Corbin & Strauss, 2008). For example, we labeled one block of data, *predictable structure,* to indicate the family participated in a handful of routines with their participation reflecting easily discerned ways of behaving. We then began the deductive process, wherein we asked questions that allowed us to segment the data into meaningful blocks. Sample questions included, *"What is predictable in the data?, What makes these predictable?"* From this process, patterns in the data were identified. We then segmented each transcript into predominant patterns. Sample patterns included the parents' *talk about Darin,* and their *justifications for events.* Next, we merged similar patterns to create categories. Sample categories included: *a typical day, child as a language user, child as a reader or writer, child as helper, and child's interests.* Once the categories stabilized, we segmented each transcript into the final categories. Then, we culled like segments into categories and pasted them into a Word document. This created one document for each category with the individual segments arranged in chronological order. Each document was read multiple times to identify themes that crossed categories. Sample themes included *parent-initiated* and *child-initiated* events. However, Darin's interest in cars and NASCAR was the subject of many of the themes and, thus, was identified as an overarching theme in the interview transcripts and the one described herein.

During Phase Three, we focused our analysis on the overarching theme: NASCAR racing. Multiple readings of these data revealed a rich data set with explicit parent descriptions of: (a) the family's interest in NASCAR racing, (b) how Darin displayed interest in this event, and (c) changes they noted in their son's participation. Also significant to the focus of our larger study, Darin's participation in this event revealed elements related to reading development identified in Alexander's (2006) lifespan model of reading, interest, knowledge, and strategic processing. At this time, we used Alexander's model as a framework to analyze Darin's non-print behavior.

We used Alexander's (2006) model for two reasons. One, it incorporates a developmental theory of reading that details the changes that occur in three essential elements (interest, knowledge, and strategic processing) of reading as they progress through the three stages of reading development (acclimation, competence, and proficiency/expertise). Two, although Alexander conceptualized the model for print-focused events and behaviors, we found the three characteristics of the model, interest, knowledge, and strategic processing, relevant for our examination of non-print-focused events—key when analyzing emergent literacy events. This paper reports the results of that analysis.

FINDINGS AND DISCUSSION

This section describes what we learned about Darin's emergent literacy learning from his parents' perceptions of their son's behavior during NASCAR racing events. As mentioned, the three elements (interest, knowledge, and strategic processing) in Alexander's (2006) lifespan model of reading provided the framework for the analysis. Alexander conceptualizes the three elements interacting to their mutual benefit; however, as she does in her article, we discuss each element separately to present a more in-depth analysis. The description of the findings related to each element proceeds as follows: explanation of the element, findings related to that element, and emergent literacy research that supports attention to this element. This section closes with a discussion of the role Darin's parents played.

Interest

Interest, states Alexander (2006), supplies the energy behind reading development. Interest incites motivation to perform a task, and that motivation promotes engagement in the task, which then leads to enhanced capabilities. She segments interest into *situational interest* and *individual interest*. Situational interest refers to elements within an environment that motivate one to engage in an activity or task. For example, a young child who typically displays little interest in an activity or event might be stimulated to participate in that event when his teacher incorporates music, hence, music becomes the enticing element. Individual interest, on the other hand, is evident when a person seeks to perform a task, such as reading a book, without prodding. Although both types of interest serve to influence behavior throughout the lifespan of reading development, the weight of their respective influence shifts across the lifespan (Alexander, 2006) with situational interest weighing more influence during the acclimation stage of reading development and individual or personal interest weighing more influence during the competence and proficiency/expertise stages.

Given that interest is the energy behind reading development, we examined how Darin displayed interest in NASCAR racing. In the first interview, Darin's mother said Darin was, "obsessed with cars…We'll come home and fix dinner. And again he'll just be playing then. You know he'll pull things out of his toy box or get cars out. Right now he's obsessed with cars."

For the three years of our study, Darin maintained interest in cars. See Table 1 for parent comments related to Darin's interest. In the first interview, his mother said he was "obsessed with cars." The second interview indicates the extension of his car interest to NASCAR racing: "He likes to watch racing. He likes to watch NASCAR." This interest in NASCAR continued, as indicated by his father's statement in the sixth and final interview: "He's still really, really into NASCAR; that's been going on for a while." For Darin, watching NASCAR meant sitting on the floor, near his father, enacting his version of NASCAR. Darin's father described his son's behavior as he watched NASCAR:

> We'll have to take that downstairs, his big (Lightening McQueen) car and that big one of (Roger Biscotty). And we have to take all of those downstairs and they form long lines down there, there's a pit row.

Darin's mother agreed, "He has a truck as a pace car. He's acting it out, he's enacting it while he's watching it, that's part of watching racing."

Table 1. Parents' Comments Related to Darin's Interest in NASCAR

1st Parent Interview	2nd Parent Interview	3rd Parent Interview	4th Parent Interview	5th Parent Interview	6th Parent Interview
Now he's obsessed with cars.	The little matchbox cars, he's very into them right now; he likes to watch racing. He likes to watch NASCAR.	After nap he will either go outside with his brother or watch TV with Dad. They like to watch NASCAR.	He watches a lot of car racing.	[He plays mostly w/] cars, cars, trains, but trains not so much.	He's still really, really into NASCAR; that's been going on for a while.
		While we're reading the paper, he plays with his blocks, or his cars, or his trains. Those are the big things now.		[We watch] two car races [weekly] between February and mid-November.	

Although other family members supported Darin's interest in cars—for example, his Uncle gave him a car video as a gift—his father was the genesis of his son's interest. By his own statements, Darin's father was an avid NASCAR fan. From the comments of both parents and videos of family interactions, we know: Darin watched NASCAR with his father; watching NASCAR occurred weekly for 10 months of the year, watching NASCAR was a family event, and that Darin played with cars by himself, but in close proximity to family. His father explained:

> There are 2-3 races a week. It's a family thing, and with Tivo the beauty of it is you can go right to getting to the going around the track without all the extraneous b.s., so that's good. And that's about the only TV he watches.

Although Darin's father provided the situational interest, additions to the environment added by his parents, and in one instance his uncle, promoted Darin's interest. These included a video, racing props (racetrack, helmet), and a variety of small toy cars. His family's purchase of these items likely stimulated Darin's interest as well signaled that his family valued his interest in cars and NASCAR. What likely began for Darin as situational interest, probably stimulated by his father's presence, appears to have developed into an individual interest as demonstrated by his independent play, repetition of play, and self-initiated play. As noted in his parents' comments, Darin's three-year-interest in cars and NASCAR was a consistent topic of his play. This continued involvement with NASCAR and cars in his play likely led to enhanced capabilities, including enhanced knowledge, described in the next section.

Research supports attention to the role interest plays in emergent literacy learning. As early as 1966, Durkin, in a seminal study of early readers, determined interest played an integral role in the experiences of the children who learned to read prior to beginning school. Parents of early readers believed their children's interest offered a legitimate pathway to reading. Whereas, parents of non-early readers believed children should be taught to read in school. Parents of early readers encouraged their children's "interest binges" (p. 137), by providing time and materials so their children could pursue projects, like creating calendars and by responding to their children's requests, such as, "Show me my name" (p. 137). In other instances, the children's interests, rather than direct parent encouragement, appeared to be the catalyst behind the children's interactions with print. For example, one mother said it was her son's interests in television weather reports that stimulated his interest in print. In fact, she said, she did not know her son could read until he began to read the words contained in television advertisements. A more recent study suggests that interests may influence the ways young children respond to literacy events. Rowe and Neitzel (2010) found that children, as young as two years old, exhibited preferred orientations (i.e., interest preferences) when participating in writing events. The children's preferences could be categorized in one of four interest orientations: conceptual, procedural, creative, and socially oriented. The children evidenced their orientations in their use of materials, their interactions with others, and their writing choices. The researchers suggested that enabling children to align their participation with their individual interest orientation might serve as an "entrée to literacy" (p. 194). Interests, Alexander (2006) states, provides the energy behind reading growth; these studies suggest interest may also serve to bootstrap emergent literacy learning. The next section elaborates on the likely outcomes when children can pursue their interests: enhanced capabilities and knowledge.

Content Domain Knowledge and Language Knowledge

The knowledge element in Alexander's (2006) model represents content domain knowledge and language knowledge. Content domain knowledge refers to how much the reader knows about the domain and topics presented within texts. Also included is what the reader knows about the reading process. For example, in the case of readers in the acclimation stage, Alexander asserts reader's knowledge of sound-symbol relationships intertwines content-domain knowledge and language knowledge with deep knowledge about a domain or topic leading to the development of more sophisticated linguistic structures to represent that knowledge. Hence, content and language knowledge are "co-facilitative" in nature (p. 2).

Darin's knowledge of the content of car racing is listed in Table 2. This knowledge is evidenced in his use of the names of aspects and objects that distinguish car racing, such as *pace car, pit stop, fresh tires,* and *pit row,* from other events involving cars. He possessed knowledge of what racecars do during a race: *They crash into walls; the pace car is first in line; they make pit stops.* He named the characters in his stories after current and former racecar drivers, such as Bobby Labonte and Mario Andretti.

Language knowledge, the second component of the knowledge characteristic, is reflected in Darin's use of literate language. Generally literate language represents language used to talk about one's language, feelings, understanding, thinking, events that occurred in the past, or objects not physically present (Pellegrini, 2001). One aspect of literate language demonstrated by Darin was

Table 2. Content and Linguistic Knowledge Exhibited by Darin during Interactions with Cars and Trains Gathered from Parent Interviews

Evidence of Content Knowledge	Evidence of Literate Language
NASCAR, fresh tires; pace car; pit stop; helmet; names of drivers; pit row pace car	The other morning he ran in & gave me this whole saga about how the leader ran into the wall, big crash, fresh tires.
Race cars: don't fly; get fresh tires during pit stops; crash into walls	Knowledge of the purpose and components of narratives

an ability to talk about events in the past. In the fourth interview, Darin's father recounted a story Darin told him that morning. The story was a retelling of one he had created earlier in the morning: "I was taking a shower this morning, and he ran in and gave me this whole saga about how the leader ran into the wall and there was a big crash and he tells me all of this." Listening, Darin's mother explained the emergency, "He needed some fresh tires."

Darin's use of language to talk about his understanding provides additional evidence of his use of literate language. In this excerpt from the sixth interview, Darin's mother's comments allude to two examples of Darin's use of literate language to reflect his understanding. She stated,

> He used to make me ask him who drives the number 33 car because he would get mad because I would ask him cars that nobody drove, that there isn't a driver for, but I don't know anything about the sport. It's kind of silly because he knows all of them and I don't know any of them, but he wants me to quiz him on the different racers.

In the first example, Darin's annoyance with his mother's inaccurate information suggests his ability to use his understanding of NASCAR as a measure of another's understanding. In the second example, Darin's request for his mother to quiz him suggests his ability to think about understanding as something that can be evaluated or quizzed.

Darin's knowledge of narrative, specifically narrative reasoning, is the second linguistic element implied in his parents' comments. (Note: All Darin's narratives discussed by his parents were oral and/or demonstrated through play, not written.) From his parents' descriptions, we know that his stories revolved around a car-racing theme, included racecar events, and featured racecar drivers. Darin's narrative knowledge also reflects his strategic processing, discussed more in the next section.

A focus on emergent literacy learners' content and language knowledge finds support in the emergent literacy research literature. Both have been investigative topics of researchers interested in emergent learners' comprehension development. Breadth of content domain knowledge has been shown to influence preschool children's comprehension. To illustrate, Chi and Koeske (1983) describe a four-year-old boy's ability to make sophisticated inferences when asked questions about dinosaurs, a topic about which he possessed a lot of knowledge. When Paris, Carpenter, Paris, and Hamilton (2005) discussed this study, they attributed the child's exceptional comprehension abilities to the child's breadth of dinosaur knowledge. Such breadth led to the formation of complex cognitive networks that created more efficient processing of information.

Narrative, according to Kavanaugh and Engle (1998), is a distinctive mode of communication that gives young children access to the social-emotional world. Via narratives, children garner understanding of the events, people, norms, and values of the extant culture (Kavanaugh & Engel, 1998). As described by Kavanaugh and Engel, narratives: (a) can be verbal or written, (b) cohere around a central idea or topic, (c) contain content that is either real or contrived, (d) represent something meaningful to its author, and (e) include characters (p. 89). Paris et al. (2005) identify narrative reasoning as a strong predictor of children's reading comprehension. Clay (2001) identified children's knowledge of how stories work, what she called *storying*, as a critical processing system that could support children's formal literacy learning.

Two aspects of language—literate language and knowledge of narrative—were especially relevant to this study. As stated previously, literate language represents language used to talk about language, feelings, understanding, thinking, events that occurred in the past, or objects not physically present. Literate language holds a unique place in emergent literacy learning. Pellegrini and Galda (1993) as well as Olson (1996) found that the use of literate language by emergent literacy learners predicted later reading success. A young child's use of literate language is considered a precursor to meta-cognitive-meta linguistic knowledge (Pellegrini, 2001). Olson (1996) draws a distinction between conceptions of traditional reading and emergent literacy learning. Typically, he asserts, the former is a set of component skills and the latter equates to literate language. Snow (1983) discussed the importance of young children's use of decontextualized speech, or speech removed from the "concrete here and now" (p. 175), an early reference to what is now called literate language. Darin's experiences suggest that language development, so important to his literacy development, is inherently tied to his interests. More evidence of his narrative and linguistic knowledge reflects strategic processing, discussed in the next section.

Strategic Processing

Strategic processing, the third characteristic in Alexander's (2006) model, refers to procedures enacted by an individual to solve reading problems and to monitor one's reading. *Surface level* strategies and *deep processing* strategies comprise strategic processing in her model. Readers apply surface level strategies to assist their access to a text (e.g., previewing headings and subheadings in an expository text before reading a text). Readers apply deep processing strategies to personalize or transform knowledge (e.g., creating a concept map after reading a text).

Table 3 provides examples of surface level strategies used by Darin to gain access to information from the environment and to build his knowledge. Darin's parents' comments suggest he gained access to information about racecars from watching races on television and watching videos, and from being with his father.

Deep processing strategies used by Darin included making transformations, narrating, extending information, and personalizing and making information his own. He moved from real (live race car racing on TV) to not real (interactions with his cars). Table 3 provides examples of his use of procedures to personalize his knowledge. For example, he transformed the concrete objects in his environment to build tracks for his cars to transform the information from the television. In this case, he used the 3-D blocks from his own environment to transform what he saw on television. Plus, he used oral language to transform the inanimate objects (cars) into characters in his personally constructed narratives.

Narrative, as suggested by his parents' comments, was Darin's communicative organizational structure of choice. Their descriptions of Darin's narratives evidence Darin's deep processing. His narratives contained elements characteristic of narratives. Those characteristics include theme (car racing), characters (drivers and cars), and events (lining up to race, racing, crashing into walls, making pit stops, getting fresh tires) (Kavanaugh & Engel, 1998). Darin used narrating to transform his knowledge of cars and NASCAR racing. As early as the second interview, his parents mentioned Darin's narratives: "He's acting it [car racing] out. He's acting it out. He's enacting what he's watching on TV." In the third interview, Darin's mother explained, "He kind of adopts those stories, makes up dialogue because he watches a lot of car racing." By the end of three years, this pattern continued. His mother stated, "He plays with his cars and sometimes narrates too and that's based on the NASCAR. He acts out races like he watches TV." In addition to transforming

Table 3. Parent References to Darin's NASCAR-Related Behavior that Suggest Strategic Processing

	Surface Level Strategies: Build Knowledge		Deep Processing Strategies: Suggest Personalization of Knowledge		
Input	Practice	Transformations	Narrating: Special Kind Transformation	Extensions	Critical Processes
He watches NASCAR 2-3 times a week.	It's like anything he likes; he wants to do it over and over again.	He builds the most amazing tracks that use every piece of track.	He makes up elaborate narratives about the car race he's having.	He narrates stories to himself.	He made me ask him who drives the number 33 car; he got mad 'cause I asked about cars nobody drove.
He wants me to quiz him on the racers.	He's enacting what he sees on TV.		He's acting it [the race] out; he's enacting what he sees on TV.	He makes up elaborate narrative.	
	He spends a lot of time, a lot of time building train tracks.	He adopts stories [from NASCAR].	He kind of adopts those stories for his own; makes up dialogue between the trains and stuff; also because if he watches a lot of car racing, he'll do the cars around; I was taking a shower this morning; he ran in and gave me this whole saga about how the leader ran into the wall; there was a big crash; he tells me all of this. And he needed fresh tires.	He sometimes sings.	
		He uses helmets, cars; tracks.	He plays w/ his cars and sometimes narrates based on NASCAR.	He draws cars.	
		He plays on the floor; lines them up [cars]; one is the pace car.	Dad: We watch a lot of car racing; he gets his little cars out; he has stories about who is going to pit row, who got spun out and hit the wall, who wins the race; they'll go on a long time. Mom: It's commentary.		
			He doesn't have a specific script, but he will narrate, ya know, 'this is Bobby Labonte, this is Mario Andretti' which he has picked up from the cars video; this is someone from the truck series, the Nationwide series, and the Cup series; they are all together; they are racing and, 'Oh no! Bobby Labonte spun, caution on the track, caution on the track.' Or we'll ask, 'Do you know who is winning the race?' Or, 'Who won the race?'		
			He has a truck as a pace car. He's acting it out, he's enacting it while he's watching it, that's part of watching racing		

the knowledge he gained into narratives, he also displays evidence of extending that knowledge. For example, his mother stated, "he draws cars sometime." We don't know if he drew the cars as part of a racing scenario.

Support for considering strategic processing in the behavior of young emergent literacy learners comes from research that examines ties between children's play and literacy. Play, according to some authorities, is the ultimate child-friendly procedure for accessing information (Roskos & Christie, 2000). Children access the real world via play. In fact, Vandenberg (2004) states children's "signaling, '*This is play*' [reflects] a transformational act where, real experiences are rendered 'not real,' the serious made playful" (p.56). This type of play, Vandenberg states, enables children to lift personal experiences from the ongoing context to allow further examination, experimentation, and consolidation of those experiences. Socio-cultural theories proffer an explanation of how play provides children access to their unique cultural world. Specifically, Vygotsky (1966, 1978,) theorized that during play children try out roles, scripts, and actions they have observed others exhibit. In effect, play, as theorized by Vygotsky, creates a zone of proximal development whereas they can try out behaviors they have yet to internalize. In Darin's case, playing with cars and recreating car-racing narratives supported his strategic processing.

Understanding narrative and story structure correlate to later reading comprehension (Oakhill & Cain, 2007). Evidence indicates that these understandings do develop prior to comprehension of print (Oakhill & Cain). Narrative likely aids in the coherence of ideas, which in turn, aids working memory, which Paris and Hamilton (2009) assert aids reading comprehension. Play, when tailored after real events experienced by the child, is the ultimate transformational procedure (Oakhill & Cain).

The Parents' Role in Darin's Literacy Learning

The influence of Darin's family cannot be overstated. Watching NASCAR racing was a ritual in Darin's family, occurring frequently, two to three times a week for ten months a year. Darin's family, his core social group, supported Darin's car racing play. They demonstrated support by providing the objects and props to embellish his play (e.g., cars, helmet, racecar tracks). They supplied venues for input to expand his play (e.g., car racing video, televised NASCAR races). They provided the physical context for the play, (e.g., space on the floor next to his father in the TV room or the dining room). And they accommodated his play (e.g., carrying "all of those [cars] downstairs").

Families are children's first teachers and often their presence serves to create situational interest in an activity. Through daily routines, young children are introduced to the world. By participating beside others, often members of their family, young children come to share and understand the goals (purposes) that guide the participants' actions and the procedures (means) used to accomplish the activity's goals (Wells, 1999). Thus, children reap important cultural benefits from their early, close relationships, most notably the meaning and use of linguistic symbols.

Darin's interest in NASCAR supplied the momentum that fueled his progress along the path to literacy development. Along the way and mediated by his play, Darin's accumulated knowledge was expressed in his use of literate language, narration, and application of strategic processing. Obviously Darin's father influenced his interest in NASCAR and both parents encouraged that interest. This level of support provided Darin the opportunity to develop and express understanding in ways similar to, as well as different from, what he experienced which, in turn, led to his acquisition of the threads that support emergent literacy learning: interests, knowledge, and strategic processing (Alexander, 2006).

CONCLUDING THOUGHTS

Case study research, like the one described here, provides an in-depth look at a topic or person of interest. Such depth allows others to gain insights about the study focus that investigations using other paradigms cannot reveal. Given these strengths, findings generated from this phenomenological case study must be viewed within its limitations. Insights gained about this European American, middle-class child may not reflect the experiences or responses of other children, even children who share his background. The experiences Darin's parents presented likely reflect only a sample of the routines and rituals in their life. And, Darin's parents' interpretations were subjective and may reflect personal preferences.

In closing, our examination of Darin's behavior adds support for an expanded view of contexts and activities that promote children's literacy development. Heath (1982) was one of the first to document the different pathways children travel in the early years of their literacy development. The children she described, like Darin, displayed competence in areas that mirrored the ways and means valued by their respective families and communities.

Darin's parents were our informants. We learned about Darin's interest from his parents because we asked a simple question, "How does your family spend time together?" Their responses to that question deepened our understanding of Darin's unique emergent literacy journey.

AUTHORS' NOTE

This research was funded by Georgia State University and the Thomas Family Foundation.

REFERENCES

Alexander, P. A. (2006). The path to competence: A lifespan developmental perspective on reading. *Journal of Literacy Research, 37,* 413-436.

Barton, D., Hamilton, M., & Ivanic, R. (2000). *Situated literacies: Theorising reading and writing in context.* London, England: Routledge.

Chi, M. T. H., & Koeske, R. D. (1983). Network representations of a child's dinosaur knowledge. *Developmental Psychology, 19,* 29-39.

Clay, M. M. (1991). *Becoming literate: The construction of inner control.* Mahwah, NJ: Heinemann.

Clay, M. M. (1998). *By different paths to common outcomes.* York, ME: Stenhouse.

Clay, M. M. (2001). *Change over time in children's literacy development.* Portsmouth, NH: Heinemann.

Corbin, J. Strauss, & Strauss, A. (2008). Basics of qualitative research (3rd ed.). Los Angeles, CA: Sage.

Crotty, M. (1998). *The foundations of social research.* St. Leonards, Australia: Allen & Unwin.

Doake, D. (1985). Reading-like behavior: Its role in learning to read. In A. Jaggar & T. Burke-Smith (Eds.), *Observing the language learner* (pp. 82–98). Newark, DE: International Reading Association; Urbana, IL: National Council of Teachers of English.

Dooley, C. M. (2010). Emergent comprehension in young children. *The Reading Teacher, 64,* 120-130. DOI:10.1598/RT.64.2.4

Dooley, C. M., & Matthews, M. W. (2009). Emergent comprehension: Understanding comprehension development among young literacy learners.

Dooley, C. M., Matthews, M. W., Matthews, L., & Champion, R. (2009). Emergent comprehension: Preschool children's learning and intentions. *National Reading Conference Yearbook, 58*, 261-276.

Durkin, D. (1966). *Children who read early*. New York, NY: Teachers College Press.

Ferreiro, E., & Teberosky, A. (1982). *Literacy before schooling*. Exeter, NH: Heinemann.

Goodman, K. S., & Goodman, Y. M. (2009). Helping readers make sense of print: Research that supports a whole language pedagogy. In S. E. Israel & G. G. Duffy (Eds.), *Handbook of research on reading comprehension* (pp. 91–114). New York, NY: Routledge.

Heath, S. B. (1982). *Ways with Words*. Cambridge, UK: Cambridge University Press.

Jackson, K. M. (2005). *Rituals and patterns in children's lives*. Madison, WI: University of Wisconsin Press.

Kavanaugh, R. D., & Engel, S. (1998). The development of pretense and narrative in early childhood. In O. N. Saracho & B. Spodek (Eds.), *Multiple perspectives on play in early childhood education.* (pp.80-99). Albany, NY: State University of New York Press.

Oakhill, J., & Cain, K. (2007). Introduction to comprehension development. In K. Cain & J. Oakhill (Eds.), *Children's comprehension problems in oral and written language: A cognitive perspective* (pp. 3-40). New York, NY: Guilford Press.

Olson, D. (1977). From utterance to text: The bias of language in speech and writing. *Harvard Educational Review, 47*, 257-281.

Paris, S. G. (2005). Reinterpreting the development of reading skills. *Reading Research Quarterly, 40*, 184-202. DOI: 10.1598/RRQ.40.2.3

Paris, S. G., Carpenter, R. D., Paris, A. H., & Hamilton, E. E. (2005). Spurious and genuine correlates of children's reading comprehension. In S. G. Paris, & S. A. Stahl (Eds.), *Children's reading comprehension and assessment* (pp. 131-160). Mahwah, NJ: Erlbaum.

Paris, S. G., & Hamilton, E. E. (2009). The development of children's reading comprehension. In S. E. Israel, & G. G. Duffy (Eds.), *Handbook of research on reading comprehension* (pp. 32-53). New York, NY: Rutledge, Taylor & Francis.

Paris, S., & Paris, S. G. (2003). Assessing narrative comprehension in young children. *Reading Research Quarterly, 38*, 36-76. DOI: 10.1598/RRQ.38.1.3

Pellegrini, A. D., & Galda, L. (1993). Ten years after: A reexamination of symbolic play and literacy research. *Reading Research Quarterly, 28*, 162-175.

Pellegrini, A. D. (2001). Some theoretical and methodological considerations in studying literacy in social context. In S. B. Neuman & D. Dickinson (Eds.), *Handbook of early literacy research* (pp. 54-65). New York, NY: Guilford Press.

Rogoff, B. (1998). Cognition as a collaborative process. In W. Damon (Series Ed.) & D. Kuhn & R. S. Siegler (Vol. Eds.), *Handbook of child psychology: Vol. 2. Cognition, perception, and language* (5th ed., pp. 679-744). New York, NY: Wiley.

Rogoff, B. (2003). *The cultural nature of human development*. New York, NY: Oxford University Press.

Roskos, K. A., & Christie, J. F. (2000). *Play and literacy in early childhood*. Mahway, NJ: Erlbaum.

Rowe, D. W., Neitzel, C. (2010). Interest and agency in two- and three-year-olds' participation in emergent writing. *Reading Research Quarterly, 45*, 169-195.

Snow, C. E. (1983). Literacy and language: Relationships during the preschool years. *Harvard Educational Review, 53*, 165-189.

Strommen, L. T., & Mates, B. F. (1997). What readers do: Young children's ideas about the nature of reading. *The Reading Teacher, 51*, 98–107.

Sugarman, S. (2005). Playing the game: Rituals in children's games. In K. M. Jackson (Ed.). *Rituals and patterns in children's lives* (pp. 124-138). Madison, WI: The University of Wisconsin Press.

Sulzby, E. (1985). Children's emergent reading of favorite storybooks: A developmental study. *Reading Research Quarterly, 20*, 458–481. DOI:10.1598/RRQ.20.4.4

Sulzby, E. (1991). Assessment of emergent literacy: Storybook reading. *The Reading Teacher, 44*, 498–500.

Teale, W. H., (1986). Home background and young children's literacy development. In W. H. Teale & E. Sulzby (Eds.), *Emergent literacy: writing and reading* (pp. 173-206). Norwood, NJ: Ablex Publishing Corporation.

Teale, W. H., & Sulzby, E. (1986). Introduction: Emergent literacy as a perspective for examining how young children become writers and readers. In W. H. Teale & E. Sulzby (Eds.), *Emergent literacy: writing and reading* (pp. VIII-XXV). Norwood, NJ: Ablex Publishing Corporation.

Tomasello, M., Carpenter, M., Call, J., Behne, T., & Moll, H. (2005). Understanding and sharing intentions: The origins of cultural cognition. *Behavioral and Brain Sciences, 28*, 675-735. DOI:10.1017/S0140525X05000129

van Manen, M. (1990). *Researching Lived Experience: Human Science for Action Sensitive Pedagogy.* Albany, NY: State University of New York Press.

Vandenberg, B. (2004). Real and not real: A vital developmental dichotomy. In E. F. Zigler, D. G. Singer, & S. J. Bishop-Josef (Eds.), *Children's play: The roots of reading* (pp. 49-58). Washington, DC: Zero to Three Press.

Vygotsky, L. (1966). Play and its role in the mental development of the child. *Soviet Psychology, 12*, 62-76. (Original work published 1933).

Vygotsky, L. S. (1978). *Mind in society: The development of higher psychological processes.* Cambridge, MA: Harvard University Press.

Wells, G. (1999). *Dialogic Inquiry: Towards a Socio-cultural practice and theory of education.* Cambridge, UK: Cambridge University Press.

Werstch, J. V. (1991). *Voices of the mind: Sociocultural approach to mediated action.* Boston: Harvard University Press.

Spaces for Academic and Interpersonal Growth in a Primary Literacy Workshop Classroom

Jo Worthy
Annamary L. Consalvo
Katie W. Russell
Treavor Bogard
The University of Texas at Austin

When we asked Mae Graham to choose a metaphor for her teaching, she chose "mom," without hesitation. "A better mom than I am, because I'm very hovering. You know, just on the side. I want you to do it, but I'm here for you." Continuing the metaphor, she described her classroom: "You know, it feels like a home environment. I know what they're interested in; I encourage them to bring in their interests and work together."

Mae is a second-grade teacher considered exemplary by the faculty in our university, her school and district, and the parents of her students. Numerous educational researchers have concluded that the social climate, positive teacher-student interactions, and instructional support (Hamre & Pianta, 2001; Nye, Konstantopolous, & Hedges, 2004; Stuhlman & Pianta, 2009), as well as high academic expectations and attention to students' lived experiences (Ladson-Billings, 1995b) provided by exemplary teachers are highly related to students' learning and achievement. Studies of effective and exemplary literacy teachers—reviewed in the next section—have reached similar conclusions, along with findings more specific to literacy (Allington & Johnston, 2001; Pressley, Allington, Wharton-McDonald, Block, & Morrow, 2001). This research provides valuable information about the characteristics of exemplary teachers and classrooms. However, few studies provide in-depth portraits of exemplary/effective teachers.

The current study adds to effective teaching research with an academic-year-long case study drawing on multiple data sources, including 38 classroom observations. We addressed this research question: How does Mae provide opportunities for students' academic and interpersonal development through literacy instruction? The research is rooted in literature and theory on effective literacy teaching, culturally relevant pedagogy, and dialogue.

LITERATURE AND THEORY

Effective/Exemplary Literacy Teaching

Cross-national studies in grades kindergarten through four have uncovered some common characteristics of highly effective literacy teachers and their instruction. In the classrooms of accomplished K-3 teachers studied by Taylor, Pearson, and Walpole (2000), teachers used explicit instruction and higher-level questioning, and they coached students in applying strategies in their independent reading. The students of the most accomplished teachers had ample time to practice reading independently, often writing in response to their reading, and demonstrated engagement and on-task behavior. Small-group rather than whole-group instruction was the norm in these classrooms.

309

In studies of exemplary teachers in grade one (Pressley, Allington, Wharton-McDonald, Block, & Morrow, 2001) and four (Allington & Johnston, 2001), teachers reported using a variety of research-supported literacy practices, including read-alouds, process writing, curriculum integration, thematic instruction, and explicit teaching. Their classrooms were filled with print and well-chosen reading materials. Students selected their own books and writing topics, making instruction personally relevant. Classroom environments were warm and supportive, with an appropriate balance of success and challenge in instruction and materials, which aided in developing students' self-confidence and independence. Students were engaged in productive learning, such as connected reading, process writing, and integrated skills instruction with appropriate teacher support. The talk in exemplary classrooms was respectful and interactive, with students having ample opportunities to voice their thoughts. Rather than using a common program or instructional method, teachers at both grade levels used a variety of teaching practices and materials in unique and expert ways. Teachers believed learning is a social process and had high expectations for students' achievement and self-regulation; thus, they structured their classrooms around individualized and small group instruction and fostered student responsibility for learning.

In writing about both the first- and fourth-grade studies reviewed earlier, Allington (2004) highlighted features of exemplary classrooms that contributed to students' literacy development and progress, including time to read and write throughout the school day; an abundance of appropriately challenging and relevant text materials; active, explicit, responsive instruction; and longer, more complex instructional tasks integrated across the curriculum.

Research and theory in culturally responsive pedagogy implicates many of the same characteristics found in effective/exemplary teacher research, including high academic expectations; student collaboration and responsibility for learning; supportive classroom environments; teachers' deep content knowledge; respect for students' ideas; and getting to know students personally. Other characteristics of culturally responsive teachers and classrooms add important nuances and extend beyond those discussed in the effective teacher literature.

Culturally Responsive/Relevant Pedagogy

Culturally responsive pedagogy (CRP) recognizes the importance of including students' culture in all aspects of learning (Ladson-Billings, 1994). According to Gay (2000), culturally responsive teaching "is based on the assumption that when academic knowledge and skills are situated within the lived experiences and frames of reference of students, they are more personally meaningful, have higher interest appeal, and are learned more easily and thoroughly" (p. 106). Academic success is a central tenet of CRP; knowing students and their families is essential for providing the instruction and environment needed to foster success. According to Ladson-Billings (1995b), culturally relevant teachers believe knowledge is actively constructed and shared among students and teachers. They see students as having expertise and as being responsible for their own and their peers' success, and they arrange their classrooms so students can share knowledge and collaborate. Finally, culturally relevant teachers are committed to helping students develop and maintain competence in their own culture and to helping students develop a "critical consciousness through which they challenge the status quo of the current social order" (Ladson-Billings, 1995a, p. 160).

Classroom Talk and Dialogue

Meaningful classroom talk is identified as important in both exemplary/effective classrooms and culturally relevant pedagogy. In the book *Choice Words*, Johnston (2004) used data from Allington and Johnston's (2001) study to show how exemplary teachers used language to influence students' learning, agency, and positive identity development. Classroom talk was purposeful and meaningful, emphasizing reflection and inquiry rather than known answers. The concepts of shared meaning and active construction of knowledge during classroom talk, common to both CRP and exemplary teacher research, are also foundational to Bohm's (1996) view of dialogue. Important aspects of dialogue according to Bohm are that there is no pre-established purpose or agenda, that the talk that produces shared meanings among the participants, and that no speaker or idea is excluded. Bohm contrasts dialogue with discussion, which "emphasizes the idea of analysis, where there may be many points of view, and where everybody is presenting a different one—analyzing and breaking it up" (p. 7). In many discussions, according to Bohm, the participants take turns speaking but are mainly interested in making their own points and convincing others to agree with their ideas. In contrast, the spirit of dialogue is to enter a conversation with an open mind, actively listening to the thoughts of all participants, and developing shared meaning through thoughtful, open-ended conversation. Bohm asserts that, although it takes time and practice, true dialogue has potential to foster positive social interaction, understanding, and tolerance.

METHODS

Miller Elementary School serves a middle-income neighborhood in a mid-size city in the southwest. The student population of about 350 is 69% White, 24% Latino, 4% African American, and 3% Asian. Mae Graham (all names are pseudonyms) has a reputation among the faculty in our university as one of the finest teachers in the large urban district that surrounds us. She has been recognized for exemplary teaching by her school and district, and her students consistently achieve above the school and district average in reading and math, the only subjects for which data is available. At the time of the study, Mae had been teaching a total of 19 years in first grade and second grade at the current school and previously in fifth grade at a school serving an urban, high-poverty community. Mae's second-grade general education and special education inclusion classroom included 19 students: 4 Latino, 1 African American, 1 Middle Eastern, and 13 European American.

The author and a doctoral student—both former elementary teachers—collected the data for the study. Two doctoral students assisted in data analysis. We were participant observers in the classroom from the end of August through the end of May, during the 2007-2008 school year. Our major focus was the two-hour literacy block, which included read-aloud and reading and writing workshop. Although Mae read aloud across the curriculum, we focused on the after-lunch read-aloud, in which she usually read a novel, chosen for its age-appropriateness and relevance to students. Mae used a reading and writing workshop approach, modeled on Atwell's (1987) *In the Middle: New Understanding about Writing, Reading, and Learning*, in which students read from self-selected books of interest and wrote about chosen topics. She taught strategy mini-lessons and assessed, coached, and conferred with students about their reading and writing in individual and heterogeneous small group meetings. Students shared their writing and reading informally during workshop times and in scheduled sessions. Although her official schedule included 45 to 50 minutes each of separate, back-to-back times for reading workshop and writing workshop, in practice, students could be seen reading or writing during either time period. We also observed "morning menu," a 20- to 30-minute time when students worked on self-selected cross-curricular projects individually, in pairs, or in small collaborative groups.

Data Collection and Analysis

We used an ethnographic approach to data collection (Dyson & Genishi, 2005; Erlandson, Harris, Skipper, & Allen, 1993), spending intensive and extensive time as participant-observers in Mae's classroom, and gathering data from multiple sources. We observed a total of 38 days, taking ethnographic field notes, and extending the notes after each observation (Emerson, Fretz, & Shaw, 1995). We videotaped 18 of the observations and used a modified form of multimodal transcriptions, noting teacher and student gestures, facial expressions, sounds, actions, as well as movement when visible on the tape (Nelson, Hull, & Roche-Smith, 2008). Data also included transcriptions and notes from three formal interviews and many informal conversations with Mae, along with notes from numerous informal conversations with students. During data collection, we wrote regular analytic memos and met together to share our emerging interpretations of the data. During interviews and informal conversations with Mae, we shared transcripts, videos, and our developing hypotheses and asked for her feedback.

We began by open-coding the entire set of data to capture recurring and salient patterns (Graue & Walsh, 1998), consisting of both comparable examples and examples of variation. Through a recursive process of group discussion, data analysis, and reading of research and theory, we began to develop categories that described how Mae provided for students' academic and interpersonal or social development. We continued the process of coding, defining and refining the categories, until we reached the point of saturation and ultimately agreed on three themes.

RESULTS, CONCLUSIONS, AND INTERPRETATIONS

The overarching theme we found in analyzing the data was that Mae constructed instructional, curricular, and personalized spaces in both physical and metaphoric senses and gave students room within them to develop academically and interpersonally. First, through read-alouds of high quality, age-appropriate literature, Mae gave students space to consider and wrestle with complex issues and personal concerns through open-ended dialogue. Second, through reading and writing workshop and "morning menu," students were afforded spaces to engage in purposeful work—to follow their interests, choose materials, projects, and collaborators, and work at appropriate levels of challenge with Mae's guidance. Third, the curriculum and instructional structures of Mae's classroom opened spaces for her to learn about her students as scholars and people and to develop personalized curriculum, instruction, and support based on that knowledge.

Spaces for Meaningful Dialogue

In the classrooms of exemplary and culturally relevant teachers, we observed that read-aloud discussions and other talk in Mae's classroom were characterized by a high proportion of student talk, student-initiated ideas, and shared meaning (Allington & Johnston, 2001; Johnston, 2004; Ladson-Billings, 1995b), as illustrated in the following transcript excerpt. While Mae was reading a chapter from *Ereth's Birthday* (Avi, 2001), a character's comment led to a discussion initiated by Edward:

Mae:	(reading from the text): "Of course you should, said Marty, "The weak always have to help the strong. We're the important ones."
Edward:	No!
Mae:	Who said no? What are you saying no to Edward?
Edward:	The weak don't always have to help the strong because if they're a criminal or something, that might make it worse
Elena:	And it's kinda the opposite. The strong should help the weak.
Trey:	It's not that, they shouldn't open it because Ereth is still weak. I mean like, that is not true. The weak don't have to help the strong.
Mae:	Allie, what are you thinking?
Allie:	He might not be telling the truth. He might start hunting them again.
Mae:	Yeah. I wouldn't want to trust him. Roger, thanks for raising your hand. What are you thinking?
Roger:	I have two predictions. I think that they're gonna let him out, but when he tries to get Ereth he's gonna land on the snowmobile. (video transcript, February 13, 2008)

The conversation continued with students commenting about Roger's prediction and Mae continuing with the read-aloud. In the spirit of dialogue and reflective classroom talk, Mae did not lead the students in a particular direction; instead she stepped back and allowed the students space to consider the dilemma presented in the text (Bohm, 1996; Johnston, 2004).

Read-alouds also provided spaces for students to engage in dialogue about issues important to young children, including family and friend relationships and age-appropriate ethical issues and dilemmas, such as whether to help those who treat others badly (*Ereth's Birthday*, Avi, 2001), using "special powers" for good and evil purposes (*Matilda*, Dahl, 1988), and whether it is ever okay to take what doesn't belong to you (*Fantastic Mr. Fox*, Dahl, 2007). For example, in *Trumpet of the Swans* (White, 1970), a father swan (a cob) steals a trumpet so his mute son can have a voice, and Mae engaged students in reflecting on the ethical implications of this act, as shown in the following transcript.

Mae:	Chapter 9 is called "The Trumpet." (Reading from the text): "As the cob flew toward Billings on its powerful wide wings, all sorts of troublesome thoughts whirled in his head. The cob had never gone looking for a trumpet before. He had no money to pay for a trumpet.... "This is a strange adventure," he said to himself. "Yet, it is a noble quest. I will do anything to help my son Louis. Even if I run into real trouble."
Mae:	Put your heads down and hide your eyes. Raise your hand if you know your mom or dad would do anything for you even if that meant they were running into real trouble? (About 8 hands are raised).
Edward:	Don't know.

Mae:	Hands down. Raise your hand if you would do anything for your mom or dad or sister or brother even if you know it was going to get you into some real trouble. (Several hands are raised)
Edward:	Depends on what it is.
Allie:	Yeah. Depends on what it is.
Mae:	Alright. Hands down, heads up. Let's listen and see what happens with Louis' dad. (video transcript, February 21, 2008)

In this discussion, as in other similar discussions we observed, there was no heavy-handed moralistic agenda or push for a specific answer—the dilemma was simply posed as food for thought (Bohm, 1996).

The read-aloud time was also a space for open dialogue about personal experiences and feelings. Mae modeled this openness from the beginning of the year by sharing personal information about herself and her family as well as her thoughts and feelings as she read books to the students. As the year progressed, we observed students freely sharing their own thoughts and emotions in response to literature, as in the following transcript excerpt from April. The discussion followed a conversation in which Mae described a possible future read-aloud book that contained scary events, and she surveyed students about whether they wanted her to read it. The conversation was lengthy, and Mae was ready to move on so even though several students were still raising their hands to talk, she asked them to lower them. However, Robert insisted he needed to share:

Robert:	Wait, wait, wait!
Mae:	(with mock exasperation) Well Robert, what is it?
Robert:	Well, it's kind of a connection to what Roger said, but I just like I uh, um, um, it makes me really sad, like when I was listening to *The Lightning Thief* (Riordan, 2006) where um, Percy's mom gets choked by the minotaur, it made me really sad because I didn't want to lose my mom.
Mae:	I know. Sometimes fiction's a little too close to home, isn't it?
Lydia:	Me too.
Mae:	Just like in Ereth's birthday when the mother fox dies and leaves those kits, it just breaks my heart. Gena, what do you have to say?
Gena:	Um, this is something like that (inaudible) a dad dies, a mom dies (inaudible). I hope my mom and dad doesn't die.
Mae:	Yeah. Thanks for waiting, Edward.
Edward:	I have a connection to that. Once I read um, *Frankenstein*, and it was sad 'cause um, Frankenstein kept on killing his creator's friends and family. And also Harry Potter also is kinda like that because in the seventh book a lot of his friends die.
Mae:	It starts out sad, doesn't it, Harry Potter? How many stories do we know that are fantastic stories, but they start out sad. Ellie, what are you thinking? (video transcript, April 10, 2008)

Ellie shared that she was often afraid before going to sleep and that reading usually helped. In response to Ellie's remarks, Lydia shared her own strategy for comforting nighttime fears. "Sometimes at night, whenever my eyes trick me, I sorta pull up the covers because I feel much,

much better if I can't see because then I feel real scared." The discussion continued as other students shared books with traumatic events, other worries and fears, and other comfort strategies. Dutro (2008) asserts such "deeply personal responses" should be taken seriously in literature discussions, yet opportunities for students to talk about traumas and other emotionally weighty issues are rare (p. 426). Although conversations such as these took time, Mae felt they were important, as she explained: "It seems like we relate a lot of our daily lives to our read-aloud at times, so I try to give them room to make those kinds of personal connections. And it's a bonding time." (Interview, April 2008). The read-aloud space Mae provided for students to respond personally also gave her opportunities to learn more about her students' interests, beliefs, values, experiences, and motives, in accordance with culturally responsive teaching (Gay, 2000).

Spaces for Purposeful, Relevant Work

Reading and writing workshops gave students choice and responsibility for their own learning, as well as fostering a collaborative environment in which students read together and shared and developed writing and project ideas. The following example from a writing workshop observation illustrates the way Mae's workshop approach provided students with space to write in the way authors do—pausing to think, rehearsing ideas, and sharing with peers during the process of composing. Robert and some of the other students were creating their own myths after Mae had read aloud myths and legends from several different cultures.

> Robert sits on the bench with his arms folded, staring into space. Abruptly, he turns and jots something in his writer's notebook. He goes to Riley's table and flips through a book of myths, all the while talking to himself and making faces. He returns to the bench to write, this time for several minutes. Molly asks if she can sit next to him. He glances at her writing and asks her a question about the god she is writing about, which she quickly answers and goes back to writing. Then he tells her about his own god: "Mine is kind of like a dragon. He eats fire…" After the brief conversation, he alternately writes and mumbles to himself like he's rehearsing what he's going to write ("Ah, the minotaur!" "Scary." "s-c"). He sharpens his pencil, returns to the bench, and writes feverishly for several minutes. (field notes, November 21, 2007)

Mae explained that she started using writing workshop during her student teaching because her cooperating teacher's team was trying it just after Atwell's (1987) *In the Middle: New Understanding about Writing, Reading and Learning* was published. Mae added reading workshop when she began teaching fifth grade in the early 1990s and has continued using both because they allow choice and self-pacing and afford "everyone dignity without pigeon holing" (Interview, October 14, 2007). During workshops, we consistently observed a high level of engagement, with all students working in appropriate instructional materials; achievement levels were not highlighted, as they are in instruction based on ability grouping.

Regardless of their skill level, students were able to work on projects that were relevant and purposeful to them. For example, Tyisha's major interest was her family—particularly her grandmother, with whom she was very close, and the baby sister her mother was expecting soon. Despite her special education identification as developmentally delayed (her literacy skills were similar to those of a late pre-kindergarten student), Tyisha published several writing projects with support and even worked on some independently. She made a birthday card for her grandmother and then published a story about the birthday party, wrote about family memories and the anticipation she felt about the new birth, and made a welcome home poster for her mother and baby sister. Mae also gave her space to share her work and excitement with the class.

Mae described the cross-curricular project time she called "morning menu" as something that started "organically" as a way to give students more time to read or to finish writing, science, or math work. Gradually, students began proposing ideas for independent and collaborative projects. During an observation of morning menu, one researcher wrote: "It is a buzz of activity, with students at their desks, computers, and around the room working on different activities. Mae is floating around the room and meeting with different students.… " (field notes, October 19, 2007). During the observation, two boys and a girl were exploring a fan site for "High School Musical" and writing letters to their favorite cast members. Two boys were writing the directions and drawing cartoon figures for a game they were constructing about the *Spiderwick Chronicles* series (e.g., *The Field Guide,* Black & DiTerlizzi, 2003). Two girls were working together to make a bird mobile, using information they had learned from a bird-watching trip with one of their fathers, a field guide to Texas birds, and various websites. A boy and a girl were exploring NASA's "Astronomy Picture of the Day" website in preparation for a research project. At the end of the observation, the researcher wrote: "Wow! This was an incredible 30 minutes! The students all worked independently and everyone was completely engaged. I kept looking for one student who wasn't being productive and failed completely" (field notes, October 19, 2007).

In ways we found reminiscent of descriptions of culturally relevant classrooms (Ladson-Billings, 1994), the workshops and morning menu fostered student responsibility for their own and their peers' learning and gave students frequent opportunities to share knowledge and expertise. In addition, these structures afforded spaces for Mae to gather knowledge of students' home lives, interests, and personal concerns as well as their academic needs as she moved around to assess and assist individuals and groups. Combined with what she learned from hearing students talk during read-aloud discussions, informal classroom interactions, and from her close relationships with students' families, Mae intentionally built curriculum that addressed students' academic needs and capitalized on their lived experiences.

Spaces for Personalized Instruction

Using her knowledge of students' academic skills and interests, Mae personalized instruction for her students, including those who needed academic support. For example, Rubén—a student labeled learning disabled and diagnosed with attention deficit disorder—was having trouble finding accessible reading materials that engaged his interest, in spite of the remarkable quantity and variety of books in Mae's classroom library. Based on her conferences and assessments with Rubén, and knowing he enjoyed information text, Mae tried several text series with him. The most successful was her multi-grade-level collection of *Scholastic News,* a newspaper for elementary students, which Rubén read exclusively for several weeks and excitedly shared with other students before branching out to other information books. Similarly, writing topics did not come easily for Lydia. Even when Mae brainstormed possibilities and sat with her to get her started, Lydia would often write only a few words in her notebook during writing workshop. Mae conferred with Lydia's father, suggesting he go through family photo albums and artifacts. He began helping her write about family experiences at home, and she continued this writing at school.

In interviews with Mae, she said she considered the workshop approach a "sort of inclusion model in a way" (interview, October 14, 2007), in that the students with special education labels in her class could participate in the same ways as other students. Instead of being pulled out to go to the resource room or being instructed in special reading programs that often have questionable efficacy (Allington, 1994), Mae was able to address their needs mostly in her classroom. For example, three students in her class—two with Down's syndrome and another with developmental delays—were emerging readers with 20 words or fewer in their sight vocabularies at the beginning of the year. Mae assessed their reading skills and interests, collected pattern books for them to read and reread during workshop, and continued to help them choose appropriate reading material as they became more independent. They participated in readers theater with other students, playing parts in *Frog and Toad are Friends* (Lobel, 1979) at the end of the year. As Mae commented, "They just fit in so beautifully because everybody's just doing their own thing. They are growing so well…" (interview, April 7, 2008).

Mae was able to work with students who needed extra support in this intense manner because she had spent the early weeks of school building her workshop environment—one in which students had become accustomed to working with appropriate, relevant materials and topics and taking responsibility for their learning as students in the classrooms of effective and culturally relevant teachers do (Allington & Johnston, 2001; Ladson-Billings, 1994; Pressley et al., 2001). Through status checks, she knew what each student was working on every day, and they worked mostly independently as Mae moved from student-to-student or group-to-group to confer and assist while she scanned the room to check on students' activity and behavior.

Mae also used her knowledge of students' home lives to make instruction relevant and personal, as well as appropriate (Gay, 2000). In daily interactions and discussions, for example, we often heard her make a comment about a student's parent, sibling, or pet in relation to a book or other shared experience. She also based teaching decisions on what she knew about students' personal lives. For example, Mae knew Roger's family had recently experienced a death, which had caused extreme anxiety for Roger. Consequently, Mae decided to reconsider her plan to read a book that involved a kidnapping and to consult students about it. Without singling out Roger, she described the book to the class, explaining that it involved a "friendly kidnapping" but acknowledging the story events could be scary to some students. Then she conducted a survey, as shown in the following transcript:

Mae: Please be honest, and raise your hand if it would be upsetting to you or if you would be scared at night when you got home or when you're alone if we were to read a book about kidnapping. (Several students, including Roger, raise their hands). All right. Hands down, heads up. Then in that case, I'm going to tell you about the book because a lot of kids would be bothered, and I'm not going to read a book that's going to bother you, but I will tell you about the book because in a couple of years, it'll be a great fit for you to read on your own.

Mae describes the book and then Roger raises his hand to speak.

Roger: I sort of have a book like that, called *Everything on a Waffle* (Horvath, 2008) (Roger and other students giggle), and I read the back, but my mom said I couldn't read it because the girl loses her parents, so I didn't.

Mae: You know, sometimes these topics are very hard for us to take, aren't they?
            Even though we know that it's fiction the whole time, it's just not something
            we need to be worrying about right now. (video transcript, April 10, 2007)

In an informal conversation about this exchange, Mae told us she had read the book about
kidnapping to prior classes and had not fully considered that it might be so scary to some students.
Thus, in addition to giving Roger and other students an opportunity to "opt out" of listening to a
potentially frightening book, she said she learned a valuable lesson about consulting students when
choosing read-aloud books.

The theme of personalized instruction was also evident during discussions when Mae
responded to students differentially, based on her understanding of their ways of being (Compton-
Lilly, 2008). She actively solicited participation from students who did not often share during
discussions, making it clear through body language, verbal modeling, and explicit instructions that
others needed to listen respectfully. For example, Ellie was a student labeled gifted who spoke very
softly, with numerous pauses and stammers. She rarely spoke in class discussions early in the year
because she had become accustomed to negative comments from other students in her previous
years in school. In our October interview with Mae, she told us, "I wish [Ellie] were a little more
open because we could learn so much from her." Mae deliberately opened spaces for Ellie to share
more by frequently asking her to talk to the class about what she had been reading and thinking,
repeating her contributions and asking for clarification if needed. During a fall observation, the
class was discussing "A Musical Instrument" by Elizabeth Barrett Browning as cited in Carl's (1991)
poetry collection, *Eric Carle's Dragons, Dragons*. The poem contains the line, "the sun on the hill
forgot to die" (p. 28). Ellie raised her hand and made a comment in a voice so soft it was inaudible
on the videotape, but Mae heard it and asked her to elaborate.

Mae: Ellie, in that book, do you think the sun forgot to die, because it was still
            high in the sky?

Ellie: It was, um, one of um uh, um, well um, well um, it will take a while for me
            to explain. Well um (long pause). Fairies control (long pause) and they used
            feathers to (long pause) they um, um um, then they escaped fairy land, and
            um they were causing um trouble, and… (video transcript, November 21,
            2008)

Ellie talked for more than three additional minutes, with Mae watching her intently and twice
asking for clarification. Among her many pauses and fillers, Ellie was able to explain her relevant
connection to the poem. In an informal conversation with Mae, when we showed her the videotape
of the discussion, she commented, "Well, she's brilliant. I mean, you know, she has so much to
share. Today she actually got it out within two ums" (Personal communication, January 2007). We
observed that Mae often seized moments such as these during read-aloud time to help a student
develop an idea. She asserted it was important for all students to have such opportunities to build
confidence and develop their thinking as well as to build a classroom community in which all voices
and ideas were heard and respected (Bohm, 1996).

CONCLUSIONS AND IMPORTANCE OF THE STUDY

Large-scale studies of high-quality and exemplary teachers correlate teacher and classroom characteristics with student achievement (Hamre & Pianta, 2001; Nye, Konstantopolous, & Hedges, 2004; Stuhlman & Pianta, 2009). Multiple case studies of exemplary literacy teachers and culturally relevant teachers (Ladson-Billings, 1994) provide more nuanced descriptions of classroom instruction and interactions (Allington & Johnston, 2001; Pressley et al., 2001; Taylor, Pearson, & Walpole, 2000). However, few studies provide in-depth, ethnographic portraits of exemplary teachers over an extended period of time—an entire school year. Through this research, we were able to highlight complexities that would not be as evident in a shorter period of time or with fewer observations. We were thus able to offer rich detail about Mae's classroom environment, in which achievement, agency, responsibility, personal interests, purposeful work, and social interaction were valued for all students. Further, because Mae's classroom included students with identified learning challenges, we were able to shine a light on the ways in which this exemplary teacher addressed a range of academic and social needs. The workshop and morning menu afforded Mae time, opportunity, and flexibility to assess and gather information about her students and to use this information in personalizing instruction and providing all her students opportunities to develop academically and socially.

Previous research in text discussion considers student engagement, negotiation of meaning, personal and intertextual connections, and talk about complex issues inspired by literature (Clarke & Whitney, 2009; Moller, 2002; Silvers, 2001). We observed each of these responses in the discussions in Mae's classroom, yet previous research does not fully address the kind of open-ended talk we saw in Mae's classroom. Bohm's (1996) work gave us a frame for interpreting the agenda-free, open-ended dialogue we observed that gave students space and time to freely voice deeply personal thoughts and emotions in response to literature. The talk served to strengthen the classroom community and provide Mae with insights into students' lives, which further aided in personalizing instruction for them.

IMPLICATIONS

We found the workshop and morning menu, as well as the read-aloud discussion, central to Mae's practice and to her goal of providing room for students to grow academically and interpersonally. Yet, research on the effectiveness of workshop approaches and open-ended dialogue is severely limited. Consequently, these kinds of spaces—and the time taken to build them—are rare in schools, as some educational stakeholders in the current accountability-focused climate might see them as enrichment rather than essential to students' achievement (Assaf, 2008; Bomer, 2005). To accrue a body of evidence convincing to a larger audience of education stakeholders, including policymakers, we call for research on these practices using a variety of methodological approaches.

REFERENCES

Allington, R. L., (2004). What I've learned about effective reading instruction from elementary classroom teachers. *The Phi Delta Kappan, 83,* 740-747.

Allington, R. L., & Johnston, P. H. (2001). *Reading to learn: Lessons from exemplary fourth-grade classrooms.* New York, NY: Guilford.

Allington, R. L. (1994). What's special about special reading programs for children who find learning to read difficult? *Journal of Reading Behavior, 26,* 95-103.

Assaf, L. (2008). Professional identity of a reading teacher: Responding to high-stakes testing pressures. *Teachers and Teaching: Theory and Practice, 14,* 239-252.

Atwell, N. (1987). *In the middle: New understanding about writing, reading, and learning* (1st ed.). Portsmouth, NH: Heinemann.

Avi, B. F. (2001). *Ereth's birthday.* New York, NY: HarperCollins.

Black, H., & DiTerlizzi, T. (2003). *The field guide.* In H. Black & T. DiTerlizzi (Eds.), *The Spiderwick Chronicles, Book 1.* New York, NY: Simon & Schuster.

Bohm, D. (1996). *On dialogue.* London, England: Routledge.

Bomer, K. (2005). Missing the children: When politics and programs impede our teaching. *Language Arts, 82,* 168-176.

Carle, E. (1991). *Eric Carle's dragons, dragons & other creatures that never were.* New York, NY: Philomel.

Clarke, L. W., & Whitney, E. (2009). Walking in their shoes: Using multiple-perspectives texts as a bridge to critical literacy. *The Reading Teacher, 62,* 530-534.

Compton-Lilly, C. (2008). Teaching struggling readers: Capitalizing on diversity for effective learning. *The Reading Teacher, 61,* 668-672.

Dahl, R. (1988). *Matilda.* New York, NY: Viking.

Dahl, R. (2007). *Fantastic Mr. Fox.* New York, NY: Penguin.

Dutro, E. (2008). "That's why I was crying on this book:" Trauma as testimony in children's responses to literature. *Changing English, 15,* 423-434.

Dyson, A., & Genishi, C. (2005). *On the Case. Approaches to language and literacy research.* New York, NY: Teachers College Press.

Emerson, R., Fretz, R. I., & Shaw, L. L. (1995). *Writing ethnographic fieldnotes.* Chicago, IL: University of Chicago Press.

Erlandson, D. A., Harris, E. L., Skipper, B. L., & Allen, S. D. (1993). *Doing naturalistic inquiry.* Newbury Park, CA: Sage.

Gay, G. (2000). *Culturally responsive teaching.* New York, NY: Teachers College Press.

Graue, M. E., & Walsh, D. J. (1998). *Studying children in context: Theories, methods and ethics.* Thousand Oaks, CA: Sage.

Hamre, B. K., & Pianta, R. C. (2001). Early teacher-child relationships and the trajectory of children's school outcomes through eighth grade. *Child Development, 72,* 625-638.

Horvath, P. (2008). *Everything on a waffle.* New York, NY: Square Fish.

Johnston, P. (2004). *Choice words: How our language affects children's learning.* Portland, ME: Stenhouse.

Ladson-Billings, G. (1994). *The dreamkeepers.* San Francisco, CA: Jossey-Bass.

Ladson-Billings, G. (1995a). But that's just good teaching! The case for culturally relevant pedagogy. *Theory into Practice, 34,* 159-165.

Ladson-Billings, G. (1995b). Toward a theory of culturally relevant pedagogy. *American Educational Research Journal, 32,* 465-491.

Lobel, A. (1979). *Frog and toad are friends.* New York, NY: HarperCollins.

Moller, K. (2002). Providing support for dialogue in literature discussions about social justice. *Language Arts, 79,* 467-477.

Nelson, M. E., Hull, G. A., & Roche-Smith, J. (2008). Challenges of multimedia self-presentation: Taking, and mistaking the show on the road. *Written Communication, 25,* 415-440.

Nye, B., Konstantopoulos, S., & Hedges, L. (2004). How large are teacher effects? *Educational Evaluation and Policy Analysis, 26,* 237–257.

Pressley, M., Allington, R. L., Wharton-McDonald, R., Block, C. C., & Morrow, L. M. (2001). *Learning to read: Lessons from exemplary first-grade classrooms.* New York: Guilford.

Riordon, R. (2006). *The lightning thief.* New York, NY: Hyperion.

Silvers, P. (2001). Critical reflection in the elementary grades: A new dimension in literature discussions. *Language Arts, 78*, 556-563.

Stuhlman, M. W., & Pianta, R. C. (2009). Profiles of educational quality in first grade. *The Elementary School Journal, 109*, 323-342.

Taylor, B. M., Pearson, P. D., & Walpole, S. (2000). Effective schools and accomplished teachers: Lessons about primary grade reading instruction in low-income schools. *Elementary School Journal, 101*, 121-165.

White, E. B. (1970). *The trumpet of the swan.* New York, NY: Harper & Row.

"Dude, It's the Milky Way!": An Exploration of Students' Approaches to Informational Text

Beth Maloch
Angie Zapata
The University of Texas at Austin

Adela examines the cover of *Don't Know Much About the Solar System,* by Kenneth C. Davis, turns around to share the pages with a student behind her, and begins to read. She interrupts her reading to say, "Whoa, Jupiter is big!" Down the hall, SeEun opens to the page in her book on Earth, studies it for a moment, then flips back to Mercury, then Venus, then Earth, then quickly flips until she gets to the page on Saturn. And, across the hall, Sonny marvels at an image of Mercury's largest crater in the *Scholastic Atlas of Space.*

Interested in understanding how young children navigate and make sense of informational texts, we observed these third-graders and their peers for a period of seven months. We spent time in three classrooms led by teachers dedicated to the inclusion of informational texts. Our analysis across those seven months suggested that informational texts made their way into these classrooms primarily as part of classroom inquiry units—units of study centered on particular broad topics or themes and characterized by students' individual inquiries within this broad topic. This manuscript reports our analysis of one such unit, focused on the solar system, taught in all three classrooms over a period of six to eight weeks, in which each student was invited to select and research a planet using multiple informational sources. Focusing our attention on students' interactions with these sources/texts, we examined the question—How do third-graders engage with informational texts within the context of a classroom inquiry?

LITERATURE REVIEW

Duke (2003) defines informational texts as texts written with "the primary purpose of conveying information about the natural and social world...and having particular text features to accomplish this purpose" (p. 14). In recent years, researchers have become increasingly interested in how informational texts are or are not taken up in primary classrooms. Ten years ago, Duke (2000) noted the scarcity of informational texts in first-grade classrooms, both in physical availability of texts and time spent with these texts. Today, while there is some indication that informational texts are increasing in availability (in basal readers, for example, Moss [2008]), it is likely that informational texts are still not readily available in many primary classrooms (Jeong, Gaffney, & Choi, 2010).

The reasons for including informational texts in primary classrooms are many and well established. First, informational texts can be motivating for young children, tapping into their curiosity about the world around them. Caswell and Duke (1998) found that this motivational aspect can spur overall literacy development as children are drawn into reading through their interest in informational texts. Second, informational texts have real-world relevance. For example, Harvey (2002) reported that 80 to 90 percent of out-of-school reading is nonfiction or informational.

Third, young children often struggle with informational texts. Chall (1983) has speculated that the "fourth grade slump" might be partly related to the shift students typically make at that age into texts that are more expository in nature. Drawing on research and linking to educational policy, Pearson (2004) argued that "it is competence with expository reading, not narrative reading, that most concerns educators and future employers" (p. 222). Fourth, from the work of Pappas and others (e.g., Pappas, 1991; Purcell-Gates, Duke, & Martineau, 2007; Wollman-Bonilla, 2000), we know that young children are capable of learning the features and structures of informational text and that their comprehension of these texts can be improved (Williams et al., 2005). Together, these studies make clear that informational texts belong in primary classrooms.

Few studies, however, document teachers' and students' work with informational texts in primary classrooms (Maloch, 2008; Palmer & Stewart, 2003; Purcell-Gates et al., 2007; Smolkin & Donovan, 2000). Overall, these studies suggest the importance of providing students multiple opportunities for engagement with text within text-rich and instructionally supportive environments. In fact, Purcell-Gates et al. (2007) found that students' authentic opportunities to engage with informational texts were more important to students' growth than explicit teaching of text features. These findings suggest the importance of coming to a better understanding of how young children engage with informational texts during these authentic encounters. Our study contributes to the literature by offering a detailed examination of young children's interactions with and around informational texts.

Theoretically, we approached these classrooms from a sociocultural perspective on learning (Mercer, 1995; Vygotsky, 1978; Wertsch, 1991). Accordingly, we view learning as a culturally sensitive and interactive process in which both teachers and students play a part. Learning occurs as a matter of apprenticeship into valued practices, rather than as an accumulation of skills and strategies (Lave & Wenger, 1991). Our analytic attention, therefore, was drawn to not just the individual student but to the activity itself, which included the students (often more than one), the various written texts, and the dialogue that occurred as a part of the activity. We were interested in the kinds of textual practices performed by young children as they engaged in joint activity around informational texts—joint activity as a class (in that they were engaged in a shared inquiry about the solar system) and joint activity around individual texts as these "individual" encounters occurred in very close proximity to their peers, and as such, became joint encounters with and around informational texts.

CLASSROOM CONTEXT

All three classrooms regularly engaged in classroom inquiry units around science and social studies topics. For the solar system unit, teachers followed a structure similar to their other units and were quite intentional in the ways they scaffolded students' independent research experiences. First, teachers flooded the room with informational texts related to the solar system, and in particular, various planets. In addition to these in-the-hand print resources, the teachers also invited students to consult Internet resources including informational articles found on-line and video resources, i.e., United Streaming. All three teachers reported great efforts in searching and obtaining quality nonfiction literature that was both high interest and at an accessible level for each of their students.

Our observations suggested that the teachers were successful in these efforts, with each teacher providing, on average, fifty to sixty high quality books of varying reading levels related to the solar system unit.

Second, the teachers read to the students from multiple texts about planets and the solar system, invited expert speakers, and planned a "star party" students could voluntarily attend one evening to gaze at and learn about the night sky. The teachers frequently opened the fifty-minute classroom inquiry session with a read-aloud of a picture book about the solar system, a viewing and discussion of an online movie about the solar system, or a guided reading of a brief selection from an informational piece about the solar system in order to demonstrate and guide students though informational text reading and research. Two of the teachers—Jane and Jessica—guided the students through a whole-class demonstration of inquiry around a planet in which the teacher modeled how the students might draw information from and across nonfiction texts. For example, Jane led the entire group in research about the sun—guided by the same "big" questions asked of the students later (in their individual research), reading texts aloud and adding information to their joint chart, as well as searching the Internet and watching United Streaming videos. Karen modeled the navigation and note-taking from informational texts, but did not carry out a comprehensive demonstration focused on one particular planet.

Third, the teachers invited the students to select and pursue individual research of particular planets. Students consulted self-selected texts (including trade books, Internet articles, and video), reading and collecting information that would best answer the questions provided by the teacher in the form of a note-taking packet. Students actively used this packet to record the particular facts they deemed worthwhile. The focus questions in this packet included such questions as: What are the physical features of your planet?, What are the myths and legends of your planet?, and How was your planet named? During this independent work time, our teachers conferred with students individually or in small groups to receive and scaffold their learning and note-taking processes. In some classrooms, a whole-group share would conclude the inquiry time, providing a platform for students to offer a status update on their progress. Culminating in a final project, the children created planet brochures inviting imaginary visitors to their planet; these brochures were shared at the conclusion of the unit during a "travel convention" attended by parents, former (and future) teachers, and other students.

METHOD

This interpretive study examines data collected over a period of eight weeks during classroom inquiry units in three different classrooms. Our intentional focus on this unit emerged from ongoing analysis of the larger data set that suggested the importance of classroom inquiry units as contexts for informational text use. Participants included three teachers—Jane and Jessica, in their fourth years of teaching, and Karen, in her third year of teaching (pseudonyms are used throughout). We selected these teachers because our previous interactions with them suggested their enthusiastic integration of informational texts. Their principal and our faculty colleagues (who had placed interns in their classrooms) also recommended them to us as exemplary. The participating classrooms (ranging in size from 18-22) included students who were ethnically and socioeconomically diverse. The school was located in an urban school district in central Texas. Its assigned zone cuts across the center of the city, drawing from homeless shelters, international university housing, downtown living, predominantly Latino *barrios*, historically African American communities, and affluent neighborhoods. Of the 53 participating students, six were African American, six were Asian, 18 were Latino (all of whom speak English fluently), and 23 were European American. There were 30 boys and 23 girls.

Data Collection

Across the eight weeks, we observed (as observer/participants) in each classroom two to four days a week on average, documenting (through video/audio records and photos) students' work with nonfiction trade books, with Internet articles, and with web-based video (i.e., United Streaming). Data collection also included interviews with the teacher and students, photo documentation of evolving classroom charts, and collection of artifacts (e.g., lesson plans, teacher's notes, students' research notes). We interviewed each teacher twice, following a structured protocol, asking them questions about their overall philosophies of teaching, their views on their integration of informational texts, and their reflections on how the year had gone (in the final interview). We initiated student interviews more informally as conversations around the texts students were reading and the tasks they were engaged in. The data corpus analyzed for this manuscript totals over 30 hours of video/audio documentation of student research, observational field notes (from 48 observations), photos, and student artifacts.

Data Analysis

Data analysis was inductive, using the constant-comparative method (Strauss & Corbin, 1990), and occurred throughout data collection. Following data collection, analysis occurred in three phases. In phase one, both researchers independently read and open-coded the field notes (Strauss & Corbin, 1990) with an eye toward both teacher and student uses of informational texts. Preliminary codes were then discussed and compiled into categories and emergent themes. While this early analysis generated a number of themes related to both teachers' and students' uses of informational texts, this manuscript reports on our analysis of how *students* made use of informational text. To that end, phase two involved more systematic analysis of students' approaches to informational texts. In this phase, the lead researcher went back through the data from all three classrooms, coding the data line by line, and moving back and forth between the field note data and the videotaped archives of these observations. Using the initial categories as guides, the researcher cut up and sorted the data accordingly, and modified, merged, and deleted categories as necessary to fit the data. The analysis process during this phase could be described as recursive and iterative as we moved between the analytic categories, the field note data, the video and audiotaped archives, and existing research literature to determine categories and themes grounded in the data and triangulate findings. The final categories generated and refined during this phase are provided in Tables 1 and 2.

In the final phase of analysis, both researchers worked to conceptualize how these categories fit together into overarching themes. Also during this time, both researchers pulled selected excerpts from the data to check the credibility of our categories and themes.

Before moving into findings, two limitations of this study should be mentioned. First, this study's findings are limited to the particular contexts in which this study took place. Second, this

Table 1. Social Contexts of Informational Text Reading

Category	Definition	Relationship to teachers' instruction/support
Social: Response	Peers spontaneously share information they've learned or graphics from informational text	All three teachers planned for whole-group sharing time (Jane and Karen brought students together at the end of every research time; Jane did this periodically as well). Jessica used the RAN chart to conduct conversations around the information that students were gathering from books. Karen: Students worked individually, and Karen discouraged sharing until the end-of-period sharing time. Her students did share quite often in spite of this. Jane: Had the end-of-period share time, but students shared throughout their research period Jessica: Very much encouraged sharing and support amongst peers. Because she had them arranged in groups already, there was less spontaneous sharing/responses because they were experiencing the learning together. Occasionally, students shared across groups.
Social: Support	Peers support one another's learning. Includes support in: navigation of text, sharing resources (mainly books), and content/fact checking	None of the teachers seemed to emphasize the idea of peer support explicitly. However, Jessica, in particular, emphasized community and peer support more generally (across the year). Also, Jessica placed students into groups for their research rather than having them work individually. This structure resulted in more evidences of peer support in her classroom.

study relies primarily on observational, artifact, and interview data. It does not measure student outcomes, and therefore, it is difficult to ascertain the degree to which these practices influenced students' literacy growth.

FINDINGS

Two prominent themes surfaced in our analysis of the eight-week unit: (a) the social nature of informational text reading, and (b) students' varying approaches to text.

Informational Texts as Social Stimulus

The most salient of all of our themes was students' social involvement with one another during their "independent" informational text exploration. The engagement with informational texts seemed to function in these three classrooms as a social stimulus—prompting text-centered interactions among students. The motivational qualities of these texts, previously discussed by Caswell and Duke (1998), were clearly evident as students spontaneously shared with one another newly found information and interesting graphics, shared resources and information, and debated the qualities of their respective planets. This theme was displayed prominently in all three classrooms, evident in almost every instance of student-focused data. We identified two categories within this theme: (a) social response, and (b) social support.

Table 2. Student Approaches to Informational Text

Category (student)	Definition	Relationship to Instruction
Approach: Steeping	Readers examine information text to build familiarity with the topic of inquiry and with little attention to note-taking	Jessica encouraged the students to "read first for fun." Karen tells her students that on their first day of (book) research they'll read "just for fun." The second day of research she tells them they'll read like detectives. Jane doesn't suggest a time of reading for fun; she starts the first day by reminding them about copyright dates and how to skim/scan
Approach: Focused exploration	Readers selectively read the text, using questions as a guide	Jane and Jessica model this type of approach during their whole-group instruction. They read a text (usually paragraph by paragraph) and note particular interesting facts. Then, they decide where the information will go. Karen doesn't model note-taking with the note-taking guide. She only explains the note-taking guide.
Approach: Searching	Readers search texts for answers to specific questions	Karen does a few demonstrations (fairly minimal) of searching for information. Using the table of contents to "zone in" on the information you're trying to find.

Social response. In social response, students spontaneously shared their responses and learning from the informational texts. Many times, this social "reaching out" occurred quite briefly, as in the following example.

> Sonny is flipping through *Our Solar System* (Simon, 1992), flips past a picture of the Milky Way, then immediately turns back to that page, studies the picture and reads the caption aloud – "Milky Way Galaxy." He points to the photo and says to Denny, "Dude, this is the Milky Way!" Sonny shows Denny the picture and reads the caption again. Both boys go back to reading their own books (2/17/09; Jane's classroom).

We observed multiple instances of this kind—students sharing information or graphics with their peers, often in these short-lived interactions (e.g., "Oh my gosh, did you know . . . ?"; "Wow, look at this picture!"). These interactional episodes indicated to us the ways in which informational texts, along with a shared focus for inquiry, seemed to spur social response.

Students also invited their peers into a joint exploration of a text. Below, Amber attempts to bring Miriam into her reading of *The Third Planet: Exploring the Earth from Space* (Ride & O'Shaughnessy, 2004).

> Amber says to Miriam, "Do you see that? Do you see that? That's on earth (pointing to the book)". Miriam leans over and says, "That's kinda freaky," then goes back to her own note-taking. Amber turns the page to one that displays a photo of the southern lights ("aurora australis"). She says, "Oh my gosh, Miriam, look at this!" Miriam continues examining her own book, and Amber says, "This is beautiful (smiling); Oh my gosh, Miriam, you've gotta look at this (putting her hand over her mouth)". Miriam leans over and comments on it, saying, "Oh

> those are like the things that ** ** I don't remember what they're called." Next,
> Amber calls the teacher over to look at it (2/18/09; Karen's classroom).

Here, as Amber tries to draw Miriam into her text, her first attempt is met by a casual, seemingly tossed off, "That's freaky." Amber then elevates her response—one that also seems to be truly a reaction to what is on the page—in volume and animation. Miriam, in response, more fully turns her attention to Amber, stopping her own reading to study this picture with her peer. This exchange and the others displayed in this section demonstrate the value of an appreciative other in students' work with informational text. Such conversations may invite students into further inspection and exploration of the texts and their contents, as we discuss in the next section.

As evidenced in all of these examples, graphics (such as photographs, diagrams, tables, or other informational visuals) were quite often the source of response. While students regularly commented on information learned through the actual text in books or on-line, the graphics in the texts seemed particularly likely to elicit sharing or interaction around the text. Whereas earlier examples illustrated students' reactions to photos, the excerpt below shows Naomi examining a table inside the front cover of Seymour Simon's *Our Solar System* (1992) when two other students invite themselves into the reading.

> Amelia, looking over at Naomi across the table, says, "What's that?" and leans
> across desk to see the table. Denny also leans in and they all study the table briefly.
> Next, the teacher comes back and begins going through the table with Naomi
> (2/17/09; Jane's classroom).

Naomi's public examination of this information-rich table (one that included much of the information needed for their research packets) invited the participation of two of her more academically successful peers. By holding a book that was of great interest to her peers, the exploration of informational texts offered Naomi an opportunity to be an information-bearer rather than information-receiver.

In summary, our data suggest that providing opportunities for students to share information with one another may be an important part of informational text learning. Further, informational text reading, within a socially rich context, seems to offer possibilities for students to positively re-position themselves in relation to content and to their peers.

Social support. Students' social engagement around informational texts also included what we called "social support" when students assisted or supported one another in their reading of informational texts or research. This support happened in several ways. First, students shared resources with each other. Across all three classrooms, we regularly observed students passing along relevant books or recommending particularly rich websites.

Second, although not as common as resource sharing, we observed students sharing information about another's planet. For example, in Jane's classroom (2/10/09), Samuel reported to Tony, "Your planet was the first one to get discovered." Tony, expressing interest in this information that was new to him, walked over to Samuel's table and they began looking through the book together. In Karen's classroom, Josh showed us a fact he had recorded in his research packet, one that "Alexis found in a book." We considered this information-sharing an indication that students (at least some of them) were reading with an eye toward their peer's research, and not just their own.

Some students seemed to see their peers as resources and invited this kind of information sharing, as we see in the example below.

> Ben walks by another table and says, "Do you know who discovered Venus?" Miriam tells him that it was Galileo. Ben, seemingly satisfied, walks back to his table. Antonio comments to Miriam, "He was like the first person to discover all the planets." Miriam notes, "He thought Neptune was a star," and Antonio follows with, "He thought Pluto was a planet. It used to be a planet, until they figured out it was a dwarf planet." (2/18/09; Karen's classroom)

Here, Ben's question launches this table into a brief conversation about discovery and also highlights the connections students are finding across planets. In Jessica's classroom, students researching the same planet worked together, and as a result, we found more information sharing of this kind in her classroom. For example, in February 2009, Byun was sitting next to another student researching the same planet (i.e., Mars) who pointed out information about one of Mars' moons—Phobos—saying "this moon is only 17 miles long." Byun leaned in to see the book, read the names of two moons, Phobos and Deimos, and then recorded the information in his research packet.

Third, students sometimes helped each other navigate through and make sense of informational text. For example, in Karen's classroom, Marisa attempted to use a table of contents to find information. When the table of contents did not tell her where she could find this particular information (about the mythology of her planet), she seemed at a loss for another strategy. Hannah, sitting next to her, offered the idea of using the index, and helped her look up the information in the index. We observed only a few episodes of this kind, perhaps because many of the students seemed already quite proficient with basic navigational skills in these texts.

More apparent in our data were students' conversations around text that served to clarify or qualify what students were reading. For example, the following transcript occurred as two students read from a website (www.kidsastronomy.com/uranus.htm). The text from the website is included in italics and the full sentences read: *Uranus was the lord of the skies, and husband of Earth. He was also the king of the gods until his son Saturn overthrew him.*

Student 1: *Uranus was the lord of the skies, and husband* What?

S2: What? Husband of Earth?

S1: Yeah, people think Earth is a girl.

S2: I know, it probably is. Mother Earth.

S1: Yeah, that's pretty weird. Uranus is husband of Earth?

S2: Uranus is husband of Earth?

S1: Wait, *he was also king of the gods, until his son Saturn overthrew him.*

S2: (Pause) Zeus is the king of the gods, isn't he?

S1: Well, I don't know, I guess. That's pretty amazing.

S2: So, he was king of the gods until he got too old, and then Saturn became king of the gods, right?

S1: I guess

S2:   (to another group) Did you know that Uranus was king of the gods, but then Saturn became king of the gods?

(Jessica's classroom, 2/11/09)

In this excerpt, we see these two students reading and processing the text out loud as they go. As mentioned earlier, students in Jessica's classroom were assigned to work in groups and, as a result, this kind of on-line collaboration was more readily apparent in her classroom. These two students engaged in a joint retelling of sorts, reading and retelling to make sure they understood what they had read (a strategy promoted heavily by Jessica).

Students also played clarifying roles for one another as they spontaneously shared information they were learning. For example, in Jane's classroom (2/17/09), a student shared information with Samuel, saying, "Oh cool, it [Uranus] has 27 moons, and it has 11 rings." Samuel responds with what seems to be an important qualification, "It *may* be 11 rings." His own reading of the research suggested that the number of rings visible on a particular planet seemed to change as technology had become more advanced.

These episodes, and others like it, suggest the potential of allowing students to collaborate and freely share with one another as they engage in informational text learning and research. Our data indicate that students, when given the opportunity, engaged in socially supportive behaviors, sharing information and resources, assisting in text navigation, or helping each other process through text. We speculated that, in these moments, students were supporting each other in their meaning-making of informational texts. However, while some students engaged in such behaviors, not all of them did. We speculate that there is still much potential for capitalizing on students' inclination toward socially rich text learning.

Student Approaches to Text

A second theme evident in the data was that students varied—from each other, and from day to day—in their approaches to informational texts. Some students sat engrossed in particular texts, reading and sharing what they learned, with very little attention to note-taking. Others searched texts for particular bits of information, using informational texts as a means to an end. And, most of the time, students explored informational texts somewhere in between complete engrossment and intentional searching. In this stance, students read informational texts, guided by their focusing research questions (assigned by their teachers). Initially, our analysis led us toward developing profiles of readers, but further examination suggested that children did not take on just one stance or approach to text, but rather moved along a continuum of approaches ranging from steeping/browsing to focused exploration to searching/hunting (see figure 1). Their uptake of these approaches seemed to be related to the instructional focus of their teacher, the structure and difficulty level of the text, where students were in the research process (just beginning or finishing up), and with whom they were working. In that way, we conceptualized these approaches as being on a continuum, along which students moved, sometimes quite fluidly, during the course of their research. Of these three approaches, students spent the most *time* engaged in focused exploring, although there were more instances of the searching approach (these instances were shorter in duration, but they occurred more frequently). The steeping approach was the least common approach taken up by the students. We will now describe each of these stances or approaches.

Figure 1. Students' Approaches to Informational Text

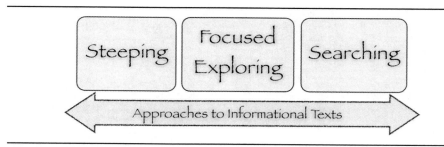

Steeping. The approach to text that we called *steeping* was most apparent in the first days of the inquiry unit, although it surfaced for particular children across the study. Based on the data, we identified the students as engaging in steeping when readers examined information text to build familiarity with the topic of inquiry and with little attention to note-taking. Below, an excerpt from our field notes shows Haewon, who seems to be "steeping" in informational text.

> Haewon sits quietly at the round table, reading through a book called *Neptune* (1997), by Seymour Simon (2/20/09; Jessica's classroom).

Many of the students who engaged in steeping, however, were not sitting quietly by themselves. Most of them were engaged with one another and with the texts in the socially rich ways described in the previous section, excitedly sharing what they found with others. Interestingly, the amount of time spent on this approach was relatively brief in all of the classrooms. We speculate that the brevity of steeping was related to the way the instructional unit was designed along with the importance of the task laid out for the children—that of reading and taking notes on their planet, guided by a series of focusing questions. Our observations suggested that students often seemed drawn to a steeping sort of approach, but then moved into a guided exploration or hunting stance as they were reminded (by their peers or by their teacher) of the task at hand. We see this in the following example from our field notes.

> Byun is reading *Seeing Red: The Planet Mars* (Loewen, 2008) and says, "Gross." Thomas leans over to see what he's looking at. Byun tells him that when you look at Mars with no telescope, they called it the "naked eye." All three boys sitting at the table agree that it is gross. Byun goes back to reading for a moment, then says, "Wait, how cold is it there?" Then pulls out his note-taking packet, looks through it, settles on physical characteristics and records the temperature of Mars (2/25/09, Jessica's classroom).

In this example, we see Byun briefly engaged in what seems to be a steeping stance towards text, reading and responding to the text, building knowledge about Mars. He responded briefly, and humorously, to one piece of information and shared it with his peers sitting close by. A check of his note-taking packet indicated no notes taken during this time. Then, he quickly moved back into a stance in which he explored the text, guided by his focusing questions. We found this move in and out of stances quite typical across the three classrooms.

We hypothesize that the steeping phase of research and exploring informational texts offered opportunities to, well, steep in the richness of these texts and the information. It was during these times that the children immersed themselves in information, and we suggest may have been a time for them to build up content knowledge about space and about their planet, in particular. There was also evidence that this steeping phase was important to their later research. For example, the next excerpt occurred as Ingrid and Ethel worked together on studying Venus.

> Ingrid gets up, retrieves a book, and opens to the last page in the book titled *Updated Venus*, a page that holds a series of "quick facts" provided in boxes. When (researcher) asked her how they knew to open that page, Ethel told her, "The first time we went through the whole book, and this time, she (Ingrid) just remembered." (2/17/09; Jessica's classroom)

Here, Ingrid returned to a page that she had found in previous days when she and Ethel spent time in open exploration of these books. Steeping, in this case, allowed them to become familiar with what books were available, the information that was in them, and facilitated their navigation back to this information.

Focused Exploring. A second approach that students took up in relation to informational text was what we called *focused exploring*. In this approach, students selectively read the text, using questions as a guide. The following examples illustrate this approach:

> Hayoung reads linearly through pages 2-3. After she reads the sentence, "Like Jupiter, Saturn is made up mostly of gasses," she sets the book aside and picks up her note-taking guide and says something about "what your planet is made of" (referencing a guiding question). (2/23/09; Jessica's classroom)

> Miriam reads, "Neptune is the smallest . . . and farthest from the sun. Oh Wow facts." (2/18/09, Karen's classroom)

> Melissa and Youngseo read and figured out where the information should go, "Ok, blue clouds are lowest...now, where do we put that?"

As is evident in these examples, students read through the text in this approach, then matched what they had learned or found with the appropriate guiding question or area. This approach to text was the one modeled by two of the three teachers in their pre-research instructional time. In whole-group settings, Jane and Jessica read through informational text with the guiding questions displayed, stopped (or had the students stop them) when they found interesting information, and then decided on an appropriate place to record the information. Because of the instructional emphasis on this approach, it was not surprising that many of the students took up this stance towards the informational texts.

Searching. A third approach that students took up in relation to informational texts was one we called *searching*. In this approach, as its name suggests, students searched for particular bits of information. This stance towards text, almost as common as the *focused exploring* approach, occurred more often as students progressed in their research. That is, after they moved through steeping and guided exploring, they often ended their research by taking up a searching stance to answer those final few questions. However, while we observed this broad progression in students' research, it is important to note that this stance also surfaced throughout their research, and not just at the end.

This approach toward text necessarily involved the readers in heavier use of the navigational text features, such as table of contents and index, as we see in the following example.

> (Researcher) asks Ethel what she's doing now as she observes her looking at the table of contents. She tells (researcher) that she is looking specifically for the distance the earth is from Venus, that they found out how far away Venus is from the Sun, but not from Earth. She said that all they know is that Venus is closest to the Earth. (2/17/09; Jessica's classroom)

Episodes like this one, in which students searched texts for specific information, were common. We regularly observed this searching behavior while students were on the Internet, as they typed in particular questions to websites such as "Ask.Com," and while they were exploring trade books (e.g., "I just used it to know when Earth was discovered," "We need to find out how far Saturn is from Earth."). Students were making use of these informational texts as resources—using the books/texts as a means to an end. This approach to text was quite different from the *steeping* approach that many students started with.

Interestingly, this searching approach also exposed limitations in students' understandings about navigating informational texts.

> Amber is searching for the answer to a question, "How many earth days?", and skips through the pages. Then, she decides to try the Table of Contents, and looks for it, but this book doesn't have one. Frustrated, she slams the book down and picks up another one. (2/18/09, Karen's classroom)

> Marisa attempts to use the table of contents to find information on mythology. Unable to find it in the table of contents, she stops searching. (2/27/09, Karen's classroom)

In the above examples, students sometimes struggled with finding information if the text did not include the common feature—table of contents—or if this feature did not yield enough information. Their teacher, Karen, also noted students' frustrations with texts that did not include these typical features, reporting: "That's when the world comes crashing down. When they can't find the index and they can't find the table of contents, 'What do I do? Am I supposed to read this cover to cover? What steps do I take here?'" For us, these gaps indicated places for potential instruction around the searching strategies that extend beyond use of text features such as table of contents and index.

DISCUSSION

In conclusion, we argue that the approaches taken up by these third-graders in response to informational texts should not be understood as rigid profiles, but instead as situated social/textual practices enacted within particular discursive environments and particular instructional demands. The students' approaches were shaped, at least in part, by the instructional practices being emphasized and the teachers' curricular choice of a shared inquiry unit. We wonder, for example, if social interactions of this kind would be as common if the children were all reading about different topics instead of different planets within an overarching consideration of a system. For students, this period of time was not one in which they freely explored informational texts to pursue information related to questions of their own choosing. They did, indeed, select a particular planet for in-depth study, but across all classrooms, these inquiries were guided by teacher-generated questions that directed students toward particular information. Our analysis exposed the ways in which these students approached informational texts according to this particular frame, albeit a frame that is not uncommon in primary classrooms.

Our findings indicate, that within this particular context, engagement with informational texts could not be separated from engagement with one another. In a reciprocal way, the informational texts prompted social interactions and, in turn, the social interactions seemed to support students' engagement with the text. Informational text seemed to act as a social stimulus, prompting conversations with peers in response to newly learned information or interesting graphics. In this way, our work joins other researchers, such as Dyson (1993), who highlight the social nature of literacy and learning. In this study, the students' talk seemed to demonstrate a desire to share, to respond, to inquire, and to challenge when in community with their peers. Research on informational text often focuses on how children learn to find, understand, and evaluate important information from texts (Smolkin & Donovan, 2000; Williams et al., 2005). While research of that kind is necessary and important, this study invites a different way of thinking about informational text-based learning and suggests that the motivational draw of informational texts (Caswell & Duke, 1998) may have a social outlet when students have space to explore and talk about texts.

These findings have implications for how teachers integrate informational texts into classrooms, suggesting that students may need extended time and space as they explore informational texts— social room to navigate texts in collaboration with their peers, supporting and responding to each other as prompted by the texts and their graphics and/or by each other. Perhaps providing time and space for rich interactions around informational texts allows students opportunities to do the kind of social *and* cognitive work they need to do with informational texts.

The students' varying approaches to text suggested students' different purposes—some purposes aligning with classroom intentions, and others aligning more with personal goals. In these contexts, the obligations of the classroom assignment moved students towards a particular approach toward informational texts, and in some ways, away from their own purposes for these texts. While acknowledging the necessity of providing structure to students' research endeavors as well as time constraints inherent in the tightly packed days of elementary classrooms, we want to suggest here the promise of steeping as an approach and the danger of clamping down so tightly on the research process in classrooms (in the interest of providing structure). This clamping down can limit the possibilities for steeping, space for students to spend time exploring their own questions as they inquire and respond aesthetically to the texts. Our research suggests that within this space, students may also interact with their peers in a way that affords opportunities for these interactions to become, effectively, scaffolds for their reading and navigation of text.

REFERENCES

Caswell, L., & Duke, N. (1998). Non-narrative as catalyst for literacy development. *Language Arts, 75*, 108-117.
Chall, J. S. (1983). *Stages of reading development.* New York, NY: McGraw-Hill.
Chrismer, M. (2008). *Venus.* Danbury, CT: Children's Press.

Davis, K. C. (2004). Don't know much about the solar system. New York, NY: HarperCollins.

Duke, N. K. (2000). 3.6 minutes per day: The scarcity of informational texts in first grade. *Reading Research Quarterly, 35*(2), 202-224.

Duke, N. K. (2003). Information books in early childhood. *Young Children, 58*(2), 14-20.

Duke, N. K., & Kays, J. (1998). "Can I say 'once upon a time?'" Kindergarten children developing knowledge of information book language. *Early Childhood Research Quarterly, 2,* 275-300.

Dyson, A. H. (1993). *Social worlds of children learning to write in an urban primary school.* New York, NY: Teachers College Press.

Harvey, S. (2002). Nonfiction inquiry: Using real reading and writing to explore the world. *Language Arts, 80,* 12-22.

Jeong, J., Gaffney, J., and Choi, H. (2010) Availability and Use of Informational Texts in Second-, Third-, and Fourth-Grade Classrooms. *Research in the Teaching of English, 44*(4), 435-456.

Kids Know It Network (2011). Astronomy for Kids. Retrieved Feb. 11, 2009 from http://www.kidsastronomy.com

Lave, J., & Wenger, E. (1991) *Situated learning: Legitimate peripheral participation.* Cambridge, UK: Cambridge University Press.

Loewen, N. (2008). *Seeing Red: The Planet Mars.* Bloomington, MN: Picture Window Books.

Mercer, N. (1995). *Guiding the construction of knowledge.* Bristol, PA: Multilingual Matters, Ltd.

Maloch, B. (2008). Beyond exposure: The use of informational text in a second grade classroom. *Research in the Teaching of English, 42,* 315-362.

Moss, B. (2008). The information text gap: The mismatch between non-narrative text types in basal readers and 2009 NAEP recommended guidelines. *Journal of Literacy Research, 40,* 201-219.

Oyler, C. (1996). Sharing authority: Student initiations during teacher-led read-alouds of information books. *Teaching and Teacher Education, 12,* 149-160.

Palmer, R. G., & Stewart, R. (2003). Nonfiction trade book use in primary grades. *Reading Teacher, 57,* 38-48.

Pappas, C. (1991). Fostering full access to literacy by including information books. *Language Arts, 68,* 449-462.

Pearson, D. (2004). Reading Wars, *Educational Policy,* 18, 216-252.

Purcell-Gates, V., Duke, N. K., & Martineau, J. A. (2007). Learning to read and write genre-specific text: Roles of authentic experience and explicit teaching. *Reading Research Quarterly, 42,* 8-45.

Ride, S., & O'Shaughnessy, T. (2004). *The Third Planet: Exploring the Earth from Space.* San Diego, CA: Imaginary Lines, Inc.

Scholastic. (2005). *Scholastic atlas of space.* New York, NY: Scholastic.

Simon, S. (1992). *Our Solar System.* New York, NY: Harper Collins Publishers.

Simon, S. (1997). *Neptune.* New York, NY: Harper Collins Publishers.

Smolkin, L. B., & Donovan, C. A. (2000). *The contexts of comprehension: Information book read alouds and comprehension acquisition.* Center for the Improvement of Early Reading Achievement Report #2-009. Ann Arbor, MI: University of Michigan.

Strauss, A., & Corbin, J. (1990). *Basics of qualitative research: Grounded theory and procedures and techniques.* Newbury Park, CA: Sage.

Vygotsky, L. S. (1978). *Mind in society:* The development of higher psychological processes. Cambridge, MA: Harvard University Press.

Wertsch, J. V. (1991). *Voices of the mind:* A sociocultural approach to mediated action. Cambridge, MA: Harvard University Press.

Williams, J., Hall, K., Lauer, K., Stafford, K., DeCisto, L., & deCani, J. (2005). Expository text comprehension in the primary grade classroom. *Journal of Educational Psychology, 97,* 538-550.

Wollman-Bonilla, J. E. (2000). Teaching Science Writing to First Graders: Genre Learning and Recontextualization. *Research in the Teaching of English, 35,* 35-65.

Yopp, & Yopp (2000). Sharing informational text with young children. *Reading Teacher, 53,* 410-423.

Meaningful and Significant Texts for Adolescent Readers: Tensions in Text Selection Policies

Leslie S. Rush
University of Wyoming

Gwynne Ellen Ash
Jane Saunders
Jodi Patrick Holschuh
Texas State University-San Marcos

Jessica Ford
University of Wyoming

Working with a consortium of charter middle schools in Atlanta, one member of our team (Gwynne) was asked if *Animal Farm* (Orwell, 1951) was an appropriate novel for fifth-grade students. Stunned, she replied, as politely as she could, that she did not think *Animal Farm* was an appropriate novel for fifth grade for a variety of reasons, including students' lack of knowledge about the Bolshevik Revolution and the early Soviet Period. She then asked why they were considering *Animal Farm* for fifth graders. The middle school educators said they wanted all of their students to read great works of literature.

The schools in this consortium have student bodies in which 60% of the students are reading below grade level, 80% receive free and reduced lunch, and 100% are African American. The school has a "high academic press" (Lee & Smith, 1999), hoping to accelerate all students' growth so they are accepted at and given scholarships to exclusive public and private high schools and later colleges. However, reading scores were not making the accelerated progress teachers had hoped. The teachers, most of whom had no formal coursework in literacy instruction, thought *Animal Farm* might be the key to accelerated literacy growth in fifth graders. The students were assigned *Animal Farm*; even with a great amount of teaching, the teacher acknowledged the students did not understand it. That semester students also read *The Watsons Go To Birmingham—1963* (Curtis, 1995), a book Gwynne recommended and which she believed students would connect. This, at times light and at times somber, Newbery Honor Book, a tale of an African American family's visit to the deep south during violent and turbulent times, brings up questions of racism, sibling and family relationships, and identity. The students read *The Watsons Go To Birmingham—1963*; they understood it because it mirrored their lives and echoed their humor (McNair, 2008; Tatum 2008a). The teachers wondered at how much students loved the book.

In our roles as middle- and high-school teacher educators, we see this tension between books that are seen as meaningful for their academic worth by teachers and policy makers and those that students find meaningful being played out in classrooms and schools across the country. School districts create book lists, filled with canonical texts (Stallworth, Gibbons, & Fauber, 2006), but often the adolescents assigned to read them do not feel connected to them (Franzak, 2008). In spite of this, some argue that canonical texts are *gatekeeping texts*, essential for making sure all students have the cultural capital necessary to be successful in high-performing high schools and post-secondary institutions (Schoenbach, Greenleaf, Cziko, & Hurwitz, 1999). Those in favor of the traditional canon suggest that Young Adult (YA) and popular texts alone neither give students the background knowledge necessary for post-secondary studies (Greenleaf, Schoenbach, Cziko, &

Mueller, 2002; Pike, 2003; Schoenbach et al., 1999), nor the rich text required for students to make deep connections with the text. Others suggest that YA and popular texts are anathema to literature and to literary study itself (Stotsky, 2010a).

Simultaneously, many have suggested students' responses to texts are positioned by their racial, ethnic, social, cultural, linguistic, gender, and other identities (Clarke, 2006; Galda, & Beach, 2004; Tatum, 2008a, 2008b). However, arguments for texts that connect to students' racial, ethnic, social, cultural, linguistic, and gendered identities (Brooks & Hampton, 2005; Dubb, 2007; McNair, 2008; Morrell, 2000; Tatum, 2008b; Tribunella, 2007) often clash with arguments for scaffolding students' understanding of canonical texts (Greenleaf et al., 2001; Pike, 2003; Simon, 2008; Schoenbach et al., 1999). Some even go so far as to suggest canonical texts themselves are central to the ability to understand complex texts (Stotsky, 2010a).

Tatum (2008b) argues that students' textual lineages consist of "texts that move them to feel differently about themselves, affect their views of themselves, or move them to some action in their current time and space" (p. 10). Tatum found that most students saw value in texts with characters within both their gender and ethnicity and, although students might branch out across one or the other, they rarely branched across both. The changing demographics of the United States suggest that in terms of identity, texts written by white males might fail to connect with many students on that basis alone. Nevertheless, a recent study of 142 Alabama high school English teachers demonstrated that even an expanded canon of 23, mostly 19th and 20th century texts, included only three works by women (Harper Lee, Emily Brontë, and Lorraine Hansberry) of which one, Hansberry, is an author of color (Stallworth et al., 2006).

In this article, we present two perspectives on text choices for English language arts courses in the upper grades. The first perspective is provided by the recently released Common Core State Standards for English/Language Arts (Common Core State Standards, 2010); the second is the perspective provided by a report of a recent survey of English teachers regarding their text choices (Stotsky, 2010a). We then present our suggestions for policy and practice related to text choice and future research in this area.

THE RISE OF THE COMMON CORE STANDARDS

In some cases (Morrell, 2000; Pike, 2003; Simon, 2008; Tatum, 2008b), the arguments for books that students can relate to and books that carry cultural capital are not seen as incompatible. Morrell, Tatum, and others suggest mediating the tension through a combination of canonical and meaningful texts. A synthesis of text types may be an answer, yet integrating canonical, YA, and popular texts requires teachers to be much more than just teachers of literature.

The tensions English language arts teachers feel—torn between being teachers of literature and teachers of literacy—have also been well documented. For example, Franzak (2008) demonstrated that readers who struggled in a high-performing high school were further marginalized by an English curriculum that focused on canonical texts and literary study, at the expense of literacy strategies. Likewise, in their study of a high school program to prepare students for collegiate reading and writing tasks, Moss and Bordelon (2007) suggested that opportunities were lost by pushing twelfth-grade students reading on the seventh-grade level into demanding text without providing appropriate instructional scaffolding. Others have suggested the key to post-secondary success for middle and secondary literacy learners lies in tying literary theory to response-based literacy instruction (Eckert, 2008).

Enter the Common Core State Standards. The National Governors Association Center for Best Practices (NGA Center) and the Council of Chief State School Officers (CCSSO) coordinated the state-led Common Core State Standards (CCSS) effort that reflects a collaboration among "teachers, administrators, and experts, to provide a clear and consistent framework to prepare our children for college and the workforce" (Common Core State Standards Initiative, 2010). These k-12 standards are aligned with the College and Career Readiness Standards (CCR) and delineate the knowledge and skills students should possess for a successful transition into entry-level employment, university, or workforce training programs. After the initial writing of standards, the NGA Center and CCSSO requested and received feedback from various organizations and groups like teacher organizations, university professors, educators, civil rights groups, and experts in language learners and students with disabilities in an effort to refine the language and wording of each standard.

All but two states, Texas and Alaska, took part in the development of the Common Core State Standards Initiative. Materials provided by the Initiative advocate the creation of common standards to "provide a greater opportunity to share experiences and best practices within and across states that will improve our ability to best serve the needs of students" (Common Core State Standards Initiative, 2010). While the standards are not a curriculum—this point is emphasized throughout the website and in ancillary materials provided by the Initiative—they offer teachers a roadmap in terms of knowledge and skills students should have at a particular grade level, which will aid teachers in developing appropriately rigorous lesson plans and units of study.

SEARCHING FOR COMMON GROUND: WHAT THE COMMON CORE STANDARDS SAY ABOUT TEXT SELECTION

Although CCSS offer "Sample Performance Tasks" as exemplars of how teachers might approach the study of a particular piece of literature, these tasks are offered as models rather than mandates. One instance of this is found in the grades 9-10 Reading Standards, where a performance task suggests that students examine the purpose and point of view present in Martin Luther King, Jr.'s "I Have a Dream Speech," (1963) and consider the rhetorical devices present in the speech that forward these goals. Among a list of Key Takeaways from the English Language Arts/Reading Standards is a required "progressive development of reading comprehension" (Common Core State Standards Initiative, 2010) and the assignment of increasingly complex texts drawn from both contemporary and classical literature, and including a wide array of informational texts. Although the CCSS suggest certain categories of texts, such as classic myths and stories, primary documents, and classic works of literature, the Standards defer to school districts and states to determine which literature and readings are appropriate and/or required for local populations.

In terms of identifying appropriate texts for particular grade levels, the CCSS Initiative provides supporting materials and includes representative reading materials for English language arts, history/social studies, science, mathematics, and technical subjects and sample performance tasks. Reading materials are grade-banded (e.g., 4-5; 6-8; 9-10; 11-College and Career Readiness) and broken out into categories for each content area. For English language arts, these are "stories, poetry, drama, informational texts;" for history/social studies, science, mathematics, and technical subjects there are exemplars of readings, both paper and digital, under the heading of "informational texts." Grade-level determinations are made based on both quantitative and qualitative measurements, and additional support for approaching reading with English language learners and students with disabilities are readily available as resources/ancillary documents posted to the CCSS website.

After reading the recommended text resources and exemplar reading lists provided by the Common Core State Standards, several questions surface: To what degree do the Common Core State Standards rely on canonical texts as opposed to multicultural or more contemporary texts? What types of digital resources are highlighted? Do the readings help students "build knowledge, gain insights, explore possibilities, and broaden their perspective" as is suggested by the Key Takeaways document included in the Draft of the K-12 Common Core State Standards for English Language Arts (Common Core State Standards Initiative, 2010)?

After exploring the reading lists and excerpts for each of the grade levels from 4-5, 6-8, 9-10, and 11-CCR, it is clear that the preponderance of texts suggested as exemplars are classic or canonical texts and are readily available in textbook anthologies commonly used in English language arts classrooms. For example, Lewis Carroll's *Alice's Adventures in Wonderland* (reprint, 1997) is suggested as an exemplar for grades 4-5, Louisa May Alcott's *Little Women* (reprint, 2011) is suggested as an exemplar for grades 6-8, and Geoffrey Chaucer's *The Canterbury Tales* (reprint, 2008) is suggested as an exemplar for grades 11-12.

Although contemporary and multicultural texts are included for each of the grade-band levels, these texts are smaller in number and in some instances have become part of the literary canon. For example, for grades 4-5, Christopher Paul Curtis' (1999) novel, *Bud, Not Buddy* is listed as an exemplar; for grades 6-8, Mildred Taylor's (2004) novel *Roll of Thunder, Hear My Cry*; for grades 9-10, Chinua Achebe's (reprint, 1994) novel *Things Fall Apart*; and for grades 11-12, Zora Neale Hurston's (reprint, 2006) novel *Their Eyes Were Watching God*.

Although digital literacy is a necessary tool for contemporary students, the CCSS resource lists include only a smattering of web-based readings for each grade level, and these are largely confined to informational texts. We provide two examples of such digital texts below.

- An online inventory and description of invasive plants, which is also available in pdf format (California Invasive Plant Council, 2010).
- An online map and table showing U. S. zones and suggested home insulation levels (U. S. Environmental Protection Agency/U. S. Department of Energy, 2010).

It is possible that because this is considered a "recommended" list, the writers chose only a few digital texts to stand as exemplar texts. Also, because websites are historically unstable and often produce dead links over time, the writers might have decided to leave the selection of digital texts up to individual schools and educators.

In regard to the question, "Do the Common Core State Standards readings help students 'build knowledge, gain insights, explore possibilities, and broaden their perspective' over time," it is difficult to assess the absence of the passage of time and the use and critique of practicing teachers. Critiques and compliments are already available from the educational community about CCSS and the literary choices excerpted and highlighted in the CCSS Appendix documents. Stotsky (2010a) expresses concern that the creation of CCSS is a step toward a nationalized curriculum and one that favors "non-analytical approaches" (p. 31) to the study of literature that will handicap students as they move toward college admission. Interestingly enough, she employs the work of E. D. Hirsch, Jr., who has written in support of CCSS (Hirsch, 2010/2011), to support the claim that the Core Standards will devolve into a "skills-driven" (Stotsky, 2010a, p. 32) approach, thus increasing the likelihood that secondary students will find themselves ill-prepared or capable of college-level work. Like Hirsch, Jr., many from the educational research community (Darling-Hammond, 2010/2011; Finn Jr. & Petrilli, 2010) are supportive of CCSS even though they are not always in accord on other educational issues. What this suggests is that the Common Core, and the increasingly challenging texts that are present in English language arts content area as well as in social studies, math, science, and technology studies, provides a workable set of standards to assist teachers, school districts, and states in developing curricula that become more complex while preparing students for entry into the workforce, university, or technical training centers after graduating from public schools.

RESISTING THE COMMON GROUND: THE CANONICAL BACKLASH

As noted, the Common Core Standards were not well received by some; the standards were criticized for not including enough traditional literary texts and for including a large number of non-fiction texts in the English curriculum. In 2010, one leading critic, Sandra Stosky, published a report in the Association of Literary Scholars, Critics, and Writers' (ALSCW) publication, *Forum*, entitled, "Literary Study in Grades 9, 10, and 11: A National Survey" (Stotsky, 2010a). *Forum* is described by the ALSCW as, "an imprint on literary advocacy and public policy, issued on an occasional basis and with the approval of the ALSCW Council" (ALSCW, n.d., para. 1). Although describing itself as non-political, the ALSCW is aligned with the National Association of Scholars (as is Stotsky), and considers its mission "to insist upon the literary nature of the teaching of literature" (ALSCW, n.d., Mission Goal 7).

Sandra Stotsky is the Endowed Chair in Teacher Quality at the University of Arkansas and was one of six educators featured in the *New York Times* commentary on the National Standards (Stotsky, 2009). She served on the state of Massachusetts's Common Core validation committee, although she chose not to sign off on the final version, arguing:

> In my judgment, Common Core's standards for grades 6-12 do not reflect the core knowledge needed for authentic college-level work and do not frame the literary and cultural knowledge one would expect of graduates from an American high school. (Stotsky, 2010b, bullet point 1)

Even with this stated bias, her non-peer-reviewed study, meant to counter the Common Core Standards, has been given great credence by the press (e.g., Heitin, 2010; Leef, 2011; Johnson, 2011), teachers (e.g., English Companion Ning: http://englishcompanion.ning.com), and policy-makers (e.g., The John William Pope Center for Higher Education Policy http://www.popecenter. org).

In her piece (funded by the National Endowment for the Humanities, The University of Arkansas, and the Lynde and Harry Bradley Foundation and sponsored by the ALSCW, the Concord Review, and the California Reading and Literature Project), Stotsky (2010a) purports to be replicating earlier studies by Applebee (1989) and Squire and Applebee (1968). These two earlier studies, conducted by surveying high school department chairs or curriculum coordinators, sought to gather information on which texts were being read in which grades (9-12) in the United States.

However, in the introduction to the discussion of her survey of grade 9-11 classroom teachers, Stotsky condemns the quality of literature that high school students currently read. This condemnation is based on an internally conducted study of the most frequently taken tests in Accelerated Reader (AR) on the high school level (Stotsky, 2010a, p. 8). Using information indicating that of 1500 high school students (designated by Accelerated Reader to be in the top 10% of reading achievement), 332 took an AR test on *Twilight* (Meyer, 2005), 325 on *Breaking Dawn* (Meyer, 2008), and 116 on *To Kill a Mockingbird* (Lee, reprint 1988), Stotsky concludes that students *chose* Meyer's works, but they were likely *assigned* Lee's works (an assertion unsupported by her data). In general, the inclusion of AR data (which are not widely used in high schools) and its use to describe the reading habits of a nation of high school students is puzzling. However, when Stotsky reveals she is using the AR readability formula, Advantage/TASA Open Standard for Readability (ATOS) for calculating the difficulty for all books discussed in her piece, the connection seems clearer (p. 38). Although she acknowledges there are concerns with using readability formulas for evaluating the actual difficulty of literary works, she notes that she chose the formula because it adjusts difficulty based on the length of the text "adjusted upward for longer books and downward for shorter books" (p. 39). This choice is problematic, as book length is not necessarily a primary indicator for text difficulty. For example, ATOS equates the difficulty of *The Crucible* (Miller, reprint, 1976) with that of *Twilight* (Meyer, 2005). Additionally, the following texts are rated as below a high school reading level by ATOS: *The Crucible* (Miller, reprint 1976) (4.9), *Of Mice and Men* (Steinbeck, reprint, 2002) (4.5), *Night* (Wiesel, reprint 2006) (4.8), *The Great Gatsby* (Fitzgerald, reprint 1999) (7.3), *Lord of the Flies* (Golding, reprint 2003) (5.0), *Huckleberry Finn* (Twain, reprint 2011) (6.7), *Animal Farm* (Orwell, 1951) (7.3), and *Antigone* (Sophocles, reprint 2005) (5.3).

Many researchers might question the validity of the report from these two unsupported propositions alone (the number of AR tests taken reflects what students both choose and are assigned to read and that ATOS is a valid measure of difficulty for literary texts because it rates longer books as more difficult). However, as noted previously, the report has been widely read, and is becoming influential in discussions of both the Common Core Standards and secondary text selection. With these two conclusions and an American College Testing (ACT) recommendation that students read more challenging materials to be prepared for college level instruction, Stotsky (2010a) sets the stage for presenting her survey.

With two research questions: (a) What book-length works of fiction, poetry, drama, and non-fiction are assigned by teachers in grades 9-11 in standard or honors courses?, and (b) Which approach(es) do teachers use for the literature they assign and how much time do they allot to literary study? (that is not discussed in this piece), she surveyed (as best we can ascertain because the methodology is not clearly described and is only included in Appendices) 406 teachers via telephone, a web-based survey, or a mailed survey. Some portions of the survey are reproduced, but some details, such as the prompts used to elicit teachers' pedagogical approaches, are missing. The number of teachers in the original sample is unclear; 1500 were contacted initially, then when the response rate was low, "we added additional teachers" to the database, although no specific number is given (p. 38). Finally, an additional 1300 teachers were mailed surveys. How many teachers completed the survey via the various means is not reported, and there is no internal comparison among data collected in these different ways.

Regardless of methodological concerns, Stotsky (2010a) calls this "a representative sample" (p. 39) and goes on to draw the conclusion that only four commonly assigned books are on a high school reading level (according to ATOS): *Julius Caesar* (Shakespeare, reprint 2010), *The Odyssey* (Homer, reprint 2011), *The Scarlet Letter* (Hawthorne, reprint 2011), and *Macbeth* (Shakespeare, reprint 2010). As a result, she states:

> little is left of a coherent and progressive literature curriculum with respect to two of its major functions—to acquaint students with the literary and civic heritage of English-speaking people, and to develop an understanding and use of the language needed for college coursework. (p. 14)

Following this conclusion, she presents a data table, which she suggests demonstrates the differences in the assignment of quality literature from Applebee's 1989 study to hers in 2009. Although she acknowledges:

> For purposes of comparison, it is important to note that his study included all the different types of classes in grades 9-12…, not just standard and honors courses in grades 9-11…. Moreover, his unit of analysis was the school, not individual courses. Thus, his study picked up the maximum assignment of the titles on a school-wide basis, not a profile of what the average student likely reads…. (p.14)

She then asserts, "it is reasonable to conclude that significant changes have taken place" (p. 14). But is it? If we go deeply into Applebee's (1989) study, we find he reported data by track. See Table 1.

We also find that if we use an apples-to-apples comparison of higher-level tracks, a comparison that includes information about how many texts in Applebee's study were assigned in Grade 12 (which was not included, inexplicably) in Stotsky's survey, we find the belief that significant changes have taken place unreasonable.

Table 1. Applebee's (1989) Most Frequently Assigned Texts Reported by Track

Higher-level Track Text Choices	Percent of Schools Reporting this Text Choice	Lower-level Track Text Choices	Percent of Schools Reporting this Text Choice
Romeo & Juliet	44%	Of Mice and Men	25%
Macbeth	44%	The Outsiders	23%
Huckleberry Finn	38%	The Pearl	21%
To Kill a Mockingbird	35%	Romeo and Juliet	17%
Julius Caesar	34%	Macbeth	17%
Hamlet	34%	The Pigman	14%
Scarlet Letter	34%	To Kill a Mockingbird	13%
Great Gatsby	31%	Julius Caesar	13%
Lord of the Flies	28%	Call of the Wild	13%
The Crucible	28%	Diary of a Young Girl	12%

Table 2. A Comparison of Stotsky's (2009) and Applebee's (1989) Higher-level Track Findings

Higher-Level Track Text Choices	Percent of Schools Reporting this Text Choice in Applebee (1989)	Percent of Schools Reporting this Text Choice in Stotsky (2009)
Romeo & Juliet	44%	33%
Macbeth*	44%	8 %
The Adventures of Huckleberry Finn	38%	13%
To Kill a Mockingbird	35%	30%
Julius Caesar	34%	22%
Hamlet**	34%	5%
The Scarlet Letter	34%	11%
The Great Gatsby	31%	15%
The Lord of the Flies	28%	13%
The Crucible	28%	59%

* 54% in grade 12 (Applebee, 1989)
** 45% in grade 12 (Applebee, 1989)

Certainly changes have taken place (including a great increase in teachers assigning *The Crucible*), and there has been a decline in the assignment of some texts. However, teachers do not seem to be fleeing Shakespeare and works that reflect the "literary and civic heritage of English-speaking people" at the rate Stotsky purports.

In reviewing text selection policies for middle and secondary schools, we are concerned by the assumptions that underlie Stotsky's study (that literary reading is key to college success) and the conclusions drawn, often without supporting data, from a flawed piece of research (that to improve students' college and career preparation, we must assign more canonical, literary text). Although ACT's (2006) college readiness report suggests the clearest discriminator between students who are prepared for college-level work and those who are not is the ability to comprehend complex texts, there is no indication the texts are solely literary. Poor readers face difficult challenges in courses with heavy text demands (Simpson & Nist, 2000), but those courses often involve reading complex expository, discipline-based text and the synthesis of text information with class-based lecture and discussion. Recognizing this, the ACT (2006) calls on high schools to increase the level and amount of reading instruction in all high school courses, not just in English or remedial courses and they call on states to address text complexity in state standards. The Common Core, however, does promote the notion that reading must go beyond the English classroom and reading must comprise more than literature. We hope teachers, districts, and policy-makers do their own close reading of Stotsky's report before using its findings in text-selection decisions.

MEETING IN THE MIDDLE: MEDIATING STUDENTS' NEEDS AND TEXT-SELECTION POLICY

Educators in the United States are concerned about how to help struggling readers in middle and high school classrooms (Greenleaf et. al., 2001). Crocco and Costigan (2007) found that, because of mandated testing and the resulting narrowing of curricular choices, teachers do not have room in the curriculum to be creative and to create relationships with their students. This narrowing of curriculum means it is less likely teachers and students will have meaningful literacy experiences within the classroom. Curricula that focus on the canon do not necessarily enable students to engage and connect meaningfully with texts. Many students cannot read canonical texts with deep understanding because they find the texts boring or because teachers have not appropriately scaffolded reading to facilitate these connections (Tatum, 2008c).

Perhaps one thing educators can all agree on is that we want students to be active and effective readers, to be critical thinkers, and to learn both how to read a variety of texts and how to choose texts that will best suit their needs. Based on our discussion here, and on our understanding of the needs of students and the competing desires of policy makers, we have developed the following suggestions for teachers, department heads, curriculum coordinators, and others who are responsible for choosing texts and developing policies around choosing texts. In addition, we provide some suggestions for future research in the area of text selection.

Use Available Resources to Develop Policy Statements on Text Choices

We recommend teachers, curriculum directors, and administrators use resources that are available to them in regard to text choice. These resources might include the Common Core State Standards' recommendations (Common Core State Standards Initiative, 2010), as well as those provided by the National Council of Teachers of English and the International Reading Association (NCTE/IRA, 1996). A policy that attends to students' needs and interests and provides for increasing levels of text complexity and demand, as well as one that is coherent in terms of the community in which schools are located, has the opportunity to meet the needs of all stakeholders. Such a policy will ensure text choices can stand against banning or censorship attacks as well as voiced concerns about text and instructional rigor. In addition, it is our belief that the process of developing such a policy will assist in preventing self-censorship by teachers.

Put Students' Needs at the Center

If we choose texts for students by focusing on what students need to be effective citizens of the world, we move away from imagining certain texts are required reading for all students. What we are advocating here is to begin with the student as the center of text choice, rather than beginning with the text at the center of the process of choosing texts.

Paying attention to students' needs, and even students' desires, means we should be developing collections of texts that are varied in genre and format. Fiction, non-fiction; classics and young adult literature; poetry and prose; digital and paper texts—all of these will suit some students' needs and desires. No one category will provide what all students need. Thus, as we develop lists of texts for students, we must build in variety and invite a diversity that reflects the ever-burgeoning media available.

In addition, paying attention to students' needs involves consideration of development of student skills. Thus, we may want to think of text choices using the metaphor of bridges or ladders (Lesesne, 2010). Both metaphors allow teachers and other knowledgeable parties to provide students with experiences with texts that build skills required for more difficult texts.

We suggest text choices begin with the collection of data on students' backgrounds, cultural heritage, funds of knowledge (Moll, Amanti, Negg, & Gonzalez, 2005; Moll & Gonzalez, 2004), interests, and reading choices or motivation to read. Once collected, these data can be used by school district personnel to make text choices that balance the needs and interests of students with other driving forces, such as standards, curriculum, culture, and community. A culturally responsive approach to text selection will give all students a sense of pride in their cultural backgrounds, a chance to learn through learning styles that will work for each student, and to instill in students the understanding that their culture is one of their strengths (Morgan, 2009).

Recognize the Complex Nature of Text Choices

A variety of means exist to determine text difficulty. Teachers in schools use methods ranging from simplistic sentence/syllable ratios to lists of grade-level ranges developed at some point in the history of a school. We like to advocate for a method for choosing texts that takes into consideration not only the word-level and sentence-level difficulty of a text, but also more qualitative considerations, such as students' familiarity with the context and background of a text; complexity of ideas and concepts in a text; and sophistication or specialized knowledge required by a text.

The Common Core State Standards provides a roadmap for how stakeholders might approach text selection. Their recommended works include both challenging canonical texts as well as high-interest, culturally relevant and/or contemporary texts. However, we should not rely on any one list to support the learning needs of all adolescents. Instead, knowledgeable participants in text selection activities should consider students' needs, text complexity, and available resources to develop text choices that are malleable, wide-ranging, and representative of the populations being served.

IMPLICATIONS FOR FURTHER RESEARCH

Our analysis of Stotsky's (2010a) survey research indicates it is time for an independent, nationwide survey of teachers' text choices. We hope such a survey will be complemented by collection and analysis of additional corroborating data. Such data sources may include interviews with teachers and school district or state curriculum coordinators who can provide explanations of how text-choice decisions are made, observations of teaching techniques used with chosen texts, and documents created by schools, districts, and states in the process of text choice.

In addition, researchers should delve more deeply into the oft-repeated claim that reading literary classics is a necessary part of preparation for success in college. Much of the argument for the literary canon is based on this assumption, one for which we find little support in the literature. If college reading requires certain types of skills, how might those skills be best supported in high schools?

With the growing level of cultural and linguistic diversity in our country, we question the impetus to narrow curricular choices. One way to address concerns about high drop-out rates and to create more seamless transition to college and the workplace is to focus on student engagement by providing a wide array of text choices and to arrange those texts so increasing complexity is allied with increasing potential for academic growth. We are also concerned that, with the move toward standardization, many teachers will feel bound to use canonical books that may not reflect their students' needs. We believe the field should remain vigilant against policies that make text choices less inclusive for today's students.

REFERENCES

Achebe, C. (reprint, 1994). *Things fall apart.* New York, NY: Anchor.

ACT (2006). Reading between the lines: What the ACT reveals about college readiness in reading. Retrieved from http://www.act.org/research

Alcott, L. M. (reprint, 2011). *Little women.* Toronto, Canada: University of Toronto Libraries.

Applebee, A. N. (1989). *A study of book-length works taught in high school English programs.* (Report Number 12). Albany, NY: Center for the Learning and Teaching of Literature.

Association of Literary Scholars, Critics, and Writers (n.d.). *Publications.* Retrieved from http://www.bu.edu/literary/publications/

Brooks, W., & Hampton, G. (2005). Safe discussions rather than first hand encounters: Adolescents examine racism through one historical fiction text. *Children's Literature in Education, 36,* 83-98.

California Invasive Plant Council. (2010). Invasive plant inventory. Retrieved from http://www.cal-ipc.org/ip/inventory/index.php.

Carroll, L. (reprint, 2011). *Alice's adventures in Wonderland.* New York, NY: Superior Publishing.

Clarke, L. W. (2006). Power through voicing others: Girls' positioning of boys in literature discussion circles. *Journal of Literacy Research, 38,* 53-79.

Chaucer, G. (reprint, 2008). *The Canterbury tales.* New York, NY: Oxford University Press.

Common Core State Standards Initiative (2010). Retrieved from http://www.corestandards.org/the-standards.

Crocco, M. S., & Costigan, A. T. (2007). The narrowing of curriculum and pedagogy in the age of accountability. *Urban Education, 42,* 512-532.

Curtis, C. P. (1995). *The Watsons go to Birmingham—1963.* New York, NY: Delacorte Press.

Curtis, C. P. (1999). *Bud, not Buddy.* New York, NY: Delacorte Press.

Darling-Hammond, L. (2010/2011). Soaring systems: High flyers all have equitable funding, shared curriculum, and quality teaching. *American Educator, 20-23, 53.*

Dubb, C. R. (2007). Adolescent journeys: Finding female authority in "The Rain Catchers" and "The House on Mango Street." *Children's Literature in Education, 38,* 219-232.

Eckert, L. S. (2008). Bridging the pedagogical gap: Intersections between literary and reading theories in secondary and postsecondary literacy instruction. *Journal of Adolescent & Adult Literacy 52,* 110-118.

Finn Jr., C., & Petrilli, M. (2010, July 22, 2010). The common core curriculum: National education standards that even conservatives can love. Retrieved from http://www.nationalreview.com/articles/243517/common-core-curriculum-chester-e-finn-jr

Fitzgerald, F. S. (reprint, 1999). *The Great Gatsby.* New York, NY: Scribner.

Franzak, J. K. (2008). On the margins in a high-performing high school: Policy and the struggling reader. *Research in the Teaching of English, 42,* 466-505.

Galda, L., & Beach, R. (2004). Response to literature as cultural activity. In R. Ruddell and N. Unrau (Eds.), *Theoretical Models and Processes of Reading (5th ed., pp. 852-869).* Newark, DE: International Reading Association.

Golding, W. (reprint, 2003). *Lord of the flies.* New York, NY: Perigree.

Greenleaf, C. L., Schoenbach, R., Cziko, C., & Mueller, F. L. (2001). Apprenticing adolescent readers to academic literacy. *Harvard Educational Review, 71,* 79-130.

Hawthorne, N. (reprint, 2011). *The scarlet letter.* New York, NY: Tribeca.

Heitin, L. (2010). Study challenges "idiosyncratic" reading selections. *Education Week.* Retrieved from http://www.edweek.org/tm/articles/2010/10/28/alscwlitstudy.html

Hirsch Jr., E. D. (2010/2011). Beyond comprehension: We have yet to adopt a common core curriculum that builds knowledge grade by grade—but we need to. *American Educator, 30-36.*

Homer. (reprint, 2011). *The odyssey.* New York, NY: Simon & Brown.

Hurston, Z. N. (reprint, 2006). *Their eyes were watching God.* New York, NY: Harper.

Johnson, T. (2011). Nought 101 [Web log post]. Retrieved from http://blogs.burlingtonfreepress.com/highered/tag/sandra-stotsky/

McNair, J. C. (2008). "I May Be Crackin', But Um Fackin'": Racial humor in "The Watsons Go To Birmingham—1963." *Children's Literature in Education, 39,* 201-212.

King, M. L. K., Jr. (1963). *I have a dream* speech. Retrieved from http://www.mlkonline.net/dream.html.

Lee, H. (reprint, 1988). *To kill a mockingbird.* New York, NY: Popular Library.

Lee, V. E., & Smith, J. B. (1999). Social support and achievement for young adolescents in Chicago: The role of school academic press. *American Educational Research Journal, 36,* 907-945.

Leef, G. (2011). Sandra Stotsky on the erosion of educational standards [Online column]. Retrieved from http://www.nationalreview.com/phi-beta-cons/258555/sandra-stotsky-erosion-educational-standards-george-leef

Lesesne, T. (2010). *Reading ladders: Leading students from where they are to where we'd like them to be.* Portsmouth, NH: Heinemann.

Meyer, S. (2005). *Twilight.* New York, NY: Little Brown.

Meyer, S. (2008). *Breaking dawn.* New York, NY: Little Brown.

Miller, A. (reprint, 1976). *The crucible.* New York, NY: Penguin.

Moll, L., Amanti, C., Neff, D., & Gonzalez, N. (2005). Funds of Knowledge for Teaching: Using a Qualitative Approach to Connect Homes and Classrooms. In N. Gonzalez, L. Moll, & C. Amanti (Eds.), *Funds of Knowledge: Theorizing Practices in Households, Communities, and Classrooms* (pp. 71-87). Mahwah, NJ: Elrbaum.

Moll, L., & Gonzalez, N. (2004). Engaging life: A funds of knowledge approach to multicultural education. In J. Banks & C. Banks (Eds.), *Handbook of Research on Multicultural Education* (pp. 699-715). San Francisco, CA: Jossey-Bass.

Morgan, H. (2009). What every teacher needs to know to teach Native American students. *Multicultural Education, 16,* 10-12.

Morrell, E. (2000, April). *Curriculum and popular culture: Building bridges and making waves.* Unpublished paper presented at the annual meeting of the American Educational Research Association, New Orleans, LA.

Moss, B., & Bordelon, S. (2007). Preparing students for college-level reading and writing: Implementing a rhetoric and writing class in the senior year. *Reading Research and Instruction, 46,* 197-221.

National Council of Teachers of English/International Reading Association. (1996). *Standards for the English Language Arts.* Retrieved from *http://www.ncte.org/library/NCTEFiles/Resources/Books/Sample/StandardsDoc.pdf.*

Orwell, G. (1951). *Animal farm: A fairy story.* New York, NY: Penguin.

Pike, M. A. (2003). The canon in the classroom: Students' experiences of texts from other times. *Journal of Curriculum Studies, 35,* 355-370.

Schoenbach, R., Greenleaf, C., Cziko, C., & Hurwitz, L. (1999). *Reading for understanding: A guide to improving reading in middle and high school classrooms.* San Francisco, CA: Jossey-Bass.

Shakespeare, W. (reprint, 2010). *Julius Caesar.* New York, NY: CreateSpace.

Shakespeare, W. (reprint, 2010). *Macbeth.* New York: CreateSpace.

Simon, L. (2008). "I wouldn't choose it, but I don't regret reading it": Scaffolding students' engagement with complex texts. *Journal of Adolescent & Adult Literacy, 52,* 134-143.

Simpson, M. L., & Nist, S. L. (2000). An update on strategic learning: It's more than textbook reading strategies. *Journal of Adolescent and Adult Literacy, 43,* 528-541.

Sophocles. (reprint, 2005). *Antigone.* New York, NY: Prestwick House.

Stallworth, B. J., Gibbons, L., & Fauber, L. (2006). It's not on the list: An exploration of teachers' perspectives on using multicultural literature. *Journal of Adolescent and Adult Literacy, 49,* 478-489.

Steinbeck, J. (reprint, 2002). *Of mice and men.* New York, NY: Penguin.

Stotsky, S. (2010a). Literary study in grades 9, 10, and 11: A national survey. *Forum: A Publication of the Association of Literary Scholars, Critics, and Writers, 4.*

Stotsky, S. (2010b). *Letter to the Massachusetts Board of Elementary and Secondary Education.* Retrieved from http://www.doe.mass.edu/boe/docs/0710/item1.html?printscreen=yes&section=stotsky

Stotsky, S. (2009, September 22). More complex than simple English. The National Academic Standards: The first test. *The New York Times.* Retrieved from http://nytimes.com

Squire, J., & Applebee, R. (1968). *High school English instruction today: The national study of high school English programs.* Urbana, IL: National Council of Teachers of English.

Tatum, A. W. (2008a). Adolescents and texts: Overserved or underserved? *English Journal, 98,* 82-85.

Tatum, A. W. (2008b). Discussing texts with adolescents in culturally responsive ways. In K. A. Hinchman & H. K. Sheridan-Thomas (Eds.), *Best Practices in Adolescent Literacy Instruction* (pp. 3-19). New York, NY: Guilford.

Tatum, A. W. (2008c). Toward a more anatomically complete model of literacy instruction: A focus on African American male adolescents and texts. *Harvard Educational Review, 78,* 155-180.

Taylor, M. D. (2004). *Roll of thunder, hear my cry.* New York, NY: Puffin.

Tribunella, E. L. (2007). Institutionalizing "The Outsiders": YA literature, social class, and the American faith in education. *Children's Literature in Education, 38*, 87-101.

Twain, M. (reprint, 2011). *The adventures of Huckleberry Finn.* New York, NY: Simon and Brown.

U.S. Environmental Protection Agency/U.S. Department of Energy (2010). Recommended levels of insulation. Retrieved from http://www.energystar.gov/index.cfm?c=home_sealing.hm_improvement_insulation_table.

Wiesel, E. (reprint, 2006). *Night.* New York, NY: Hill and Wang.

Donald J. Leu
Neag Chair of Literacy and Technology
Neag School of Education
University of Connecticut

Section IV: New Literacies—
Enriching Research and Theory

The Internet and other information and communication technologies (ICTs) have generated new literacies, regularly redefining both literacy and life in the 21st century (Lankshear & Knobel, 2006). It is also important to understand that new literacies are not just new today; they are continuously new (Castek, Leu, Coiro, Gort, Henry, & Lima, 2008). New ICTs appear nearly every day, requiring additional literacies for their effective use. In theoretical terms, literacy has become a deictic construct (Leu, 2000; Warschauer, 2006), its meaning continually changing as the technologies for literacy change.

To study literacy as a deictic construct demands theoretical frameworks that adapt rapidly to the diverse nature of those changes, yet provide adequate stability to be useful. To that end, a dual-level New Literacies Theory (Leu, O'Byrne, Zawilinski, McVerry, & Everett-Cacopardo, 2009) is emerging.

New Literacies theory works on two levels: uppercase (New Literacies) and lowercase (new literacies). Multiple, lowercase theories explore either a specific area of new literacies, such as the social communicative transactions occurring with text messaging (e.g., Lewis & Fabos, 2005), a focused disciplinary base, such as the semiotics of multimodality in online media (e.g., Kress, 2003; 2010), or a particular research perspective (e.g., Street, 2003). Common findings across multiple lines of work inform the broader New Literacies theory. Thus, this approach to theory building believes that collaborative groups who bring diverse, multiple perspectives to problems will find the best solutions (Coiro, Knobel, Lankshear, & Leu, 2008; Page, 2007). This permits everyone to fully explore their unique, lowercase perspective of new literacies, as we build a larger, common, and uppercase New Literacies theory.

The articles in this section reflect the rapidly changing and diverse work currently taking place at the lowercase level. Consistent with New Literacies theory, you will find that most employ multiple theoretical frameworks to inform their research.

The new literacies of online reading comprehension (Coiro, 2003; Leu, Kinzer, Coiro, & Cammack, 2004) is one lower-case theory. Previous work has come from more of a cognitive perspective, trying to understand the skills, strategies, and dispositions required for effective online reading comprehension (Castek, 2008; Coiro & Dobler, 2007; Henry, 2007). Coiro, Castek, & Guzniczak advance this area in important ways by exploring online reading comprehension from a social interaction perspective. This study helps us to better understand how two adolescent readers engage in meaning construction as they read online together, weaving together offline reading strategies as well as additional online reading strategies. It also supports findings from other work showing the benefits to learning when two students collaboratively read online together and discuss their reading within an argumentation framework (Kiili, Laurinen, & Marttunen, 2010; Marttunen & Laurinen, 2007).

In a study of online discussion, Lee et al. bring an important new theoretical construct to the table, showing how resistance positively affects learning in online discussions. The authors define resistance as, "...the struggles that a learner experiences when encountering new ideas that are not easily aligned with prior beliefs or that seem to contradict cherished ideas, and yet that eventuate in a deeper understanding." This analysis of online discussion among graduate students demonstrates how frequently resistance occurs when cultural norms support challenging ideas in constructive ways. It also shows how resistance is an important catalyst for learning.

Miller analyzes multimodal literacies during video composing. Using multiple theoretical lenses based on Bakhtin (1981), Kress (2010), and Lankshear & Knobel (2006), this study documents the outcomes of multi-modal video composing from students' perspectives. It shows how transmediation, or the translation of meaning from one sign system (literary texts) to another (multimodal video), generates a richer understanding, including new stances toward interpreting print texts.

The preceding studies analyzed students engaged in new literacies. They point to important changes in the classroom. How knowledgeable are undergraduate teachers in preparation with using online new literacies? Kim, McTigue, & Helfeldt's study found that, "…current education underclassmen possess neither sufficient awareness nor sufficient mastery of new literacies skills necessary for them to teach these skills to their future students." This work suggests that we have important opportunities to expand the teacher education curriculum in the years ahead.

There is an important lack of lowercase new literacies research and theory in family contexts. Fortunately, intriguing studies are just appearing, such as the one you will read by Lewis. This shows how an African American mother used digital tools to develop awareness, agency, and apprenticeship at home, creating important new relationships and social practices with her sons. Lewis combines several theoretical lenses to inform this work: New Literacies Studies, digital literacies, and multimodality.

Enjoy this section. As you read, you will encounter the diverse ways in which each of these investigations into lower-case new literacies is helping us to build a richer, more complex, and more complete understanding of the new literacies that are shaping our lives and, in turn, are being shaped by them. Together, this research helps us to build a broader, more diverse, and more complete, New Literacies theory.

REFERENCES

Bakhtin, M. M. (1981). *The dialogic imagination: Four essays by M. M. Bakhtin.* (M. Holquist, Ed.; C. Emerson & M. Holquist, Trans.). Austin, TX: University of Texas Press.

Castek, J. (2008). *How do 4th and 5th grade students acquire the new literacies of online reading comprehension? Exploring the contexts that facilitate learning.* Unpublished doctoral dissertation, University of Connecticut.

Castek, J., Leu, D. J., Jr., Coiro, J., Gort, M., Henry, L. A., & Lima, C. (2008). Developing new literacies among multilingual learners in the elementary grades. In L. Parker (Ed.) *Technology-mediated learning environments for young English learners: Connections in and out of school.* (111-153). Mahwah, NJ. Lawrence Erlbaum Associates.

Coiro, J. (2003). Reading Comprehension on the Internet: Expanding our understanding of reading comprehension to encompass new literacies. *The Reading Teacher, 56,* 458-464.

Coiro, J., & Dobler, E. (2007). Exploring the online reading comprehension strategies used by sixth-grade skilled readers to search for and locate information on the Internet. *Reading Research Quarterly, 42,* 214–257.

Coiro, J., Knobel, M., Lankshear, C., & Leu, D. J. (2008). Central issues in new literacies and new literacies research. In J. Coiro, M. Knobel, C. Lankshear, & D. J. Leu. (Eds.), *The handbook of research in new literacies* (pp. 1–22). Mahwah, NJ: Lawrence Erlbaum.

Henry, L. (2006). SEARCHing for an answer: The critical role of new literacies while reading on the Internet. *Reading Teacher, 59,* 614–627.

Kiili, C., Laurinen, L., & Marttunen, M. (2010). Working on understanding: Collaborative reading patterns on the Web. Paper presented at the Annual Meeting of the American Educational Research Association 2010, Denver.

Kress, G. (2003). *Literacy in the new media age.* London, UK: Routledge.

Kress, G. (2010). *Multimodality: A social semiotic approach to contemporary communication.* New York, NY: Routledge.

Lankshear, C., & Knobel, M. (2006). *New literacies* (2nd ed.). Maidenhead, UK: Open University Press.

Lewis, C., & Fabos, B. (2005). Instant messaging, literacies, and social identities. *Reading Research Quarterly, 40*, 470–501.

Leu, D. J. (2000). Literacy and technology: Deictic consequences for literacy education in an information age. In M. L. Kamil, P. B. Mosenthal, P. D. Pearson, & R. Barr (Eds.), *Handbook of reading research* (Vol. 3, pp. 743–770). Mahwah, NJ: Lawrence Erlbaum.

Leu, D. J., Everett-Cacopardo, H., Zawilinski, Z., McVerry, J. G., & O'Byrne, W. I. (in press). In C. A. Chapelle (Ed.), *The encyclopedia of applied linguistics.* Oxford, UK: Wiley-Blackwell.

Leu, D. J., Jr., Kinzer, C. K., Coiro, J., & Cammack, D. (2004). Toward a theory of new literacies emerging from the Internet and other information and communication technologies. In R. B. Ruddell & N. Unrau (Eds.), *Theoretical models and processes of reading* (5th ed., pp. 1568–1611). Newark, DE: International Reading Association. Retrieved from http://www.readingonline.org/ newliteracies/ lit_index.asp?HREF=/newliteracies/leu

Leu, D. J., O'Byrne, W. I., Zawilinski, L., McVerry, J. G., & Everett-Cacopardo, H. (2009). Leu, Leu, D. J., O'Byrne, W. I., Zawilinski, L., McVerry, J. G., & Everett-Cacopardo, H. (2009). Expanding the new literacies conversation. *Educational Researcher, 38,* 264-269.

Marttunen, M., & Laurinen, L. (2007). Collaborative learning through chat discussions and argument diagrams in secondary school. *Journal of Research on Technology in Education, 40*(1), 109–126.

Street, B. (2003). What's new in new literacy studies? *Current Issues in Comparative Education, 5*(2), 1–14.

Warschauer, M. (2006). Literacy and technology: Bridging the divide. In D. Gibbs and K.-L. Krause (Eds.), *Cyberlines 2: Languages and cultures of the Internet* (pp. 163-174). Albert Park, Australia: James Nicholas.

Uncovering Online Reading Comprehension Processes: Two Adolescents Reading Independently and Collaboratively on the Internet

Julie Coiro
University of Rhode Island

Jill Castek
University of California, Berkeley

Lizabeth Guzniczak
Oakland University

New technologies are constantly changing the landscapes of reading and writing (Coiro, Knobel, Lankshear, & Leu, 2008; Dalton & Proctor, 2008). In addition, transactions and social interactions that facilitate readers' comprehension of print (e.g., Almasi, McKeown, & Beck, 1996; Rosenblatt, 1998) have begun to take on new meaning in complex, online environments (Selfe & Hawisher, 2004; Wyatt-Smith & Elkins, 2008). To learn how individuals are meeting the demands of a 21st century knowledge society, research in a variety of disciplines has shifted attention away from information recall and transmission and toward the construction of personal understanding and co-construction of new knowledge (Assessment and Teaching of 21st Century Skills, 2008; Bransford, Brown, & Cocking, 2000; Wells, 2007). This study seeks to uncover the nature of constructive meaning-making processes as revealed by two skilled adolescent readers engaged in both independent and collaborative online reading situations.

THEORETICAL FRAMEWORKS

We approached this work through three theoretical lenses that conceptualize reading in terms of overlapping dimensions of individual cognition and social interaction. First, our conceptions of reading comprehension are grounded in constructivist theories that posit accomplished readers are actively constructive as they interact with and respond to information in text while reading for a particular purpose (see Kintsch, 1988; Pressley & Afflerbach, 1995; Rosenblatt, 1998). Accordingly, expert readers use a range of strategic cognitive processes to select, organize, connect, and evaluate what they read. More recently, Alexander and Fox (2004) reported that the emergence of a greater range of text types introduces additional dimensions to this set of cognitive reading strategies that continue to reshape perceptions of readers and the reading process. To adequately describe these new forms of reading, Afflerbach and Cho (2008) highlighted the need for additional research that explicitly connects patterns of online reading strategy use to existing models of reading and thinking. Thus, the present study seeks to build on Pressley and Afflerbach's (1995) compendium of constructively responsive reading comprehension strategies with an expanded framework that incorporates processes drawn from contemporary think-aloud studies of online reading comprehension (e.g., Coiro & Dobler, 2007; Schmar-Dobler, 2003; Zhang & Duke, 2008).

Secondly, this study was informed by a new literacies perspective of online reading comprehension that frames reading comprehension as a web-based inquiry process involving skills and strategies for locating, evaluating, synthesizing, and communicating information on the Internet (Leu, Kinzer, Coiro, & Cammack, 2004; Leu, O'Byrne, Zawilinski, McVerry, & Everett-Cacopardo, 2009). Previously developed models of the cognitive reading strategies needed to comprehend printed texts do not sufficiently characterize the complex and unique processes required to locate, evaluate, and comprehend information found on the Internet (see Coiro [in press]; Hartman, Morsink, & Zheng, 2010).

Third, we drew from sociocultural perspectives that view text comprehension as a consequence of working as part of a social group (Schwandt, 1994; Mercer, 1995). Accordingly, we approached this study with the assumption that social interaction contributes to individual development (Vygotsky, 1978) and, further, that technology, as a cultural artifact, can play a key role in mediating social activity (Crafton & Burke, 1994; Wells, 2007). Consequently, this study seeks to examine how two students employed online reading comprehension processes first, independently, and later as partners, as they read and responded to two inquiry prompts.

LITERATURE REVIEW

Reading Comprehension and Verbal Protocol Analysis

In the 1980s and 1990s, much attention was paid to analyzing think-aloud protocols as readers interacted with offline (or printed) texts (see Ericsson & Simon, 1993). As a result, contemporary research and instruction in reading comprehension is grounded in a robust understanding of how skilled readers integrate cognitive reading processes, self-regulated monitoring strategies, and personal knowledge as they construct meaning from offline texts (see Pressley & Afflerbach, 1995; Kucan & Beck, 1997). However, this work was based on studies conducted before widespread Internet use and is not informed by research that characterizes the nature of online reading comprehension. In fact, Afflerbach and Cho (2008) surmised that there likely exist specific strategies critical for successful online reading that have yet to be widely investigated or documented. Thus, it becomes important to update models of reading comprehension to encompass results from think-aloud protocols as readers interact with complex online texts for a range of purposes.

Individual Reading Patterns in Online Environments

Findings from a handful of think-aloud studies of online reading comprehension have emerged to inform work in this area. For example, Schmar-Dobler (2003) and Coiro and Dobler (2007) employed concurrent think-aloud protocols and retrospective interviews with adolescent readers and revealed similar and more complex strategies involving navigation, prior knowledge sources, inferential reasoning strategies, and self-regulated reading processes.

More recently, in an effort to update Pressley and Afflerbach's (1995) model of constructively responsive reading strategies used by accomplished readers when reading offline text, Afflerbach and Cho (2008) synthesized results of 46 think-aloud protocol studies focused on reading strategy use during intertextual, hypertext, and Internet reading. Their analyses revealed many overlaps with offline reading comprehension, but the authors also proposed an entirely new category of online reading processes, *realizing and constructing potential texts to read*. This category represents "accomplished readers' strategic approaches to reducing uncertainty, determining the most appropriate reading path, and managing a shifting problem space" (p. 212).

Results of two recent think-aloud studies with skilled adults (Zhang & Duke 2008) and adolescent readers (Cho, 2010) specified a set of unique reading strategies that might very well fit in this new category. These reading strategies included generating digital queries; applying prior knowledge of search engines and websites; monitoring one's reading pathways and speed in relation to his/her online reading purposes; determining a suitable reading order; and constructing individualized paths to accessing useful resources. The present study seeks to characterize additional processes of reading comprehension that adolescent readers use as they read online and formulate a response to two researcher-posed information problems.

Collaborative Reading Patterns in Online Environments

In addition to understanding how individuals construct their personal understanding of complex texts, national standards indicate that informal academic discussions, such as those that take place when students collaborate to answer questions, build understanding, and solve problems, are an important focus of the next generation of language arts, literacy, and content area standards (Common Core State Standards Initiative, 2010). Since small groups of students are often assigned to work together to complete school-based inquiry tasks (Smith, Sheppard, Johnson, & Johnson, 2005), it makes sense to learn more about how collaborative online reading situations may influence strategy use, comprehension, and knowledge construction.

Researchers have used think-aloud protocols during paired or small-group reading to explore relationships between social interaction and offline reading (Anderson & Roit, 1993), online reading (Castek, 2008; Dillenbourg & Schneider, 1995) or online discussions (Kim, Anderson, Nguyen-Jahiel, & Archodidou, 2007). However, to our knowledge, no studies have applied Pressley and Afflerbach's (1995) model of constructively responsive reading for individual readers to consider the extent to which these same comprehension processes play out when two adolescents work as partners to solve an inquiry problem online. Consequently, to add to our understanding of constructively responsive reading strategies observed while reading offline texts, the present study sought to explore how two adolescent readers constructed and co-constructed meaning and formulated responses to inquiry tasks, as they first worked online independently, and then with a partner.

METHODS

Participants

Participants for this case study (Yin, 2009) were purposely selected (Merriam, 2009) from a seventh-grade science classroom of 35 students located in a suburban public school in the midwestern United States. Demographics for this middle school population were 80% Caucasian, 12.5% Asian, 4% African American, 2.5% Hispanic, and 2% multi-racial. Initially, twelve students volunteered to participate in the study. From this sample, the teacher was asked to recommend those students with strong academic histories and strong verbal skills in order to achieve rich verbal protocols. Of the twelve volunteers, the teacher recommended six students (four girls and two boys) as strong academic achievers who also possessed strong verbal skills; these students were likely to provide insights into the types of constructively responsive strategies about which we were interested in learning. This preliminary study reports our analysis of data from two of these six students, Abby and Starfish (pseudonyms).

At the time of the study, Abby typically received As or Bs in all academic areas and her standardized reading and writing scores on the 6th grade state achievement test placed her at the state's Advanced level (or Level 1) in offline reading ability. Abby's science teacher described her as highly verbal, well organized, and a good listener. Starfish was also considered a high achiever in all curriculum areas and, like Abby, was classified as Level 1 on the 6th grade state standardized test for reading and writing. Starfish's teacher considered her to be quiet and studious, yet verbally expressive when engaged in academic tasks.

Data Collection

Each student met with a researcher outside of class in the school library to participate in two video-recorded online reading sessions, one individual and one collaborative, in which data were collected using a think-aloud protocol (Pressley & Afflerbach, 1995). Camtasia screen capture software (www.camtasia.com) was used to simultaneously record all on-screen reading actions, verbal think-alouds, and verbal/non-verbal interactions with the text and each other (e.g., nodding, smiling, expressing confusion with facial gestures). For both sessions, a frontal view of each reader was also captured with a camera mounted on the computer (see Figure 1).

In the first online reading session, Abby and Starfish each worked individually (and at separate times) to answer the following prompt: *Should land be set aside to preserve the leatherback sea turtle?* Prior to the session, the researcher read a brief set of directions about how to think aloud while completing the task. Then, students were instructed to think aloud while they independently researched information online that would allow them to make an informed response to the prompt. Immediately after the reading session, each student participated in a short reflective interview about what they learned.

On a subsequent day, Abby and Starfish were paired together to complete a collaborative online task in which they were asked to research a topic, and come to consensus about, a second prompt: *What caused the downfall of the ancient Mayan civilization?* Again, the researcher explained the procedures for thinking

Figure 1. Screenshot of Abby and Starfish's Camtasia Screen Capture Recording that Documented Their Onscreen Reading Actions, Verbal Think-Alouds, and Non-Verbal Interactions with the Text

aloud and responding to the prompt. Students were reminded to think aloud as they collaboratively worked to comprehend the range of information they encountered online and construct a response. After completing the collaborative prompt, Abby and Starfish jointly participated in a short reflective interview about what they learned. No time limit was given in either online reading session, but Abby and Starfish's individual reading sessions lasted 33 minutes and 32.5 minutes, respectively, while their collaborative reading session lasted 27.5 minutes.

For all of the data collection, one researcher was always present. Most of the time, the students were able to think aloud as they completed the tasks with little prompting from the researcher. However, occasionally, when more clarification was needed, or when a student seemed confused, the researcher intervened with an open-ended question such as "Tell me what you are thinking now" or "What do you think that means?" Responses to researcher-prompted questions of this sort were coded separately, and were not included in counts of spontaneous (e.g., unprompted) reading comprehension strategies we observed the two readers using.

Data Analysis

Analysis took place in several phases. Initially, we independently reviewed the Camtasia screen-capture recordings of Starfish and Abby's individual reading sessions to get a general sense of how each reader completed the online reading prompt about leatherback sea turtles. Next, transcripts were created that documented all verbal responses and online reading actions (e.g., scrolling, typing search terms, clicking on hyperlinks) made by the students during each session. Because each reader was free to explore any location on the Internet, the website address and actual web text was inserted into the transcript. This provided a way to connect verbal responses, and any relevant non-verbal actions, to particular sections of online text students read. Finally, all verbal responses and associated reading actions were parsed into individual semantic units (Aviv, 2001), which were defined as any discrete and meaningful response to the text.

Once the transcripts were complete, data were analyzed using an abductive reasoning approach (Morgan, 2007). Analysis of the individual reading sessions began with a theory-driven, deductive coding structure derived from a combination of constructively responsive reading strategies observed in verbal protocols of printed text comprehension (Pressley & Afflerbach, 1995) and additional reading strategies observed in protocols of online text comprehension (see Afflerbach & Cho, 2008, 2009; Coiro & Dobler, 2007; Schmar-Dobler 2003; Zhang & Duke, 2008). Then as new patterns emerged, data-driven inductive procedures (Bogdan & Biklen, 2003) were used to revise the coding scheme in order to more accurately represent the set of online reading processes we observed in the present study.

Initially, all three researchers analyzed transcriptions for Abby's individual session to assess the validity of the coding scheme. Researchers met to further refine categories and code definitions, and adjust the coding scheme terminology. Then, each researcher independently coded the transcript from Starfish's individual session. The researchers agreed on 91% of the 172 codes for Abby at the category level (and 82% at the sub-process level) and on 94% of the 175 codes for Starfish at the category level (and 89% at the sub-process level), which demonstrated adequate reliability (Krippendorff, 2003). The resulting coding system of constructively responsive online reading comprehension strategies (see Appendix A) consisted of 56 sub-processes (observed in verbal responses and/or performance indicators). These codes were organized under 11 categories of reading comprehension processes and three broad clusters (before-, during-, and after-reading processes). These sub-processes included strategies similar to those observed in studies of offline text comprehension (as denoted by superscript 1 in Appendix A) and additional strategies observed in online reading contexts (as denoted by superscript 2). Two additional sub-processes, observed when students responded to researcher questions or comments, were categorized as "Confirming or Clarifying." The inclusion of this extra coding category reflects Mercer's (1995) notion that dialogues between the researcher and participant can strongly influence a participant's performance in tasks, and thus, should be treated as "part of the object of study" (p. 3) (see also Elbers, 1991).

Next, the complex coding scheme of constructively responsive online reading strategies was applied to the transcriptions from the collaborative reading task, with researchers coding each partner's individual meaning units using the same process used to code students' individual reading sessions. In this phase, researchers agreed on 92% of the 162 codes at the category level and 83% at the sub-process level. In the last phase of analysis, we examined the quantity of each student's contributions and the nature of what they contributed in both the individual and collaborative reading sessions. We sought to explore whether student interactions within a collaborative dyad would mirror the patterns identified during individual online reading or if different patterns would emerge.

FINDINGS

Constructively Responsive Reading Processes Observed in the Individual Reading Task

Abby. According to the coding categories in Appendix A, Abby's protocol revealed that her predominant interactions with the text (71%) involved determining important ideas (63%) and evaluating online text (8%). Abby used her ability to read aloud, read silently, and paraphrase key ideas in 110 of her total 172 interactions. In addition, Abby made 14 evaluative statements, or reactions, to the text as she read. The protocol excerpt that follows reveals Abby's ability to determine what is important about sea turtles and personally respond to these ideas with evaluative comments such as "this is interesting" and "just strange":

> [*Reading silently where text says: "HABITAT: The leatherback is the most pelagic of the sea turtles. Adult females require sandy nesting beaches backed with vegetation and sloped sufficiently so the crawl to dry sand is not too far. The preferred beaches have proximity to deep water and generally rough seas."*] This is interesting ... the habitat are sandy nesting beaches with vegetation, and their preferred beaches are to have deep waters and generally rough seas. [*Looks toward researcher*] That's just strange ... because they just lay their eggs on the beaches and then just have time to go to the water.

As depicted in Figure 2, Abby's online reading patterns showed evidence of thoughtful integration processes. She expressed important ideas in familiar terms in order to draw a conclusion about what she read. For example, while silently reading a lengthy section under the heading "Conservation Accomplishments" which detailed a range of publications (e.g., booklets, videos, posters, and newsletters) produced by Greenpeace, the National Audubon society, and others, Abby interpreted the text and concluded:

> So, the government is like trying to help the turtles. [*Reads silently for 10 seconds,*

Figure 2. Abby's Frequency of Constructively Responsive Online Reading Strategy Use During the Individual Reading Session

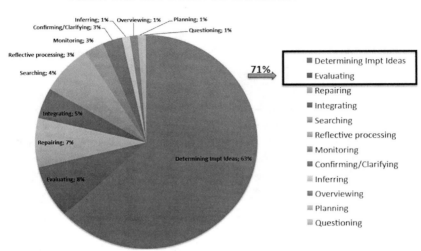

ABBY: THE THOUGHTFUL GATHERER

Inferring; 1% Overviewing; 1% Planning; 1%
Confirming/Clarifying; 3% Questioning; 1%
Monitoring; 3%
Reflective processing; 3%
Searching; 4%
Integrating; 5%
Repairing; 7%
Determining Impt Ideas; 63%
Evaluating; 8%

71%

- Determining Impt Ideas
- Evaluating
- Repairing
- Integrating
- Searching
- Reflective processing
- Monitoring
- Confirming/Clarifying
- Inferring
- Overviewing
- Planning
- Questioning

eventually thinking aloud as she reads/skims] They have printed more materials about the sea turtle so we can learn more about them and what works and everything. [*Reads silently for 15 seconds*] Now the turtles have a great deal of attention, so...they are helping them out—now the general public is aware and they are helping them.

Based on Abby's responsive patterns of gathering, processing, and evaluating online text, we described her as "The Thoughtful Gatherer." Notably, while Abby spent 76% of her individual reading time determining, evaluating, and integrating important ideas (typically conceived as offline reading processes), an additional 15% of her online processing involved searching, monitoring her reading pathways, and repairing those pathways when needed. An excerpt that illustrates these processes is included below, wherein Abby generated an initial search, carefully scrutinized a set of Google search results, determined whether certain parts of a text were relevant to her purpose, and then used this information to repair the direction of her hyperlink selections before she finally settled on a webpage relevant to the task:

Abby: I'm going to type in Leatherback Sea Turtles [*Generates her search terms, clicks the search button, and scrutinizes the returned list of search results. After scanning a descriptive annotation that led to a "Sea Turtle Factsheet"*]...No, cuz that's [*the information*] on all of them [*the other websites*]. [*Shifting her attention to a different search result, following the link, scanning the website for a second, and then quickly clicking the back button*]

Researcher: Okay, so you decided not to go there either.

Abby: No...because it had a bunch of other turtles too [*suggesting that the website was not specific to leatherback sea turtles. Clicks the back button to return to* search results list and selects the third link] Let's see here…ok [begins skimming new website under section about Sea Turtle Habitats].

Starfish. If Abby was "The Thoughtful Gatherer" when she independently read on the Internet, then Starfish might best be described as "The Aesthetic Summarizer." Of Starfish's 175 total responses, 77% of the codes related to determining important ideas (50%), integrating (16%), and evaluating (11%) online text (see Figure 3). However, Starfish often responded to information in an aesthetic manner, expressing concern and empathy as she read. Instances when Starfish reacted emotionally as she read and integrated important details about the nesting practices and lifespan of leatherback sea turtles are denoted in bold and underlined:

Starfish: [*reading aloud*]: Only about one in a thousand leatherback hatchlings survive to adulthood. **That's kind of sad.** [*paraphrasing*] Eggs—they die because of humans. [*comments outside of reading—appears to be considering the prompt*]: So we should leave them alone so that they don't die because they are getting extinct because we are killing them. We should leave them on land so we can get more sea turtles. [*paraphrasing*]: Eggs are taken by humans by their nest…[*paraphrasing*]: Many leatherbacks are victims of fishing lines and nets, or they are hit by boats. **That's pretty sad too.** [*paraphrasing*]: Eleven pounds of plastic in their stomach from falling in the water. **That's a lot! That's kind of really sad that we're doing that to them.** There is all this plastic.

Researcher: Do you think that's a problem for them?

Starfish: Yeah. Well, the more plastic they get, the closer they are to dying, and that's when they're getting a lower population and now they are endangered… **That's not good.**

Figure 3. Starfish's Frequency of Constructively Responsive Online Reading Strategy Use During the Individual Reading Session

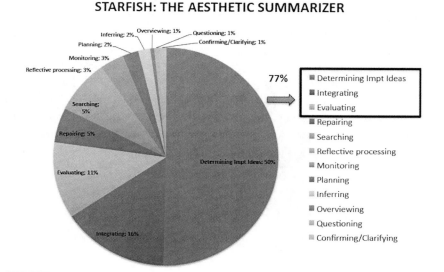

Another responsive reading pattern that characterized Starfish's use of integration strategies was observed when she stopped reading, summarized key points from what she read across multiple sections of text, and then constructed an interpretation from that summary. Evidence of this strategic integration is apparent in the protocol excerpt above when she states, "the more plastic they get, the closer they are to dying." In that instance, Starfish appeared to summarize in her own words a series of cause and effect relationships (informed by what she read). In short, she gathered that growing amounts of plastic in the ocean increases the risk of sea turtles dying, which in turn decreases the sea turtle population in the world, and ultimately causes them to be endangered. Frequently, as illustrated here, Starfish reacted emotionally to her constructed summary and expressed a personal evaluation (e.g. "that's not good"). Hence, our characterization of Starfish as "The Aesthetic Summarizer."

Similar to Abby, Starfish spent an additional 13% of her online reading time searching, monitoring, and repairing her understanding of and pathways through online text. Evidence of how Starfish monitored and repaired her comprehension as she negotiated multiple online texts was revealed in a combination of online reading actions and think-aloud verbalizations as illustrated in the following two examples:

- [*Skimming her school's library website for a link to a search engine*]: I can't find the page with Google on it—I'll just type it [the address] in.
- [*Pausing after revisiting a section of text and reading silently*]: I'm kind of like, rereading all of this stuff… I'm wondering about what kinds of things we can do to help them other than just opening up some shoreline for them…Oh, here we go [*sees the heading "Conversation Efforts" and begins reading silently*].

Student responses to the individual reading prompt. In the analysis of students' online reading processes, responses to the prompt were also considered. These responses were formulated to answer the prompt: *Should land be set aside to preserve the leatherback sea turtle?* In Abby's summary, she presented an informed decision, which included several details from her reading to support her reasoning: "I think that, right now, we actually should have a private beach for the turtles. Um…If they just lay it on the beaches, then other people will kick the eggs, and the fisherman will eat them and everything. But if we just have a private beach like just for the turtles, no one would go on it and then the eggs could hatch, and there would be a lot more of them."

Compared to Abby, Starfish provided a much shorter summary, but she successfully addressed the question and offered two pieces of evidence to support her reasoning: "Yes, land should be set aside, because it should be set aside away from…so they can be protected from animals, and predators, so they could have a perfect place to live." Interestingly, Starfish's response lacked the emotional complexity her thinking revealed as she read online. This suggests to researchers and educators alike the importance of examining readers' during-reading processes for richer evidence of their comprehension.

Constructively Responsive Reading Processes Observed in the Collaborative Reading Task

Abby. When reading collaboratively with Starfish to determine what caused the downfall of the Mayan Civilization, Abby spoke 51% of the time in a total of 82 oral statements (see Table 1). She employed processes from all 12 categories of online reading strategies identified in our coding scheme, with instances of integrating being coded most frequently (32% of her total contributions).

Two instances where Abby *integrated*, or *synthesized* ideas from different parts of the text and interpreted them in relation to the task were observed as follows.

After reading together from a website about a possible plague that caused disease, and then paraphrasing information about how the Mayan culture thrived until the Spanish monarchy took over, Abby interpreted: "They [the Spanish] probably killed a lot, so that would be another reason of the downfall." Similarly, while skimming information at a website about how the Mayans made sacrificial killings to their gods, Abby shared with Starfish her interpretation in relation to their efforts to determine what caused the downfall of the Mayan civilization: "It [human sacrifices] didn't lead to it, but it contributed to it."

The second more frequently coded strategy in Abby's transcript was *determining important ideas*. Twenty three percent of Abby's total contributions were coded in this way and involved skimming portions of text and paraphrasing orally to her partner. An additional 9% of Abby's comments in the paired reading session involved confirming/clarifying statements for which she confirmed her partner's thinking with comments such as "Yeah" or "I think so" or clarified her own thinking by responding to her partner's question. For example, Starfish asked, "Now where is Guatemala?" and Abby replied, "That's by Mexico, isn't it?"

Other common strategies that Abby used included *evaluating*, or reacting to the text (e.g., "Oh, that's cool!" after viewing a photo of the Mayan ruins), and *monitoring* the relevance of a text in relation to their purpose (e.g., I'm thinking this isn't very helpful). Both processes comprised 7% of Abby's total coded segments. The remaining categories of strategies that Abby used in the paired reading session are summarized in Table 1.

Starfish. When reading collaboratively with Abby, Starfish spoke 49% of the time, making a total of 81 oral statements. She employed 11 of the 12 categories of online reading strategies and, like Abby, her most frequently observed strategy was *integrating* (31% of her total contributions

Table 1. Distribution of Constructively Responsive Online Reading Strategy Use by Category, Reading Session, and Participant

Strategy Coding Category	Individual Reading Sessions		Paired Reading Session		
	Abby (Individual)	Starfish (Individual)	Abby (Paired)	Starfish (Paired)	TOTAL (Paired)
Planning	1 (1%)	4 (2%)	2 (2%)	2 (2%)	4 (2%)
Searching	7 (4%)	8 (5%)	2 (2%)	2 (2%)	4 (2%)
Overviewing	1 (1%)	1 (1%)	1 (1%)	0 (0%)	0 (0%)
Determining Impt. Ideas	110 (64%)	88 (50%)	19 (23%)	11 (14%)	30 (18%)
Inferring	1 (1%)	4 (2%)	3 (4%)	2 (2%)	5 (3%)
Integrating	8 (5%)	27 (16%)	26 (32%)	25 (31%)	51 (31%)
Questioning	1 (1%)	1 (1%)	3 (4%)	4 (5%)	7 (4%)
Evaluating	14 (8%)	20 (11%)	6 (7%)	2 (2%)	8 (5%)
Monitoring	5 (3%)	6 (3%)	6 (7%)	3 (4%)	9 (6%)
Repairing	13 (8%)	9 (5%)	3 (4%)	5 (6%)	8 (5%)
Reflective Processing	6 (3%)	6 (4%)	4 (5%)	12 (15%)	16 (10%)
Confirming/Clarifying	5 (3%)	2 (1%)	7 (9%)	13 (16%)	21 (13%)
TOTAL	172 (100%)	175 (100%)	82 (100%)	81 (100%)	163 (100%)

to the dialogue). A coded segment demonstrating Starfish's ability to integrate ideas from different parts of the text to address the task follows.

Starfish: [*reading aloud: "The stone carvings at some sites show ball players with severed human heads dangling from their belts. Do these carvings depict what happened to the losers of a war? What is known is that the ball was a metaphor for the movement of the sun, and by extension also of the moon and stars."*] So, the movement of the sun—whenever the sun moved, they had to sacrifice a person.

Starfish was observed validating Abby's thinking during their collaboration 16% of the time. Statements were coded as validating, for example, when Starfish confirmed Abby's confusion with hyperlinks that led to an irrelevant advertisement ("Yeah, it does things like that sometimes") or when she validated an interpretation Abby made about the text ("Right, like it's coming from the earth").

Reflective processing was another strategy Starfish used frequently, 15% of the time. This strategy was coded when Starfish, together with Abby, deliberately paused to reflect, regroup, and summarize the information they collected so far. In essence, Starfish often paused to create a cumulative list of factors (across multiple websites) that contributed to the downfall of the Mayan civilization. This was demonstrated by comments such as: "So, let's go over this again. Okay…we have droughts, and disease, and other, and the Spanish, and erosion."

Also like Abby, Starfish was frequently observed *determining important ideas* (14% of her total responses). For example, Starfish silently read a paragraph and then paraphrased the most important information that related to the dyad's overall goal: "It [the Mayan Civilization] collapsed in the 9th century …and the towns and cities were abandoned."

When Abby and Starfish worked collaboratively to gather information about the Ancient Mayan civilization task, they built on one another's ideas, and would often integrate, or come to a shared understanding together, in ways that seemed to help them stay focused on their purpose. The excerpt that follows reveals the social nature of their collaborative reading activity, where confirmatory statements were made as part of the spontaneous dialogue between the two readers.

Abby: Oh, okay [*she emphatically reads aloud*]. The reason for the downfall of the Maya is unknown. However there are several possible reasons for their downfall including soil exhaustion, water loss, and erosion…

Starfish: [*smiles proudly*] It's kind of like the dinosaur!

Abby: [*smiles and shakes head…unintelligible*] I wouldn't have thought of that.

Starfish: [*continues reading*] Other possibilities include catastrophes such as earthquakes and hurricanes, and disease.

Looking across Abby and Starfish's overall contributions to collaborative reading in Table 1, Abby appeared to take the lead when it came to *interpreting* and Starfish appeared to take responsibility for *summarizing* what they had learned and determining whether more information was needed to address the prompt. While both of these strategies were crucial to meeting their final goal, their conscious or unconscious division of responsibilities allowed each student to focus on different aspects and contribute something vitally important, yet different than their partner. In this way, their collaboration was mutually beneficial.

Student responses to the collaborative reading prompt. The prompt did not have one clear or obvious correct answer, yet the students persisted in collecting information from multiple websites to address it. As Abby and Starfish navigated across websites, they co-constructed a list of contributing factors. When asked to sum up what caused the downfall of the Mayan civilization, they both shared what they had learned in an informed and confident manner.

Abby:	We think a lot of things contributed to it. There wasn't just one thing. We think that disease, erosion, the Spanish civilization
Starfish:	[*Starfish interrupts, to say some of the list*] civilization killed it, and like droughts, and like other natural disasters like hurricanes, earthquakes.
Abby:	and also their religion, they sacrificed one person every day so that took a lot of them.
Starfish:	Yeah, and water and food shortages.
Researcher:	So you felt it wasn't just one thing—that there were a lot of contributing factors.

Starfish and Abby together: Yeah.

In contrast to the responses these students offered in response to the individual prompt, which were less complete, their collective response to the collaborative prompt was more thorough and detailed. This difference in quality suggests that collaboration during online reading may have led to a comprehensive understanding and supported recall of pertinent details.

Reflective interview. Though our findings suggested there might have been some positive benefits associated with reading online collaboratively, we felt it important to collect students' perspectives to come to a richer understanding. During the reflective interview, following the collaborative prompt, students were asked, "How was working in pairs different from working by yourself? What do you think was similar and what do you think was different?" Both students indicated that working together was more beneficial and made the task easier to accomplish.

Abby:	I think it was easier, because you wouldn't have to remind me because you'd [*indicating Starfish*] say it, so then I'd...
Starfish:	I couldn't have remembered all of those things.
Abby:	Yeah, and like, I didn't remember the sacrifice and then she said it.

DISCUSSION AND NEXT STEPS

Results of our analyses revealed that in both the individual and paired online reading sessions, two skilled online readers frequently engaged in determining important ideas, integrating, evaluating, and reflecting while responding to informational prompts on the Internet. These patterns are similar to those outlined in Pressley and Afflerbach's (1995) compendium of reading strategies clustered around processes of identifying and learning text content, monitoring, and evaluating observed when readers interact with offline texts. In addition, we found evidence that both readers frequently engaged in new dimensions of planning, searching, monitoring, and repairing as they negotiated multiple online texts. These data provide tangible examples consistent with Afflerbach and Cho's (2008; 2009) notion that processes of "realizing and constructing potential texts to read" are dynamically interwoven with more traditionally conceived reading processes. This finding is important for researchers, who examine online reading, and teachers, who teach online reading, to consider since it suggests that an expanded set of strategies appears to be required when reading online. The additional online strategies identified and labeled in our coding scheme may provide guidance for researchers who seek to expand this work. This expanded coding scheme may also inform teachers who seek to design instruction around a bank of useful online reading strategies.

We also sought to explore whether students' interactions within a collaborative dyad would mirror the patterns identified during individual online reading or if different patterns would emerge. Results revealed qualitative differences in patterns of strategy use among students reading individually and in pairs and additional qualitative differences in the pair's collective response to the prompt. When reading individually, Abby was characterized as "The Thoughtful Gatherer" who carefully chose relevant sections of text to attend to and gathered pertinent information as she read. Starfish was termed "The Aesthetic Summarizer" who often expressed concern or empathy as she read. However, when reading in collaboration, those tendencies appeared to shift. For example, in contrast to her performance during the individual task where she was observed *integrating* 5% of the time, Abby *integrated* much more frequently when reading online collaboratively, 32% of the time. Starfish's tendency to *integrate* increased as well from 16% of the time when reading individually to 31% of the time when reading collaboratively. This pattern suggests that as the dialogue unfolded, Starfish was modeling integration for Abby, with Abby ultimately taking up this strategy as her own. Through the act of collaboration, Abby appeared to gradually take on a new role as "The Purposeful Summarizer."

With Abby actively integrating as the pair read, Starfish appeared to become more active in monitoring the pair's reading by engaging in reflective processing 15% of the time and confirming/clarifying 16% of the time. These strategies were rarely coded in Starfish's individual reading session where she engaged in reflective processing only 4% of the time and confirming/clarifying only 1% of the time. This pattern of strategy use may have emerged naturally due to the increased opportunity to work collaboratively. However, Starfish more actively monitored as the pair read collaboratively, and thus took on a new role of "The Reflective Analyzer." Together, Abby and Starfish appeared more efficient in reading reflectively and responding to the prompt.

Consequently, these findings suggest that opportunities to co-construct meaning and responses to prompts that require students to read on the Internet may foster more efficient and productive comprehension of online informational texts—even among readers who are skilled at comprehending online texts independently. This is consistent with work that suggests discussion and shared decision-making facilitates knowledge construction and deeper levels of understanding (Dillenbourg & Schneider, 1995; Mercer, 1995).

As we grapple to understand the constantly changing textual landscape of the digital world we inhabit, we acknowledge that additional research is needed. Our next study will analyze group interaction and functions of collaborative talk through microgenetic lenses (e.g., Rogoff, 2003) and explore the connections between constructivist and sociocultural perspectives of reading comprehension (see Cobb, 1994). Our sample will include additional pairs of students, particularly those who come to partnerships with different background knowledge and varying levels of strategy use. This trajectory of work will guide the field to better understand the talents and strategies required to read skillfully when immersed in the diverse and continually evolving reading contexts found online.

REFERENCES

Afflerbach, P. A. & Cho, B-Y. (2008). Identifying and describing constructively responsive comprehension strategies in new and traditional forms of reading. In S. Israel & G. Duffy (Eds.), *Handbook of reading comprehension research*. (pp. 69-90). Mahwah, NJ: Erlbaum.

Afflerbach, P. A. & Cho, B-Y. (2009). Determining and describing reading strategies: Internet and traditional forms of reading. In Waters, H. S., & Schneider, W. (Eds.), *Metacognition, strategy use, and instruction* (pp. 201-225). New York, NY: Guilford Press.

Alexander, P. A. & Fox, E. (2004). Historical perspectives on reading research and practice. In R. B. Ruddell & N. J. Unrau. (Eds.). *Theoretical models and processes of reading, fifth edition* (33-59). Newark, DE: International Reading Association.

Almasi, J. F., McKeown, M. G., & Beck, I. L. (1996). The nature of engaged reading in classroom discussions of literature. *Journal of Literacy Research, 28*(1), 107-146.

Anderson, V. & Roit, M. (1993). Planning and implementing collaborative strategy instruction for delayed readers in grades 6-10. *The Elementary School Journal, 94*(2), 121-137.

Assessment and Teaching of 21ˢᵗ Century Skills [ATC21S]. (2008, September 1). *Transforming Education: Assessing and Teaching the Skills Needed in the 21st Century: A Call to Action*. Intel, Microsoft and Cisco Education Taskforce. Retrieved March 14, 2010 from http://www.atc21s.org/GetAssets.axd?FilePath=/Assets/Files/699792fd-4d41-44f2-8208-cbb3fccb6572.pdf

Aviv, R. (2001). Educational performance of ALN via content analysis. *Journal of Asynchronous Learning Networks, (4)*2, 53-72.

Bogdan, R. C., & Biklen, S. K. (2003). *Qualitative research for education: An introduction to theories and methods,* (4th ed.). Boston, MA: Allyn & Bacon.

Bransford, J., Brown, A., & Cocking, R. (2000). *How People Learn: Brain, Mind, and Experience & School*. Washington, DC: National Academy Press.

Castek, J. (2008). How do 4th and 5th grade students acquire the new literacies of online reading comprehension? Exploring the contexts that facilitate learning. Unpublished doctoral dissertation: University of Connecticut.

Cho, B-Y. (2010, December 3). *A study of adolescents' constructive strategy use in a critical Internet reading task*. Paper presented at the annual meeting of the Literacy Research Association, Fort Worth, TX.

Cobb, P. (1994). Where is the mind? Constructivist and sociocultural perspectives on mathematical development. *Educational Researcher, 23*(7), 13-20.

Coiro, J. & Dobler, E. (2007). Exploring the online comprehension strategies used by sixth-grade skilled readers to search for and locate information on the Internet. *Reading Research Quarterly, 42*, 214-257.

Coiro, J. (in press). Predicting reading comprehension on the Internet: Contributions of offline reading skills, online reading skills, and prior knowledge. *Journal of Literacy Research*.

Coiro, J., Knobel, M., Lankshear, C., & Leu, D. J. (2008). Central issues in new literacies and new literacies research. In J. Coiro, M. Knobel, C. Lankshear, and D. J. Leu. *The handbook of research in new literacies.* (pp. 1-22) Mahwah, NJ: Erlbaum.

Common Core State Standards Initiative. (2010). *Key points in English Language Arts*. Retrieved December 22, 2010 from http://www.corestandards.org/about-the-standards/key-points-in-english-language-arts

Crafton, L. & Burke, C. (1994). Inquiry-based evaluation: Teachers and students reflecting together. *Primary Voices, 2*(2), 2-7.

Dalton, B. & Proctor, C. P. (2008). The changing landscape of text and comprehension in the age of new literacies. In J. Coiro, M. Knobel, C., Lankshear, & D. J. Leu. (Eds.), *Handbook of research on new literacies*. Mahwah, NJ: Lawrence Erlbaum Associates.

Dillenbourg, P. & Schneider, D. (1995). *Collaborative learning and the Internet*. Retrieved December 15, 2010 from http://tecfa.unige.ch/tecfa/research/CMC/colla/icc

Elbers, E. (1991). The development of competence in its social context. *Educational Psychology Review, 3*(2), 73-93.

Ericsson, K., & Simon, H. (1993). *Protocol analysis: Verbal reports as data*. Cambridge, MA: MIT Press.

Hartman, D. K., Morsink, P. M., & Zheng, J. (2010). From print to pixels: The evolution of cognitive conceptions of reading comprehension. In E. A. Baker (Ed.). *The new literacies: Multiple perspectives on research and practice* (pp. 131-164). New York, NY: Guilford Press.

Kim, I-H., Anderson, R. C., Nguyen-Jahiel, K., & Archodidou, A. (2007). Discourse patterns during children's collaborative online discussions. *The Journal of The Learning Sciences, 16(3)*, 333-370.

Kintsch, W. (1988). The role of knowledge in discourse comprehension: A construction-integration model, *Psychological Review, 95*, 163-182.

Krippendorff, K. H. (2003). *Content analysis: An introduction to its methodology, 2nd edition.* Thousand Oaks, CA: Sage Publications.

Kucan, L. & Beck, I. L. (1997). Thinking aloud and reading comprehension research: Inquiry, instruction, and social interaction. *Review of Educational Research, 67(3)*, 271-299.

Leu, D. J., Jr., Kinzer, C.K., Coiro, J., & Cammack, D. (2004). Toward a theory of new literacies emerging from the Internet and other ICT. In R. B. Ruddell & N. Unrau (Eds.), *Theoretical Models and Processes of Reading*, Fifth Edition (1568-1611). Newark, DE: International Reading Association.

Leu, D. J., O'Byrne, W. I., Zawilinski, L., McVerry, J. G., & Everett-Cacopardo, H. (2009). Expanding the new literacies conversation. *Educational Researcher, 38(4)*, 264-269.

Mercer, N. (1995). *The guided construction of knowledge: Talk amongst teachers and learners.* Philadelphia, PA: Multilingual Matters Ltd.

Merriam, S. (2009). Qualitative research: A guide to design and implementation. San Francisco, CA: Jossey-Bass.

Morgan, D. L. (2007). Paradigms lost and pragmatism regained: Methodological implications of combining qualitative and quantitative methods. *Journal of Mixed Methods Research, 1*(1), 48-76.

Pressley, M. & Afflerbach, P. A. (1995). *Verbal protocols of reading: The nature of constructively responsive reading.* Hillsdale, NJ: Erlbaum.

Rogoff, B. (2003). *The cultural nature of human development.* Oxford and New York: Oxford University Press.

Rosenblatt, L. (1998). *The transactional theory of reading and writing.* In R. Ruddell, M. R. Ruddell, & H. Singer (Eds.), Theoretical models and processes of reading, 4th Edition. (pp. 864-893). Newark, DE: International Reading Association.

Schmar-Dobler, E. (2003, September). Reading on the Internet: The link between literacy and technology. *Journal of Adolescent & Adult Literacy, 47*(1).

Schwandt, T. A. (1994). Constructivist, interpretivist approaches to human inquiry. In N. K. Denzin & Y. S. Lincoln (Eds.), *Handbook of qualitative research* (pp. 118-137). Thousand Oaks, CA: Sage.

Selfe, C. L., & Hawisher, G. E. (2004). *Literate lives in the information age: Narratives of literacy from the United States.* Mahwah, NJ: Lawrence Erlbaum Associates.

Smith, K. A., Sheppard, S. D., Johnson, D. W., & Johnson, R. T. (2005). Pedagogies of engagement: Classroom-based practices. *Journal of Engineering Education, 94*(1), 1-15.

Vygotsky, L. S. (1978). *Mind and society: The development of higher psychological processes.* Cambridge, MA: Harvard University Press.

Wells, G. (2007). Semiotic mediation, dialogue, and the construction of knowledge. *Human Development, 50*, 244-274.

Wyatt-Smith, C. & Elkins, J. (2008). *Multimodal reading and comprehension in online environments.* In J. Coiro, M. Knobel, C. Lankshear, & D. J. Leu, (Eds.). *Handbook of research in new literacies.* Mahwah, NJ: Erlbaum.

Yin, R. K. (2009). *Case study research, design and methods.* Thousand Oaks, CA: Sage Publications.

Zhang, S. & Duke, N. K. (2008). Strategies for internet reading with different reading purposes: A descriptive study of twelve good internet readers. *Journal of Literacy Research, 40*(1), 128-162

APPENDIX A

Coding Scheme for Constructively Responsive Online Reading Processes

PRE-READING	DURING READING (continued)
Planning	**Integrating**
• Activating prior knowledge[1]	• Interpreting[1]
• Anticipating the search[2]	• Supporting interpretation[1]
• Planning the search[2]	• Reconsidering interpretation[1]
• Identifying search goals[2]	• Reconsidering prior knowledge[1]
Searching	• Summarizing for meaning[1]
• Generating a search[2]	• Synthesizing[1]
• Scrutinizing search result link utility[2]	• Remembering[1]
• Scrutinizing website link utility[2]	**Evaluating**
• Predicting hyperlink utility[2]	• Evaluating utility[1]
• Generating alternative hyperlink inferences[2]	• Evaluating accuracy[1]
• Searching to overview[2]	• Evaluating author's level of expertise[1]
Overviewing	• Evaluating author's perspective[1]
• Overviewing[1]	• Reacting[2]
• Sampling initial texts[1]	**Monitoring**
DURING READING (within a website)	• Monitoring understanding[1]
Determining Important Ideas	• Monitoring strategy use[1]
• Adjusting[1]	• Verbalizing strategy use[1]
• Reading aloud[1]	• Monitoring reading pathways[2]
• Reading silently[1]	**Repairing**
• Skimming[1]	• Changing reading strategy[1]
• Predicting[1]	• Changing reading path[2]
• Paraphrasing accurately[1]	• Reconsidering alternative search[2]
• Paraphrasing with misconception[2]	• Selecting additional websites from search results[2]
• Following with cursor[2]	• Conducting extended search[2]
• Highlighting with cursor[2]	• Conducting alternative search[2]
• Discussing website images[2]	**Confirming/Clarifying** (in response to researcher or partner questions/comments)
• Avoiding text[2]	• Providing confirmation[2]
• Sequencing hypertexts[2]	• Providing clarification[2]
Questioning	**POST-READING**
• Asking questions about text meaning[1]	**Reflecting**
• Clarifying text meaning[1]	• Reflective processing[1]
• Determining word meaning[1]	• Planning to use knowledge[1]
• Conversing with the author[1]	
Inferring	
• Inferring[1]	
• Connecting key ideas within text[1]	
• Connecting key ideas to self[1]	
• Connecting key ideas across texts[2]	

[1]Constructively responsive reading processes observed by Pressley & Afflerbach (1995)
[2]Additional processes observed in contemporary think-aloud studies of online reading comprehension

Resistance Phenomena in Collaborative Online Discussions

SoonAh Lee
Diane L. Schallert
Kwangok Song
The University of Texas at Austin

Yangjoo Park
Seoul National University

Yueh-hui Vanessa Chiang
Stanford University

Jane S. Vogler
The University of Texas at Austin

Michelle E. Jordan
Arizona State University

Ji-Eun Lee
The University of Texas at Austin

An-Chih Janne Cheng
DePaul University

Anke Z. Sanders
Jeong-bin Park
The University of Texas at Austin

> Thinkers must hear several voices within their heads representing contrastive perspectives on an issue. The ability and disposition to take more than one perspective arises from participating in discussions with others who hold different perspectives. (Anderson, Nguyen-Jahiel, McNurlen, Archodidou, Kim, Reznitskaya, Tillmanns, & Gilbert, 2001, p. 2)

Within a broader framework of what it means for students to learn from participating in online discussions, we focused in this project on the role that resistance plays in how students engage with the ideas presented in such a collaborative activity. In using the term *resistance*, we acknowledge that it may generally connote such negative aspects as are associated with uncooperative attitudes or rejection experienced by clients in psychotherapy, citizens in revolutionary states, or students in educational settings. Indeed, Torrance (1950) reviewed previous work portraying college students' experience of resistance as a negative cognitive and emotional reaction that hinders learning and as similar to struggling, feeling challenged, or lacking motivation. By contrast, our interest in what we are calling *resistance* was in line with Torrance's own perspective on the phenomenon, and had a broader purview, encompassing the kind of resistance that accompanies and fosters learning. In such a view, resistance includes the struggles that a learner experiences when encountering new ideas that are not easily aligned with prior beliefs or that seem to contradict cherished ideas, and yet that eventuate in a deeper understanding. By looking at online discussion among advanced graduate students discussing new and complex ideas in their fields, we hoped to contribute to a more nuanced understanding of the learning process through a focus on the likely resistance they would exhibit.

As we review in the next section, many studies about conceptual change have reported that doubting and resisting previous conceptions is indispensible to the process of conceptual change. Learners often resist change when new ideas are dissonant with the conceptions they already have about themselves or their worlds, resisting until they can find a way to harmonize with the new ideas by changing their old conceptions. Additionally, conflict in forming new ideas is likely when a learner interacts with others who bring different perspectives. Illeris (2004; 2007) recently claimed that resistance is an active and conscious response to a learning situation, representing an important potential for accommodative and transformative learning. Thus, as reflected in the quote from Anderson et al. (2001) with which we began, we saw collaborative classroom discussions as fruitful sites in which to examine resistance because of their affordance for change and interaction. In this, we were informed by three lines of work.

RESISTANCE AND LEARNING

A first line of influence on our ideas came from views of learning as resulting from conflict with one's current knowledge, from what Piaget (1926) called *disequilibration*, and what Chan, Burtis, and Bereiter (1997) called *explicit knowledge building*. Conceptual change occurs when learners come to realize that the new information encountered actually conflicts with their current views. The process of considering explanations for the conflicting information, a process often grounded in collaborative meaning-making activities, is instrumental in leading to change. In a recent essay on the nature of learning, Alexander, Schallert, and Reynolds (2009) described how learning can occur even in situations when an individual initially may feel reluctance to entertain a new idea. Discussion with others, in such a situation, may be a particularly effective way to shape new interpretations, making conflict a useful tool in learning (Almasi, 1995).

Simply setting students up for a discussion does not guarantee that they will actively exchange ideas and engage in meaning-making. It is *how* students react to expressed ideas, negotiate with multiple voices, and make their own meaning that is crucial to collaborative discussions. Thus, when someone in a discussion says something with which others express agreement without adding anything new to the idea, little can be learned from the discussion. By contrast, when someone says something to which a fellow group member responds, "I see what you mean, but what about...," a possibility of learning something new opens up. In our project, a phrase such as "but what about..." was coded as an expression of *resistance* in a discussion.

A second construct we brought in was related to the context in which we wanted to study the phenomenon of resistance, the online classroom discussions of graduate students taking an advanced course. A relevant theoretical description of this context would portray the students as acquiring the disciplinary discourse practices of their field (Bartholomae, 1985; Bazerman, 1985; Berkenkotter, Huckin, & Ackerman, 1988; Casanave & Li, 2008). As newcomers to the academic fields they were pursuing, these students were learning the conventions of how to read critically, how to express their ideas, and how to respond to others' views. In academic disciplines, conflict and argument are typically highly valued discourse practices for advancing the field, and students are encouraged to take on such practices early in their studies. In our project, we were interested in how graduate students would show their emerging understanding of how to keep an academic conversation going at a sophisticated level.

RESISTANCE AND COLLABORATIVE DISCUSSION

Like Anderson, Chinn, Chang, Waggoner, and Yi (1997) and their work on *collaborative reasoning*, we were interested in how students learn to work together in a collaborative task that involves considering alternative points of view and developing meaning through an intellectual discussion. A classroom activity that asks students to discuss what they have read may easily foster expressions of resistance when the text they are discussing is difficult, either because the ideas presented are new, complicated, or expressed in language with which they are not familiar, or because it conflicts with their previously established ways of understanding the world.

Such dialogical views of discourse are grounded ultimately in Bakhtin's (1981) theoretical views of language and related to classic notions of how language and conversations work (de Beaugrande & Dressler, 1981; Grice, 1975; Halliday, 1975) as well as to newer views of discourse (Gee, 2008; Street, 2005). For Bakhtin, every utterance carries with it echoes of past utterances to which it is a response, and it calls forth or predicts a future response. As individuals share words in a developing dialogue, they construct a sense of what others mean through their "answering words." To these ideas can be added the notion of how rules of conversation necessitate that each contribution add something new at the moment it is made in the developing conversational topic (Grice, 1975). Finally, we were influenced by Gee's idea of discourse as representing a toolkit made up of ways of expressing ideas as well as sets of attitudes, beliefs, and cultural stances represented among individuals. Whenever students are set the task of discussing new ideas, ideas they are newly formulating from assigned readings, conflicts are likely to arise as contrasting values, beliefs, and cultural models are revealed in their words.

Although resistance per se has rarely been examined in classroom discourse research, the role of academic conflict has been explored as a means to facilitate learning. For example, studying discussion groups that involved conflict, Johnson and Johnson (1985) compared how students learned when assigned to one of three groups all focused on controversial issues: (1) a collaborative learning group that had the goal of coming to an agreement or finding a solution; (2) a debate group with students arguing for or against a position with the goal of winning the debate; and (3) an individual learning group who read about the controversial issue on their own. Johnson and Johnson found that the two groups involved in interaction experienced more positive changes on several affective and attitudinal measures than the students in the individual learning group. These results suggest that when students argue against or take an oppositional position, they can still learn from the facilitative, constructive, and productive discussion that occurs, and restructure their position in the course of the discussion. Other researchers have discussed the importance of conflicts or disagreements for keeping participants engaged in knowledge building and dynamic change (Matusov, 1996; Mercer, 1995; Smolka, De Goes, & Pino, 1995).

RESISTANCE IN ONLINE DISCUSSION

Finally, we drew from the research on the use of online computer-mediated discussion (CMD) in learning environments, and paid particular attention to the several ways that researchers, though rarely explicitly, had made a connection to the construct of resistance. One such aspect relates to the potentials and limitations of CMD as an environment for scholarly and academic collaboration (Faigley, 1992; Fauske & Wade, 2003-2004), with participants experiencing chaos and confusion, not only because of their lack of familiarity with the medium but also because of the challenge of keeping up with the swiftly moving conversation on complex concepts and ideas (Jordan et al., 2007; Schallert, Reed, & the D-Team, 2003-2004). Commenting on beneficial aspects of CMD, Astleitner (2002) claimed that CMD made it comfortable for participants to take the risk of putting their ideas into the public domain and to express uncertainty and disagreement. The more democratic environment of CMD can foster argumentation for knowledge building, reducing the influence of social, cultural, and institutional categories and stratifications on participants' engagement in the discussion (Bonk & King, 1998; Dubrovsky, Kiesler, & Sethna, 1991; Wade & Fauske, 2004). Finally, online discussions can provide a medium through which participants share resistance to authoritative and powerful social and institutional systems while supporting each others' thoughts (Pena-Shaff, Martin, & Gay, 2001; Spears, Lea, Corneliussen, Postmess, & Harr (2002).

OUR STUDY

In this project, we explored students' expressed resistance during collaborative learning from online discussions. Rather than focusing on the effect of conflict on what Alexander et al. (2009) called the *product* of learning, we attempted to explore how resistance, as a complex psychological and linguistic mechanism, would play a role in the *process* of students' meaning-making in classroom online discussions. In this, we were guided by two broad research questions: what is the relationship of resistance to learning in online discussion?, and beyond individual messages, how does resistance affect the dynamics of a developing topic of conversation?

METHOD

Participants and Context

Participants were the 24 students (19 women and 5 men; 8 of international status) taking a graduate course that incorporated online discussion as a regular part of course activities. As the course dealt with the psychology of language in use, it attracted students from different disciplinary areas in education, the liberal arts, and communication. The teacher, Donna (a pseudonym; all names have been changed), had used online discussion as a regular activity in this and similar courses for more than 10 years.

These online activities took the form of both synchronous and asynchronous computer-mediated discussions. For the three synchronous discussions, the students and teacher moved to a computer lab during the last 35 to 45 minutes of class to continue their discussion, hosted on an online program that allowed an individual to read chronological postings in a public window and to compose a message privately, before posting it. By contrast, the three asynchronous discussions replaced face-to-face meetings. Hosted on the web-based course management system (Blackboard), these discussions were "in session" over the span of 36 to 40 hours with a general assignment of posting at least three comments (although most students posted more). The teacher assigned the students to two or three groups, changing membership for each discussion, so that by the end of the semester, students had interacted online with everyone else in the class.

Directions encouraged the students to discuss theoretical concepts and empirical findings as presented in the three or four articles assigned for each meeting. These articles came from the published body of work in the field and presented for most students new, complex, and nuanced ideas. The goal of the activity, as stated by Donna, was to help students understand concepts more deeply by sharing their own responses to the articles and negotiating the meaning of ideas together. No specific form of talk, such as disputational or critical, seemed privileged by Donna. Instead, the type of discussion she valued can be described as constructive student-centered talk where students and the teacher actively engage in collaborative meaning-making.

Data Sources

For the purpose of this study, we decided to focus on the groups' discussions in the last session of each mode (synchronous and asynchronous) because we wanted to capture the students' discourse practices once they had become familiar with the online medium. For each mode, we then chose the discussions of two groups based on an initial reading that led us to identify one group as showing much resistance and one group with much less seeming resistance. Thus, our data sources included the written transcripts produced by four groups in both kinds of online discussions. Also, we constructed coherence graphs from each transcript (see Figure 1). As described in Schallert, Lissi, Reed, Dodson, Benton, and Hopkins (1996), a coherence graph allows one to reconstruct visually the topical threads that connect messages to each other in a discussion. This is particularly useful for synchronous discussions because there are no topic indicators as participants post their messages.

Data Analysis

In order to explore resistance phenomena in classroom discourse, we took an inductive, interpretive, and naturalistic approach. Using the tools of constant comparison (Corbin & Strauss, 2008), we developed emergent categories from data rather than testing the validity of established concepts and presumed relationships. Representing an interpretivist stance (Lincoln & Guba, 1985; Erlandson, Harris, Skipper, & Allen, 1993; von Wright, 1971), our study was an inquiry for promoting an understanding rather than for providing an explanation of the ways that students expressed and benefitted from resistance in classroom discussion. Finally, our study involved microgenetic analysis of discourse, which meant for us an attempt to understand the practices of participants as revealed in the words they chose to express their ideas.

Our data analysis consisted of three phases. In the first phase, we developed a coding scheme to capture and differentiate nuances of resistance through a dialectic and iterative process of individual coding, consensus discussion, and re-checking against the data. The process began by tasking the members of our research team individually to look for emergent categories of resistance, concentrating on one synchronous transcript. Through an iterative process of discussion as a team

Figure 1. An Example of a Coherence Graph[1]

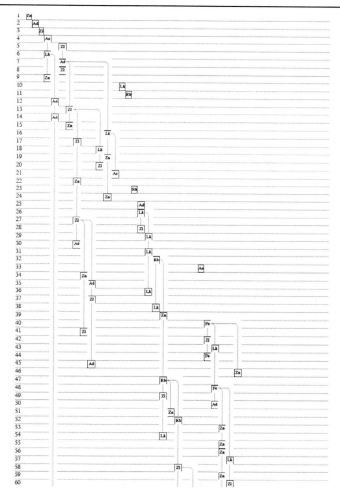

[1]Letters in small boxes come from the names of the authors of each posting. Numbers indicate the chronology of postings. Lines between boxes show that one posting was in response to an earlier posting.

and re-checking as individuals, we identified several emergent categories of how resistance can be expressed drawing on our general knowledge of linguistic expressions and our interpretation of how the ideas were developing in the discussion (open coding). We then went through the same process with one asynchronous transcript. Each dimension created from open coding was constantly compared and contrasted to find similarities and differences to other dimensions (axial coding). Through consensus building informed by the data, we developed a final coding scheme with two major dimensions made up of several categories. The two dimensions represented *what* was being resisted (with seven categories representing resistance to content, resistance to participation, and meta-resistance) and *how* this resistance was being expressed (with three categories). Table 1 lists

Table 1. Resistance Coding Scheme

Dimension	Category			Description	Example from transcripts
"What" Code (What a writer is resisting)	Content Resistance	R1		Resistance to author(s)' idea	This article made some good points but I was unsatisfied with it in a lot of way. I thought that the way it was framed, "insider" versus "outsider" was too broad. (Isaac)
		R2		Resistance to peer(s)' idea	But, Janice, if there is no standard testing, what are we going to use to test students' performance, and with what are we going to decide whether the students are qualified for higher study? (Ya-wen)
		R3		Resistance to a certain issue in education	I think standardized testing also inhibits our ability to use innovative approaches and empower students to make more choices, as well as to use more modern ways of teaching and communicating. (Janice)
	Participation Resistance	R4		Resistance to being positioned	Sorry if my comment was insensitive. I was referring to the students in the article, Rachel, who wrote about shooting someone in her poem. (Beatrice)
		R5		Resistance to tools	I hate all the typing. When I have an idea I just want to blurt it out. I have to restrain myself from doing it here! (Renee)
		R6		Resistance to a certain feature of discussion (flow, speed, direction, etc.)	Politeness is a learned communication procedure..now can we move on? (Luke)
	Meta Resistance	R7		Talking about resistance itself	As an undergrad, I was on my own as far as figuring out how I was "supposed to be writing" and I even experienced some of the resistance Fox talks about. (Linda)
"How" Code (How a writer is resisting)	ER			Explicit (direct) Resistance	Yes, it's a good example of a study with good data, but you can't generalize it. (Zena)
	IR			Implicit (indirect) Resistance	Seems like we need a whole lot more, huh? Like getting teachers to have high expectations for all kids, I would guess. (Cathy)
	RR			Ironic Resistance	Right, Rose, because they may invest the time to try something new and it may not even work. (Renee)

the two dimensions with their sub-categories, along with definitions and examples drawn from the transcripts. Every message in the four focal discussions was coded for both dimensions according to this coding scheme (on average 75% agreement across pairs of coders; all disagreements were resolved by whole-team consensus).

The second phase of data analysis was focused on understanding of the association of expressed resistance with students' learning. Here, we used categories of learning that we had developed in previous research (Jordan, Schallert, & the D-Team, 2008), using a consensual and iterative process much like the one with which the resistance codes were developed. These learning codes are listed in Table 2 (first column) along with short definitions. Coding for learning obeyed several decision rules: (a) the learning in a message could come either from course readings or from other participants' messages in the discussion; (b) learning had to refer to something recently new to a person and could not refer only to something that had been learned in the past; and (c) simple "I agree" statements were ignored because we could not tell, unless accompanied by further elaboration, whether the person was agreeing because of old or because of new knowledge. (We acknowledge the overlap between our full set of resistance codes and the learning category we had earlier developed, called *L3- constructive resistance*. As a learning code, *constructive resistance* referred

Table 2. Number of Messages With/Without Resistance and Different Types of Learning

Learning codes*	With Resistance	No Resistance	Total
L1 – Noticing: Initial recognition or noticing of a new idea; considering the idea	12	29	41
L2 – Struggling: Struggling with understanding of an idea or a concept; questioning its application	5	24	30
L3 – Constructive resistance: Resisting a new idea and arguing against it	44	0	44
L4 – Idea expanding: Refining prior knowledge based on new concepts (e.g., clarifying, specifying)	32	36	68
L5 – Idea application: Re-interpreting life experiences in light of a new concept	19	36	55
L6 – Naming: Applying a newly learned label to a life experience or prior knowledge	0	0	0
L7 – Connecting to other disciplinary knowledge: Making intertextual connections to other articles	4	6	10
L8 – Metacognitive assessment of utility of idea: Evaluating the value of a new idea or its utility	2	3	5
L9 – Proposing a new idea: Offering an idea going beyond those existing in a reading or discussion	14	20	34
Total	125	165	

*Learning codes come from Jordan et al., 2008

Table 3. Occurrence of Resistance and Learning

Discussion	Total # of Messages	Number and % of Message With:			
3rd Synch. (Grp. 1)	153	Resistance	36 (23.5%)	With Learning	28 (77.8%)
				No Learning	8
		No Resistance	117 (76.5%)	With Learning	53
				No Learning	64
3rd Synch. (Grp. 3)	145	Resistance	46 (31.7%)	With Learning	41 (89.1%)
				No Learning	5
		No Resistance	99 (68.3%)	With Learning	54
				No Learning	45
3rd Asynch. (Grp. 2)	64	Resistance	34 (53.1%)	With Learning	26 (76.5%)
				No Learning	8
		No Resistance	30 (46.9%)	With Learning	22
				No Learning	8
3rd Asynch. (Grp. 3)	38	Resistance	16 (42.1%)	With Learning	16 (100%)
				No Learning	0
		No Resistance	22 (57.9%)	With Learning	15
				No Learning	7

Note: Resistance or Learning could be included more than once in one message.

not to a way of expressing resistance but to indicators of an individual changing his/her mind by arguing against a new idea.) A final step in this second phase was to annotate the coherence graphs with both learning and resistance codes, allowing us to look for patterns in their association within threads and across each discussion.

The third phase of data analysis was focused on developing an understanding of how expressed resistance influenced the dynamics of the discussion. Through several iterations, the four transcripts and their coherence graphs were characterized by what happened when students showed much or little resistance, and were explicit or indirect in their expressions of resistance.

FINDINGS

Findings are presented in two parts, focused first on the frequency of expressed resistance and its association with learning, and second on resistance in the dynamics of CMD.

Part 1: Resistance and Learning

Here, we organize our findings in terms of three conclusions supported by our data.

Students frequently expressed resistance as they engaged in online classroom discussion. As shown in Table 3, in light of all possible speech acts that could be expressed in a message, resistance was a frequent occurrence in all discussions for these students, varying from a little less than one quarter of the messages in one synchronous discussion to slightly more than half of the messages in one asynchronous discussion. That there was so much resistance evident in the asynchronous discussions (53.1% and 42.1% compared to 23.5% and 31.7% in the synchronous discussions) is understandable given that messages were typically much longer than in synchronous discussions, thus affording a message writer more opportunity to express resistance. When only the codes of content resistance (R1, R2, and R3) are counted, the amount of resistance expressions remains notable, ranging from 18% to 29%.

Such prevalence of resistance might imply that the conversations were rife with confrontational and barbed comments. On the contrary, although there were a few comments that could seem pointed and argumentative, students generally remained congenial, friendly, and on-task even when they explicitly expressed their resistance to peers' or authors' ideas or to how the discussion itself was developing. These graduate students were impressive in their use of language to express their disagreement smoothly and politely. The following exchange between two students in a synchronous discussion is typical of how students expressed their resistance to each others' ideas. In a topical thread about the dangers associated with young people using the website Myspace, Luke expressed his disagreement with Zelda's concerns about the use of technological tools in the classroom. Zelda had described how a student at the school where she taught had "*posted herself and her boobs to the world.*" (Note that we underline the words that indicate some resistance and provide in parentheses the particular resistance coding the words received.) Luke responded: *If it is "her" site, and her parents don't mind, then maybe it shouldn't be an issue…but why not use another tool that is less conducive to the use of images?* Zelda responded: *Luke, definitely, I could use other forms but like Cathy said in class, there is so much legality involved that it puts us in a conundrum.* We coded Luke's post as explicitly expressing resistance to Zelda's own post (R2), and Zelda's response as an implicit expression of resistance to Luke's suggestion (R2), even though she began by "*definitely*" agreeing with him. In an example from an asynchronous discussion, Isaac included his resistance to the authors of the article being discussed: *Did anybody else have a problem with this article? If the authors want to start a discussion about who has a voice in academia and who does not, comparing the writing of a PhD student in philosophy to that of a freshman (major undecided?) seems a little manipulative to me* (R1: resisting author's ideas, explicit). In the message, he questioned whether there might not be a confounding factor represented in the authors' research design, inviting others at the same time possibly to change his mind about the issue.

Resistance often accompanies students' learning. We found that resistance was highly related to occurrences of learning. The last column in Table 3 shows how frequently resistance co-occurred with learning, as 77% to 100% of resistant messages were also coded as reflecting some sort of learning. The excerpt in Table 4 shows how students' expressed resistance seemed to accompany a positive willingness to consider different points of view and to make learning happen. When students wrote messages showing much resistance, they seemed as much hoping to get others to respond from a different angle as wanting to persuade others of their own views.

In the spirit of testing our conclusions by checking for counterexamples, we carefully examined all messages coded with resistance but not coded as reflecting learning and found that *content resistance* was more likely related to occurrences of learning than *participation resistance*. In

Group 1's synchronous discussion, of eight resistant messages without learning, three were coded as showing resistance to the flow of discussion (R6), and one message was coded as resistance to being positioned (R4). Although the other four messages were related to issues regarding content (coded as either R1: resisting author ideas, or R2: resisting peer ideas), they each had special characteristics that made sense of the fact that they showed resistance but no learning (e.g., an initiation of a problem posted early in a topic's development, a short answer to a peer's question, or a question to clarify a peer's ideas). In the other synchronous discussion, of five resistant messages with no learning, none showed resistance to content (four were coded as R5: resisting the tools, and one as R4: resisting being positioned).

A similar pattern was found for one asynchronous discussion, and we could not find any counterexample in the other asynchronous discussion. In the asynchronous discussion of Group 2, the messages coded as showing resistance but no learning were either not directly related to the content of readings or course concepts, or they were short comments that showed resistance to an author's or peer's ideas (R1 or R2) but so short as not to show if any learning had occurred (as when Isaac posted, "*That was a nice post! But, I have to object to calling reading articles 'a huge obstacle' for second language writers!*"). Thus, the more useful form of resistant messages for students' learning seemed to include their own opposing claims along with appreciation of an author's or a peer's point, and actually, the percentages of co-occurrence of learning and resistance increased

Table 4. An Example of Interconnected Postings Showing Co-occurrence of Learning and Resistance

---

Fred: [having written two long paragraphs, he concludes] *Acceptance in the culture, the emotional toll, the economic challenges, etc. all have a major impact on literacy. I think it is hard for me now to see literacy as a construct in itself. It must be tied to the culture.* (**R7, explicit**). *This makes me want to go back and re-read some of our past articles with this viewpoint.*

Changho: [having written some introduction] *Usually, we think that literacy is something about learning how to write (let's talk about just writing). However, as Fred pointed out, it's about learning how to write "correctly"* (**R3, explicit**). *The Moje's gangster writers are writing well, but incorrectly. This correctness belongs to a culture* [he goes on for 5 more lines].

Donna: *Right! You and Fred are adding an interesting point here. I am predicting that Fred will say to you that he likes what you are saying, but objects to one little word in what you say, Changho, the word "incorrectly"* (**R2, implicit**). *He'd say that it's not that the gangster kids write incorrectly* [she goes on for 10 more lines].

Fred: *Thank you Donna, you read my mind* (**R2, ironic**). *I think we have to understand that our academic view of "correct" or "good" writing is subjective to what the collective majority view as correct or good. Literacy in itself does not hold values, it reflects value.* [He then continues with about 20 more lines of text.]

Changho: *Thank you, Donna and Fred, for elaborating ideas. I said that the correctness belongs to a culture. That means the incorrectness is also cultural product* (**R4, explicit**). *As Fred mentioned, the power system is one of the main factors that may determine which ones are correct while others are not.*

to an incidence of 83% to 100% across the four discussions (from 77% to 100%) when we only considered students' messages coded as content resistance (R1, R2, or R3).

In Table 2, we summarize how resistance was distributed across the different forms of learning for the four discussions. We want to focus first on the lines of data associated with L2 and L3. As we had expected, all of the messages coded with the learning code of "constructive resistance," L3, received resistance (R) codes. When we had developed our learning codes in our previous research (Jordan et al., 2008), we considered that a student resisting a new idea and arguing against it was showing a form of learning. Therefore, it is not surprising that the 44 messages showing constructive resistance as a form of learning would receive some form of resistance coding. By contrast, the distribution of resistance/no resistance for the L2 "struggling" messages may seem surprising at first blush, with such a disproportionate preference for no resistance. However, this puzzling finding becomes clear if we return to our definition of *resistance*, a matter of accepting or rejecting ideas, not an issue of understanding an idea. Thus, to struggle (L2) with an idea involves trying hard to understand something that is not clear, a process that differs from feeling a sense of not wanting to go along with an idea. We only had five messages showing L2 and resistance as coincident, all from synchronous postings. And, of these five, two cases received a resistance code and a learning code, respectively, in different parts of the message (as when Andrea posted, "*Don't know much about it* (L2). *I keep hearing a peer talk about it in my Discourse Analysis class… and TIME has just run out!* [R6: resistance to a feature of the discussion, implicit] *Talk to ya'all later!*"). The other three cases were all coded as implicit resistant messages to a peer's idea.

Although the relationship between resistance and L2 (struggling) and L3 (constructive resistance) were in line with expectations, the patterns of resistance for L1 (noticing), L4 (idea expanding), L5 (idea application), and L9 (proposing a new idea) were interesting exactly because they went against what we expected. For L1, we had expected that *noticing* would not be associated with any kind of resistance. Of the 12 messages coded as L1, eight came from the asynchronous discussions and all showed *noticing* in one part of a long message and resistance in a different paragraph. We only had four instances when resistance occurred in the same part of the message as *noticing*, and in all cases, resistance was followed by an elaboration of ideas. As for the relationship between L5 and resistance, we had thought that idea application would perhaps simply involve providing an example from one's daily life or from society at large to illustrate an idea with which one agrees. Instead, we had half of the L5 messages also coded as showing resistance. We postulate that students might resist an idea by presenting a very particular example, as a strategy for arguing their point. A good example is a message in one of the asynchronous discussions by SunYoung about being accused of plagiarism when working on a group project. After a very long and heartfelt description of what had happened, she wrote "*I also can experience and learn how the dominant value or discipline easily makes the other 'wrong' rather than 'different'*" (R3: resistance to an educational issue, explicit).

We were also surprised that there was as much resistance with L4 (idea expansion) and L9 (proposal of a new idea) as these kinds of learning imply that the learner is taking an idea and running with it. However, we came to see idea expansion as an expression of wanting to say something new in a conversation using words that juxtapose a contribution to what has been said already, thereby earning a resistance code. Similarly, it is possible that a new idea may be introduced because the learner is not in agreement with previously expressed ideas that have been mentioned either by the article or by peers, and offers something new in contrast to what has come before. Such language might get coded as resistance. Andrea's post exemplifies a co-occurrence of L9 with resistance: "*I think we shouldn't generalize across groups … I can see politeness as being something that changes depending on context* (R1: resistance to authors' ideas, explicit)." Thus, resistance, particularly resistance to content, generally co-occurred with learning, and this was true across different kinds of learning as revealed in all four transcripts.

Expressions of resistance may reflect cultural norms of academic conversations. Resistance may be a natural part of Discourse in a graduate course, a social norm needed in order to carry on an academic conversation by clarifying ideas or bringing up something new. With each utterance, it becomes necessary to show how one's new contribution is to be distinguished from what others have said so far, and this push from conversational norms may "naturally" bring out resistance. Furthermore, in advanced educational settings, especially in doctoral studies, it is expected of students that they will come to know how to show their understanding of theory by being able to critique and advance these theories or find practical applications for the theories that extend into new intellectual territory. This form of academic conversation is culturally valued and encouraged. Especially in graduate courses, professors as representatives of the discipline encourage students as newcomers to learn how to express resistance, and in response, graduate students may feel the need to show their emerging expertise at "talking the talk."

Of our participants, Soonja showed the most resistance across the four discussions we analyzed, a propensity she exhibited in all the online discussions in which she took part. From the 145 messages making up the synchronous discussion of Group 3, Soonja posted 61—21 of which received some sort of resistance code. These 21 messages represented a little less than half of all resistance messages (47) produced by the group (made up of eight participants). It is possible that Soonja may have authentically objected to particular ideas and wanted others to help her understand alternatives or to make explicit her own ideas. We are suggesting that instead (or in addition), she may have been expressing resistance in order to trigger lively talk.

For example, Soonja initiated one thread by asking a question: "*Have you guys all noticed any differences between electronic and traditional ways of communication?*" In response, two subtopics developed, one that was about a comparison of face-to-face and online discussion and a second that was about whether online communication would hinder young people's social development. To the first subtopic, Soonja posted five messages that all received codes of resistance to peers (R2) and then a final compromise saying that there must be both similarities and differences between the two forms of discussion. Here, she seemed to use resistance as an intentional prompt for talk. For the second subtopic, she was the only one to take the position that young people can learn social skills online, and she continued to argue with peers showing resistance nine times to each of their points. Thus for her, resistance seemed a way both to foster her own thinking and to perform the intellectual "game" of seeing different sides of an issue. Although not to the degree that Soonja exhibited, others also showed differences in the degree to which they were likely to express resistance, seeming to adopt the discourse style of an academic discussion. In spite of these individual predilections, resistance was nevertheless a social phenomenon that called for responses from others, whether with or without expressed resistance.

Part 2: Resistance and the Dynamics of Discussions

Having discussed how resistance worked at the message level, we turn in this part of our findings to an exploration of the influence that resistance in a message has on other messages in the discussion. Like any oral conversation, an online discussion takes place over time with messages building on ideas and responding to previously posted messages. For this part of our data analysis, we relied heavily on the coherence graphs, with their depiction of threads representing the topics that were emerging as students discussed the assigned readings and course concepts. Our focus in this section, then, is on how resistance expressed in one message in one thread affected the thread's development, its dynamic flow, summarized into three themes.

Whether resistance will be expressed in a thread is related to the nature of a topic. From the coherence graphs, we found that resistance was distributed differently across threads within any one discussion. Some threads included only a few messages with resistance codes, but other threads had more than half of the messages coded as expressing some sort of resistance. For example, a thread about Moje's article had all messages except for one coded with some kind of resistance. Andrea's message, posted third in the thread, seemed pivotal in how she showed resistance both to the author and to Doris who had posted a message right before hers. Doris had mentioned that she had found it hard to accept Moje's ideas in general, and in response, Andrea wrote how compelling an argument Moje had made about the relationship between gangster youths' use of literacy practices and their identity construction (resistance to peer, R2). At the same time, Andrea raised an objection to Moje, expressing her doubts that teachers could invite gang members' unsanctioned literacy practices into the classroom (resistance to the author, R1). In this way, Andrea shaped two sides of the topic, pro-Moje and con-Moje, that then influenced the discussion as other students expressed their opinions about Moje's ideas taking up one side or the other. Andrea's message seemed to have the effect of making it safe to express resistance.

Although the two-sidedness of a topic may contribute to more expressions of resistance, we found it interesting that students also expressed resistance when they were all on the same side of an issue. For example, in a thread about one article, almost all the students agreed with the authors' idea that teachers should give students authority in constructing their own knowledge. However, in sharing stories about their own frustrating experiences in past writing classes, students expressed how they had felt silenced (R7: talking about resistance), showing resistance to the underlying system (R3). In addition, they sometimes debated the causes or attributions of a problem, even though they agreed that something was a problem. These "hot button" issues in themselves seemed to create room for resistance among students.

Resistance develops differently within threads. We identified two broad patterns by which the development of resistance tended to proceed within a thread. One pattern showed a preliminary phase of exploration and a collaborative growth of resistance. In one thread, Fred brought up a complex question with resistance to the authors of one article. His message received a flurry of responses expressing appreciation of his comment but also indicating that students were not fully understanding his question (Andrea—*"That's deep, Fred…☺My head is about to explode"*; Zena—*"I'm trying to formulate my thoughts into words, Fred"*; Rebecca—*"Good points…Let me think more on this"*). Only after 14 of these messages was there a first expression of implicit resistance followed thereafter by 15 examples of explicit and implicit resistance in 31 messages. Thus, it seemed that students needed to understand what the initial message was saying, in an exploration phase, before resisting it. Additionally, the resistance seemed to be a collaborative product with different students expressing resistance and all but one group member posting to the thread. Resistance did not appear as isolated messages simply showing disagreement. Instead, the messages seemed to weave different points of view, making the discussion deeper, and contributing to a collaborative understanding and knowledge building.

Another interesting pattern of resistance involved the following: after several resistance messages, a student would offer a compromise or a synthesis, and this comment would trigger another resistance message including idea expansion or suggestion of a new idea. For example, in one synchronous discussion, after Mehmet's and Soonja's resistance messages, Janice posted a compromise: *"I think we also need to consider that the most efficient way for one student to learn may not be the most efficient way for another."* Her post received two responses, one of which was coded as expressing resistance. These two patterns were similar in that both contributed to thread development, and ultimately to enriching the discussion.

Table 5. Threads of the Four Online Discussions Showing the Effect of Resistance Expressed Early Rather Than Late [1]

	Total # of Threads	Total # of threads with resistance early on	Thread number	Total # of messages	Messages with resistance	
					# of messages	% of messages
Synch. Grp. 1	6	3	1	6	1	16.7
			2	20	1	10.0
			3	17	8	47.5
			4	16	1	6.2
			5	26	5	31.3
			6	47	18	38.3
Synch. Grp.3	4	3	1	31	6	19.4
			2	46	13	28.3
			3	16	5	31.3
			4	42	23	54.8
Asynch. Grp. 2	4	4	1	15	6	40.0
			2	14	12	85.7
			3	18	8	44.4
			4	15	6	40.0
Asynch. Grp. 3	3	2	1	15	8	53.3
			2	10	4	40.0
			3	13	4	30.8

[1]Threads that are shaded met the criterion of having an early message coded with resistance.

Resistance has a snowball effect on a thread. The term *snowball effect* is a metaphor created by Anderson et al. (2001) to refer to the phenomenon that a useful argument stratagem used by one child can spread to other children with increasing frequency in classroom talk. For us, we looked to see whether the expression of resistance would increase across a thread. Note that in our use of the idea of a snowball effect, we were simply looking for whether resistance of any type, and not particular words that expressed resistance, would more likely than not follow a previous resistance expression. In Table 5, we show how much resistance was found in threads that showed resistance in the first four messages. Threads that had resistance early on were more likely to have resistance later on than threads that had no early resistance: 12 of the 17 threads had resistance early on, and 30% to 85% of the messages within those 12 threads were coded as resistant. By contrast, of the five threads that had no resistance early on, only one had resistance in more than 30% of its messages, and this thread had a resistance expression in its fifth post.

We interpreted this phenomenon as showing that the students were influenced by their fellow group members' expressions of resistance. As graduate students, they seemed to know the value of exchanging ideas with each other in a discussion, and of making a conversation lively. Their use of resistance seemed to function as a tool for this purpose, the occasion of their meaning-making of ideas. Relevantly, we recognize that in some threads, several successive messages were coded with meta-resistance (R7) or resistance to tools (R5); once one student shared his or her own experience of college writing classes or began to complain about the online discussion tool, other students expressed sympathy and added their own experiences or opinions. We saw such mirroring as a sign of students' willingness to collaborate in meaning-making.

DISCUSSION

In this study, we examined the kinds of resistance that occurred in graduate students' online discussions and how resistance influenced the students' collaborative knowledge building and the conversation itself. A contribution of the study is that it represented a look at *resistance*, a construct that has received relatively little attention in the field of education although its importance has been discussed since the 1950s. Also, we focused on the function of resistance in a collaborative meaning-making activity, not simply on its operation in individual learning.

Results indicated that in online classroom discussion, our participants expressed a substantial amount of resistance as they interacted with each other. We also found that resistance expressed in students' messages was closely associated with several aspects of learning as students pursued ways of dialoguing with each other to extend and deepen their understanding of disciplinary texts collaboratively. Students' expression of resistance was influenced by the nature of topics. For example, when the topic of the discussion allowed multiple levels of discussion points, students expressed resistance not only to the central topic but also to other issues that the topic allowed them to see. We also saw that the development of resistance in a topical thread could take one of at least two broad patterns: (a) participants explored and clarified the meaning of a message before expressing resistance as they developed a topic; and (b) participants began with resistance followed by compromise and synthesis that would then trigger more resistance.

In our microanalysis of these CMD postings, resistance did not seem centered on negative emotions or reluctance to engage. Instead, the way these graduate students and their teacher expressed resistance was invariably friendly, polite, and inviting. Thus, resistance can contribute to an open and productive discussion that allows students to explore new concepts and ideas for their academic growth, functioning as an initiator of change, the initial impetus to considering new ideas, a catalyst for learning. Like children trained in collaborative reasoning, we saw these much older students consider each others' points of view, argue for a position based on their reading, think more deeply and critically about complex issues, and thereby learn.

Resistance functioned as a psychological tool that helped students seek a deeper understanding of the course's theoretical concepts, educational issues, and methodological approaches. Thus, our findings supported Illeris' (2004) point that resistance "constitutes symptoms of strong personal forces and engagement" (p. 87) even though it can at the same time be annoying and inappropriate. Resistance also played a role as a discourse tool that facilitated collaborative meaning-making. When no resistance is expressed in a conversation, it can sometimes mean that its participants do not recognize a mismatch among conflicting ideas. In other words, expressed resistance can be seen as an indicator of students' critical thinking and active making meaning. In our data, resistance was expressed in various ways and contributed to different discourse patterns and to keeping the discussion going at a sophisticated level.

We close by re-stating that resistance is not always a productive aspect of classroom talk. Although resistance has a great potential for fostering learning, acting as a resource to encourage critical thinking and conceptual change, it is often difficult for students and even teachers to deal with resistance that is expressed in argumentative ways. Future research is needed on how the teacher can foster the expression of reasoning in discussion (cf. Anderson et al., 2001) and allow room for students' resistance, even inspiring it with an appreciation for its legitimacy and guidance for its appropriate expression.

REFERENCES

Alexander, P. A., Schallert, D. L., & Reynolds, R. E. (2009). What is learning anyway?: A topographical perspective considered. *Educational Psychologist, 44*, 176-192.

Almasi, J. (1995). The nature of fourth graders' sociocognitive conflicts in peer-led and teacher-led discussions of literature. *Reading Research Quarterly, 30*, 314-351.

Anderson, R. C., Chinn, C., Chang, J., Waggoner, M., & Yi, H. (1997). On the logical integrity of children's arguments. *Cognition & Instruction, 15*, 135-167.

Anderson, R. C., Nguyen-Jahiel, K., McNurlen, B., Archodidou, A., Kim, S.-Y., Reznitskaya, A., Tillmanns, M., & Gilbert, L. (2001). The snowball phenomenon: Spread of ways of talking and ways of thinking across groups of children. *Cognition & Instruction, 19*, 1-46.

Astleitner, H. (2002). Teaching critical thinking online. *Journal of Instructional Psychology, 29*, 53-76.

Bakhtin, M. (1981). *Dialogic imagination: Four essays.* Austin, TX: University of Texas Press.

Bartholomae, D. (1985). Inventing the university. In M. Rose (Ed.), *When a writer can't write* (pp. 134-165). New York, NY: Guilford Press.

Bazerman, C. (1985). Physicists reading physics: Schema-laden purposes and purpose-laden schema. *Written Communication, 2*, 3-34.

Berkenkotter, C., Huckin, T., & Ackerman, J. (1988). Convention, conversations, and the writer: Case study of a student in a rhetoric Ph.D. program. *Research in the Teaching of English, 22*, 9-44.

Bonk, C. J., & King, K. S. (Eds.) (1998). *Electronic collaborators: Learner-centered technologies for literacy, apprenticeship, and discourse.* Mahwah, NJ: Erlbaum.

Casanave, C. P., & Li, X. (Eds.) (2008). *Learning the literacy practice of graduate school: Insiders' reflection on academic enculturation.* Ann Arbor, MI: University of Michigan Press.

Chan, C., Burtis, J., & Bereiter, C. (1997). Knowledge building as a mediator of conflict in conceptual change. *Cognition & Instruction, 15*, 1-40.

Corbin, J. M., & Strauss, A. M. (2008). *Basics of qualitative research: Techniques and procedures for developing grounded theory.* Los Angeles, CA: Sage Publications.

de Beaugrande, R., & Dressler, W. U. (1981). *Introduction to text linguistics.* London, UK: Longman.

Dubrovsky, V. J., Kiesler, S., & Sethna, B. N. (1991). The equalization phenomenon: Status effects in computer-mediated and face-to-face decision-making groups. *Human Computer Interaction, 6*, 119-146.

Erlandson, D. A., Harris, E. L., Skipper, B. L., & Allen, S. D. (1993). *Doing naturalistic inquiry: A guide to methods.* Newbury Park, CA: Sage.

Faigley, L. (1992). *Fragments of rationality: Postmodernity and the subject of composition.* Pittsburgh, PA: University of Pittsburgh Press.

Fauske, J., & Wade, S. E. (2003-2004). Research to practice online: Conditions that foster democracy, community, and critical thinking in computer-mediated discussions. *Journal of Research on Technology in Education, 36*(2), 137-153.

Gee, J. P. (2008). *Social linguistics and literacies: Ideology in discourses* (3rd ed.). New York, NY: Routledge.

Grice, H. P. (1975). Logic and conversation. In P. Cole & J. Morgan (Eds.), *Syntax and semantics* (Vol. 3, pp. 41-58). New York, NY: Academic Press.

Halliday, M. A. (1975). *Learning how to mean: Explorations in the development of language.* London, UK: Edward Arnold.

Illeris, K. (2004). Transformative learning in the perspective of a comprehensive learning theory. *Journal of Transformative Education, 2*(2), 79-89.

Illeris, K. (2007). *How we learn: Learning and nonlearning in school and beyond.* London, UK: Routledge.

Johnson, D. W., & Johnson, R. T. (1985). Classroom conflict: Controversy versus debate in learning groups. *American Educational Research Journal, 22*, 237-256.

Jordan, M., Schallert, D. L., Cheng, A., Park, Y., Lee, H., Chen, Y., Yang, M., Chu, R., & Chang, Y. (2007). Seeking self-organization in classroom computer-mediated discussion through a complex adaptive systems lens. *National Reading Conference Yearbook, 56*, 304-318. Oak Creek, WI: National Reading Conference.

Jordan, M. E., Schallert, D. L., & the D-Team. (2008). *Expressing uncertainty in computer-mediated discourse: Language as a marker of intellectual work.* Paper presented at the annual meeting of the National Reading Conference, Orlando, FL.

Kuhn, D., & Goh, W. W. L. (2005). Arguing on the computer. In T. Koschmann, D. Suthers, & T. W. Chan (Eds.), *Computer supported collaborative learning 2005: The next 10 years* (pp. 125-134). Mahwah, NJ: Erlbaum.

Matusov, E. (1996). Intersubjectivity without agreement. *Mind, Culture, and Activity, 3*, 25-45.

Mercer, N. (1995). *The guided construction of knowledge.* Clevedon, UK: Multilingual Matters.

Lincoln, Y. S., & Guba, E. G. (1985). *Naturalistic inquiry.* Newbury Park, CA: Sage Publications.

Pena-Shaff, J., Martin, W., & Gay, G. (2001). An epistemological framework for analyzing student interactions in computer-mediated environments. *Journal of Interactive Learning Research, 12*(1), 41-68.

Piaget, J. (1926). *The language and thought of the child.* New York, NY: Harcourt.

Schallert, D. L., Lissi, M. R., Reed, J. H., Dodson, M. M., Benton, R. E., & Hopkins, L. F. (1996). How coherence is socially constructed in oral and written classroom discussions of reading assignments. In K. Hinchman, D. J. Leu, & C. K. Kinzer (Eds.), *Forty-fourth Yearbook of the National Reading Conference.* Chicago, IL: NCR Inc.

Schallert, D., Reed, J. H., & the D-Team. (2003-2004). Intellectual, motivational, textual, and cultural considerations in teaching and learning with computer-mediated discussion. *Journal of Research on Technology in Education, 36*(2), 104-118.

Smolka, A. L. B., De Goes, M. C. R., & Pino, A. (1995). The construction of the subject: A persistent question. In J. V. Wertsch, P. D. Rio, & A. Alvarez (Eds.), *Sociocultural studies of mind* (pp. 165–84). Cambridge, UK: Cambridge University Press.

Spears, R., Lea, M., Corneliussen, R., Postmes, T., & Harr, W. T. (2002). Computer-mediated communication as a channel for social resistance: The strategic side of SIDE. *Small Group Research, 33*, 555-574.

Street, B. V. (2005). New literacies, new times: How do we describe and teach the forms of literacy knowledge, skills, and values people need for new times? *Yearbook of the National Reading Conference, 55,* 21-42.

Torrance, P. (1950). The phenomenon of resistance in learning. *Journal of Abnormal & Social Psychology, 15,* 592-597.

von Wright, G. H. (1971). *Explanation and understanding.* Ithaca, NY: Cornell University Press.

Wade, S. E., & Fauske, J. R. (2004). Dialogue online: Prospective teachers' discourse strategies in computer-mediated discussions. *Reading Research Quarterly, 39,* 134-160.

Transmediating with Multimodal Literacies: Adolescents' Literature Learning through DV Composing

Suzanne M. Miller
University at Buffalo, SUNY

The argument that media and mass culture are becoming more sophisticated and demanding (Gee, 2003, 2004; Jenkins, 2006; Johnson, 2005) suggests that media-savvy adolescents may have new cognitive resources to bring to school. Games, movies, and even some television shows challenge participants to fill in information gaps that characterize new media "texts." The resulting puzzlement leads to a reflective search for answers (Dewey, 1933/2010) through repeated viewings and consulting with other audience members. In response, some active viewers also create and publish content for Web 2.0 in fan-fiction, videos, blogs, adapted games, etc., which drives a new "participatory culture" (Jenkins, 2006). This "flow of content across multiple media platforms" (Jenkins, p. 2) occurs "in the brains" of participants through their social interaction with others and with texts. From a sociocultural perspective, this engagement with networked others and media texts can lead to mastery of new textual practices and, thereby, to extended cognitive development (Kozulin, 1998; Vygotsky, 1978; Wertsch, 1998).

Increasingly in digital practices outside of school, adolescent youth actively compose such meaning through new kinds of texts in their social worlds (Lenhart, Madden, Smith, & Macgill, 2007; Lenhart, Purcell, Smith, & Zickuhr, 2010). When they have opportunities to use new digital, cultural tools for learning in school, students draw on this media learning (Mills, 2010). Like all of us, adolescents take the bits and pieces of media and transform them "into resources through which we make sense of our everyday lives" (Jenkins, 2006, p. 4). In the digital world of information overload, no one can know everything, but everyone knows something: "We can put the pieces together if we pool our resources and combine our skills" (Jenkins, p. 4) to interpret texts in media and in the world.

Recent research suggests that by drawing on such collaborative meaning-making, multimodal media resources, and digital composing tools, students and teachers have created new kinds of contexts to mediate content learning and identity making (e.g., Miller, 2008; Miller, 2010b; Miller, Blondell, Cercone, & Goss, in review). In these classroom studies, the distributed intelligence and accessible social support for a "shared endeavor" that operate as "affinity spaces" in the participatory culture out of school (Gee, 2003) emerged in school. These classroom affinity spaces provided access to digital composing tools, multiple modes of representation, and peer support—with the addition of teachers and curricular texts as available resources. In the current study, I examined students' accounts of multimodal composing with digital video where evidence suggested classroom affinity spaces emerged. Specifically, the present study addresses the question of what student learning occurred in these urban classrooms when English teachers initiated student digital video composing about literature.

REVIEW OF THEORY AND RESEARCH

Through the technological and cultural contexts of the past two decades, the notion of literacy in professional organizations has significantly shifted from the traditional sense of reading and writing *only* print text *to* an expanded sense of reading and writing multiple forms of nonprint texts, as well (International Reading Association [IRA], 2001; National Council of Teachers of English [NCTE], 2005). Support for this view comes from interdisciplinary theory and research grounded in sociocultural and literacy scholarship, and relevant research in psychology, new literacies, social semiotics, media, and English studies.

Teaching and Learning of Literature

The social practice of reading literature can be seen as a cultural tool to promote ways of thinking and making sense of the world (e.g., Kozulin, 1998). When reading a literary text, interpretations are shaped by experiences in cultural groups. In the literature classroom, socioculturally grounded research suggests that in activities which give students interpretive agency and provide support through mediation to complete challenging tasks, students learn ways of reading, talking, thinking and making meaning: sociocultural and emotional-cognitive development is at stake as adolescents engage with literature, especially in dialogic conversation with the interpretations of others (e.g., Applebee, Langer, Nystrand & Gamoran, 2003; Langer, 1996; Lee, 2003; Miller, 2003).

These studies draw on Bakhtin's (as cited in Holquist & Liapunov, 1982) theory of dialogue as the nature of language-in-use, and his parallel concern with issues of dialogic forms of consciousness for creating meaning in literature and in life. In brief, Bakhtin demonstrates that the forms of language people use have been learned from others. Such social languages "are specific points of view on the world, forms for conceptualizing the world in words" (p. 291). To work against the dangers of the monologic mind trapped in one social language, unable to engage multiple perspectives or interpretations, Bakhtin argued the need to consider one of our social languages in terms of another to create a new dialogic perspective that prompts thinking critically about worldviews. Adapting this theory to explain literacy practices, Gee (2004) argues that along with uses of language (discourses), people learn the ways of acting, talking, reading, writing, and thinking appropriate to and identified with a particular social group (Discourses). In Bakhtin's view, the literary text offers rich opportunities to materialize and examine these Discourses, because it both materializes and promotes a dialogue of perspectives and, thereby, serves as a cultural tool for promoting such dialogic reflection (also, Kozulin, 1998).

Multimodal Representation in Theory & Practice

A conceptually similar argument is articulated by Kress (2010) in his summary of decades of work on a social-semiotic theory of multimodal communication and representation. He argues that using only one authoritative representation of the world in language/print constitutes a "monomodally conceived world" (p. 27). Digital tools, in contrast, provide easy access to representational elements that are multimodal. That is, visual, audio, spatial and gestural modes of representation, along with writing and speaking (Kress, 2010; also New London Group, 1996). From his critical analysis of communicative practices and current media, Kress demonstrates that "signs" made with different resources and modes are "the expression of the interest of socially formed individuals who, with these signs, *realize*—give outward appearance to—their meanings, using culturally available semiotic resources" (p. 10). Vygotsky (1971, 1978), too, argued that besides language, mediational means/cultural tools include multimodal texts such as drawings, maps, and works of art. In this view, "New mediational means transform mediated action" (Wertsch, 1998, p. 25), leading to the question of how the new mediational means of digital video (DV) composing might transform learning in school.

A related line of research situated in the sociocultural theoretical framework, New Literacy Studies (NLS), generally defines literacy practices as ways of communicating within a social group "through the medium of encoded texts" (Lankshear & Knobel, 2006, p. 68). Research in schools illustrates the inclination of even young students to draw on multimodal texts (drawing, drama, media) as resources to mediate their written composing/encoding (Dyson, 1999, 2004). Studies of bringing print and other representational modes together document successes when teachers work to support students and recognize their identity-making lifeworlds (everyday experiences) in their media/literacy practices (e.g., Alvermann, 2010; Knobel & Lankshear, 2010; Snyder & Beavis, 2004; Pahl & Rowsell, 2005). A review of studies of using new digital literacies in urban schools, however, suggested systemic problems in schools serving students living in poverty: researchers found "routine practices that militate against the effective integration of digital tools in literacy curriculum" (Mills, 2010, p. 262).

Digital Video Composing in Schools

Technological advances in hardware and connectivity have made capturing, editing, and distributing DV widely and cheaply accessible, leading educational forecasters to cite DV as an emerging technology that will "significantly impact the choices of learning-focused organizations" (*The Horizon Report*, 2008, p. 3). During one month, December 2007, Internet users in the U.S. watched over 10 billion videos online (Lipsman, 2008). Existing classroom research suggests potential for DV composing as a learning tool for teachers and students. Focusing on using DV composing in English teacher education, Miller (2007) traced teachers' experiences of design—"engaging in purposeful orchestration of modes to create meaning" from the curriculum (p. 66)—and found a shift in their pedagogical stances toward valuing multimodal representations as a literacy practice (see also McVee, Bailey & Shanahan, 2008). In a media studies class adolescent youth designing DV to orchestrate multiple modes used meaning-making activities that paralleled written composing processes (Bruce, 2009). A study of students' accounts of their DV composing across schools has not yet been conducted.

A growing body of research situated in classrooms provides evidence that DV composing can be a multimodal learning tool that leads to increased student engagement and learning (Miller, 2007, 2008; Miller & Borowicz, 2005, 2007; Blondell, 2009; Borowicz, 2005; Costello, 2010; Lauricella, 2006). Ethnographic case studies of teachers integrating DV composing into subject-area classes have shown mixed results. In a longitudinal study Miller, Hughes & Knips (in press) documented the developing multimodal pedagogy of an urban social studies teacher using DV composing as a learning tool that increased student achievement in U.S. History. Borowicz (2005) traced one teacher using DV composing with literature and found thoughtful attention of some urban students to meaning-making and then their disengagement as the teacher turned back to a test-prep only curriculum. Costello (2010) demonstrated both the promise of DV composing and the problems when an English teacher treated the activity as a privilege only for the well behaved in the "tight ship" of his urban school. Other studies documented the gradual changes in teachers struggling to engage students with DV composing assignments that were initially too constrained (Blondell, 2009) or overly teacher determined (Bailey, 2009; Goss, 2009; Cercone, 2009). Cercone (2010) traced the influence on students of a tech-savvy teacher's pedagogy, focusing on student composing and identity-making in what he called the "new literacies classroom." Identity is involved in DV design because "the outcome of Designing is new meaning, something through which meaning makers remake themselves" (Cope & Kalantzis, 2000, p. 23).

From these ongoing analyses of enactments of DV composing as a student-learning tool in the classrooms, my colleagues and I have elaborated a research-based model of *multimodal literacy pedagogy* that has 4 major interactive principles (Miller, McVee, Thompson, & Boyd, 2008; also Miller, 2007, 2008, 2010a, b). Teachers who have transformed themselves and their classrooms to enact student multimodal composing on curricular concepts have these transacting principles in common: they (a) design social spaces for mediating student multimodal composing activities; (b) co-construct with students authentic purposes for these composing activities about curricular concepts; (c) focus explicit attention to multimodal design and critique of multimodal texts; and (d) persistently open opportunities for students to draw on their identities and "lifeworlds." Miller (2010b) takes up specifically the importance of one component: teachers' co-constructing authentic purpose for DV composing in classrooms. In that process, several teachers reframed their practice and their students' learning, leading to the conclusion that negotiating purposeful activity may be the "engine" of transformation for teachers and students.

Across these studies researchers found that learning to use and to teach DV composing about curricular concepts sometimes induced changes in teachers' epistemologies and social practices that promoted changes in their pedagogies and opportunities for student learning (Miller & Borowicz, 2006; Miller, 2007, 2008, 2010a, b). To better understand such change, education needs research documenting outcomes of new literacy practices in school from students' perspectives—particularly how youth feel, if they are more engaged in classrooms, and what youth learn about content, about literacy practices, and about their identities and positions in the world (Moje, 2009). This study addresses the call for examination of student perspectives on their engagement in content learning with new digital tools.

RESEARCH QUESTIONS

This analysis is part of a larger study of students' effortful attention to curricular learning as a result of using new cultural tools. The present study focuses on urban students' accounts of their DV composing in English classrooms to provide an understanding of their literature learning. The study addressed the following question: What student learning occurs when English teachers initiate and mediate student DV composing about literature? By examining students' perceptions of their use of multimodal composing as a literacy-learning tool across 11 English classrooms, I hope to contribute to our understanding of new literacies and literature learning in schools.

METHODOLOGY

School Context

The 11 English classrooms were located in an urban school district in the northeast. The school system had 70 schools, serving predominantly high-poverty communities, with 82% of families eligible for free or reduced-cost lunches. The multi-ethnic community is reflected in the school population with a Black majority, both African Americans and African immigrants (57%); Whites of western European origin (24%); Hispanic (15%); and American Indian, Alaskan, Asian, or Pacific Islander (3%). In 2009 the graduation rate among all students was 53%. In response to performance on the English language arts (ELA) state graduation test, the district mandated a test-practice approach to teaching English. The ELA exam required two essays about literature, so writing about literature became a special target of concern.

Participants

Secondary teachers in a DV composing professional development were invited to participate through the school districts' instructional technology (IT) departments. Teachers learned to make DVs on curricular topics in familiar media genres, such as poetry videos, movie trailers, and public service announcements. Continued support for teacher participants occurred through the university team collaborators visiting classrooms during DV-composing activities. I identified all of the urban Grade 7-12 English teachers who had completed the DV-composing professional development, were still teaching in the district, were not teaching scripted curricula, and who had completed a student-created DV-composing project related to literature. These criteria produced 11 English teachers (seven females, four males). Teaching experience ranged from 2 to 21 years. The criteria for selection of 29 focal students from teachers' classes included a range of engagement in typical class activities and reflecting the ethnicity and gender in the class. The research team interviewed 1-4 students from each class; the two classes with only one student interview had unusual circumstances (i.e., interviews the last day of school). See Appendix for student details.

Data Collection

Interview data for this study were collected over a 3-year period from 2006-2009 by the research team that included Miller, as project director, and graduate research assistants who were all experienced English teachers. The purpose of interviewing for the grounded theory study was to ask students to reconstruct their experiences with DV-composing in English class. Questions prompted for stories about their experiences in the class, including accounts of their process of DV composing (e.g., How did your group come up with the idea? What was your favorite part?). The interview protocol served as a framework, allowing for flexibility of pursuing topics students introduced. Follow-up questions to probe answers (Could you say more about the editing you did?) were part of the protocol. In almost every instance, students were clearly shaping at the point of utterance (Britton, 1993), voicing thoughts they had not verbalized before, indexed by self-talk (e.g., "How do I explain this?") and checking for understanding (e.g., "You know?"). Each interview was digitally recorded with the student's assent and permission of his/her parents. The recordings were transcribed verbatim and reviewed by the interviewer for accuracy.

Data Analysis

I completed an analysis of each verbatim transcript of student interviews, using the constant-comparative method (Strauss & Corbin, 1998) to identify categories that represented the students' experiences of literature and DV composing, including their perceptions about the process of engagement, affordances and limitations, and those comments revealing identity-making and content learning. Reviewing and annotating my analytic and theoretical memos provided another source of categories in a process sometimes called axial coding. The next close reading of the interviews provided a check on the preliminary categories as related to the research questions, resulting in some categories being subsumed into other ones, some re-named to be inclusive of additional evidence, and some newly introduced. I developed an initial pattern explanation for the data trends and themes. In this phase I used the patterns to integrate the themes into propositions that formed a theory grounded in the empirical data of this study. To do justice to the theme of students' content learning, in this report I focus only on that aspect of the analysis.

FINDINGS

Portraying a print text meaning in another sign system is an example of transmediating, a semiotic concept referring to the act of translating meaning from one sign system to another (Siegel, 1995). Findings suggest that this translation generated depth of focus and opportunity for reflection as students composed/created/invented connections between the original literary text and the emerging multimodal text of the digital video.

Transmediating Text with DV: From "Just Words" to Reading for "Meaning"

For some students, the DV-composing assignment led them to new ways of reading and understanding literature. The campaign ad with its persuasive purpose prompted Chantal's 10th grade group to revisit *Julius Caesar* (Shakespeare, 1599/1998) to find support for their candidate for Emperor. Chantal explained that she "definitely understood the play more…because we had to find examples of why we thought [Brutus] would be a good leader, so we took examples from the play and that helped me understand the situation that Brutus was in." [Note: I quote students verbatim in order to maintain their speaking voices, which contain markers of student dialect and vernacular, appropriate to the informal context we tried to create for the interviews.] They interpreted the details about Brutus to create a script for their political ad: "After reading it and then actually acting it out ….[it] kinda gave me a better idea of who these people were." Chantal reflected on how revisiting texts and performance were better for her than writing: "When you write, you kinda get a visual picture, but they're just words. And then when you actually shoot the film, you get to be in the action of seeing what you're doing and how it's gonna end up." The transmediating of acting allowed "just words" to become "what you're doing," an embodying of the interpreted scenes ("to be in the action") that seemed to make the characters "real": "It definitely, like I said, showed us what type of person they are, what kind of personality they had." Her favorite scene showed the audience listening with great attention to the words Brutus was speaking, showing one of his strengths. Interpreting and inferring from drama, especially Shakespeare, is a challenge for most students. Chantal "learned how to understand a play better," contending that her multimodal inquiry developed her ability to read and learn from plays.

Natalie narrated a surprising story of learning. In the beginning of reading *Their Eyes Were Watching God* (Hurston, 1937/2000), she told her teacher, "I hate this book." Usually in Ms. Gorski's 11th grade English class Natalie described herself as "lazy" and "slouching all the time" when "we read books and we do the worksheets." Ms. Gorski found an audio book to play in class to ease the difficulties of reading dialect; they stopped to discuss meanings. At the end, the assignment asked Natalie and other students to transform the book into a thematic "found" poem from lines they selected from the text—on the broad theme of self-discovery. Re-reading with the purpose of understanding whether Janie was still "looking for love" by the end changed the experience for Natalie into an inquiry—she found herself "digging deeper" into the text "'cause I wanted to know how [Janie] was feeling." Her re-reading and reflection were prompted by DV composing and her search for Janie's feelings: "Was she ready to call it quits? You couldn't just find out how that was just by reading the book and then saying, 'Yeah. I know what it was.' You have to go through certain chapters and find out what was going on with her. I think I kinda learned from that….You have to find deep in there and find words that helped her find love."

After her inquiry back into the text, Natalie made her poetry video. She explained the difference for her in this approach to literature: "We're reading books and we're just basically just digging more into the book and being creative with it instead of just reading a book, taking a test on it…[DV] helps me to understand the curriculum of English." In seeking to create images that matched the words and her sense of their meaning, she said, "I think my favorite part is when [we] took—trees blowing and all that. I liked that a lot because it kinda matched that line when [Janie] was looking and waiting, really. It kinda matched perfectly." This aesthetic response to the combined words and images as symbolic seemed to animate Natalie's connection to and interpretation of the book. The whole encounter appeared to be a critical experience for her: in working with a group and then designing her own DV, Natalie learned, "Everything means something"—for her, a new vision of literature and the world.

Thematic Abstraction in DV Meta-Texts

In these classes DV composing helped students to understand thematic abstraction, a fundamental way of thinking about texts and experience.

Beyond the literal in texts and meta-texts. Through her poetry video on *Their Eyes Were Watching God* (Hurston, 1937/2000), Kiara said she learned something new: "Doing this helped me understand English a lot more …everything's not gonna be literal, so you really have to think about stuff more." Likewise Nevin talked about how he'd explain learning about literature in DV composing: "You gotta think outside the box, basically, because everything you see is not …literal… When we're in English class, when we read the story—like when we read *The Giver*—we know that there's not gonna really be no man that's gonna' touch our bats and give us memories."

Thinking beyond the literal was built into the DV assignments Nevin did in Ms. Watson's class. For the first video she asked students to read two flash fiction stories and come up with a "controlling idea" as the topic for their DV. In that video Nevin recalled, "What's the controlling idea we came up with? Like, what we were trying to get to is like the littlest thing could change your life." To demonstrate this theme, Nevin's group acted out a short scene from each story to show

how incidents supported that idea. Tracing this theme across two texts is the same kind of thinking required in the state graduation exam essays, but in this case, the students created the thematic "lens" and supported it multimodally.

Then, in his group's video on *The Giver* (1996), they used that kind of thinking in response to a teacher-provided thematic statement about bravery. Nevin's detailed account of the thinking behind that video demonstrated his ability to provide an abstract reading by constructing an example of "bravery" as solving a moral dilemma by "obeying your conscience":

> We did bravery and obeying your conscience. And at first we had to do just like a regular person [outside the book] obeying their conscience, so we gave—so, what we did was have James in the corner like he was homeless. And I was the conscience and I whispered into Andrea's ear basically—'cause you know how they say your conscience is the little person in your head … and she like then—example of her conscience—and she gave him water, signifying that she was obeying her conscience and giving him a drink.

Nevin's control of the concept of "signifying" was impressive. We asked him to explain the example in order to understand how he constructed the elaborated argument:

> In the end, it related in a lot of ways. In one way, giving food to the homeless, that's trying to help them. And the Giver [Jonas] saving Gabriel, he was trying to help him… From [the homeless example], we went to where Jonas was in the war games and how he told all them to stop, but they—he knew they didn't understand, but that was leading up to what happened in the end where he realized that that wasn't the place for him and he took the baby and left… I mean Jonas leaving the community, it would have hurt him in the—for the short time, but in the long term, it would have helped him 'cause now they got free will, which they didn't have before.

His distinction between short- and long-term effects shows nuance to his thinking. He traces the thematic abstraction across different scenes in the text and performs intertextual thinking and thematic clarity as an extension of the literary text. In the sense that their DV was a text that added to and completed *The Giver* (1996) for them, it was a meta-text for Nevin and his group, one that connected back to the lifeworld that included homelessness. They learned about the thinking needed for constructing an essay for the exam, but much more.

Mindset for thematic abstraction. Ms. Sanders assigned her seniors the task of using a structure from the sonnets to create their own Shakespearean-like quatrain and then to create a poetry video about it. Hazel liked English, but Shakespeare was not easy: "I like poems and I like literature and stuff but I really couldn't understand Shakespeare… You know reading Shakespeare, ain't nobody understand that." Hazel described her group's process: "We only had to come up with four lines, two couplets. We figured two words should rhyme [in] each one, so it was about a boy and a girl and his love for her. In the first part it was good; they were happy. And in the second part he left and it was sad. But it was kind of like a contrast." This account shows Hazel's ability to use disciplinary terms (i.e., couplets) and the structure of the sonnet, with its turn of mood and a revelation. In her video Hazel was particularly pleased with how they communicated a troubling aspect of love in the abstract, rather than love between two people:

> When we put it all together we just used different people and it was like every

line was a different boy and a different girl. So it wasn't just one boy and one girl, both happy and then both sad. But it was like one and then another and then another and then another. It was cool.... You got to understand it not only from just one boy and one girl being happy and then sad or just one relationship after another, [but] different people.

This clever representation of a repeating cycle of love and loss fits well with Shakespeare's complex depictions of love in the sonnets. Hazel described another group's poem showing her appreciation of their physical representation of thematic abstraction: "This other poem, it had like a timeless theme and it showed how [the camera] was like going all around but it was, like, he was in still pictures and I thought that was so cool." In the end, Hazel saw the purpose for the assignment as "to teach everybody that they can not only write a poem but understand it and teach everyone else to understand it too." She did well on her Shakespeare test ("got a 98") and said making the poetry video helped: "It wasn't exactly Shakespeare, but it was just getting the gist of everything. Like I had to put my mind in a set where, okay, this is not actually what it seems or it's not literally the sky is dark or something like that. It probably meant like a dark, sad emotion or something. I had to connect the two." The "gist" seemed to be Hazel's understanding of an expectant mindset that questioned images for potential symbolic meaning and required active readers "to connect" the literal image with representational possibilities. This insight provided her with a workable strategy for approaching literary texts and possible abstract themes.

Students' multimodal composing on literature generated a new appreciation for the rewards of this active stance and sustained attention to print texts through multimodal reflection on print meaning. By using modes to engage more of their bodies in materially and conceptually composing interpretations; delving into symbolic thinking and abstract meaning; re-reading deeply with purpose; and drawing on and reading their lifeworlds with thematic intent, students developed their thinking and learning through their transmediating efforts in DV composing. In the words of Kress (2010), their "transformative engagements" led to learning, an expansion of their "semiotic/conceptual resources."

Transmediating DV Composing to the Written Essay

The clearest example of the relationship between DV composing and essay writing came from Ms. Watson's class. Her DV assignments actively served to scaffold the structure of the thematic essay in a way that engaged students, but also focused attention to the thinking and organization involved in this written form. As described earlier, the first DV assignment asked students to create a thematic link between two flash fiction pieces and then make a DV to show it. The second DV assignment asked students to respond to a teacher-provided theme (critical lens) and asked students to illustrate it with examples from life and from *The Giver* (1996). Her student Nevin was quite clear about the wisdom of this mediation:

I learned that writing most of these essays that we have to write for the English III exams are easier than they seem. Like, when somebody explaining something to you, you just getting words on how to write words, but the video gave us another example. So, instead of getting words we got actions to go along with the words, so it helped us understand.

Only in this class did students suggest that the graduation essays "were easier than they seem." Nevin's reasoning that other modes—actions, images, sounds—provided a better mediation than a within-mode explanation—"getting words on how to write words"—seems to be a rational explanation.

The thematic abstraction Nevin was supporting in his DV on *The Giver* (1996), served him well as he wrote a critical lens on the theme of strengths. He was able to flexibly reason about these abstractions: "What we did was about bravery, but this one is about strengths and bravery is a strength. So I basically just switched it around from basically talking about bravery to adding bravery and courage into a strength." Framing bravery and courage as a moral strength was a thoughtful move. From there he drew on the thematic video he and his group had composed to guide his essay:

> Like now that I'm writing the essays right after we did that [DV], it helped me understand them more…Like with—like 'cause with the essay, especially with the one that I'm doing now with the critical lens 'cause we had to pick out a certain part about *The Giver* and 'cause acting it out helped me write my critical lens 'cause that's all I had to basically do is go back and think about, okay, what'd we do with the video? And I remember it, okay, this thing and this—I just took the scene and made it as my body, my body paragraph.

Using the DV as a mental model for the essay, with scene corresponding to paragraph, mediated his writing multimodally; his acting served as a kinesthetic reminder to use the scene as "my body paragraph." The sense of embodied memory and cognition is strong in his description.

Nevin drew a sharp distinction between this essay and how he had approached earlier ones: "Whatever the statement is before, we used to really sit there and think like, okay—like, I used to basically write a summary of the whole story." This plot-summary strategy was such a widespread stand-in for thematic abstraction and analysis in student essays, that it appeared on the state rubric as the description for a score of 2 (not passing) on a 6-point scale. What Nevin learned from the DV composing seems relatively simple—unless you do not understand it:

> The first one that we did on *The Giver*, I learned to base both body paragraphs on your statement….but now I see just pull out a specific *part* of the story. Summarize the story real quick like, basically, the main character and what happened. And, once you do that, find a *part* in the story that best suits the quote and use the literary elements just to back you.

Nevin's move from a plot-driven to a theme-driven essay was what made the essay much easier than he had thought it was. With some effort to shape at the point of utterance, he also provided a conclusion that elaborated what he learned: "And doing the video project, we acted out, basically, the way the literary elements… the way that they helped—basically, the way that they helped us prove why that part of the story relates to the quote." Here, Nevin seems to realize the persuasive purpose of the essay that makes his own thinking relevant to the writing, and he completes the account of what makes the written argument—the explanation of "why that part of the story relates to the quote." In all, Nevin has learned through his DV composing to structure his written essay, explain abstractions like strength as inclusive of bravery and following conscience, and use explanation to connect an example to a claim or theme.

This idea that DV composing mediates written composing also showed up from Tacita, who was in the same class. She narrated a similar kind of learning. In talking about DV composing and critical lens composing, she explained: "We learn how to use the digital camera and we learn how to edit things out that we didn't want in our video….It helped me understand the controlling idea better. [How'd it do that?] Because I never understood what it was until I did the video." This terminology of "controlling idea" was one of many concepts that teachers used to try to teach thematic abstraction to students. In using this term in the DV assignment, Ms. Watson engaged students' effortful attention to its use as a guiding idea in the DV. Before doing the video Tacita admits, "I never understood what it was." As an 11th grader scheduled to take the ELA exam, Tacita must have heard the term many times. Perhaps, like Nevin, she was "just getting words on how to write words," in a way that did not help her to understand. She says, in fact, " I ain't never know what it [controlling idea] was FOR. I thought the essays was stupid." After finishing the DV, she was able to explain the intertextual intent of the critical lens (thematic) essay:

> In controlling idea, you got to compare the two stories and find out if they got the same controlling idea—you've got to see if they've got the same controlling idea and stuff. In the critical lens, you've got to find two stories that go with the quote, agree or disagree with the quote. [DV] made me **understand** the essays more.

Her DV composing required active thinking that carried over to thinking about print and written texts. A more knowledgeable Tacita understood the purpose, finally, for controlling idea: "The essays are important because if you want to know what the two stories is talking about, then you— or to show what they talking about, then [you show] what's the point?"

In other classes students felt more confident about writing critical lens essays after composing DVs on a literary text. After making her poetry video on *Their Eyes Were Watching God* (1937/2000), Natalie felt, "I would definitely use that on a critical lens question because now I know a lot about the book. I've learned so much about it. And I can just right off the bat tell every single detail about the book." Because in that class students transmediated the book to a thematic poem and the poem to a poetry video, Natalie had "spent more time with it than any other book that we've done." Dax saw that, "With your essay and with your video you have to have thought before you start it" and in both you need to "perform, meaning writing it down," and finally put "your ideas in a very creative way where it all runs together and makes sense." In the context where writing was too often seen as not requiring thinking, this account offers a process parallel to DV composing that includes a role for student ideas and performance organized for coherence ("makes sense").

DISCUSSION AND IMPLICATIONS

Students' accounts of their engagement in challenging DV-composing assignments showed that transmediating (Siegel, 2005) with multimodal tools developed students' understandings of specific texts and of literature as a tool for reflection, as well as creating new stances towards reading print texts and writing about them. They learned new ways of immersive reading and thinking to create new content (a meta-text) about literary text; they learned strategies for making meaning from text and the world through analysis, synthesis, symbolic/metaphoric thinking, and thematic abstraction. Many students were able to speak of their learning in remarkable detail. They exhibited signs of "knowing how" and "mastery" in that they could "use a mediational means with facility"

(Wertsch, 1998, p. 50-51). The abilities of, for example, Natalie, Hazel, and Nevin to describe the persuasive academic social language related to arguing with examples demonstrated that they knew how to use the conceptual tools they referenced and had learned strategies for making sense of poetry, drama and novel. The expansion of culturally available resources in school expanded students' semiotically available resources and, thereby, their habits of mind.

The importance of social identity in a classroom of adolescents cannot be overstated. Not only do constructed stories of one's identity have "strong emotional resonance," identities are also "a key means through which people care about and care for what is going on around them" (Holland, 1998, p. 5). As Dax, Chantal, Natalie, and others became multimodal inquirers and composers, they construed a new sense of self as creative, technologically savvy, and able to "dig into" and understand even difficult text. They learned to conceptualize the world in words in a new-to-them Academic Discourse. As they engaged in and cared about "authoring the world," they at the same time were "becoming" more (Bakhtin as cited in Holquist & Liapunov, 1982; Kozulin, 1998).

The findings are related to one long-term DV-composing project. The field needs more studies of student responses to and learning from various forms of multimodal composing across contexts. While the findings reveal something about teacher approaches to DV composing in literature classes, additional examinations of the pedagogies of teachers could contribute to a framework for a multimodal literacy pedagogy (e.g., Miller, 2010 a, b; Miller & McVee, in press).

Drawing on biological/neuroscience research and Vygotskian theories of conceptual development, Kalantzis and Cope (2008) focus on "the enormous flexibility and generativity of the human symbol making systems of language, image, sound, touch, gesture and space" (p. 152). Findings in this study demonstrate that in mediated DV composing, diverse students, including those who struggled in school, responded with effortful attention and, through their collaborative composing, learned new ways of reading and thinking. They drew on their cognitive resources developed in media out of school to materialize their thinking in digital video. This finding can be explained in part by the "profound growth in human capacities" resulting when these multimodal forms of representation "relate to each other, forming structures or systems of symbol-to-symbol relationships" (p. 152). From this view, multimodal composing serves as a transformative tool for learning: it can be seen as one of "the new basics" of "New Learning," necessitated by rapid changes in technology and culture in a digital world.

AUTHOR'S NOTE

I am grateful to the research assistants who have been instrumental in the City Voices, City Visions Digital Video Composing project, especially Monica Blondell, James Cercone, Stephen Goss, and Merridy Knips. This study was funded, in part, by the John R. Oishei Foundation.

REFERENCES

Alvermann, D. E. (2002). *Adolescents and literacies in digital world*. New York, NY: Peter Lang.
Alvermann, D. E. (2010). *Adolescents' online literacies: Connecting classrooms, digital media, & popular culture.* New York, NY: Peter Lang.
Applebee, A., Langer, J. A., Nystrand, M. & Gamoran, A. (2003). Discussion-based approaches to developing understanding: Classroom instruction and student performance in middle and high school English, *American Educational Research Journal, 40,* 685-730.
Bailey, N. M. (2009). 'It makes it more real': Teaching new literacies in a secondary English classroom. *English Education, 41,* pp. 207-234.

Barton, D., & Hamilton, E. (1998). *Local literacies: Reading and writing in one community.* London, UK: Routledge.

Blondell, M., (2009). *An English teacher's design of digital video composing in an urban high school: Impacts on student engagement and learning.* Unpublished doctoral dissertation, University at Buffalo, State University of New York.

Borowicz, S. (2005). *Embracing lives through the video lens: An exploration of literacy teaching and learning with digital video technology in an urban secondary English classroom.* Unpublished doctoral dissertation, University at Buffalo.

Britton, J. (1993). *Language and learning: The importance of speech in children's development* (2nd ed.). Portsmouth, NH: Boynton/Cook Publishers. (Original work published 1970).

Bruce, D. L. (2009). Writing with visual images: Examining the video composition processes of high school students. *Research in the Teaching of English, 43,* 426-450.

Buckingham, D. (2008). Introducing identity. In D. Buckingham (Ed.), *Youth, identity, and digital media* (pp. 1-22). Cambridge, MA: Massachusetts Institute of Technology Press.

Buckingham, D. (2009). *Youth, identity, and digital media.* Cambridge, MA: Massachusetts Institute of Technology Press.

Cercone, J. (2009, November). *Negotiating teacher growth: Adapting digital video composing in an urban classroom.* Paper presented at annual conference of the National Council of Teacher of English. Philadelphia, PA.

Cercone, J. (2010). *Learning English in new times: The participatory design spaces of the new literacies classroom.* Unpublished doctoral dissertation, University at Buffalo.

Cope, B., & Kalantzis, M. (2000). Multiliteracies: The beginning of an idea. In B. Cope & M. Kalantzis (Eds.), *Multiliteracies: Literacy learning and the design of social futures* (pp. 3–8). London, UK: Routledge.

Costello, A. (2010). Silencing stories: The triumphs and tensions of multimodal teaching and learning in an urban context. In P. Albers & J. Sanders (Eds.) *Literacies, the arts and multimodality* (pp. 234-254). Urbana, IL: National Council of Teachers of English.

Creswell, J. W. (2006). *Qualitative inquiry and research design: Choosing among five traditions.* Thousand Oaks, CA: Sage.

Dewey, J. (2010). *How we think: A restatement of the relation of reflective thinking to the educative process.* New York, NY: Booktree. (Original work published in 1933.)

Dyson, A. H. (1999). Coach Bombay's kids learn to write: Children's appropriation of media material for school literacy. *Research in the teaching of English, 33,* 367-397.

Dyson, A. H. (2004). Diversity as a "handful": Toward re-theorizing the basics. *Research in the teaching of English, 39,* 211-214.

Gee, J. P. (2003). *What video games have to teach us about learning and literacy.* New York, NY: Palgrave Macmillan.

Gee, J. P. (2004). *Situated language and learning: A critique of traditional schooling.* London, UK: Routledge.

Goss, S. (2009, November). *Between theory and practice: Teacher stance and multimodal literacies in the classroom.* Paper presented at annual conference of the National Council of Teachers of English, Philadelphia, PA.

The Horizon Report (2008). Austin, TX: The New Media Consortium.

Holland, D., Lachiocotte, W., Skinner, D., & Cain, C. (1998). *Identity and agency in cultural worlds.* Cambridge, MA: Harvard University Press.

Holquist, M., & Liapunov, V. (Eds.). (1982). *The dialogic imagination: Four essays by M. M. Bakhtin* (V. Liapunov & M. Holquist, Trans.). Austin, TX: University of Texas Press.

Hurston, Z. N. (1937/2000). *Their eyes were watching God.* New York, NY: Harper Collins.

International Reading Association. (2001). *Integrating literacy and technology in the curriculum: A position statement.* Retrieved from http://www.reading.org/resources/issues/positions_technology.html

Jenkins, H. (2006). *Convergence culture: Where old and new media collide.* New York, NY: New York University Press.

Johnson, S. (2005). *Everything bad is good for you: How today's popular culture is actually making us smarter.* New York, NY: Riverhead Books.

Kalantzis, M., & Cope, B. (2008). *New learning: Elements of a science of learning.* Cambridge, MA: Cambridge University Press.

Knobel, M. & Lankshear, C. (2010). *DIY Media: Creating, sharing, and learning with new technologies.* New York, NY: Peter Lang.

Kozulin, A. (1998). *Psychological tools: A sociocultural approach to education.* Cambridge, MA: Harvard University Press.

Kress, G. (2010). *Multimodality: A social semiotic approach to contemporary communication.* New York, NY: Routledge.

Langer, J. (1996). *Envisioning literature: Literary understanding and literature instruction,* New York, NY: Teachers College Press.

Lankshear, C., & Knobel, M. (2006). *New Literacies: Everyday practices and classroom learning* (2nd). Berkshire, England: Open University Press.

Lauricella, A. M. (2006). *Digital video production as a tool for learning; Exploring multiple text documents in an urban social studies classroom.* Unpublished doctoral dissertation, University at Buffalo, Statue University of New York.

Lee, C. D. (2003). Cultural modeling: CHAT as a lens for understanding instructional discourse based on African American English discourse patterns. In A. Kozulin, B. Gindis, V. Ageyev, & S. Miller (Eds.), *Vygotsky's educational theory in cultural context* (pp. 393-410). Cambridge, MA: Cambridge University Press.

Lenhart, A., Madden, M., Smith, A., & Macgill, A. (2007). *Teens and social media.* Retrieved from Pew Internet & American Life Project website: http://www.pewinternet.org/Reports/2007/Teens-and-Social-Media/1-Summary-of-Findings.aspx

Lenhart, A., Purcell, K., Smith, A. & Zickuhr, K. (2010). *Social media and mobile Internet use among teens and young adults.* Retrieved from Pew Internet & American Life Project website: http://www.pewinternet.org/~/media//Files/Reports/2010/PIP_Social_Media_and_Young_Adults_Report_Final_with_toplines.pdf

Leu, D. J., Jr., Kinzer, C. K., Coiro, J., & Cammack, D. W. (2004). Toward a theory of new literacies emerging from the Internet and other information and communication technologies. In R. B. Ruddell & N. J. Unrau (Eds.), *Theoretical models and processes of reading* (pp. 1570–1613). Newark, DE: International Reading Association.

Lipsman, A. (2008). U. S. Internet users viewed 10 billion videos online in record-breaking month of December according to comScore Video Metrix [Comscore Press Release]. Retrieved from http://www.comscore.com/press/release.asp?press=2051

Lowry, L. (1996) *The Giver.* New York, NY: Dell Laurel Leaf.

McVee, M., Bailey, N., & Shanahan, L. (2008). Using digital media to interpret poetry: Spiderman meets Walt Whitman. *Research in the Teaching of English, 43,* 112-143.

Miller, S. M. (2003). How literature discussion shapes thinking: Teaching/learning habits of the heart and mind. In A. Kozulin, V. Ageyev, S. Miller, B. Gindis. (Eds.) *Vygotsky's educational theory in cultural context* (pp. 289-316). Cambridge, England: Cambridge University Press.

Miller, S. M. (2007). English teacher learning for new times: Digital video composing as multimodal literacy practice. *English Education, 40,* 64-83.

Miller, S. M. (2008). Teacher learning for new times: Repurposing new multimodal literacies and digital-video composing for schools. In J. Flood, S. B. Heath, & D. Lapp (Eds.), *Handbook of research on teaching literacy through the communicative and visual arts,* (Vol.2, pp. 441-460). New York, NY: Erlbaum and the International Reading Association.

Miller, S. M. (2010a). Towards a multimodal literacy pedagogy: Digital video composing as 21st century literacy. In P. Albers & J. Sanders (Eds.) *Literacies, art, and multimodality,* (pp. 254-281). Urbana-Champaign, IL: National Council of Teachers of English.

Miller, S. M. (2010b). Reframing multimodal composing for student learning: Lessons on purpose from the Buffalo DV project. *Contemporary Issues in Technology and Teacher Education, 10,* 197-219. Retrieved from: http://www.citejournal.org/vol10/iss2/maintoc.cfm

Miller, S. M., & Borowicz, S. (2005). City Voices, City Visions: Digital video as literacy/learning supertool in urban classrooms. In L. Johnson, M. Finn, & R. Lewis (Eds.), *Urban education with an attitude* (pp. 87-105). Albany, NY: State University of New York Press.

Miller, S. M., & Borowicz, S. (2007). New literacies with an attitude: Transformative teacher education through digital video learning tools. In Finn, M. & Finn, P. (Eds.), *Teacher education with an attitude* (pp. 111-126). Albany, NY: State University of New York Press.

Miller, S. M., Blondell, M., Cercone, J., & Goss, S. (under review). Multimodal composing through literature: Effortful attention, immersive reading, and digital video meta-texts in mediated classroom learning.

Miller, S. M., & McVee, M. (in press). *Multimodal composing in classrooms: Learning and teaching in a digital world.* New York, NY: Routledge.

Miller, S. M., Hughes, K., & Knips, M. (In press). Teacher knowledge-in-action: Enacting multimodal literacy pedagogy for DV composing. In S. Kadjer & C. Young (Eds.) *Research on technological pedagogical content knowledge in English classrooms.* Charlotte, NC: Academic Information Press.

Miller, S., McVee, M., Boyd, F., & Thompson, M. K. (2008, March). *Why multimodal literacy practice? Lessons from students, teachers and teacher educators.* Symposium conducted at the annual conference of the American Educational Research Association, New York, NY.

Mills, K. A. (2010). A review of the 'Digital Turn' in the New Literacy Studies. *Review of Educational Research, 80,* 246-271.

Moje, E. B. (2009). Standpoints: A call for new research on new and multi-literacies. *Research in the Teaching of English, 43,* 348-362.

Moran, J., Ferdig, R. E., Pearson, P. D., Wardrop, J. & Blomeyer, R. L. (2008). Technology and reading performance in the middle-school grades: A meta-analysis with recommendations for policy and practice. *Journal of Literacy Research, 40,* 6-58.

National Council of Teachers of English (2005). *NCTE position statement on multimodal literacies.* Retrieved from http://www.ncte.org/positions/statements/multimodalliteracies

National Council of Teachers of English (2008). *NCTE position statement: Definition of 21st century literacies.* Retrieved from: http://www.ncte.org/positions/statements/21stcentdefinition.

New London Group. (1996). A pedagogy of multiliteracies: Designing social futures. *Harvard Educational Review, 66,* 60-92.

Pahl, K., & Rowsell, J. (2005). *Literacy and education: Understanding the New Literacy Studies in the classroom.* Thousand Oaks, CA: Sage.

Shakespeare, W. (1599/1998). Rosen, B., & Rosen, W. (Eds.). *Julius Caesar* (Signet Classic Shakespeare). Logan, IA: Perfection Learning Company.

Siegel, M. (1995). More than words: The generative power of transmediation for learning. *Canadian Journal of Education / Revue canadienne de l'éducation, 1,* 455-475.

Snyder, I. & Beavis, C. (2004). *Doing literacy online: Teaching, learning and playing in an electronic world.* Creskill, NJ: Hampton Press.

Strauss, A. & Corbin, J. (1998). *Basics of qualitative research techniques and procedures for developing grounded theory* (2nd ed.). Thousand Oaks, CA: Sage.

Vygotsky, L. S. (1971). *The psychology of art.* Cambridge, MA: MIT Press.

Vygotsky. L. S. (1978). *Mind in society: The development of higher psychological processes.* Cambridge, MA: Harvard University Press.

Wertsch, J. V. (1998). *Mind as Action.* New York, NY: Oxford University Press.

APPENDIX

Table 1. Focal Students[1] Interviewed in English Classes using DV Composing

Name	Grade, School	Student about Teacher	Self-Identity[2]
Mr. Lange			
Casey	7 urban	"Gave us confidence" in making DV; told students to not be nervous and have fun	Leader in his DV group; often bored with school, esp. taking notes— classes "like chewing the same piece of gum over & over"
Lakesha	7 urban	Noted he brought in DV example when students didn't understand what to do; doesn't give the answer – makes her wish "I could do better"	School can be boring and seems to be a lot about grades. If learning isn't fun, she will "doze" and "daydream". When learning is fun, will be "trying to take part"; grades imp.
Luke	7 urban	Taught Luke things he didn't know about DV	School is "just staring at the board"; likes to work with the computer

Name	Grade, School	Student about Teacher	Self-Identity[2]
Mr. Bradley			
Bill	9 urban	"A little strict" and "screaming a little when people are talking" except during DV	Acts in DVs; Feels "great because I'm up on the computer"
Allen	9 urban	"He's really good to us and he helps us work"	Does his homework, doesn't think it's too much; likes to do DV in groups
Gerald	9 urban	Mostly do workbooks & write essays; with DV he gives a model & suggestions	Does well with writing essays—95%—but "I just don't like writing"
Jasmine	9 urban	"No clue" why he said their poetry video could only have objects in it.	Feels 9th graders get "so much homework"; likes "hands on" "active" aspects of DV
Greg	9 urban	Happy when we do DV, "nice about it," "puts it on the website"	Watches class DVs on website; Likes to write, but it's "tiring"
Mr. Zane			
Chantal	10 urban	Teacher gave examples of genre and how to use literary evidence	Received good grades but thought writing was boring; Leader in DV. {kept to herself about her academics--friends with Ss who weren't turning in assignments}
Ms. Morgan			
Charles	10 urban	Gave students excellent speeches to choose from; integrated DV into her speaking and listening unit.	Learned to use anime in his videos fr online community & global "friends"; leader in group, trying to support Ss & teachers; makes DV at home
Ms. Michaels			
Sasha	11 urban	Gives guideline, encouragement, and "backs out" to let us work together	"1 year in the U.S."; advocates DV to help kids learn; role as editor; studied animation, graphic design & video in his country
Samantha	11 urban	It was fun & interesting that we got to make a movie…and it counted for a grade.	"Work together and you always succeed"; "I acted and directed" and a little bit of everything [English Language Learner]
Sally	11 urban	Teacher shared her own ideas with the students. "And told us what we were going to do, and put us in a good direction."	"Passed the ELA exam"; works with her friend as partner; did video and voiceover; wishes diverse students got along [English Language Learner]
Ms. Winsome			
Conrad	11 urban	Getting us ready for the exam; did lots of essay writing; gave me poetry contest flyers; Kept a blog with last year's videos posted	Loves writing poetry; football player; "72% on ELA exam"; out with injuries for weeks
Anthony	11 urban	Preparing us for the ELA Exam; promised they'd do a DV, but she went on maternity leave	"Visual learner," "got 78% on ELA exam"; does better in Soc. St "where we make movies"
Jane	11 urban	"Mellow," "firm," "everybody respected her"	Always liked Eng—"creating something bigger than yourself"; writes poetry; "failed Eng 9"

Name	Grade, School	Student about Teacher	Self-Identity[2]
Ms. Watson			
Nevin	11 urban	Helped us plan, film, edit, gave advice—"and it worked out."	"Talkative" gets him "in trouble"; "I'm a krumper*, I gotta be energetic"; "I'm just good at writing"; "I don't try too hard in school" [teacher: problem student who disrupts with his talking]
Tacita	11 urban	Teacher helped plan, acted in films, assisted with filming	Liked how she could make her DV look like *Law and Order*; wishes ethnic/racial groups could get along better; {got in arguments with her teacher}
Ms. Peters			
Omar	11 urban	Teacher should "make sure we have like the right equipment... like flash drives and stuff right here so we can save [video] so no mistakes can happen like this. They should have more computers and more room for us. And more time available to make the videos."	Watched DV online, now "can create them"; last year an A student, this year B; works on computer at home til 2 am "to learn more"; wishes could use computer more school-just study hall; graduating senior
Zack	11 urban	Teacher Helped with ideas; "Most of the students lost their videos because they gave them to the teacher and the teacher lost them. Or some other students came and recorded over them. So they could be more careful about it."	Never made a DV before, now making one at home; liked editing DV best; kept re-doing the video when the teacher lost his group's footage
Ms. Gorski			
Kiara	11 urban	"She's a fun teacher." Helped with putting ideas together in the DV projects; Asked about meanings to help students "get into" the novel	"Learning is fun to me sometimes"; likes "trying new things"; found editing "exciting"; liked the novel after she came to understand it; [took care of her siblings at home]
Carlos	11 urban	"The teacher is always a good help when it comes to like the video projects, [she's] right there, and everybody's working together and it's like a group effort, it's not just you."	Likes football; has done DV before in Eng class; wishes had DV in math & science; liked the novel *Their Eyes Were Watching God (TEWWG)*
Natalie	11 urban	Hopes to have Ms Gorski again next year; she has "personality" "all bubbly" "pumped us up to do DV" "one of my favorite English teachers	Was "lazy"; trying to learn from group member how to "just focus more instead of just slouching all the time"; Learned more about *TEWWG* than any other novel
Gavin	10 urban	Helped out to get them going on the movie trailer and to think about symbolism	Above average student, does his work; felt school work "gots to get done"; a lot of English work "boring," but okay with him

Name	Grade, School	Student about Teacher	Self-Identity[2]
Mr. Garvey			
Miguel	12 urban	"He kind of came as a referee and just stood there and helped us and I learned how to make two out of one, how to make one out of two from him because he always say, "Okay, how can we make this work together? How can we do this to be one?" I learned that from him... He's like a mentor to everybody."	Did videos in 11th gr history; in U.S. 5yrs.; Leader in his group, pushed for quality; wants to be a teacher [needs a 5th yr to finish high school because he was failing other classes]
Dax	12 urban	Cool enough to sit down and talk about ideas for DV; gave feedback on drafts of the videos	"English usually boring beyond all reason"; "worst subject"; did DV in Social Studies year before; Was "a barbarian with technology"; DV made me think. "learned a lot"; feel like "a tree growing roots"
Al	12 urban	"The freedom to basically know that he'll – as long as he knows that you're getting your work done he doesn't bother you"	Watches cop shows, loves *Law & Order*, stayed after school to do a lot of editing; had conflicts with his DV group; "not the best English student"; English "boring beyond all belief"; "I wanna become a cop"
Ms. Sanders			
Lynne	12 urban	"The teacher doesn't necessarily feed you everything. The process of learning you have to do it on yourself and you have to get information from others so you have to make sure you work well with other people in your group or you won't be successful."	Did videos in 10th grade Social Studies; never heard of DV in English, but learned about imagery in doing hers
Hazel	12 urban	"She actually opened up the door on a video project. And this is the first time I actually heard of an English teacher doing something like that so I thought that was cool. She actually took the chance and it worked out great."	Did videos in 10th grade social studies; leader in her group; wanted to be a teacher, now wants to be an Miller; accepted to private college but can't afford it; waiting for state college

[1]Focal students in classes were chosen to include diverse perspectives along the lines of gender, race, ethnicity, participation, and course grades. Only those returning parental permission were interviewed.

[2]Primary identity statements made by students in their interviews, sometimes in response to the question "How do you describe yourself as a student?" and sometimes as they talked about their experiences in school and in the class. [Anything in brackets is from the teacher.] {In a few cases, information from observations of research team are included in {} to provide more context.}

**As Nevin defined krumping: "It's a religious dance that originated in Africa...as war chants and it's a positive outlook, outlet your energy and stay out of the streets. And it relieves certain stress."

A Comparison of Education, Business, and Engineering Underclass Students' Internet Use and Their Experience, Confidence, and Competence in Using New Literacies of the Internet

Suyeon Kim
Erin McTigue
Jack Helfeldt
Texas A&M University

The recent shift from print-dominated text reading to online reading has redefined the skills needed to be fully literate. While it may be assumed that young people, who have grown up with the Internet, may be fully prepared to navigate new literacies of the Internet, exposure does not guarantee mastery. In this study, we explored incoming teachers' (who have grown up with the Internet) skills and experiences with new literacies of the Internet and compared them to their peers in other areas of study. It is critical for teacher-preparation programs to understand current pre-service teachers' strengths and weaknesses in this area in order to revise curriculum and learning experiences accordingly.

RATIONALE FOR THE STUDY

Recent evidence (Estarbrook & Rainie, 2007; Facebook, 2011; Horrigan, 2009; Lee, Leung, & So, 2004; Leu, Kinzer, Coiro, & Cammack, 2004) indicates that the Internet has become increasingly central in people's personal and professional lives. Due to increased Wi-Fi Internet access, individuals now search, collect, and share vast amounts of information with few geographic constraints. According to Horrigan (2009), 56% of Americans went online via wireless devices in 2009. In addition, more than 500 million Facebook users shared information and interacted with "friends" in virtual communities (Facebook, 2011). Beyond personal use, the Internet has become essential in most workplaces and professions. For example, a recent survey among engineers indicated that they depend heavily on the Internet for many job-related tasks such as locating components (83%), seeking product information (81%), and conducting research (79%) (Electronic Design News, 2008).

Currently, as "digital natives" who are "native speakers of the digital language of computers, video games, and Internet" (Prensky, 2001, p. 1), the majority of today's pre-service teachers have had opportunities to use the Internet throughout their school-aged years. For example, in 2005, 94% of public schools reported that their instructional rooms had Internet access (NCES, 2005). In that same year, 87% of all middle and high school students in the U.S. reported that they used the Internet (Rainie & Hitlin, 2005).

Despite their being "digital natives," current pre-service teachers may not be fully competent in using new literacies of the Internet because they have likely developed the knowledge, skills, and dispositions informally. New literacies of the Internet are defined as the skills that "allow us to use the Internet...to identify important questions, locate information, critically evaluate the usefulness of that information, synthesize information to answer those questions, and then communicate the answers to others" (Leu, et. al., 2004, p.1572). In contrast to reading hard copy or print text, there are many more decisions that Internet readers must make, such as deciding which links to follow or bypass (Leu, et al., 2004). However, typical reading programs in K-12 focus on reading print text so students may not receive formal instruction in this area. Accordingly, beginning pre-service teachers may not differ from younger individuals who proved to be too "accepting" of texts they read on the Internet as reflected by nearly 90% of high-performing seventh-graders who believed false information presented on a website dedicated to the Pacific Northwest tree octopus (Leu, et al., 2007).

The purpose of the current survey research was to investigate beginning pre-service teachers': a) Internet use, b) their experiences in acquiring and using new literacies of the Internet during their high school years, and c) their *perceived confidence* and *performed competence* in locating and evaluating Internet-based information. In addition, we compared these dispositions and skills to their same-aged peers in the academic disciplines of business and engineering so as to determine whether education, business, and engineering majors enter college with the same or uniquely different levels of skills and dispositions associated with new literacies. The majors of business and engineering were selected because for the past five years business students and education students entered into university with similar mean standardized test scores (e.g., SAT), whereas engineering students entered with significantly higher standardized test scores (College Board, 2008). Additionally, all three professional areas have increasingly required job-related use of the Internet (Connect Ohio, 2008; Electronic Design, 2008).

THEORETICAL FRAMEWORK

There are differences between print-based text and electronic text (McKenna, 2001; McKenna, Reinking, Labbo, & Kieffer, 1999; Reinking, 1992), including primarily that electronic texts are often nonlinear (McKenna, 2001). Previous research (McDonald & Stevenson, 1996; McKnight, Dillion, & Richardson, 1990) reported that people performed better with the linear type texts than with the non-linear hypertexts. However, the construct of "new literacies" has been interpreted differently by various scholars (Coiro, Knobel, Lankshear, & Leu, 2008). Some scholars and researchers have described new literacies as social practices (Street, 1998) or multi-literacies (New London Group, 1996). This study is based on a new literacies perspective that defines new literacies as, not simply the skills for Internet reading, but more broadly, as the skills needed to adapt to evolving information technologies (Leu, et al., 2004). Leu, Kinzer, Coiro, and Cammack (2004) provided a set of 10 guiding principles of new literacies that can provide a basis for research in this area. Five of the 10 principles that specifically guided our study on underclass students' Internet use and their experience, confidence, and competence in using new literacy skills were: a) the Internet and other ICTs are crucial for literacy in an information age; b) fundamental literacies are included within new literacies, however, additional literacy skills are required to fully use the Internet and other ICTs; c) critical literacies are important in new literacies of the Internet because anyone can publish on the Internet; d) new types of strategic knowledge are important to use new literacies effectively; and e) the teacher's role becomes more important in students' new literacy learning.

RELATED RESEARCH

Today's children are deemed digital natives and are therefore assumed to be tech-savvy due to their widespread uses of technology. According to Rideout, Foehr, and Roberts (2010), social networking was the most popular computer activity among individuals between the ages of 8 and 18. In 2006, approximately 90% of American teens reported using the Internet, nearly 64% of American teens reported creating online content, and 39% of American online teenagers shared creative contents, such as photos, with others (Lenhart, Madden, McGill, & Smith, 2007). Further, 64% of middle and high school students in the US participated in content creation activities such as creating web pages or writing online journals on the Internet (Lenhart, et al., 2007).

However, widespread use of the Internet for the purposes mentioned above does not automatically insure the development of proficiency in new literacies of the Internet. Differences between traditional literacies and new literacies of the Internet derive from the disparate nature of the texts: Traditional literacy is "about print on a page or decoding and making sense of words, images and other content .... They are the words and pictures students read and pore over that are contained in textbooks, in novels, on standardized tests, and even in comic books" (Miners & Pascopella, 2007, p.12). In traditional literacies, every reader is provided with the same information, in the same order, through the intentionality of the author. In contrast to paper-based texts, online texts are often nonlinear and quite flexible because they can be updated and changed more quickly and easily. A Web page consists of hypertexts and hypermedia. A rich hypertext is constructed by many pages and links that connect each page (Bolter, 1998). Hypermedia consisting of multiple representations and multimedia such as icons, animated symbols, graphics, and video clips that typically provide additional ways of conveying meaning (Coiro & Doubler, 2007) can also become a distraction for some readers (Coiro, 2003).

Therefore, new literacies of the Internet require not only foundational reading skills, but also additional skills and strategies (Miners & Pascopella, 2007). Like print reading, decoding and fluency are also important for skimming large amounts of text and scanning in order to locate target information (Eagleton & Doubler, 2007). Vocabulary knowledge is needed to understand the topic of the websites and terms used for navigating on the Web (e.g., search engine, back button), and also for formulating effective keywords to enter in a search engine (Eagleton & Doubler, 2007). Comprehension on the Internet requires skills beyond those needed for traditional texts and often emphasizes certain traditional skills to a greater degree. For example, to locate information on the Web, the user must know how to use a search engine, how to read search engine results, or how to quickly read a webpage to select the best link to get appropriate information (Leu, et al., 2008). Because anyone can publish on the Web, the role of critical reading and thinking is more important than ever (Leu et al., 2004; Leu et al., 2008). With print texts, critical reading is also important, but the process of publishing texts is more rigorous with editors serving as a form of gate-keepers. Students have demonstrated difficulties in locating information on the Internet in an efficient manner (Leu, et al., 2008), and in selecting and using effective keywords for searching (Kuiper & Volman, 2008). Research involving undergraduate students in Austria has reported that they felt comfortable but were not competent in finding information on the Internet (Albion, 2007; Genrich, Roberts, & Grist, 2006).

METHODS

Participants

Freshman and sophomore students majoring in education, business, and engineering at a public university in the Southwestern United States were recruited to participate in this study. The sample of 706 subjects (132 education underclassmen, 239 business underclassmen, and 335 engineering underclassmen) was proportionate and representative of the total number of students enrolled in these three majors. The vast majority of the students (99.7%) were between 18 to 25 years of age, and slightly more than half (53%) were female.

Instrumentation

The online Survey of Undergraduate Students' New Literacies (SUSNL) instrument created for this study was based on surveys used in previous research (Henry, 2007; Kumar & Kaur, 2006) in the field. The SUSNL consisted of 34 items that were completed by all participants. Survey questions were developed and organized to attain information regarding participants': a) demographics, b) confidence in using new literacies, c) competence in locating and evaluating Internet-based information, d) purpose and frequency of Internet use, and e) experiences with learning and using new Internet literacies.

Four items assessing the participants' purposes for Internet use were adapted from Kumar and Kaur's (2006) *Survey for Internet Users*. In addition, 18 items that inquired about students' demographics and appropriately assessed their Internet access, Internet use, and ability to locate and evaluate Internet-based information were adapted from Henry's (2007) *Digital Divide Measurement Scale for Students* (DDMS-S).

In order to measure participant confidence in using new literacies of the Internet, we designed seven items, each with a five-point Likert scale with choices ranging from strongly disagree to strongly agree. Three of these items related to locating information on the Internet: a) using keywords with a search engine, b) locating information within the search results, and c) locating information within the webpage. Four of the items measured confidence in evaluating the: a) accuracy, b) relevance, c) bias, d) reliability of information on the Internet. The highest total possible confidence score was 35 points.

We measured participants' competence to locate and evaluate information on a series of tasks adapted from Henry's (2007) DDMS-S. The 14 tasks consisted of six items related to locating information on the Internet (e.g., You are searching on the Internet for information about Jupiter's atmosphere. You have obtained the following Google search engine results. What would probably be the most useful link for the specific information that you are seeking?) and eight items pertaining to evaluating information on the Internet (e.g., A 10-year-old student is going to write a report about ancient Egypt. She is looking for information that is reliable. Among the Google search results below, which site would you recommend her to go to first?).

One item designed to assess participants' awareness of learning experiences with new literacies directly reflected Leu, Leu, and Coiro's (2004) description of effective instructional models for teaching efficient Internet use, namely Internet workshop, Internet inquiry, and Webquest activities.

Validation of the SUNSL was accomplished by employing the commonly used procedures of item revision, content validation, and pilot testing which were also used by Henry (2007) to validate the DDMS-S. As in the DDMS-S, we incorporated and adapted actual images of Webpages so that students' experiences during completion of the competency performance items for locating and evaluating experiences would be authentic. Content validation of the SUSNL was accomplished by an expert panel of literacy and educational technology professors that included a past president of the International Society for Technology in Education (ISTE). The panel judged whether the items measured the content, skills, and constructs central to this investigation and suggested item revisions. In addition, undergraduate students, not involved in the study, participated in pilot testing that also provided feedback and suggestions for re-wording or clarifying survey items. The Cronbach's alpha reflecting the overall reliability of the SUSNL was 0.69.

Data Collection Procedures

Academic advisors in the three colleges identified the required freshman- and sophomore-level courses in the respective majors. Then, when feasible, the first author visited classes and presented a scripted explanation of the purpose for the survey and the study. When this was not possible, instructors sent their students an explanatory e-mail containing the scripted explanation along with the link to the survey. Two weeks after the initial explanation of the study, student advising listserves were used to send a follow-up e-mail, including the link to the survey, to all underclass students in these majors. Students were offered no direct incentive for participation. However, participating students could choose to provide their e-mail addresses in order to enter a drawing for gift cards to a local book store.

Data Analysis

Frequency counts and percentages were used to descriptively present the results reflecting Internet use, access, and awareness of instructional experiences for learning Internet skills and strategies. To further analyze and compare the counts of categorical responses between groups associated with these topics, chi-square tests (Sirkin, 2006) were computed. For the survey items that students were asked to choose a single answer from multiple categories, we collapsed the students' responses into two categories and ran 3x2 chi-square tests to insure that the expected counts in 80% of the cells would be greater than five (Morgan, Leech, Gloechner, & Barrett, 2004).

If the p-value for each question was significant, we conducted 2x2 chi-square tests to compare each of three possible comparisons—a) education and business students, b) education and engineering students, and c) business and engineering students. If the p-value was not significant but the cells included expected counts that were not greater than five, we ran 2x2 chi-square tests for each of the three groups and determined the differences by Yates's continuity correction.

Means and standard deviations were used to descriptively present the numerical data reflecting the confidence and competence scores associated with participants' abilities to locate and evaluate information on the Internet. To further analyze the numerical data, we employed univariate analysis of variance (ANOVA) procedures to compare the participants across the three majors. For each of the academic majors, we also computed the Pearson correlation that is used with two normal variables (Morgan et al., 2004) to analyze the relationship between confidence and competence for the two domains of locating and evaluating information on the Internet.

RESULTS

Internet Use

Research question 1. During their high school years, to what extent did education, business, and engineering underclassmen differ in their Internet use?

In regards to overall frequency of Internet use, 70% of engineering, 71% of education, and 78% of business underclassmen used the Internet daily during high school (see Table 1). The chi-square analysis revealed no significant differences between the majors. Pertaining to the number of hours of Internet use per week while in high school, 71% of education, 83% of engineering, and 85% of business underclassmen used the Internet for at least five hours a week (see Table 1). Another chi-square analysis revealed that significantly fewer education underclassmen spent five or more hours per week using the Internet than both business underclassmen (χ^2 =11.06, df =1, N=371, p= .001) and engineering underclassmen (χ^2 =8.61, df =1, N=467, p= .003).

With regards to the required Internet use during high school classes, 53% of education and business majors and 57% of engineering majors reported they were required to use the Internet in class at least once per week (see Table 1). There were no significant differences among the majors in terms of in-class Internet use. With respect to their Internet use required for high school assignments, 69% of engineering majors, 70% of education majors, and 81% of business majors indicated they were required to use the Internet outside of school at least once per week (see Table 1). A chi-square analysis revealed that business underclassmen reported using the Internet to complete outside assignments significantly more often than both education underclassmen (χ^2 =6.34, df=1, N=371, p= .01) and engineering underclassmen (χ^2 =10.35, df =1, N=574, p= .001). Education and engineering underclassmen did not differ significantly from each other in their outside-of-school use of the Internet to complete assignments beyond the classroom.

Pertaining to the purposes of Internet use while in high school, underclassmen frequently used the Internet for school-related research (93-95%); entertainment (86-93%); social networking (85-87%); communication (81-84%); and music, video, or podcast downloads (71-81%). However, they used the Internet rarely to create websites (2-10%) (see Table 1). In terms of group differences, business underclassmen used the Internet significantly more often than education underclassmen for the three purposes of: a) reading news (χ^2 =6.90, df =1, N=371, p= .009); b) downloading music, videos, or podcasts (χ^2 =5.58, df =1, N=371, p= .02); and c) creating websites (χ^2 =4.94, df =1, N=371, p= .03). Engineering majors used the Internet to create websites significantly more often than education majors (χ^2 =10.36, df =1, N=467, p= .001). Regarding Internet connectivity, 97% of engineering, 99% of education, and 100% of business underclassmen reported having Internet access when they lived with their parents (see Table 1). In terms of methods used for learning Internet skills, underclassmen in all majors used the "trial and error" method more frequently than any other learning methods (see Table 1). However, business majors (χ^2 =5.87, df =1, N=371, p= .02) and engineering majors (χ^2 =14.97, df =1, N=467, p< .001) used the trial and error method more often than education majors. Moreover, education underclassmen reported receiving teacher instruction and parent or peer guidance for learning Internet skills significantly more often

Table 1. Number and Percent of Underclassmen's High School-Related Internet Use

		N (%) Education UC	N (%) Business UC	N (%) Engineering UC
Overall frequency of Internet use	Less than every day	39(29.5%)	52(21.8%)	99(29.6%)
	Every day	93(70.5%)	187(78.2%)	236(70.4%)
Hours a week of Internet use	Less than 5 hours a week	39(29.5%)	36(15.1%)	58(17.3%)
	5 hours a week or more	93(70.5%)	203(84.9%)	277(82.7%)
Internet use required during class	Less than once a week	62(47%)	104(43.5%)	158(47.2%)
	Once a week and more	70(53%)	135(56.5%)	177(52.8%)
Internet use required for school assignments	Less than once a week	40(30.3%)	45(18.8%)	103(30.7%)
	Once a week and more	92(69.7%)	194(81.2%)	232(69.3%)
Purposes of Internet use	Research for schoolwork	125(94.7%)	226(94.6%)	311(92.8%)
	Entertainment	114(86.4%)	219(91.6%)	312(93.1%)
	E-learning	18(13.6%)	37(15.5%)	70(20.9%)
	Communication	111(84.1%)	194(81.2%)	271(80.9%)
	Shopping	69(52.3%)	131(54.8%)	156(46.6%)
	News	58(43.9%)	139(58.2%)	173(51.6%)
	Social networking	115(87.1%)	204(85.4%)	284(84.8%)
	Online banking	41(31.1%)	79(33.1%)	136(40.6%)
	Downloads	93(70.5%)	194(81.2%)	235(70.1%)
	Website creation	2(1.5%)	16(6.7%)	35(10.4%)
Internet connection at home	Not connected	1(0.8%)	1(0.4%)	10(3%)
	Connected	131(99.2%)	238(99.6%)	325(97%)
Methods of learning Internet skills	The trial and error method	107(81.1%)	215(90%)	312(93%)
	Teacher instruction	98(74.2%)	152(63.6%)	133(39.7%)
	Guidance from parents and peers	102(77.3%)	159(66.5%)	173(51.6%)
	Books or online tutorials	17(12.9%)	32(13.4%)	68(20.3%)

than business underclassmen (χ^2 =4.38, *df* =1, N=371, p= .04; χ^2 =4.71, *df* =1, N=371, p= .03 respectively) and engineering underclassmen (χ^2 =45.19, *df* =1, N=467, p< .001; χ^2 =25.69, *df* =1, N=467, p< .001 respectively).

Experience with Using New Literacies of the Internet

Research question 2. During their high school years, to what extent did education, business, and engineering underclassmen differ in their experiences with using specific instructional activities for learning new literacies of the Internet?

Between 20% and 27% of underclassmen completed Internet workshops, 35% to 49% used Internet inquiry, and 28% to 43% experienced Webquest activities (see Table 2). Underclassmen did not differ significantly from each other in their experiences with Internet workshop. Education underclassmen reported receiving more Internet inquiry instruction than either business

Table 2. Number and percent of underclassmen's experience with using new literacies of the Internet—Internet workshop, Internet inquiry, and Webquest

	N (%) Education UC	N (%) Business UC	N (%) Engineering UC
Internet Workshop	36(27.3%)	62(25.9%)	67(20%)
Internet Inquiry	65(49.2%)	89(37.2%)	116(34.6%)
Webquest	57(43.2%)	90(37.7%)	94(28.1%)

underclassmen (χ^2 =5.05, df =1, N=371, p= .03) or engineering underclassmen (χ^2 =8.52, df =1, N=467, p= .004). Education majors did not differ from business majors in completing Webquest activities, but they did report completing significantly more Webquest activities than engineering majors (χ^2 =9.9, df =1, N=467, p= .002).

Confidence and Competence in Using New Literacies of the Internet

Research question 1. To what extent do education, business, and engineering underclassmen differ in their perceived confidence in locating and evaluating information on the Internet?

As mentioned previously, the highest total possible confidence score was 35 points. Group mean scores ranged from 27.43 to 28.79 (Education majors: M=27.43, SD=3.75; Business majors: M=28.02, SD=3.35; Engineering majors: M=28.79, SD=3.86) indicating that all majors were confident in their overall abilities to locate and evaluate information on the Internet.

The seven items were also sub-grouped into two domains of confidence in locating information (three items) and confidence in evaluating information (four items) in order to compare these skills. Table 3 presents the means and standard deviations for the three groups' confidence ratings on each domain. The highest possible score for locating information on the Internet was 15 points, and the highest possible score for evaluating information was 20 points.

The summed scores were used as dependent variables to conduct ANOVA tests comparing the three groups. The ANOVA tests resulted in significant differences among the three majors' confidence for both locating information (F (2,703)= 4.88, p = .008) and evaluating information (F (2,703)= 6.15, p = .002) on the Internet. Post hoc Sidak tests revealed that engineering underclassmen were more confident than education underclassmen in both locating and evaluating information on the Internet. No other differences between groups were significant, indicating that education and business underclassmen reflected comparable levels of confidence in locating and evaluating information on the Internet.

Research question 2. To what extent do education, business, and engineering underclassmen differ in their competence in locating and evaluating information on the Internet?

Table 3. Means and Standard Deviations of Underclassmen's Confidence in Locating and Evaluating Information on the Internet

	Education UC	Business UC	Engineering UC
Confidence to locate	M=12.58 SD=1.75	M=12.77 SD=1.64	M=13.08 SD=1.75
Confidence to evaluate	M=14.86 SD=2.53	M=15.25 SD=2.24	M=15.70 SD=2.61

We measured competence by students' performance on a series of 14 tasks. The total mean scores for competence attained by education, business, and engineering underclassmen were 6.75, 6.96, and 7.47 respectively out of a total possible score of 14 points. As mentioned previously, six items related to locating information on the Internet and eight items pertained to evaluating information on the Internet. Table 4 presents the means and standard deviations of the participants' competence in each domain of locating and evaluating information on the Internet.

Table 4. Means and Standard Deviations of Underclassmen's Competence in Locating and Evaluating Information on the Internet

	Education UC	Business UC	Engineering UC
Competence to locate	M=3.89 SD=1.26	M=3.84 SD=1.29	M=4.10 SD=1.24
Competence to evaluate	M=2.86 SD=1.11	M=3.12 SD=1.17	M=3.37 SD=1.31

The ANOVA results in significant differences in competence scores among the three groups in both locating information (F (2,703)=3.16, p= .04) and evaluating information (F (2,703)=8.90, p< .001) on the Internet. Follow up post hoc tests, Sidak and Games-Howell indicated that engineering underclassmen were significantly more competent than business underclassmen in locating and evaluating information on the Internet. Engineering underclassmen were significantly more competent than education underclassmen in evaluating information on the Internet. However, education and business underclassmen did not differ significantly from each other in locating and evaluating information on the Internet. Education and engineering underclassmen did not differ significantly from each other in locating information on the Internet.

Research question 3. Is education, business, and engineering underclassmen's confidence related to their competence in locating and evaluating information on the Internet?

By using summed scores, Pearson correlation analyses were conducted for each domain of locating and evaluating information on the Internet. In terms of locating information on the Internet, only education majors' confidence in locating information on the Internet was positively and moderately correlated with their demonstrated competence in locating information on the Internet (education majors: r(130)= .32, p< .001). The confidence-competence correlation in locating information for business majors (r(237)= .08, p= .23) and for engineering majors (r(333)= .03, p= .59) were not significant. With regards to evaluating information on the Internet, only engineering major's confidence and their demonstrated competence in evaluating information on the Internet were positively and moderately correlated (r(333)= .12, p = .03). The confidence-competence correlations for evaluating information on the Internet were not significant for education underclassmen (r(130)= .13, p= .14) and for business underclassmen (r(237)= .02, p= .79).

DISCUSSION

As expected, the present study revealed that during their high school years, education, business, and engineering underclassmen were familiar with using the Internet. Specifically, between 70% and 78% of underclassmen in the three different groups used the Internet daily and between 70% and 85% of underclassmen spent at least five hours a week using the Internet. Between 69% and 81% of underclassmen in these three groups were required to use the Internet outside of class for completing their school assignments and nearly all the students had Internet access in their homes. The groups of students reported using the Internet frequently for research (93-95%), social networking (85-87%), entertainment (86-93%), and communication (81-84%). In summary, these findings indicate that these underclassmen are digital natives who have grown up with Internet use integrated into their lives.

The students' frequent use of the Internet during their high school probably contributed to their feelings of confidence in using new literacies of the Internet for both locating and evaluating information. Within the construct of overall confidence, however, students reported higher confidence in locating information than in evaluating information on the Internet. This is a notable finding because evaluating information is arguably a more complex task than locating information.

Additionally, when making comparisons across the three groups of majors, education students were less confident than engineering students in locating and evaluating information on the Internet. However, a lower confidence in their skill level is not necessarily a deficit. Instead, this disparity in confidence between the groups may indicate that education students are more realistic regarding their abilities in this manner since they reported receiving teacher instruction and guidance from others about using the Internet more often than students in the other two groups. The discrepancy in confidence may also result from differing amounts of exposure to the Internet during high school years because engineering students reported significantly more hours of weekly Internet use during high school than their education counterparts. This finding has multiple implications. First, teachers in general should recognize that there may be great variability within the group of digital natives when it comes to their prior experience with the Internet. Additionally, for instructors of pre-service education students, it is important to be aware that their students may not enter college with the same levels of confidence and experience with Internet skills as their more technically oriented peers.

Regarding competence, the present study found that overall no group of underclassmen demonstrated a high level of competence in locating or evaluating information on the Internet. Out of a possible score of 14 points for the online location and evaluation of information performance tasks, the overall mean score for the three groups of underclassmen was 7.06, with group means of 6.75 for education, 6.96 for business, and 7.47 for engineering. These results appear to be somewhat comparable to those reported by Henry (2007), where the mean for middle school subjects' online performance scores was 5.40 out of 14 and the mean of teachers' scores was 7.51 out of 14. Such results indicate that a great need persists for more explicit teaching of new literacy skills in the primary and secondary grades. Additionally, it indicates that current education underclassmen possess neither sufficient awareness nor sufficient mastery of new literacies skills necessary for them to teach these skills to their future students.

In the current study, all participants struggled more on items pertaining to the evaluation of information than those related to the location of information. These results are consistent with Henry's (2007) research indicating that middle school students had particular difficulty evaluating the biased nature of information. These results indicate the importance of teaching students strategies for effectively evaluating information on the Internet. These evaluation skills include triangulating content from multiple sources, examining author information, updating information, as well as considering the domain types (e.g., .com, .gov, .edu). Further, the similarity between the results of the current study and Henry's work in 2007 indicates that similar challenges of using new literacies of the Internet persist, regardless of age.

The present study also found that education, business, and engineering students' confidence and competence in using new literacies of the Internet were more often not related as only two of six comparisons were significant. Only engineering students reflected a direct, positive correlation between their confidence and competence in *evaluating* information on the Internet, and only education students reflected a positive correlation between their confidence and competence in *locating* information on the Internet. However, neither of these positive correlations (r= .12 and r= .32 respectively) can be considered as strong. Overall, these results imply that students' high levels of confidence were not generally demonstrated in their competence with using new literacies of the Internet. Stated in another way, the students were largely unaware of what they did not know or could not do with regards to their Internet use.

The results of the current study corroborated the results of earlier studies (Albion, 2007; Genich, Roberts, & Gist, 2006) that reported approximately 90% of first-year undergraduate students possessed great confidence in their abilities to complete Internet reading assignments and using search engines to find information. However, when most of the students in these studies participated in actual lab sessions, they did not perform successfully on tasks of locating information on the Internet. The results of these earlier studies along with the findings of the current study reveal that college students tend to overestimate their abilities to critically read on the Internet.

This apparent disconnect between college students' confidence and competence in using new literacies implies that they are not metacognitively aware of their reading processes on the Internet. Most likely these students would benefit from further instructional opportunities in order to become more tech-savvy, critical readers who use their new literacies of the Internet appropriately and more effectively. However, if college students are overly confident, and correspondingly unaware of their lack of skills, they will probably not independently seek instructional opportunities to improve their skills, so this instruction needs to be carefully planned and systematically implemented within their collegiate programs of study.

With regards to education students in particular, the results of the present study indicate that education students may need more support and instruction in learning to use new literacies of the Internet than their engineering peers. While education underclassmen reported that they received more teacher instruction in learning Internet skills and completed more Internet inquiry and Webquest activities than engineering underclassmen, their competence still lagged behind in certain skills. Possibly, while education underclassmen had more school-based instructional experiences for learning new literacies of the Internet, they were still insufficient to master the essential Internet literacy skills. In contrast, the engineering students who reportedly had even fewer and probably less sufficient in-school learning experiences might be more self-directed in their learning because they reported using more trial and error approaches to acquire Internet skills than the education students.

LIMITATIONS

The results of the current study may not be generalizable to all university students in the United States. While the sample size was relatively large, the students were recruited from one university in the southwestern region of the United States. However, because we sampled students from three distinct majors, the results can be used informatively with students in these other fields.

This study, as well as survey research in general, is largely dependent upon self-report data. The SUSNL instrument used in the current study also assessed student competence in locating and evaluating information on the Internet with performance tasks in addition to self-report items.

IMPLICATIONS

This study suggests that schools must provide students with more effective instruction in using new literacies of the Internet, particularly in the evaluation of information. According to the results of this study, many high schools required students to use the Internet for outside-of-class assignments such as homework. However, only 53-57% of the underclassmen reported that they were required to use the Internet at least once a week in class. This indicates that teachers may be assuming that students possess sufficient competence to independently use the Internet in an effective manner. Underclassmen also reported their limited experiences in completing instructional activities such as Internet workshop, Internet inquiry, or Webquests. Thus, many of the students' Internet skills appear to have been formed informally, or "on their own." In light of the general lack of college students' competence in locating and evaluating information on the Internet, K-12 schools must provide more effective new Internet literacy skills instruction to students, especially before requiring them to use the Internet independently to complete schoolwork outside of class.

This study also raises implications for further research involving senior-level university students. It is quite evident that the students in the current study did not enter the university with the essential skills pertaining to new literacies of the Internet. Inquiries into the competence of senior-level students are warranted to determine whether the students are acquiring these essential skills during their college studies. If they are, that will be valuable information to possess. However, if university seniors perform in a manner similar to the university freshmen and sophomores in this study, then it will become imperative for colleges and universities to planfully and explicitly incorporate the development of these skills into their core curricula as well as their program majors not just for future teachers, but for all future professionals who will become increasingly dependent on using the Internet efficiently in the workplace.

In terms of teacher education, further research is needed to investigate the types of courses and experiences that are most effective in developing pre-service teachers' abilities to not only learn and efficiently use new literacies of the Internet, but to acquire the pedagogical content knowledge that will enable them to effectively implement strategies to teach new literacies of the Internet.

REFERENCES

Albion, P. (2007). Student teachers' confidence and competence for finding information on the Internet. In R. Carlsen et al. (Eds.), *Proceedings of society for information technology & teacher education international conference 2007.* Retrieved from http://eprints.usq.edu.au/2099/1/infolit.pdf

Bolter, J. D. (1998). Hypertext and the question of visual literacy. In D. Reinking, M. C. McKenna, L. D. Labbo, & R. D. Kieffer (Eds.), *Handbook of literacy and technology: Transformations in a post-typographic world.* Mahwah, NJ: Erlbaum.

Coiro, J. (2003). Reading comprehension on the Internet: Expanding our understanding of reading comprehension to encompass new literacies. *Reading Teacher, 56,* 458-464.

Coiro, J. & Doubler, E. (2007). Exploring the online reading comprehension strategies used by sixth-grade skilled readers to search for and locate information on the Internet. *Reading Quarterly, 42*(2), 214-257.

Coiro, J., Knobel, M., Lankshear, C., & Leu, D. (Eds.). (2008). *Handbook of research on new literacies.* Mahwah, NJ: Lawrence Erlbaum.

College Board (2008). *2008 College bound seniors: Total group pile report.* Retrieved from http://professionals. collegeboard.com/data-reports-research/sat/cb-seniors-2008

Connect Ohio. (2008). Connect Ohio 2008 Business technology assessment. Retrieved from http://www. slideshare.net/reinventlivecom/ohio-business-technology-survey

Eagleton. M. B., & Doubler, E. (2007). *Reading the Web: Strategies for Internet inquiry.* New York, NY: Guilford Press.

Electronic Design News. (2008). Engineers rely on the Internet for product information. *Electronic Design.* Retrieved from http://electronicdesign.com/Articles/Index.cfm?AD=1&ArticleID=20161

Estarbrook L., & Rainie, L. (2007). *In search of solutions: How people use the Internet, libraries, and agencies to find help.* Washington, DC: Pew Internet and American Life Project. Retrieved from http://www. pewinternet.org/-/media/Files/Reports /2007/Pew_UI_LibrariesReport.pdf.pdf

Facebook. (2011). People on facebook. Retrieved from http://www.facebook.com/press/Info.php?statistics

Genrich, R., Roberts, D., & Grist, S. (2006). *Y generation students fail with Google.* Paper presented at the 17th Australasian Conference on Information Systems, Adelaide, Australia.

Henry, L. A. (2007). Exploring new literacies pedagogy and online reading comprehension among middle school students and teachers: Issues of social equity or social exclusion? Available from ProQuest Dissertations and Theses database. (UMI NO. AAT3282520)

Horrigan, J. (2009). *Wireless Internet use.* Washington, DC: Pew Internet and American Life Project. Retrieved from http://www.pewInternet.org/Reports/2009/12-Wireless-Internet-Use.aspx

Kuiper, E., & Volman, M. (2008). The web as a source of information for students in K-12 education. In J. Coiro, M. Knobel, C. Lankshear, & D. Leu (Eds.), *Handbook of research on new literacies.* Mahwah, NJ: Lawrence Erlbaum.

Kumar, R., & Kaur, A. (2006). Internet use by teachers and students in engineering colleges of Punjab, Haryana, and Himachal Pradesh states of India: An analysis. *Electronic Journal of Academic and Special Librarianship, 7*(1), Retrieved from http://southernlibrarianship.icaap.org/content/v07n01/kumar_r01. htmhttp://southernlibrarianship.icaap.org/content/v07n01/kumar_r01.htm

Lee, P., Leung, L., & So, C. (2004). *Impact and issues in new media: Toward intelligent societies.* Cresskill, NJ: Hampton.

Lenhart, A., Madden, M., McGill, A. R., & Smith, A. (2007). *Teens and social media: The use of social media gains a greater foothold in teen life as they embrace the conversational nature of interactive online media.* Washington, DC: Pew Internet and American Life Project. Retrieved from http://www.pewInternet. org/-/media//Files/Reports/2007/PIP_Teens_Social_Media_Final.pdf.pdf

Leu, D., Coiro, J., Castek, J., Hartman, D., Henry, L., & Reinking, D. (2008). Research on instruction and assessment in the new literacies of online reading comprehension. In C. C. Block & S. R. Parris (Eds.). *Comprehension instruction: Research-based best practices.* New York, NY: Guilford Press.

Leu, D. J., Kinzer, C. K., Coiro, J. L., & Cammack, D. W. (2004). Toward a theory of new literacies and other information and communication technologies. In R. B. Ruddell & N. J. Unrau (Eds.), *Theoretical models and processes of reading* (pp. 1570-1613). Newark, DE: International Reading Association.

Leu, D. J., Leu, D. D., & Coiro, J. (2004). *Teaching with the Internet K-12: New literacies for new times.* Norwood, MA: Christopher-Gordon Publishers, Inc.

Leu, D. J., Reinking, D., Carter, A., Castek, J., Coiro, J., Henry, L. A., Malloy, J., Robbins, K., Rogers, A., & Zawilinski, L. (2007). *Defining online reading comprehension: Using think aloud verbal protocols to refine a preliminary model of Internet reading comprehension processes.* Paper presented at The American Educational Research Association. Chicago, IL.

McDonald, S. & Stevenson, R. J. (1996). Disorientation in hypertext: The effect of three text structures on navigation performance. *Applied Ergonomics, 27*(1), 61-68.

McKenna, M.C. (2001). The new world of electronic text. *Library Talk, 14*(5), 30-31.

McKenna, M.C., Reinking, D., Labbo, L. D., & Kieffer, R. D. (1999). The electronic transformation of literacy and its implications for the struggling reader. *Reading and Writing Quarterly: Overcoming Learning Difficulties, 15,* 111-126.

McKnight, C., Dillon, A., & Richardson, J. (1990). A comparison of linear and hypertext formats in information retrieval. In R. McAleese and C. Green (Eds.), *Hypertext: State of the art* (pp.10-19). Oxford, England: Intellect.

Miners, Z., & Pascopella, A. (2007). New literacies. District Administration, *43*(10), 26-34. Retrieved from http://www.readingrockets.org/article/21208

Morgan, G. A., Leech, N. L., Gloechner, G. W., & Barrett, K. C. (2004). *SPSS for introductory statistics.* Clifton, NJ: LEA.

National Center for Education Statistics. (2005). *Internet access in public schools and classrooms: 1994-2005.* Retrieved from http://nces.ed.gov/pubs2007/2007020.pdf

New London Group. (1996). A pedagogy of multiliteracies: Designing social futures. *Harvard Educational Review, 66*(1), 60-92.

Prensky, M. (2001). Digital natives, digital immigrants. *On the Horizon, 9*(5), 1-6. Retrieved from http://www.marcprensky.com/writing/Prensky%20-%20Digital%20Natives,%20Digital%20Immigrants%20-%20Part1.pdf

Rainie, L., & Hitlin, P. (2005). *The Internet at school.* Washington, DC: Pew Internet and American Life Project. Retrieved from http://www.pewInternet.org/Reports/2005/The-Internet-at-School.aspx

Reinking, D. (1992). Differences between electronic and printed texts: An agenda for research. *Journal of Educational Multimedia and Hypermedia, 1*(1), 11-24.

Rideout, V. J., Foehr, U. G., & Roberts, D. F. (2010). *Generation M2: Media in the lives of 8- to 18-year-olds.* Menlo Park, CA: Henry J. Kaiser Family Foundation.

Sirkin, M. (2006). *Statistics for the social sciences.* London, England: Sage.

Street, B. (1998). New literacies in theory and practice: What are the implications for language in education? *Linguistics and Education, 10*(1), 1-24.

APPENDIX

Survey of Undergraduate Students' New Literacies (SUSNL) for Education Underclass Students

Question 1.

I am a

❏ Male   ❏ Female

Question 2.

Please select the option that best describes you.

❏ American Indian   ❏ Hispanic American

❏ Asian American   ❏ White

❏ Black or African American   ❏ Other (Please specify)_____

Question 3.

My academic major is

❏ PreK-6th grades education

❏ 4-8th grades language arts/social studies

❏ 4-8th grades math/science education

❏ Other (Please specify) _____

Question 4.

I was born

❏ Before 1981

❏ Between 1989 and 1990

❏ Between 1981 and 1984

❏ Between 1991 and 1992

❏ Between 1985 and 1988

Question 5.

I am a

❏ Freshman (Class of 2013)

❏ Junior (Class of 2011)

❏ Sophomore (Class of 2012)

❏ Senior (Class of 2010)

Question 6.

I am confident in using appropriate key words with a search engine to locate information on the Internet.

❏ Strongly Disagree   ❏ Disagree   ❏ Neither Agree nor Disagree   ❏ Agree   ❏ Strongly Agree

Question 7.

I am confident in locating the most relevant information within the search results.

❏ Strongly Disagree   ❏ Disagree   ❏ Neither Agree nor Disagree   ❏ Agree   ❏ Strongly Agree

Question 8.

I am confident in locating the most useful information within a webpage.

❏ Strongly Disagree   ❏ Disagree   ❏ Neither Agree nor Disagree   ❏ Agree   ❏ Strongly Agree

Question 9.

I am confident in evaluating the accuracy of information on the Internet (that means evaluating whether information on the Internet is correct or incorrect).

❏ Strongly Disagree   ❏ Disagree   ❏ Neither Agree nor Disagree   ❏ Agree   ❏ Strongly Agree

Question 10.

I am confident in evaluating the relevance of information on the Internet.

❏ Strongly Disagree   ❏ Disagree   ❏ Neither Agree nor Disagree   ❏ Agree   ❏ Strongly Agree

Question 11.

I am confident in evaluating the bias of information on the Internet.

❏ Strongly Disagree   ❏ Disagree   ❏ Neither Agree nor Disagree   ❏ Agree   ❏ Strongly Agree

Question 12.

I am confident in evaluating the reliability of information on the Internet (that means evaluating whether information and information sources on the Internet are trustworthy or plausible).

❏ Strongly Disagree   ❏ Disagree   ❏ Neither Agree nor Disagree   ❏ Agree   ❏ Strongly Agree

Question 13.

How did Oprah Winfrey get started with her talk show?

You want to find the answer to this question. What would be the best way to search the Internet for an answer?

❏ A. Go to Google and search for Amazon.com

❏ B. Go to Google and search using the words "How did Oprah Winfrey get started with her talk show?"

❏ C. Go to Google and search using the words "Oprah Winfrey career"

❏ D. Type in www.talkshowstars.com in the Google address bar

❏ E. Type in www.oprahwinfreycareer.com in the Google address bar

Question 14.

A 10-year-old student is going to write a report about ancient Egypt. She is looking for information that is reliable. Among the Google search results below, which site would you recommend her to go to first?

A. **Ancient Egypt** Travel & Vacation Tours
You see the most outstanding attractions of **Ancient Egypt**. Cairo, Nile Cruise experience between Luxor & Aswan, Abu Simbel....
www. africapoint.com/tours1/egyptour. htm-27k- Cached – Similar pages

B. **Ancient Egypt** Thematic Unit
Focus: Students will become familiar with **Ancient Egypt** and expand their... Collection of books relating to Ancient Egypt (See Related Literature at the ...
www. libsci.sc.edu/miler/Egypt.htm-18k – Cached –Similar pages

C. The **Ancient Egypt** Site
The history, language and culture of **Ancient Egypt** by Egyptologist Jacques Kinnaer.
www. ancient-egypt.org/-5k – Cached –Similar pages

D. **Ancient Egypt** Web
More than a dozen illustrated reports written by primary students.
www. /hitchams.suffolk.sch.uk/Egypt /- Similar pages

E. **Ancient Egypt** – Wikipedia, the free encyclopedia
Ancient Egypt was an ancient civilization of eastern North Africa, concentrated along the lower reaches of the Nile River in what is now the modern country ...
en.wikipedia.org/wiki/Ancient Egypt - Cached

❏ A. Ancient Egypt Travel & Vacation Tour

❏ B. Ancient Egypt Thematic Unit

❏ C. The Ancient Egypt Site

❏ D. Ancient Egypt Web

❏ E. Ancient Egypt-Wikipedia, the free encyclopedia

Question 15.

You are searching for reliable websites about the rainforest like the one in the picture below. If you had to predict which link would most probably lead to the MOST reliable information about rainforests, which link would you pick?

❑ A. www.davesite.com/rainforest

❑ B. www. rainforest-australia.net

❑ C. www.usmith.edu/rainforest/~jpeters/savetheforest.html

❑ D. www.rain-tree.com/schoolreports.htm

Question 16.

You are searching on the Internet for information about Jupiter's atmosphere.

You have obtained the following Google search engine results. What would probably be the most useful link for the specific information that you are seeking?

A **The Planet Jupiter**
The **planet Jupiter** is shown in the adjacent Hubble Space Telescope true-color image (Ref).
Jupiter is by far the largest of the planets. ...
csep10.phys.utk.edu/astr161/lect/jupiter/jupiter.html - 4k - Cached - Similar pages

B **Jupiter - MSN Encarta**
Great books about your topic, **Jupiter (planet)**, selected by Encarta editors ... **Jupiter (planet)**,
fifth **planet** from the Sun and the largest **planet** in the ...
encarta.msn.com/encyclopedia_761564261/Jupiter_(planet).html - 44k -
Cached - Similar pages

C **Jupiter, planet Jupiter, discover planet Jupiter, Jupiter the ...**
Space.com explains **Jupiter, planet Jupiter, discover planet Jupiter, Jupiter** the planet, the
planet Jupiter.
www.space.com/jupiter/ - 26k - Cached - Similar pages

D **StarChild: The planet Jupiter**
This **planet** is made mostly of hydrogen and helium gases. **Jupiter** gives off two times more
heat than it gets from the Sun. It shines very brightly in the ...
starchild.gsfc.nasa.gov/docs/StarChild/solar_system_level1/jupiter.html - 8k -
Cached - Similar pages

❑ A. The Planet Jupiter

❑ B. Jupiter-MSN Encarta

❑ C. Jupiter, planet Jupiter, discover planet, Jupiter the…

❑ D. StarChild: The planet Jupiter

Question 17.

You want to find a list of award-winning books written by the author of The Chronicles of Prydain. On the website below, which link would you choose first?

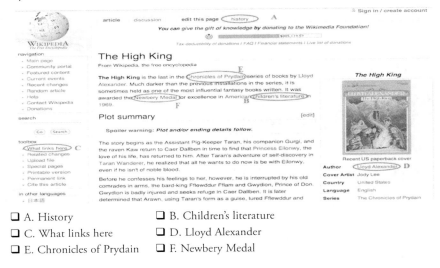

- ❑ A. History
- ❑ C. What links here
- ❑ E. Chronicles of Prydain
- ❑ B. Children's literature
- ❑ D. Lloyd Alexander
- ❑ F. Newbery Medal

Question 18.

You have found the following website for the Anne Frank Center, USA. Where would you locate the street address of the center on the website?

- ❑ A. about us
- ❑ B. our exhibits
- ❑ C. news & media updates
- ❑ D. the anne frank house, amsterdam

Question 19.

You want to find the name of the C.E.O of the Burger King company. In the following Google search engine results, which would be the most reliable site to visit to find out the name of the person?

A. Burger King® 7:22am
TM & © 2007 Burger King Brands, Inc. (USA only). TM & © 2007 Burger King Corporation (Outside USA). All rights reserved. ...
www. burgerking.com/-3k- Jan 4, 2007 - Cached –Similar pages

B. Burger King- Wikipedia, the free encyclopedia
Hungry Jack's is a franchisee of Burger King that owns, operates and franchises over 300 ... As a result of Burger King's actions, Hungry Jacks Pty. ...
en.wikipedia.org/wiki/ Burger _ King – 135k - Cached –Similar pages

C. Burger King- Phoenix, AZ, 85004-Citysearch
Come to Citysearch to get information, directions, and reviews on Burger King and other Restaurants in Phoenix.
Phoenix.citysearch.com/profile/32310306?landing=1&query=&brand=synd_flightview – 34k - Cached –Similar pages

D. Burger King Calories and Calorie Counter
Burger King Menu (Web Address: http://www.bk.com/) (Please click on a menu item below to view the nutritional breakdown) ...
www. chowbaby.com/fastfood/ fast_food_nutrition.asp?ff_restid=1011-141k - Cached –Similar pages

E. Burger King – SourceWatch
Burger King, based in Miami, Florida, USA, is the world's second largest hamburger chain (behind McDonald's). The company has "more than 11200 restaurants ...
sourcewatch.org/index.php?title=Burger_King - Cached -Similar pages

❑ A. Burger King

❑ B. Burger King-Wikipedia, the free encyclopedia

❑ C. Burger King-Phoenix, AZ, 85004-Citysearch

❑ D. Burger King Calories and Calorie Counter

❑ E. Burger King-Source Watch

Question 20.

You are looking for information about what it was like to be a soldier during the Civil War. From the website below, what would be the best way to proceed?

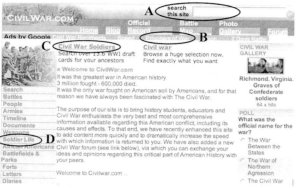

❑ A. Type the words "a soldier at war" in the Search This Site search engine

❑ B. Click on "Prisoners of War"

❑ C. Click on "Civil war soldiers"

❑ D. Click on "Soldier Life"

Question 21.

What is the best way to check if the information on the following web page is correct?

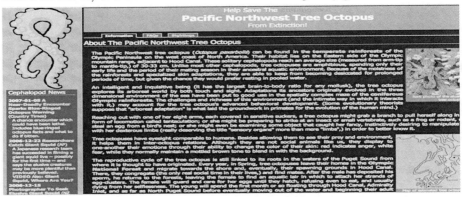

❏ A. Check if all the links work.

❏ B. Check to see if there is an email address for the person who created the site.

❏ C. Look at the copyright information.

❏ D. Check to see if the octopus is on an endangered species list on another site.

❏ E. Check the date on which the web page has been updated.

Question 22.

You are looking for information about the lost city of Atlantis. You typed the word "Atlantis" in the Google search bar. You got the results below. What key words should you use to get better results with another search?

❏ A. Atlantis NOT vacation

❏ B. Atlantis OR City

❏ C. Atlantis Caribbean

❏ D. Atlantis city

❏ E. Atlantis NOT Island

❏ F. Atlantis and Cyprus

Question 23.

You have a bank account with Bank of America. You received the message below on email. What should you do?

☐ A. Click on the link in the email to log into your account and check Alert history
☐ B. Sign in through the link in the email to see if your account is locked
☐ C. Google Bank of America phishing
☐ D. Go to the bank and check your balance
☐ E. Send a reply to the email message

Question 24.

What clue indicates that you probably cannot trust the following website?

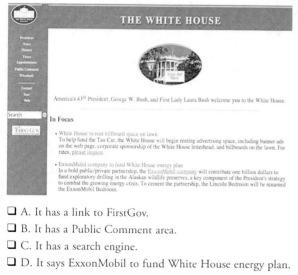

☐ A. It has a link to FirstGov.
☐ B. It has a Public Comment area.
☐ C. It has a search engine.
☐ D. It says ExxonMobil to fund White House energy plan.

Question 25.
Where would you go to see if the news story below is true or false?

CANADIAN MAN RAISES ENORMOUS 80 ib, 60-inch CAT

❏ A. www.images.google.com   ❏ B. www.snopes.com
❏ C. www.falsephotos.net   ❏ D. www.IsItTrue.com

Question 26.

You are doing a project on the Martin Luther King holiday. You have found the following site. Now where should you go first?

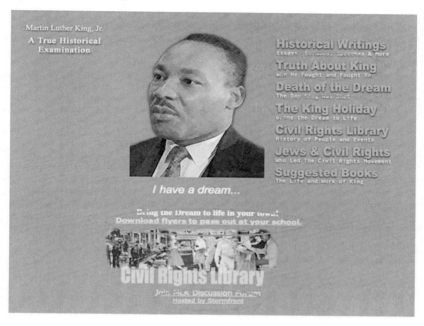

☐ A. Truth About King   ☐ B. The King Holiday
☐ C. Download flyers to pass out at your school   ☐ D. Hosted by Stormfront

Question 27.

What kind of Internet connection did you have when you lived with your parents?
☐ Telephone dial up Internet   ☐ High speed Internet   ☐ I didn't have Internet connection

Question 28.

When you were of high school age, how often did you use the Internet?
☐ Less than once a month   ☐ Once a month   ☐ 2-3 times a month
☐ Once a week   ☐ 2-5 times a week ☐ Every day

Question 29.

When you were a high school aged person, how many hours did you spend in a week to use the Internet?
☐ Less 5 hours a week   ☐ 5-14 hours a week
☐ 15-35 hours a week   ☐ Over 35 hours a week

Question 30.

How did you acquire or learn your Internet skills? Please click on all of the items that apply.

❏ Trial and error method

❏ Teacher instruction in K-12

❏ Guidance from parents and peers

❏ Courses in university

❏ Self-instruction using books or online tutorials

Question 31.

When you were a high school aged person, for what purpose(s) did you use the Internet? Please click on all of the items that apply.

❏ Research for school assignments

❏ Entertainment

❏ E-learning

❏ Communication

❏ Shopping

❏ News

❏ Social networking

❏ Online banking

❏ Downloading music, videos, or podcasts

❏ Creating websites

❏ Other (Please specify)

Question 32.

When you were a high school aged student, how often had you been required to use the Internet during class?

❏ Never   ❏ Less than once a month

❏ Once a week   ❏ A few times each week

❏ Once a day   ❏ Several times a day

Question 33.

When you were a high school aged student, how often had you been required to use the Internet for school assignments?

❏ Never   ❏ Less than once a month

❏ Once a week   ❏ A few times each week

❏ Once a day   ❏ Several times a day

Question 34.

Which of the following activities did you complete in high school? Please click on all of the items that apply.

❑ INTERNET WORKSHOP activity in which you explored information on the assigned website for a lesson and shared your discoveries, questions, and new literacy strategies with classmates.

❑ INTERNET INQUIRY activity in which you: 1) generated a question to explore, 2) located information relevant the idea on the Internet, 3) evaluated the information, 4) composed a presentation of the information, and 5) shared the information.

❑ WEBQUEST activity in which you or a group of classmates were provided with 1) an introduction, 2) a task description, 3) the process description, 4) online information resources to use, 5) guidance about organizing the information collected in completing the task, and 6) a concluding activity.

Family Digital Literacies: A Case of Awareness, Agency, and Apprenticeship of One African American Family

Tisha Y. Lewis
Georgia State University

We are a hands-on family. We have to do the task to really, really know it, and by having to do this, it's causing us to work more and more together, which allows our moods to intertwine, interact, and join one another and become unified as one. (*Larnee*)

INTRODUCTION

The ways individuals use computers in the home have dramatically changed the ways we communicate, respond to information, and learn (Hawisher, Selfe, Moraski, & Pearson, 2004). Individuals have become hooked on connecting to the world on a daily basis, thereby causing a large amount of families' time to be mediated through the Internet (Bruce, 2002). However, many may not recognize the underlying factors that occur when individuals rely on, are inundated with, or even consumed by the technology. For instance, a number of researchers have explored digital literacies or media-related literacy practices (Alvermann, 2002; 2010; Bruce, 2002; Cammack, 2002; Chandler-Olcott & Mahar, 2003; Jacobs, 2006; Kirkland, 2009; Lankshear & Knobel, 2008; Lewis & Fabos, 2005; Mahar, 2002; Marsh, 2006; Marsh & Thompson, 2001); these studies examine issues such as the influence of pop culture, instant messaging, digital literacies, and multimodalities in online communities. However, there is a limited amount of research that focuses on family literacy and digital literacy practices (Ba, Tally, & Tsikalas, 2002; Marsh, 2006; Marsh & Thompson, 2001). This study describes how digital literacy influences families and how they talk, think, value, and identify themselves on a daily basis.

The opening quote by Larnee Ali, an African American divorced mother of four sons, signifies how Larnee defined "family," "learning," and "community" in her home. She manages her family by the way she interacts with them socially and digitally through tools, and teaches them how to function in and out of the home. Raising three young men in an urban neighborhood (one of the sons lived with his grandmother), Larnee is the cornerstone of what makes this family function on a daily basis. The purpose of this study is to illustrate how this mother used digital literacies to manage her life and the lives of her two sons—Gerard and David—through awareness, agency, and apprenticeship on a daily basis. (The other two sons were not officially involved in the study). More specifically, I emphasize the ways in which Larnee's initiation and engagement in multimodal literacy learning tasks with her sons reveal how they shaped and were simultaneously shaped by digital literacy practices. I define digital literacies as multiple and interactive practices, mediated by technological tools such as the computer, cell phones, instant messaging (IMing), and video games that involve reading, writing, language, and exchanging information in online environments.

It is important to recognize that there is a shortage of literacy-related studies that detail African American families' relationships to digital literacies that overlooks and neglects their rich practices, voices, and experiences. These examinations make this research significant to family literacy research, as well as in creating a springboard for researchers to rethink family literacy practices in the digital age in the home and in classrooms. Therefore, I focus on two questions: (a) In what ways do awareness, agency, and apprenticeship play a role in the ways an African American mother engages in digital literacies with her sons?, and (b) What is the relationship between a mother, her sons, and digital literacies?

REVIEW OF RELEVANT LITERATURE

The field of family literacy has offered significant insight into family literacy practices in the home (Cairney & Ruge, 1998; Compton-Lilly, Rogers, & Lewis, [in press, January 2012]; Edwards, Pleasants, & Franklin, 1999; Edwards, 2004; Heath, 1983; Rogers, 2002; Taylor, 1983; Taylor & Dorsey-Gaines, 1988). These studies examined the emergence of children's understanding of the nature and functions of literacy practices. Family literacy researchers have identified discursive and unique literacy patterns among families and barriers between home and school, especially for children from lower socioeconomic backgrounds (Compton-Lilly, 2003; Lareau, 1989; McCarthey, 1997; Purcell-Gates, 1995). While these studies have raised awareness of how families understand literacy, family literacy is changing and research must focus on the new ways that families interact with one another and engage in complex literacy practices through digital technologies.

Ba, Tally, and Tsikalas (2002) examined nine low-income and 10 middle-income African American and Latino families' use of "home computing practices" that influenced their social, technological, and school environments. The authors found unique ways that children were being impacted at home: their use of computers, the length of time children spent online, the family's ability to connect to the Internet, and the number of computers in the home and its location. Low-income families did not have money or credit cards to pay for Internet access. This concern resulted in these families not being as fluent with certain computer tools or terminology as were their middle-income counterparts. Ba et al.'s (2002) study influenced the researchers to identify ways for low-income families to have the resources to not only gain access but maintain access, to be and stay computer literate. In addition, the researchers found that the children developed basic literacy skills when online.

Hawisher et al. (2004) have explored the literacy narratives of two women, an African American and European American, born in different cultures and generational times. The authors highlight how the women came to acquire and develop the literacies of technology, using contexts as the cultural ecology of literacy and focusing on how the relationships between individuals and technology evolved.

Through the lens of New Literacy Studies, Marsh (2006) examined three studies that involved young children's engagement in digital literacy practices in the home. Marsh drew from Cairney and Ruge's (1998) framework of four distinct purposes for literacy in the homes of 27 Australian families: (a) "literacy for establishing or maintaining relationships," (b) "literacy for accessing or displaying information," (c) "literacy for pleasure or self-expression," and (d) "literacy for skills development." Marsh focused on popular culture, media, and new technologies and how these tools affected the literacy experiences of young children in the home. Marsh identified that the young children's literacy practices evolved over time and were no longer isolated social practices but were embedded in communicative practices that specifically related to popular culture, media, and new technologies in the home.

Under the auspices of New Literacy Studies and Multimodality, researchers examined the ways families and adolescents engaged in literacy practices. Each of the aforementioned studies incorporates strands of literacy research that reveal how social practices in family spaces are uniquely complex based on their resources, interest, and purpose.

To underscore the power of how digital literacy tools, such as the computer, have a place and fulfill a need in individuals' lives, Turkle (1984; 2005) examined how individuals engage and interact with computational technologies as a way for them to work through identity issues, to help resolve personal issues, and even develop a greater need for intimacy. What unites these studies are the basis of a consistent interrelationship between individuals and the technological tool and what happens when a cultural change has been adapted to an environment (Steward, 1972). Building on work that has explored the use of technologies/digital literacies in the home, this paper investigates how an African American mother uses digital literacy practices to mediate awareness, agency, and apprenticeship within her family.

THEORETICAL PERSPECTIVES

Perspectives of Digital Literacies

According to Bawden (2008), digital literacy has been referred to as information literacy, computer literacy, media literacy, network literacy, and e-literacy. In addition, Paul Gilster (1997) introduced "digital literacy" as "the ability to understand and use information in multiple formats from a wide range of sources when it is presented via computer" (p. 1).

Sociocultural theorists realize that because digital literacy consists of a "myriad of social practices and conceptions of engaging in meaning-making mediated by texts that are produced, received, distributed, exchanged, etc.," the ways we engage in situated practices and make meaning when relating to texts, must be understood as *digital literacies* (Lankshear & Knobel, 2008, p. 5). The social practices take multiple forms as relating to blogs, video games, text messages, online social network pages, discussion forums, Internet memes, and so on. In this context, it makes more sense to refer to digital literacies not as a singular social practice, but as a multiplicity of social practices. This shift encourages researchers to analyze unique social practices, including families' everyday practices and popular culture sites that have become an increasingly significant part of how individuals learn and make meaning in on- and offline environments (Lankshear & Knobel, 2008).

New Literacy Studies and Multimodality

This study applies New Literacy Studies (NLS) and multimodality as lenses by which to consider social practices in literacy. Theories of NLS views literacy as social and semiotic practices (Barton & Hamilton, 1998, 2000; New London Group, 1996; Street, 1995). What is social about NLS is that this line of research does not only focus on the acquisition of skills of just reading and writing, but explores how all literacies exist, are multiple, and extend through time and space and through relations of power. NLS questions what counts as literacy and "whose literacies" are dominant, marginalized, and resistant (Street, 1995; 2003). Semiotic practices focuses on the different things that take on meaning (i.e., signs, symbols, images, objects) in a practice (Gee, 2003).

Multimodality highlights multiple modes of meaning (Kress & van Leeuwen, 2001). Multimodality involves visual, linguistic, oral, gestural, and spatial modes of meaning that occur simultaneously (Kress & van Leeuwen, 2001). It allows us to look at the ways various modes are integrated in multimodal texts. Sociocultural researchers acknowledge that all literacies are multimodal because all texts rely on some element of linguistic, visual, or spatial cues that involve various modes of meaning and representation (Kress & van Leeuwen, 2001).

NLS and multimodality intersect in critical ways for this investigation. While NLS researchers are attempting to explore and understand what individuals *do* with everyday social practices, researchers interested in multimodalities are exploring the "tools" and modes of meaning that individuals are *using* in everyday social practices (Kress & Street, 2006). As researchers, our role is to find the link to what individuals do and how they use tools in their everyday literacy practices that produce, reproduce, and shape digital literacies in the home. To portray the most important constructs relative to NLS and multimodality, I describe Larnee's experiences with digital literacies with her sons as integrated within a myriad of social practices around digital tools.

Cultural Ecology

Although there is a lack of research relating to family literacy and digital literacies, in particular among African Americans, a few studies have focused on individuals' relational involvement with computers/digital literacies that suggest how the world rapidly changes, emerges, and accumulates around us (Hawisher et al., 2004). A *cultural ecology approach* (Steward, 1972) describes the relationship and adaptation between the nature and culture in human societies. For this study, I adapted this approach by examining individuals using computer technologies as a cultural phenomenon (Hawisher et al., 2004). To illustrate, Hawisher et al. (2004) highlight how the literacy narratives of two women, African American and European American, came to acquire and develop the literacies of technology. Using a framework of cultural ecology of literacy, the researchers focused on how the relationships between individuals and technology evolved as they adopted computers as literacy tools in multiple environments relating to race, class, gender, politics, and economics.

Perspectives on digital literacies, the use of NLS and multimodality to define the use and social practices of digital tools, along with a cultural ecology approach, enabled me to capture the layered and nuanced ways the participants in this study engaged in digital literacy practices. Each of these perspectives is needed in order to understand how individuals use digital tools in different contexts for different purposes that not only guide the way they engage in these practices, but also how these tools allow them to produce, interpret, and create meaning in their lives and relationships.

METHODS

Participants

One African American family from an urban community participated in this study through purposive sampling (Patton, 1990). I met the Ali family at an after-school program where three of Larnee's sons attended. I was the reading specialist and taught each of her sons for over two years. I identified the family based on the following criteria: (a) the family members were avid digital literacy users and had access to digital literacies on a daily basis, and (b) a substantial amount of rapport was already established between me and the family.

Data Collection

I collected data on an ongoing basis for over three months from July to October 2007 in the Ali household (Lewis, 2009). Given the nature of my relationship with the family, they offered additional data for up to a year. I collected data by the following methods: structured, semistructured, and unstructured interviews, participant observations, and audio and video recording. These methods were used simultaneously. In addition, a guided "digital walk," digital photo collages, e-mail discussions, and artifact collections were used to document what this family did with digital literacies in the home. I conducted interviews with the mother once a week for an average of 60-90 minutes, and 30-60 minutes with her nine-year-old son, Gerard over a course of three months. Interview questions were modified based on Larnee's responses and consisted of general to specific questions regarding her and her family's digital literacy practices. In addition, I also conducted ongoing interviews with Larnee about things she might do or say concerning digital literacies. Larnee's 17-year-old son, David, lived at his grandmother's house, but often visited the home and contributed to the study.

I visited Larnee's home twice a week to obtain further data about her sons' and their mother's use of digital tools. I observed all activities and practices in Larnee's bedroom, where the only computer in the home was located. Observations gave me the opportunity to learn about the family's behaviors and practices that made sense in their worlds. I took field notes of the observations and related them to interview questions (Merriam, 2001). In my observational field notes, I captured pertinent information that provided significance to my study relating to: (a) the context, (b) the participants' behaviors, and (c) my behavior as researcher. For instance, I detailed how Larnee utilized one computer with her son, where she positioned the computer and the television in her room, and how Larnee's bed and the television were focal points of attraction and attention in this context.

Last, I acknowledged my behavior and stance, as researcher, by documenting data in a reflective journal. I identified similarities and differences in how I would engage in particular situations with certain family members. I recognized ways to address sensitive questions and practices that I observed in the home that became important in this study. In addition, I examined my own biases and assumptions of Larnee's socio-economic status and her use and alliance to digital tools in the home.

Data Analysis

I analyzed the data continually, recursively, and simultaneously with data collection. I began with an analysis of transcripts, field notes, videotapes, and audiotapes to develop categories, themes, and patterns that reflected the research questions (Creswell, 1998; Merriam, 2001; Miles & Huberman, 1994). For instance, I read and reread through transcripts with and without the audiotapes, made margin notes and questions, and developed codes to help make sense of the data. I continued transcribing audio- and videotapes and color-coding the interviews.

I used Mediated Discourse Analysis (MDA) to examine social actions in real-time activities (Scollon, 2001a). MDA allowed me to analyze the ways the Ali family constructed meaning through real-time interactions with texts, tools, and one another while engaging in digitally embedded literacy practices. MDA, theoretically and methodologically utilized within ethnographic research, allowed me to actively become a part of the Alis' everyday lives and actions in their home. Using its five concepts: *Mediated Action, Site of Engagement, Nexus of Practice, Practice,* and *Mediational Means* (Scollon, 2001) allowed me to capture how Larnee made sense of her practices in the meaning-making process and created a springboard into multiple modes of meaning, talk, learning, and action (Norris & Jones, 2005; Scollon, 2001).

RESULTS

Larnee's struggles come from a world that is foreign to many. She is a divorced mother of four sons, is unemployed, a recipient of government assistance, was physically and sexually abused as a child, and lives with a painful, rare skin disease—epidermolysis bullosa (EB), the same disease that took the life of her younger sister many years ago. Larnee exhibits traits of self-determination, morality, and independence in her everyday conversations and practices. On a daily basis, she shifts her attention to the digital world through gaming, instant messaging, texting, and talking on her cell phone. These digital literacy practices guide and influence her decisions. She engaged in digital literacy practices to fill the void of childhood hurts. It is through these literacy practices that I identified three themes in which she created an *awareness* of digital tools for and with her sons, and through her disease to the online community, exerted her own *agency* in and throughout digital literacies, and participated in *apprenticeship* models with her son through digital literacy practices. For this paper, I highlight each of these themes separately, although they all intermingle to identify ways in which Larnee's use of digital literacy practices helps her make sense of her life.

Awareness

Larnee plays the role of initiator and communicator with her sons and her online community. For instance, Larnee created a blog for herself and Gerard, but also invited me into their discussions on www.blogger.com. She provided me with the log-in names and passwords to interact equally with her and Gerard. She felt that this would be an added bonus for the three of us to communicate, share, engage, and openly address our thoughts about the technologies/digital literacies we use on a daily basis. Larnee took the lead, in a gentle way, by making us aware of the rules she created for us to utilize the blog. For example, she informed Gerard and me of the following: "We are encouraged to post as frequently as we can. We should respond to each other's comments and thoughts, and no one is allowed to edit any of the posts without permission from the group." Rule number three was quite important to Larnee; she wanted this virtual space to be "safe, not judged, and respected" (e-mail transcript, 8/27/07).

Norton-Meier (2004) used this same format to interpret how children took control of their identity constructions when they negotiated rules in innovative ways online. Larnee's rules, like those reported by Norton-Meier, reveal how she used the activity of blogging as a way of creating affinity spaces for online communication with regulations and a sense of community. Creating rules gave her the acceptance of doing something positive and enticing at the same time, but also compensating skills that she was not otherwise privy to knowing. She also became in charge and was accountable for the identity constructions she chose to create on the blog. She also created choice, power, and community to make sense in a safe environment.

The following quotation explained how family literacy practices surrounding digital literacies became a participatory practice that involved a shared purpose or activity with others (Lankshear & Knobel, 2008):

> I can't even tell you how much fun this blogging thing has been for Gerard and myself. Outside of doing things around the house I have been at this computer nonstop. We have watched the sun rise and fall at our computer, and have enjoyed each and every moment of it. This blog has really brought me and all my boys closer. *(Larnee)*

This quotation demonstrated Larnee's consistent interaction with Gerard and how she tried innovative practices to introduce new digital tools to him. By voluntarily creating a blog, she became the initiator and made Gerard aware of the unconventional ways that they could communicate and participate with each other despite the fact that they only had one computer.

Further evidence demonstrated ways in which Larnee raised a level of consciousness about her sons' digital literacy practices. One day, I received an e-mail from Larnee, who had voluntarily asked her sons to participate in asking some questions about their digital literacy practices: "Hey Ms. T, I was just asking the boys these questions (see Table 1) just to see if we all felt the same way about DL. Hope this helps" (8/13/07). This activity was initiated by Larnee, who allowed me to become aware of her son's digital literacy practices, but to also open up discussions about what would occur if these digital literacies/tools were not prevalent in their everyday practices.

In addition, Larnee also felt responsible to share her experiences and create an awareness of her illness and its conditions with others in online chat rooms and websites specifically geared to those who have epidermolysis bullosa (EB, Nabs, EBwomen and www.EBinfoworld.com). Her online friends dealt with the same illness and were seeking a confidant. She felt safe in "this virtual world" where she was not judged, nor would she have to explain her scars and burns when she was out in public. She used this online space to not only vent, offer companionship, and find social support, with the intent to be heard and understood, but to introduce newcomers into her conversations about the symptoms of the disease and in seeking advice or resources. Larnee spent time on the Internet researching medical procedures and medicines that she had to take in order to manage her illness. When Larnee engaged in digital literacies, she positioned and repositioned herself, to create new ways of being that generated new identities in the practice and in her life.

Table 1. Sons' Answers About Digital Literacy

Date/ Time	Larnee's sons/ age	What does digital literacy mean to you?	What digital literacies do you own? How often do you use them?	In this family do you think [digital literacy] shapes us? How? or How not? Would we communicate?	How do you think our family would be if we had no digital literacies? What would we do for fun? How would we communicate?
Wednesday, November 21, 2007 @ 2:39pm	*Gerard* 10 years old	Digital literacy is for something to use for research or to just have fun with it.	I own a computer and I use it a lot.	No. Because there is more than life than digital literacy.	Our family would have to tell stories to have fun and we would have to take the train to meet each other.
Saturday, November 24, 2007 @ 9:39pm	*Romeo* 11 years old	Digital literacy means we really don't need electronics, but I think it's just a extra privilege.	One of the things that I use is my PS2, and I use it mostly every day.	In this family I don't think that technology shapes us because think about if we didn't have technology we would still survive.	I think our family would have to use candles [and] flashlights for fun. I think we can tell stories and tell what our dreams were about, and I think we can communicate by sending notes to each other.
Saturday, November 24, 2007 @ 6:34pm	*David* 18 years old	Digital Literacy means how well you can use technology.	I have tons of them from iPod to Xbox.	It shapes us more than we realize. We plan whole days around technology. You even get mad when the internet or cable goes out.	We would just do what people did before technology— go out, and see plays.

Agency

Larnee's intellects are not contingent on how much she knows in an institutionalized setting but, rather come from her everyday ideas and practices shared in her home and community. Collins (1990) argues that there is much to learn from an African American woman's knowledge. Collins acknowledged that "African American women not commonly certified as 'intellectuals' by academic institutions have long functioned as intellectuals by representing the interests of Black women as a group and fostering Black feminist thought" (p. 15). For instance, during my first interview with Larnee, she expressed her comfort with computers as "a little more than a novice." In fact, Larnee boasted about having taken a computer repair course and knowing how to disassemble and assemble a computer. This practice demonstrated how Larnee used her knowledge and skills

Table 2. MDA and Motherboard Chart

Time Stamps	MDA Concepts	Video Still	Multimodality	Verbal Discourse
0:20:46:03- 0:22:20:00	Nexus of Practice "The intersection or linkage of multiple practices such that some group comes to recognize 'the same set' of actions…a recognizable grouping of a set of mediated actions" (Scallon, 2001) [Explaining the terminology and functions of the Computer Unit to Tisha; taking out parts of the computer unit]		(5a) Larnee touches the motherboard (5b) Tisha touches the equipment that look like AA batteries (5c) Larnee's voice lowers and is very serious	(5a) L: This is the Motherboard. (5b) T: What are these things? (5c) L: Roadblocks for me, personally is not finishing school. That's a major roadblock for me because it's not my fault that I wasn't in school, I was taken out of school.

when engaging in digital literacy practices with her sons despite the fact that she had not obtained her GED. She exclaimed, "I CAN BUILD a computer. I actually took some classes for computer repair… [building a computer] is the easiest thing. Let me tell you. It's much easier than learning the software" (semi-structured interview, 7/24/07).

This activity demonstrated Larnee's sense of agency. According to Moje and Lewis (2007), agency refers to the "strategic making and remaking of selves, identities, activities, relationships, cultural tools and resources and histories, as embedded within relations of power" (p. 18). Larnee was "remaking" and redefining parts of herself, through disassembling a computer, to show that she had other skills and strengths that gave her a sense of self (Matlow, 2000; Moje & Lewis, 2007). For example, I captured how Larnee demonstrated agentic roles when she disassembled a computer unit using mediated discourse analysis (see Table 2).

For two hours without sitting, Larnee demonstrated dissembling the computer unit, taking out each piece of equipment with care, as a doctor operating in an emergency room, even though the computer was not operational. Table 2 illustrates how she described the computer unit while using various modalities (i.e., pointing to the equipment) to emphasize unique ways she made sense of her past and present histories.

For instance, Larnee prided herself in knowing the purpose of the computer motherboard as being the primary functional unit of the computer, but she also recognized the symbolism of her role as the mother of four sons. "I call myself 'The Motherboard;' I have always linked anything electronic with the way the human body works, but the one electronic thing that I most identify with is 'The Motherboard.'" Here, Larnee attributed other functions to the motherboard, as a mother of four sons, a provider, a consumer, and an agent for change; she embodied the motherboard as a symbol for her life. For Larnee, engaging in digital literacies was more than multiple and interactive practices traveling through technological tools, but it actually is a way of supporting her agentic self.

In addition, Larnee demonstrated how agency was constructed through her interactions with her sons' digital literacy practices. In the home, Larnee is the "rock" for her sons. Despite her physical, financial, and emotional challenges, it is apparent that she loves them and will do anything to protect them, especially from what they view on the computer, which is strategically positioned in her room. She explained the reason why she chose to have the computer in her room, thus demonstrating overarching themes of safety, proximity, and management. Larnee kept her sons safe by making sure that she was aware of their whereabouts at all times. "I have the computer in my room because I can't trust people—other people. I'm so protective of my children. If some IM popped up and it had something inappropriate, I would have a fit! When they get a little older I may get their own computer or move the computer to another room, but for right now, I can watch them from right here" (semi-structured interview, 7/24/07).

Larnee opens up her bedroom to her sons by providing them with the space to be physically connected to her and their digital literacy practices. They are in the same room at the same time, sometimes without conversation or engagement, yet they are still a part of the same social practice. In other words, the culture of the Ali household allowed family members to congregate physically and digitally and share cultural interests and languages from their primary discourse. Larnee introduced a digital culture in which her and her sons' connections around digital literacies are shaped by the very holds, satisfactions, and reassurances she experiences while operating in her agentic roles (Turkle, 2005).

Larnee's "relationship" with the computer and other digital literacy tools empowered her, giving her the agency she never felt as a child. Overall, her ability to disassemble a computer unit suggested her need and desire to acquire a skill that she could use to teach her sons, or to become tech support for her family and friends. Larnee's experiences reinforce Lewis and Fabos' (2005) argument that "it is not the computer or the Internet itself that is central to literacy, but the way that these tools of technology shape social relations and practices" (p. 475). Similarly, Turkle (2005) argues against the common view that the computer is "just a tool": "We must look beyond all the things the computer does *for* us to what using it does *to* us as people" (p. 3). Turkle's concept of the computer as "second self," or as part of our social and psychological lives" suggests that individuals' experiences with computers change the ways they think, function, and act in the world (p. 1). Clearly Larnee's sense of agency gave her opportunities to make and remake herself and her identities, and still created a space to learn new practices, skills, and discourses with her sons.

Apprenticeships

Larnee and her sons' digital literacy practices enhanced their modes of problem solving, provided dialogue between a mother and sons around a digital tool, and showed how the dynamics of family relationships changed a mother and sons as "digital immigrants" (a person not born into the digital world but who has accepted many of the functions that technology offers) and "digital natives" ("native speakers" of the digital era of using video games, computers, and the Internet)

(Prensky, 2001). Vygotsky (1978) reminds us that apprenticeship occurs when individuals are engaged in activities that involve learning and/or understanding a particular cultural practice with the assistance of a more experienced other. This definition was reinforced by Larnee's digital literacy practices on a daily basis with her sons. Consequently, Larnee's learning relationship with her sons involved symmetrical and asymmetrical power structures that shifted apprenticeship models.

The power structures shifted and influenced the family relationships when Larnee enlisted the help of her 17-year-old son David to transfer a file from her computer to my e-mail account. During Larnee and David's interaction, they engaged in symmetrical and asymmetrical power relationships. The discourse between the two appeared to be tense at times as Larnee related her frustration to David when she was unable to make the tool work. David remained calm and attempted to assist Larnee step-by-step. The back-and-forth verbal and nonverbal gestures showed how their roles shifted throughout the interaction.

David appeared to be the dominant one in knowing how to troubleshoot the computer. He provided directives to guide Larnee through the process as a teacher would do to a student. David's gentle informal lessons and explanations of how to send attachments through AOL to my Yahoo account challenged, guided, and supported Larnee's skills in this valued activity. David sat in Larnee's chair with his back hunched forward and turned to the side. He was not sitting directly in front of the computer, but his position was inviting as he faced Larnee.

Meanwhile, Larnee's tone was stern and dominant with linguistic expressions. Standing to his right, while David simultaneously worked on the computer, Larnee moved around and tilted over David to point to the computer screen. Larnee's language and body movements became authoritative when pointing to the screen, leaning over and shifting one arm to both arms behind her back, placing her hands on her waist, or folding her arms across her chest. Commands such as: "Wait," "Do," "Here," "Open up the mail," and "Close that up," positioned Larnee as the authoritative one as she coached David throughout the activity. Larnee would also lift her hands in surrender mode, saying comments like, "I did that" . . . "but I didn't know" and putting her hands on her hips, showing her frustrations openly. The following excerpt showed the interaction between the two around this practice.

L: Go right here. Open up the mail and go to that one. Then go to some of the ones that Gerard sent to me.

D: Right here?

L: You gotta open it up and then you're gonna forward them to her (Tisha).

D: Just send it?

L: Yeah. OK...wait, wait click keep as new, cause I gotta put 'em all in a file. OK exit out and go to the next one.

D: That's what I'm trying do OK, where's it at where is it? OK and I can send later... Attach Files! You attach the file.

L: I know, I tried to do that and Tisha said she couldn't get it.

D: I just gotta find it. Go back to the main computer.... Or you can like, send more than one attached files...You can't send out more than that...

Larnee and David reciprocally apprenticed one another. Their interactions revealed symmetrical power relationships where both individuals felt that they were offering assistance in the correct way by instructing and showing the other how to find a file, what to expect, or what to do next. Their apprenticeship was not the traditional asymmetrical relationship in which an expert apprentices a novice, as described by Vygotsky (1978) and Rogoff (1990). In the traditional model, one person knows more than the other and literally teaches and helps the apprentice become a more skilled partner. Rather in Larnee's case, she was the initiator of digital literacies in the home, who first began to adopt the apprentice role of learner in an attempt to solve problems with David. Once Larnee learned how to send the attachment, she immediately switched roles from student to teacher. At one time, she gave him time to work on the computer without any talking. There was only the multiple clicking and scrolling of the mouse. During a moment in this activity, she said, "Let me see something real quick," and took the mouse while standing over David. With the mouse in her hand, there was a level of comfort as she stood with her right leg out, leaning over with her left arm behind her back. In this practice, mother and son reciprocally positioned themselves and each other as knowledgeable or as engaged in a collaborative practice or inquiry in a symmetrical power relationship. Larnee had the opportunity to remake herself through this practice that not only took her mind off of the medicine, frequent hospital visits, and constant bandaging of her scars, but allowed her to become the apprentice and teacher and spend quality time with her son. This type of apprenticeship within the family was mediated through digital literacies.

CONCLUSION AND IMPLICATIONS

The goal of this study was to understand and acknowledge, from an emic perspective, how unique and complex digital literacy practices extend and transform family literacies. Larnee's family provided only one insight into the complex relationship of how, for a variety of reasons, families use digital literacies as mediating tools to make sense of themselves.

Larnee's story of awareness, agency, and apprenticeship through digital literacies demonstrated how aspects of her life shaped her engagement with others in digital spaces. The themes awareness, agency, and apprenticeships are descriptive of family literacy practices and their use of digital tools. As a result, this study has raised significant points of new ways to examine family literacy and new literacies in the 21st century. Having access to digital tools in the home helped mediate awareness, agency, and apprenticeship in the Ali household. For instance, Larnee became the initiator and recipient of introducing her sons to digital tools at home and when using the social chat rooms to bring awareness to her online friends battling epidermolysis bullosa. In addition, Larnee has demonstrated ways of making and remaking herself through her activities, identities, relationships, and histories by creating a blog for her younger son, disassembling a computer unit, and troubleshooting with her older son.

Larnee and her sons' interactions with the blog, in particular, provide a contrast to Ba et al.'s (2002) study. The authors found that low-income African American parents were not comfortable touching the computer, let alone troubleshooting or modeling certain features on the computer with their children. Rather, their work suggested other activities to bring the families together. Larnee and Gerard were not concerned that there was only one computer or that they had to switch places in order to type responses on the blog. Instead, they were interested in engaging with one another in this practice, which debunks the idea that low-income families do not engage in meaningful activities with family members or that low-income families are not knowledgeable about digital technologies in their homes.

In any relationship, there are issues of power. Larnee and David addressed these issues when Larnee needed David's assistance to troubleshoot on the computer. The study explored how they interchangeably apprenticed each other in a seesaw of symmetrical and asymmetrical power relationships. These practices changed the dynamics of the family's relationships around digital literacy practices when Larnee and David conceded authority to teach the other on the computer at different times. This sort of relationship was not common in traditional literacies because the older generation possessed the expertise that the younger needed to acquire. With the rapid change of digital literacies, both generations are acquiring different aspects of the technology at the same time and can have complementary knowledge. Therefore, digital literacy practices support an empowering reciprocal relationship in the teaching and learning experience.

We learn that digital literacies were never intended to be a static practice. Instead, it was meant to shape and mold our ways of thinking, to form our communities, and to communicate in social spaces with others (Barton et al., 2007; Lewis & Fabos, 2005; Turkle, 2005). We also take from Larnee's story how imperative it is to create springboards for further questions and discussions on the importance of constructing a new education and new literacies for today's students. Taylor (1983) argues that "no single, narrow definition of 'family literacy' can do justice to the richness and complexity of families, and into the multiple literacies, including often unrecognized local literacies, that are a part of their everyday lives" (p. 4). The Ali family has defined family literacy in ways that are mediated by social contexts that influence what they bring to communal learning settings every day. They demonstrated how engagement with digital literacies changes family dynamics. This study showed how a family's digital literacy practices influenced family relations.

REFERENCES

Alvermann, D. E. (2002). *Adolescents and literacies in a digital world.* New York, NY: Peter Lang.

Alvermann, D. E. (2010). *Adolescents' online literacies: Connecting classrooms, digital media, and pop culture.* New York, NY: Peter Lang.

Ba, H., Tally, W., & Tsikalas, K. (2002). Investigating children's emerging digital literacies. *Journal of Technology, Learning and Assessment, 1*(4), 1–48.

Barton, D., & Hamilton, M. (1998). *Local literacies: Reading and writing in one community.* London, England: Routledge.

Barton, D., & Hamilton, M. (2000). Literacy practices. In D. Barton, M. Hamilton, & R. Ivanič (Eds.), *Situated literacies: Reading and writing in context* (pp. 7–15). London, England: Routledge.

Barton, D., Ivanič, R., Appleby, Y., Hodge, R., & Tusting, K. (2007). *Literacy, lives and learning.* London, England: Routledge.

Bawden, D. (2008). Origins and concepts of digital literacy. In C. Lankshear & M. Knobel (Eds.), *Digital literacies: Concepts, policies and paradoxes* (pp. 15–32). New York, NY: Peter Lang.

Bruce, B. C. (2002). Diversity and critical social engagement: How changing technologies enable new modes of literacy in changing circumstances. In D. E. Alvermann (Ed.), *Adolescents and literacies in a digital world* (pp. 1–18). New York, NY: Peter Lang.

Cairney, T. H., & Ruge, J. (1998). *Community literacy practices and schooling: Towards effective support for students.* Canberra, Australia: DEET.

Cammack, D. W. (2002). Literacy, technology, and a room of her own: Analyzing adolescent girls' online conversations from historical and technological literacy perspectives. In D. L. Schallert, C. M. Fairbanks, J. Worthy, B. Maloch, & J. V. Hoffman (Eds.), *51st Yearbook of the National Reading Conference* (pp. 129–141). Oak Creek, WI: National Reading Conference.

Chandler-Olcott, K., & Mahar, D. (2003). "Tech-savviness" meets multiliteracies: Exploring adolescent girls' technology-mediated literacy practices. *Reading Research Quarterly, 38,* 356–385.

Collins, P. H. (1990). *Black feminist thought: Knowledge, consciousness and the politics of empowerment.* New York, NY: Routledge.

Compton-Lilly, C. (2003). *Reading families: The literate lives of urban children.* New York, NY: Teachers College Press.

Compton-Lilly, C., Rogers, R., & Lewis, T. Y. (in press, January 2012). Analyzing diversity epistemologies: An integrative critical literature review of family literacy scholarship. *Reading Research Quarterly.*

Creswell, J. W. (1998). *Qualitative inquiry and research design: Choosing among five traditions.* Thousand Oaks, CA: Sage.

Edwards, P. A. (2004). *Children's literacy development: Making it happen through school, family, and community involvement.* Boston, MA: Allyn & Bacon.

Edwards, P. A., Pleasants, H. M., & Franklin, S. H. (1999). *A path to follow: Learning to listen to parents.* Portsmouth, NH: Heinemann.

Gee, J. P. (2003) *What video games have to teach us about learning and literacy.* New York, NY: Palgrave Macmillan.

Gilster, P. (1997). *Digital literacy.* New York, NY: Wiley.

Hawisher, G., & Selfe, C., Moraski, B., & Pearson, M. (2004). Becoming literate in the information age: Cultural ecologies and the literacies of technology. *College Composition and Communication 55,* 642-692.

Heath, S. B. (1983). *Ways with words: Language, life, and work in communities and classrooms.* Cambridge, England: Cambridge University Press.

Jacobs, G. (2006). Fast times and digital literacy: Participation roles and portfolio construction within instant messaging. *Journal of Literacy Research, 38,* 171–196.

Kirkland, D. (2009). Shaping the digital pen: Media literacy, youth culture, and MySpace. *Youth Media Reporter,* pp. 188-200. Retrieved from http://www.youthmediareporter.org/docs/D.Kirkland.pdf

Kress, G., & Street, B. (2006). Foreword. In K. Pahl & J. Rowell (Eds.), *Travel notes from the New Literacy Studies: Instances of practice* (pp. vii–x). Clevedon, England: Multilingual Matters Ltd.

Kress, G., & van Leeuwen, T. J. (2001). *Multimodal discourse: The modes and media of contemporary communication.* London, England: Arnold.

Lankshear, C., & Knobel, M. (2008). *Digital literacies: Concepts, policies and practices.* New York, NY: Peter Lang.

Lareau, A. (1989). *Home advantage: Social class and parental intervention in elementary education.* London, England: Falmer.

Lewis, C., & Fabos, B. (2005). Instant messaging, literacies, and social identities. *Reading Research Quarterly, 40,* 470–501.

Lewis, T. Y. (2009). Family literacy and digital literacies: A redefined approach to examining social practices of an African-American family. Unpublished dissertation. University at Albany, State University of New York, Albany, NY.

Mahar, D. (2002). An uncharted journey: Three adolescent technology experts navigate the school system. In D. L. Schallert, C. M. Fairbanks, J. Worthy, B. Maloch, & J. V. Hoffman (Eds.), *51st Yearbook of the National Reading Conference* (pp. 287–297). Oak Creek, WI: National Reading Conference.

Marsh, J. (2006). Global, local/public, private: Young children's engagement in digital literacy practices in the home. In K. Pahl & J. Rowsell (Eds.), *Travel notes from the New Literacy Studies: Instances of practice* (pp. 19–38). Clevedon, England: Multilingual Matters Ltd.

Marsh, J., & Thompson, P. (2001). Parental involvement in literacy development: Using media texts. *Journal of Research in Reading, 24,* 266–278.

Matlow, E. (2000). Women, computers and a sense of self. Cutting Edge: Women's Research Group (Ed.). *Digital desires: Language, identity and new technologies* (pp. 167–183). New York, NY: Tauris.

McCarthey, S. (1997). Connecting home and school literacy practices in classrooms with diverse populations. *Journal of Literacy Research, 29,* 145–182.

Merriam, S. B. (2001). Qualitative research and case study applications in education: Revised and expanded from case study research in education. San Francisco, CA: Jossey-Bass.

Miles, M. B., & Huberman, A. M. (1994). *Qualitative data analysis: An expanded sourcebook* (2nd ed.). Thousand Oaks, CA: Sage.

Moje, E., & Lewis, C. (2007). Examining opportunities to learn literacy: The role of critical sociocultural literacy research. In C. Lewis, P. E. Enciso, & E. B. Moje (Eds.), *Reframing sociocultural research on literacy: Identity, agency, and power* (pp. 15–48). Mahwah, NJ: Erlbaum.

New London Group. (1996). A pedagogy of multiliteracies: Designing social futures. *Harvard Educational Review, 66*(1), 69–92.

Norris, S., & Jones, R. (Eds.) (2005). *Discourse in action: Introduction to mediated discourse analysis*. London, England: Routledge.=

Norton-Meier, L. (2004). A technology user's bill of rights: Lessons learned in chat rooms. *Journal of Adolescent and Adult Literacy, 47*, 606–608.

Patton, M. Q. (1990). *Qualitative evaluation and research methods* (2nd ed.). Newbury Park, CA: Sage Publications.

Prensky, M. (2001). Digital natives, digital immigrants. *On the Horizon, 9*, 1–6.

Purcell-Gates, V. (1995). *Other people's words: The cycle of low literacy*. Cambridge, MA: Harvard University Press.

Rogers, R. (2002). Between contexts: A critical analysis of family literacy, discursive practices, and literate subjectivities. *Reading Research Quarterly, 37*, 248-277.

Rogoff, B. (1990). *Apprenticeship in thinking: Cognitive development in social context*. New York, NY: Oxford University Press.

Scollon, R. (2001). Action and text: Towards an integrated understanding of the place of text in social (inter) action, mediation discourse analysis and the problem of social action. In R. Wodak & M. Meyer (Eds.), *Methods of critical discourse analysis* (pp. 139–183). London, England: Sage.

Steward, J. H. (1972). *Theory of culture change: The methodology of multilinear evolution*. Champaign, IL: University of Illinois Press.

Street, B. (1995). *Social literacies: Critical approaches to literacy in development, ethnography and education*. New York. NY: Longman.

Street, B. (2003). What's "new" in New Literacy Studies? Critical approaches to literacy in theory and practice. *Current Issues in Comparative Education, 5*, 77-91.

Taylor, D. (1983). *Family literacy: Young children learning to read and write*. Portsmouth, NH: Heinemann.

Taylor, D., & Dorsey-Gaines, C. (1988). *Growing up literate: Learning from inner-city families*. Portsmouth, NH: Heinemann.

Turkle, S. (1984). *The second self: Computers and the human spirit*. New York, NY: Simon & Shuster.

Turkle, S. (2005). *The second self: Computers and the human spirit* (20th anniversary ed.). Cambridge, MA: MIT Press.

Vygotsky, L. S. (1978). *Mind in society: The development of higher psychological processes*. Cambridge, MA: Harvard University Press.